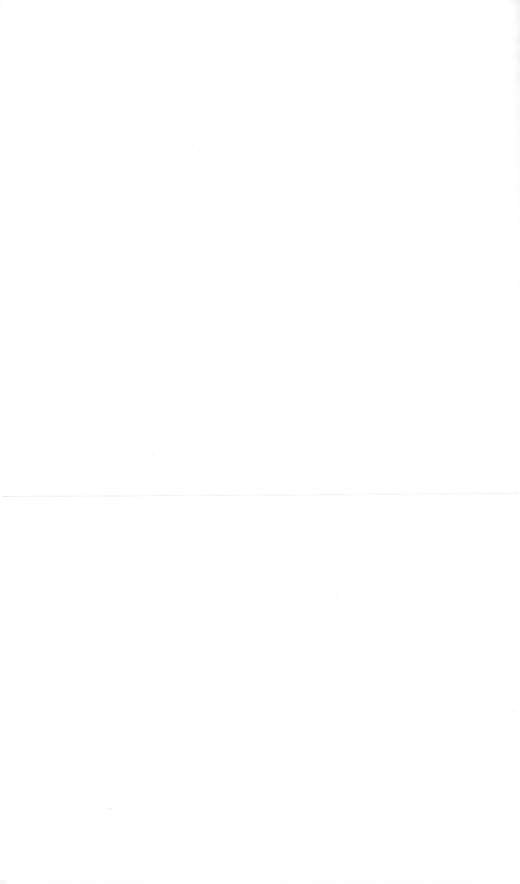

The Automobile
in American History
and Culture

**Recent Titles in
American Popular Culture**

The Automobile in American History and Culture

A REFERENCE GUIDE

Michael L. Berger

American Popular Culture
M. Thomas Inge, Series Editor

GREENWOOD PRESS
Westport, Connecticut • London

Library of Congress Cataloging-in-Publication Data

Berger, Michael L., 1943-
    The automobile in American history and culture : a reference guide / Michael L. Berger.
       p.   cm.—(American popular culture, ISSN 0193–6859)
    Includes bibliographical references and index.
    ISBN 0–313–24558–4 (alk. paper)
    1. Automobiles—United States.   2. Automobile industry and trade—United States.
    3. United States—Social life and customs.   I. Title. II. Series.
    TL23.B43   2001
    016.629222'0973—dc21   00–064049

British Library Cataloguing in Publication Data is available.

Copyright © 2001 by Michael L. Berger

Library of Congress Catalog Card Number: 00–064049
ISBN: 0–313–24558–4
ISSN: 0193–6859

First published in 2001

Greenwood Press, 88 Post Road West, Westport, CT 06881
An imprint of Greenwood Publishing Group, Inc.
www.greenwood.com

Printed in the United States of America

The paper used in this book complies with the
Permanent Paper Standard issued by the National
Information Standards Organization (Z39.48–1984).

10 9 8 7 6 5 4 3 2 1

Copyright Acknowledgment

Portions of the introduction first appeared in Michael L. Berger and Maurice Duke, "The Automobile," in M. Thomas Inge, ed., *Handbook of American Popular Culture,* 3 vols., 2nd ed. (Westport, Conn.: Greenwood Press, 1989), pp. 107–110. Copyright © 1989 by M. Thomas Inge.
Reproduced with permission of Greenwood Publishing Group, Inc., Westport, CT.

For my parents,
Ethel J. and Clarence Q. Berger,
who taught me the value of the written word

Contents

Preface

The Automobile in American History and Culture is part of a Greenwood Press series designed to provide evaluative surveys of bibliographic material in selected aspects of American popular culture. Nonetheless, it should be complete enough to serve as a thorough introduction to the many dimensions of automotive studies, providing multiple starting points for novices and professionals alike who wish to do research on a given topic. Hopefully, even advanced scholars will find some material here with which they were previously unfamiliar. Since the majority of the works cited are of a scholarly nature and thus have footnotes and a bibliography, even a single item is capable of creating a multiplier effect.

Unlike bibliographic lists, which simply categorize works under subject headings, or annotated bibliographies, which follow a similar format but add some descriptive material immediately following the citation, this guide links together a multiple number of books in a sequence of narrative essays. Those essays not only explain the nature of an individual work but place it in a broader context within the field of American automotive studies. As such, this guide should be of assistance both in the conceptualization and in the completion of previously formulated research studies. In addition, those researchers who have an interest in a general area of automotive studies but have not yet settled on a specific topic should find this guide to be valuable. It provides a resource with which to examine the entire field and its structure before deciding which particular subject to investigate in depth. One of the advantages of this essay approach is that the chapters and the sections of which they are composed have a narrative integrity that allows them to be read either individually or as a portion of a larger overview of the field.

Besides providing an introduction to the literature in the field of automotive studies, it is hoped that this guide will make a second significant contribution in the form of the schema created for it. In attempting to organize the vast amount of material, the author has found it necessary to design a unique structural framework, or schema, within which to discuss it. Hopefully, that framework will be helpful to others looking for ways of organizing their work and for insights into the relationships that exist among various topics. Such a schema also may assist researchers in a particular area of automotive studies to more discretely define their specialty and provide a framework for the organization of new publications as they appear.

In sum, if *The Automobile in American History and Culture* fosters additional research regarding the nature and significance of the motor car's impact on American history and life, it may be said to have succeeded in its purpose. In the eyes of many, serious study in this field, other than of a business or biographic nature, began in 1965 with the publication of John B. Rae's *The Automobile: A Brief History*. Thus, automotive studies as a field of scholarship is only a little over a generation old. It seems appropriate that the publication of this guide closely follows a number of anniversary celebrations commemorating the centennial of the automobile in the United States. Hopefully, both will lead to a renewed interest in, and expansion of, research and publication regarding what some consider to be the most significant technological artifact of the 20th century.

SELECTIVITY

Any user of a reference guide such as this is entitled to know the criteria by which items were selected for inclusion. The most obvious criterion was that an item be concerned with the social, economic, and political impact of the automobile on American history and life. For the purpose of this guide, "automobile" is defined as a self-propelled, multi-purpose vehicle used for personal (as opposed to commercial) transportation. Thus, one will find little here on bicycles, buses, and trucks, even though the history of each intersects with that of the motor car. While such vehicles as motorcycles or snowmobiles might seem to fit our definition, they are excluded because they are not generally viewed as multi-purpose vehicles, but rather primarily as recreational ones.

In the same vein, this guide makes no attempt to include the literature concerned with associated industries, such as the rubber and petrochemical ones, and the people connected with them, except insofar as they *directly* impact on a singular event in automotive history, such as the oil embargoes of the 1970s. Similarly, except in that it has *specific* social or economic implications, there is no discussion of civil engineering topics such as road, bridge, or tunnel construction; traffic management; road repair and maintenance (including snow removal); or industrial design.

As noted above, the primary purpose of this guide is to further research relative to the influence of the motor car on American history and life. Thus, every effort has been made to include all relevant books that would be classified as scholarly in nature. In most cases, this meant that the work had to evidence a research base, that it built upon earlier scholarship. Footnotes and a bibliography were taken as indicators of this status. As a result, primary source materials; sales and technical literature related to the automobile and its industry; government and corporate reports; polemics and other writing of a transitory or ephemeral nature (including the results of experimental research); non-fiction written primarily for the juvenile market; and "how-to" materials of whatever type have generally been excluded.

In addition, many books written for the auto enthusiast audience have been included. These works often contain some information that might be of interest to the scholar, and they often examine topics that have not yet been the subject of a full-length monograph. No attempt has been made to include all such books, since their sheer number would have so overwhelmed this guide as to make it unwieldy. (It has been estimated that thousands of additional items would thereby be eligible for inclusion.)

Finally, those books that had a very limited press run and/or have become scarce with the passage of time have generally been excluded. Where the author had reason to believe a book was not generally available, that specific volume has not been cited since it would be counterproductive to the purpose of this guide, which is to encourage and facilitate the work of the novice automotive historian.

Despite these exclusions, the centrally important works for each topic (published through 1999) ought to be discussed herein. In addition, some works that do *not* meet the criteria described earlier also are included if they are generally considered to be "classics" in the field, if they have won a book award, if the stature of the author justifies it, or if they treat a significant topic regarding which there has been no or insufficient scholarly attention. As noted earlier, one of the purposes of this guide is to help remedy the last named situation.

Undoubtedly, a few works that some might consider significant have been omitted. No reference guide, no matter how extensive, could hope to cite and describe all of the books written about the automobile. To have continued to search for additional items to include would have been counterproductive for two reasons. First, the law of diminishing returns comes into play. Second and probably more importantly, with the continual appearance of new works, it is ultimately impossible to reach closure. (I have learned that lesson all too well over the past decade and a half.) Nonetheless, the author would welcome correspondence regarding possible additional entries and suggestions regarding the organizational structure of the guide for a possible supplement or second edition.

ORGANIZATION

The guide begins with a brief, introductory, historical overview of the history of the automobile in the United States. The main body of the work then consists of twelve chapters, eleven of which are devoted to a different aspect of the automobile's impact on American history and life. These chapters are further subdivided into a multiple number of sections, each of which is written to be a self-contained, bibliographic essay. In the twelfth chapter, the major reference books (as opposed to monographs) and periodicals in the field are organized and described. These chapters are followed by two appendixes: (1) a selected chronology of American automotive history events and (2) an essay describing the major automotive research collections in the United States.

Despite efforts to create as logical a division of the material as possible, there is an unavoidable arbitrariness to the placement of some of the works. For instance, does an examination of books concerning car safety most properly belong in Chapter 4, as part of a discussion of automotive design and engineering, or in Chapter 11, as a socioeconomic problem involving the automobile? Why not include these books in the health section of Chapter 6? While some might argue for discussing the car safety books in all three chapters, the result would be a much longer, more redundant, and duplicative work, and thus ultimately a decision had to be made as to the most "appropriate" placement. In the author's opinion, it was in Chapter 11.

For that reason, every attempt has been made to include chapter cross-references in the text whenever appropriate, and occasionally material appearing in one chapter is reprinted in another. Naturally, as with all books, the reader also is advised to consult the table of contents and the indexes, which will direct her or him to the relevant page(s). In this regard, two separate indexes have been provided: author and subject. Hopefully, the inclusion of the former index, one often omitted from reference works of this type, will prove to be especially useful for novices who may be familiar with the names of scholars in the field but not the titles of the works that they have authored.

LITERARY CONVENTIONS

A brief explanation needs to be given of the "literary conventions" employed in the following chapters. In general, for each topic, books devoted exclusively to the subject are described first, followed by book chapters found in more general anthologies. To conserve space, when there are more than two authors, only the first author is cited in the narrative followed by the designation *et al.* Similarly, when a work is written "with the assistance" of another person, usually only the primary author is noted in the text. In both cases, a more complete listing of authorship can be found in the chapter bibliography. Finally, an author's full middle name is given only when it is necessary to distinguish him or her from another individual, most commonly when it is the maiden name of a female author.

In most cases, the full title of the work is provided in the text. Not only does this clarify the nature of the contents, but it often avoids the necessity of further describing the work, except for an evaluative word or phrase, and thereby helped keep the length of the guide within manageable proportions. (The assumption here, of course, is that the reader will note and reflect on the title without further prompting.) Nonetheless, redundant subtitles are not included and lengthy archaic titles have been shortened in the narrative. The full title of such books, of course, appears in the chapter bibliography.

As a general rule, the first edition of a book is cited unless substantial revisions were subsequently made. However, in those cases where a dissertation was later published as a book, the latter is named since, more often than not, it is a revised version of the former.

Throughout the guide, reference is made to books that have been honored with awards from professional associations. Most of these works received either the Nicholas-Joseph Cugnot Award from the Society of Automotive Historians (SAH) or the Thomas McKean Memorial Cup from the Antique Automobile Club of America (AACA). Both awards recognize the best book in automotive history for a particular year. Occasionally, the honor will be cited in the narrative without reference to the association, the title of the award will be foreshortened, or, in the case of the McKean, it will be called an "award" rather than a "cup." (The McKean Cup is actually given now in the form of an engraved sterling-silver serving tray.)

Finally, as noted above, there is a bibliography at the end of each chapter. Each of these combines the books cited in a given chapter into a single, continuous listing, with entries ordered alphabetically by first author. Anthology book chapters described individually in the text are *not* listed separately in the bibliographies but are instead subsumed under the name of the editor and the complete collection. Although this guide is limited to commercially published books, occasionally a magazine or journal article is mentioned to provide historical background information. With the exception of thematic issues, wherein automotive related articles constitute the majority of the contents, citations for periodicals or serials are not included in the chapter bibliographies. The bibliographies for the two appendices are slightly different, in that they include the reference works on which the text was based in addition to books cited in the narrative.

Acknowledgments

A volume of this magnitude can never be the product of a single person's efforts. During the seventeen years it took to research and write *The Automobile in American History and Culture*, numerous people willingly gave of their time and expertise to assist me in what often seemed an endless task. My colleagues at St. Mary's College of Maryland and Beaver College, now Arcadia University, evidenced a degree of collegiality that made me proud to be part of those academic communities. Among those who were most helpful was Leslie Milner who, while she was Inter-Library Loan Librarian at St. Mary's, secured numerous books and articles for me during the crucial early years when the structure and scope of this work were determined. My two administrative assistants, M. Linda Vallandingham of St. Mary's and Marie T. Gallagher of Arcadia, provided yeoman service at key points in this book's preparation. Their aid and support went far beyond what might have been expected. On the faculty side, Henry Rosemont, Jr., Reeves Distinguished Professor of Liberal Arts at St. Mary's, was a constant source of encouragement and good advice. I value greatly the collegial relationship we have shared and the personal friendship that has developed over the past twenty-five years.

Special thanks are due to Ann Ranieri, the Head of Technical Services at Arcadia's Atwood Library, who gave unstintingly of her time and energy. I will always be grateful for her expertise in library science and her ability to maintain a positive attitude while responding to what must have appeared to be an unending stream of bibliographic queries and questions.

I also wish to express my appreciation to the editors at Greenwood Press: Cynthia Harris, Marilyn Brownstein, Lynn Taylor, George F. Butler, and Alicia S. Merritt, each of whom exhibited extraordinary patience and understanding during the lengthy gestation period of this guide. I am particularly grateful to Pamela St. Clair for her support and encouragement during the final three years. In addition, from inception to completion, M. Thomas Inge, Blackwell Professor of the Humanities at Randolph-Macon College, proved to be a most supportive series editor and provided that much-needed "statement of closure" all non-fiction authors require to prevent them from continuing to research forever.

A work of this nature and breath is prone to contain minor errors and inconsistencies, which can be especially vexing to the neophyte researcher who must necessarily take what is written on faith. Therefore, I owe a special debt of gratitude to John Donohue of Rainsford Type, whose painstaking and thorough review of the manuscript eliminated many flaws and thereby greatly enhanced the quality of this guide. I publicly thank him and add the caveat that I alone am responsible for whatever inadvertent errors remain.

Finally, this work would never have been completed if it had not been for the advice and steadfast support of my wife, Linda Cannizzo Berger. It was she, at several critical points when the work languished for months on end, who convinced me not to abandon this project, who applied her keen judgment to help resolve issues and problems related to this project, and who accepted with a commendable equanimity my need to disappear after dinner and on weekends to work on "the book." Thank you, Linda!

Introduction

HISTORICAL OUTLINE*

Although people had dreamed of a self-propelled vehicle for centuries, it was not until the end of the 19th century that a practical road machine capable of sustained distances emerged for general use. Historians disagree on the actual inventor of the first American automobile. However, credit is usually given to the brothers Charles E. and J. Frank Duryea for the successful development (1893) and marketing of the gasoline motor car that most resembles the one in use today. The Duryeas' success was abetted by their victory in the first American automobile race, held in 1895. This event was sponsored by the *Chicago Times-Herald* and thus resulted in considerable publicity for the new means of transportation. The brothers used this free advertising to successfully launch their auto manufacturing company. Indeed, the fact that their car had progeny separates the Duryeas' efforts from others of this period.

When the automobile first appeared, it was treated variously as an object of curiosity, a plaything for the rich, a tinkering project for inventors, and a new customer for the neighborhood blacksmith. It came in a bewildering variety of sizes, shapes, and engine types. The primary difference, though, was in the means of propulsion: electricity, steam, or gasoline.

Although there was a fair degree of initial interest in electric and steam vehicles, the contest between them and gasoline ones was uneven. Cars that ran on gasoline possessed power that was comparable to that of steamers and were capable of greater sustained speed. In addition, gasoline automobiles could travel

*Portions of this introduction first appeared in Michael L. Berger and Maurice Duke, "The Automobile," in M. Thomas Inge, ed., *Handbook of American Popular Culture*, 3 vols., 2nd ed. (Westport, Conn.: Greenwood Press, 1989), pp. 107–110.

farther than the other two types without refueling. They also were reasonably simple to operate, capable of being repaired by anyone familiar with internal combustion engines, and, by the standards of the day, non-polluting. Early questions regarding the widespread availability of gasoline were answered by the discovery of significant domestic oil reserves in Texas in 1901. As a result, by 1905, 86% of the cars being produced were gasoline ones.

Races, such as the Vanderbilt Cup road races of 1904–1916; reliability runs, like the Glidden Tours held between 1905 and 1913; and successful cross-country automobile trips, beginning in 1903 with that of Dr. H. Nelson Jackson, all helped establish the reliability of the automobile and advertise its superiority, in many respects, to horse-drawn transportation.

Although still not completely trustworthy from a mechanical standpoint, automobiles soon became popular among the wealthy for day trips and longer-duration vacations, giving rise, incidentally, to a number of early automobile travel narratives and novels. Motorized Americans began to explore places that a mere decade or two before had been beyond the range of the traveler, who had to rely on the horse, the ship, and/or the train. The automobile had begun to shrink the size of a continent on whose vastness and inexhaustibleness explorers had commented since the 16th century.

Such travel, however, would not have been possible without the road improvements that accompanied the technological development of the automobile. The impetus for the former came first from the bicycle craze of the 1880s and 1890s and then the Good Roads Movement that followed it. That movement was primarily concerned with constructing good farm-to-market roads, which would allow farmers to avoid the allegedly abusive railroads if they so chose. At the same time, public interest in long-distance and cross-country touring and transportation led to the formation of the Lincoln Highway Association in 1913, with its goal of creating a transcontinental roadway.

By 1916 the political pressure exerted by the highway lobby was sufficient to lead to the passage of the Federal Aid Road Act, which provided some $75 million for improving rural post roads. This act was especially significant since it marked the introduction of the federal government into the business of financing motor highways. It was followed by a series of laws providing matching grants to the states for the purpose of creating a national system of interconnected roads. During the same period, both the federal and state governments discovered the efficacy of making the users help pay for the construction and upkeep of these highways through taxes on gasoline, and by 1929 they had become the chief source of money for such construction.

Mass production of automobiles, pioneered first by Ransom E. Olds and his curved-dash Oldsmobile (1902) and then to a greater extent by Henry Ford and his Model T (1908), ushered in a new era of American attitudes and convictions regarding the motor car. Both Ford and Olds showed that a mechanically efficient automobile, produced and sold at a moderate price, could still be the source of significant profits for the manufacturer if purchased in sufficient quantities.

Although there was some early resistance to the motor car, especially in rural areas, once its economic and social usefulness had been demonstrated, this hostility disappeared. By 1910 the United States had more cars on (and off) the road than any other nation. With the unlimited production capabilities provided by the moving assembly line and the ready availability of raw materials, the dream of mass automotive ownership was about to become reality.

The reasons for the popularity of the automobile were many. First, it had proven itself to be technically reliable. This was especially true of Ford's Model T. A progressive simplicity of operation accompanied this reliability, an important aspect of which was the introduction of the electric starter by Cadillac in 1912. The necessity of "turning over" the gasoline engine by hand had been a major deterrent for women drivers. Second, studies seemed to show that the new mode of transportation was less expensive, longer lasting, and easier to maintain than the horse. Early in its history, the automobile also was seen as helping to provide a cleaner environment. In New York City, where 2.5 million pounds of horse manure had to be removed daily, the citizens hailed the mechanized vehicle, which seemingly left nothing but evaporating smoke in its wake.

Third, the majority of middle-class American families, not just the wealthy, had the financial ability to purchase a car if they desired to do so, especially with the introduction of installment payment plans. Finally, there seemed to be a good match between the nature of motor travel and what was perceived to be the national character. The individualism and personal mobility that Americans always had valued had found a new means of expression, and a new "escape valve" had been discovered for the stresses of modern society, especially those resulting from urbanization.

The synergy between the car and traditional American values may also help to explain the incredible lack of restrictive governmental regulation of either motor travel or the automotive industry until the late 1960s. In fact, quite the reverse was true, as a series of laws and regulations aided the development of the automotive industry and subsidized the highways on which cars traveled.

In the beginning, car manufacturing was often simply an assembly operation. A wide variety of companies were able to produce automobiles as a sideline by combining key components (engines, chassis, carriage bodies, etc.) produced by others. It was frequently difficult to tell one make from another, and in some cases the name badge was the principal variation.

With time, motor cars became more differentiated from their predecessor (they were no longer "horseless carriages") and more specialized and individualized in their appearance and engineering. As a result, automotive manufacturing required more capital and technical expertise. With the greater financial investment and increasing consumer demand and expectancies regarding delivery, it became necessary to establish relationships that bound suppliers of raw materials and parts to those who were becoming true manufacturers of automobiles. In addition, to assure the most efficient and profitable sales of these vehicles, franchise systems of dedicated dealers were created on a nationwide basis.

As a result, the period 1908–1917 witnessed the first big shakeout in domestic automotive manufacturing. By the time of American entry into World War I, Henry Ford and his company had captured over 40% of the American market for new cars. Ford's primacy made it increasingly difficult for others to compete with him. While General Motors, with about one-fifth of the market, was financially healthy, by 1917 there were only 118 independent companies remaining, and a drift toward oligarchy in the industry was apparent.

Following World War I, both the joys and woes of owning an automobile became known to a wider spectrum of Americans. Although sudden death or permanent injury might lurk around the next curve, not to mention the emerging noise and pollution problems, Americans continued to respond positively to the car and the new lifestyle that accompanied it. In 1923 the Ford Model T Runabout was selling at an all-time low of $265. Four years later, more than half of American families owned cars. By the end of the 1920s, automotive manufacturing was the largest American industry, whether one measured it in terms of product value, number of employees, or amount of materials (raw and semifinished) consumed.

The seemingly insatiable demand for automobiles led to a number of industrial developments in the 1920s that were destined to determine the shape of the industry for decades to come. Unable to undersell Ford's Model T, General Motors (GM), under Alfred P. Sloan Jr.'s leadership, introduced a series of innovations calculated to increase its share of the market. To appeal to as broad a range of buyers as possible, GM created quasi-autonomous divisions, each specializing in car models for a particular income bracket. As a result, GM was able to offer a full line of cars designed, manufactured, and marketed under a single corporate strategy.

To attract buyers who had difficulty saving the money to purchase an automobile, GM offered and popularized (but did not originate) the installment or time payment plan through its GMAC subsidiary, thus both widening the market and introducing a new source of revenue for the manufacturer—interest from loans. By 1925 GM was selling 65% of its cars on time and was able to surpass Ford in sales four years later. In the latter part of the decade, GM introduced the concept of an "annual model," thereby making the introduction of technological and design innovations easier and the unchanging Model T increasingly obsolete. Much to his credit, Sloan realized that Americans were ready for something beyond a dependable, utilitarian machine. He understood the concept of conspicuous consumption, in which such factors as style, speed, power, comfort, and convenience played major roles.

Chrysler Corporation, itself a creation of the 1920s, followed GM's lead and prospered as well, although to a lesser extent. Even Henry Ford, with his notorious lack of sound accounting principles, could not fail to observe the slippage in his company's share of the market. In 1921 Ford sold 55% of the cars in the United States. By 1929 that figure had fallen to just 31%. Even the replacement of the Model T with the much more contemporary Model A could not reverse the company's fortunes, and by 1937 both GM and Chrysler were selling more cars than Ford.

As the automobile increasingly became part of the American way of life, it became an instrument of social change. For instance, family life was altered in a number of significant ways. Thus, the traditional family dinner and subsequent neighborhood stroll faced severe competition from "going for a spin" in the automobile. Furthermore, the latter activity did not always involve all members of the family, thus adding a divisive force not previously there. Similarly, the sanctity of the Sabbath and the attendant church events found themselves challenged by the idea of communing with nature by virtue of a Sunday drive.

Parents and the local community could no longer exert the same moral hold on its young people as they had in the past, since the car allowed the latter to escape the prying eyes of adults to whom they were known. Not only could the automobile offer swift transportation to a distant town or city, but it also could serve as a parlor or bedroom on wheels. The resulting revolution in social and sexual mores, while difficult to document, is almost impossible to refute. In fairness, the car could just as easily contribute to family bonding. For example, the after-meal and Sunday drives and the opportunity to visit more often with distant relatives could provide a new means for strengthening family unity. In this area, as well as others, the social consequences of the motor car were not foreordained but rather were the result of the sum total of millions of individual decisions.

In any case, the 1920s witnessed a homogenization of the population to an extent unknown before, as regional, sectional, and rural–urban differences were subordinated to a mass culture of which the automobile was an integral part. The car allowed city and country residents to share in the leisure-time opportunities available in each other's world and to participate in previously unheard of numbers. Entertainment and recreation based on mass participation, such as attendance at motion picture theaters and vacations at mountain and sea resorts, enjoyed significant growth. At the same time, individualized leisure pursuits such as fishing and hunting came within range for a broader portion of the population.

Major beneficiaries of this new means of motorized transportation were the women of America, especially those living in rural areas. With the advent of the mechanically reliable car, women had at their disposal a form of transportation with a measure of privacy, safety, and speed unmatched by any means of public transit. The automobile provided a means by which women could escape their homebound existence without neglecting their traditional domestic responsibilities. Their range of mobility began to approach that of men, and the sphere of their activities expanded accordingly. Thus, they were able to develop and take advantage of new employment opportunities outside the home, form geographically extensive social clubs for philanthropic or recreational pursuits, or just get away from the house or apartment for an hour or two of reflection, shopping, or culture.

Finally, the automobile itself was responsible for the introduction of a new form of entertainment—motor racing. As previously mentioned, road racing developed along with the car and remained popular until the demise of the Vanderbilt Cup in 1916. Much more important was the emergence of closed-circuit track racing. Whether on dirt, wooden boards, brick, or concrete, such racing was a significant addition to the panoply of professional sports available to Americans seeking amusement during the 1920s. Although the Indianapolis 500, which originated in 1911, was the most famous, thousands of lesser races were run everywhere, from small county fairgrounds, to big-city "velodromes."

At the same time that the motor car was instrumental in bringing about social change, it also was altering the American economic and physical landscape. The auto's ability to quickly traverse relatively great distances favored the expansion of town and city economic centers to the detriment of the neighborhood and village ones. While rural dwellers might bemoan the loss of the convenient crossroads establishments like the country store and village church, they welcomed the consolidated schools, the town hospitals, and generally the economies of scale that such centralization made possible.

This preference for accessibility and affordability influenced the evolution of roadside accommodations and restaurants. Motorists began to demand and expect the provision of roadside services that would cater to their needs. In some respects, this required only a modification of establishments that had served the horse-and-buggy trade. More often, it meant the introduction of new types of businesses. Thus, hotels began to give way to auto camps, tourist cabins, and eventually the modern "motel." (The introduction of that word in our vocabulary showed that not even the language would remain unaffected by the cultural revolution brought forth by the automobile.) Service stations, garages, auto parts stores, and other car-related business operations emerged.

By the 1920s, the "drive-in market" had made its appearance in California, and by the early 1930s drive-in restaurants and true suburban shopping centers had been built in Kansas City and Dallas. Increasingly, roadside establishments were specifically designed for the motorized customer. Thus, they were designed to be commercial islands in seas of parking, accessible by broad driveway tributaries. Unique building designs were introduced to catch the attention of the passing motorist, often mimicking in terms of design and materials the automobile itself.

Such architectural change was not limited to commercial structures. The mass acceptance of the automobile affected the design of private houses as well, leading to such developments as the "motorcentric" home and attached garages. At the same time, suburban developments were planned with the assumption that the car would be the major mode of transportation for their inhabitants. No longer was it necessary for one to live near where one worked or to depend on public transit. City dwellers in increasing numbers found that they could live outside urban areas and motor to work, thus helping to create America's vast and sprawling suburbs. Prior to the automobile, such "country life" was limited to communities adjacent to the rail and trolley lines emanating from the downtown area. Now, the vast areas between these lines could profitably be developed.

The older towns and cities, built to function in a horse-and-buggy era, found themselves faced with severe traffic congestion and parking problems. In response to these problems, the emerging new field of city planning recommended wider streets, narrower sidewalks, and longer blocks. But rather than solve the problems, these "solutions" only made matters worse. The broadened roads invited more traffic into the already congested central business district, while at the same time they erected barriers between neighborhoods or cut them into small pieces.

Despite the fact that the decade of the 1920s witnessed a mounting number of automotive fatalities, neither the general public nor the auto manufacturers seemed very concerned with safety. The American love affair with the car had begun in earnest, and there were too many related benefits to be very concerned with the possibility that one might be killed on the highway. So committed had Americans become to a motorized lifestyle that while in 1920 they still owned twice as many horses as automobiles, by 1930 the reverse was true.

Although the depression that began in 1929 brought the period of unbridled social and economic change to a close, the car remained an important part of American life during the 1930s. At one end of the economic spectrum, the car was often for the poor the last refuge against the elements—the possession that was never sold, best exemplified by the Joad family's behavior in John Steinbeck's 1939 novel *The Grapes of Wrath*.

The vast American middle class continued to set new records for motorized travel, as the automobile often provided the only means of recreation for them. However, vehicle registrations fell a bit, and new car purchases plummeted.

The lack of a middle-class market spelled the death knell for those "independent" car manufacturers that had built their businesses on such buyers in the 1920s. Production fell by 75% during the period 1929–1932, and the result was a further evolution toward oligarchy in the industry.

For the rich, a new era of American luxury cars was introduced with the appearance of the Cord, Duesenberg, and sixteen-cylinder Cadillac. Styling became increasingly important during the 1930s as manufacturers attempted to use yearly model changes, more powerful engines, and national ad campaigns to sell cars.

The 1930s was also a significant period in automotive history because it saw the first successful unionization of workers in the car industry. Aided by the passage of the National Labor Relations Act in 1935, the introduction of the tactic of the "sit-down" strike, and auto workers' unwillingness to buckle under to intimidation and violence, the United Automobile Workers (UAW) was able to unionize Chrysler and General Motors in 1937 and Ford in 1941. From that time forth, workers became an integral part of the automotive power structure.

The coming of the Second World War brought production of new cars to a standstill, as auto manufacturers retooled to produce airplane engines and military vehicles, something they had first done in 1917. Experiencing gasoline shortages for the first time, Americans now had to queue up to receive rationing stickers. "Is this trip necessary?" became the question of radio newscasters and politicians alike.

Following World War II, the pent-up demand for cars, when combined with postwar prosperity, led to record sales in the late 1940s and the decade of the 1950s. During the latter period, often termed the "golden age" of the American automobile, cars became longer, wider, heavier, and more powerful. By the mid-1950s, the average car weighed 4,000 pounds, was over six feet wide, and was eighteen feet long—providing ample opportunity for automotive design and styling to became more outlandish (witness the tail fin craze) and for available options to multiply to extreme. Horsepower ratings reached new highs for mass-produced automobiles, with figures in the 300-range not uncommon. These latter developments would lead to the so-called muscle cars of the late 1960s.

This fascination of the American public with cars per se also found new means of expression. The cars of yesteryear began reappearing on the nation's roads, having been reworked in various "customized" ways, "souped" up, and/or transformed into "hot rods" for use on "drag strips," with their youthful creators maintaining that the cars reflected their innermost personalities. The authentic restoration of old cars gained in popularity as a hobby, with devotees apparently oblivious to the costs, and organizations like the Antique Automobile Club of America established judging criteria for competitive meets.

Cars also became more numerous; by 1955 there were over 52 million on the road, with two-car families no longer viewed as unusual. Multi-lane freeways, turnpike toll roads, and interstates took the place of prewar, undivided highways, which now became relegated to secondary road status, the so-called blue highways featured in William Least Heat Moon's best-seller of the early 1980s. The passage of the Interstate Highway Act (1956) created the Highway Trust Fund, the proceeds of which were dedicated to funding 90% of the cost of the projected 41,000 miles of the new, mostly toll-free interstate highway system.

More cars and better roads led to significant demographic changes in the postwar period. They abetted the flight of the middle class from the cities to the suburbs, thereby seriously diminishing the tax base of the former and contributing to economic problems with which the United States is still wrestling. They also were a factor in the increasing residential segregation of the urban poor, especially African Americans, who for social and/or economic reasons could not move to the new middle- and upper-class suburban neighborhoods.

At the same time, these motorized suburbs were developing unique configurations of businesses. The emergence of commercial "strips," where commercial establishments of every sort were built along the roadside with little regard to planning or aesthetics, was a common phenomenon. Soon, where the population warranted it, such stores began to be clustered in shopping centers and malls, complementing and eventually surpassing the strips in economic importance.

Following the population to the suburbs, these shopping centers and malls frequently contained branches of the retail stores that had defined the city center and increasingly obviated the need for suburbanites to travel to the latter for personal shopping. As a result, in city after city, the downtown shopping area fell upon hard times.

As more and more retail stores and manufacturing plants moved to the suburbs, they increasingly brought with them the middle-class workers who could afford to move to the hinterland. Thus, social preferences and economic determinism combined to cause significant demographic changes.

The automobile was also responsible for the emergence of a range of enterprises that catered exclusively to the motorized customer. Although such establishments were sometimes found in urban areas, they were most common in suburban areas. Thus, the 1950s saw the full flowering of outdoor drive-in movie theaters, dubbed "passion pits" by their critics; drive-in restaurants, where car-bound customers were often served by waitresses on roller skates; drive-in churches; and even drive-in funeral parlors.

While America's so-called love affair with the car continued unabated into the early 1960s, by the middle of that decade some serious disenchantment with the automobile began to appear. Critics pointed to the car as a major contributor to environmental pollution, as fundamentally "unsafe at any speed," and as the instrument of 50 million unnecessary deaths and countless injuries each year. Unable to prod the car manufacturers into voluntary corrective action and finding itself the recipient of increasing public pressure, the federal government abandoned its previous laissez-faire attitude toward the automotive industry and its products. Congress began to regulate cars and, in a sense, dictate design, in the same manner as it had previously for other modes of transportation, leading to the passage of the Motor Vehicle Air Pollution Act of 1965 and the National Traffic and Motor Vehicle Safety Act of 1966.

Nonetheless, the 1960s saw a proliferation of car models and the introduction of a number of specialty automobiles, such as the only truly high-performance American sports car, the Chevrolet Corvette, and "personal cars," such as the Ford Mustang, which in size and styling looked like a sports car but lacked the power and handling of the real thing. The popularity of automobile racing as a spectator sport grew enormously, new forms emerged, and greater commercialization occurred as it became a multi-million-dollar entertainment industry. Aspects that had long been considered exclusively European in nature, most notably grand prix motor racing, began to achieve a level of acceptance that would make them important elements of American automobile culture in the years to come.

Seemingly forever seeking vehicular freedom, many Americans in the 1960s yearned to leave the restricted confines of the highway for "off-road" adventures. Jeeps enjoyed a renaissance; specially produced "recreation vehicles," or RVs as they soon began to be called, made their appearance and were commercially

xxvi INTRODUCTION

successful; and motorized camping gained in popularity to the extent that national and state parks were no longer able to effectively handle the demand.

At the same time, to counter a relatively successful early foreign invasion of the American car market that had begun in the mid-1950s and has never really ceased, the Big Three introduced so-called compact models. It was clear that a small, but significant, percentage of car buyers preferred these smaller, more maneuverable, and relatively inexpensive vehicles.

By the early 1970s cars were owned by 83% of American families, manufacturers could not keep up with demand, and the car's central place in American life seemed assured for the foreseeable future. However, before the end of the decade, Americans would be seriously questioning the role of the automobile (and its industry) in their lives and their dependence on it. The oil embargo of 1973–1974 forced them to face the prospect that fossil fuels might soon be depleted and the reality of gasoline prices that doubled before they leveled off. Americans witnessed the cost of new cars increase twofold and sometimes threefold, and buyers experienced what was dubbed "sticker shock." Moreover, the motor car continued to be cited as a major contributor to environmental pollution and urban congestion and decay. National leaders began to discuss severely restricting automobile use, mandating the replacement of the internal combustion engine with more ecologically acceptable alternatives, and even totally prohibiting car use in certain areas.

However, such stringent regulation and engineering innovations were never adopted. Oil "shortages" eased, and gasoline prices actually went down. Inflation moderated, and the price of new cars stabilized (though admittedly at the highest level ever). Federal and state emission control laws forced car manufacturers to produce less-polluting vehicles capable of better gasoline mileage. But most important of all, the American public made it very clear that it wanted to keep private automobiles and the lifestyle that they had helped create, irrespective of the social, economic, and political costs involved.

That commitment, however, did not necessarily entail an unswerving loyalty to American-made cars. Most of the domestically produced compacts of the early 1960s had evolved into conventionally sized and equipped vehicles by the end of the decade. Not surprisingly, import sales rose again. They had been better positioned than Detroit for the oil embargoes of the 1970s, which placed a premium on smaller, fuel-efficient vehicles. More importantly, the American public increasingly perceived the cars of Detroit as mechanically inferior to those imported from abroad. By the mid-1970s, Detroit's market share had fallen to less than 80%, and at least one of the Big Three—Chrysler—technically went bankrupt, surviving only with the assistance of a large loan from the federal government engineered by Chrysler's new president, Lee Iacocca.

The response of American car manufacturers to the import challenge, which by the 1980s had come to be seen as largely Japanese in nature, was to raise worker productivity at home, while depending more heavily on overseas subsidiaries for materials and parts. Of the two, the productivity emphasis proved to be the more troublesome. Growing worker alienation, which had begun to manifest itself in absenteeism and substance abuse, had led to significant quality control problems. At the same time, relatively high salaries and fringe benefit packages for which the UAW had fought over the years made American cars relatively expensive to produce even when they were qualitatively equal or superior to the imports.

The key question in the late 1980s for American manufacturers was whether they could find ways to produce a better vehicle at a cheaper price while satisfying worker demands. In response, techniques such as total quality management (TQM), where workers are involved in plant decision making, were adopted, and entire new divisions, such as General Motors' Saturn, were created to allow for a fresh start with the latest production techniques. It also became clear to Detroit that yearly styling changes were no longer enough to satisfy the contemporary car buyer. American automotive engineering had to match and surpass the post–World War II advances made in Europe and Asia.

The dependence on overseas suppliers for many of the car's components, including entire engines, meant that, in a sense, American companies had returned to their early roots, functioning essentially as assemblers, rather than manufacturers, of automobiles. As a result, it became increasingly difficult to determine exactly what constituted an "American" car. The situation became more complex when Japanese auto makers, such as Honda and Toyota, established manufacturing plants in the United States. As more than one observer noted, by the 1990s the industry as a whole seemed well on its way to becoming an international oligarchy producing a limited number of multinational or "world" cars, the exact origins of which were unknown to the average buyer.

Nonetheless, new manufacturing techniques and labor–management relationships increased productivity and led to a situation where American car companies began once again to match their foreign rivals in terms of quality. At the same time, worldwide economic developments led to a situation where the price of the Asian vehicles began to rise. Thus, by 1992 Ford Taurus had become the best-selling car in the United States, ending the three-year domination of the Honda Accord in that category. By the end of the century, American-badged automobiles were operating on a relatively even playing field with their overseas competitors.

The resurgence of the American automotive industry, when combined with the growing global manufacturing interdependence mentioned earlier, led to a spate of acquisitions and mergers such as would have been undreamed of a decade earlier. Thus, the Ford Motor Company purchased or gained controlling interest in such traditional giants as Britain's Jaguar and Sweden's Volvo, and Chrysler merged with Daimler-Benz of Germany to become DaimlerChrysler. What these developments would eventually mean to the worldwide industry and the American consumer was uncertain as the 21st century began.

What was clear by the year 2000 was that Americans were prepared to cast off their economically and ecologically determined preference for smaller cars, something that had dominated the last third of the century, and began to purchase larger cars in significant numbers once again. Aided by boom times within the American economy and the relative stability of gasoline prices, this reversal in consumer buying habits made itself known most visibly by the American response to the introduction of the "sport utility vehicle," or SUV. The latter owed its origins to the Jeep and earlier off-road vehicles, but, despite its appearance and alleged engineering capabilities, it was clearly meant to be a new form of passenger car for wealthy suburbanites, the logical successor to the station wagon and the minivan.

The purchase of SUVs and a higher demand for luxury cars were powered by the increasing use of the technique of leasing a vehicle as opposed to purchasing it outright or on time. Thus, millions of Americans came to "rent" new vehicles for periods of two or three years, paying a monthly fee no higher than the monthly payments they formerly had made on a new car in return for agreeing to have it serviced regularly. At the end of the lease, they returned the car to the dealer—often in exchange for a new one, and the cycle began anew. These previously leased cars, in turn, began to flood the used car market and change its very nature, as the quality of such vehicles began to be guaranteed in a manner never true before.

The growth in the sales of SUVs and luxury cars, vehicles with low miles-per-gallon (mpg) figures, was partially dependent on the availability of gasoline and the relative stability (and occasional declines) in its price. However, Americans had never really lessened their reliance on foreign oil; indeed, it had increased by the end of the century to a level higher than in the 1970s, making the car industry and the American economy in general increasingly dependent on the whims of the oil-exporting nations and the latter's ability to act in concert through such organizations as the Organization of Petroleum Exporting Countries (OPEC).

While the fragility of oil imports had led General Motors to gamble on the introduction of a production electric passenger car in the late 1990s, its cost and limited range led to meager sales beyond those mandated for state vehicles in the West. More promising were signs that several Japanese manufacturers would market so-called hybrid autos early in the new century—cars that combined electric propulsion with the standard internal combustion engine, thus reducing dependence on gasoline.

PART I

General Industrial Histories
and Biographies

CHAPTER 1

Histories of the Automobile
and Automotive Manufacturing

GENERAL HISTORIES

Histories of specific automotive companies, biographies of the people involved
in their development, and popular accounts of the car's impact on American life
were common by the 1920s. However, it was not until 1965, with the publication
of John B. Rae's *The American Automobile: A Brief History*, that there appears
a *scholarly* treatment that combines in a single volume an analysis of the social,
economic, and political dimensions of this subject. Rae's work opened up the
field to serious study, and the next fifteen years saw the publication of several
important works of interest to serious historians, beginning with James J. Flink's
America Adopts the Automobile, 1895–1910, which explores how the introduction and growth of the automobile industry altered the socioeconomic milieu of
the time. Flink's book was followed by Rae's *The Road and Car in American
Life*, probably the best account of how the interplay between automobiles and
highways had influenced the economic and social lives of urban, suburban, and
rural Americans through the 1960s and, as such, is essentially optimistic about
the car's impact. A counterpoint to this Rae volume is a second, even more
influential book by Flink, entitled *The Car Culture*, which presents a brilliant,
though decidedly critical, three-stage (1896–1910, 1910–1950, 1950–1975) historical synthesis of the automobile's influence on American history and life.
Flink concludes with the revisionist view that the automobile is now (1975)
viewed as a social problem, whereas in the middle period it was idolized and
became the center of a consumption economy.

Predating the second Flink volume and in some respects as significant as
Rae's initial book was Reynold W. Wik's *Henry Ford and Grass-roots America*,
the first scholarly study of the automobile's socioeconomic impact on a specific

subgroup of Americans—rural residents. Wik's volume was followed by the end of the decade by Michael L. Berger's *The Devil Wagon in God's Country: The Automobile and Social Change in Rural America, 1893–1929* and Howard L. Preston's *Automobile Age Atlanta: The Making of a Southern Metropolis, 1900–1935.* Both of these volumes are described in more detail elsewhere in this chapter.

The scholarly movement that Rae set in motion in 1965 with his "brief history" reached a type of fruition with the publication of James Flink's *The Automobile Age* in 1988. Hailed by reviewers as a definitive treatment of the subject, Professor Flink's book is a comprehensive history that masterfully combines analysis of both industrial developments and societal impacts. While Flink's emphasis is on the American experience, he does a fine job of placing it in worldwide perspective. *The Automobile Age* should be the starting point for most serious students of the subject.

As noted, Flink's work represents a maturation of the field of automotive history. The next decade was to see a further flowering of the genre. In 1990 there appeared Peter J. Ling's *America and the Automobile: Technology, Reform and Social Change,* which, like Flink's initial 1970 book, analyzed the automobile in the context of the Progressive Era (defined as the years 1893–1923), paying special attention to the practical, daily applications that private citizens found for their cars. Separate chapters treat the impact of the automobile on rural America, the creation of an interstate highway system, and the evolution of the suburbs, among other topics. Ling concludes that it was not the auto that changed life in the United States, but rather our capitalistic economic system.

In 1977 and 1983 two pioneering collections of essays were published that helped define the field and identify potentially rich areas for future sociocultural research. These volumes are *Automobiles in American Life,* edited by Charles L. Sanford, and *The Automobile and American Culture,* edited by David L. Lewis and Laurence Goldstein. Both are wide-ranging books, particularly noteworthy for their investigation of a number of social issues ignored or casually treated by previous histories. Of the two, Sanford's is the more traditional, with primary emphasis on the human dimensions of economic issues. Nonetheless, most of the readings wrestle with the question of social costs and benefits, with topics as diverse as the assembly line, automotive design, and possible motorized replacements for the car.

The more recent Lewis and Goldstein volume was an innovative one in that it was the first to include scholarly research exploring the car's influence on the cultural mainstream. Thus, essays are included that analyze that influence on art, music, film, literature, and poetry. In addition, such social concerns as sex, the status of women and teenagers, and the symbolic dimensions of the automobile are treated. It was also one of the first collections to include fictional treatments of the motor car.

Somewhat similar efforts have been the result of decisions by scholarly journals to devote an issue to the theme of the automobile. Included in this category would be the November 1924 issue (Vol. 116) of *The Annals of the American Academy of Political and Social Science*, entitled "The Automobile: Its Province and Its Problems," edited by Clyde L. King, whose chapters describing the impact of the automobile on the American way of life in the early 1920s become more valuable with time; the summer 1974 issue (Vol. 8, No. 1) of the *Journal of Popular Culture*, which contains a sixty-three-page thematic section entitled "Automobiles," edited by David J. Neuman; the combined fall 1980/winter 1981 number (Vol. 19, No. 4/Vol. 20, No. 1) of the *Michigan Quarterly Review*, a 350-page issue entitled "The Automobile and American Culture," which subsequently was republished, with a few new essays added, as the Lewis and Goldstein volume cited above; and "The Automobile in America," a special thematic section in the winter 1986 issue of the *Wilson Quarterly*. Individual articles from all four collections are cited in the appropriate chapter(s) of this guide.

Finally, some mention needs to be made of the pioneering sociological works of Robert S. Lynd and Helen M. Lynd: *Middletown: A Study in Contemporary American Culture* (1929) and *Middletown in Transition: A Study in Cultural Conflicts* (1937), both of which analyze the automobile's impact on the community of Muncie, Indiana.

Popular, as opposed to scholarly, histories of the automobile began appearing as early as 1900 with Gardner D. Hiscox's *Horseless Vehicles, Automobiles, Motorcycles: Operated by Steam, Hydro-Carbon, Electric and Pneumatic Motors*, followed in 1905 by Robert T. Sloss' *The Book of the Automobile: A Practical Volume Devoted to the History, Construction, Use and Care of Motor Cars and to the Subject of Motoring in America*, and contine to the present. Listed alphabetically by author, some of the pre-1970 works that contain significant amounts of socioeconomic information are Rudolph E. Anderson's *The Story of the American Automobile: Highlights and Sidelights*; Reginald M. Cleveland and S.T. Williamson's *The Road Is Yours: The Story of the Automobile and the Men behind It*; David L. Cohn's *Combustion on Wheels: An Informal History of the Automobile Age*; Frank Donovan's *Wheels for a Nation*; C.B. Glasscock's *The Gasoline Age: The Story of the Men Who Made It*; Frank E. Hill's *The Automobile: How It Came, Grew, and Has Changed Our Lives*; Hiram P. Maxim's *Horseless Carriage Days*; M.M. Musselman's *Get a Horse!: The Story of the Automobile in America*; and a pamphlet by Franklin M. Reck, *A Car Traveling People: How the Automobile Has Changed the Life of Americans—A Study of Social Effects*, published by the Automobile Manufacturer's Association and espousing an incredibly positive view of developments. Of these books, the Cohn and Donovan volumes will probably prove most valuable to the social or cultural historian, although the Cleveland and Williamson volume is good popular history as well.

Popular histories continued to be published in the 1970s, 1980s, and 1990s benefiting from the concurrent scholarly research and evidencing much more concern with sociocultural questions than their predecessors. Among the more notable works have been *Behind the Wheel: The Magic and Manners of Early Motoring*, by Lord Montagu of Beaulieu and F. Wilson McComb; *Early Days on the Road: An Illustrated History, 1819–1941*, another book by Lord Montagu, with G.N. Georgano as the coauthor, which devotes approximately half its pages to the worldwide evolution of the passenger car; and *100 Years on the Road: A Social History of the Car*, by Raymond Flower and Michael W. Jones. All three of these books deliver what they promise, although with a heavily European emphasis. A recent contribution to this genre is *Driving Passion: The Psychology of the Car*, the work of two British psychologists, Peter Marsh and Peter Collett. It is one of the first book-length works to concentrate exclusively on the psychological satisfactions associated with car ownership and driving.

More specifically American in focus are Walter J. Boyne's *Power behind the Wheel: Creativity and the Evolution of the Automobile*, possibly the best written of the recent popular histories (a Literary Guild selection), certainly one of the better-illustrated ones, and stronger on the history of design and technology than on social impacts; Derek Jewell's *Man and Motor: The 20th Century Love Affair*, which attempts to show how our infatuation with the car has influenced every aspect of our lives, from literature to engineering; Leon Mandel's *Driven: The American Four-Wheeled Love Affair*, in which the author applies his version of social psychology to analyze what he sees as the multivariate impact of the car; Julian Pettifer and Nigel Turner's *Automania: Man and the Motor Car*, an international overview of the auto's influence on several areas usually ignored in such volumes (e.g., courtship, music, movies, death, and third world nations); and Stephen W. Sears' *The American Heritage History of the Automobile in America*, a lavishly produced and extremely well illustrated volume and winner of the Thomas McKean Award and judged by many to be the premier enthusiast overview available. Frank Oppel's *Motoring in America: The Early Years* is a wonderful collection of magazine articles from 1900 to 1910 that explore how the public reacted to the automobile as it began to impact on their daily lives, to the technological innovations, and to motor races and recreational touring, among other things. The most recent work in this genre is Nick Georgano's *The American Automobile: A Centenary, 1893–1993*, a grand, heavily illustrated survey of major industrial and technological developments, plus important figures, in the automobile's evolution. It won the Society of Automotive Historians' 1992 Cugnot Award for the best book in the field of automotive history.

The years of pioneer motoring were memorable events for the participants, and the result has been a considerable number of personal accounts and reminiscences, though of varying quality. Some of the better works in this genre, listed alphabetically by author, are Harold B. Chase's *Auto-biography: Recollections of a Pioneer Motorist, 1896–1911; Two Thousand Miles on an Automobile: Being a Desultory Narrative of a Trip through New England, New York, Canada and the West*, a 1902 volume by the anonymous "Chauffeur"; Stanley W. Ellis' *Smogless Days: Adventures in Ten Stanley Steamers*; William B. Gross' *From San Diego, California to Washington, D.C.: Being a Descriptive*

Account of the First Official Trip by Automobile over the Southern National Highway; Walter H. James' *Joys and Sorrows of an Automobilist*, in which a college professor relates his 1918 transition from horse-drawn to motorized transportation; Eugene W. Lewis' *Motor Memories: A Saga of Whirling Gears*, the autobiography of an early car parts salesman and a participant in the initial launching of the Hudson; Stephen Longstreet's *The Boy in the Model T: A Journey in the Just Gone Past*, childhood recollections by the author of an earlier official history of the Studebaker Corporation; Bellamy Partridge's *Fill 'er Up!: The Story of Fifty Years of Motoring*, which concentrates on the author's adventures in a small New York town and on a 1912 cross-country trip; Alice Huyler Ramsey's *Veil, Duster, and Tire Iron*, remembrances by the first woman to successfully drive coast to coast; and C.G. Sinsabaugh's *Who, Me?: Forty Years of Automobile History*, by a man who spent most of his working life as editor of various automotive magazines. (Personal accounts of early motor touring undertaken as a recreational pursuit are found in Chapter 8.)

Not surprisingly, auto manufacturers soon realized the public relations value of associating their marque(s) with one of these early exploits—provided it was successful. (They attempted to make use of early motor racing in much the same manner.) Using incredibly descriptive (and heavy-handed) titles, which were not totally untypical of the era in general, the companies gladly published these accounts themselves. Two instances of such merchandising would be the publication in 1908 by the Packard Motor Car Company of Jacob M. Murdock's *A Family Tour from Ocean to Ocean: Being an Account of the First Amateur Motor Car Journey from the Pacific to the Atlantic, Whereby J.M. Murdock and Family, in Their 1908 Packard "Thirty" Touring Car, Incidentally Broke the Transcontinental Record* and *5000 Miles Overland, Wonderful Performance of a Wonderful Car, The Story of Miss Scott's Journey Overland*, published in 1910 by—not surprisingly—the Overland Automobile Company and purporting to be the first such trip by a woman driving alone.

For some, motoring remained an adventure (and an opportunity for publication) through the 1920s and into the early 1930s, as witnessed by John T. Faris' *Roaming American Highways*, the story of a transcontinental motor trip at the close of the decade, and Lewis S. Gannett's *Sweet Land*, a collection of essays and observations based on a journey of over 8,600 miles. There also are a number of good, secondary accounts of early historic trips, such as Ralph N. Hill's *The Mad Doctor's Drive: Being an Account of the 1st Auto Trip across the United States of America, San Francisco to New York, 1903, or, Sixty-Three Days on a Winton Motor Carriage*.

Historic and nostalgic interest in the pre-depression era of motoring has led to the publication of a number of loosely organized collections of photographs, advertisements, "trivia" lists, and short narratives. While the absence of footnotes and other trappings of research can make such volumes frustrating for the scholar, those willing to "read" the photographs and analyze the narrative will often find valuable information. Some of the better works in this genre are two books by Floyd Clymer, *Those Wonderful Old Automobiles* and the *Treasury of Early American Automobiles, 1877–1925*; Robert F. Karolevitz' *This Was Pioneer Motoring: An Album of Nostalgic Automobilia!*; and Philip Van Doren Stern's *A Pictorial History of the Automobile: As Seen in Motor Magazine, 1903–1953*.

During this early period of American automotive history, one vehicle became so dominant that it almost became synonymous for motoring during these years. That vehicle was the Model T Ford, of which over 15 million were produced between 1908 and 1927. The most scholarly book devoted exclusively to the Model T is Philip Van Doren Stern's *Tin Lizzie: The Story of the Fabulous Model T Ford*. Although relatively brief (180 pages), this volume does a fine job of presenting the essential facts *and* capturing the flavor of what the "T" meant to America for almost two decades, including period photographs and original drawings by Charles Harper. There also are a number of well-researched and heavily illustrated popular histories. Probably the best of this genre is Bruce W. McCalley's *Model T Ford: The Car That Changed the World*, a veritable visual and technical encyclopedia of information and winner of the Antique Automobile Club of America's 1994 Thomas McKean Memorial Cup. Ray Miller and Bruce McCalley's earlier *From Here to Obscurity: A Look at the Changes in an Unchanging Car, 1909–1927* also is very good. Although best classified as a nostalgic coffee-table book, Floyd Clymer's *Henry's Wonderful Model T, 1908–1927* is, nonetheless, full of factual information as well as excellent photographs and early advertisements. In the same vein is his earlier *Floyd Clymer's Historical Motor Scrapbook: Ford Model T Edition* and *Floyd Clymer's Model T Memories: Including the Ubiquitous Model T, by Les Henry*. Both contain Clymer's reminiscences of his experiences with that car, and the latter volume reprints Leslie Henry's well-known "Ubiquitous" essay as well. Joseph Floyd Clymer devoted most of his life to the automobile, and he could be viewed as one of its first historians.

The Model T was really more than a car; it was a true legend that directly touched the lives of millions of Americans for over two decades. Thus, it is not surprising that the demise of the Tin Lizzie brought forth an outpouring of eulogies, in much the same way that the death of a good friend would. Preeminent among such statements was *Farewell to the Model T*, by E.B. White and Richard L. Strout, writing under the pseudonym Lee Strout White. "Obituaries" were published in almost all of the national periodicals and major newspapers, including *The New Yorker* and *The New York Times Magazine*.

Although Americans have not always acknowledged it, the socioeconomic impact of the automobile as a vehicle is inseparable from the roads that it traverses. The first scholarly road conference held after World War II recognized this fact, as can be seen throughout its published proceedings, *Highways in Our National Life: A Symposium*, edited by Jean Labatut and Wheaton J. Lane. Lewis Mumford in *The Highway and the City* and John B. Rae in the previously mentioned *The Road and the Car in American Life* start from the same premise but reach very different conclusions regarding the benefits (Rae) and drawbacks (Mumford) of highway development. A less scholarly, though nonetheless valuable, work is Christy Borth's *Mankind on the Move: The Story of Highways*, with its dual emphasis on both the construction (men and methods) and consequences of American road building.

More recently, there has been renewed interest in this topic. Phil Patton's *Open Road: A Celebration of the American Highway* is a historical overview of the entire subject, with considerable attention to how the American lifestyle was changed by the growth of the interstate system. In a more popular vein, but still worthwhile, is *Automerica: A Trip Down U.S. Highways from World War II to the Future*, by the Ant Farm Design Group, an eclectic combination of nostalgia and insightful contemporary observations. For a more detailed discussion of the multiple impacts of roads and highways on American life, see the relevant sections of Chapters 8, 10, and 11 in this guide.

REGIONAL, LOCAL, AND STATE HISTORIES

Since automotive history is a relatively new scholarly subdiscipline, the work that has been done to date has been primarily national in focus. Nonetheless, a growing number of pioneering books investigate the impact of the automobile on American local history and life through World War II. Studies of the "contemporary" postwar period, especially those that concentrate on demographic changes and city planning, are covered in Chapter 6; and those that concern state and regional transportation issues, in Chapter 10.

When one considers the social and economic impact of the automobile in the years before the depression, the regions most affected were the rural, not the urban or suburban, ones. In the study of these regions one finds some of the best historical monographs concerning the motorization of the United States. The pioneering work in this regard was Norman T. Moline's *Mobility and the Small Town, 1900–1930: Transportation Change in Oregon, Illinois*, published in 1971 as a University of Chicago geographical research paper. Moline's work is one of those little gems that appear without fanfare but earn themselves a permanent place in historical literature by the nature and quality of their presentation. It is particularly valuable in terms of its discussion of the automotively induced emergence of new travel patterns and concepts of time and distance. Moline's study was followed by Reynold W. Wik's broader *Henry Ford and Grass-roots America*, with its insightful observations regarding rural responses to both Ford's inventions and his ideas. A "cousin" of the Wik book is Michael L. Berger's later *The Devil Wagon in God's Country: The Automobile and Social Change in Rural America, 1893–1929*. Berger's focus is on the modifications in such social institutions as the family, the school, and the church among farmers and residents of small towns. In this regard, his work was pathbreaking, and these topics are deserving of further study. Finally, John A. Jakle's *The American Small Town: Twentieth-Century Place Images* shows how perceptions of varying social and economic aspects of the small town were modified as the major mode of transportation changed from the railroad to the motor car. With the exception of Moline, there are few significant case studies of the automobile's influence on specific rural towns or localities. The size and relative insignificance of an individual small town have worked against entire books being devoted to the car's influence on life in a specific locality. Those studies that exist are relatively brief periodical accounts.

The first historical survey devoted exclusively to the impact of the car on urban America did not appear until 1979. Howard L. Preston's *Automobile Age Atlanta: The Making of a Southern Metropolis, 1900–1935* was a pioneering volume at the time and still deserves reading for its insightful analysis of how the car influenced the growth and planning of one of the nation's premier southern metropolitan areas. In 1986 David J. St. Clair's *The Motorization of American Cities* marked the first publication of a study that was national in scope. While qualitatively excellent, St. Clair's small volume is unfortunately limited to a discussion of the auto industry's attempts to create an economic and political environment in which personal transportation would triumph over mass transit. Building upon his doctoral work, Clay McShane's excellent *Down the Asphalt Path: The Automobile and the American City* explores the multifaceted relationship between the car and urbanization prior to World War I, with special attention to how the concept and physical design of the American city were changed. For a brief, though scholarly, overview of the car's impact on one region of the United States, see David R. Goldfield and Blaine A. Brownell's "The Automobile and the City in the American South," in *The Economic and Social Effects of the Spread of Motor Vehicles*, edited by Theo Barker.

Of all the American cities, most scholars would agree that Los Angeles, for better or worse, has been the one whose physical development has been most affected by the motor car. Not surprisingly, studies of that city are plentiful. An excellent general introduction to the history of the city and its transportation is Robert M. Fogelson's *The Fragmented Metropolis: Los Angeles, 1850–1930*. More specific is Scott L. Bottles' *The Making of the Modern City: Los Angeles and the Automobile, 1900–1950*, with its "pro-auto" explanation of why the car replaced public transit as the chief means of personal transportation and its analysis of the spatial reorganization of the city that was the result. Finally, worthy of examination, if only for its renowned author, is the chapter on Los Angeles in Sam Bass Warner Jr.'s *The Urban Wilderness: A History of the American City*.

Like Los Angeles, Detroit found itself transformed by the automobile. But in the latter, the changes had more of an effect on the nature of the city than on its physical appearance. Although it was not inevitable, metropolitan Detroit soon became the base for the Big Three auto makers. The best historical overview of how that happened is Robert G. Szudarek's *How Detroit Became the Automotive Capital: 100th Anniversary*, in which the author uses historical profiles of over 125 companies to explain the evolution of the automobile industry in Michigan. Arthur Pound's *The Automobile and an American City* further develops some of the points made in his earlier, more general histories of Detroit but focuses more exclusively on the car's impact on the development of that city. Finally, Norman Beasley's *Made in Detroit* offers a history of cars made in that city through the mid-1950s.

To a lesser extent, the city of Flint, Michigan, experienced many of the same developments as Detroit. Home of the Buick Motor Company since 1903, the histories of Flint and that car manufacturer have been inseparably intertwined. For the story of both through World War II, see Carl Crow's *The City of Flint Grows Up*. Approximately a decade later, George H. Maines' *Men, a City, and a Buick* appeared. Neither is a particularly scholarly work.

Other major cities have been the subject of more general studies regarding the social and economic impact of the automobile. Howard Preston's *Automobile Age Atlanta* already has been mentioned. Also worthy of examination is *Four Wheels—No Brakes: A History of Automobiles in St. Louis and the Part that City Has Taken in the Development of the Automobile*, a collection of eighty-six essays on the automobile industry in St. Louis first published in 1930 by the St. Louis Society Automotive Pioneers. In addition to essays on individual makes and "one-off" vehicles, this 320-page volume also has essays on dealers, motoring organizations, and competitive events. Joel A. Tarr's *Transportation Innovation and Changing Spatial Patterns in Pittsburgh, 1850–1934*, a pamphlet in the Essays in Public Works History series, examines first the streetcar's, and then the automobile's, effect on population distribution, journey-to-work patterns, and the growth of the central business district, including building development, industrial location, and traffic patterns.

Curiously, there is no book-length work devoted exclusively to the history of the automobile's impact on suburban America. For studies of the phenomenon of suburbanization, which necessarily discuss the role of the car, see Chapter 6.

Finally, a few works attempt to study the impact of the car or automotive manufacturing on a statewide level. Most of these are periodical accounts, but see Horace J. Cranmer's *New Jersey in the Automobile Age: A History of Transportation* for an example of a book-length treatment.

HISTORIES OF THE AUTOMOTIVE INDUSTRY

This section is concerned with studies that investigate the development of the automotive industry per se, including changes in its structure and organization over time. Treated elsewhere in more detail are three related topics: labor–management relations (Chapter 3), domestic and foreign sales competition (Chapter 3), and government regulation (Chapter 10).

An aphorism usually attributed to former General Motors President Charles E. Wilson states that "What's good for GM is good for the nation." While that statement's veracity is open to question, the implication that the health of the American economy is highly dependent on the automobile industry is not.

Therefore, the organization, structure, and functioning of that industry have been subjected to careful scrutiny from its earliest years. Shortly after consumer demand brought forth mass production, there was the 1916 publication of *The Romance of the Automobile Industry*, edited by James R. Doolittle. Doolittle was followed a year later by Herbert L. Barber's *Story of the Automobile: Its History and Development from 1760 to 1917, with an Analysis of the Standing and Prospects of the Automobile Industry*. Leonard P. Ayres' *The Automobile Industry and Its Future* appeared in 1921. Premature as all three were from a scholarly perspective, the Doolittle, Barber, and Ayres volumes signaled the importance of this new 20th-century industry.

The 1920s is often viewed as the final decade of the pioneering period, the time when independent manufacturers could still easily launch successful new cars and companies. It is also the decade during which mass ownership of automobiles became a reality. Thus, it is not surprising that when the University of Michigan inaugurated its Michigan Business Studies series in 1926, it chose Clare E. Griffin's pathbreaking *The Life History of Automobiles* to be the first volume. Another excellent contemporary study from this period, published in 1928, is Ralph C. Epstein's *The Automobile Industry: Its Economic and Commercial Development*, an important enough volume that it was considered "well worth reading" by John B. Rae in the mid-1960s and was reprinted in 1972. Also good are Lawrence H. Seltzer's *A Financial History of the American Automobile Industry* (1928) and Theodore F. MacManus and Norman Beasley's 1929 *Men, Money, and Motors: The Drama of the Automobile* (1929).

Noteworthy in terms of its being another indicator of the recognition of the importance of the automobile in American life was the 1923 publication by *National Geographic* of William J. Showalter's seventy-four-page article entitled "The Automobile Industry: An American Art That Has Revolutionized Methods in Manufacturing and Transformed Transportation."

By this time, it also had become clear that the center of the automotive industry would be in Detroit and its suburbs. In the beginning, manufacturing plants seemed to sprout (and wither) almost everywhere. By 1910, however, Detroit had established its preeminence for reasons well described in George S. May's incredibly detailed *A Most Unique Machine: The Michigan Origins of the American Automobile Industry*, the classic work on this subject. Similar in concept is James P. Edmonds' much earlier (1942) *Development of the Automobile and Gasoline Engine in Michigan*.

Although Detroit is often used as a synonym for car manufacturing in the United States, other cities, regions, and states were the home for individual auto companies and clusters of them, at least until 1950. Books and pamphlets exploring this phenomenon for a particular area include (listed alphabetically by author) James F. Bellamy's *Cars Made in Upstate New York*, a survey of over 200 makes manufactured in that state through 1938; Richard A. and Nancy L. Fraser's *A History of Maine Built Automobiles*; Wallace S. Huffman *et al.*, *Indiana Built Automobiles*, a thirty-two-page pamphlet consisting largely of motor vehicle lists, ads, and photographs that the Huffmans have compiled; Robert E. Ireland's *Entering the Auto Age: The Early Automobile in North Carolina, 1900–1930*, an interesting account of the unique challenges faced by automotive entrepreneurs in the South, with special attention to the Anderson Motor Company; Curt McConnell's *Great Cars of the Great Plains*, a well-written, detailed, nicely illustrated history of five midwestern car companies (Great Smith, Luverne, Patriot, Spaulding, and Moon) and the communities where they were manufactured during the first three decades of the automotive industry, winner of the AACA's 1995 McKean Cup for excellence in automotive research; *Wisconsin Cars and Trucks: A Centenary*, edited by Val Quant, an exhaustive treatment of motor vehicles manufactured in that state (including American Motors/ Chrysler, Nash, Kissel, and Case), together with chapters on component manufacturers and Wisconsin license plates; Rector R. Seal's *Maryland Automobile History, 1900 to 1942*, a nicely illustrated volume that briefly describes twenty-four manufacturers and eight Baltimore automobile shows and lists Baltimore automobile dealers; Hayden Shepley's *Automobiles Built in Essex County, Mass.*, a brief (62-page) history of sixty automotive companies and individuals who built cars in that Massachusetts county from 1866 through 1976; the St. Louis Society Automotive Pioneers' *Four Wheels—No Brakes*, a collection of eighty-six essays on the automotive industry in St. Louis first published in 1930 (this 320-page volume also has essays on dealerships and motoring associations); and Richard Wager's *Golden Wheels: The Story of the Automobiles Made in Cleveland and Northeastern Ohio, 1892–1932*, a publication of the Western Reserve Historical Society that chronicles well with an informative text and accompanying pictures the 118 makes produced in a region that once rivaled Detroit in this regard.

In addition, the Big Three Detroit companies established component manufacturing and complete assembly plants for particular models at other locations in the United States. For example, there was a General Motors facility in North Tarrytown, New York, for the better part of the 20th century. These plants often carried with them significant economic benefits for the community in which they were located, and thus there was intense competition among areas to attract and retain such industry. This competition was intensified in the 1980s and 1990s, when Japanese and European car companies established assembly facilities in the United States at a time of international corporate flight. An excellent collection of essays, *The Politics of Industrial Recruitment: Japanese Automobile Investment and Economic Development in the American States*, edited by Ernest J. Yanarella and William C. Green, explores the phenomenon of foreign industrial recruitment and its consequences for six states in the Midwest.

Initially preeminent among the Detroit manufacturers was the Ford Motor Company. However, neither Ford nor its later giant competitors probably would have succeeded to the degree that they did had they been required to pay royalties to George B. Selden, who claimed exclusive patents on certain key elements of the automobile. That this did not happen is largely due to legal actions led by Henry Ford against Selden. The fascinating story of this prerequisite for later industrial development is well told in William Greenleaf's *Monopoly on Wheels: Henry Ford and the Selden Automobile Patent Suit*, which is an analysis of the history of the legal maneuvers that finally made the automobile common property. James J. Flink calls Greenleaf's work "the most complete and scholarly study of the Selden patent controversy."

Due to the economic depression, the 1930s was not a particularly productive period either for the industry or for historians concerned with it. The most significant exception to this observation was John W. Scoville's heavily statistical and meritorious *Behavior of the Automobile Industry in Depression*, published in 1936.

During the 1930s the number of firms producing cars dropped precipitously. Nonetheless, the fact that so many companies survived and, indeed, prospered, indicated both the strength of the industry and its promise for the future. In this regard, Edward D. Kennedy's classic 1941 book, *The Automobile Industry: The Coming of Age of Capitalism's Favorite Child*, is still worth reading. Rich in anecdotes, it remained the standard work well into the 1950s—and some would say until the 1960s and 1970s writings of John Rae and James Flink. Three other roughly contemporaneous studies are C.B. Glasscock's *The Gasoline Age: The Story of the Men Who Made It* (1937), a solid history of the industry that emphasizes the individuals involved; Andrew T. Court's *Men, Methods and Machines in Automobile Manufacturing* (1939), which includes a discussion of labor–management relations then, written from the manufacturer's perspective; and the U.S. Federal Trade Commission's *Report on Motor Vehicle Industry* (1939), which is a government study of auto company management occasioned by dealer complaints in the 1930s.

Several more recent studies examine this same pre-1950 economic growth of the automobile industry from a historical perspective. The best of this group is Donald F. Davis' *Conspicuous Production: Automobiles and Elites in Detroit, 1899–1933*. Davis argues convincingly that members of that city's economic and political elite, for nearsighted social reasons, invested primarily in companies producing luxury (as opposed to mass-market) cars, decisions that eventually hurt their status when such vehicles proved to be economically less successful.

The 1950s are seen by many as the "golden age" of the automobile in America, with absolute and per capita car sales hitting new heights, styling on a rampage, and the auto becoming a part of *every* aspect of American life, with drive-in restaurants, movies, churches, and funeral parlors. Not surprisingly, these developments brought forth a new wave of interest in the history of the car and the automotive industry during their first half-century. The most significant of the earliest of these general studies was John B. Rae's *American Automobile Manufacturers: The First Forty Years*, an excellent historical account of the importance of leadership in the industry from 1895 to 1935. Also worth investigating from this same period is Merrill Denison's *The Power to Go: The*

Story of the Automotive Industry which, while uneven in quality, is still the source of much valuable information. Richard Crabb's *Birth of a Giant: The Men and Incidents That Gave America the Motorcar* also is recommended. Despite its somewhat misleading title, Crabb's book is a late 1960s history of the automobile industry that won the AACA's McKean Cup. Less impressive is Philip H. Smith's *Wheels within Wheels: A Short History of American Motor Car Manufacturing*, with its emphases on the technical, economic, and political.

The post–World War II period also marks the beginning of a series of studies that attempt to analyze the hierarchical organization and managerial techniques that have been and are being applied in the automotive industry. Christy Borth's *Masters of Mass Production* explores organizational innovations in the automotive industry and the people responsible for them. Peter F. Drucker analyzes how the corporation evolved, with special attention to the automobile industry, in *The Concept of Corporation*. (The same author's *Innovation and Entrepreneurship*, with its automotive examples, is pertinent here as well.)

Other excellent studies—drawn from the 1960s and 1970s—are *Giant Enterprise: Ford, General Motors, and the Automobile Industry*, by Alfred D. Chandler Jr., a successful blend of original source material and editorial comment concerning the contributions of technology, market demand, management, and labor in the history of industrial growth; Charles E. Edwards' *Dynamics of the United States Automobile Industry*, with its emphasis on the sales, engineering, and production problems of the decade following World War II and special attention to the American Motors and Studebaker–Packard mergers; and Lawrence J. White's *The Automobile Industry since 1945*, a pioneering 1971 critique that accuses car manufacturers of collusion and excess profit taking while at the same time ignoring operational efficiency, technological improvements, and questions regarding car safety and air pollution. Much the same criticisms were still being leveled a decade later by Brock Yates in his more popular (in more ways than one) *The Decline and Fall of the American Automobile Industry*. Of lesser value, but nonetheless worthwhile, is John B. Schnapp's textlike *Corporate Strategies of the Automotive Manufacturers*.

The year 1996 marked the 100th anniversary of the American automobile industry, as measured from the incorporation of the Duryea Motor Wagon Company, the first automotive manufacturer in the United States to produce and sell multiple (six) copies of the same motorized vehicle. By the mid-1990s, the automobile had become less controversial than it was a decade or two earlier and, thus, this centennial was celebrated with the publication of a number of books that pay tribute to the accomplishments of the industry. Among those works, Frank Coffey and Joseph Layden's *America on Wheels: The First Hundred Years, 1896–1996* clearly is the best. A companion volume to the Public Broadcasting System (PBS) special of the same name, it offers a detailed, authoritative account, backed by archival photographs, original documents, and insightful observations by pioneers and current leaders of the automotive industry. More in the enthusiast vein is *Wheels in Motion: The American Auto-*

mobile Industry's First Century by Gerald Perschbacher, a heavy illustrated volume that pays due attention to both the people and the technology that created a manufacturing giant that came to dominate the American economy. Finally, it should be noted that many of the trade journals devoted entire issues to the centennial. See, for example, the May 1996 issue of *Ward's Auto World* with its theme "Quite a Ride, 1896–1996."

In a more general vein are a number of works that compare and contrast the organization and administration of a select group of industries, one of which is usually the automotive. Listed in chronological order of their original publication, these would include *The Age of Big Business: A Chronicle of the Captains of Industry* (1919), by Burton J. Hendrick; *The Iron Man in Industry* (1922), by Arthur Pound, which, like Hendrick, is interesting because of its early publication date and its emphasis on the contributions of individual personalities; *The Age of Enterprise: A Social History of Industrial America* (1942), by Thomas C. Cochran and William Miller; Roger Burlingame's *Backgrounds of Power* (1949), with its analysis of the social impact of mass production; *Small Enterprise and Oligopoly: A Study of the Butter, Flour, Automobile, and Glass Container Industries*, by Harold G. Vatter, an analysis of the oligarchical growth of the automotive industry in comparison with others, paying special attention to the failure of the post–World War II Kaiser–Frazer effort; *Innovation and Capital Formation in Some American Industries* (1956), by William R. McLaurin, which covers only the years to 1940; *The Development of American Industries: Their Economic Significance* (1959), edited by John G. Glover and Rudolph L. Lagai, which has sections on both the automobile and travel industries; Alfred D. Chandler Jr.'s *Strategy and Structure: Chapters in the History of American Industrial Enterprise* (1962), a classic study of what has worked in industrial organization; *Explorations in Enterprise* (1965), edited by Hugh G.J. Aitken, with its unifying theme that entrepreneurial spirit and organizational abilities lead to societal adoption of new technologies, not the inventions themselves; and Paul Baran and Paul Sweezy, *Monopoly Capital: An Essay on the American Economic and Social Order* (1966), which analyzes the historic significance of the automobile industry on the American economy.

More recently, we have Thomas Cochran's *Social Change in America: The Twentieth Century* (1972), similar in approach to Baran and Sweezy (above); *Business Enterprise and Economic Change* (1973), edited by Louis P. Cain and Paul J. Uselding, which contains an interesting essay entitled "Style Change and the Automobile Industry during the Roaring Twenties," by Robert P. Thomas; Alfred D. Chandler Jr.'s *The Visible Hand: The Managerial Revolution in American Business* (1977); David A. Hounshell's Dexter Prize-winning *From the American System to Mass Production, 1800–1932: The Development of Manufacturing Technology in the United States* (1984), a third of which is devoted to the development and historical impact of the original Ford assembly line and its successors; *The Structure of American Industry: Some Case Studies* (1984), edited by Walter Adams, which includes Lawrence J. White's "The Automobile

Industry"; and Mansel G. Blackford and K. Austin Kerr's text *Business Enterprise in American History* (1986), which uses General Motors as a case study and is particularly good on government–business relations.

Finally, the 1970s marks a watershed in the history of the American automobile industry, during which changes in market conditions and foreign competition forced the car manufacturers to rethink the nature of their methods and products. William J. Abernathy has written an excellent study of one specific problem area: *The Productivity Dilemma: Roadblock to Innovation in the Automobile Industry*, which focuses on the difficulties of innovating in a system based on mass production. More general, though highly recommended, is Davis Dyer *et al.*'s *Changing Alliances: The Harvard Business School Project on the Auto Industry and the American Economy*, with its argument that competition is now between national "enterprise systems," not individual companies, and thus only systematic change designed to enhance cooperation will avert further decline in the industry. More recently, Raphael Kaplinsky and Kurt Hoffman have placed the issues in international perspective by comparing developments in the United States with those in Japan and Europe in their *Driving Force: The Global Restructuring of Technology, Labor, and Investment in the Automobile and Components Industry*. By the early 1990s, Detroit had seemingly turned things around and was successfully competing with its Asian manufacturing rivals. Pulitzer Prize-winning authors Paul Ingrassia and Joseph B. White attempt to explain this amazing turnaround in *Comeback: The Fall and Rise of the American Automobile Industry*, which, while a complex and insightful behind-the-scenes account of developments in the 1980s and 1990s, unfortunately does a better job of explaining the reasons behind the decline than those of the turnaround.

HISTORIES OF INDIVIDUAL COMPANIES

The Big Three American automobile companies that dominate domestic production today were creations of the 1920s, well after a number of the marques that they absorbed had begun producing automobiles. Therefore, it is appropriate to include in this section works that trace the history of certain individual marques, as well as books that treat the parent company as a whole. Although countless books that fit that description have been published for the auto "enthusiast" or "buff" market, relatively few volumes can claim to be serious scholarly literature. The books cited below focus more on the company as an organization than as a personification of one or more individuals who ran it. The latter approach is more common within the genre of biography, and such works are described in Chapter 2. Since the distinction between these two categories is not as sharp as one might wish, readers interested in the history of a particular automotive firm are urged to consult both this chapter and the next.

In terms of company history surveys, for General Motors we have Arthur Pound's early (1934) *The Turning Wheel: The Story of General Motors through*

Twenty-Five Years, 1908–1933, which, while an "authorized" account, was still being strongly recommended by John B. Rae some thirty years later, partially because Pound was the last scholar to be granted anything approaching free access to the company's records. Ed Cray's 1980 *Chrome Colossus: General Motors and Its Times* concentrates on an analysis of the administrative organization and market strategies of that giant. More recently, there is Maryann Keller's *Rude Awakening: The Rise, Fall, and Struggle for Recovery of General Motors*, which is at its best when discussing the attempts of this once-unparalleled leader of the industry to adapt to the exigencies of the new international competition of the past two decades.

In a more specific vein, scholars have analyzed corporate management at General Motors in a number of historical studies, such as Arthur J. Kuhn's comprehensive *GM Passes Ford, 1918–1938: Designing the General Motors Performance-Control System*, which attempts to explain how General Motors, using managerial techniques introduced by Alfred P. Sloan Jr., surpassed the previously nearly monopolistic Ford organization in terms of sales and profits. Other works concerned with particular aspects of GM's corporate history include *Managerial Innovation at General Motors*, a collection of articles written between 1922 and 1927 and edited by Alfred D. Chandler Jr., describing selected aspects of GM's administration and management at that time; the same author's *Strategy and Structure: Chapters in the History of Industrial Enterprise* and *Giant Enterprise: Ford, General Motors, and the Automobile Industry*; and Peter F. Drucker's *The Concept of Corporation*, each of which includes Alfred Sloan's reorganization of General Motors as one of its prime examples. The most recent study of management at GM is Doron P. Levin's *Irreconcilable Differences: Ross Perot versus General Motors*, an investigation of the ill-fated, multibillion-dollar merger between Perot's Electronic Data Systems and GM under Roger Smith, a highly unlikely alliance between very different companies and powerful, strong-willed managers.

Within the last two decades, General Motors, like the other two large auto makers, periodically has been the subject of public scorn. A highly critical and, in some regards, pioneering analysis of management in the 1970s was J. Patrick Wright's *On a Clear Day You Can See General Motors: John Z. De Lorean's Look inside the Automotive Giant*, which became a best-seller and helped make De Lorean a nationally known figure. In a somewhat similar vein is Edward Ayres' *What's Good for GM . . .*, although the criticism goes beyond economic issues to include questions of social responsibility as well.

General Motors was the product of a series of mergers and corporate takeovers. As such, its history incorporates that of a number of companies that enjoyed varying periods of independent existence. Significant histories for six of the companies that are now divisions of General Motors exist: Terry B. Dunham and Lawrence R. Gustin's *The Buick: A Complete History*, covering the years 1903–1993 and the most comprehensive history ever published of this marque; Maurice D. Hendry's *Cadillac, Standard of the World: The Complete History*, written with the editors of *Automobile Quarterly* magazine, which has been revised and updated by David Holls and John Heilig to bring the story up to 1996 and includes a supplemental history of the LaSalle marque; and two by Beverly Rae Kimes, *Chevrolet: A History from 1911* (to 1980) and *Oldsmobile: The First Seventy-Five Years*, the former written with Robert C. Ackerson and the latter with Richard M. Langworth. All four books are part of the prestigious *Automobile Quarterly* Marque History book series. In addition, see Helen Earley and Jim Walkinshaw's McKean Award-winning *Setting the Pace*, a heavily illustrated centennial history of Oldsmobile (1897–1997) containing extensive excerpts from interviews with people who worked for the company and comprehensive data tables. Finally, Thomas E. Bonsall's *Pontiac!: They Built Excitement* is the best work on that vehicle. Winner of the Cugnot Award, it is an entertaining, well-balanced history that covers the years 1926 to 1992.

Researchers interested in additional survey histories of those firms will need to rely upon the voluminous enthusiast literature. Among better works in that regard, cited alphabetically by marque, are Richard M. Langworth and Jan P. Norbye's *The Complete History of General Motors, 1908–1986*; Thomas E. Bonsall's *Cadillac: The American Standard*; LeRoi Smith and Tony Hossain's *Cadillac*; *Chevrolet, 1911–1985*, by Richard M. Langworth *et al.*; a special 1995 issue (Vol. 34, No. 4) of *Automobile Quarterly* devoted to topics in Chevrolet history; Doug Bell's *Early Chevrolet History*, which covers the years 1912 to 1928; Thomas E. Bonsall's *Pontiac: The Complete History, 1926–1986*; and Richard L. Busenkell's chronologically more limited, but technically more detailed, *Pontiac since 1945* (to 1988).

The Ford Motor Company has been the subject of the premier automobile company history to date, a three-volume work by Allan Nevins and Frank E. Hill, individually titled *Ford: The Times, the Man, the Company*, covering the years up to 1915; *Ford: Expansion and Challenge, 1915–1933*; and *Ford: Decline and Rebirth, 1933–1962*. John B. Rae called this multivolume achievement "the great classic in this field," and in some respects it may have stifled further purely corporate histories of Ford.

Unlike Chrysler and GM, most historians have found the history of Ford to be inseparable from the family that founded and still controls it. The result has been a number of excellent biographical studies, which are described in Chapter 2 and should be consulted by anyone interested in the history of the company. The most recent book in that genre, Robert Lacey's *Ford: The Men and the Machine*, deserves mention here since it attempts to balance family and company histories in one massive volume, although personalities serve to give this account its focus.

Although the Ford Motor Company had flourished, like the industry as a whole, in the decades following World War II, by the early 1980s it found itself in serious economic trouble. Unexciting designs, production problems, and foreign competition had taken their toll. In a bold attempt to resurrect itself, Ford launched the radically styled Taurus and Sable models, introduced total quality management techniques, and redefined its relationships with its employees and customers. The gamble paid off, and by 1987 Ford was showing historically high profits. The story of this turnaround is enthusiastically told in *Reinventing the Wheels: Ford's Spectacular Comeback*, by Alton F. Doody and Ron Bingaman, and *Taurus: The Making of the Car That Saved Ford*, by Eric Taub, which is more a case study of how the company decided to introduce a new product and the design, manufacturing, and sales challenges that followed. Emboldened by its success and spurred on by a desire to overtake the sales of the Toyota Camry, Ford undertook a radical redesign of the Taurus in the mid-1990s. A fascinating account of that project is *Car: A Drama of the American Workplace*, by Mary Walton, a book that offers keen insights into the design/manufacturing process and the influence of management style on it, written by an author who was present to observe both.

On the level of individual divisions/marques, Thomas E. Bonsall has written the outstanding *The Lincoln Motorcar: The Complete History of an American Classic*, the story of the car and the company from 1919 through 1993, which won both the Society of Automotive Historians' (SAH) Cugnot Award and the AACA's McKean Cup when the original edition was published in 1981 and has become the standard reference work for this marque. Also good is Beverly Rae Kimes' *The Golden Anniversary of the Lincoln Motorcar, 1921–1971*, another *Automobile Quarterly* Marque History book. Mercury has been less well treated, although John A. Gunnell's *55 Years of Mercury: The Complete History of the Big "M"* does offer a celebration of significant models. The short-lived, but legendary, Edsel is the subject of Robert Daines' *Edsel: The Motor Industry's Titanic*. Hailed by Ford at its introduction as "a most exciting star" for which "a whole new market is ready to bloom," the Edsel lasted only three production years and resulted in the greatest loss ever sustained by an automobile manufacturer, even though Daines believes it was not really a bad car and may have been a victim of circumstances beyond the company's control.

Worthwhile enthusiast literature concerning the Ford Motor Company and its products include George H. Dammann's *Illustrated History of Ford, 1903–1970* and the updated edition, *90 Years of Ford*, really as much an encyclopedia as a photographic history; Beverly Rae Kimes' *The Cars That Henry Ford Built: A 75th Anniversary Tribute to America's Most Remembered Automobiles*, a brief (136-page) survey covering from the Quadricycle to the V-8 and a portrait of the automotive pioneer during those years; *Ford: 1903–1984*, by David L. Lewis *et al.*, a solid, year-by-year company history; and *Ford: The Complete History* (to 1990), written by the auto editors of *Consumer Guide*, who received a Cugnot Award of Distinction for exceptional merit from the Society of Automotive Historians for it.

For Chrysler, the best recent work is Steve Jeffreys' *Management and Managed: Fifty Years of Crisis at Chrysler*, which focuses on labor–management relations in the context of the broader history of that corporation. Although Chrysler traditionally has taken a back seat to Ford and General Motors, recently it has been the most interesting company of the Big Three. Chrysler's near-bankruptcy in the late 1970s, the so-called federal government bailout, and its subsequent reemergence as a powerful company under Lee Iacocca are the stuff from which a multitude of books can be, and were, written. Probably the best in this regard is *New Deals: The Chrysler Revival and the American System*, by Robert B. Reich and John D. Donahue, which places the bailout within the broader context of whether and when the federal government should interfere with the free market economy. Other books worth reading include *Going for Broke: The Chrysler Story*, by Michael Moritz and Barrett Seaman, and *Bailout: America's Billion Dollar Gamble on the New Chrysler Corporation*, by Reginald Stuart, both of which were written for a more general audience than the book by Reich and Donahue.

Two of the better and more recent Chrysler Corporation histories written primarily for the auto enthusiast are a special issue of *Automobile Quarterly* (Vol. 32, No. 4), which provides a complete history of Chrysler from its beginnings in the 1920s through the mid-1990s and features articles on Chrysler design, engineering, racing, advertising, and Walter P. himself; and *The Complete History of the Chrysler Corporation, 1924–1985*, by Richard M. Langworth and the editors of *Consumer Guide*.

Major historical studies of the individual marques that compose Chrysler Corporation are rare, with the most notable recent volume being *Dodge Dynasty: The Car and the Family That Rocked Detroit*, by Caroline Latham and David Agresta, who provide a lively popular history that emphasizes the individuals involved more than the vehicles; Thomas McPherson's *The Dodge Story* (through 1975); Don Butler's *The Plymouth–DeSoto Story*; and the more chronologically and textually restricted *Plymouth, 1946–1959*, by Jim Benjaminson.

For a brief period from the mid-1950s to the mid-1960s, it appeared as if the newly formed American Motors Corporation (Hudson, Nash, Rambler, and Jeep) might challenge the hegemony of the Big Three. However, that was not to be, and sales of American Motors cars subsequently remained modest and ultimately unprofitable, despite a partial merger with the French manufacturer Renault. In the late 1980s, the financially troubled company was absorbed by Chrysler and evolved into its Jeep/Eagle Division. Unfortunately, there is no truly scholarly study of American Motors. The best available work is a profusely illustrated popular history by Patrick R. Foster entitled *American Motors: The Last Independent*, a company history that focuses on both the people who were American Motors and the cars that they sold during the years 1954 to 1987. Additional information is available in general manufacturing histories, especially Charles E. Edwards' *Dynamics of the United States Automobile Industry*.

Moving to the major independent manufacturers, Studebaker is the company that has been most extensively studied. Given Studebaker's long history, beginning in the 19th century as a carriage maker, such attention is not surprising. The best comprehensive history of the company is Donald T. Critchlow's *Studebaker: The Life and Death of an American Corporation*, a book that focuses on the company's corporate tradition, managerial dynamics, and the nature of competition in the automotive industry through 1963. Also worthy of examination is Thomas Bonsall's *The Rise & Fall of Studebaker*, which, while intended for the enthusiast market, is nonetheless comprehensive, authoritative, and stylishly written. The first significant study of the company to include some of the automobile years was Albert R. Erskine's *History of the Studebaker Corporation*, published in 1924. Kathleen A. Smallzreid and Dorothy J. Roberts carry the story of the Studebaker organization and especially the family up to 1942 in their *More Than You Promise: A Small Business at Work in Society*, a positive work that tends to minimize the company's business problems in the early 1930s. Edwin Corle's biography *John Studebaker: An American Dream* includes a great deal on the company established by John and his brothers. Stephen Longstreet's *A Century on Wheels: The Story of Studebaker*, is a good, but brief, popular history aimed at the general reader that tends to be more positive than it should be regarding events in the early 1950s and unfortunately lacks an index. Most recently, we have the retrospective *Studebaker: Less Than They Promised*, by Michael Beatty *et al.*, a bittersweet, illustrated history of the company through its closure in 1963, with special attention to its relationship to the city of South Bend, Indiana. Although only sixty pages in length, this book is meritorious for the issues that it raises regarding community–industry relations and the fine collection of archival photographs that it presents. Despite these volumes, the definitive narrative history of Studebaker is yet to be written.

Another major independent marque was Packard, which in the middle third of the 20th century was a worthwhile challenger to Cadillac, Lincoln Continental, and Chrysler Imperial for recognition as the best luxury car made in the United States. The most extensive study of that challenger is *Packard: A History of the Motor Car and the Company*, edited by Beverly Rae Kimes, a monumental, 828-page book in the *Automobile Quarterly* Marque History series that won the SAH's Cugnot Award in 1978 and that *Road & Track* magazine noted is "researched to almost fanatical depths." *Packard*, by George Dammann and Jim Wren, is another complete and detailed history of that car company, heavily illustrated with 1,200 photographs from the Packard factory archives. *Packard*, by Dennis Adler, is probably the most concise (156-page) history available, supplemented by excellent archival photographs. Gwil Griffiths' *Packard: A History in Ads, 1903–1956* provides an interesting approach to the subject. Finally, in *The Fall of the Packard Motor Car Company*, James A. Ward analyzes why the company declined in the years following World War II and ceased production in 1956 despite a general boom in the automobile industry.

A third major independent which, like Packard, was marketed as a luxury vehicle, was Duesenberg. The best history of the latter, even though it encompasses two related marques as well, is Griffith Borgeson's *Errett Lobban Cord, His Empire, His Motorcars: Auburn, Cord, Duesenberg*, a massive and lavish volume from *Automobile Quarterly* that matches in style and scope the magnificence of the cars themselves. J.L. Elbert's *Duesenberg: The Mightiest Amer-*

ican Motor Car was the first (1951) major work concerning that marque and still considered the best by many; Fred Roe's *Duesenberg: The Pursuit of Perfection* is excellent as well, one of the first books to win both the SAH's Cugnot Award as the best book in the field of automotive history (for 1993) and the AACA's Thomas McKean Memorial Cup and a storehouse of detailed information and illustrations. Also of interest are *The Duesenberg*, by Louis W. Steinwedel and J. Herbert Newport, the latter a designer of that car and the man who succeeded Gordon Buehrig (see Chapter 2) at Duesenberg; and the Cugnot Award-winning special issue of *Automobile Quarterly* (Vol. 30, No. 4) devoted to Duesenberg.

Other independents, listed here in alphabetical order by marque, have been featured in R. Thomas Willson's *The First Hundred Years, 1853–1953: Baker Raulang*, a history of probably the most successful makers of electric cars (Baker Electric and Rauch & Lang Electric), which remained in production under a variety of corporate arrangements from 1899 to 1928; Richard P. Scharchburg's *Carriages without Horses: J. Frank Duryea and the Birth of the American Automobile Industry*, a publication of the Society of Automotive Engineers and also a recipient of the Cugnot Award and McKean Cup, which relates the history of the Duryea Motor Wagon Company, the first automobile firm in the United States, and its successor, the Stevens-Duryea Company, maker of luxury cars; J. Frank Duryea's autobiographical *America's First Automobile* and *Who Designed and Built Those Duryea Cars?*; Buckminster Fuller and Robert Marks' description of the evolution and demise of the Dymaxion car (1933–1935) in *The Dymaxion World of Buckminster Fuller*; Sinclair Powell's *The Franklin Automobile Company: The History of the Innovative Firm, Its Founders, the Vehicles It Produced (1902–1934) and the People Who Built Them*, an extensive and thoroughly researched work on a make of luxury cars that was the most successful air-cooled automobile in American history; Michael Keller's *The Graham Legacy: Graham-Paige to 1932*, a well-written and comprehensive study of the Graham brothers (Joseph, Robert, and Ray) and the popular cars their company produced beginning in 1927 (and surviving until 1941); Richard M. Langworth's Cugnot Award-winning *Kaiser-Frazer: The Last Onslaught on Detroit*, the story of an ill-fated, decade-long attempt to gain a foothold in the post–World War II American automotive marketplace; George Hanley and Stacey Hanley's *The Marmon Heritage*, an encyclopedically complete, 608-page work that tells the story of the Marmon and Marmon–Herrington firms and another winner of the Cugnot Award; Charles T. Pearson's *The Indomitable Tin Goose: The True Story of Preston Tucker and His Car*; and Philip S. Egan's *Design and Destiny: The Making of the Tucker Automobile*, a car that, like Kaiser-Frazer, was a post–World II attempt to introduce an automobile innovative in both styling and engineering to successfully compete with Detroit and a story interesting enough to be filmed as a major motion picture in the late 1980s. Egan, who was a member of the team that designed the Tucker, relates his experiences with both the car and Preston Tucker himself.

There also are a number of good works on the history of other independent manufacturers, although these are aimed primarily at the auto enthusiast reader. See, for instance, William T. Cameron's *The Cameron Story*, which tells the story of two brothers who built some 3,500 cars in six states between 1901 and 1920; Don Butler's *The History of Hudson* which, while essentially a photographic history of the models and not the company, is still the best comprehensive treatment of any of the marques that eventually became part of the American Motors Corporation; Val Quandt's description of the history of *The Classic Kissel*, a car produced from 1907 to 1931, which established itself as one of the finer quality independents; Mark Ralston's *Pierce-Arrow: The Golden Age*, a massive 828-page volume with 1,200 illustrations, including hundreds of factory photographs, of the marque that was for a while the most expensive car in the world; Brooks T. Brierley's *There Is No Mistaking a Pierce-Arrow*, a much briefer work that, nonetheless, does a fine job of placing the cars and the company in the larger context of life in the first third of the 20th century; Arthur W. Souttler's *The American Rolls-Royce*, the history of a British attempt to seize a share of the luxury car market during the 1920s; *The Splendid Stutz: The Cars, Companies, People and Races*, edited by Raymond E. Katzell, the first attempt at a comprehensive history (1911–1934) of that legendary marque; and J.[ames] H. Valentine's *The Tourist from California*, a brief (48-page) history of a company that built mostly custom-built automobiles and, despite being plagued by rapidly changing ownership and management, was the largest producer of motor vehicles in the far West during the period of its existence (1902–1910).

Although they often amount to little more than an illustrated collection of publicity releases, the automotive companies periodically publish self-histories, usually to commemorate some chronological epoch. There are, however, a few significant exceptions to this observation, among them being the *American Motors Family Album*, written by John A. Conde in 1976, which more fully develops the 1961 *Rambler Family Album*; Chrysler's *Chrysler Corporation: The Story of An American Company*, which covers the first thirty years (1925–1955) of that firm; *A Pictorial History of Chrysler Corporation Cars*, published in 1973; the Ford Motor Company's *Ford at Fifty, 1903–1953; General Motors: The First 75 Years of Transportation Products*, written under the auspices of the General Motors Corporation by the editors of *Automobile Quarterly* magazine; *Buick's First Half-Century*, produced by General Motors and covering the years 1903–1953; and GM's *The Chevrolet Story, 1911–1967*; Pope's *The Pope Manufacturing Company: An Industrial Achievement*, published in 1907, one of the few in-house histories of an important pioneer auto manufacturer and still the only book-length treatment of that company; the Studebaker Corporation's *100 Years on the Road* (1952); and the White Motor Company's *The Albatross: A Quarter Century of White Transportation*, a 1925 work that details the history of a defunct firm now better known for its subsequent manufacture of trucks.

BIBLIOGRAPHY

Abernathy, William J. *The Productivity Dilemma: Roadblock to Innovation in the Automobile Industry.* Baltimore: Johns Hopkins University Press, 1978.

Adams, Walter, ed. *The Structure of American Industry: Some Case Studies.* New York: Macmillan, 1984.

Adler, Dennis. *Packard.* Osceola, Wisc.: 1998.

Aitken, Hugh G.J., ed. *Explorations in Enterprise.* Cambridge, Mass.: Harvard University Press, 1965.

American Motors Corporation. *Rambler Family Album.* Detroit: American Motors Corporation, 1961.

Anderson, Rudolph E. *The Story of the American Automobile: Highlights and Sidelights.* Washington, D.C.: Public Affairs Press, 1950.

Ant Farm Design Group. *Automerica: A Trip Down U.S. Highways from World War II to the Future.* New York: E.P. Dutton, 1976.

Automobile Quarterly Magazine, Editors of. *General Motors: The First 75 Years of Transportation Products.* Kutztown, Pa.: Automobile Quarterly, 1983.

Ayres, Edward. *What's Good for GM . . .* Nashville: Aurora, 1970.

Ayres, Leonard P. *The Automobile Industry and Its Future.* Cleveland: Cleveland Trust Company, 1921.

Baran, Paul, and Paul Sweezy. *Monopoly Capital: An Essay on the American Economic and Social Order.* New York: Monthly Review Press, 1966.

Barber, Herbert L. *Story of the Automobile: Its History and Development from 1760 to 1917, with an Analysis of the Standing and Prospects of the Automobile Industry.* Chicago: A.J. Munson, 1917.

Barker, Theo, ed. *The Economic and Social Effects of the Spread of Motor Vehicles: An International Centenary Tribute.* London: Macmillan, 1987.

Beasley, Norman. *Made in Detroit.* New York: G.P. Putnam's Sons, 1957.

Beatty, Michael, Patrick Furlong, and Loren Pennington. *Studebaker: Less than They Promised.* South Bend, Ind.: and books, 1984.

Belasco, Warren J. *Americans on the Road: From Autocamp to Motel, 1910–1945.* Cambridge, Mass.: MIT Press, 1979.

Bell, Doug. *Early Chevrolet History.* Los Angeles: Floyd Clymer, 1966.

Bellamy, James F. *Cars Made in Upstate New York.* Red Creek, N.Y.: Squire Hill, 1989.

Benjaminson, Jim. *Plymouth, 1946–1959.* Osceola, Wisc.: Motorbooks International, 1994.

Berger, Michael L. *The Devil Wagon in God's Country: The Automobile and Social Change in Rural America, 1893–1929.* Hamden, Conn.: Archon Books, 1979.

Blackford, Mansel G., and K. Austin Kerr. *Business Enterprise in American History.* Boston: Houghton Mifflin, 1986.

Bonsall, Thomas E. *Cadillac: The American Standard.* Baltimore: Stony Run Press, 1993.

Bonsall, Thomas E. *The Lincoln Motorcar: The Complete History of an American Classic.* Rev. ed. Baltimore: Stony Run Press, 1993.

Bonsall, Thomas E. *Pontiac: The Complete History, 1926–1986.* 2nd ed. Baltimore: Bookman Dan, 1986.

Bonsall, Thomas E. *Pontiac!: They Built Excitement.* Baltimore: Stony Run Press, 1991.

Bonsall, Thomas E. *The Rise & Fall of Studebaker.* Baltimore: Stony Run Press, 1996.

Borgeson, Griffith. *Errett Lobban Cord, His Empire, His Motorcars: Auburn, Cord, Duesenberg.* Princeton, N.J.: Automobile Quarterly, 1984.

Borth, Christy. *Mankind on the Move: The Story of Highways.* Washington, D.C.: Automotive Safety Foundation, 1969.

Borth, Christy. *Masters of Mass Production.* Indianapolis: Bobbs-Merrill, 1945.

Bottles, Scott L. *The Making of the Modern City: Los Angeles and the Automobile, 1900–1950.* Los Angeles: University of California Press, 1984.

Boyne, Walter J. *Power behind the Wheel: Creativity and the Evolution of the Automobile.* New York: Stewart, Tabori, & Chang, 1989.

Brierley, Brooks T. *There Is No Mistaking a Pierce-Arrow.* Coconut Grove, Fla.: Garrett and Stringer, 1986.

Burlingame, Roger. *Backgrounds of Power: The Human Story of Mass Production.* New York: Scribner, 1949.

Busenkell, Richard L. *Pontiac since 1945.* New York: Norton, 1989.

Butler, Don. *The History of Hudson.* Sarasota, Fla.: Crestline Books, 1982.

Butler, Don. *The Plymouth-DeSoto Story.* Osceola, Wisc.: Motorbooks International, 1992.

Cain, Louis P., and Paul J. Uselding, eds. *Business Enterprise and Economic Change.* Kent, Ohio: Kent State University Press, 1973.

Cameron, William T. *The Cameron Story.* Tucson: International Society for Vehicle Preservation, 1990.

Chandler, Alfred D., Jr. *Giant Enterprise: Ford, General Motors, and the Automobile Industry.* New York: Harcourt, Brace, & World, 1964.

Chandler, Alfred D., Jr. *Strategy and Structure: Chapters in the History of Industrial Enterprise.* Cambridge, Mass.: MIT Press, 1962.

Chandler, Alfred D., Jr. *The Visible Hand: The Managerial Revolution in American Business.* Cambridge, Mass.: Belknap Press, 1977.

Chandler, Alfred D., Jr., ed. *Managerial Innovation at General Motors.* New York: Arno Press, 1979.

Chase, Harold B. *Auto-biography: Recollections of a Pioneer Motorist, 1896–1911.* New York: Pageant Press, 1955.

"Chauffeur." *Two Thousand Miles on an Automobile: Being a Desultory Narrative of a Trip through New England, New York, Canada and the West.* Philadelphia: J.B Lippincott, 1902.

Chrysler Corporation. *Chrysler Corporation: The Story of an American Company.* Detroit: Chrysler Corporation, Department of Public Relations, 1955.

Chrysler Corporation. *A Pictorial History of Chrysler Corporation Cars.* Rev. ed. Detroit: Chrysler Corporation, 1973.

Cleveland, Reginald M., and S.T. Williamson. *The Road Is Yours: The Story of the Automobile and the Men behind It.* New York: Greystone Press, 1951.

Clymer, Floyd. *Floyd Clymer's Historical Motor Scrapbook: Ford Model T Edition.* Los Angeles: Author, 1954.

Clymer, Floyd. *Floyd Clymer's Model T Memories: Including the Ubiquitous Model T, by Les Henry.* Los Angeles: Author, [194-].

Clymer, Floyd. *Those Wonderful Old Automobiles.* New York: Bonanza Books, 1963.

Clymer, Floyd. *Treasury of Early American Automobiles, 1877–1925.* New York: Bonanza Books, 1950.

Cochran, Thomas C. *Social Change in America: The Twentieth Century.* New York: Harper and Row, 1972.

Cochran, Thomas C., and William Miller. *The Age of Enterprise: A Social History of Industrial America.* Rev. ed. New York: Harper, 1961.

Coffey, Frank, and Joseph Layden. *America on Wheels: The First 100 Years, 1896–1996.* Santa Monica, Calif.: General Publishing Group, 1996.

Cohn, David L. *Combustion on Wheels: An Informal History of the Automobile Age.* Boston: Houghton Mifflin, 1944.

Conde, John A. *The American Motors Family Album.* Detroit: American Motors Corporation, Public Relations Department, 1976.

Consumer Guide, Auto Editors of. *Ford: The Complete History.* Lincolnwood, Ill.: Publications International, 1990.

Corle, Edwin. *John Studebaker: An American Dream.* New York: E.P. Dutton, 1949.

Court, Andrew T. *Men, Methods and Machines in Automobile Manufacturing.* New York: Automobile Manufacturers' Association, 1939.

Crabb, Richard. *Birth of a Giant: The Men and Incidents That Gave America the Motorcar.* Philadelphia: Chilton, 1976.

Cranmer, Horace J. *New Jersey in the Automobile Age: A History of Transportation.* Princeton, N.J.: Van Nostrand, 1964.

Cray, Ed. *Chrome Colossus: General Motors and Its Times.* New York: McGraw-Hill, 1980.

Critchlow, Donald T. *Studebaker: The Life and Death of an American Corporation.* Bloomington: Indiana University Press, 1997.

Crow, Carl. *The City of Flint Grows Up: The Success Story of an American Community.* New York: Harper, 1945.

Daines, Robert. *Edsel: The Motor Industry's Titanic.* London: Academy, 1994.

Dammann, George H. *90 Years of Ford.* Osceola, Wisc.: Motorbooks International, 1993.

Dammann, George H., and Jim Wren. *Packard.* Osceola, Wisc.: Motorbooks International, 1996.

Davis, Donald F. *Conspicuous Production: Automobiles and Elites in Detroit, 1899–1933.* Philadelphia: Temple University Press, 1988.

Denison, Merrill. *The Power to Go: The Story of the Automotive Industry.* Garden City, N.Y.: Doubleday, 1956.

Donovan, Frank. *Wheels for a Nation.* New York: Thomas Y. Crowell, 1965.

Doody, Alton F., and Ron Bingaman. *Reinventing the Wheels: Ford's Spectacular Comeback.* Cambridge, Mass.: Ballinger, 1988.

Doolittle, James R., ed. *The Romance of the Automobile Industry.* New York: Klebold Press, 1916.

Drucker, Peter F. *The Concept of Corporation.* New Brunswick, N.J.: Transaction Publishers, 1993.

Drucker, Peter F. *Innovation and Entrepreneurship: Practice and Principles.* New York: Harper & Row, 1985.

Dunham, Terry B., and Lawrence R. Gustin. *The Buick: A Complete History.* Updated ed. Princeton, N.J.: Princeton Publishing, 1996.

Duryea, J. Frank. *America's First Automobile.* Springfield, Mass.: D.M. Macaulay, 1942.

Duryea, J. Frank. *Who Designed and Built Those Early Duryea Cars: Answered in Ten Deadly Parallels by J. Frank Duryea.* Madison, Conn.: n.p., 1944.

Dyer, Davis, Malcolm S. Salter, and Alan M. Webber. *Changing Alliances: The Harvard*

Business School Project on the Auto Industry and the American Economy. Boston: Harvard Business School Press, 1987.

Earley, Helen, and Jim Walkinshaw. *Setting the Pace.* East Lansing, Mich.: Earley Enterprises, 1996.

Edmonds, James P. *Development of the Automobile and Gasoline Engine in Michigan.* Lansing, Mich.: Franklin DeKleine, 1942.

Edwards, Charles E. *Dynamics of the United States Automobile Industry.* Columbia: University of South Carolina Press, 1965.

Egan, Philip S. *Design and Destiny: The Making of the Tucker Automobile.* Orange, Calif.: ON THE MARK Publications, 1989.

Elbert, J.L. *Duesenberg: Mightiest American Motor Car.* Rev. ed. Arcadia, Calif.: Post-Era Books, 1975.

Ellis, Stanley W. *Smogless Days: Adventures in Ten Stanley Steamers.* Burbank, Calif.: Howell-North Books, 1971.

Epstein, Ralph C. *The Automobile Industry: Its Economic and Commercial Development.* Chicago: A.W. Shaw, 1928.

Erskine, Albert R. *History of the Studebaker Corporation.* South Bend, Ind.: Studebaker Corporation, 1924.

Faris, John T. *Roaming American Highways.* New York: Farrar & Rinehart, 1931.

Flink, James J. *America Adopts the Automobile, 1895–1910.* Cambridge, Mass.: MIT Press, 1970.

Flink, James J. *The Automobile Age.* Cambridge, Mass.: MIT Press, 1988.

Flink, James J. *The Car Culture.* Cambridge, Mass.: MIT Press, 1975.

Flower, Raymond, and Michael W. James. *100 Years on the Road: A Social History of the Car.* New York: McGraw-Hill, 1981.

Fogelson, Robert M. *The Fragmented Metropolis: Los Angeles, 1850–1930.* Cambridge, Mass.: Harvard University Press, 1967.

Ford Motor Company. *Ford at Fifty, 1903–1953.* New York: Simon & Schuster, 1953.

Foster, Patrick R. *American Motors: The Last Independent.* Iola, Wisc.: Krause, 1993.

Fraser, Richard A., and Nancy L. Fraser. *A History of Maine Built Automobiles.* East Poland, Me.: Authors, 1991.

Fuller, R. Buckminster, and Robert Marks. *The Dymaxion World of Buckminster Fuller.* Garden City, N.Y.: Anchor Books, 1973.

Gannett, Lewis S. *Sweet Land.* New York: Doubleday, Doran, 1934.

General Motors Corporation. *Buick's First Half-Century.* Detroit: General Motors Corporation, Buick Motor Division, 1952.

General Motors Corporation. *The Chevrolet Story: 1911–1970.* Detroit: General Motors Corporation, Chevrolet Motor Division, 1969.

Georgano, G.N. *The American Automobile: A Centenary, 1893–1993.* New York: Smithmark, 1992.

Glasscock, Carl B. *The Gasoline Age: The Story of the Men Who Made It.* Indianapolis: Bobbs-Merrill, 1937.

Glover, John G., and Rudolph L. Lagai, eds. *The Development of American Industries: Their Economic Significance.* New York: Simmons-Boardman, 1959.

Greenleaf, William. *Monopoly on Wheels: Henry Ford and the Selden Automobile Patent Suit.* Detroit: Wayne State University Press, 1961.

Griffin, C[lare] E. *The Life History of Automobiles.* Ann Arbor: University of Michigan, Graduate School of Business Administration, Bureau of Business Research, 1926.

Griffiths, Gwil. *Packard: A History in Ads 1903–1956.* Lutherville, Md.: Author, 1970.

Gross, William B. *From San Diego, California to Washington, D.C.: Being a Descriptive Account of the First Official Trip by Automobile over the Southern National Highway.* San Diego: Frye & Smith, 1916.

Gunnell, John. *55 Years of Mercury: The Complete History of the Big "M."* Iola, Wisc.: Krause, 1994.

Hanley, George, and Stacey Hanley. *The Marmon Heritage.* Rochester, Mich.: Doyle Hyde, 1990.

Hendrick, Burton J. *The Age of Big Business: A Chronicle of the Captains of Industry.* New Haven, Conn.: Yale University Press, 1919.

Hendry, Maurice D., and the Editors of Automobile Quarterly. *Cadillac, Standard of the World: The Complete History.* 5th ed. Kutztown, Pa.: Automobile Quarterly, 1996.

Hill, Frank E. *The Automobile: How It Came, Grew, and Has Changed Our Lives.* New York: Dodd, Mead, 1967.

Hill, Ralph N. *The Mad Doctor's Drive: Being an Account of the 1st Auto Trip across the United States of America, San Francisco to New York, 1903, or Sixty-Three Days on a Winton Motor Carriage.* Brattleboro, Vt.: Stephen Green Press, 1964.

Hiscox, Gardner D. *Horseless Vehicles, Automobiles, Motorcycles: Operated by Steam, Hydro-Carbon, Electric and Pneumatic Motors.* New York: Scientific American, 1900.

Hounshell, David A. *From the American System to Mass Production, 1800–1932: The Development of Manufacturing Technology in the U.S.* Baltimore: Johns Hopkins University Press, 1984.

Huffman, Wallace S., with David A. Huffman and Harry V. Huffman, compilers. *Indiana Built Motor Vehicles.* Centennial ed. Indianapolis: Indiana Historical Society, 1994.

Ingrassia, Paul, and Joseph B. White. *Comeback: The Fall and Rise of the American Automobile Industry.* New York: Simon & Schuster, 1994.

Ireland, Robert E. *Entering the Auto Age: The Early Automobile in North Carolina, 1900–1930.* Raleigh: North Carolina Department of Cultural Resources, Division of Archives and History, 1990.

Jakle, John A. *The American Small Town: Twentieth-Century Place Images.* Hamden, Conn.: Archon Books, 1982.

James, Walter H. *Joys and Sorrows of an Automobilist: Being an Authentic Account of the Writer's Experiences Written for His Own Satisfaction, but Free to Be Read by Anyone Who Wants to Read It.* Mount Shasta, Calif.: Earth Heart, 1992.

Jeffreys, Steve. *Management and Managed: Fifty Years of Crisis at Chrysler.* New York: Cambridge University Press, 1986.

Jewell, Derek. *Man and Motor: The 20th Century Love Affair.* New York: Walker, 1967.

Kaplinsky, Raphael, and Kurt Hoffman. *Driving Force: The Global Restructuring of Technology, Labor, and Investment in the Automobile and Components Industry.* Boulder, Colo.: Westview Press, 1988.

Karolevitz, Robert F. *This Was Pioneer Motoring: An Album of Nostalgic Automobilia!* Seattle: Superior, 1968.

Katzell, Raymond A., ed. *The Splendid Stutz: The Cars, Companies, People and Races.* Wilbraham, Mass.: The Stutz Club, 1996.

Keller, Maryann. *Rude Awakening: The Rise, Fall, and Struggle for Recovery of General Motors*. New York: William Morrow, 1989.

Keller, Michael. *The Graham Legacy: Graham-Paige to 1932*. Paducah, Ky.: Turner, 1999.

Kennedy, Edward D. *The Automobile Industry: The Coming of Age of Capitalism's Favorite Child*. New York: Reynal & Hitchcock, 1941.

Kimes, Beverly Rae. *The Cars That Henry Ford Built: A 75th Anniversary Tribute to America's Most Remembered Automobiles*. Princeton, N.J.: Princeton Publishing, 1978.

Kimes, Beverly Rae. *The Golden Anniversary of the Lincoln Motorcar, 1921–1971*. New York: Automobile Quarterly, 1970.

Kimes, Beverly Rae, ed. *Packard: A History of the Motor Car and the Company*. Kutztown, Pa.: Automobile Quarterly, 1978.

Kimes, Beverly Rae, and Robert C. Ackerson. *Chevrolet: A History from 1911*. 2nd ed. Kutztown, Pa.: Automobile Quarterly, 1986.

Kimes, Beverly Rae, and Richard M. Langworth. *Oldsmobile: The First Seventy-Five Years*. New York: Automobile Quarterly, 1972.

Kuhn, Arthur J. *GM Passes Ford, 1918–1938: Designing the General Motors Performance-Control System*. University Park: Pennsylvania State University Press, 1986.

Labatut, Jean, and Wheaton J. Lane, eds. *Highways in Our National Life: A Symposium*. Princeton, N.J.: Princeton University Press, 1950.

Lacey, Robert. *Ford: The Men and the Machine*. Boston: Little, Brown, 1986.

Langworth, Richard M. *Kaiser-Frazer: The Last Onslaught on Detroit*. Kutztown, Pa.: Automobile Quarterly, 1975.

Langworth, Richard M., and the Editors of Consumer Guide. *The Complete History of Chrysler Corporation, 1924–1985*. New York: Beekman House, 1985.

Langworth, Richard M., and Jan P. Norbye. *The Complete History of General Motors, 1908–1986*. New York: Beekman House, 1986.

Langworth, Richard M., Jan P. Norbye, and the Editors of Consumer Guide. *Chevrolet, 1911–1985*. New York: Beekman House, 1984.

Latham, Caroline, and David Agresta. *Dodge Dynasty: The Car and the Family That Rocked Detroit*. New York: Harcourt Brace Jovanovich, 1989.

Levin, Doron P. *Irreconcilable Differences: Ross Perot versus General Motors*. Boston: Little, Brown, 1989.

Lewis, David L., and Laurence Goldstein, eds. *The Automobile and American Culture*. Ann Arbor: University of Michigan Press, 1983.

Lewis, David L., Mike McCarville, Lorin Sorensen, and the Auto Editors of Consumer Guide. *Ford: 1903–1984*. New York: Beekman House, 1983.

Lewis, Eugene W. *Motor Memories: A Saga of Whirling Gears*. Detroit: Alved, 1947.

Ling, Peter J. *America and the Automobile: Technology, Reform and Social Change*. Manchester, Eng.: Manchester University Press, 1990.

Longstreet, Stephen. *The Boy in the Model T: A Journey in the Just Gone Past*. New York: Simon & Schuster, 1956.

Longstreet, Stephen. *A Century on Wheels: The Story of Studebaker*. Westport, Conn.: Greenwood Press, 1970.

Lynd, Robert S., and Helen M. Lynd. *Middletown: A Study in Contemporary American Culture*. New York: Harcourt, Brace, & World, 1929.

Lynd, Robert S., and Helen M. Lynd. *Middletown in Transition: A Study in Cultural Conflicts.* New York: Harcourt, Brace, & World, 1937.

MacManus, Theodore F., and Norman Beasley. *Men, Money, and Motors: The Drama of the Automobile.* New York: Harper & Brothers, 1929.

Maines, George H. *Men, a City, and a Buick, 1903–1953: An Account of How Buick, and Later General Motors, Grew Up in Flint, from the Records and Personal Recollections of George Humphrey Maines.* Flint, Mich.: Advertisers Press, 1953.

Mandel, Leon. *Driven: The American Four-Wheeled Love Affair.* New York: Stein & Day, 1977.

Marsh, Peter, and Peter Collett. *Driving Passion: The Psychology of the Car.* Boston: Faber & Faber, 1987.

Marvin, Keith, Alvin J. Arnhem, and Henry Blommel. *What Was the McFarlan?* New York: A.J. Arnheim, 1967.

Marvin, Keith, and Arthur L. Homan. *The Dagmar and the Moller Motor Car Company: An Automotive Enigma.* Troy, N.Y.: Automobilists of the Upper Hudson Valley, 1960.

Maxim, Hiram P. *Horseless Carriage Days.* New York: Harper & Brothers, 1937.

May, George S. *A Most Unique Machine: The Michigan Origins of the American Automobile Industry.* Grand Rapids, Mich.: William B. Eerdmans, 1975.

McCalley, Bruce W. *Model T Ford: The Car that Changed the World.* Iola, Wisc.: Krause, 1994.

McConnell, Curt. *Great Cars of the Great Plains.* Lincoln: University of Nebraska Press, 1995.

McLaurin, William R. *Innovation and Capital Formation in Some American Industries.* Chicago: University of Chicago Press, 1956.

McPherson, Thomas. *The Dodge Story.* Osceola, Wisc.: Motorbooks International, 1992.

McShane, Clay. *Down the Asphalt Path: The Automobile and the American City.* New York: Columbia University Press, 1994.

Miller, Ray, and Bruce McCalley. *From Here to Obscurity: A Look at the Changes in an Unchanging Car, 1909–1927.* Oceanside, Calif.: Evergreen Press, 1971.

Moline, Norman T. *Mobility and the Small Town, 1900–1930: Transportation Change in Oregon, Illinois.* Chicago: University of Chicago, Department of Geography, 1971.

Montagu of Beaulieu, Baron Edward, and G.N. Georgano. *Early Days on the Road: An Illustrated History, 1819–1941.* New York: Universe, 1976.

Montagu of Beaulieu, Lord Edward, and F. Wilson McComb. *Behind the Wheel: The Magic and Manners of Early Motoring.* New York: Paddington Press, 1977.

Moritz, Michael, and Barrett Seaman. *Going for Broke: The Chrysler Story.* Garden City, N.Y.: Doubleday, 1981.

Mumford, Lewis. *The Highway and the City.* New York: Harcourt, Brace, & World, 1963.

Murdock, Jacob M. *A Family Tour from Ocean to Ocean: Being an Account of the First Amateur Motor Car Journey from the Pacific to the Atlantic, Whereby J.M. Murdock and Family, in Their 1908 Packard "Thirty" Touring Car, Incidentally Broke the Transcontinental Record.* Detroit: Packard Motor Car Co., 1908.

Musselman, M.M. *Get a Horse!: The Story of the Automobile in America.* Philadelphia: J.B. Lippincott, 1950.

Nevins, Allan. *Ford: The Times, the Man, the Company*. New York: Charles Scribner's Sons, 1954.

Nevins, Allan, and Frank E. Hill. *Ford: Decline and Rebirth, 1933–1962*. New York: Charles Scribner's Sons, 1963.

Nevins, Allan, and Frank E. Hill. *Ford: Expansion and Challenge, 1915–1933*. New York: Charles Scribner's Sons, 1957.

Oppel, Frank, ed. *Motoring in America: The Early Years*. Secaucus, N.J.: Castle Books, 1989.

Overland Automobile Company. *5000 Miles Overland. Wonderful Performance of a Wonderful Car. The Story of Miss Scott's Journey Overland*. Toledo: Overland Automobile Company, 1910.

Partridge, Bellamy. *Fill 'er Up!: The Story of Fifty Years of Motoring*. New York: Clymer, 1959.

Patton, Phil. *Song of the Open Road: A Celebration of the American Highway*. New York: Simon & Schuster, 1986.

Pearson, Charles T. *The Indomitable Tin Goose: The True Story of Preston Tucker and His Car*. New York: Abelard-Schuman, 1960.

Perschbacher, Gerald. *Wheels in Motion: The American Automobile Industry's First Century*. Iola, Wisc.: Krause, 1996.

Pettifer, Julian, and Nigel Turner. *Automania: Man and the Motor Car*. Boston: Little, Brown, 1984.

Pope Manufacturing Co. *The Pope Manufacturing Company: An Industrial Achievement*. Hartford, Conn.: Pope Manufacturing, 1907.

Pound, Arthur. *The Automobile and an American City*. Detroit: Wayne State University Press, 1962.

Pound, Arthur. *The Iron Man in Industry: An Outline of the Social Significance of Automatic Machinery*. Boston: Atlantic Monthly, 1922.

Pound, Arthur. *The Turning Wheel: The Story of General Motors through Twenty-Five Years, 1908–1933*. Garden City, N.Y.: Doubleday, Doran, 1934.

Powell, Sinclair. *The Franklin Automobile Company: The History of the Innovative Firm, Its Founders, the Vehicles It Produced (1902–1934) and the People Who Built Them*. Warrendale, Pa.: Society of Automotive Engineers, 1999.

Preston, Howard L. *Automobile Age Atlanta: The Making of a Southern Metropolis, 1900–1935*. Athens: University of Georgia Press, 1979.

Quandt, Val. *The Classic Kissel*. Amherst, Wisc.: Palmer, 1991.

Quandt, Val, ed. *Wisconsin Cars and Trucks: A Centenary*. Amherst, Wisc.: Palmer Publications for the Wisconsin Chapter, Society of Automotive Historians, 1998.

"Quite a Ride: 1896–1996." *Ward's Auto World* 32 (May 1996): 28–164.

Rae, John B. *The American Automobile: A Brief History*. Chicago: University of Chicago Press, 1965.

Rae, John B. *American Automobile Manufacturers: The First Forty Years*. Philadelphia: Chilton, 1959.

Rae, John B. *The Road and the Car in American Life*. Cambridge, Mass.: MIT Press, 1971.

Ralston, Mark. *Pierce Arrow: The Golden Age*. Lafayette, Ind.: Author, 1984.

Ramsey, Alice Huyler. *Veil, Duster, and Tire Iron*. Covina, Calif.: Castle Press, 1961.

Reck, Franklin M. *A Car Traveling People: How the Automobile Has Changed the Life of Americans—A Study of Social Effects*. Detroit: Automobile Manufacturers Association, 1945.

Reich, Robert B., and John D. Donahue. *New Deals: The Chrysler Revival and the American System*. New York: Times Books, 1985.

Roe, Fred. *Duesenberg: The Pursuit of Perfection*. London: Dalton Watson, 1986.

St. Clair, David J. *The Motorization of American Cities*. New York: Praeger, 1986.

St. Louis Society Automotive Pioneers. *Four Wheels—No Brakes: A History of Automobiles in St. Louis and the Part that City Has Taken in the Development of the Automobile*. St. Louis: St. Louis Society Automotive Pioneers, 1930.

Sanford, Charles L., ed. *Automobiles in American Life*. Troy, N.Y.: Center for the Study of the Human Dimensions of Science and Technology, 1977.

Scharchburg, Richard P. *Carriages without Horses: J. Frank Duryea and the Birth of the American Automobile Industry*. Warrendale, Pa.: Society of Automotive Engineers, 1993.

Schnapp, John B. *Corporate Strategies of the Automotive Manufacturers*. Lexington, Mass.: D.C. Heath, 1979.

Scoville, John W. *Behavior of the Automobile Industry in Depression*. New York: Econometric Society, 1936.

Seal, Rector R. *Maryland Automobile History, 1900 to 1942*. Chicago: Adams Press, 1985.

Sears, Stephen W. *The American Heritage History of the Automobile in America*. New York: American Heritage, 1977.

Seltzer, Lawrence H. *A Financial History of the American Automobile Industry*. Boston: Houghton Mifflin, 1928.

Shank, William H. *History of the York Pullman Automobile, 1903–1917*. York, Pa.: Historical Society of York County, 1970.

Shepley, Hayden R. *Automobiles Built in Essex County, Mass.* Beverly, Mass.: Paulard Printing, 1976.

Sinsabaugh, C.G. *Who, Me?: Forty Years of Automobile History*. Detroit: Arnold-Powers, 1940.

Sloss, Robert T. *The Book of the Automobile: A Practical Volume Devoted to the History, Construction, Use and Care of Motor Cars and to the Subject of Motoring in America*. New York: D. Appleton, 1905.

Smallzreid, Kathleen A., and Dorothy J. Roberts. *More Than You Promise: A Small Business at Work in Society*. New York: Harper & Brothers, 1942.

Smith, LeRoi, and Tony Hossain. *Cadillac*. New York: Crescent Books, 1983.

Smith, Philip H. *Wheels within Wheels: A Short History of American Motor Car Manufacturing*. 2nd ed., rev. New York: Funk & Wagnalls, 1970.

Souttler, Arthur W. *The American Rolls-Royce*. Providence, R.I.: Mowbray, 1976.

Steinwedel, Louis W., and J. Herbert Newport. *The Duesenberg*. New York: W.W. Norton, 1983.

Stern, Philip Van Doren. *A Pictorial History of the Automobile, As Seen in Motor Magazine, 1903–1953*. New York: Viking Press, 1953.

Stern, Philip Van Doren. *Tin Lizzie: The Story of the Fabulous Model T Ford*. New York: Simon & Schuster, 1955.

Stuart, Reginald. *Bailout: America's Billion Dollar Gamble on the New Chrysler Corporation*. South Bend, Ind.: and books, 1981.

Studebaker Corporation. *100 Years on the Road*. South Bend, Ind.: Studebaker Corporation, 1952.

Szudarek, Robert G. *How Detroit Became the Automotive Capital: 100th Anniversary*. Detroit: Typocraft, 1996.

Tarr, Joel A. *Transportation Innovation and Changing Spatial Patterns in Pittsburgh, 1850–1934*. Chicago: Public Works Historical Society, 1978.

Taub, Eric. *Taurus: The Making of the Car That Saved Ford*. New York: Dutton, 1991.

U.S. Federal Trade Commission. *Report on the Motor Vehicle Industry*. Washington, D.C.: Government Printing Office, 1939.

Valentine, J[ames] H. *The Tourist from California*. Los Angeles: Author, 1990.

Vatter, Harold G. *Small Enterprise and Oligopoly: A Study of the Butter, Flour, Automobile, and Glass Container Industries*. Corvallis: Oregon State College Press, 1955.

Wager, Richard. *Golden Wheels: The Story of the Automobiles Made in Cleveland and Northeastern Ohio, 1892–1932*. 2nd ed., rev. Cleveland: J.T. Zubal, with the cooperation of the Western Reserve Historical Society, 1986.

Walton, Mary. *Car: A Drama of the American Workplace*. New York: W.W. Norton, 1997.

Ward, James A. *The Fall of the Packard Motor Car Company*. Stanford, Calif.: Stanford University Press, 1995.

Warner, Sam Bass, Jr. *The Urban Wilderness: A History of the American City*. New York: Harper & Row, 1972.

Weldon, Chichester P. *The New Departure Classics*. Canaan, N.H.: Phoenix, 1986.

White, Lawrence J. *The Automobile Industry since 1945*. Cambridge: Harvard University Press, 1971.

White, Lee Strout [E.B. White, with Richard L. Strout]. *Farewell to the Model T*. New York: G.P. Putnam's Sons, 1936.

White Motor Corporation. *The Albatross: A Quarter Century of White Transportation, 1900–1925*. Cleveland: White Motor Corporation, 1925.

Wik, Reynold W. *Henry Ford and Grass-roots America*. Ann Arbor: University of Michigan Press, 1972.

Willson, R. Thomas. *The First Hundred Years, 1853–1953: Baker Raulang*. Cleveland: Author, 1953.

Wright, J. Patrick. *On a Clear Day You Can See General Motors: John Z. De Lorean's Look inside the Automotive Giant*. New York: Avon Books, 1980.

Wurster, Nina B. *The Welch Tourist*. Ann Arbor, Mich.: Washtenaw Historical Society, 1954.

Yanarella, Ernest J., and William C. Green, eds. *The Politics of Industrial Recruitment: Japanese Automobile Investment and Economic Development in the American States*. Westport, Conn.: Greenwood Press, 1990.

Yates, Brock. *The Decline and Fall of the American Automobile Industry*. New York: Empire Books, 1983.

CHAPTER 2

Famous Automotive Personalities

In this chapter, we will be concerned with works that are biographical in nature. Obviously, all of the people chosen for inclusion are known for some significant contribution to automotive history. They are grouped under four generic headings: Early Inventors and Entrepreneurs, Corporate Managers and Labor Organizers, Engineers and Designers, and Racing Drivers. In addition to the material cited below, the reader should investigate the section or sections of the guide that pertain to developments in that aspect of automotive history in which the person was active.

EARLY INVENTORS AND ENTREPRENEURS

Although scholars might disagree on the exact dates, there was a pioneering period in American automotive history that lasted from the early 1890s to the end of World War I. By 1918 the mass-produced, gasoline-powered automobile, represented by the Model T Ford, had begun to dominate the market. Subsequently, automobile manufacturing became a true industry, and the contributors to its development largely refined the car's power plant and design and/or increasingly organized the management and labor required for its production. Accordingly, this first section is concerned with those pioneers who were active during the period 1890–1920 in the role of automotive inventor or entrepreneur or both.

Few would question that Henry Ford was one of the most important people in the first half of the 20th century. The economic and social impact of his motor cars, especially the Model T, was enormous. In addition, he chose, rightly or wrongly, to apply his economic wealth and power to political and religious questions as well, and his influence was significant in these areas, too.

Therefore, it is not surprising that the life and work of Henry Ford have been, and continue to be, the subjects of scholarly study. The best place to begin is probably with Allan Nevins' three-volume Ford history. Written in collaboration with Frank E. Hill, these volumes cover developments from Ford's birth to 1962. The story begins with *Ford: The Times, the Man, the Company* (to 1915), which historian John B. Rae has observed is "the great classic in this field." Volume 2 is entitled *Ford: Expansion and Challenge, 1915–1933*, and Volume 3 is *Ford: Decline and Rebirth, 1933–1962*. Together they provide as fine and comprehensive an introduction to the subject as is currently available, although the emphasis at times tends to be more on company history than Ford biography. Supplementing the Nevins trilogy are a number of fine one-volume biographies of Henry Ford. The oldest of these is *The Legend of Henry Ford*, written by Keith Sward and published in 1948. It is arguably the first truly scholarly appraisal and still worth reading because of both its emphasis on Ford as a man and his treatment of labor relations. However, this controversial book should be used with caution, given the author's desire to destroy the "myth" of Henry Ford. Probably a better choice would be Roger Burlingame's 1954 *Henry Ford: A Great Life in Brief*, the best short biography available. Most recently, we have Carol Gelderman's *Henry Ford: The Wayward Capitalist*, a well-researched and balanced account of the man, with particular attention to the complexities of his personality.

Some of the biographies concentrate on a particular aspect of Ford's life or character. Given the overwhelming task of treating all facets of his life in a single volume, such specialization makes sense and has resulted in a number of excellent studies. For a massive, detailed study of Ford and the public relations image created by the company up to 1932, see David L. Lewis' Cugnot Award-winning *The Public Image of Henry Ford: An American Folk Hero and His Company*. Lewis' work is an excellent biography, objective in its approach, and the most successful analysis of selected aspects of Henry Ford's character. Ford's appeal to, and influence on, rural Americans, to whom he became a regional icon in the 1920s, are well treated by Reynold W. Wik in his *Henry Ford and Grass-roots America*. This book is a good, specific application of some of the more general observations made by Lewis.

Following a different approach, Anne Jardim's *The First Henry Ford: A Study in Personality and Business Leadership* attempts to analyze Ford's business decisions using Freudian psychoanalytic theory. While Jardim deserves credit for trying a new approach to explain Ford's personality, her thesis is never really proven, and this failure is compounded by the inclusion of many historical errors. In the same genre is David E. Nye's *Henry Ford: "Ignorant Idealist,"* also a psychohistory, in which the author theorizes that Ford's belief in reincarnation provides an explanation for his publicly stated ideas and behavior.

Finally, for a largely visual account of Ford during his early years, supplemented with lengthy, informative captions, see Sidney Olson's *Young Henry Ford: A Picture History of the First Forty Years*. In the same regard, Charles

B. King's *Psychic Reminiscences* is interesting. A contemporary automotive pioneer, King offers remembrances of Ford in the beginning years of experimentation and invention.

Booton Herndon's *Ford: An Unconventional Biography of the Men and Their Times*, published in 1969, was one of the first books to blend together the lives of Henry Ford and his grandson, Henry Ford II, with more attention to the latter. The author's emphasis is on personalities, with the intergenerational struggle for control of the company particularly well done. Somewhat similar in focus is James Brough's *The Ford Dynasty: An American Story*. Finally, there is Robert Lacey's 1986 *Ford: The Men and the Machine*. Probably the best of all the family histories to date, Lacey provides a colorful narrative of the public and private lives of Henry, Edsel, Henry Ford II, and the Ford women. The section dealing with Henry II contains an interesting defense of his business acumen in response to accusations made by Lee Iacocca in his autobiography.

Ford's impact on American life was so significant and so swift that full-blown biographies of the man, though admittedly of the popular (as opposed to scholarly) variety, began to appear as early as 1917. Several of these are worth examining, both for what they say about Henry Ford and for what they tell us about American perceptions of the man at the height of his success. One of the earliest is Rose Wilder Lane's *Henry Ford's Own Story: How a Farmer Boy Rose to the Power That Goes with Many Millions, Yet Never Lost Touch with Humanity*. Entitled as only a book published before 1920 could be, it is popular myth making of the World War I era. In addition, see James M. Miller's *The Amazing Story of Henry Ford: The Ideal American and World's Most Famous Private Citizen*, an incredibly one-sided portrait from the early 1920s that is blatantly anti-Semitic as well; and William Stidger's *Henry Ford: The Man and His Motives* (1923), which, despite the somewhat negative-sounding title, is a very positive, largely uncritical view of the man. Allan L. Benson's *The New Henry Ford* (1923) is another myth-making book, which nonetheless is good in terms of developments immediately following the First World War. Interesting in that they were written during a watershed period for Ford and the company (the transition from the Model T to the Model A) are Gamaliel Bradford's *The Quick and the Dead*, Jonathan N. Leonard's *The Tragedy of Henry Ford*, Ralph H. Graves' *The Triumph of an Idea: The Story of Henry Ford*, and Charles Merz's *And Then Came Ford*. These volumes were the last of the early biographical efforts. The Bradford, Leonard, and Merz books also have been described as "some of the better portraits" by Ford biographer David E. Nye.

Henry Ford himself was a surprisingly prolific author, at least for a man with the corporate responsibilities that he had. Often collaborating with freelance writer Samuel Crowther, he authored some seven major books and numerous articles from the early 1920s until his death in 1947. Of these, the most important are probably three works written at four-year intervals beginning in 1922: *My Life and Work, Today and Tomorrow*, and *Moving Forward*. Combined, they form a type of multi-volume autobiography in which Ford analyzes his business success and proselytizes for the personal philosophy that he believes made it possible. Each was essentially written by Crowther based on interviews with Ford, and each was carefully reviewed by the public relations department of the company. As a result, their historical accuracy is open to question.

Two other works of interest are Ford's *My Philosophy of Industry: An Authorized Interview with Fay Leone Faurote* and *Things I've Been Thinking About*. The former is really a collection of essays on industrialism and its social impact reprinted from an earlier magazine series. Faurote had ingratiated herself earlier with Ford by writing a highly laudatory account of his production methods in 1915. *Things*, written in 1936, is valuable for the insights that it provides into Ford's ideas in the years after his virtual monopoly of the inexpensive car market had been shattered and talk of war was once again troubling the isolationist in him. Finally, some note should be taken of *The Case against the Little White Slaver*, a collection of four pamphlets written in 1916 by Henry Ford in an effort to convince adolescent boys not to use tobacco in any form. Ford was a man of strong opinions, and tobacco was definitely something that he abhorred.

Members of Henry Ford's family have either written their autobiographies or been the subject of biographies written by others, and two deserve mention in this section to the extent that they intersect with Henry's own life. Readers interested in gaining some perspective on Henry's wife, Clara Bryant Ford, are directed to the only full-scale biography of her life, *The Believer: The Life Story of Mrs. Henry Ford*, by Louise Clancy and Florence Davies. In addition, Ford R. Bryan's recent *The Fords of Dearborn: An Illustrated History* is a collection of essays spotlighting the various branches of the extended Ford family, from 1820 to 1950, with particular attention to their interaction with the most famous member of the clan.

Given the large number of people who worked for the Ford Motor Company, it should come as no surprise that some of those people would have written accounts of their lives that contain biographical information regarding Henry Ford. Probably the most significant reminiscence is that of Harry Bennett, who headed the infamous Service Department. Ostensibly concerned with internal personnel matters, Bennett's operation functioned more like the secret police in a totalitarian state, and he wielded enormous influence in the company and over Henry Ford for thirty years. With the assistance of Paul Marcus, he authored *We Never Called Him Henry*. Readers expecting to find new information and unique insights in this volume will be disappointed, as this loyal Ford friend and employee provides neither. Another longtime employee of Ford was Charles E. Sorensen, whose autobiographical *My Forty Years with Ford* is both interesting and valuable, although the veracity of parts of it has been questioned, particularly in terms of the author's role in certain key events. Samuel S. Marquis' *Henry Ford: An Interpretation*, published in 1923, is a personal evaluation of Ford by a man who directed the company's controversial Sociological Department after World War I and whose job was to "improve" the lifestyles of

Ford workers and their families. Finally, there is William A. Simonds' *Henry Ford: His Life, His Work, His Genius*, a largely uncritical work by a man who spent most of his career at Ford. (Simonds was also the author of an earlier, 1929 biography, entitled *Henry Ford—Motor Genius*.) Ford R. Bryan, in *Henry's Lieutenants*, profiles the lives and careers of Bennett, Sorensen, Marquis, James Couzens, William S. Knudsen, and thirty-two others who served as the elder Henry Ford's assistants and, as such, is a useful reference work in this regard.

There also are a few popular accounts of Henry Ford's life that deserve attention. One of the best of this genre is William C. Richards' *The Last Billionaire: Henry Ford*. Written in 1948, newspaperman Richards' account focuses on the 1930s and 1940s and is full of entertaining anecdotes. In a very different vein is John C. Dahlinger's *The Secret Life of Henry Ford*, written in collaboration with Frances S. Leighton. Dahlinger maintains that he is Ford's illegitimate son and presents an interesting "family" history. Dahlinger's claims are of doubtful veracity, given what we know of Ford's lifestyle.

Two aspects of Ford's non-automotive life have received the most attention from historians: his personal diplomatic initiatives during World War I and his negative attitudes toward the Jewish people. In regard to the former, Ford believed that he could bring an end to the war, and in 1915 he sent his so-called Peace Ship across the Atlantic to achieve that mission. The story of that failed venture has been explored in three full-length books. Easily the best is Barbara S. Kraft's *The Peace Ship: Henry Ford's Pacifist Adventure in the First World War*, a well-researched, lively, and balanced scholarly work. The two other volumes fall more in the category of memoirs. There is the more contemporaneous (1925) and politically oriented account of Louis P. Lochner, *Henry Ford: America's Don Quixote*, issued by the leftist International Publishers. Lochner was a young newsman who sailed aboard the ship. Burnet Hershey's *The Odyssey of Henry Ford and the Great Peace Ship*, written a half century after he, too, participated as a cub reporter in the adventure, adds little except for the "color" and personalities aboard ship.

In a related activity, Ford was persuaded by President Woodrow Wilson to run for the U.S. Senate from Michigan in 1918. Wilson hoped, thereby, to gain another vote in support of the establishment of the League of Nations. Ford was a reluctant Democratic candidate who said little during the campaign except to indicate his support for Prohibition, woman suffrage, and the repeal of the patent law. In the end, Ford lost a close election to Republican Truman Newberry, whose supporters did an effective job of undermining the Ford family mystique. The full story of this episode is told in Spencer Ervin's *Henry Ford versus Truman Newberry: The Famous Senate Election Contest*.

The second aspect, Ford's anti-Semitism, has been the subject of numerous articles and is covered in each of the biographical works cited above. The most detailed treatment of this dark side of Ford's personality is found in Albert Lee's *Henry Ford and the Jews*. Readers interested in gaining firsthand insight into

Ford's views in this regard should see *The International Jew*, which was published in four parts by the Dearborn Publishing Company over the years 1920–1922. Dearborn Publishing was part of the Ford industrial empire, and its editorial decisions and policy were clearly under Henry Ford's control. The anti-Semitic editorial policy of its *Dearborn Independent* had become so controversial by 1922 that "exposé" books began to appear that year. See, for instance, E.G. Pipp's *The Real Henry Ford*. Pipp was the first editor of the *Independent*, who quit his position to protest the newspaper's treatment of Jews. He wrote a second volume along similar lines in 1926, entitled *Henry Ford: Both Sides of Him.*

A third aspect of Henry Ford's non-automotive life that has been the focus of some study is his philanthropy, especially Ford's establishment of Greenfield Village in Dearborn, Michigan. The best overview of the roots and development of this aspect of Ford family affairs is William Greenleaf's *From These Beginnings: The Early Philanthropies of Henry and Edsel Ford, 1911–1936*, which emphasizes how, why, and to whom the Fords gave away millions prior to establishing and endowing the Ford Foundation. With Greenfield, Henry Ford attempted to create a nostalgic village museum that would showcase significant aspects of American life and history, especially those associated with a 19th-century rural existence. In 1938 William A. Simonds, a longtime Ford employee, published the first book devoted to the subject, entitled *Henry Ford and Greenfield Village*. Aimed at the general reader, it is essentially a public relations piece, containing no criticism of the man or this particular venture.

Finally, some mention should be made of Ford's circle of friends, one or more of whom participated in a series of well-publicized "camping trips," which actually lacked few of the comforts of home. The camaraderie that developed from these trips and other social occasions is the subject of James D. Newton's *Uncommon Friends: Life with Thomas Edison, Henry Ford, Harvey Firestone, Alexis Carrel & Charles Lindbergh.*

As important as Henry Ford was to the development of auto America, many other people played significant roles and have been the subject of biographical accounts. One of Ford's early rivals was Ransom E. Olds. In fact, credit for the first mass-produced, low-priced, American motor vehicle goes to Olds for his curved-dash Oldsmobile, rather than to Henry Ford and his Model T. Even though he sold the Olds Motor Works, the Oldsmobile name, and production facilities to others in 1903, he later founded and led Reo Motors and remained active in the automotive industry for some forty years. The best and most complete biography of his life is George S. May's *R.E. Olds: Auto Industry Pioneer.* Other good, earlier biographies are Glenn A. Niemeyer's *The Automotive Career of Ransom E. Olds*, with its emphasis on his business career, and Duane A. Yarnell's *Auto Pioneering: A Remarkable Story of Ransom Eli Olds, Father of Oldsmobile and Reo*, which primarily provides Olds' (not necessarily accurate) view of the history that he helped make. For an insider's perspective on the development of the original Olds Motor Works, see Frederick L. Smith's autobiographical *Motoring Down a Quarter Century*. This pamphlet, published in 1928, contains the interesting reminiscences of one of Olds' first company presidents.

Of the other pioneers, brothers figure prominently—the Duryeas, Studebakers, and Dodges. Of the two Duryeas, Charles has attracted more biographical attention than his brother, Frank, since the former was (rightly or wrongly) originally credited with the mechanical ideas behind the car that they created—the first practical, American-made, gasoline-powered vehicle that produced progeny. The best biography of the former is *Charles E. Duryea—Automaker*, a relatively slim volume by George S. May. Although neither of the two brothers even wrote a full-length autobiography, Charles did author two early practical treatises on cars and motoring, *Handbook of the Automobile* (1906) and *The Automobile Book* (1916), the latter written with James E. Homans. Following his brother's death, Frank wrote *America's First Automobile*, an account of the pioneering years in which he plays a larger role than most historians had previously portrayed. This latter judgment was given significant support by the publication in 1993 of *Carriages without Horses: J. Frank Duryea and the Birth of the American Automobile Industry*, beautifully written by Richard P. Scharchburg and winner of the SAH's Cugnot Award as the best book in the field of automotive history that year; it is the definitive work not just on Frank but on Charles and the cars that they manufactured both together and separately in conjunction with others.

One of the few firms that successfully made the transition from buggy manufacture to the production of motor vehicles was Studebaker, which continued to produce its own line of cars in the United States until 1963. The best biography of the most significant brother is Edwin Corle's *John Studebaker: An American Dream*, which appeared in 1949. An especially meritorious aspect of this work is its heavy citation of excerpts from Studebaker's personal journal. There is also one study of the company that contains substantial biographical information, Kathleen A. Smallzreid and Dorothy J. Roberts' *More Than You Promise: A Small Business at Work in Society*.

In regard to the Dodge brothers and their heirs, whose lives were sometimes akin to a modern-day soap opera, one should examine two books by Jean Maddern Pitrone: *The Dodges: The Auto Family Fortune and Misfortune*, coauthored with Joan Potter Elwart, and *Tangled Web: The Legacy of Auto Pioneer John F. Dodge*. The former was the first serious biography of John and Horace Dodge and their families and carries the story through four generations. The latter focuses on the question of whether the first child born to John and Matilda Dodge had a Siamese twin sister—a truly bizarre tale, yet one that was the subject of court litigation for five years in the late 1980s. Aimed more at the general reader is *Dodge Dynasty: The Car and Family That Rocked Detroit*, by Caroline Latham and David Agresta. In somewhat of a docudrama style, the authors tell the story of the founding of the company, its growth under the brothers' tutelage, and the internal family battles that ultimately caused its sale.

Unfortunately, most of the other pioneers of this period have not had full-length, commercially produced biographies published concerning their lives. Two important exceptions are *Alloys and Automobiles: The Life of Elwood Haynes*, by Ralph D. Gray, and *Famous but Forgotten: The Story of Alexander Winton, Automotive Pioneer and Industrialist*, by Thomas F. Saal and Bernard J. Golias. Both works won the AACA's Thomas McKean Cup for the most significant automotive book in the year of its publication. Gray's is an excellent account of one of the premier inventor-entrepreneurs of the first quarter of this century. Haynes was responsible not only for the Haynes and the Haynes–Apperson motor cars but also for the development of several metallic alloys (hence the title of Gray's book). Haynes himself in 1914 wrote *The Complete Motorist*, a Haynes Automobile Company history (to date) with due attention to the contributions of its founder. For their part, Saal and Golias have done justice to Alexander Winton, an automotive pioneer whose contributions had indeed been "forgotten." He was a man whose company produced popular, high-quality vehicles for twenty-seven years (1898–1924) that distinguished themselves both on the road and on the racetrack. In addition, Winton was responsible for some 100 patents during the years when the automobile was evolving technologically and even made contributions to the adaptation of the diesel engine to trains.

In addition, there are a small number of good, but less distinguished works. Charles B. King, who drove his first successful car on the streets of Detroit in 1896—the year that Ford accomplished the same feat with his "Quadricycle"— wrote a brief autobiography entitled *A Golden Anniversary, 1895–1945* and the aforementioned *Psychic Reminiscences*. King had previously helped form the American Motor League, an organization that lobbied for road improvements in the late 1890s, and was subsequently responsible for organizing two automobile manufacturing concerns before he retired from the business in 1916. Hiram Percy Maxim, another early inventor of a motor car (1895), has left a highly readable autobiography entitled *Horseless Carriage Days*, in which he recounts the early days of "motor carriage" construction at the Pope Manufacturing Company. John Gary Anderson, founder of the Anderson Motor Company (1916–1925), relates the history of one of the most successful cars manufactured in the South (Rock Hill, South Carolina) in his *Autobiography*. Finally, there is *Victor W. Pagé: Automotive and Aviation Pioneer*, in which author Frank C. Derato recounts the life of a man who tried three times to manufacture motor vehicles but never got beyond the prototype stage. Pagé was more successful as an author, writing nearly 100 books and countless magazine articles concerning automobiles, and serving for a time as automotive editor for *Scientific American*.

Besides these auto/biographies, short career histories of various automotive pioneers also can be found in collections consisting of a series of individual chapters on specific individuals. In this category would be such works as *Automotive Giants of America: Men Who Are Making Our Motor Industry*, written by B.C. Forbes and O.D. Foster and published in 1926, and Richard Crabb's *Birth of a Giant: The Men and Incidents That Gave America the Motorcar*, a more recent and comprehensive work that attempts (with mixed success) to weave chapter-length biographies together to form a history of the early automotive industry. George B. Selden, the man whose patent control over automotive manufacturing was finally broken by Henry Ford, is the subject of a chapter in L. Sprague DeCamp's *The Heroic Age of American Invention*.

Finally, some mention needs to made of Clessie L. Cummins, whose fame lies more in his industrial and entrepreneurial efforts on behalf of the diesel engine than in his being an automotive pioneer. Cummins has left us his autobiographical *My Days with the Diesel: The Memoirs of Clessie L. Cummins, Father of the Highway Diesel*, in which he describes his efforts (often bizarre) in the first third of the 20th century to publicize and market that engine for automobile, bus, and truck use. Cummins' work evidences the strengths and weaknesses that one would expect from a book of memoirs. Of a more scholarly nature is *The Diesel Odyssey of Clessie Cummins*, by Lyle Cummins, Clessie's son. Lyle's effort benefits especially from its broader chronological and technical coverage, as well as his use of the records of the Cummins Engine Company.

Curiously forgotten has been Albert A. Pope, an extremely successful bicycle manufacturer, who turned his talents to a number of automobiles that bore his name, at least in hyphenated form, such as the Pope–Hartford, the Pope–Toledo, and the Pope–Waverly. Also deserving, and still lacking, book-length biographical treatment are the Stanley brothers, Frederic and August (Augie) Duesenberg, and Benjamin Briscoe.

CORPORATE MANAGERS AND LABOR ORGANIZERS

While the exploits of automotive pioneers were crucial to the initial acceptance of the automobile in American life, the corporate managers and labor organizers were largely responsible for developing the multimillion-dollar automotive corporations that we know today. So different were the pioneering and nurturing roles that only one man really excelled at both—Henry Ford. In a very real sense, that explains Ford's preeminence in automotive history. Readers interested in Henry Ford as a company executive should examine the pertinent sections of the biographies described in the first section of this chapter.

In terms of corporate management, the presidency of the Ford Motor Company was transferred from Henry to his son Edsel in 1919. However, Henry continued to exert such oversight over the company that it was not until grandson Henry Ford II took over in 1945 that we begin to see some independent leadership. Although this namesake has been, and continues to be, studied in a number of corporate histories (see, for instance, the Brough and Lacey volumes cited in the earlier section), Henry Ford II has had only one serious biography devoted solely to himself, and that a critical one, by Victor Lasky. Entitled *Never Complain, Never Explain: The Story of Henry Ford II*, the emphasis here is more on his lifestyle than his management technique, and Lasky's objectivity is open to question. Booton Herndon's previously cited *Ford: An Unconventional*

Biography of the Men and Their Times, while it covers all three Ford Company family presidents, is primarily a biography of Henry II and better balanced than the Lasky account. Walter Hayes' *Henry: A Life of Henry Ford II* is nothing more than an uncritical tribute from a man who was public relations adviser to Ford.

Beyond the Ford family, a number of men were not directly involved in the pre–World War I pioneer days but instead entered the field in the 1920s and 1930s to serve as true corporate managers. Of this group, three men saw their name used for a make of motor car: Walter P. Chrysler, William C. Durant, and Errett Lobban Cord. Chrysler, who worked at Buick, Willys, and Maxwell-Chalmers (a predecessor of the Chrysler Corporation), wrote his autobiography in installments for the *Saturday Evening Post* in 1937, and these were published, with a postscript, in book form in 1950 as *Life of an American Workman*. Written with Boyden Sparkes, this work has been praised by reviewers for its insight, accuracy, and readability. Chrysler's personal character is the focus of a chapter entitled "Personality and Good Practical Judgement," written by Thomas C. Cochran, which appears in John A. Garraty's *The Unforgettable Americans*. Despite Chrysler's sizable achievements with three automotive companies, as late as 1999 he had not yet been the subject of a scholarly biography.

When we think of automobile corporations today, we envision gigantic operations producing a range of makes and an even larger diversity of models. Such was not always the case. In fact, to the mid-1920s, a single company manufacturing cars under more than one name was exceptional. This was all changed by William C. Durant. Durant brought together some twenty-odd companies to form the General Motors Corporation in 1908–1909, a company he was to head and then lose control of twice by 1920, with a stop at Chevrolet along the way. One of the truly great American entrepreneurs, Durant was a man with a compelling personality and a life history to match. The premier biography of Durant is Bernard A. Weisberger's comprehensive *The Dream Maker: William C. Durant, Founder of General Motors*. An earlier, also excellent biography was written by Lawrence R. Gustin, entitled *Billy Durant: Creator of General Motors*. It relies heavily on an autobiographical manuscript and personal papers left by Durant, along with interviews with his wife, two of his personal secretaries, and others. Gustin was awarded the Thomas McKean Cup for this work, symbolizing his outstanding contributions to automotive history. Finally, one should read Margery Durant's *My Father* for the detail that it provides regarding the events of Durant's non-commercial life, even though the late automotive historian John B. Rae called it merely a "work of filial piety."

If Durant assembled the pieces and created a functioning entity, Alfred P. Sloan Jr., as president of General Motors from 1923 to 1937, fine-tuned and expanded the operation to the point where it was the single largest corporation in the world. Fortunately for the historian, Sloan has written two autobiographical accounts of his experiences, spaced some twenty years apart. The first, published in 1941 and written with the assistance of Boyden Sparkes, is entitled

Adventures of a White-Collar Man. In 1963, a second, more comprehensive volume appeared, *My Years with General Motors.* Another winner of the Mc-Kean Cup, the latter is particularly interesting in terms of its discussion of the reorganization of GM and Sloan's innovative management policies that guided it.

Another president of General Motors deserving of mention is William S. Knudsen, who earlier helped engineer what many believed was impossible—the demise of the Model T Ford as a result of an inability to compete with another car, in this case, General Motors' Chevrolet. Norman Beasley's *Knudsen: A Biography,* although it lacks footnotes and a bibliography, is really the only decent account of a man who also provided exemplary service overseeing production management for the federal government during World War II.

Although his star was in ascendancy for a briefer period of time, none shone brighter than that of Errett Lobban Cord. His cars became design classics in their age and formed part of what may have been, car for car, the most prestigious automotive corporation ever formed—the Cord Corporation, which made Auburn, Cord, and Duesenberg. The definitive biography of this man is Griffith Borgeson's *Errett Lobban Cord, His Empire, His Motor Cars: Auburn, Cord, Duesenberg.* True to the subject and his creations, this book is a graphic work of art, beautifully illustrated, bound in genuine leather, and printed in a limited edition; it sold in the year of its publication (1984) for $325!

Nonetheless, having a car named after oneself is not by itself a very good measure of a person's contributions to automotive history. Several individuals were "indispensable" in terms of the development of their companies and yet never received such public recognition. Chief among them might be Henry M. Leland, who formed the Cadillac and later Lincoln Motor Companies and was one of the first, and probably the greatest, advocate of the use of standardized parts in automobiles. His story has been well told by his daughter-in-law, Mrs. Wilfred C. Leland, in *Master of Precision: Henry M. Leland,* a past winner of the Thomas McKean Cup. Written with the assistance of Minnie Dubbs Millbrook, this book recounts the life of one of the industry's great innovators and does so in a surprisingly scholarly and well-balanced manner. Equally important was Charles E. Sorensen, a Ford Motor Company executive who remained on the good side of Henry Ford for a longer time than anyone with the exception of Clara. In the mid-1950s, he wrote with the assistance of Samuel T. Williamson a personally revealing autobiography entitled *My Forty Years with Ford,* which provides significant observations on the inner workings of the company, especially for the period prior to the 1920s.

The Second World War caused the temporary suspension of the production of automobiles for private use and created a pent-up demand for new cars in 1945. Many felt that the times were propitious for launching new automotive companies. While all eventually failed, two stand out not only for the cars they produced but for the men who headed them: Henry J. Kaiser and Preston T. Tucker. Easily the best biography of Kaiser is Mark S. Foster's well-written and well-researched *Henry J. Kaiser: Builder in the Modern American West*. Foster's biographical treatment covers not only the Kaiser–Fraser Motors effort but the more successful post–World War II ventures in aluminum, steel, and plastics as well. Also worthy of attention is *Henry J. Kaiser, Western Colossus: An Insider's View*, a celebratory account by Albert P. Heiner, who worked for Kaiser as a public relations officer and was an eyewitness to many of the events described.

Tucker has been the subject of less scholarly scrutiny. The best account of his life is Philip S. Egan's brief *Design and Destiny: The Making of the Tucker Automobile*. Egan, who was assistant chief designer at Tucker, provides an insider's observations on both the car and the man who brought it into being. An earlier biography, *The Indomitable Tin Goose: The True Story of Preston Tucker and His Car*, was written by Charles T. Pearson, who directed Tucker's public relations efforts. Although his objectivity might be questioned, Pearson resurrects the theory that Tucker was done in by a conspiracy of Detroit auto makers and their Washington, D.C., allies. Regardless, Tucker remains somewhat of a mystery today, considered a prophet by some and a flimflam man by others.

In terms of more recent automotive history, two men have dominated the headlines and been the subject of the most writing: John Z. DeLorean and Lee A. Iacocca. While widely different in temperament and accomplishments, both men represent the professional manager whose loyalty is not necessarily to one company but rather to achieving success wherever he finds himself in the industry as a whole. Thus, DeLorean made his name with General Motors before his much-publicized resignation and subsequent ill-fated attempt to launch his own automobile company. Similarly, Iacocca was the fair-haired boy at Ford before running afoul of Henry Ford II, moving on to Chrysler, where he successfully oversaw the resurrection of that bankrupt car maker.

Although John DeLorean's meteoric rise within the corporate structure of General Motors was well known within the business world, he first became a public celebrity with the publication of *On a Clear Day You Can See General Motors: John Z. DeLorean's Look inside the Automotive Giant*, written with his cooperation by J. Patrick Wright. Insider exposés of billion-dollar corporations are rare, and that fact, together with GM's attempts to block circulation of the book, guaranteed a wide audience for this account of alleged mismanagement of the then number one auto maker in the world.

As DeLorean moved and changed roles from corporate "bad boy" to automotive entrepreneur, his social and business activities continued to draw media coverage. One result was a spate of books that appeared shortly before his 1983 trial on charges of selling illicit drugs for the purpose of propping up the economically ailing DeLorean Motor Corporation. (He subsequently was acquitted when the jury ruled that government agents had engaged in entrapment.) At this time *Dream Maker: The Rise and Fall of John Z. DeLorean*, written by Ivan Fallon and James Srodes, appeared, a highly critical account by two financial writers that emphasizes the economic problems of the later years with DeLorean

Motor over the accomplishments at GM. Similar in both tone and concept is Hillel Levin's 1983 *Grand Delusions: The Cosmic Career of John DeLorean*. Also published the same year was John Lamm's *DeLorean: Stainless Steel Illusion*, which emphasizes the origins and development of the car more than the man behind it, though in terms of the latter, Lamm is much more positive than Fallon and Srodes. (The metallic allusion [or illusion] in the title referred to the material from which the body of the DeLorean motor car was made.) Two years later, DeLorean tried his hand at autobiographical writing, authoring (with the help of Ted Schwarz) *DeLorean*, both a history of his life and an ultimately unsuccessful attempt to explain and justify his controversial actions to fund the DeLorean Motor Corporation. In this regard, *The DeLorean Tapes*, edited by Paul Eddy, provides transcripts of seventy-nine of the secret Federal Bureau of Investigation (FBI) recordings that led to his illegal drugs indictment. Given the publicity surrounding DeLorean's adventures, it is not surprising that his associates began to write books on their experiences with him. One of the more interesting of these is William Haddad's *Hard Driving: My Years with John DeLorean*. Haddad, who was a consultant to DeLorean for fifteen years, has concluded that he and others were taken in by the supposed dreams of a man who was really a con artist at heart.

Easily the most significant leader of Chrysler since the company's founder has been Lee Iacocca, whose *Iacocca: An Autobiography* is must reading for a better understanding of the resurrection of that company *and* the role that Iacocca played at Ford previously. Published in 1984, it immediately appeared on the *New York Times* best-seller list, moving to the number one rank and remaining on the list for eighty-eight weeks. Written with William Novak, Iacocca's life story reads like the American Dream, and his rebuilding of Chrysler is one of the great success stories of an era better known for Detroit's failures. Iacocca's celebrity status led almost immediately to a spate of books concerning him. While his autobiography was still on the best-seller list, *Iacocca: America's Most Dynamic Businessman*, by David Abodaher, became a paperback best-seller of its own. Abodaher, a former employee of Chrysler's advertising agency, draws upon personal interviews with members of Iacocca's immediate family and combines that information with in-depth research to produce what the *Library Journal* calls "a stimulating biography . . . an excellent history."

As a result of his success at Chrysler, Iacocca's reputation soared. As might be expected, the time was also right for an exposé of the man, and Peter Wyden attempted to present an unflattering portrait in *The Unknown Iacocca: An Unauthorized Biography*. Based on extensive interviews, Wyden does present the "darker" side of Iacocca's personality and business practices but still reaches essentially positive conclusions regarding his subject. More recently, Doron P. Levin's *Behind the Wheel at Chrysler: The Iacocca Legacy* provides a valuable reinterpretation of how Iacocca turned the company around, arguing that it was more a question of personality and image than fundamental reform. Levin's book was termed "fascinating and terribly important" by a reviewer for the *New York Times.*

Somewhat similar to Iacocca in the way that he breathed new life into an old company was George W. Romney. In an age when Detroit cars were getting bigger by the year, Romney made the bold move of introducing a line of compact cars in the mid-1950s. They found a ready, albeit limited, market, and Romney was able to bring American Motors from the red into the black. Like Iacocca, his success captured the public's imagination, to such an extent that he actually ran for the Republican presidential nomination. The most complete biography of George Romney is Tom Mahoney's laudatory *The Story of George Romney: Builder, Salesman, Crusader,* which portrays his life as "a modern American success saga." Published as it was in 1960, it covers his life only up through the middle of his tenure as head of American Motors, with his political career and six years as governor of Michigan yet to come. T. George Harris' *Romney's Way: A Man and an Idea* completes the story, at least through 1967.

Lesser, though still significant, contributions to the American automobile industry were made by a number of other men. In this regard, the life of Roy D. Chapin is particularly interesting. Chapin, whose managerial skills were probably equivalent to those of many mentioned previously, chose to apply his talents to the Hudson Motor Company, which he helped form in 1909 and served until his death in 1936. For a good biography of the man, see J.C. Long's *Roy D. Chapin,* a family-authorized biography that is still the standard reference. Another in that same category was James S. Couzens who, as business manager, became about as powerful as one could become in the Ford organization during the life of Henry and later served as mayor of Detroit and in the U.S. Senate. For his story, see Harry Barnard's *Independent Man: The Life of Senator James Couzens.*

The life of one of the consummate industrial managers of the first half of the twentieth century, Ernest R. Breech, has been explored by J. Mel Hickerson in his *Ernie Breech: The Story of His Remarkable Career at General Motors, Ford and TWA.* Breech was one of those persons whose administrative skills were so carefully honed that they were transferable from one corporate giant to another. Breech was not the only individual whose career encompassed the automotive as well as one or more other industries. Edward V. "Eddie" Rickenbacker, the World War I flying ace and later chief executive officer (CEO) of Eastern Air Lines, found himself the titular head of a short-lived (1922–1927) car company bearing his name. The history of that venture is explored in his 1967 autobiography, *Rickenbacker,* and in a lengthy chapter in Finis Farr's *Rickenbacker's Luck: An American Life.* Finally, there was Walter Carpenter, CEO at Du Pont and an important director at General Motors (working with Alfred Sloan) whose professional life is studied in *Strictly Business: Walter Carpenter at Du Pont and General Motors,* by Charles W. Cheape. Carpenter's career personified, as one reviewer called it, "the transition from owner management to professional management." As the archetypical "organization man" from 1919 to 1962, Carpenter's career provides important insights into American corporate culture in the middle third of the 20th century, as well as the unique relationship that existed between Du Pont and GM.

Turning to more contemporary figures, there is Robert S. McNamara, one of the so-called Whiz Kids hired by the Ford Motor Company after World War II. He helped introduce a form of systematic management that brought that company back into the black and furthered an automotive career that culminated in his being selected as Ford president. Deborah Shapley's *Promise and Power: The Life and Times of Robert McNamara* is the most recent and best biography of this man. Henry L. Trewhitt's *McNamara*, published twenty years earlier, is also good. Both books cover his tumultuous years as secretary of defense (1961–1968) as well. Ross Perot, unsuccessful candidate for president of the United States in 1992 and 1996, is at the center of Doron P. Levin's *Irreconcilable Differences: Ross Perot versus General Motors*, which tells the story of the merger of Perot's Electronic Data Systems (EDS) with GM in the 1980s, the sharp differences between Perot, who had become the largest holder of GM stock, and CEO Roger Smith over corporate policy, and the eventual $700 million buyout of Perot. Todd Mason's *Perot: An Unauthorized Biography* is broader in coverage, a relatively evenhanded (though essentially critical) account of Perot's life as a maverick businessmen, including his David and Goliath struggle with GM. Roger Smith, chairman of the General Motors Corporation during the 1980s, is the subject of Albert Lee's *Call Me Roger*. Like Iacocca and Romney, Smith saw himself faced with a corporate challenge, in his case preparing GM for competition into the 21st century. According to Lee's analysis, Smith essentially failed in this regard, and thus this biography by a former GM speechwriter is a generally critical one.

The rise of large automotive corporations and the concomitant emergence of corporate managers also saw the inevitable development of organized labor and the rise of leaders in that area. Of the men involved in the initial organizing efforts and later, the work of Walter P. Reuther clearly was the most significant. As a result, Reuther has been the object of much biographical writing. The best work is Nelson Lichtenstein's *The Most Dangerous Man in Detroit: Walter Reuther and the Fate of American Labor*, which does a fine job of chronicling the life of a man who served as president of the United Automobile Workers from 1946 to 1970 and relating it to the rise and decline of the American labor movement. John Barnard's *Walter Reuther and the Rise of the Auto Workers* provides a good general introduction to the subject but is somewhat simplistic in its approach and lacks footnotes for further exploration. A more detailed and in-depth study that is better written is Frank Cormier and William J. Eaton's *Reuther*, published in 1970, a year after his death, which favorably highlights his skills as collective bargainer and union leader. An earlier, though still valuable, work is Irving Howe and B.J. Widick's *UAW and Walter Reuther*, an excellent history of the union written from the labor perspective but largely unsuccessful in terms of placing that union in a larger societal context.

In addition, see *The Brothers Reuther and the Story of the UAW: A Memoir*, by Victor G. Reuther, Walter's brother and coworker in the union. Though Reuther's account is clearly biased and adds little of a factual nature, he does present in a dramatic fashion the struggle to organize all automotive workers (and a union for them) and includes the type of vignettes that add color to the historical record. Finally, Eldorous L. Dayton's *Walter P. Reuther: The Autocrat of the Bargaining Table*, while yet another biographical account, is a book with a significant difference. Dayton takes a decidedly negative view of his subject and sees Reuther and unionism as a threat to the free enterprise system.

Certainly, no one man can rightfully be given full credit for an achievement as enormous as the unionization of American automotive workers. Fortunately, we have some biographical works by others who were actively involved in the movement. Clayton M. Fountain, who for years worked with Walter Reuther in the UAW, has written *Union Guy*, memoirs written from the perspective of a rank-and-file union organizer. Similarly autobiographical in nature is Wyndham Mortimer's *Organize! My Life as a Union Man*, by a man who was once vice-president of the UAW. Margaret Collingsworth Nowak's *Two Who Were There: A Biography of Stanley Nowak*, tells the story of the Polish-American UAW pioneer and, later, the first labor legislator in Michigan and his wife. Finally, Philip Bonosky's *Brother Bill McKie: Building the Union at Ford* provides a highly favorable account of the activities of one of the better-known communist labor organizers.

Finally, some mention should be made of a pioneering work that chronicles the life not of a labor leader but rather of an ordinary workman. Norman Best's autobiographical *A Celebration of Work* is the story of a man who spent almost fifty years as a blue-collar worker, primarily as a highway construction laborer, and the philosophy of economic democracy that he espouses.

ENGINEERS AND DESIGNERS

By the end of the 19th century, inventors both in the United States and abroad had proven the feasibility of a self-propelled, road vehicle that could be used for private transportation. In a sense, from that time until today, the further development of the automobile has been in the hands of two different, yet related, groups of people—engineers and designers. The former have largely concerned themselves with developing the power plant under the hood, although some attention also has been given to such other considerations as steering mechanisms, brakes, and interior comfort. The latter have tried to make the cars more "attractive" to the potential buyer and have been aided in their work by the adoption of the idea of yearly model changes and, more recently, the attention to aerodynamic styling.

Within the engineering group, the person who has been most heavily studied is Charles F. Kettering, "Boss" to his friends. Kettering, who was head of research at General Motors for twenty-seven years, is most famous for his introduction of the electric self-starter, although that was one of the earliest (1911) in a long line of accomplishments that also included quick-drying lacquer, four-wheel brakes, two-way shock absorbers, and ethyl (octane-boosting) gasoline. The most recent and undoubtedly the best biography is by Stuart W. Leslie. Entitled *Boss Kettering: Wizard of General Motors*, this 1983 book is an interesting and scholarly portrayal of an American engineer/inventor who may be second only to Thomas Edison in importance in that category. An earlier biography of considerable merit is Thomas A. Boyd's *Professional Amateur: The Biography of Charles Franklin Kettering*. Boyd was one of Kettering's close business associates, and the resulting work, while largely uncritical, does offer personal insights regarding Kettering's personality and research work unavailable elsewhere. Boyd is also responsible for *Prophet of Progress: The Speeches of Charles F. Kettering*, which he edited.

Other than Kettering, automotive engineers have not received the attention that they deserve. The reason for this may be that "pure" engineers are rare in automotive history. Much more common is what John B. Rae calls the "engineer-entrepreneur," a person who has both the mechanism and the market in mind when he or she does his or her work. Henry Leland, mentioned in the previous section of this chapter, would be a good example of such an individual, as would Henry Ford. A third would be Carl G. Fisher. His Prest-O-Lite Company was a pioneer in early automotive headlights and starting systems. Fisher's interest in test tracks led to the construction of the Indianapolis Motor Speedway and, in 1911, the 500-mile race that made that venue famous. He also was a leader in the movement for good roads and interstate highways and is generally credited with being the prime mover behind the transcontinental Lincoln Highway and the subsequent Dixie Highway. The best biography of this "practical visionary" is *The Pacesetter: The Untold Story of Carl Fisher*, by Jerry Fisher, which won the AACA's McKean Memorial Cup for 1998.

A number of other men have made more discrete contributions to the mechanical development of the automobile and have been the subject of at least a single, book-length manuscript devoted to their lives. These include Robert J. Casey's *Mr. Clutch: The Story of George William Borg*, whose success in automotive parts went far beyond the clutch; J. Edward Christie's brief biography of his father, *Steel Steeds Christie: A Memoir of J. Walter Christie*, a man who did pioneering work on the front-wheel drive car; *The Unreasonable American: Francis W. Davis, Inventor of Power Steering*, by Houston Branch and Wendell Smith; F.C. Kelly's *David Ross: Modern Pioneer*, the latter being the inventor of a type of steering gear extensively adopted in the automotive industry between the two world wars; *One Man's Vision: The Life of Automotive Pioneer Ralph R. Teetor*, a biography by his daughter Marjorie Teetor Meyer of the blind inventor of cruise control and president of the Perfect Circle Corporation, manufacturers of world-famous oil-regulating piston rings; and *T.A. Willard: Wizard of the Storage Battery*, as author Edna Robb Webster calls the man who perfected the electric storage battery, which is still an integral part of a car's ignition system.

The number of scholarly studies of designers, while somewhat greater than that of engineers, is still sparser than one would imagine, particularly given the attention paid by American automotive producers and consumers to car styling. Of those designers who have achieved fame, Harley J. Earl is probably the best known. Earl was a longtime chief of the Styling Section at General Motors and is credited with such innovations as the hardtop and the quad taillight, with its separate lights for breaking, turning, and backing; the tail fin, to say nothing of the original 1950s Chevrolet Corvettes. The best biographies of the man are two by Stephen Bayley: *Harley Earl*, a comprehensive account of his life and significance to post–World War II automotive design, and the earlier, lavishly illustrated, but brief, *Harley Earl and the Dream Machine*.

Second only to Earl in prominence and longevity was Gordon M. Buehrig, the man responsible for such inspirational cars as the Duesenberg Model J, the Auburn Boattail, the Cord 810 and 812, the Stutz, and the Continental Mark II. Buehrig's autobiography is cleverly titled *Rolling Sculpture: A Designer and His Work* and is fascinating and well illustrated. Also prominent during the era of so-called classic cars was W. Dorwin Teague, who recently wrote his autobiography, *Industrial Designer: The Artist as Engineer*. Although Teague was a prolific inventor and stylist, his body design for the legendary Marmon sixteen-cylinder motor car of the early 1930s was his finest achievement.

Paul Jodard's *Raymond Loewy* is the biography of a man responsible for a wide variety of mid-20th-century innovative vehicle designs, such as streamlined trains for the Pennsylvania Railroad, the interior of the Skylab space craft, and, most importantly from our perspective, cars for Studebaker, including the Avanti. Similarly, John Bridges' *Bob Bourke Designs for Studebaker* chronicles the career of a man who played a key role in the designs created for that company in the early and mid-1950s. Finally, there is journeyman designer Bob Thomas' brief autobiography *Confessions of an Automotive Stylist*. Thomas worked for three years with Harley Earl at General Motors and also at Ford, Hudson, and Lincoln, making contributions to the original Lincoln Continental, its successors at Ford, and the ill-fated Pinto.

An additional source of information on the lives of significant engineers and designers can be "survey" books on this subject. For American designers, the best and most recent work is *Art of the American Automobile: The Greatest Stylists and Their Work*, written by Nick Georgano with photography by Nicky Wright. Careers of *all* the important stylists from the late 1920s to the present are described and illustrated, including Gordon Buehrig, Howard Darrin, Harley Earl, Virgil Exner, Raymond Loewy, Bill Mitchell, and Dick Teague. Other volumes, such as *Automobile Design: Twelve Great Designers and Their Work*, edited by Ronald Barker and Anthony Harding, and *The World's Great Automobile Stylists*, by John Tipler, tend to be predominantly European in coverage. However, Barker and Harding include chapters on American engineers Henry

M. Leland (written by Maurice D. Hendry) and Harry Miller (by Griffith Borgeson), and Tipler profiles Frank Costin, Bill Mitchell, and Harley Earl.

Finally, some mention should be made of those individuals whose contributions to automotive design and engineering have been the result of competition racing. (The lives of the men and women who drive those cars are discussed in the next section, and motor racing as a sport is the focus of Chapter 9.) Biographical volumes exist for four of these racing designer/engineers: Carroll Shelby, Harry A. Miller, Briggs Cunningham, and Roy Richter. Shelby's autobiography "as told to" John Bentley has appeared under several titles and in different editions, the original being called *The Cobra Story* after the most famous of his creations. An excellent book, it provides both a chronicle of Shelby's life through 1965 and a history of the racing and production cars that have borne his name.

The life and achievements of Harry A. Miller, whose cars dominated oval track racing during the years between the two world wars, have been described in two good biographies. Of these, Griffith Borgeson and Patricia Borgeson's *Miller*, published in cooperation with the Smithsonian Institution, is the best, covering as it does not only the life (1875–1943) of this highly successful automotive engineer but also the engines, the cars, and the competition history of the Miller-powered cars—all in under 150 pages! Cars equipped with his innovative engines won the Indianapolis 500 thirty-nine times, and power plants derived from his original designs were still being used in race cars in the 1980s. Mark L. Dees' *The Miller Dynasty*, an earlier biography, has recently been updated and remains an excellent source of technical data.

Cunningham: The Life and Cars of Briggs Swift Cunningham, by Dean Batchelor and Albert R. Bochroch, recounts the career of a man and a team that built a series of exciting vehicles that dominated American sports car racing in the mid-1950s but never attained their greatest goal—winning the Le Mans twenty-four-hour race. Cunningham is also known for a significant California automotive museum that carried his name from 1966 to 1986.

Less known by the general public but possibly more influential in the 1930s and 1940s, was Roy Richter. He began his automotive career as a midget car driver and went on to become the owner of Bell Auto Parts, the country's first "speed shop," where he developed and manufactured such well-known racing paraphernalia as the Bell helmet and the Cragar S/S custom wheel. His story is recounted in *Roy Richter: Striving for Excellence*, by Art Bagnall.

RACING DRIVERS

In Chapter 9, we shall examine the literature on the sport of automobile racing. Here, our concern is with those American men—and some women— who earned their living driving those cars and, in so doing, became famous personalities. In the United States, oval track (as opposed to road) racing has been the dominant form of the sport. In that regard, possibly the most versatile driver and certainly one of the greatest is Mario Andretti, winner of the Indi-

anapolis 500, the Daytona 500, and three U.S Auto Club (USAC) champion-
ships. Andretti's life has been chronicled twice by Lyle K. Engel, first in *Mario
Andretti: The Man Who Can Win Any Kind of Race* and again in *Mario Andretti:
World Driving Champion*, an accolade that he garnered in 1978, the last of only
two Americans to achieve that distinction. A biography by Bill Libby, entitled
Andretti, also appeared at the time of his Indy triumph. Andretti himself has
been involved in no less than three autobiographical projects: *What's It Like
Out There?*, written in 1970 with Bob Collins; *Mario Andretti: World Champion*, coauthored with Nigel Roebuck; and, most recently, *Andretti*, written just
before he retired in 1994, which focuses more on Mario the person and his
family than on the cars he drove.

Another individual who has succeeded in varying types of racing is A.J. Foyt,
who has been a first-place finisher at Indianapolis a record-setting four times, a
six-time USAC champion, and a Daytona 500 winner. Foyt is the author (with
William Neely) of one of the best racing autobiographies, his award-winning
A.J.: My Life as America's Greatest Race Car Driver, an unglamorized account
of the life of a man who won over $4 million. In addition to this autobiography,
readers should also examine Bill Libby's *A.J. Foyt: Racing Champion*.

Brothers who both race are not uncommon in professional circles. One of
best "families" are the Unsers, Bobby and Al, who have had great success at
Indianapolis (where they have won a combined seven times) and on the USAC
circuit (one or the other has been the annual champion five times). Their lives
have been chronicled in two dual biographies, one by Joe Scalzo, entitled *The
Unbelievable Unsers*, and the other by Gordon Kirby, entitled *Unser: An American Family Portrait*. With the assistance of Scalzo, Bobby has written his autobiography, *The Bobby Unser Story*.

While his career was somewhat briefer and more circumscribed than the previously mentioned drivers, Phil Hill earned himself a permanent listing in the
record books. *Phil Hill: Yankee Champion, First American to Win the Driving
Championship of the World*, the title of a biography by William F. Nolan, explains why Hill has that distinction. He won the Grand Prix championship in
1961, at a time when American participation, let alone victory, in that type of
racing was rare.

For the story of an individual who made a successful career of driving in
Indianapolis-type and stock car races, see the ubiquitous Bill Libby's insightful
Parnelli: A Story of Auto-Racing, an account of the life of Rufus Parnell Jones
beginning with his 1963 Indy 500 victory. A well-written look at a man who
has been involved in all aspects of motor racing, from driver to car owner to
business entrepreneur (STP Corporation), is Anthony (Andy) Granatelli's autobiography, *They Call Me Mister 500*. One of the more colorful and probably
the most successful of American drivers abroad was the late Peter Revson, heir
to the Revlon cosmetics fortune. With the assistance of Leon Mandel, he wrote
his autobiography, entitled *Speed with Style: The Autobiography of Peter Revson*, published the year (1974) of his tragic death while practicing for the South

African Grand Prix. In the book, Revson traces the development of his racing career, concentrating on his years as a Formula 1 driver. Finally, Gordon Kirby's *Bobby Rahal: The Graceful Champion* is the biography of the only Indy car driver to win the Championship Auto Racing Team's (CART) championship three times (1986, 1987, and 1992), a man whose career also included an Indianapolis 500 victory and experience in Canadian–American (Can-Am) and Formula 1 racing.

The lives of a number of drivers less well known to the general public but nonetheless significant in terms of American motor racing history also have been found worthy of book-length treatment. For example, see *The Jim Gilmore Story: Alone in the Crowd* by William Neely. Gilmore successfully raced Indy-type cars for twenty years. *Adventure on Wheels: The Autobiography of a Road Racing Champion*, by John Fitch (with William F. Nolan), also is worth reading. Fitch was a successful sports car driver of the early 1950s. Sam Posey's auto-biographical *The Mudge Pond Express* describes his Trans-American and Can-Am exploits in the late 1960s and early 1970s. *The Unfair Advantage* is Mark Donohue's autobiographical account of a driver best remembered for his victories in the Can-Am Challenge Cup and as driver for the (Roger) Penske racing team. *Tattersall—The Legend*, written by Ed Watson and Dennis Newlyn, covers the career of midget auto racing's Bob Tattersall. *In like a Lamb . . . Out like a Lion: The Story of John Buffum* recounts the career of a man whom *Road & Track* magazine has called "the most famous American rally driver ever" and is written by his longtime codriver, Tom Grimshaw. *Safe at Any Speed: The Great Double Career of Joie Chitwood*, by Jim Russell and Ed Watson, describes the life of a man who, after establishing himself as one of the nation's foremost sprint car drivers, went on to greater fame as a thrill and stunt driver show artist. Finally, there is Hal Higdon's *Summer of Triumph*, which chronicles both Jimmy Caruthers' racing career and his battle against terminal cancer.

The individuals mentioned so far might all be termed "contemporary" drivers. For the remembrances of a man who began as a board-track racer, won the 1925 Indianapolis 500, and was twice National Driving Champion (1925 and 1927), see Peter DePaolo's ingeniously named *Wall Smacker: The Saga of the Speedway*. An excellent biography of a driver of the next decade is Russ Catlin's *The Life of Ted Horn: American Racing Champion*, whose career spanned the years 1931 to 1948, ending in a fatal track accident just as he was about to garner his third straight American championship. The autobiography of Wilbur Shaw, entitled *Gentlemen, Start Your Engines*, tells the story of a man who began racing in the 1920s on dirt tracks, was three times a champion at Indianapolis (1937, 1939, and 1940), was president of the Indianapolis Motor Speedway, and continued to race until his 1954 death in a plane crash. His life also is the subject of a chapter in John Bentley's *The Devil behind Them*. Finally, for insights into a "racing" career of another type, see Lee Lott's *The Legend of Lucky Lee Lott and His Hell Drivers*. Lott was a stunt car driver who began crashing cars at county fairs in the 1920s and destroyed nearly 18,000 vehicles by the time his career was over.

While Indianapolis-type, Formula 1, and Grand Prix racing get the majority of media attention, stock car racing is the most popular American form of this sport, and the generally acknowledged "king" of that form is Richard Petty. Petty so dominated the National Association for Stock Car Auto Racing (NASCAR) circuit that he achieved victory in 200 races—an unprecedented number—and won the Winston Cup seven times! He also finished first six times in the Daytona 500. Petty's success led to a situation where over the years there were no less than four "autobiographies" by the man: *Grand National: The Autobiography of Richard Petty* (1971); *King of the Road* (1977); *"King Richard": The Richard Petty Story* (1977), written with the assistance of Bill Libby; and *King Richard I: Autobiography of America's Greatest Auto Racer* (1986), coauthored with William Neely. For a more traditional biographical treatment, see Richard Benyo's *The Book of Richard Petty*.

The lives of other prominent NASCAR drivers (past and present) have been given book-length treatment. *Cale: The Hazardous Life and Times of the World's Greatest Stock Car Driver* is the autobiography of William Caleb "Cale" Yarborough, written with the assistance of the omnipresent William Neely. Beside winning the Winston Cup three times in the late 1970s, Yarborough was a four-time winner of the Daytona 500. *Junior Johnson: Brave in Life*, by Tom Higgins and Steve Waid, chronicles the personal and professional life of one of the legendary NASCAR pioneers. *Dale Earnhardt: Rear View Mirror*, by the editors of the *Charlotte Observer*, features highlights from the career of a seven-time Winston Cup champion. *Rusty Wallace: The Decision to Win*, by Bob Zeller with Rusty Wallace, and *Rusty Wallace: Racer*, by Kenny Kane and Gerald Martin, offer insights into the career of a man who by 1997 had become the fourth highest stock car money winner of all time. *Mark Martin: Driven to Race*, by Bob Zeller, is the biography of another driver who has consistently finished in the money. Finally, the life of the newest NASCAR superstar and three-time Winston Cup champion is the subject of Gary L. Thomas' *Jeff Gordon: An Unauthorized Biography*.

In addition to stock car racing, Americans have made a big money sport out of professional drag racing. For a look at the life of one of the premier practitioners of this art and the first man to achieve 200 miles per hour on a drag strip, see Don Garlits' 1967 autobiography, *King of the Dragsters: The Story of Big Daddy "Don" Garlits*, written with Brock Yates; later updated versions (1978 and 1990) of the same work retitled *"Big Daddy": The Autobiography of Don Garlits; Close Calls* (1984), written with Darryl E. Hicks; and, most recently, the two-volume *Big Daddy: A Career Pictorial*, written by Garlits and Michael Mikulice, a photographic reference work that carries the story through 1994. Of these, the 1990 *"Big Daddy"* is the best, both in terms of content and for capturing the "spirit" of drag racing. Garlits also is one of three drivers featured in *Superdrivers: Three Auto Racing Champions*, by Bill Libby. The others are Rodger Ward, winner of the Indy 500, and Lee Petty (father of Richard), three-time winner of the Winston Cup and the first victor in the Daytona 500.

Good biographies also exist for three other dragsters: *Art Arfons: Fastest Man on Wheels*, by Frederick Katz; *The Loner: The Story of a Drag Racer* (Tony Nancy), by Tom Madigan; and *Six Seconds to Glory: Don Prudhomme's Greatest Drag Race*, by Hal Higdon.

While women race car drivers remain somewhat of a novelty, they have been a continuing part of the racing scene since the early 1950s. One of the better-known woman drivers is drag racer Shirley "Cha Cha" Muldowney, whose life is briefly sketched by Pat Jordan in "Cha-Cha and Her Time Machine," a chapter in the book *Broken Patterns*, and by Tony Sakkis in *Drag Racing Legends* (see below).

Beside these biographical accounts of individual drivers, a multitude of books present "capsule" biographies of the people and their machines. The best general work, in that it covers all types of racing and gives ample coverage to American drivers, is *Winners: A Who's Who of Motor Racing Champions*, edited by Brian Laban. Unfortunately, its 1981 publication date makes it more a historical record than a contemporary biographic reference.

Most of the other books in this category follow a thematic approach. Among these volumes are four concerned with the Indianapolis 500: Brock Yates' *Famous Indianapolis Cars and Drivers*, a well-illustrated volume covering the years 1909–1959; Billy Libby's *Champions of the Indianapolis 500: The Men Who Have Won More than Once*; Phil Berger and Larry Bortstein's *The Boys of Indy*, in which twelve who have competed in the race tell of their experiences; and Tony Sakkis' *Indy Racing Legends*, which profiles twenty-five individuals from Barney Oldfield to Emerson Fittipaldi.

Other books in the capsule biographies genre that concern uniquely American forms of racing are *Drag Racing Legends*, by Tony Sakkis, which features profiles of thirty drivers, builders, promoters, and mechanics, including such greats as Don Garlits, Shirley Muldowney, and Don Prudhomme; Ross R. Olney's *Kings of the Drag Strip*, which presents brief accounts of the lives of a number of participants on the drag racing circuit; and David A. Fetherston's *Heroes of Hot Rodding*, a volume that sketches the careers and contributions of thirty-one men (including Craig Breedlove, Don Garlits, Ed Iskenderian, Wally Parks, and Dean Moon), many of whom later achieved national fame in one form of racing or another, and one woman—Linda Vaughn.

Readers interested in stock car (NASCAR) racing should read John Craft's *Legends of Stock Car Racing*, which covers past and present drivers (from the 1960s into the 1990s), NASCAR founder Bill France, and car builders; Bill Center and Bob Moore's *NASCAR: 50 Greatest Drivers*, a collection of brief profiles ranging from those of legendary pioneers like Junior Johnson and Buck Baker, to contemporary Winston Cup stars such as Dale Earnhardt and Jeff Gordon; and probably the best of the group, Peter Golenbock's *The Last Lap: The Life and Times of NASCAR's Legendary Heroes*, which offers biographical studies of race car drivers who died before their time, based on interviews with other drivers, crew members, and families.

Other drivers who have achieved fame are featured in the following idiosyncratic works. Giles Tippette's *The Brave Men* contains a large section devoted to USAC (now CART) racing in the 1960s and early 1970s, with particular attention to Roger McCluskey. For a general introduction to the people (and venues) involved in dirt track racing in the 1960s and 1970s, see John Sawyer's *The Dusty Heroes*. S.C.H. Davis' *Atalanta* offers a collection of short biographies of women racers. Finally, there is Ross Olney's *Auto Racing's Young Lions*, which traces the careers of seven sons of successful drivers.

In addition, see *The Guinness Complete Grand Prix Who's Who*, by Steve Small, and *Grand Prix Greats*, by Nigel Roebuck. The former features biographies of every driver (over 400 of them) who participated in a World Championship race from 1950 to 1993. The latter focuses on the exploits of twenty-five of the greatest drivers in that series. Although the emphasis is predictably European, there is a fine chapter on Mario Andretti.

Some mention needs to be made in this section about the men who competed primarily not against others but rather against the clock, in the continuing battle to set the world land speed record (WLSR). Chapter 9 of this guide covers the racing contests themselves. Here we are concerned with biographical accounts of the men involved. For brief introductions to many of these men, see Paul Clifton's *The Fastest Men on Earth* and Brock Yates' *Racers and Drivers: The Fastest Men and Cars from Barney Oldfield to Craig Breedlove*.

Probably the best known and certainly the most colorful of these individuals was Berna Eli "Barney" Oldfield. William F. Nolan has written the best biography to date, *Barney Oldfield: The Life and Times of America's Legendary Speed King*. The lives of most of the other pioneers, such as Ralph DePalma and Fred H. Marriott, are described only in collections of racing biographies such as the Clifton and Yates volumes mentioned above.

While the speeds of the "pioneers" were impressive by contemporary standards (Marriott reached 128 mph in 1906), they pale into insignificance when compared with today's record holders, who travel faster on land than many planes do in the air. Of these, the most famous American is undoubtedly Craig Breedlove. Racing at the Bonneville Salt Flats in Utah, Breedlove has held (and lost) the WLSR title no less than five times, finally attaining a speed slightly in excess of 600 miles per hour. In 1971, with Bill Neely, he wrote his autobiography, entitled *Spirit of America: Winning the World's Land Speed Record*. (Spirit of America is the name that Breedlove has given to the succession of rocket-powered cars he has driven.) Prior to Breedlove, the most famous post–World War II American attempts to establish a new WLSR were by Mickey Thompson. *Challenger: Mickey Thompson's Own Story of His Life of Speed*, written with the assistance of Griffith Borgeson, recounts his ultimately futile quest in his four-engined *Challenger I*.

While the drivers themselves are usually the ones who garner the headlines and are the subjects of the preceding books, some attention has been given to the men and women who are part of the teams behind every successful race effort. Gene Banning's *Speedway: Half a Century of Racing with Art Sparks*, chronicles the career of an engineer who designed and built cars and engine parts for oval-track racing from the late 1920s into the 1970s, including significant successes at Indianapolis. *The Certain Sound: Thirty Years of Motor Racing* is a fine autobiography by John Wyer, who was a racing team manager from the 1950s into the early 1970s, including oversight of the famous Ford GT40 victory at Le Mans. A view from the "pit," as opposed to behind the wheel, is provided by Clint Brawner and Joe Scalzo in the award-winning *Indy 500 Mechanic*. *The Bobby, the Babe, and Me* is the autobiography of Hershel Winfred "Herk" Edwards, the chief mechanic for the Bobby Special, which, driven by "Babe" Stapp, was a fixture at the old Ascot Speedway in California. *Boss: The Bill Stroppe Story*, by Tom Madigan, traces the engineering career of one of the more important contributors to the success of a number of Ford racing teams, most notably at Le Mans (with the GT40) and Indianapolis. Finally, *Life at the Limit: Triumph and Tragedy in Formula One* is another interesting autobiography, this one chronicling the career of Sid Watkins, a neurosurgeon who for over thirty years attended to the medical needs of drivers hurt in racing accidents.

BIBLIOGRAPHY

Abodaher, David. *Iacocca: America's Most Dynamic Businessman*. New York: Zebra Books, 1985.

Anderson, John G. *Autobiography*. Rock Hill, S.C.: Record Publishing, 1937.

Andretti, Mario, edited by Mark Vancil. *Andretti*. San Francisco: Collins Publishers, 1994.

Andretti, Mario, with Nigel Roebuck. *Mario Andretti: World Champion*. London: Hamlyn, 1979.

Andretti, Mario, and Bob Collins. *What's It Like Out There?* Chicago: Henry Regnery, 1970.

Bagnall, Art. *Roy Richter: Striving for Excellence*. Los Alamitos, Calif.: Art Bagnall Publishing, 1990.

Banning, Gene. *Speedway: Half a Century of Racing with Art Sparks*. Escondido, Calif.: Spartus Enterprises, 1983.

Barker, Ronald, and Anthony Harding, eds. *Automobile Design: Twelve Great Designers and Their Work*. 2nd ed. Warrendale, Pa.: Society of Automotive Engineers, 1992.

Barnard, Harry. *Independent Man: The Life of Senator James Couzens*. New York: Charles Scribner's Sons, 1958.

Barnard, John. *Walter Reuther and the Rise of the Auto Workers*. Boston: Little, Brown, 1983.

Batchelor, Dean, and Albert R. Bochroch. *Cunningham: The Life and Cars of Briggs Swift Cunningham*. Osceola, Wisc.: Motorbooks International, 1993.

Bayley, Stephen. *Harley Earl*. New York: Taplinger, 1991.

Bayley, Stephen. *Harley Earl and the Dream Machine*. New York: Knopf, 1983.

Beasley, Norman. *Knudsen: A Biography*. New York: McGraw-Hill, 1947.

Bennett, Harry, as told to Paul Marcus. *We Never Called Him Henry*. New York: Fawcett, 1951.

Benson, Allan L. *The New Henry Ford*. New York: Funk and Wagnalls, 1923.

Bentele, Max. *Engine Revolutions: The Autobiography of Max Bentele*. Warrendale, Pa.: Society of Automotive Engineers, 1991.

Bentley, John. *The Devil behind Them: Nine Dedicated Drivers Who Made Racing History*. Englewood Cliffs, N.J.: Prentice-Hall, 1958.

Benyo, Richard. *The Book of Richard Petty*. Alexandria, Va.: Lopez Automotive Group, 1976.

Berger, Phil, and Larry Bortstein. *The Boys of Indy*. New York: Sterling, 1977.

Best, Norman, edited by William G. Robbin. *A Celebration of Work*. Lincoln: University of Nebraska Press, 1990.

Bonosky, Philip. *Brother Bill McKie: Building the Union at Ford*. New York: International Publishers, 1953.

Borgeson, Griffith. *Errett Lobban Cord, His Empire, His Motor Cars: Auburn, Cord, Duesenberg*. Princeton, N.J.: Automobile Quarterly Publications, 1984.

Borgeson, Griffith, and Patricia Borgeson. *Miller*. Osceola, Wisc.: Motorbooks International, 1993.

Borgeson, Griffith, with the Smithsonian Institution. *Miller*. Osceola, Wisc.: Motorbooks International, 1993.

Boyd, Thomas A. *Professional Amateur: The Biography of Charles Franklin Kettering*. New York: E.P. Dutton, 1957.

Boyd, Thomas A., ed. *Prophet of Progress: The Speeches of Charles F. Kettering*. New York: E.P. Dutton, 1961.

Bradford, Gamaliel. *The Quick and the Dead*. Boston: Houghton Mifflin, 1937.

Branch, Houston, and Wendell Smith. *The Unreasonable American: Francis W. Davis, Inventor of Power Steering*. Washington, D.C.: Acropolis, 1968.

Brawner, Clint, and Joe Scalzo. *Indy 500 Mechanic*. Radnor, Pa.: Chilton, 1975.

Breedlove, Craig, with Bill Neely. *Spirit of America: Winning the World's Land Speed Record*. Chicago: Henry Regnery, 1971.

Bridges, John. *Bob Bourke Designs for Studebaker*. Nashville: J.B. Enterprises, 1984.

Brough, James. *The Ford Dynasty: An American Story*. Garden City, N.Y.: Doubleday, 1977.

Bryan, Ford R. *The Fords of Dearborn: An Illustrated History*. Detroit: Wayne State University Press, 1989.

Bryan, Ford R. *Henry's Lieutenants*. Detroit: Wayne State University Press, 1993.

Buehrig, Gordon M., with William S. Jackson. *Rolling Sculpture: A Designer and His Work*. Newfoundland, N.J.: Haessner, 1975.

Burlingame, Robert. *Henry Ford: A Great Life in Brief*. New York: Knopf, 1954.

Bush, Vannevar. *Charles F. Kettering (1876–1958)*. Philadelphia: American Philosophical Society, 1959.

Casey, Robert J. *Mr. Clutch: The Story of George William Borg*. Indianapolis: Bobbs-Merrill, 1948.

Catlin, Russ. *The Life of Ted Horn: American Racing Champion*. Los Angeles: Clymer Publishing, 1949.

Center, Bill, and Bob Moore. *NASCAR: 50 Greatest Drivers*. New York: HarperHorizon, 1998.

Charlotte Observer, Editors of. *Dale Earnhardt: Rear View Mirror*. Champaign, Ill.: Sports Publishing, 1998.

Cheape, Charles W. *Strictly Business: Walter Carpenter at Du Pont and General Motors*. Baltimore: Johns Hopkins University Press, 1995.

Christie, Edward J. *Steel Steeds Christie: A Memoir of J. Walter Christie*. Manhattan, Kans.: Sunflower University Press, 1985.

Chrysler, Walter P., with Boyden Sparkes. *Life of an American Workman*. New York: Dodd, 1950.

Clancy, Louise, and Florence Davies. *The Believer: The Life Story of Mrs. Henry Ford*. New York: Coward-McCann, 1960.

Clifton, Paul. *The Fastest Men on Earth*. New York: John Day, 1966.

Corle, Edwin. *John Studebaker: An American Dream*. New York: E.P. Dutton, 1949.

Cormier, Frank, and William J. Eaton. *Reuther*. Englewood Cliffs, N.J.: Prentice-Hall, 1970.

Crabb, Richard. *Birth of a Giant: The Men and Incidents That Gave America the Motorcar*. Philadelphia: Chilton, 1969.

Craft, John. *Legends of Stock Car Racing*. Osceola, Wisc.: Motorbooks International, 1995.

Cummins, Lyle. *The Diesel Odyssey of Clessie Cummins*. Wilsonville, Ore.: Carnot Press, 1998.

Cummins, Clessie L. *My Days with the Diesel: The Memoirs of Clessie L. Cummins, Father of the Highway Diesel*. Philadelphia: Chilton, 1967.

Dahlinger, John C., as told to Frances S. Leighton. *The Secret Life of Henry Ford*. Indianapolis: Bobbs-Merrill, 1978.

Davis, S.C.H. *Atalanta*. London: G.T. Foulis, 1955.

Dayton, Eldorous L. *Walter P. Reuther: The Autocrat of the Bargaining Table*. New York: Devin-Adair, 1958.

Dearborn Publishing Co. *The International Jew*. 4 vols. Dearborn, Mich.: Dearborn, 1920–1922.

DeCamp, L. Sprague. *The Heroic Age of American Invention*. Garden City, N.Y.: Doubleday, 1961.

Dees, Mark L. *The Miller Dynasty*. 2nd ed., rev. Moorpark, Calif.: Hippodrome, 1994.

DeLorean, John Z., and Ted Schwarz. *DeLorean*. Grand Rapids, Mich.: Zondervan, 1985.

DePaolo, Peter. *Wall Smacker: The Saga of the Speedway*. Brooklyn: Braunworth, 1935.

Derato, Frank C. *Victor W. Pagé: Automotive and Aviation Pioneer*. Norwalk, Conn.: Cranbury, 1991.

Donohue, Mark, with Paul Van Valkenburg. *The Unfair Advantage*. New York: Dodd, Mead, 1975.

Durant, Margery. *My Father*. New York: G.P. Putnam's Sons, 1929.

Duryea, Charles E. *Handbook of the Automobile*. New York: American Motor League, 1906.

Duryea, Charles E., and James E. Homans. *The Automobile Book*. New York: Sturgis & Walton, 1916.

Duryea, J. Frank. *America's First Automobile*. Springfield, Mass.: Donald M. Macauley, 1942.

Eddy, Paul, ed. *The DeLorean Tapes: The Evidence, The Sunday Times Insight*. London: Collins, 1984.

Edwards, Herk, as told to Earl C. Fabritz. *The Bobby, the Babe, and Me: The Herk Edwards Story*. Marshall, Ind.: Witness Productions, 1994.

Egan, Philip S. *Design and Destiny: The Making of the Tucker Automobile*. Orange, Calif.: ON THE MARK Publications, 1989.

Engel, Lyle K. *Mario Andretti: The Man Who Can Win Any Kind of Race*. New York: Arco, 1970.

Engel, Lyle K. *Mario Andretti: World Driving Champion*. New York: Arco, 1979.

Ervin, Spencer. *Henry Ford versus Truman Newberry: The Famous Senate Election Contest*. New York: Richard R. Smith, 1935.

Fallon, Ivan, and James Srodes. *Dream Maker: The Rise and Fall of John Z. DeLorean*. New York: G.P. Putnam's Sons, 1983.

Farr, Finis. *Rickenbacker's Luck: An American Life*. Boston: Houghton Mifflin, 1979.

Fetherston, David A. *Heroes of Hot Rodding*. Osceola, Wisc.: Motorbooks International, 1992.

Fisher, Jerry M. *The Pacesetter: The Untold Story of Carl Fisher*. Fort Bragg, Calif.: Lost Coast Press, 1998.

Fitch, John, with William F. Nolan. *Adventure on Wheels: The Autobiography of a Road Racing Champion*. New York: G.P. Putnam's Sons, 1959.

Forbes, B[ertie] C., and O[rline] D. Foster. *Automotive Giants of America: Men Who Are Making Our Motor Industry*. New York: B.C. Forbes, 1926.

Ford, Henry. *The Case against the Little White Slaver*. Ann Arbor: Historical Society of Michigan, 1992.

Ford, Henry. *My Philosophy of Industry: An Authorized Interview with Fay Leone Faurote*. New York: Coward-McCann, 1929.

Ford, Henry. *Things I've Been Thinking About*. New York: Fleming H. Revell, 1936.

Ford, Henry, in collaboration with Samuel Crowther. *My Life and Work*. Garden City, N.Y.: Doubleday, Page, 1922.

Ford, Henry, and Samuel Crowther. *Moving Forward*. Garden City, N.Y.: Doubleday, Doran, 1930.

Ford, Henry, and Samuel Crowther. *Today and Tomorrow*. Garden City, N.Y.: Doubleday, Page, 1926.

Foster, Mark S. *Henry J. Kaiser: Builder in the Modern American West*. Austin: University of Texas Press, 1989.

Fountain, Clayton. *Union Guy*. New York: Viking Press, 1949.

Foyt, A.J., and William Neely. *A.J.: My Life as America's Greatest Race Car Driver*. New York: Warner, 1984.

Garlits, Don. *"Big Daddy": The Autobiography of Don Garlits*. Rev. ed. Seffner, Fla.: Author, 1990.

Garlits, Don, and Darryl E. Hicks. *Close Calls*. Shreveport, La: Huntington House, 1984.

Garlits, Don, and Michael Mikulice. *Big Daddy: A Career Pictorial*. 2 vols. Ocala, Fla.: Museum of Drag Racing, 1994.

Garlits, Don, and Brock Yates. *King of the Dragsters: The Story of Big Daddy "Don" Garlits*. Philadelphia: Chilton, 1967.

Garraty, John A., ed. *The Unforgettable Americans*. Great Neck, N.Y.: Channel Press, 1960.

Gelderman, Carol. *Henry Ford: The Wayward Capitalist*. New York: Dial Press, 1981.

Georgano, Nick, with photography by Nicky Wright. *Art of the American Automobile: The Greatest Stylists and Their Work*. London: PRION, 1995.

Golenbock, Peter. *The Last Lap: The Life and Times of NASCAR's Legendary Heroes*. New York: Macmillan, 1998.

Granatelli, Anthony. *They Call Me Mister 500*. Chicago: Henry Regnery, 1969.

Graves, Ralph H. *The Triumph of an Idea: The Story of Henry Ford*. New York: Doubleday, Doran, 1935.

Gray, Ralph D. *Alloys and Automobiles: The Life of Elwood Haynes*. Indianapolis: Indiana Historical Society, 1979.

Greenleaf, William. *From These Beginnings: The Early Philanthropies of Henry and Edsel Ford, 1911–1936*. Detroit: Wayne State University Press, 1964.

Grimshaw, Tom. *In like a Lamb . . . Out like a Lion: The Story of John Buffum*. Charlotte Harbor, Fla.: Tabby House, 1994.

Gustin, Lawrence R. *Billy Durant: Creator of General Motors*. Grand Rapids, Mich.: William B. Eerdmans, 1973.

Haddad, William. *Hard Driving: My Years with John DeLorean*. New York: Random House, 1985.

Harris, T. George. *Romney's Way: A Man and an Idea*. Englewood Cliffs, N.J.: Prentice-Hall, 1968.

Hayes, Walter. *Henry: A Life of Henry Ford II*. New York: Grove Weidenfeld, 1990.

Haynes, Elwood. *The Complete Motorist*. Kokomo, Ind.: Privately published, 1914.

Heiner, Albert P. *Henry J. Kaiser, Western Colossus: An Insider's View*. San Francisco: Halo Books, 1991.

Herndon, Booton. *Ford: An Unconventional Biography of the Men and Their Times*. New York: Weybright and Talley, 1969.

Hershey, Burnet. *The Odyssey of Henry Ford and the Great Peace Ship*. New York: Taplinger, 1967.

Hickerson, J. Mel. *Ernie Breech: The Story of His Remarkable Career at General Motors, Ford and TWA*. New York: Meredith Press, 1968.

Higdon, Hal. *Six Seconds to Glory: Don Prudhomme's Greatest Drag Race*. New York: G.P. Putnam's Sons, 1975.

Higdon, Hal. *Summer of Triumph*. New York: G.P. Putnam's Sons, 1977.

Higgins, Tom, and Steve Waid. *Junior Johnson: Brave in Life*. Phoenix: David Bull, 1999.

Howe, Irving, and B.J. Widick. *The UAW and Walter Reuther*. New York: Random House, 1949.

Iacocca, Lee, with William Novak. *Iacocca: An Autobiography*. New York: Bantam Books, 1984.

Jardim, Anne. *The First Henry Ford: A Study in Personality and Business Leadership*. Cambridge, Mass.: MIT Press, 1970.

Jodard, Paul. *Raymond Loewy*. New York: Taplinger, 1992.

Jordan, Pat. *Broken Patterns*. New York: Dodd, Mead, 1977.

Kane, Kenny, and Gerald Martin. *Rusty Wallace: Racer*. Tucson: Aztex, 1994.

Katz, Frederick. *Art Arfons: Fastest Man on Wheels*. New York: Routledge, 1965.

Kelly, F.C. *David Ross: Modern Pioneer*. New York: Knopf, 1946.

Kimes, Beverly Rae. *The Cars That Henry Ford Built: A 75th Anniversary Tribute to America's Most Remembered Automobiles*. Princeton, N.J.: Princeton Publishing, 1978.

King, Charles B. *A Golden Anniversary, 1895–1945*. Larchmont, N.Y.: Author, 1945.

King, Charles B. *Psychic Reminiscences*. Larchmont, N.Y.: Privately printed, 1935.

Kirby, Gordon. *Bobby Rahal: The Graceful Champion*. Phoenix: David Bull, 1999.

Kirby, Gordon. *Unser: An American Family Portrait*. Dallas: Anlon Press, 1988.

Kraft, Barbara S. *The Peace Ship: Henry Ford's Pacifist Adventure in the First World War*. New York: Macmillan, 1978.

Laban, Brian, ed. *Winners: A Who's Who of Motor Racing Champions*. London: Orbis, 1981.

Lacey, Robert. *Ford: The Men and the Machine*. Boston: Little, Brown, 1986.

Lamm, John. *DeLorean: Stainless Steel Illusion*. Santa Ana, Calif.: Newport Press, 1983.

Lane, Rose Wilder. *Henry Ford's Own Story: How a Farmer Boy Rose to the Power That Goes with Many Millions, Yet Never Lost Touch with Humanity*. Forest Hills, N.Y.: E.O. Jones, 1917.

Lasky, Victor. *Never Complain, Never Explain: The Story of Henry Ford II*. New York: Richard Marek, 1981.

Latham, Caroline, and David Agresta. *Dodge Dynasty: The Car and Family That Rocked Detroit*. New York: Harcourt Brace Jovanovich, 1989.

Lee, Albert. *Call Me Roger*. Chicago: Contemporary Books, 1988.

Lee, Albert. *Henry Ford and the Jews*. New York: Stein and Day, 1980.

Leland, Mrs. Wilfred C., with Minnie Dubbs Millbrook. *Master of Precision: Henry M. Leland*. Detroit: Wayne State University Press, 1966.

Leonard, Jonathan N. *The Tragedy of Henry Ford*. New York: G.P. Putnam's Sons, 1932.

Leslie, Stuart W. *Boss Kettering: Wizard of General Motors*. New York: Columbia University Press, 1983.

Levin, Doron P. *Behind the Wheel at Chrysler: The Iacocca Legacy*. New York: Harcourt, Brace, 1995.

Levin, Doron P. *Irreconcilable Differences: Ross Perot versus General Motors*. Boston: Little, Brown, 1989.

Levin, Hillel. *Grand Delusions: The Cosmic Career of John DeLorean*. New York: Viking Press, 1983.

Lewis, David L. *The Public Image of Henry Ford: An American Folk Hero and His Company*. Detroit: Wayne State University Press, 1976.

Libby, Bill. *A.J. Foyt: Racing Champion*. New York: Putnam, 1978.

Libby, Bill. *Andretti*. New York: Grosset and Dunlap, 1970.

Libby, Bill. *Champions of the Indianapolis 500: The Men Who Have Won More than Once*. New York: Dodd, Mead, 1976.

Libby, Bill. *Parnelli: A Story of Auto-Racing*. New York: E.P. Dutton, 1969.

Libby, Bill. *Superdrivers: Three Auto Racing Champions*. Champaign, Ill.: Garrard, 1977.

Libby, Bill, with Richard Petty. *"King Richard": The Richard Petty Story*. Garden City, N.Y.: Doubleday, 1977.

Lichtenstein, Nelson. *The Most Dangerous Man in Detroit: Walter Reuther and the Fate of American Labor*. New York: Basic Books, 1995.

Lochner, Louis P. *Henry Ford: America's Don Quixote*. New York: International Publishers, 1925.

Long, John C. *Roy D. Chapin*. Bethlehem, Pa.: Author, 1945.

Lott, Lee. *The Legend of Lucky Lee Lott and His Hell Drivers*. Osceola, Wisc.: Motorbooks International, 1994.

Madigan, Tom. *Boss: The Bill Stroppe Story*. Burbank, Calif.: Darwin Publications, 1984.

Madigan, Tom. *The Loner: The Story of a Drag Racer*. Englewood Cliffs, N.J.: Prentice-Hall, 1974.

Mahoney, Tom. *The Story of George Romney: Builder, Salesman, Crusader*. New York: Harper and Brothers, 1960.

Marquis, Samuel S. *Henry Ford: An Interpretation*. Boston: Little, Brown, 1923.

Mason, Todd. *Perot: An Unauthorized Biography*. Homewood, Ill.: Dow Jones/Irwin, 1990.

Maxim, Hiram P. *Horseless Carriage Days*. New York: Harper & Brothers, 1937.

May, George S. *Charles E. Duryea—Automaker*. Ann Arbor, Mich.: Edwards, 1973.

May, George S. *R.E. Olds: Auto Industry Pioneer*. Grand Rapids, Mich.: William B. Eerdmans, 1977.

Merz, Charles. *And Then Came Ford*. Garden City, N.Y.: Doubleday, Doran, 1929.

Meyer, Marjorie Teetor. *One Man's Vision: The Life of Automotive Pioneer Ralph R. Teetor*. Indianapolis: Guild Press of Indiana, 1995.

Miller, James M. *The Amazing Story of Henry Ford: The Ideal American and World's Most Famous Private Citizen*. Chicago: M.A. Donahue, 1922.

Mortimer, Wyndham. *Organize! My Life as a Union Man*. Boston: Beacon Press, 1971.

Neely, William. *The Jim Gilmore Story: Alone in the Crowd*. Tucson: Aztex, 1988.

Nevins, Allan, with the assistance of Frank E. Hill. *Ford: The Times, the Man, the Company*. New York: Charles Scribner's Sons, 1954.

Nevins, Allan, and Frank E. Hill. *Ford: Decline and Rebirth, 1933–1962*. New York: Charles Scribner's Sons, 1963.

Nevins, Allan, and Frank E. Hill. *Ford: Expansion and Challenge, 1915–1933*. New York: Charles Scribner's Sons, 1957.

Newton, James D. *Uncommon Friends: Life with Thomas Edison, Henry Ford, Harvey Firestone, Alexis Carrel & Charles Lindbergh*. San Diego: Harcourt, Brace, Jovanovich, 1987.

Niemeyer, Glenn A. *The Automotive Career of Ransom E. Olds*. East Lansing: Michigan State University Press, 1963.

Nolan, William F. *Barney Oldfield: The Life and Times of America's Legendary Speed King*. New York: G.P. Putnam's Sons, 1961.

Nolan, William F. *Phil Hill: Yankee Champion, First American to Win the Driving Championship of the World*. New York: G.P. Putnam's Sons, 1963.

Nowak, Margaret Collingsworth. *Two Who Were There: A Biography of Stanley Nowak*. Detroit: Wayne State University Press, 1989.

Nye, David E. *Henry Ford: "Ignorant Idealist."* Port Washington, N.Y.: Kennikat Press, 1979.

Olney, Ross R. *Auto Racing's Young Lions*. New York: G.P. Putnam's Sons, 1977.

Olney, Ross R. *Kings of the Drag Strip*. New York: G.P. Putnam's Sons, 1968.

Olson, Sidney. *Young Henry Ford: A Picture History of the First Forty Years*. Detroit: Wayne State University Press, 1963.

Pearson, Charles T. *The Indomitable Tin Goose: The True Story of Preston Tucker and His Car*. New York: Abelard-Schuman, 1960.

Petty, Richard. *Grand National: The Autobiography of Richard Petty*. Chicago: Henry Regnery, 1971.

Petty, Richard. *King of the Road*. New York: Macmillan, 1977.

Petty, Richard, and William Neely. *King Richard I: The Autobiography of America's Greatest Auto Racer.* New York: Macmillan, 1986.

Pipp, Edwin G. *Henry Ford: Both Sides of Him.* Detroit: Author, 1926.

Pipp, Edwin G. *The Real Henry Ford: Henry as I Know Him—and I Know Him.* Detroit: Pipp's Weekly, 1922.

Pitrone, Jean Maddern. *Tangled Web: The Legacy of Auto Pioneer John F. Dodge.* Hamtramck, Mich.: Avenue, 1989.

Pitrone, Jean Maddern, and Joan Potter Elwart. *The Dodges: The Auto Family Fortune and Misfortune.* South Bend, Ind.: Icarus Press, 1981.

Posey, Sam. *The Mudge Pond Express.* New York: G.P. Putnam's Sons, 1976.

Reuther, Victor G. *The Brothers Reuther and the Story of the UAW: A Memoir.* Boston: Houghton Mifflin, 1976.

Revson, Peter, and Leon Mandel. *Speed with Style: The Autobiography of Peter Revson.* Garden City, N.Y.: Doubleday, 1974.

Richards, William C. *The Last Billionaire: Henry Ford.* New York: Scribner, 1948.

Rickenbacker, Edward V. *Rickenbacker.* Englewood Cliffs, N.J.: Prentice-Hall, 1967.

Roebuck, Nigel. *Grand Prix Greats: A Personal Appreciation of 25 Famous Formula 1 Drivers.* Northants, Eng.: Patrick Stephens, 1986.

Russell, Jim, and Ed Watson. *Safe at Any Speed: The Great Double Career of Joie Chitwood.* Marshall, Ind.: Witness Productions, 1992.

Saal, Thomas F., and Bernard J. Golias. *Famous but Forgotten, the Story of Alexander Winton: Automotive Pioneer and Industrialist.* Twinsburg, Ohio: Golias Publishing, 1997.

Sakkis, Tony. *Drag Racing Legends.* Osceola, Wisc.: Motorbooks International, 1996.

Sakkis, Tony. *Indy Racing Legends.* Osceola, Wisc.: Motorbooks International, 1996.

Sawyer, John. *The Dusty Heroes.* Speedway, Ind.: Carl Hungness, 1978.

Scalzo, Joe. *The Unbelievable Unsers.* Chicago: Henry Regnery, 1971.

Scharchburg, Richard P. *Carriages without Horses: J. Frank Duryea and the Birth of the American Automobile Industry.* Warrendale, Pa.: Society of Automotive Engineers, 1993.

Shapiro, Harvey. *Faster than Sound.* South Brunswick, N.J.: A.S. Barnes, 1975.

Shapley, Deborah. *Promise and Power: The Life and Times of Robert McNamara.* Boston: Little, Brown, 1993.

Shaw, Wilbur. *Gentlemen, Start Your Engines.* New York: Coward, McCann, and Geoghegan, 1955.

Shelby, Carroll, as told to John Bentley. *The Cobra Story.* New York: Trident Press, 1965.

Simonds, William A. *Henry Ford and Greenfield Village.* Sunnyvale, Calif.: Stokes, 1938.

Simonds, William A. *Henry Ford: His Life, His Work, His Genius.* Indianapolis: Bobbs-Merrill, 1943.

Simonds, William A. *Henry Ford—Motor Genius.* Garden City, N.Y.: Doubleday, Doran, 1929.

Sloan, Alfred P., Jr. *My Years with General Motors.* Garden City, N.Y.: Doubleday, 1963.

Sloan, Alfred P., Jr., with Boyden Sparks. *Adventures of a White-Collar Man.* New York: Doubleday, Doran, 1941.

Small, Steve. *The Guinness Complete Grand Prix Who's Who.* Enfield, Middlesex, Eng.: Guinness, 1994.

Smallzreid, Kathleen A., and Dorothy J. Roberts. *More than You Promise: A Small Business at Work in Society.* New York: Harper and Brothers, 1942.

Smith, Frederick L. *Motoring Down a Quarter Century.* Detroit: Detroit Saturday Night, 1928.

Sorensen, Charles E., with Samuel T. Williamson. *My Forty Years with Ford.* New York: W.W. Norton, 1956.

Stidger, William. *Henry Ford: The Man and His Motives.* New York: George H. Doran, 1923.

Sward, Keith. *The Legend of Henry Ford.* New York: Holt, Rinehart, and Winston, 1948.

Teague, W. Dorwin. *Industrial Designer: The Artist as Engineer.* Lancaster, Pa.: Armstrong World Industries, 1998.

Thomas, Bob. *Confessions of an Automotive Stylist.* [s.l.]: R.M. Thomas, 1995.

Thomas, Gary L. *Jeff Gordon: An Unauthorized Biography.* Los Angeles: Renaissance Books, 1999.

Thompson, Mickey, with Griffith Borgeson. *Challenger: Mickey Thompson's Own Story of His Life of Speed.* Englewood Cliffs, N.J.: Prentice-Hall, 1964.

Tipler, John. *The World's Great Automobile Stylists.* New York: Mallard, 1990.

Tippette, Giles. *The Brave Men.* New York: Macmillan, 1972.

Trewhitt, Henry L. *McNamara.* New York: Harper & Row, 1971.

Unser, Bobby, and Joe Scalzo. *The Bobby Unser Story.* Garden City, N.Y.: Doubleday, 1979.

Watkins, Sid. *Life at the Limit: Triumph and Tragedy in Formula One.* Osceola, Wisc.: Motorbooks International, 1996.

Watson, Ed, and Dennis Newlyn. *Tattersall: The Legend.* Marshall, Ind.: Witness Productions, 1992.

Webster, Edna Robb. *T.A. Willard: Wizard of the Storage Battery.* Sherman Oaks, Calif.: Wilmar, 1976.

Weisberger, Bernard A. *The Dream Maker: William C. Durant, Founder of General Motors.* New York: McGraw-Hill, 1979.

Wik, Reynold W. *Henry Ford and Grass-roots America.* Ann Arbor: University of Michigan Press, 1972.

Wright, Frank Lloyd. *The Disappearing City.* New York: W.F. Payson, 1932.

Wright, J. Patrick. *On a Clear Day You Can See General Motors: John Z. DeLorean's Look inside the Automotive Giant.* New York: Avon Books, 1980.

Wyden, Peter. *The Unknown Iacocca: An Unauthorized Biography.* New York: William Morrow, 1987.

Wyer, John. *The Certain Sound: Thirty Years of Motor Racing.* Lausanne, Switz.: Automobile Year/Edita, 1985.

Yarborough, Cale, with William Neely. *Cale: The Hazardous Life and Times of the World's Greatest Stock Car Driver.* New York: Times Books, 1986.

Yarnell, Duane A. *Auto Pioneering: A Remarkable Story of Ransom Eli Olds, Father of Oldsmobile and Reo.* New York: Franklin DeKleine, 1949.

Yates, Brock. *Famous Indianapolis Cars and Drivers: Illustrated with Official Speedway Photos.* New York: Harper and Row, 1960.

Yates, Brock. *Racers and Drivers: The Fastest Men and Cars from Barney Oldfield to Craig Breedlove.* Indianapolis: Bobbs-Merrill, 1976.

Zeller, Bob. *Mark Martin: Driven to Race.* Phoenix: D. Bull, 1997.

Zeller, Bob, with Rusty Wallace. *Rusty Wallace: The Decision to Win.* Phoenix: David Bull, 1999.

CHAPTER 3

Organization, Management, and Sales within the Automotive Industry

POST-1970 ORGANIZATION, STRUCTURE, AND COMPETITION

A mid-20th-century aphorism observed that "What's good for GM is good for the nation." While that statement's veracity is open to question, the implication that the health of the American economy is highly dependent on the automobile industry is not. Therefore, the organization, structure, and functioning of that industry have been subjected to careful scrutiny from its earliest years. Books that describe and analyze events through the OPEC oil embargoes of the early 1970s are presented in Chapter 1. Here we are concerned primarily with developments in the last quarter of the 20th century.

The 1970s marked a turning point in the history of the American automobile industry. The purely national auto manufacturer capable of dictating consumer tastes became a dying breed. The type of planned obsolescence of which Vance Packard wrote in his 1960 best-seller *The Waste Makers* came under increasing attack. The domestic competition that dominated the industry for its first seventy-five years was transformed into an international economic struggle, with consolidation and reorganization the order of the day. The changes in market conditions and foreign competition forced the car manufacturers to rethink the nature of their methods and products.

For a general overview of the challenges that these changes posed, see *Downsizing Detroit: The Future of the U.S. Automobile Industry*, by N.P. Kannan *et al.*, who use a computer simulation model to conclude that the demand for cars will decline in the future and that unless current (1982) industrial and governmental policies change, they will hinder the adjustment necessary for economic survival and success. Somewhat the same conclusions were reached in a 1983 book by Brock Yates, entitled *The Decline and Fall of the American Automobile Industry*, which blames the plight of the industry on poor management, a lack of technological innovation, outdated styling, poor quality compared to foreign competition, and a general misreading of what Americans wanted in a car. On the same general subject, but written in a more popular vein, are *Running on Empty: The Future of the Automobile in an Oil Short World*, by Lester R. Brown *et al.*, and *The Death of the Automobile: The Fatal Effect of the Golden Era, 1955–1970*, by John Jerome, both of which examine the social aspects along with the financial decline of the American automotive industry. All of these works suffer from data and assumptions that are no longer applicable but are valuable for their contemporaneous views of the causes and remedies of the ills besetting the American automotive industry in the early and mid-1970s.

Other studies are more specific in focus, attempting to identify a primary reason for the decline. William J. Abernathy has written an excellent study of one specific problem area: *The Productivity Dilemma: Roadblock to Innovation in the Automobile Industry*, which focuses on the difficulties of innovating in a system based on mass production. See also Davis Dyer *et al.*, *Changing Alliances: The Harvard Business School Project on the Auto Industry and the American Economy*, with its argument that competition is now between national "enterprise systems," not individual companies, and thus only systematic change designed to enhance cooperation among labor, management, and government will avert further decline in the industry; and Clifford Winston's *Blind Intersection: Policy and the Automobile Industry*, a Brookings Institution collection of articles that argue against government intervention, placing their confidence in free enterprise and the cost competitiveness of the U.S. auto industry and, as such, might be seen as a response to the Harvard Business School study, although it is not as persuasive.

Beginning in the 1970s and continuing to the present, Japanese automobiles have challenged the products of Detroit in terms of design, quality, and efficiency. As a result, still other studies have concentrated on the impact of the Japanese "invasion" on the American new car market. Although such studies tend to become dated very quickly, valuable data and information still can be found in C.S. Chang's *The Japanese Auto Industry and the U.S. Market*, which traces the historical development of that industry from its roots prior to World War II (when Ford and GM helped), to its successful penetration of world markets (including the American) during the 1960s and 1970s, to its emergence by 1980 as the world's largest producer; John B. Rae's *Nissan/Datsun: A History of Nissan Motor Corporation in U.S.A., 1960–1980*, the last book written by Rae, generally recognized to be the father of American automotive history, particularly illuminating in terms of its analysis of the early years of entry when such cars were generally regarded as curiosities; David Halberstam's more "popular" *The Reckoning*, which compares the histories of Ford and Nissan (and their leaders) to show the cultural, political, and economic forces that led to the phenomenal Japanese success in the American market; and *Toyota: The First*

Twenty Years in the U.S.A., an in-house company history that covers the years 1957–1977.

The Japanese manufacturing model has been extensively studied in an attempt to glean methods that might be transferable to American industry. While such studies have more often than not taken the form of internal "white papers," a number of them have appeared in print. The best of this writing is exemplified by *Costs and Productivity in Automobile Production: The Challenge of Japanese Efficiency*, by Melvyn A. Fuss and Leonard Waverman, which attempts to explain the reasons behind the relative cost competitiveness of automotive production in Canada, Germany, the United States, and Japan in the years 1961 to 1984, and *Product Development Performance: Strategy, Organization, and Management in the World Auto Industry*, by Kim B. Clark and Takahiro Fujimoto, a research study that compares the development and marketing practices of car manufacturers in the United States, Europe, and Japan, showing how the Japanese were able to develop superior products and market them faster than the competition in the 1980s. *Driving Force: The Global Restructuring of Technology, Labor, and Investment in the Automobile and Components Industry*, in which authors Raphael Kaplinsky and Kurt Hoffman compare developments in the United States with those in Japan and Europe; and *The Competitive Status of the U.S. Auto Industry: A Study of the Influence of Technology in Determining International Industrial Competitive Advantage*, a study done by the Automobile Panel of the National Academy of Engineering, also are good. Taking a different tack, Robert L. Kearns, in *Zaibatsu America: How Japanese Firms Are Colonizing America*, argues (and warns) that Japanese conglomerates are using Japanese-owned construction, finance, distribution, suppliers, and services to establish a competitive edge in various sectors of American industry, including the automotive, and to corner all profits for themselves.

By the mid-1990s American car manufacturers had turned things around and were successfully competing with their Asian rivals. Pulitzer Prize-winning authors Paul Ingrassia and Joseph B. White analyze this positive development in *Comeback: The Fall and Rise of the American Automobile Industry*, which, while a complex and insightful behind-the-scenes account of events in the 1980s and 1990s, unfortunately does a better job of explaining the reasons behind the decline than those behind the turnaround. For comparative data on productivity in the automobile industry before and after the substantial organizational changes of the 1980s, see *The Harbour Report a Decade Later: Competitive Assessment of the North American Automotive Industry, 1979–1989*, a study completed by Harbour and Associates.

This comeback owed its genesis to a type of structural organization often called "lean production," a term coined by James P. Womack *et al.* in their pathbreaking 1990 book *The Machine That Changed the World*, which is based on the Massachusetts Institute of Technology's $5 million, five-year study of the future of the automobile in fourteen nations. Womack *et al.* divide the worldwide history of automotive manufacturing into three eras: craft (up to 1911), mass (1911–1961), and lean (beginning in the 1960s). The latter, pioneered by Toyota, is viewed by the authors as providing "better products in a wider variety at lower cost" by limiting the waste of human and financial resources at each stage of production. It is also seen as providing "more challenging and fulfilling work for employees at every level," by giving them more responsibility for quality control and for working as a team. *After Lean Production: Evolving Employment Practices in the World Auto Industry*, by Thomas A. Kochan *et al.*, offers essays analyzing the different experiences of Brazil, Italy, South Korea, and the United States with the implementation of Japanese-style management techniques; and *Lean Work: Empowerment and Exploitation in the Global Auto Industry*, edited by Steve Babson, provides contrasting views in the mid-1990s of the strengths and threats embedded in such a system.

Offering a decidedly negative view of the cooperative dimension of lean production is Mike Parker's "Industrial Relations Myth and Shop-Floor Reality: The 'Team Concept' in the Auto Industry," a chapter in *Industrial Democracy in America*, edited by Nelson Lichtenstein and Howell J. Harris. Similarly, *Just Another Car Factory?: Lean Production and Its Discontents*, by James W. Rinehart *et al.*, describes the souring of labor–management relations at a GM–Suzuki joint venture plant in Canada, which eventually led to a five-week strike in 1992.

Andrea Gabor's *The Man Who Discovered Quality* touches on another aspect as it explores how W. Edwards Deming brought "total quality management" (TQM) to Ford and General Motors, after having previously convinced the Japanese of the efficacy of his ideas. In *A Better Idea: Redefining the Way Americans Work*, Donald Petersen, former head of Ford Motor Company, and John Hillkirk describe that company's adoption of, and success with, Deming's ideas regarding cooperation between workers and supervisors in plant management. In addition, Jeremy Main's *Quality Wars: The Triumphs and Defeats of American Business* contains a chapter entitled "The Automakers: Almost There," in which the author describes the significant progress made in quality control during the 1980s, focusing on Ford and Saturn. Finally, for insight into how one American automotive company was able to revolutionize its manufacturing techniques when given the opportunity to start from scratch, see Joe Sherman's *In the Rings of Saturn*, an investigative reporter's story of the new General Motors Division that probably owes more to Tokyo than Detroit for its origins.

In a more specific vein, scholars have analyzed changes in management at individual companies. (The reader is directed to the relevant works cited in Chapter 1 for the historical context that they provide.) Within the last three decades, General Motors, like the other two large auto makers, periodically has been the subject of public scrutiny, sometimes scorn. A highly critical and, in some regards, pioneering analysis of management in the 1970s was J. Patrick Wright's *On a Clear Day You Can See General Motors: John Z. DeLorean's Look inside the Automotive Giant*, which became a best-seller and helped make DeLorean a nationally known figure. In a somewhat similar vein is Edward Ayres' earlier *What's Good for GM . . .* , although the criticism goes beyond economic issues to include questions of social responsibility as well. The most recent study of management at GM are Maryann Keller's *Rude Awakening: The Rise, Fall, and Struggle for Recovery of General Motors*, selected as one of the "ten-best" business books of 1989 by *Business Week* magazine, a book that is at its best when discussing the efforts of this industrial giant to adapt to the challenges of international competition in the 1970s and 1980s, and Doron P. Levin's *Irreconcilable Differences: Ross Perot versus General Motors*, an investigation of the ill-fated, multibillion-dollar merger between Perot's Electronic Data Systems and GM under Roger Smith, a highly unlikely alliance between very different companies and powerful, strong-willed managers.

Although Chrysler traditionally has taken a back seat to Ford and General Motors, recently it has been the most interesting company of the Big Three. Chrysler's near-bankruptcy in the late 1970s, the so-called federal government bailout, and its subsequent reemergence as a powerful company under Lee Iacocca are the stuff from which a multitude of books can be, and were, written. Probably the best in this regard is *New Deals: The Chrysler Revival and the American System*, by Robert B. Reich and John D. Donahue, which places the bailout within the broader context of whether and when the federal government should interfere with the free market economy. Other books worth reading on the same subject include *Going for Broke: The Chrysler Story*, by Michael Moritz and Barrett Seaman, and *Bailout: America's Billion Dollar Gamble on the New Chrysler Corporation*, by Reginald Stuart, both of which were written for a more general audience than the volume by Reich and Donahue. See also in this regard the relevant portions of the biographies of Lee Iacocca, cited in Chapter 2. Iacocca was CEO of Chrysler at this time.

Ultimately, the financial health of an auto company is dependent on its ability to sell cars. Although the Chrysler turnaround was based on the so-called K-cars, these were actually rather traditional in appearance and engineering. Not until the Plymouth Voyager and Dodge Caravan of the 1980s did the company begin to manufacture a truly innovative model—the minivan. In many respects, those cars signaled the Chrysler comeback. In that regard, see Brock Yates' *The Critical Path: Inventing an Automobile and Reinventing a Corporation*. However, by the end of the decade, Chrysler again found itself in financial difficulties but once more was rescued by a combination of new organizational and management techniques introduced by Robert A. Lutz and an exciting new product line that included the "LH" family sedan, the Jeep Grand Cherokee SUV, and the V-10 Viper sports car. This "second comeback" is described by Lutz in his *Guts: The Seven Laws of Business That Made Chrysler the World's Hottest Car Company*, a 1998 memoir that combines corporate history with managerial advice.

Ford, like Chrysler, has seen its fortunes ebb and flow in the postwar period. Its low point was reached with the failure of the Edsel in the mid-1950s, a subject treated in the design section of the next chapter. Although it recovered from that debacle and enjoyed success with its Mustang "pony car" of the mid-

1960s, its sales remained somewhat lackluster until the mid-1980s. Then, Ford began to challenge General Motors on a number of fronts. Its Taurus/Sable was, by the early 1990s, the best-selling car in the United States, wresting that title from the Japanese, and its Explorer model has become a leader in the SUV market. For a brief description of the reasons behind this reversal, see *Reinventing the Wheels: Ford's Spectacular Comeback*, by A.E. Doody and R. Bingaman.

LABOR–MANAGEMENT RELATIONS

History does not record which American auto manufacturer was the first to employ a worker and who that individual was. No doubt that event took place in the mid- to late 1890s. A decade later, there was the first major labor altercation in the fledgling industry, the Pope–Toledo strike of 1907. It was to be the harbinger of things to come. In fact, it could be argued that labor relations is the most studied single aspect of automotive history. Our focus in this section will be on the interaction between management and workers. Biographies of the lives and actions of individual automotive union leaders, especially the Reuther brothers, are described in Chapter 2. The role of labor, particularly that of the UAW, in local, state, and national politics is explored in Chapter 10.

An introduction to the breadth and diversity of this area of inquiry can be found in two anthologies. *On the Line: Essays in the History of Auto Work*, edited by Nelson Lichtenstein and Stephen Meyer, is a chronologically and topically diverse compendium, ranging from the origins of the assembly line, to the defeminization of auto work following World War II, to the role of the shop foreman. *Autowork* is a more recent collection, edited by Robert Asher and Ronald Edsforth, which explores the experiences of autoworkers and the development of labor–management relations in the years since 1913, including such topics as the "speedup," the impact of factory design on the work process, automation and the workweek, wartime activities, the treatment of dissent within the UAW, and worker sabotage.

While automotive workers are one of the most thoroughly organized labor groups in the United States, unionization came comparatively late to the industry. The best history of the pre-union years is Joyce Shaw Peterson's comprehensive *American Automobile Workers, 1900–1933*. Chronologically broader, but narrower in perspective, is David Gartman's *Auto Slavery: The Labor Process in the American Automobile Industry, 1897–1950*. Gartman views the transformation of the industry from a craft to an automated one and the concomitant "enslavement" of the worker as a result of "mechanical and organizational masters." Focusing on the years since World War II is *Management and Managed: Fifty Years of Crisis at Chrysler*, wherein author Steve Jefferys argues that, despite shop-floor resistance, management was able to co-opt workers because labor organization was structurally weaker.

A good study of the pay issue and the background to later developments in labor relations is *The Five Dollar Day: Labor Management and Social Control in the Ford Motor Company, 1908–1921*, by Stephen Meyer III. The contemporary public rationale for this unprecedented salary included such "new" ideas as "profit sharing" and a "fair decent wage," a view still reflected in Raymond-Leopold Bruckberger's 1959 *Image of America*, which hails the five dollar day as the harbinger of a positive social revolution. As the subtitle of the Meyer work indicates, the true intent may have been more insidious, as evidenced by the emergence of Ford's so-called Sociological Department, which spied on workers both in the plant and at home and fired those who did not conform to the prevailing company ideology. How that system worked at the Highland Park, Michigan, plant and in the surrounding community prior to the depression of the 1930s is analyzed in Clarence Hooker's *Life in the Shadows of the Crystal Palace, 1910–1927: Ford Workers in the Model T Era*.

Credit for successfully unionizing automotive labor ultimately went to the UAW. Given its monopoly status within the industry and the importance of that industry for American economic health, it should come as no surprise that the UAW and its leadership have been the subject of extensive scholarship.

By way of historical introduction, *A History of the Mechanics Education Society of America in Detroit, from Its Inception in 1933 through 1937*, by Harry Dahlheimer, provides a brief (61-page) study of one of the early successful automotive unions, that of tool and die workers, which was to combine with others to form the UAW. *I Remember like Today: The Auto-Lite Strike of 1934*, edited by Philip A. Korth and Margaret R. Beegle, an oral history of a 1934 job action by workers at that Toledo company, provides insights into a pioneering automotive industry strike. *Heroes of Unwritten Story: The UAW, 1934–39*, by Henry Kraus, is broader in coverage and provides a participant's balanced account of the formative years of autoworker unionization, with detailed attention to the character and actions of the workers and their leaders. Steve Babson's *Building the Union: Skilled Workers and Anglo-Gaelic Immigrants in the Rise of the UAW* provides a window on the leadership roles of two important, but diverse, elements, the aforementioned tool and die makers and the Anglo-Gaelic immigrant community, and offers insight into the intraclass dynamic that they forged. For one man's autobiographic view of these early turbulent years and of the transition that later occurred as the organization became bureaucratic and as he felt more concerned with the interests of union leaders than with those of the workers themselves, see *An Auto Worker's Journal: The UAW from Crusade to One-Party Union*, by Frank Marquart.

Also good for details on the rise of the UAW and its place in the context of the wider labor movement are the contemporaneous J. Raymond Walsh's *C.I.O.: Industrial Unionism in Action* (1937), Benjamin Stolberg's 1938 book *The Story of the CIO*, and, most recently, Robert H. Zieger's *The CIO: 1935–1955*, which won the 1996 Philip Taft Prize in Labor History and provides a thorough chronicle of the twenty-year life of an organization that effectively unionized blue-collar workers in the mass-production industries (including the automotive). The

UAW and the Congress of Industrial Organizations (CIO) were part of the movement that advocated worker organization along industry, as opposed to craft, lines.

Three specific accounts of the origins of union locals are John G. Kruchko's *The Birth of a Union Local: The History of UAW Local 674, Norwood, Ohio, 1933–1940*, which emphasizes industrial and labor relations; Peter Friedlander's *The Emergence of a UAW Local, 1936–1939: A Study in Class and Culture*, an oral history that follows a more sociological and less economic approach to the birth of that Detroit labor group; and Judith Stepan-Norris and Maurice Zeitlin's *Talking Union*, a history of UAW Local 600, which was given the herculean task in the 1930s and 1940s of organizing "the Rouge," Ford's mammoth plant on the Rouge River outside Detroit.

The development of a new tactic—the sit-down strike, whereby workers remained inactive at their posts, rather than walk a picket line outside the plant—brought the UAW to national prominence. This tactic was particularly effective in terms of preventing new workers ("scabs") from breaking the strike and eventually led to the recognition of the UAW as the workers' bargaining agent by all the major automotive manufacturers. An excellent study of the first successful strike of this type is Sidney Fine's *Sit-Down: The General Motors Strike of 1936–1937*. For an earlier and somewhat one-sided view of the same strike at the Flint, Michigan, plant by a socialist participant in it, see Henry Kraus' *The Many and the Few: A Chronicle of the Dynamic Auto Workers*. Even more biased is Joel Seidman's *Sit-Down*, a brief history of that tactic and its application in Flint, published for the Education Department of the UAW, and William Weinstone's *The Great Sit-Down Strike*. Weinstone was an officer in the Michigan Communist Party at the time. A firsthand account of the use of the same labor tactic to resolve a more recent labor–management impasse is Claude E. Hoffman's *Sit-Down in Anderson: U.A.W. Local 663, Anderson, Indiana*, an account of a job action at the Guide Lamp plant.

Sit-down strikes in particular and the unionization of the automobile industry in general did not escape the attention of contemporary labor scholars. For example, Lois MacDonald included a chapter on "Labor and Automobiles" in her 1938 *Labor Problems and the American Scene*. In a study published in 1940 by the Brookings Institution, *Labor Relations in the Automobile Industry*, William H. McPherson discusses the emergence of unionism and collective bargaining and their impact on the structure of the industry. The same author was responsible for a lengthy chapter entitled "Automobiles" in *How Collective Bargaining Works: A Survey of Experience in Leading American Industries*, edited by Harry A. Millis and published in 1942 by the Twentieth Century Fund. The chapter includes sections on the development of the industry; the organization of labor, including its attitudes, tactics, and bargaining methods; the results of collective bargaining; and contemporary problems.

Henry Ford's introduction of the automotive assembly line and then his 1914 announcement that he was going to pay his workers an unprecedented five dollars a day first brought automotive labor relations to the public's attention. Ford introduced a system that built upon the earlier work of Frederick W. Taylor. The latter's "time-and-motion studies" in the early 20th century had led to the practice of "scientific management," whereby the work process is divided and organized in such a manner that maximum efficiency is achieved, irrespective of its effect on worker happiness or creativity. "Taylorism," as it came to be known, was an attempt to make workers function like machines. Ford's assembly line was the next logical step, wherein the men became appendages to the technology itself. In that regard, see Henry Ford's *My Life and Work*; Emma Rothschild's *Paradise Lost: The Decline of the Auto-Industrial Age*; Ray Batchelor's *Henry Ford: Mass Production, Modernism and Design*; Lindy Biggs' *The Rational Factory: Architecture, Technology and Work in America's Age of Mass Production*; and Clarence Hooker's previously cited *Life in the Shadows of the Crystal Palace, 1910–1927: Ford Workers in the Model T Era*.

In addition, the following three scholarly pieces treat narrower elements of the same themes: David Gartman's "Origins of the Assembly Line and Capitalist Control of Work at Ford," in *Case Studies on the Labor Process*, edited by Andrew Zimbalist; Nelson Lichtenstein's "Life at the Rouge: A Cycle of Workers' Control," an essay on the origins and demise of a unique system of shop-floor management in *Life and Labor: Dimension of American Working-Class History*, edited by Charles Stephenson and Robert Asher; and "Fordism and the Architecture of Production," a chapter in Peter J. Ling's *America and the Automobile: Technology, Reform, and Social Change*.

The resulting worker alienation was one of the primary concerns in the automotive production process in the latter half of the 20th century. According to Ely Chinoy, by the mid-1950s assembly line workers were beginning to question their social and economic role and the hierarchically structured nature of American society, a thesis advanced in his provocative *Automobile Workers and the American Dream*, and subsequently by Harvey Swados' study *On the Line*, with its descriptions of the inhumanity of the production system. Salary enhancements and fringe benefits were never sufficient to eliminate the alienation and disenchantment that come from being a human worker in a contemporary factory. Studies by William F. Whyte a decade later, as reported in *Men at Work*, revealed similar attitudes in automotive and other industries, as did Frank Marquart's "The Auto Worker," in *Voices of Dissent: A Collection of Articles from Dissent Magazine*. See also Charles Reitell's "Machinery and Its Effects upon Workers in the Automobile Industry," a chapter in Alfred J. Chandler Jr.'s 1964 *Giant Enterprise*.

Conditions had not changed significantly by the early and mid-1970s, as witnessed by the publication of *Auto Work and Its Discontents*, edited by B.J. Widick. He still found workplace alienation and a desire for greater control over working conditions. The importance of such a mentality lies in the linkage between attitudes and productivity. Similarly, James R. Zetka Jr.'s *Militancy, Market Dynamics, and Workplace Authority: The Struggle over Labor Process*

Outcomes in the U.S. Automobile Industry, 1946 to 1973 links workplace relationships, including militancy and shop-floor authority, to factory productivity
and market fluctuations.

More recently, Bernard Doray's *From Taylorism to Fordism: A Rational
Madness* is a 1988 history of scientific management, written by an industrial
psychologist who believes that any production system that sees people and machines as one results in psychopathology. Finally, Ruth Milkman's *Farewell to
the Factory: Auto Workers in the Late Twentieth Century* documents the continuing hatred of the factory system in a case study of workers at a General
Motors plant in Linden, New Jersey, who are offered a buyout plan to quit their
jobs. The decline of the American automotive industry and the UAW in the
1980s, together with the introduction of new technology and management techniques, is seen by Milkman as compounding a historically difficult situation.

For an international approach to the subject, see *The Automobile Industry and
Its Workers: Between Fordism and Flexibility*, a collection edited by Steven
Tolliday and Jonathan Zeitlin that offers a comparative analysis of developments
in Europe, Asia, and the United States from the late 19th century to the mid-
1980s; *Breaking from Taylorism: Changing Forms of Work in the Automobile
Industry*, by Ulrich Jurgens *et al.*, which explores recent changes in the relationship between labor and management in the automotive industries of the
United States, Great Britain, and Germany; and "Americanism and Fordism," a
chapter in Antonio Gramsci's *Selections from the Prison Notebooks*, edited by
Quintin Hoare and Geoffrey N. Smith. Gramsci was an Italian communist and
political theorist writing in the early 1970s.

Not surprisingly, autoworkers themselves have written frequently and elo-
quently of their alienation on the assembly line. Among the more recent works
are *Rivethead: Tales from the Assembly Line*, by Ben Hamper, an autobiographical account of the difficulty of finding personal satisfaction and maintaining
one's humanity while doing an endlessly repetitive task "on the line" at General
Motors; *End of the Line: Autoworkers and the American Dream*, edited by
Richard Feldman and Michael Betzold, which offers thirty oral histories focusing on the identity crisis of contemporary assembly line workers and its impact
on the industry; Chen-Nan Li's essay "A Summer in the Ford Works," in *Personnel and Labor Relations: An Evolutionary Approach*, edited by Allan Nark
and John B. Miller; and Charles A. Madison's "My Seven Years of Automotive
Servitude," a chapter in *The Automobile and American Culture*, edited by David
L. Lewis and Laurence Goldstein.

Another historic area of concern is that of the socioeconomic status of different workers within the manufacturing process. Obviously, this is not a problem unique to the automotive industry. Nonetheless, it has been heavily studied
there. William H. Form, who has written extensively on automotive workers in
a multi-national context, has authored *Blue Collar Stratification: Autoworkers
in Four Countries*, which compares worker behavior and attitudes in Argentina,
India, Italy, and the United States, nations in different stages of industrialization,

and reaches conclusions that question many previous theories of the worker in industrial societies, including those of Karl Marx. Stratification, of course, extended beyond the blue-collar workers. Supervising the latter was the *Foreman on the Assembly Line*, a subject studied by Charles R. Walker *et al.*, and by Carl D. Snyder in a broader perspective, *White-Collar Workers and the UAW*.

Stratification questions frequently mask underlying class and racial tensions, which have been present since the early union-organizing days. The first book-length, published work devoted to racial policies in automotive work was Herbert R. Northrup's *The Negro in the Automobile Industry*, published in 1968. This was followed shortly by a volume coauthored by Northrup entitled *Negro Employment in Basic Industry: A Study of Racial Policies in Six Industries*, a comparative study that includes automotive manufacturing. Nonetheless, not until 1979 did an exemplary work appear in this regard, August Meier and Elliott Rudwick's *Black Detroit and the Rise of the UAW*, which is still the best history of African Americans in the automotive industry. Studies of the Hispanic American experience also have begun to appear, the best of which is Zaragosa Vargas' *Proletarians of the North: A History of Mexican Industrial Workers in Detroit and the Midwest, 1917–1933*, which offers insight not only into the Chicanos' role in the workplace and union activity during this period but also into their lives as urban immigrants.

During and after World War II, the number of black automobile workers increased significantly, for socioeconomic reasons. This was particularly true for men and women on the assembly line. As a result, race relations became a more important part of personnel matters than it had been before, and real or alleged racism was seen as being at the root of some issues and situations. Since these developments were followed quickly by the civil rights movement and the subsequent period of black activism, it should not be surprising that attempts were made to organize black automobile workers into a union of their own. The origins and activities of one such group are examined in James A. Geschwender's *Class, Race and Worker Insurgency: The League of Revolutionary Black Workers*, which focuses on trade unions and race relations in Detroit, including events surrounding the riots of 1968. In addition to Geschwender's work, Dan Georgakas and Marvin Surkin offer a study of black power politics in the workplace in their *Detroit, I Do Mind Dying: A Study in Urban Revolution*, including an insightful section on the League of Revolutionary Black Workers, and Charles Denby provides a Marxist perspective on alleged racism within the UAW in *Indignant Heart: A Black Worker's Journal*.

Although black automotive workers have faced the additional burden of having to cope with industry-wide racism, they share a concern, along with their white colleagues, that further automation and robotics will eventually eliminate their jobs on the line or, at best, marginalize them. That concern has been the subject of a short book by Samuel D.K. James, *The Impact of Cybernation Technology on Black Automotive Workers in the U.S.*

Finally, racism of another type was evident in the early 1980s, when the success of Japanese imports cut employment in the auto industry from 760,000 to 490,000. Members of the UAW launched a campaign to convince Americans to buy only American-made cars, with xenophobic overtones that sometimes led to violence against Japanese cars and even Asian Americans. This relatively brief episode in labor history is described by Dana Frank in *Buy American: The Untold Story of Economic Nationalism*, a book that traces the roots of such behavior back to the boycotts that preceded the Revolutionary War.

Women form another minority in terms of automotive plant workers. The history of workers of that gender is the subject of Nancy F. Gabin's fine study of *Feminism in the Labor Movement: Women and the United Automobile Workers, 1935–1975*. Gabin explores the many links between the women's movement and unionization, with special attention to agitation for equal, rather than differential, treatment, especially in the years following World War II. Ruth S. Meyerowitz's "Organizing the United Automobile Workers: Women Workers at the Ternstedt General Motors Parts Plant," a chapter in editor Ruth Milkman's *Women, Work and Protest*, covers the contributions that women made to the union movement from 1936 to 1950, their work experiences during those years, and the reaction of union leadership to their efforts. Nancy Gabin is also the author of "Wins and Losses: The UAW Women's Bureau after World War II, 1945–1950," a chapter in *"To Toil the Livelong Day": America's Women at Work, 1780–1980*, edited by Carol Groneman and Mary Beth Norton. The Women's Bureau had been set up in 1944 to recommend policies and programs related to the employment of women and was active in attempts to have them keep their jobs in auto plants during the postwar reconversion. The same author's earlier "Women and the United Automobile Worker's Union in the 1950's," another chapter in Ruth Milkman's *Women, Work and Protest*, focuses on developments in that decade.

The automotive industry was not the only one to provide employment opportunities for women. Thus, a number of comparative studies attempt to compare women's experience in one industrial sector to another. For instance, Mary Lindenstein Walshok's *Blue Collar Women: Pioneers on the Male Frontier* explores the significance of such work for the self-identity and future plans of women automobile upholsterers and mechanics, compared to those who chose to become machinists, welders, plumbers, and so on. Like their black male colleagues, they found increased opportunities for employment during the Second World War, often flying in the face of, but never really overcoming, entrenched stereotypes. Ruth Milkman's *Gender at Work: The Dynamics of Job Segregation by Sex during World War II* is an excellent, award-winning (the American Historical Association's Joan Kelly Memorial Prize) book on this subject, which concentrates on job segregation by gender and race in the automobile and electrical manufacturing industries that laid the foundation for later postwar employment patterns. For example, women have a higher percentage of the jobs in the auto parts industry than in assembly plants. Not surprisingly, the wages in the former are much lower than in the latter.

The wartime opportunities that existed for women were quickly eliminated when the soldiers came home and demanded the return of jobs to which they believed they were "entitled." For a radical perspective on developments in the UAW during the period 1944–1954, there is *Separated and Unequal: Discrimination against Women Workers after World War II*, written by Lyn Goldfarb *et al.* and published by the Women's Work Project of the Union for Radical Political Economics. Nonetheless, women continued to seek employment in the automotive industry and were aided in that effort by laws and court decisions beginning in the 1960s aimed at ending gender discrimination. In that regard, see Nancy Gabin's "Time Out of Mind: The UAW's Response to Female Labor Laws and Mandatory Overtime in the 1960s," a chapter in *Work Engendered*, edited by Ava Baron, that chronicles the active role played by the UAW in the fight for gender equity in employment (rather than laws designed to "protect" women) and the Equal Rights Amendment.

Given its size and importance, the automotive industry has always been viewed as fertile ground for labor radicals. While one might question whether the latter's influence has ever been as great as the public perception of it, there is no denying the fact that socialists and communists have tried to play an active role in automotive union politics. One early exemplar of such activity is Robert W. Dunn's *Labor and Automobiles*, published in 1929 by the respected and long-lived, Left-leaning International Publishers.

In 1935, two years before the UAW's successful sit-down strike at General Motors, there appeared A.J. Muste's *The Automobile Industry and Organized Labor*, a fifty-nine-page tract written by an old-guard peace agitator and published by the Christian Social Justice Fund. As it began to appear that Ford would be the most difficult auto company to unionize, the radicals made their rhetoric more specific, as in Carl Raushenbush's *Fordism, Ford and the Workers, Ford and the Community*, a sixty-four-page pamphlet published by the League for Industrial Democracy in 1937. (Ford did not sign an agreement with the UAW until 1941.) A more specific and scholarly study of the role of communists in the UAW between the two world wars is provided by Roger R. Keeran in his *The Communist Party and the Auto Workers Union*.

The internal politics of the United Auto Workers has been the subject of several important works. In *UAW Politics in the Cold War Era*, Martin Halpern argues that the rise of Walter Reuther and his supporters in the immediate postwar period and the victory of the Right over the center-left coalition were a result of the Cold War and the association of the Left with policies designed to harm American labor. For an introduction to how the auto union functioned at midcentury, a time of relative strength for Reuther and the UAW, Jack W. Stieber's *Governing the UAW* is enlightening, as is *Trade Union Politics: American Unions and Economic Change, 1960s–1990s*, edited by Glenn Perusek and Kent Worcester, which contains a chapter by the former entitled "Leadership and Opposition in the United Automobile Workers." For an in-depth look at one aspect of this governance, *Democracy and Public Review: An Analysis of the UAW Public Review Board* is recommended. Written by Jack W. Stieber and published by the Center for the Study of Democratic Institutions, this book studies the early years of a body established by the UAW to protect the rights of individual members within the union.

As the union achieved parity with management, researchers shifted their focus from historical accounts to analyzing the nature of labor–management relations and the enabling processes that had evolved. Typical of this genre of scholarship is a 1947 book by Frederick Harbison and Robert Dubin entitled *Patterns of Union–Management Relations: United Automobile Workers (CIO), General Motors, and Studebaker*, wherein the authors paint an optimistic view of what could be accomplished through the cooperation of labor with management once the unions were recognized and wages guaranteed. The use of the word "patterns" in the title is interesting, in that it later came to describe the process whereby an agreement with one company defined the perameters within which labor and management negotiated elsewhere in the industry. Research into this process continued into the early 1960s, as exemplified by Robert M. MacDonald's *Collective Bargaining in the Automobile Industry*, a work that attacks the underlying premise of the Harbison and Dubin volume, arguing that those auto companies that gave labor what it wanted were left with irresponsible unions and a diminished position in the marketplace.

By the early 1970s, a type of economic accommodation had been reached between labor and management, reflected in collective bargaining negotiations that seemed satisfactory to the latter and to most rank-and-file workers. This development is explored in Kathy El-Messidi's *The Bargain: The Story behind the Thirty Year Honeymoon of GM and the UAW* and William Serrin's *The Company and the Union: The "Civilized Relationship" of the General Motors Corporation and the United Automobile Workers*. The latter takes a critical view of the union position.

For the 1980s, we have *Shifting Gears: Changing Labor Relations in the U.S. Automobile Industry*, by Harry C. Katz, which covers such subjects as collective bargaining, wages, and the quality of work life, and *The Transformation of American Industrial Relations*, by Thomas A. Kochan *et al.*, which discusses attempts at Ford and General Motors to overcome decades of labor–management distrust. For a cross-national perspective, see Lowell Turner's *Democracy at Work: Changing World Markets and the Future of Labor Unions*, which compares the impact of new organizational models and technology on labor relations in the automotive industries of Germany and the United States, and Stavros P. Gavroglou's *Labor's Power and Industrial Performance: Automobile Production Regimes in the U.S., Germany, and Japan*, a comparative study of production politics and efficiency based on the degree to which autoworkers have been integrated into the management process.

Finally, a new dimension was added to labor–management relations when foreign car makers began to establish manufacturing plants in the United States and run them using the same techniques as in their homeland. Whether this development will or will not enhance worker motivation and diminish alienation is a question that has yet to be answered. For an introduction to this new work culture, see Terry L. Besser's *Team Toyota: Transplanting the Toyota Culture to the Camry Plant in Kentucky*; Joseph J. Fucini and Suzy Fucini's *Working for the Japanese: Inside Mazda's American Auto Plant*; David Gelsanliter's *Jump Start: Japan Comes to the Heartland* on Honda, Nissan, and Toyota "transplants"; Laurie Graham's *On the Line at Subaru–Isuzu: The Japanese Model and the American Worker*; and Choong-Soon Kim's more comprehensive *Japanese Industry in the American South*, all five of which focus on how Americans respond and adapt to the Japanese production system and management style. Finally, indicative of the impact of the Japanese approach to labor relations is "The Saturn Partnership: Co-Management and the Reinvention of the Local Union," by Saul Rubinstein, Michael Bennett, and Thomas Kochan, a chapter in *Employee Representation: Alternatives and Future Directions*, edited by Bruce E. Kaufman and Morris M. Kleiner.

MARKETING AND SALES

While many of the early automotive inventors were simply tinkering with a mechanical hobby, others were quick to see the commercial potential of a successful motor car. Even if one fell into the latter category, profitable marketing of the product required the means of production and a system for attracting customers. In this section, we concentrate on books that help explain the evolution of mass automotive sales.

Advertising and Sales Campaigns

The first newspaper and magazine car advertisements appeared simultaneously with the initial commercial production of motor cars. These early ads stressed the mechanical attributes of the particular vehicle, while usually carrying a photograph or line drawing of the car and its price. Little, if any, attention was paid to the social and/or economic benefits that might accrue from car ownership. However, by the mid-teens, like the cars, these ads became increasingly more sophisticated, assisted by companies like Campbell-Ewald, which in 1911 became the first advertising agency designed to serve the fledgling auto industry. Soon, some car ads began to be recognized as exemplars of the advertising craft. Julian L. Watkins' *The 100 Greatest Advertisements* includes seventeen concerning the automobile or auxiliary enterprises, including possibly the greatest ad of all time, Cadillac's 1915 "The Penalty of Leadership" piece. The beauty of this ad is that the message is conveyed solely in narrative form, without ever mentioning the car itself in the text, its mechanical properties, or its price. Similarly, Charles A. Goodrum and Helen Dalrymple devote an entire chapter to cars in their *Advertising in America: The First Two Hundred Years*, a serious history aimed at the lay reader that also serves as a reference work for those desiring to delve deeper. Frank Rowsome Jr.'s *They Laughed When I Sat Down: An Informal History of Advertising in Words and Pictures* also contains an interesting chapter on the automobile, including a fine collection of reproductions of period ads.

A small number of books not only present but also analyze automotive advertising exclusively. The best of these is Jane Stern and Michael Stern's *Auto Ads*, which not only reproduces the classic advertisements but places them in their sociocultural context as well. Similar in approach are Peter Roberts' *Any Colour So Long as It's Black: The First Fifty Years of Automobile Advertising*, which, although its focus is more European, has an excellent collection of early car ads, and *Ads That Put America on Wheels*, a brief survey by Eric Dregni and Karl H. Miller. The first part of Roberts' title, incidentally, is a statement attributed to Henry Ford when asked about the available color schemes for the Model T. Also good are Jim Ellis' *Billboards to Buicks* and Heon Stevenson's *Selling the Dream: Advertising the American Automobile, 1930–1980*, in both of which the emphasis is more on advertising campaigns than individual ads.

Less satisfying from a scholarly perspective but more extensive from the standpoint of specific American ads are three relatively recent volumes by Yasutoshi Ikuta: *The American Automobile: Advertising from the Antique and Classic Eras*, featuring ads from the 1920s and 1930s; *Cruise-O-Matic: Automobile Advertising of the 1950s*; and *The '60s: America Portrayed through Advertisements—Automobile*, which features ads that appeared in the mass-circulation magazines of that decade. Two earlier volumes in the same genre are *Early American Car Advertisements*, edited by Q. David Bowers, which is a collection of the most interesting ads, though not necessarily the historically most significant ones, and catalog illustrations primarily from the years 1910–1916, with commentary by the editor; and Robert F. Karolevitz's *Old-Time Autos in the Ads*, containing advertisements from 1903 into the mid-1920s. All six of these books were intended for the general audience, and each author has done a good job of collecting ads that appeared during the period in question. The accompanying narrative, however, never moves much beyond the level of factual accounting.

A number of book-length treatments also focus on more specific topics. One important study is Frank Rowsome Jr.'s *The Verse by the Side of the Road: The Story of the Burma-Shave Signs and Jingles*. The development of serial advertising signs, which told a story, sometimes, as in the case of Burma-Shave, with a humorous ending, has a history intimately linked with the automobile. In fact, their placement was directly linked to the average speed of automobile driving, and it can be argued that when cars began to travel so fast that such signs could not be read easily, they disappeared as an effective advertising medium. Another book on the same topic, Bill Vossler's *Burma-Shave: The Rhymes, the Signs, the Times*, is less a history than a reference collection of the jingles that were used from 1925 to 1955.

Two books by Mitch Frumkin focus on ads that sold the famous big, high-powered cars that were so popular from the mid-1960s to the gas shortage of the 1970s. The title of the first volume is self-explanatory: *Muscle Car Mania: An Advertising Collection, 1964–1974*. *Son of Muscle Car Mania* is a sequel covering approximately the same period.

So-called auto buffs interested in a particular car or model have fortunately helped create a demand for books that collect in a single volume the best ads for that particular marque. While these are usually short on analysis, they can be a valuable reference collection of original source material waiting to be analyzed. Some of the better works in this genre are *Corvette!: Thirty Years of Great Advertising*, a compendium of nearly all the ads from 1953 to 1983 put together by the staff of *Automobile Quarterly* magazine; Jerry Heasley's *25 Years of Mustang Advertising*, a collection of over 200 advertisements appearing in print from 1964 to 1989; Otto A. Schroeder's *Packard—Ask the Man Who Owned One*, the title itself a play on one of the most successful auto advertising lines of all time, a collection of nearly 400 ads from the company beginning in 1902 through the Second World War; Gwil Griffiths' *Packard: A History in Ads, 1903–1956* and *Packard Advertising Highlights, 1900–1956*, the latter also including a bibliography of articles on that marque; and Terry Shuler's *Volkswagen: Then, Now and Forever*, featuring the award-winning ads that captured America's fancy in the 1960s and 1970s (see below).

In addition, there have been "classic" automotive sales campaigns, as opposed to individual ads. Although the Model T Ford was an incredible success, its introduction was not accompanied by any special ad campaign. Its successor, however, the Model A, was the beneficiary of an extensive, expensive, and well-orchestrated effort. For a "labor of love" study of this campaign, see Jim Schild's *Selling the New Ford, 1927–1932*, primarily a collection of contemporary ads and periodical accounts. Perhaps better known to "baby boomers" was the series of ads that accompanied the rise of Volkswagen's "Beetle" or "Bug" to preeminence among imports during the 1960s, a campaign that made assets out of that vehicle's alleged shortcomings, including its size and seemingly unchanging design. Their story is amusingly told and illustrated in *Think Small: The Story of Those Volkswagen Ads*, by Frank Rowsome Jr.; *The New Advertising: The Great Campaigns from Avis to Volkswagen*, by Robert Glatzer, which includes the latter as one of the twenty most successful ad campaigns; *Remember Those Great Volkswagen Ads?*, by Alfredo Marcantonio et al., a British publication; and *Is the Bug Dead?: The Great Beetle Ad Campaign*, edited by Marya Dalrymple, which is derived from the Marcantonio volume. The American ad agency that handled the Volkswagen (VW) account during this period was Doyle Dane and Bernbach.

Three other successful sales campaigns are described in *Glory Days: When Horsepower and Passion Ruled Detroit: A Memoir*, by Jim Wangers, written (with Paul Zazarine) by the man responsible for selling the Pontiac GTO and the concept of muscle cars to the American public; *Mustang: Selling the Legend*, by Andy Willsheer and Bob McClurg, which goes beyond advertising to also consider promotional campaigns, spin-off products, racing exploits, and testimonials by celebrities; and *Where the Suckers Moon: An Advertising Story*, by Randall Rothenberg, which analyzes in case-study fashion the decision of Subaru of America to select a new ad agency (Wieden & Kennedy) in the early 1990s and the campaign that followed.

In addition, the following books contain significant portions devoted to automotive sales: John Philip Jones' *Does It Pay to Advertise?: Cases Illustrating Successful Brand Advertising*, which includes an analysis of the Ford Escort advertising; David A. Aaker's *Managing Brand Equity: Capitalizing on the Value of a Brand Name*, which highlights the Ford Taurus as one example of a successful use of a brand name to achieve competitive advantage; and the same author's *Building Strong Brands*, which contains a lengthy chapter on General Motors' Saturn.

Before concluding this section, it should be noted that, in addition to print advertising, other techniques have been used in connection with automotive sales campaigns. For instance, when the automobile was an innovation, many car manufacturers sponsored transcontinental motor trips as a means of proving the dependability of their vehicles and securing nationwide press coverage. They then reinforced the message by publishing pamphlet accounts, usually twenty-five to fifty pages in length, of these trips. Thus, we have Horatio N. Jackson's *From Ocean to Ocean in a Winton* (1903), Lester L. Whitman's *From Coast to Coast in a [Franklin] Motor-Car* (1905), Jacob Murdock's *A Family Tour from Ocean to Ocean* in a Packard (1908), and Amanda Preuss' *A Girl, a Record and an Oldsmobile* (1915).

This same period saw the emergence of the car "show" as a medium for selling vehicles, the First National Automobile Show having been held in New York City in 1900, with forty automobiles on exhibit. Such exhibitions continue to the present day, as witnessed by the publication of *World's Greatest Auto Show: Celebrating a Century in Chicago*, by Mitchel Frumkin and James Flammang, a heavily illustrated history of the world's longest-running show. These shows provided a "captive audience" for the wiles of the manufacturers' public relations departments. In that regard, see *Mister Javelin: Guy Hadsall at American Motors*, an autobiographical account in which Hadsall, with the assistance of Sam Fiorani and Patrick R. Foster, relates stories of his efforts on the auto show circuit, which he worked from the late 1950s to the early 1970s.

These multi-marque exhibitions were supplemented for a time by shows mounted by a single manufacturer. For insight into the nature and purpose of one company's five-decade-long effort in this regard, see Lorin Sorensen's *The Ford Shows, 1904–1948*. Bruce Berghoff's *The GM Motorama: Dream Cars of the Fifties* describes a further evolution of this technique, wherein General Motors piqued the fancy of the buying public by featuring "dream" and experimental cars, plus the latest production models, in eight traveling auto shows from 1949 through 1961. Similarly, national and world fairs and exhibitions frequently were the site of automotive displays. Probably the most famous in this regard was the General Motors' Futurama exhibit at the 1939–1940 New York World's Fair. Unfortunately, there is no book-length study of that or similar efforts.

Other techniques have been adopted from time to time to market a particular car to the American public. For instance, auto companies have produced and circulated "novelty" books, such as Elsbery W. Reynolds' *Auto Line O'Type*, a 1924 collection of poems, each of which concludes with a line plugging Studebaker. More common has been the use of promotional flyers, brochures, and, more recently, videotapes. In *Corvette Catalogs: A Visual History from 1953 to the Present Day*, Terry Jackson surveys the sales literature distributed to the public from the 1953 Motorama to the 1990s as he creates a design and engineering history of that marque. Car manufacturers also have promoted new cars by placing them in the hands of "typical" citizens and having the latter drive the vehicles in their community or across country. Such a ploy was used by Chrysler in the 1960s to push its experimental turbine car (see the next chapter) and in the 1990s to publicize the Plymouth and Dodge Neon. The story of the latter is told in *Road Trip: True Travel across America*, edited by Andrew Hoegl.

Dealerships

When a company produced only a handful of cars a year, sales could be handled by the same individuals who were actually building the car. In that respect, it was no different from the building of carriages, and indeed the upper class, who were the most likely car purchasers, probably expected such personal interaction with the automotive "craftsmen." However, once cars began to be mass-produced and mass-purchased, it no longer was practical (or safe) to have each prospective purchaser come to the factory, and the need arose for automotive dealerships and the accompanying sales force.

Unfortunately, there is no significant book-length treatment of automobile dealers in general. The best work currently available is Robert Genat's *The American Car Dealership*, an illustrated survey of the history (since the 1930s) of such establishments, including the architecture, business practices employed, and the "culture" that evolved within. Another historical account is *The Master Merchandisers: America's Auto Dealers*, by Art Spinella, a volume that falls into the "labor of love" category. Finally, Jay Ketelle's *The American Automobile Dealership: A Picture Postcard History* uses over 300 postcards in a scant ninety-six pages to portray the evolution of dealerships from 1906 to the present. The commentary, while necessarily brief, is nonetheless interesting.

Given its early preeminence, it is not surprising that Ford was in the forefront of developments in this area. One of the few exclusive treatments of one company's dealerships is Henry L. Dominguez's *The Ford Agency: A Pictorial History*, which is better than the title implies, in that an informative narrative accompanies the vintage photographs. Although restricted to one company, Dominguez is still the best work on the topic of automotive dealers.

By the mid-1920s, dealerships were important enough that companies began to produce manuals for the former's employees. Thus, in 1923 Don C. Prentiss wrote *Ford Products and Their Sale*, a series of six pocket-size "how-to" books that also included general information on the automobile industry and specifics on Ford's history and its products. Similar in approach was *Standard Retailing Procedure for Willys-Overland Merchants*, issued in 1926 by that company, which contains the telling observation that "a few years ago cars were bought, today they are sold."

Such marketing arrangements were common enough in the 1930s that dealer complaints against automobile manufacturers fueled an investigation by the U.S. Federal Trade Commission, published in 1939 as the *Report on the Motor Vehicle Industry*, it is a valuable compendium of factual data. Scholarly interest in this area seems to have been sparked by the passage of the so-called Automobile Dealers' Day in Court Act of 1956. That same year saw the publication of Charles M. Hewitt's *Automobile Franchise Agreements*, which analyzes the law and legislation governing agreements between the manufacturer and dealer from 1900 to 1955.

More recent studies of the impact of the franchise arrangement and the challenges of forging cordial relations between manufacturers and dealers include Bedros P. Pashigian's *The Distribution of Automobiles: An Economic Analysis of the Franchise System* (1961), based on a doctoral dissertation which won a Ford Foundation award, and Stewart Macaulay's *Law and the Balance of Power: The Automobile Manufacturers and Their Dealers* (1966). Broader in coverage are Thomas S. Dicke's *Franchising in America: The Development of a Business Method, 1840–1980*, which analyzes the emergence of that marketing practice in five different industries, with the automotive being represented by the Ford Model T, and Richard S. Tedlow's *New and Improved: The Story of Mass Marketing in America*, which features case histories, including that of General Motors, describing how specific corporations used ads, sales programs, franchise agreements, and wholesaling empires to carve out a larger share of their particular market. Finally, for an insider's account of how such arrangements can run amok, see Steve Lynch's *Arrogance and Accords: The Inside Story of the Honda Scandal*, the largest commercial corruption case in American history, wherein executives of the American Honda Motor Company received millions in kickbacks from automobile dealers eager to obtain additional cars and franchises in the late 1970s and 1980s, a period when the demand for Japanese imports often exceeded the supply.

As one might imagine, a voluminous amount of sales literature (as opposed to print advertising) has been, and continues to be, produced by car manufacturers. Impressive collections of such exist in libraries and museums (see Appendix 2). Unfortunately, little of this material has been reproduced for the "casual" researcher. However, there are three notable exceptions. The *1909–*

1912 Sears, Roebuck & Co. Motor Buggy Catalogue, edited by Joseph L. Schroeder Jr. and Sheldon L. Factor, is readily available, as is *Buick: "The Golden Era," 1903–1915*, by Francois Therou, a collection of sales catalogs from those years, together with selected owners' and parts manuals; and *Rolls-Royce: The Living Legend, as Reflected by a Half a Century of Contemporary British and American Sales and Institutional Literature*, which includes material spanning the period 1907 to 1958 and could prove to be a valuable collection for investigators interested in comparative marketing approaches.

Scholarly study of car salespeople is a largely untapped area of investigation. Therefore, we are dependent primarily on the autobiographical accounts and personal reminiscences of men who sold cars. One of the earliest of these autobiographies is William P. Young's *A Ford Dealer's Twenty Year Ride with the Old and New Model Ford Policies*, self-published in 1932. The two models of the title are the Models T and A. Interesting, because of the later role he played as one of the first prolific writers and publishers of automotive history, is *Floyd Clymer's Historical Motor Scrapbook: Ford Model T Edition*, in the introduction to which the author briefly recounts his personal experiences selling Ford cars. The same volume contains reprints of a number of contemporary advertisements. Martin H. Bury's *Rolling Wheels* provides reminiscences of what it was like to deal cars in the 1930s, 1940s, and early 1950s. In the same vein is John W. Richley's *Obstacles No Barrier: An Autobiography*, which recounts the author's experiences running an auto agency in York, Pennsylvania. Finally, Edward Davis' *One Man's Way* is the autobiography of the first African American automobile dealer in the United States, a man who was given a Studebaker franchise in Detroit in 1956 and a Chrysler–Plymouth one in 1963. Caution should be exercised in using all four books since they are either self- or subsidy-published, though one could argue that the lack of mass-market appeal foreordains that fate.

Consumers

Sales of cars were aided by the introduction of the practice of installment buying. First tried in 1905, such purchase agreements were so widespread by the mid-1920s that they became the subject of scholarly investigation. Two early studies of this phenomenon were William A. Grimes' *Financing Automobile Sales: By the Time-Payment Plan* and Clare E. Griffin's *The Life History of Automobiles*, both of which appeared in 1926. The latter was the first volume in the University of Michigan's newly established Michigan Business Studies series and provided the first systematic study of the car from factory to junkyard. They were followed a year later by Edwin R. Seligman's massive, two-volume work, *The Economics of Instalment Selling: A Study in Consumers' Credit, with Special Reference to the Automobile*, and Harold E. Wright's briefer *The Financing of Automobile Installment Sales*. For a contemporary view of the social and economic forces responsible for this phenomenon, placed in the broader context of American household spending, see Martha L. Olney's *Buy Now, Pay Later: Advertising, Credit, and Consumer Durables in the 1920s*. Olney maintains that Americans "spent a considerably greater proportion of their disposable incomes on consumer durables," like automobiles, in the 1920s due to changes in advertising and the availability of credit. She also posits the controversial view that production considerations and control of dealers, rather than a desire to generate consumer demand, provided the impetus for the emergence of automotive finance companies.

By the end of the 1920s, the novelty of installment purchases had worn off, but the post–World War II boom in car sales rekindled interest in everything automotive. Thus, in 1952 Clyde W. Phelps did a study of installment buying for the Commercial Credit Company of Baltimore. Entitled *The Role of the Sales Finance Companies in the American Economy*, it focused largely on automobile financing for the years 1905 to 1951 and thus provided the first brief (87-page) historical survey of that practice.

Obviously, financial considerations have never been the sole determinant of whether an individual does or does not purchase a car or a particular make or model of car. Therefore, it is not surprising that studies also have been undertaken of the attitudes and actions of the consumer. Two of the more recent valuable books on this subject are Ron P. Smith's brief *Consumer Demand for Cars in the USA*, a University of Cambridge Occasional Paper, and Kenneth Train's *Qualitative Choice Analysis: Theory, Econometrics, and an Application to Automobile Demand*, which employs mathematical models of purchasing to analyze the demand issue. An interesting older study is Gregory C. Chow's brief *Demand for Automobiles in the United States: A Study in Consumer Durables*, which was published in the mid-1950s at the height of the car craze.

Most of the scholarly writing on car ownership and sales has concerned new vehicles. For millions of Americans, however, their first car was a used one. Although sales of previously owned automobiles was a common practice from the very beginning, discussion of the systematic merchandising of such vehicles was not common until the 1920s. Probably the most valuable book in this regard is *Marketing Used Cars*, a 1929 volume by Paul G. Hoffman and James H. Greene that both criticized prevailing policies and practices and offered proposals for creating a more efficient and profitable system. (Hoffman at the time was vice president of the Studebaker Corporation.) For analysis on the same subject a little over a decade later, see Theodore H. Smith's similarly titled *The Marketing of Used Automobiles*.

FOREIGN COMPETITION

Foreign competition obviously did not begin in the 1970s with the success of Japanese imports. It had always been present to some extent, particularly in terms of luxury and sports cars. Added to this in the post–World War II period was the "compact" car, the most successful being the Volkswagen Beetle. Nonetheless, the relative share of the domestic market dominated by imports remained small until fairly recently, and therefore the major American manufacturers were relatively unconcerned.

Histories of some of the more prominent of these foreign vehicles include *The American Rolls-Royce*, by Arthur W. Souttler, a heavily illustrated, participant's history of a car that was actually manufactured in the United States; *Rolls-Royce in America*, by John W. De Campi, which includes a detailed history of the 1921–1931 production of that marque in Springfield, Massachusetts; *MG: The Sports Car America Loved First*, by Richard Knudson, a heavily illustrated, fiftieth-anniversary history of that marque with attention to cars, personalities, racing activities, and ads from 1925 to 1975; *Morgans in the Colonies: Across the Pond*, by John H. Sheally II, another photo-essay, with sections on the manufacturing process, racing competition, the different models, and restorations; John Dugdale's *Jaguar in America*, a memoir full of interesting vignettes concerning the introduction of the sports car that first caught America's fancy in the years following World War II; and the more general *British Sports Cars in America, 1946–1981*, by Jonathan A. Stein, which traces the meteoric rise and fall (in terms of American importation) of such marques as Aston Martin, Austin-Healey, Daimler, Jaguar, Lotus, MG, Morgan, Sunbeam, and Triumph.

Prior to the Japanese "invasion" of the 1970s, the best-known foreign cars in the United States were of Western European manufacture, and easily the best-selling one was the German Volkswagen Export Model, affectionately dubbed the "Beetle" by the American public. At one point, these cars constituted 70% of the cars imported into the United States. A good explanation of this phenomenon is contained in Louis W. Steinwedel's *The Beetle Book: America's 30-Year Love Affair with the "Bug."* The attachment that Americans have shown to that car (and its 1990s successor) also is the focus of the *Volkswagen Bug Book: A Celebration of Beetle Culture*, by Dan Ouellette, a collection of personal anecdotes, vintage photographs, and historical detail. An interesting scholarly essay that examines the aforementioned love affair is Harry Hammond's "The Image in American Life: Volkswagen," which appeared in *Icons of Popular Culture*, edited by Marshall Fishwick and Ray B. Browne. Finally, *Bug Tales: The 99 Most Hilarious, Outrageous and Touching Tributes Ever Compiled about the Car That Became a Cultural Icon*, by Paul A. Klebahn and Gabriella Jacobs, attests to the popularity of the Beetle in the 1960s and its anthropomorphic qualities, as does *My Bug: For Everyone Who Owned, Loved, or Shared a VW Beetle: True Tales of the Car That Defined a Generation*, edited by Michael J. Rosen.

There are many general histories of this marque, which include, but go beyond, the American experience. *Small Wonder: The Amazing Story of the Volkswagen*, by Walter H. Nelson, is the most scholarly and the best of the lot, but unfortunately it provides the history only up to the mid-1960s. Among books aimed at enthusiasts, three of the better ones are James M. Flammang's *Volks-*

wagen: Beetles, Buses & Beyond; The *Origin and Evolution of the VW Beetle*, by Terry Shuler *et al.*; and Keith Seume's *VW Beetle: A Comprehensive Illustrated History of the World's Most Popular Car*. From 1949 to 1978, over 12 million examples of this marque were produced in Germany. In February 1972, it surpassed the Model T Ford as the largest-selling car in history.

Although numerically less significant, Sweden's Volvo has shown as much staying power as the Beetle and its successors. Beginning in the mid-1950s, Volvo made a name for itself first in racing, then as a "family sports car," and most recently for its safety and durability. Although there is no scholarly study devoted exclusively to its American experience, the company itself recently issued *40 Years: The Story of Volvo's First Forty Years in America*, a broad retrospective look at its evolution in the United States.

To meet the challenge of foreign competition, American car manufacturers have sought both internal remedies, such as organizational changes (see the first part of this chapter), and external solutions, such as governmental trade agreements. In regard to the latter, one of the first pacts was negotiated with Canada in the mid-1960s. In a volume entitled *United States–Canadian Automobile Agreement: A Study in Industry Adjustment*, Henrik O. Helmers provides the history and an analysis of an accord that provided for reciprocity in terms of the duty-free importation of cars and automotive parts. Although the unique relationship between the two countries and the heavy investment by Detroit in Canadian auto plants argued against the agreement's being a prototype for future arrangements with other nations, it did show the possibilities of governmental protective assistance for the industry.

Thus, in the 1970s American car manufacturers tried to minimize the competition from abroad by restricting the number of Japanese cars entering the United States. Although federal import quotas were discussed, the American government relied successfully on moral suasion to convince the Japanese of the wisdom of limiting exports to the United States. Governmental policy issues during this period of intense competition are well analyzed in Eric Toder's *Trade Policy and the U.S. Automobile Industry*.

American car manufacturers also tried to compete by abandoning their insular practices and actively seeking international cooperative arrangements, leading to the emergence of true multi-national automotive corporations. In this regard, see the recent histories of the Big Three in Chapter 1, which include past and current attempts at cooperative production and marketing, such as Ford with Mazda, Chrysler with Mitsubishi, and General Motors with Suzuki.

This trend toward multi-nationals led to a number of significant cross-national studies of automotive manufacturing in the 1980s. Among the better ones were *The Automobile Revolution: The Impact of an Industry*, a comprehensive history of the world automobile industry during its first century, with an emphasis on the economic effects of this revolution, by Frenchman Jean-Pierre Bardou and an international team of authors; *The World Automotive Industry*, an earlier (1978) work by Gerald T. Bloomfield, which is a comprehensive economic history of manufacturing and marketing in major world centers during the period from the mid-1950s to the mid-1970s; Krish Bhaskar's *Future of the World Motor Industry*, in which the author predicts slow growth for a mature industry, leading to greater competitiveness, and the eventual domination of a few multi-national companies; *Auto Industries of Europe, U.S., and Japan*, by Richard Phillips *et al.*, a statistical comparison of the status of firms in those areas in the early 1980s, with a heavy Western European emphasis; *Car Wars: The Untold Story*, an excellent analysis of economic and managerial trends in the United States, West Germany, and Japan and how they have influenced the automotive industry and will continue to do so in the future, written by Robert Sobel.

Probably the best of the future-oriented studies during this period was *The Future of the Automobile: The Report of MIT's International Automobile Program*, by Alan Altshuler *et al.* A joint project involving experts from seven countries, it examines the world automotive industry in the mid-1980s and attempts to forecast developments in such areas as international market competition, labor–management relations, corporate organization, technical innovations, and so on. The study concludes that the automobile will maintain its role as the "prime means of personal transport," although the fortunes of individual corporations and national automotive industries may vary in the future. More recently (1993), in *Collision: GM, Toyota, Volkswagen and the Race to Own the 21st Century*, Maryann Keller maintains that each of those companies represents a distinct national culture and that all three will soon face management decisions of a type unknown in the 20th century.

Although it is somewhat beyond the range of this guide, some mention should be made of those studies that explore the impact of foreign auto manufacturers on the economy of so-called developing nations. For example, see William C. Duncan's *U.S.–Japan Automobile Diplomacy: A Study in Economic Confrontation*, a scholarly study of competition in the third world during the 1960s and early 1970s; Jack Behrman's *The Role of International Companies in Latin American Integration: Autos and Petrochemicals*; Rhys O. Jenkins' *Transnational Corporations and the Latin American Automobile Industry*; and Jenkins' *Dependent Industrialization in Latin America: The Automobile Industry in Argentina, Chile, and Mexico*, the latter three focusing on the economic impact of transnational corporations on developing countries since the mid-1950s. For a recent account of an unsuccessful attempt to engage in manufacturing abroad, see Jim Mann's *Beijing Jeep: The Short, Unhappy Romance of American Business in China*, the story not only of the American Motors Corporation attempt to produce Jeeps in that country but also of the difficulty of Americans doing business in China in the 1980s. In addition, *The Multinational Corporation and Social Policy: Special Reference to General Motors in South Africa*, edited by Richard A. Jackson, shows how foreign-owned car manufacturers can become entangled in domestic social issues within host countries as well.

Finally, for insight into how things worked when the United States exported more cars than it imported, see Mira Wilkins and Frank E. Hill's 1964 *American*

Business Abroad: Ford on Six Continents, which offers a fine overview of that company's overseas operations from 1905 to 1962; Wayne Lewchuck's *American Technology and the British Vehicle Industry*, which traces the history of technological innovations (especially those that impact on mass production) imported into Great Britain, and the same author's more recent "Fordist Technology and Britain: The Diffusion of Labor Speed-up," a chapter in *The Transfer of International Technology*, edited by David J. Jeremy; Stephen Young's more specific *Chrysler U.K.: A Corporation in Transition*; and Y.S. Hu's *The Impact of U.S. Investment in Europe: A Case Study of the Automotive and Computer Industries*. As evidence that the idea of exporting cars is as old as the industry itself, there is the *Development of Motor-Vehicle Trade Abroad*, a seventy-page "special consular report" issued by the U.S. Bureau of Foreign and Domestic Commerce in 1913. The subsequent two decades have been examined by Dudley M. Phelps in his *Effects of the Foreign Market on the Growth and Stability of the American Automobile Industry*, a doctoral dissertation that was published in 1931 and covers the growth of the export business during the previous two decades.

BIBLIOGRAPHY

Aaker, David A. *Building Strong Brands*. New York: The Free Press, 1996.

Aaker, David A. *Managing Brand Equity: Capitalizing on the Value of a Brand Name*. New York: Free Press, 1991.

Abernathy, William J. *The Productivity Dilemma: Roadblock to Innovation in the Automobile Industry*. Baltimore: Johns Hopkins University Press, 1978.

Altshuler, Alan, Martin Anderson, Daniel Jones, Daniel Roos, and James Womack. *The Future of the Automobile: The Report of MIT's International Automobile Program*. Cambridge, Mass.: MIT Press, 1984.

Asher, Robert, Ronald Edsforth, with Stephen Merlino, eds. *Autowork*. Albany: State University of New York Press, 1995.

Automobile Quarterly, Staff of. *Corvette!: Thirty Years of Great Advertising*. Princeton, N.J.: Automobile Quarterly Publications, 1983.

Ayres, Edward. *What's Good for GM* . . . Nashville: Aurora, 1970.

Babson, Steve. *Building the Union: Skilled Workers and Anglo-Gaelic Immigrants in the Rise of the UAW*. New Brunswick, N.J.: Rutgers University Press, 1991.

Babson, Steve, ed. *Lean Work: Empowerment and Exploitation in the Global Auto Industry*. Detroit: Wayne State University Press, 1995.

Bardou, Jean-Pierre *et al. The Automobile Revolution The Impact of an Industry*. Translated from the French and edited by James M. Laux. Chapel Hill: University of North Carolina Press, 1982.

Baron, Ava, ed. *Work Engendered: Toward a New History of American Labor*. Ithaca,: N.Y. Cornell University Press, 1991.

Batchelor, Ray. *Henry Ford: Mass Production, Modernism and Design*. Manchester, Eng.: Manchester University Press, 1994.

Behrman, Jack. *The Role of International Companies in Latin American Integration: Auto and Petrochemicals*. Lexington, Mass.: Heath, 1972.

Berghoff, Bruce. *The GM Motorama: Dream Cars of the Fifties*. Osceola, Wisc.: Motorbooks International, 1995.

Besser, Terry L. *Team Toyota: Transplanting the Toyota Culture to the Camry Plant in Kentucky*. Albany: State University of New York Press, 1996.

Bhaskar, Krish. *Future of the World Motor Industry*. New York: Nichols, 1980.

Biggs, Lindy. *The Rational Factory: Architecture, Technology, and Work in America's Age of Mass Production*. Baltimore: Johns Hopkins University Press, 1996.

Bloomfield, Gerald T. *The World Automotive Industry*. North Pomfret, Vt.: David & Charles, 1978.

Bowers, Q. David, ed. *Early American Car Advertisements*. New York: Bonanza Books, 1966.

Brown, Lester R., Christopher Flavin, and Colin Norman. *Running on Empty: The Future of the Automobile in an Oil Short World*. New York: W.W. Norton, 1979.

Bruckberger, Raymond-Leopold. *Image of America*. New York: Viking Press, 1959.

Bury, Martin H. *Rolling Wheels*. Philadelphia: Dorrance, 1953.

Campi, John W. de. *Rolls-Royce in America*. London: Dalton Watson, 1975.

Chandler, Alfred D., Jr., ed. *Giant Enterprise: Ford, General Motors, and the Automobile Industry*. New York: Harcourt, Brace, & World, 1964.

Chang, C.S. *The Japanese Auto Industry and the U.S. Market*. New York: Praeger, 1981.

Chinoy, Ely. *Automobile Workers and the American Dream*. 2nd ed. Urbana: University of Illinois Press, 1992.

Chow, Gregory C. *Demand for Automobiles in the United States: A Study in Consumer Durables*. Amsterdam: North-Holland, 1957.

Clark, Kim B., and Takahiro Fujimoto. *Product Development Performance: Strategy, Organization and Management in the World Auto Industry*. Cambridge: Harvard Business School Press, 1991.

Clymer, Floyd. *Floyd Clymer's Historical Motor Scrapbook: Ford Model T Edition*. Los Angeles: Clymer Publications, n.d.

Clymer, Floyd. *Henry's Wonderful Model T. 1908–1927*. New York: Bonanza Books, 1955.

Dahlheimer, Harry. *A History of the Mechanics Education Society of America in Detroit, from Its Inception in 1933 through 1937*. Detroit: Wayne University Press, 1951.

Dalrymple, Marya, ed. *Is the Bug Dead?: The Great Beetle Ad Campaign*. New York: Stewart, Tabori, and Chang, 1983.

Dammann, George H. *Illustrated History of Ford, 1903–1970*. Rev. ed. Glen Ellyn, Ill.: Crestline, 1971.

Davis, Ed. *One Man's Way*. Detroit: Author, 1979.

Denby, Charles [Matthew Ward]. *Indignant Heart: A Black Worker's Journal*. Boston: South End Press, 1978.

Dicke, Thomas S. *Franchising in America: The Development of a Business Method, 1840–1980*. Chapel Hill: University of North Carolina Press, 1994.

Dominguez, Henry L. *The Ford Agency: A Pictorial History*. Osceola, Wisc.: Motorbooks International, 1981.

Doody, Alton E., and Ron Bingaman. *Reinventing the Wheels: Ford's Spectacular Comeback*. Cambridge, Mass.: Ballinger, 1988.

Doray, Bernard. *From Taylorism to Fordism: A Rational Madness*. London: Free Association Books, 1988.

Dregni, Eric, and Karl H. Miller. *Ads That Put America on Wheels*. Osceola, Wisc.: Motorbooks International, 1996.

Dugdale, John. *Jaguar in America*. Otego, N.Y.: BritBooks, 1993.

Duncan, William C. *U.S.–Japan Automobile Diplomacy: A Study in Economic Confrontation*. Cambridge, Mass.: Ballinger, 1973.

Dunn, Robert W. *Labor and Automobiles*. New York: International Publishers, 1929.

Dyer, Davis, Malcolm S. Salter, and Alan M. Webber. *Changing Alliances: The Harvard Business School Project on the Auto Industry and the American Economy*. Boston: Harvard Business School Press, 1987.

Ellis, Jim. *Billboards to Buicks: Advertising—As I Lived It*. New York: Abelard-Schuman, 1968.

El-Messidi, Kathy. *The Bargain: The Story behind the Thirty Year Honeymoon of GM and UAW*. New York: Nellen, 1980.

Feldman, Richard, and Michael Betzold, eds. *End of the Line: Autoworkers and the American Dream*. New York: Weidenfeld & Nicolson, 1988.

Fine, Sidney. *Sit-Down: The General Motors Strike of 1936–1937*. Ann Arbor: University of Michigan Press, 1969.

Fishwick, Marshall, and Ray B. Browne, eds. *Icons of Popular Culture*. Bowling Green, Ohio: Bowling Green University Popular Press, 1970.

Flammang, James M. *Volkswagen: Beetles, Buses & Beyond*. Iola, Wisc.: Krause, 1996.

Ford, Henry. *My Life and Work*. Garden City, N.Y.: Garden City Publishing, 1926.

Ford Motor Company. *Ford at the Fair: 1933 Century of Progress World's Fair*. [s.l.]: Ford Motor Company, 1934.

Form, William H. *Blue Collar Stratification: Autoworkers in Four Countries*. Princeton, N.J.: Princeton University Press, 1976.

Frank, Dana. *Buy American: The Untold Story of Economic Nationalism*. Boston: Beacon Press, 1999.

Friedlander, Peter. *The Emergence of a UAW Local, 1936–1939: A Study in Class and Culture*. Pittsburgh: University of Pittsburgh Press, 1975.

Frumkin, Mitch. *Muscle Car Mania: An Advertising Collection, 1964–1974*. Osceola, Wisc.: Motorbooks International, 1981.

Frumkin, Mitch. *Son of Muscle Car Mania*. Osceola, Wisc.: Motorbooks International, 1982.

Frumkin, Mitchel J., and James M. Flammang. *World's Greatest Auto Show: Celebrating a Century in Chicago*. Iola, Wisc.: Krause, 1998.

Fucini, Joseph J., and Suzy Fucini. *Working for the Japanese: Inside Mazda's American Auto Plant*. New York: Free Press, 1990.

Fuss, Melvyn A., and Leonard Waverman. *Costs and Productivity in Automobile Production: The Challenge of Japanese Efficiency*. New York: Cambridge University Press, 1992.

Gabin, Nancy F. *Feminism in the Labor Movement: Women and the United Auto Workers, 1935–1975*. Ithaca, N.Y.: Cornell University Press, 1990.

Gabor, Andrea. *The Man Who Discovered Quality*. New York: Times Books, 1990.

Gartman, David. *Auto Slavery: The Labor Process in the American Automobile Industry, 1897–1950*. New Brunswick, N.J.: Rutgers University Press, 1986.

Gavroglou, Stavros P. *Labor's Power and Industrial Performance: Automobile Production Regimes in the U.S., Germany, and Japan*. New York: Garland, 1998.

Gelsanliter, David. *Jump Start: Japan Comes to the Heartland.* New York: Farrar, Straus, & Giroux, 1990.

Genat, Robert. *The American Car Dealership.* Osceola, Wisc.: MBI Publishing 1999.

Georgakas, Dan, and Marvin Surkin. *Detroit, I Do Mind Dying: A Study in Urban Revolution.* New York: St. Martin's Press, 1975.

Geschwender, James A. *Class, Race and Worker Insurgency: The League of Revolutionary Black Workers.* New York: Cambridge University Press, 1977.

Glatzer, Robert. *The New Advertising: The Great Campaigns from Avis to Volkswagen.* New York: Citadel Press, 1970.

Goldfarb, Lyn, with Julie Boddy and Nancy Wiegersma. *Separated and Unequal: Discrimination against Women Workers after World War II.* Washington, D.C.: Union for Radical Political Economics' Women's Work Project, 1976.

Goodrum, Charles A., and Helen Dalrymple. *Advertising in America: The First Two Hundred Years.* New York: Harry N. Abrams, 1990.

Graham, Laurie. *On the Line at Subaru-Isuzu: The Japanese Model and the American Worker.* Ithaca, N.Y.: ILR Press/Cornell University Press, 1995.

Gramsci, Antonio. *Selections from the Prison Notebooks.* Edited and translated by Quintin Hoare and Geoffrey N. Smith. New York: International Publishers, 1971.

Griffin, Clare. *The Life History of Automobiles.* Ann Arbor: University of Michigan, Graduate School of Business Administration, Bureau of Business Research, 1926.

Griffiths, Gwil. *Packard Advertising Highlights, 1900–1956.* Timonium, Md.: Author, 1973.

Griffiths, Gwil. *Packard: A History in Ads, 1903–1956.* Timonium, Md.: Author, 1970.

Grimes, William A. *Financing Automobile Sales: By the Time-Payment Plan.* Chicago: A.W. Shaw, 1926.

Groneman, Carol, and Mary Beth Norton, eds. *"To Toil the Livelong Day": America's Women at Work, 1780–1980.* Ithaca, N.Y.: Cornell University Press, 1987.

Hadsall, Guy, with Sam Fiorani and Patrick R. Foster. *Mister Javelin: Guy Hadsall at American Motors.* Gales Ferry, Conn.: SAH Press, 1999.

Halberstam, David. *The Reckoning.* New York: William Morrow, 1986.

Halpern, Martin. *UAW Politics in the Cold War Era.* Albany: State University of New York Press, 1988.

Hamper, Ben. *Rivethead: Tales from the Assembly Line.* New York: Warner Books, 1991.

Harbison, Frederick H., and Robert Dubin. *Patterns of Union–Management Relations: United Automobile Workers (CIO), General Motors, and Studebaker.* Chicago: Science Research Associates, 1947.

Harbour and Associates. *The Harbour Report a Decade Later: Competitive Assessment of the North American Automotive Industry, 1979–1989.* Berkley, Mich.: Harbour and Associates, 1990.

Heasley, Jerry. *25 Years of Mustang Advertising.* La Puente: California Mustang Sales and Parts, 1989.

Helmers, Henrik O. *United States–Canadian Automobile Agreement: A Study in Industry Adjustment.* Ann Arbor: Institute for International Commerce, Graduate School of Business Administration, University of Michigan, 1967.

Hewitt, Charles M. *Automobile Franchise Agreements.* Bloomington: Indiana University Press, 1956.

Hoegl, Andrew, ed. *Road Trip: True Travel across America.* New York: St. Martin's Press, 1994.

Hoffman, Claude E. *Sit-Down in Anderson: U.A.W. Local 663, Anderson, Indiana*. Detroit: Wayne State University Press, 1968.

Hoffman, Paul G., and James H. Greene. *Marketing Used Cars*. New York: Harper & Brothers, 1929.

Hooker, Clarence. *Life in the Shadows of the Crystal Palace, 1910–1927: Ford Workers in the Model T Era*. Bowling Green, Ohio: Bowling Green State University Popular Press, 1997.

Hu, Y.S. *The Impact of U.S. Investment in Europe: A Case Study of the Automotive and Computer Industries*. New York: Praeger, 1973.

Ikuta, Yasutoshi. *The American Automobile: Advertising from the Antique and Classic Eras*. San Francisco: Chronicle Books, 1988.

Ikuta, Yasutoshi. *Cruise-O-Matic: Automobile Advertising of the 1950s*. San Francisco: Chronicle Books, 1988.

Ikuta, Yasutoshi. *The '60s: America Portrayed through Advertisements—Automobile*. Tokyo: Gurapikkusha, 1989.

Ingrassia, Paul, and Joseph B. White. *Comeback: The Fall and Rise of the American Automobile Industry*. New York: Simon & Schuster, 1994.

Jackson, Horatio N. *From Ocean to Ocean in a Winton*. Cleveland: Winton Motor Carriage, 1903.

Jackson, Richard A., ed. *The Multinational Corporation and Social Policy: Special Reference to General Motors in South Africa*. New York: Praeger, 1974.

Jackson, Terry. *Corvette Catalogs: A Visual History from 1953 to the Present Day*. New York: Mallard Press, 1991.

James, Samuel D.K. *The Impact of Cybernation Technology on Black Automotive Workers in the U.S.*. Ann Arbor, Mich.: UMI Research Press, 1985.

Jefferys, Steve. *Management and Managed: Fifty Years of Crisis at Chrysler*. Cambridge: Cambridge University Press, 1986.

Jenkins, Rhys O. *Dependent Industrialization in Latin America: The Automobile Industry in Argentina, Chile, and Mexico*. New York: Praeger, 1977.

Jenkins, Rhys O. *Transnational Corporations and the Latin American Automobile Industry*. Pittsburgh: University of Pittsburgh Press, 1987.

Jeremy, David J., ed. *The Transfer of International Technology: Europe, Japan and the USA in the Twentieth Century*. Aldershot, Eng.: Elgar, 1992.

Jerome, John. *The Death of the Automobile: The Fatal Effect of the Golden Era, 1955–1970*. New York: W.W. Norton, 1972.

Jones, John P. *Does It Pay to Advertise?: Cases Illustrating Successful Brand Advertising*. Lexington, Mass.: Lexington Books, 1989.

Jurgens, Ulrich, Thomas Malsch, and Knuth Dohse. *Breaking from Taylorism: Changing Forms of Work in the Automobile Industry*. Cambridge: Cambridge University Press, 1994.

Kannan, N.P., Kathy L. Rebibo, and Donna L. Ellis. *Downsizing Detroit: The Future of the U.S. Automobile Industry*. New York: Praeger, 1982.

Kaplinsky, Raphael, and Kurt Hoffman. *Driving Force: The Global Restructuring of Technology, Labor, and Investment in the Automobile and Components Industry*. Boulder, Colo.: Westview Press, 1988.

Karolevitz, Robert F. *Old-Time Autos in the Ads*. Yankton, S.D.: Homestead, 1973.

Katz, Harry C. *Shifting Gears: Changing Labor Relations in the U.S. Automobile Industry*. Cambridge, Mass.: MIT Press, 1985.

Kaufman, Bruce E., and Morris M. Kleiner, eds. *Employee Representation: Alternatives and Future Directions.* Madison, Wisc.: Industrial Relations Research Association, 1993.

Kearns, Robert L. *Zaibatsu America: How Japanese Firms Are Colonizing America.* New York: Free Press, 1992.

Keeran, Roger. *The Communist Party and the Auto Workers Union.* Bloomington: Indiana University Press, 1980.

Keller, Maryann. *Collision: GM, Toyota, Volkswagen and the Race to Own the 21st Century.* New York: Doubleday, 1993.

Keller, Maryann. *Rude Awakening: The Rise, Fall, and Struggle for Recovery of General Motors.* New York: William Morrow, 1989.

Ketelle, Jay. *The American Automobile Dealership: A Picture Postcard History.* Amarillo, Tex.: Jay Ketelle Collectables, 1988.

Kim, Choong-Soon. *Japanese Industry in the American South.* New York: Routledge, 1995.

Klebahn, Paul A., and Gabriella Jacobs. *Bug Tales: The 99 Most Hilarious, Outrageous and Touching Tributes Ever Compiled about the Car That Became a Cultural Icon.* Cincinnati: Oval Window Press, 1999.

Knudson, Richard. *MG: The Sports Car America Loved First: An Illustrated History of MGs in the U.S.A.* Oneonta, N.Y.: Motorcars Unlimited, 1975.

Kochan, Thomas A., Harry C. Katz, and Robert B. McKersie. *The Transformation of American Industrial Relations.* New York: Basic Books, 1986.

Kochan, Thomas A., Russell D. Lansbury, and John P. MacDuffie, eds. *After Lean Production: Evolving Employment Practices in the World Auto Industry.* Ithaca, N.Y.: Cornell University Press, 1997.

Korth, Philip A., and Margaret R. Beegle. *I Remember like Today: The Auto-Lite Strike of 1934.* East Lansing: Michigan State University Press, 1988.

Kraus, Henry. *Heroes of Unwritten Story: The UAW, 1934–39.* Urbana: University of Illinois Press, 1993.

Kraus, Henry. *The Many and the Few: A Chronicle of the Dynamic Auto Workers.* 2nd ed. Urbana: University of Illinois Press, 1985.

Kruchko, John G. *The Birth of a Union Local: The History of UAW Local 674, Norwood, Ohio, 1933–1940.* Ithaca, N.Y.: New York State School of Industrial and Labor Relations, Cornell University, 1972.

Levin, Doron P. *Irreconcilable Differences: Ross Perot versus General Motors.* Boston: Little, Brown, 1989.

Lewchuk, Wayne. *American Technology and the British Vehicle Industry.* New York: Cambridge University Press, 1987.

Lewis, David L., and Laurence Goldstein, eds. *The Automobile and American Culture.* Ann Arbor: University of Michigan Press, 1983.

Lichtenstein, Nelson, and Howell J. Harris, eds. *Industrial Democracy in America: The Ambiguous Promise.* New York: Cambridge University Press, 1993.

Lichtenstein, Nelson, and Stephen Meyer III, eds. *On the Line: Essays in the History of Auto Work.* Urbana: University of Illinois Press, 1989.

Ling, Peter J. *America and the Automobile: Technology, Reform, and Social Change.* New York: Manchester University Press, 1990.

Lutz, Robert A. *Guts: The Seven Laws of Business That Made Chrysler the World's Hottest Car Company.* New York: John Wiley, 1998.

Lynch, Steve. *Arrogance and Accords: The Inside Story of the Honda Scandal.* Irving, Tex.: Pecos Press, 1997.

Macaulay, Stewart. *Law and the Balance of Power: The Automobile Manufacturers and Their Dealers.* New York: Russell Sage Foundation, 1966.

MacDonald, Lois. *Labor Problems and the American Scene.* New York: Harper and Brothers, 1938.

MacDonald, Robert M. *Collective Bargaining in the Automobile Industry: A Study of Wage Structure and Competitive Relations.* New Haven, Conn.: Yale University Press, 1963.

McPherson, William H. *Labor Relations in the Automobile Industry.* Washington, D.C.: Brookings Institution, 1940.

Main, Jeremy. *Quality Wars: The Triumphs and Defeats of American Business.* New York: Free Press, 1994.

Mann, Jim. *Beijing Jeep: The Short, Unhappy Romance of American Business in China.* New York: Simon & Schuster, 1989.

Marcantonio, Alfredo, David Abbott, and John O'Driscoll. *Remember Those Great Volkswagen Ads?* London: European Illustration, 1982.

Marquart, Frank. *An Auto Worker's Journal: The UAW from Crusade to One-Party Union.* University Park: Pennsylvania State University Press, 1975.

Meier, August, and Elliott Rudwick. *Black Detroit and the Rise of the UAW.* New York: Oxford University Press, 1979.

Meyer, Stephen, III. *The Five Dollar Day: Labor Management and Social Control in the Ford Motor Company, 1908–1921.* Albany: State University of New York Press, 1981.

Milkman, Ruth. *Farewell to the Factory: Auto Workers in the Late Twentieth Century.* Berkeley: University of California Press, 1997.

Milkman, Ruth. *Gender at Work: The Dynamics of Job Segregation by Sex during World War II.* Champaign: University of Illinois Press, 1987.

Milkman, Ruth, ed. *Women, Work and Protest: A Century of U.S. Women's Labor History.* Boston: Routledge and Kegan Paul, 1985.

Millis, Harry A., ed. *How Collective Bargaining Works: A Survey of Experience in Leading American Industries.* New York: Twentieth Century Fund, 1942.

Moritz, Michael, and Barrett Seaman. *Going for Broke: The Chrysler Story.* Garden City, N.Y.: Doubleday, 1981.

Murdock, Jacob. *A Family Tour from Ocean to Ocean.* Detroit: Packard Motor Car Co., 1908.

Muste, A.J. *The Automobile Industry and Organized Labor.* Baltimore: Christian Social Justice Fund, 1935.

Nark, Allan, and John B. Miller, eds. *Personnel and Labor Relations: An Evolutionary Approach.* New York: McGraw-Hill, 1973.

National Academy of Engineering, Committee on Technology and International Economic and Trade Issues, Automobile Panel. *The Competitive Status of the U.S. Auto Industry: A Study of the Influence of Technology in Determining International Industrial Competitive Advantage.* Washington, D.C.: National Academy Press, 1982.

Nelson, Walter H. *Small Wonder: The Amazing Story of the Volkswagen.* Boston: Little, Brown, 1967.

Northrup, Herbert R. *The Negro in the Automobile Industry*. Philadelphia: University of Pennsylvania Press, 1968.

Northrup, Herbert R. *et al. Negro Employment in Basic Industry: A Study of Racial Policies in Six Industries*. Philadelphia: University of Pennsylvania Press, 1970.

Olney, Martha L. *Buy Now, Pay Later: Advertising, Credit, and Consumer Durables in the 1920s*. Chapel Hill: University of North Carolina Press, 1991.

Ouellette, Daniel. *Volkswagen Bug Book: A Celebration of Beetle Culture*. Santa Monica, Calif.: Angel City Press, 1999.

Packard, Vance. *The Waste Makers*. New York: David McKay, 1960.

Pashigian, Bedros P. *The Distribution of Automobiles: An Economic Analysis of the Franchise System*. Englewood Cliffs, N.J.: Prentice-Hall, 1961.

Perusek, Glenn, and Kent Worcester, eds. *Trade Union Politics: American Unions and Economic Change, 1960s–1990s*. Atlantic Highlands, N.J.: Humanities Press International, 1995.

Petersen. Donald E., and John Hillkirk. *A Better Idea: Redefining the Way Americans Work*. Boston: Houghton Mifflin, 1991.

Peterson, Joyce Shaw. *American Automobile Workers, 1900–1933*. Chicago: University of Chicago Press, 1960.

Phelps, Clyde W. *The Role of the Sales Finance Companies in the American Economy*. Baltimore: Commercial Credit, 1952.

Phelps, Dudley M. *Effect of the Foreign Market on the Growth and Stability of the American Automobile Industry*. Ann Arbor: University of Michigan, School of Business Administration, Bureau of Business Research, 1931.

Phillips, Richard *et al. Auto Industries of Europe, U.S., and Japan*. Cambridge, Mass.: Ballinger, 1982.

Prentiss, Don C. *Ford Products and Their Sale: A Manual for Ford Salesmen and Dealers*. Detroit: Franklin Press, 1923.

Preuss, Amanda. *A Girl, a Record and an Oldsmobile: By the Girl Herself*. Lansing, Mich.: Olds Motor Works, 1915.

Rae, John B. *Nissan/Datsun: A History of Nissan Motor Corporation in U.S.A. 1960–1980*. New York: McGraw-Hill, 1982.

Raushenbush, Carl. *Fordism: Ford and the Workers, Ford and the Community*. New York: League for Industrial Democracy, 1937.

Reich, Robert B., and John D. Donahue. *New Deals: The Chrysler Revival and the American System*. New York: Times Books, 1985.

Reynolds, Elsbery W. *Auto Line O'Type*. [s.l.]: Book Supply Co., 1924.

Richley, John W. *Obstacles No Barrier: An Autobiography*. York, Pa.: Author, 1951.

Rinehart, James W., Christopher Huxley, and David Robertson. *Just Another Car Factory?: Lean Production and Its Discontents*. Ithaca, N.Y.: ILR Press/Cornell University, 1997.

Roberts, Peter. *Any Colour So Long as It's Black: The First Fifty Years of Automobile Advertising*. Newton Abbot (Devon), Eng.: David & Charles, 1976.

Rolls-Royce: The Living Legend, as Reflected by a Half a Century of Contemporary British and American Sales and Institutional Literature. Arcadia, Calif.: Post Motor Books, 1958.

Rosen, Michael J., ed. *My Bug: For Everyone Who Owned, Loved, or Shared a VW Beetle; True Tales of the Car That Defined a Generation*. New York: Artisan, 1999.

Rothenberg, Randall. *Where the Suckers Moon: An Advertising Story.* New York: Alfred A. Knopf, 1995.

Rothschild, Emma. *Paradise Lost: The Decline of the Auto-Industrial Age.* New York: Random House, 1973.

Rowsome, Frank, Jr. *They Laughed When I Sat Down: An Informal History of Advertising in Words and Pictures.* New York: McGraw-Hill, 1959.

Rowsome, Frank, Jr. *Think Small: The Story of Those Volkswagen Ads.* Brattleboro, Vt.: Stephen Greene Press, 1970.

Rowsome, Frank, Jr. *The Verse by the Side of the Road: The Story of the Burma-Shave Signs and Jingles.* Lexington, Mass.: Stephen Greene Press, 1965.

Schild, Jim. *Selling the New Ford, 1927–1932.* St. Louis: Author, 1982.

Schroeder, Joseph J., Jr., and Sheldon L. Factor, eds. *1909–1912 Sears, Roebuck & Co. Motor Buggy Catalogue.* Northfield, Ill.: Digest Books, 1973.

Schroeder, Otto A. *Packard—Ask the Man Who Owned One: The Life and Times of That Proud Car That Became a Way-of-Life among the American Gentry—Portrayed by Pithy Advertising from the Great Magazines, a Selection.* Arcadia, Calif.: Post-Era Books, 1974.

Seidman, Joel. *Sit-Down.* New York: League for Industrial Democracy, 1937.

Seligman, Edwin R. *The Economics of Instalment Selling: A Study in Consumers' Credit, with Special Reference to the Automobile.* 2 vols. New York: Harper & Brothers, 1927.

Serrin, William. *The Company and the Union: The "Civilized Relationship" of the General Motors Corporation and the United Automobile Workers.* New York: Alfred A. Knopf, 1973.

Seume, Keith. *VW Beetle: A Comprehensive Illustrated History of the World's Most Popular Car.* Osceola, Wisc.: Motorbooks International, 1997.

Sheally, John H., II. *Morgans in the Colonies: Across the Pond.* Virginia Beach, Va.: Jordan, 1978.

Sherman, Joe. *In the Rings of Saturn.* New York: Oxford University Press, 1993.

Shuler, Terry. *Volkswagen: Then, Now and Forever.* Indianapolis: Beeman Jorgensen, 1996.

Shuler, Terry, with Griffith Borgeson and Jerry Sloniger. *The Origins and Evolution of the VW Beetle.* Princeton, N.J.: Princeton Publishing, 1985.

Smith, Ron P. *Consumer Demand for Cars in the USA.* New York: Cambridge University Press, 1985.

Smith, Theodore H. *The Marketing of Used Automobiles.* Columbus, Ohio: Bureau of Business Research, 1941.

Snyder, Carl D. *White-Collar Workers and the UAW.* Urbana: University of Illinois Press, 1973.

Sobel, Robert. *Car Wars: The Untold Story.* New York: Dutton, 1984.

Sorensen, Lorin. *The Ford Shows, 1904–1948.* St. Helena, Calif.: Silverado, 1976.

Souttler, Arthur W. *The American Rolls-Royce: A Comprehensive History of Rolls-Royce of America.* Jacksonville Beach, Fla.: Mowbray, 1976.

Spinella, Art. *The Master Merchandisers: America's Auto Dealers.* Van Nuys, Calif.: Freed-Crown, 1978.

Stein, Jonathan A. *British Sports Cars in America, 1946–1981.* Kutztown, Pa.: Automobile Quarterly Publications, 1993.

Steinwedel, Louis W. *The Beetle Book: America's 30-Year Love Affair with the "Bug."* Englewood Cliffs, N.J.: Prentice-Hall, 1981.

Stepan-Norris, Judith, and Maurice Zeitlin. *Talking Union.* Urbana: University of Illinois Press, 1996.

Stephenson, Charles, and Robert Asher, eds. *Life and Labor: Dimensions of American Working-Class History.* Albany: State University of New York Press, 1986.

Stern, Jane, and Michael Stern. *Auto Ads.* New York: Random House, 1979.

Stevenson, Heon. *Selling the Dream: Advertising the American Automobile, 1930–1980.* London: Academy, 1995.

Stieber, Jack W. *Democracy and Public Review: An Analysis of the UAW Public Review Board.* Santa Barbara, Calif.: Center for the Study of Democratic Institutions, 1960.

Stieber, Jack W. *Governing the UAW.* New York: Wiley, 1962.

Stolberg, Benjamin. *The Story of the CIO.* New York: Viking Press, 1938.

Stuart, Reginald. *Bailout: America's Billion Dollar Gamble on the New Chrysler Corporation.* South Bend, Ind.: and books, 1981.

Swados, Harvey. *On the Line.* Boston: Little, Brown, 1957.

Tedlow, Richard S. *New and Improved: The Story of Mass Marketing in America.* New York: Basic Books, 1990.

Therou, Francois. *Buick: "The Golden Era," 1903–1915.* Brea, Calif.: Decir, 1971.

Toder, Eric J, with Nicholas S. Cardell and Ellen Burton. *Trade Policy and the U.S. Automobile Industry.* New York: Praeger, 1978.

Tolliday, Steven, and Jonathan Zeitlin, eds. *The Automobile Industry and Its Workers: Between Fordism and Flexibility.* New York: St. Martin's Press, 1987.

Toyota Motor Corporation. *Toyota: The First Twenty Years in the U.S.A.* Torrance, Calif.: Toyota Motor Sales, 1977.

Train, Kenneth. *Qualitative Choice Analysis: Theory, Econometrics, and an Application to Automobile Demand.* Cambridge: MIT Press, 1986.

Turner, Lowell. *Democracy at Work: Changing World Markets and the Future of Labor Unions.* Ithaca, N.Y.: Cornell University Press, 1991.

U.S. Bureau of Foreign and Domestic Commerce. *Development of Motor-Vehicle Trade Abroad.* Washington, D.C.: Government Printing Office, 1913.

U.S. Department of Transportation. *Effects of Federal Regulation on the Financial Structure and Performance of the Domestic Motor Vehicle Manufacturers.* Cambridge, Mass.: Transportation Systems Center, 1978.

U.S. Federal Trade Commission. *Report on Motor Vehicle Industry.* Washington, D.C.: Government Printing Office, 1939.

Vargas, Zaragosa. *Proletarians of the North: A History of Mexican Industrial Workers in Detroit and the Midwest, 1917–1933.* Berkeley: University of California Press, 1993.

Voices of Dissent: A Collection of Articles from Dissent Magazine. New York: Grove Press, 1958.

Volvo Cars of North America. *40 Years: The Story of Volvo's First Forty Years in America.* Rockleigh, N.J.: Volvo Cars of North America, 1996.

Vossler, Bill. *Burma-Shave: The Rhymes, the Signs, the Times.* St. Cloud, Minn.: North Star Press of St. Cloud, 1997.

Walker, Charles R., Robert H. Guest, and Arthur N. Turner. *Foreman on the Assembly Line.* New York: Garland, 1987.

Walsh, J. Raymond. *C.I.O.: Industrial Unionism in Action.* New York: W.W. Norton, 1937.

Walshok, Mary Lindenstein. *Blue Collar Women: Pioneers on the Male Frontier.* Garden City, N.Y.: Anchor Books, 1981.

Wangers, Jim, with Paul Zazarine, *Glory Days: When Horsepower and Passion Ruled Detroit: A Memoir.* Cambridge, Mass.: Robert Bentley, 1998.

Watkins, Julian L. *The 100 Greatest Advertisements.* New York: Dover, 1959.

Weinstone, William. *The Great Sit-Down Strike.* New York: Workers Library, 1937.

Whitman, Lester L. *From Coast to Coast in a Motor-Car.* Syracuse, N.Y.: H.H. Franklin Company, 1905.

Whyte, William F. *Men at Work.* Homewood, Ill.: Dorsey Press, 1961.

Widick, B.J., ed. *Auto Work and Its Discontents.* Baltimore: Johns Hopkins University Press, 1976.

Wilkins, Mira, and Frank E. Hill. *American Business Abroad: Ford on Six Continents.* Detroit: Wayne State University Press, 1964.

Willsheer, Andy, and Bob McClurg. *Mustang: Selling the Legend.* Osceola, Wisc.: Motorbooks International, 1997.

Willys-Overland. *Standard Retailing Procedure for Willys-Overland Merchants.* Toledo: Willys-Overland, 1926.

Winston, Clifford. *Blind Intersection: Policy and the Automobile Industry.* Washington, D.C.: Brookings Institution, 1987.

Womack, James P., Daniel T. Jones, and Daniel Roos. *The Machine That Changed the World.* New York: Rawson Associates, 1990.

Wright, Harold E. *The Financing of Automobile Installment Sales.* New York: A.W. Shaw, 1927.

Wright, J. Patrick. *On a Clear Day You Can See General Motors: John Z. DeLorean's Look inside the Automotive Giant.* New York: Avon Books, 1980.

Yates, Brock W. *The Critical Path: Inventing an Automobile and Reinventing a Corporation.* Boston: Little, Brown, 1996.

Yates, Brock W. *The Decline and Fall of the American Automobile Industry.* New York: Empire Books, 1983.

Young, Stephen. *Chrysler U.K.: A Corporation in Transition.* New York: Praeger, 1977.

Young, William P. *A Ford Dealer's Twenty Year Ride with the Old and New Model Ford Policies.* Pottstown, Pa.: Author, 1932.

Zetka, James R., Jr. *Militancy, Market Dynamics, and Workplace Authority: The Struggle over Labor Process Outcomes in the U.S. Automobile Industry, 1946 to 1973.* Albany: State University Press of New York, 1995.

Zieger, Robert H. *The CIO: 1935–1955.* Chapel Hill: University of North Carolina Press, 1995.

Zimbalist, Andrew, ed. *Case Studies on the Labor Process.* New York: Monthly Review Press, 1979.

CHAPTER 4

Automotive Engineering and Design

In this chapter, we will explore the evolution of the American automobile in terms of its engineering and design. Some have argued that today's automobiles are basically the same as those of the 1920s, in that they contain the same styling components (body, roof, hood, trunk, grill, head- and taillight assemblies, etc.) and are powered by an internal combustion engine. While essentially true, such a statement belittles the enormous refinements that have taken place in automotive engineering and design over the last three-quarters of a century. Two recent works provide excellent overviews of the changes that have taken place. The first of these is a collection of articles that appeared in the magazine *Automotive Engineering* during the centennial year (1995) of the American automobile industry. Prepared under the auspices of the Society of Automotive Engineers and entitled *The Automobile: A Century of Progress*, separate chapters explore the evolution of the various systems and component parts that create a motor car, such as the engine, the electrical system, brakes, tires, and so on. In addition, other chapters cover changes in design, comfort and convenience, and safety over time. The other work is Walter J. Boyne's *Power behind the Wheel: Creativity and the Evolution of the Automobile*, an exploration of both design and engineering that begins with a historical overview and continues with chapters on the evolution of automotive chassis and engines; car styling, both mainstream and unique; customization; and a peek at the future as seen from 1988. Boyne's book is also beautifully illustrated with classic black-and-white and contemporary color photography. In addition, J. David Powell and Richard P. Brennan's *The Automobile—Technology and Society*, a study of current (1988) automotive engineering and possible future developments, is worth examining. A technical work aimed at the educated layperson, it covers topics such as turbochargers, electric carburetion, and active suspension but also pays due attention to societal and ecological considerations like vehicle emissions and accident rates.

ENGINEERING DEVELOPMENTS

The multifaceted literature that explores the technical history of the motor car is described in this section. An excellent introduction to this subject (up to 1976) is *The Bosch Book of the Motor Car: Its Evolution and Engineering Development*, by John Day. Although it takes an international (largely British) perspective, this volume traces the history of each of the components of the passenger automobile and explains its functioning with the assistance of 400 original drawings and photographs. Among the topics covered are the engine, transmissions, suspension and steering, brakes, and electrical systems. Takashi Suzuki's *The Romance of Engines* is even broader in coverage and brings the story up to the mid-1990s in terms of the histories of steam, internal combustion, rotary, and diesel engines. In fact, Suzuki's work is particularly strong on diesel combustion theory. He also examines and supports the social and ecological responsibilities of automobile engine designers to produce more efficient and cleaner power plants.

As can be implied by the topics in the *Bosch Book*, the automobile was a complex piece of machinery from the beginning. Despite its obvious debt to existing technologies, such as the internal combustion engine and the bicycle, the public still viewed the motor car as a new invention during the years prior to World War I, one that required knowledge and training to master. As a result, during the early decades of automotive history a large number of "self-help" technical and driving manuals were published. Representative of this genre and pertinent in this context were James E. Homans, *Self-Propelled Vehicles: A Practical Treatise* (first published in 1902, with revised editions appearing through the teens); Roger B. Whitman's *Motor Car Principles* (1907); the Association of Licensed Automobile Manufacturers' *Hand Book of Gasoline Automobiles* (1909); Julian Chase's *Motor Car Operation* (1910); the two-volume, 1,328-page *Practical Treatise on Automobiles* (1909), edited by Oscar C. Schmidt; Roy A. Engelman's *Autocraft* (1914); Clyde H. Pratt's *Automobile Instructor* (1917); A.L. Dyke's *Automobile and Gasoline Encyclopedia* (1917); Victor W. Pagé's *Questions & Answers Relating to Modern Automobile Design, Construction, Driving and Repair* (1919); and the American Technical Society's *Automobile Engineering* (1920), a six-volume work (2,370 pages in all!) covering cars, motorcycles, and commercial vehicles from 1910 to the date of publication. During the first two decades of the 20th century, books such as those cited in this paragraph frequently carried lengthy and rambling subtitles. Readers interested in those subtitles can find them in the bibliography appended to this chapter.

As indicated by the title of a 1900 book by Gardner D. Hiscox—*Horseless Vehicles, Automobiles, Motorcycles: Operated by Steam, Hydro-Carbon, Elec-*

tric and Pneumatic Motors—early automobiles could be driven by a variety of means of propulsion. Of these, the three most popular were gasoline, steam, and electric. Gasoline vehicles were/are powered by internal combustion engines, the development and evolution of which Lyle Cummins Jr. describes in his *Internal Fire*. Cummins offers a scholarly, yet readable, history for the years 1763 to 1900, with attention to both the technical advances and the people responsible for them. In addition, Lynwood Bryant's "The Internal Combustion Engine" and, particularly, John B. Rae's "Internal Combustion Engine on Wheels," two chapters in *Technology in Western Civilization*, edited by Melvin Kranzberg and Carroll W. Pursell Jr., offer good, brief historical accounts. Finally, in *Paths of Innovation: Technological Change in 20th-Century America*, David C. Mowery and Nathan Rosenberg use the internal combustion engine as one of three case studies to analyze how and why scientific knowledge has been translated into technological innovation during the contemporary period and the economic consequences that have resulted therefrom.

A variation of the internal combustion engine was developed in Germany by Rudolf Diesel in the late 1890s. Lyle Cummins' *Diesel's Engine: Volume One— From Conception to 1918* is both a biography of Rudolf Diesel and a well-researched history of the invention and marketing of the engine that now bears his name. (Lyle Cummins is the youngest son of Clessie Cummins, cofounder of Cummins Engine—see below.) Although born in Europe, the engine was quickly imported to the United States, a development described in the American Diesel Enterprise section of Cummins' book and in *The Engine That Could: 75 Years of Values-Driven Change at Cummins Engine Company*, by Jeffrey L. Cruikshank and David B. Sicilia, the success story of the premier independent producer of diesel engines in the United States. Nonetheless, diesel automobiles (as opposed to commercial vehicles) have not enjoyed much popularity in the United States, except for a period that coincided with the international petroleum embargoes of the 1970s. Diesel-powered vehicles of that period are exhaustively examined in Jan P. Norbye's *Modern Diesel Cars*.

The steam engine has an even longer history than that of the gasoline-fired, internal combustion engine. However, since the period of its use as a means of automotive propulsion was relatively short, only books concerned with the development of steam-powered motor vehicles are discussed here. For the early history of such vehicles, see "The Failure of the Steam Automobile" chapter in Clay McShane's scholarly *Down the Asphalt Path: The Automobile and the American City*, which does an especially good job of explaining why it failed commercially; John H. Bacon's *American Steam Car Pioneers: A Scrapbook*, a collection of personal remembrances and newspaper accounts from the turn of the century; John Bentley's brief *Oldtime Steam Cars*, a make-by-make (Stanley, White, Locomobile, etc.) history of the rise and fall of the steam car in the United States; *Floyd Clymer's Historical Motor Scrapbook of Steam Cars*, especially the chapter entitled "The Stanley Steamer" by Ray Stanley; Thomas S. Derr's *The Modern Steam Car and Its Background*, originally published in 1932, which contains chapters on the history of the steam engine and steam cars as well as a description of contemporary vehicles of the early 1930s; *History of Steam Cars, 1770–1970*, an analysis of the strengths and weaknesses of two centuries of vehicles on both sides of the Atlantic by Lord Montagu of Beaulieu and Anthony Bird; and David Burgess Wise's brief (96-page) *Steam on the Road*, similar in concept and execution to the previously cited Montagu and Bird work.

Until very recently, there was far less available on electric cars, possibly because they had the briefest history and the smallest degree of impact. However, renewed interest in the possibility of battery-powered vehicles to lessen American dependence on foreign oil and the decision by General Motors to actually market an electric car led to increased publication in this area. Two major works appeared in the mid-1990s: *History of the Electric Automobile: Battery-Only Powered Cars*, by Ernest H. Wakefield, published by the Society of Automotive Engineers, and *Taking Charge: The Electric Automobile in America*, by Michael B. Schiffer *et al.*, a publication of the Smithsonian Institution. Wakefield's, the more comprehensive of the two, takes an international approach, beginning with efforts in the 1880s, studies the so-called golden age of 1895–1905 in detail, traces technological developments and corporate histories through the mid-1930s, surveys the unproductive next four decades until the Electric Vehicle Act of 1976, and then concentrates on contemporary developments. Written by an engineer who took part in some of the developments described, *History of the Electric Automobile* is ultimately more satisfying as a technical encyclopedia than a historical survey. Schiffer, an anthropologist, traces the production of electric vehicles from 1895 to 1920 and the economic battle with gasoline and steam. He maintains that cultural factors, especially the association with women, not technological considerations, led to the electrics' demise. Advertising for such vehicles often featured women at the wheel and, therefore, electrics were seen as "unmanly." Given the mores of the day, such a perception hurt sales. The volume also contains a positive prognosis for the future of the electric vehicle in the United States, based on technological advances and environmental legislation. An earlier book, Sheldon R. Shacket's 1981 *The Complete Book of Electric Vehicles*, provides both a history of such vehicles and a technological description of how they function. Shacket's work is particularly interesting for its coverage of home-built electric vehicles and its prognosis of the future.

The story of the first modern, battery-powered production automobile—the General Motors EV 1—and the technological challenges and internal political obstacles that had to be overcome is told in Michael Shnayerson's *The Car That Could: The Inside Story of GM's Revolutionary Electric Vehicle*. A less successful venture is the subject of Joe Sherman's *Charging Ahead*, wherein the author relates the history of the Solectria Corporation and its founder, James Worden. Despite funding from the Pentagon and Boston Edison Company and the development of a battery-powered electric car in 1996 capable of traveling

374 miles on a single charge, Solectria had yet to produce a single commercial vehicle by 1998. Lobbying by Detroit's Big Three car makers had successfully killed the zero-emission mandate in California, a mandate that would have required that 2% of the cars sold in that state produce no emissions by 1998. Thus, the expected market for electric vehicles in California and other western states was severely undercut. Finally, for one man's "pioneering" experience with a 1991 electric car, Noel Perrin's *Solo: Life with an Electric Car* is fascinating, as he describes both an ill-fated attempt at a trans-continental trip from California to Vermont and his subsequent successful use of the car for commuting to work.

In addition to electricity, other means of automotive propulsion have continued to be advanced in the years since World War II, especially when the gasoline-fired, internal combustion engine has come under attack as a polluter and/or a contributor to American dependence on foreign oil. Sometimes, this has led to suggestions that we return to some *earlier* propulsion technologies—particularly steam and electricity—whose development, some maintained, had been cut short by the wholesale adoption of the gasoline engine. Books on modern electric cars are described above. For steam, see Gary Levine's *The Car Solution: The Steam Engine Comes of Age*, which is both a brief history of the steam car and a 1970s polemic pleading for a return to such automobiles as a solution to the multiple crises of energy and air and noise pollution, and Andrew Jamison's *The Steam-Powered Automobile: An Answer to Air Pollution*, similar in concept to Levine but more focused on one environmental problem.

In addition, automotive engineers have sought alternatives to the traditional, piston-driven, internal combustion engine. In fact, this quest began at the very beginning of automotive history. See Rudi Volti's "Alternative Internal Combustion Engines, 1900–1915" in this regard, a chapter in *Automotive Engineering in a Dead End*, edited by Mikael Håard. Citing the loss of fuel efficiency in contemporary engines due to modifications aimed at lessening air pollution, engineers have tried to develop a more efficient means of automotive propulsion. One outcome of this quest was the introduction of the Wankel rotary engine in the early 1970s, the subject of Harris E. Dark's *Wankel Rotary Engine: Introduction & Guide*, which provides the history and mechanics of that innovation, together with a comparison to the piston engine. Similar in concept are Nicholas Faith's *The Wankel Engine: The Story of the Revolutionary Rotary Engine*; Karl E. Ludvigsen's *Wankel Engines, A–Z*; and Jan P. Norbye's *The Wankel Engine*. Felix Wankel's engine, wherein rotors inside a chamber replace pistons and cylinders and in one continuous movement accomplish fuel intake, combustion, and gas expulsion, has fascinated engineers and manufacturers since its invention in the mid-1950s. While such engines are much lighter than piston ones and run far more smoothly, they have yet to replace traditional engines due to lingering questions regarding reliability and economy.

There also has been interest in an alternative power plant that had been conceived as early as 1791 and experimented with in cars in the mid-1950s—the gas turbine engine. Unfortunately, there is no book-length treatment of this subject. The same period saw the emergence of the naive belief that nuclear power plants would one day be installed in cars. In 1958 the Ford Motor Company announced plans to build such a vehicle, which they dubbed the Nucleon. The best, albeit very brief, discussion of this short-lived phenomenon within the broader framework of road transportation in general is in Joseph J. Corn and Brian Horrigan's *Yesterday's Tomorrows: Past Visions of the American Future*. Other futuristic ideas concerning automotive propulsion include using air in a jet-like manner to "push" the vehicle and, in some cases, provide levitation above the ground.

Of late, there has been interest in the feasibility of constructing vehicles that would be powered by solar energy and thus energy-saving and relatively pollution-free. By the end of the 1980s, there were enough solar-powered vehicles to make races possible featuring an international collection of entrants. The Society of Automotive Engineers' *GM Sunraycer Case History* is the story of the vehicle that won the 1987 World Solar Challenge race, complete with technical details from the engineers who developed it. Chester R. Kyle's *Racing with the Sun: The 1990 World Solar Challenge* is similar in concept, describing the race held across Australia that year, together with in-depth descriptions of the individual cars. For an account of one company's attempt to develop a commercially viable, solar-powered engine, see Mark Shelton's *The Next Great Thing: The Sun, the Stirling Engine, and the Drive to Change the World*, the story of William Beale and Sunpower, Inc.

Finally, the mid-1990s saw the emergence of plans for the manufacture of so-called hybrid automobiles, the joining together of multiple means of propulsion, often a combination of an internal combustion engine and an electric motor. (This is actually a rather old idea. The Woods dual-powered car was manufactured during 1917–1918 but proved to be a commercial failure.) In a contemporary hybrid vehicle, a computer determines when the gasoline engine must be used, and this engine internally recharges the batteries. Hybrids promise greater fuel economy and reduced emissions in comparison to traditional internal combustion cars, while delivering a significantly enlarged range of operation over pure electrics. Toyota actually produced and exported a gasoline/electric hybrid to the United States in 2000. The best reference on this general subject is Ernest H. Wakefield's *History of the Electric Automobile: Hybrid Electric Vehicles*. In addition to extensive coverage of what the author terms "petro-electric" vehicles, he explores the possibility of flywheel-electric, gas turbine-electric, and solar-electric cars. There also are separate chapters on the Stirling engine and on solar race car design. Wakefield hopes that competition among the latter will lead to discoveries with commercial applications. For an earlier, less technical discussion of this concept, see Robert J. Traister's 1982 *All About Electric & Hybrid Cars*.

Although historically, Americans have seemed more interested in design than engineering considerations, there were a number of notable exceptions to this generalization beginning in the middle third of the 20th century. Doug Bell's *Cast Iron Wonder* is a history of the six-cylinder engine that powered Chevrolets from 1929 to 1953. Ray Miller and Glenn Embree's *The V-8 Affair: An Illustrated History of the Pre-War Ford V-8* covers in words and over 1,000 pictures developments from the introduction of this engine in 1932 down to 1942. Similarly, Lorin Sorensen tells the story of *The Classy Ford V8* in a photo history of the legendary "flathead" engine that powered Fords and Mercurys of varying stripes up through the 1950s. More general is Michael Frostick's *V8*, an illustrated survey of cars powered by that engine configuration. Finally, Roy A. Schneider's *Sixteen Cylinder Motorcars: An Illustrated History* tells the story of the great behemoths of the 1930s built by Cadillac, Marmon, and Peerless.

These engines were followed by a new breed that put the "muscle" in muscle cars (see below). Two of these achieved legendary status. Anthony Young tells the story of the development of the *Chevrolet Small-Block V-8*, an engine that proved popular both with the general public and with professional racers. Young's *Hemi: History of the Chrysler Hemi V-8 Engine and Hemi-Powered Cars* is similar in approach, although it benefits from interviews with contemporary engineers. Production Hemi-powered muscle cars boasted 426-horsepower engines in the 1960s and 1970s. Also worthy of attention are two other engine histories by the same author: *Chevrolet Big-Block Muscle Cars* (from 1958 to 1976) and *Ford Hi-Po V-8 Muscle Cars* (from the 1930s to the contemporary period). Finally, more general coverage is provided in such volumes as Martyn L. Schorr's *Mopar: The Performance Years 1962–1972*, with its focus on Chrysler Corporation cars.

Contributions of Racing Cars

In much the same way that the space program has developed technologies for use on land by the average citizen, so also has the development of racing cars contributed significantly to the evolution of the passenger automobile. In fact, the very nature of automotive racing—to build the fastest, most maneuverable vehicle—brings forth constant innovations in this area. Our concern in this section will be with the cars themselves as a type; racing as a sport and individual models that achieved success within it are treated in Chapter 9.

Many books treat the historical development of the racing car as a generic form. Given the topic, such volumes frequently have a heavily European emphasis to them, especially for the first half-century. Among the better works, listed alphabetically by author, are Griffith Borgeson's *The Golden Age of the American Racing Car*, which superbly examines the evolution of race car technology and the men responsible for it during the years 1910–1929—winner of the AACA's McKean Award; Piero Casucci's *Racing Cars*, a comprehensive history through the 1970s, emphasizing the accomplishments of individual vehicles; *The Racing Car: Development and Design*, by Cecil Clutton *et al.*, although dated by virtue of its early 1960s publication date; Alex Gabbard's

Vintage & Historic Racing Cars, which traces developments from the early 1900s to the post–World War II era; and G[eorge] N. Georgano's *A Source Book of Racing and Sports Cars*, which studies 100 vehicles to show design and engineering changes from 1899 to 1972.

Racing cars are frequently classified and written about according to a characteristic design and/or engine type, such as "Indy," "Grand Prix," and "Formula 1" vehicles. Here, too, there is a plethora of volumes to choose from, often with a worldwide focus. The following books, grouped by type, all make solid contributions to the study of their subject: Roger Huntington's *Design & Development of the Indy Car*, an engineer's history of technical advances associated with the Indianapolis 500 from the beginning through the 1970s, and Tony Sakkis' similarly titled *Anatomy & Development of the Indy Car*, another technical history, this one emphasizing aerodynamics and handling rather than engines.

Laurence Pomeroy's two-volume *The Grand Prix Car, 1906–1953* is generally considered to be *the* classic on this topic, although it obviously now contains only half the story. A continuation volume, *The Grand Prix Car, 1954–1966*, written by L.J.K. Setright, takes the story up to the introduction of the Formula 1 vehicles. Complementing Setright and chronologically moving beyond him are two more recent volumes by Doug Nye, *The Autocourse History of the Grand Prix Car, 1945–65* and *The Autocourse History of the Grand Prix Car, 1966–91*, which provide technical and competition histories of those years, focusing on the evolution of the cars themselves, complete with factory blueprints, cutaway drawings, and detailed photographs. Finally, chronologically more specific is Doug Nye and Geoff Goddard's *Classic Racing Cars: The Post-War Front-Engined GP Cars*, an exploration of the development and performance of those vehicles.

By the mid-1980s, the Formula One (F1) racing car introduced twenty years earlier had evolved into an aerodynamic, 800-horsepower, turbocharged vehicle that was the dominant model type on the Grand Prix circuit. For historical and technical information on this car, see Howdy Holmes and Don Alexander's *Formula Car Technology*, winner of the 1980 American Association of Racing Book Writers and Authors (AARBWA) Book Award; Sal Incandela's *Anatomy and Development of the Formula One Racing Car from 1975*, a survey and explanation of the technological design and engine evolution of F1 cars to 1985; Alan Henry's similar *Grand Prix Car Design and Technology in the 1980s*, which actually covers the years 1977 to 1987 in Formula 1 design; Nigel MacKnight's *Technology of the F1 Car* (with coverage of wind tunnel testing; fuel, electrical, and suspension systems; and the design of the cockpit); and David Tremayne's *The Science of Speed: Today's Fascinating Hi-Tech World of Formula 1*, with its emphasis on recent engineering and design innovations and interviews with the individuals who brought those "winning-edge" changes to fruition.

A part of this F1 history is often referred to as the "turbo era," which lasted from the mid-1960s to the late 1980s. During that period, especially from 1977 on, racing cars equipped with turbochargers were so dominant that they threatened to change the nature of motor racing and were eventually banned in 1988 from F1 competition. There are two good surveys of this phenomenon: Ian Bamsey's *A History of the Turbo-Charged Racing Car*, which is strong both on the racing record and on the engineering developments that accompanied it, and Alan Henry's *The Turbo Years: Grand Prix Racing's Battle for Power*, similar to Bamsey but also including interviews with key personalities. Behram Kapadia's *The Turbo Decade* is a photo history of the years 1977–1988. The concept of turbocharging also was adapted to production models, beginning in the United States with the 1962 Corvair Monza Spider. Graham Robson's *Turbo: An A–Z of Turbocharged Cars* is an analysis of the design and engineering features of a collection of the more important models.

Formula 1 cars are clearly the upper crust of racing vehicles. At the other end of the spectrum is a type of racer built around a modified 1,200cc Volkswagen Beetle chassis. Most popular in the 1960s and 1970s, there still were races in this class into the 1990s. Their story is told in *The Racing Bugs: Formula Vee and Super Vee*, by Ross R. Olney and Ron Grable, and *Formula Vee/Super Vee: Racing, History, and Chassis/Engine Prep*, by Andrew L. Schupack, both of which chronicle how modified Volkswagen Beetles were raced for fun and profit.

The specific racing engines and the companies that manufactured them sometimes have been the subject of attention, as in *Continental: Its Motors and People*, by William Wagner, a comprehensive history of one of this country's major manufacturers of engines (or "motors," as they were then known), covering over eighty years of developments, beginning with a two-cycle gasoline engine in 1902 through its heyday as the power behind not just racing cars but aircraft as well. During the first half of this century, it was not unusual for car manufacturers to buy engines from companies like Continental that specialized in their production.

In the decades following World War I, pioneer mechanics developed increasingly powerful engines, many of which made their public debuts in racing cars. See, for example, Mark L. Dees' excellent and technically detailed *The Miller Dynasty*, the story of Henry Arminius Miller (1875–1943), whose cars and engines dominated American oval track (dirt and board) racing during the years between World Wars I and II. Griffith Borgeson's more recent *Miller*, published in cooperation with the Smithsonian Institution, is similar in concept to the Dees book, with attention given to the man, his exceptionally engineered racing cars, and his twin-cam, four-cylinder racing engines. These engines were decades ahead of their time and were the predecessors of the legendary Offenhauser engines. From the mid-1930s through the 1970s, the Offenhauser, or "Offy," engine and its descendants dominated every type of automotive racing. The history of the men who designed, built, and raced it is comprehensively told in George E. White's *Offenhauser*, which garnered the AACA's 1996 Thomas McKean Award.

In addition, George Peters and Henri Greuter authored *Novi—The Legendary Indianapolis Race Car*, the story of a series of racing cars of the 1940s and 1950s and the 450-horsepower engine (the Novi supercharged V-8) designed by Leo Goossen and Bud Winfield that powered them. John Blunsden's *The Power to Win* is an award-winning (Montagu Trophy) history of the design, development, and achievements of the legendary Ford Cosworth V-8 engine during the years 1967–1982, when it was adapted for use in Indy, Formula 1, and endurance racing. Finally, Griffith Borgeson's authoritative *The Classic Twin-Cam Engine* recounts its history from prewar beginnings through the 1970s, with considerable attention to technical details and the personalities responsible for the evolution of the "thoroughbred" racing engine.

Finally, there are several non-technical overviews of the design and engineering of contemporary race cars. Some of the better ones are Alan Henry's *The Quest for Speed: Modern Racing Car Design and Technology*, with its focus on Formula 1 and Indy vehicles; Forbes Aird's *Race Car Chassis: Design and Construction*, a survey of frame development and function from the ladder-type to the composites, and the same author's *Aerodynamics for Racing and Performance Cars*, an explanation of the theory and an application of the principles first explored in the streamlining movement of the 1930s (see below); John F. Katz' similar *Race Car Aerodynamics: Designing for Speed*; and Terry Jackson's *Anatomy of Speed: Inside the World's Great Race Cars*, with its emphasis on how such cars are prepared for and technically function in competition.

For more technical observations on contemporary engineering and design characteristics and their impact, see *Race Car Vehicle Dynamics*, by William F. Milliken and Douglas L. Milliken, a comprehensive overview of specific theories and principles that are applied to race car design; *Design of Racing and High Performance Engines*, edited by Joseph Harralson, which focuses on the basic principles of such design and their impact on a car's effectiveness in competition; and Paul van Valkenburg's *Race Car Engineering & Mechanics*, a wide-ranging exploration of all aspects of race car technology.

Other Engineering Innovations

As implied in the titles of some of the books previously cited in this chapter, not all automotive engineering innovations have been confined to the motor itself. For each car model, engineers have had to decide how to transfer the power from the engine to the wheels. For a fine overview of this subject, see Philip G. Gott's *Changing Gears: The Development of the Automotive Transmission*, which traces the history of this engineering challenge from the turn of the 20th century to 1990, with due attention to the social dimensions, especially of automatic transmission. Gott won the 1993 Engineering Historian Award from the American Society of Mechanical Engineers (ASME) for this work.

A continuing question in the history of automotive engineering has been with which set(s) of wheels to drive a car. Although Americans are most familiar with rear-wheel drive automobiles, other types have equally long histories. See, for instance, *The Complete Handbook of Front Wheel Drive Cars*, by Jan P. Norbye, an international treatment of the development and evolution of the technology involved in such vehicles, together with chapters devoted to the cars of specific American, European, and Japanese manufacturers.

Another variation is that of four-wheel drive, wherein the power train is capable of turning all of the wheels, not just the front or rear two. In a sense the car is both pushed and pulled, thus providing the maximum traction possible. While the first successful American car equipped with four-wheel drive was introduced in 1908, its post–World War II application to jeeps, off-road vehicles, and SUVs is responsible for its current popularity. A good introductory history of the subject from an international perspective is provided in Jack Jackson's *Four Wheel Drive*, although the information on "current" models is now dated. Older (1954) but still informative is Howard W. Troyer's *The Four Wheel Drive Story*, a history of the FWD Company.

Significant improvements and innovations also have been made in instrumentation, automotive finishes, lights, body construction, the brake system, heating and cooling, and so on. For an in-depth look at one of these aspects, see David Holland's *Dashboards*. He provides fascinating, double-page photographs of each example and explanatory text for the instrument panels of over fifty different cars, dating from 1904 to 1973 and ranging from the simplicity of a few dials to a complexity that approaches that of an airplane cockpit. Although the focus is heavily British, a Model T Ford, a Chrysler Imperial from the 1930s, a New Yorker from the 1950s, a Cord 812, a 1955 Chevrolet Corvette, and a Jeep are included. Jack Gieck's *Riding on Air: A History of Air Suspension* traces the evolution of a technology that has improved vehicular comfort since the mid-19th century, with special attention to the challenges of adapting that technology to the passenger automobile. Finally, an interesting little book dedicated to the proposition that many automotive engineering innovations are not as new as they claim to be is Stanley K. Yost's *They Don't Build Cars Like They Used To!*, which won the AACA's Thomas McKean Award. Among the earlier developments that Yost cites are an adjustable steering wheel on the 1904 Marr, automatic transmission in the 1907 Sturtevant, coil springs supporting the 1910 Brush, and the rotary engine of the 1917 Eagle-Macomber.

Before leaving this section on engineering, it should be noted that, particularly in the first third of the 20th century, individual engineers were often responsible for significant advances. Biographies and autobiographies of these people are described in Chapter 2. See, for instance, Charles F. Kettering (inventor of the electric self-starter), Henry M. Leland (interchangeable parts), William Borg (the clutch), Francis W. Davis (power steering), Max Bentele (engines, including the Wankel), and Ralph R. Teetor (cruise control). In this regard, Ingo Seiff's *The Great Classics: Automobile Engineering in the Golden Age* focuses on the contributions of an international cast that includes Henry Ford and Henry M. Leland.

By the 1920s large automobile manufacturers had established their own in-house engineering departments. See, for example, Carl Breer's *The Birth of Chrysler Corporation and Its Engineering Legacy*. Breer, together with Owen Skelton and Fred Zeder, worked together as an engineering team for thirty-five years, originally at Studebaker and then moving to Chrysler. At the latter, their many technical innovations established Chrysler's unparalleled reputation for engineering excellence during the middle third of the 20th century. In a similar vein, but far less significant as a historical reference, is G.E. "Bud" Adams' self-published *Bedtime Stories for Young Engineers: 40 Years in Product Design and Engineering at Ford Motor Co*. At least one of the Big Three—General Motors—has attempted to systematically train its own engineers. The story of the first half century of that effort is told by Clarence H. Young and Robert E. Tuttle in *The Years 1919–1969: A History of the General Motors Institute*, a fully accredited college with a narrowly focused curriculum.

Finally, it should be noted that engineering advances have never been totally self-contained within a particular company—or nation, for that matter. There has been technological cross-fertilization from the earliest days of the automobile, a topic explored in Peter J. Hughill's "Technology Diffusion in the World Automobile Industry, 1885–1995," a chapter in *The Transfer and Transformation of Ideas and Material Culture*, a book that he and D. Bruce Dickson edited.

DESIGN AND STYLING

The attention that Americans have devoted to the design and styling of their automobiles is unique among the tools that they use on a daily basis. Whereas economy and performance have been the preeminent selling points for kitchen appliances, radios, and televisions, styling has been an important consideration in the purchase of an automobile since the 1920s, and often the paramount one.

This was not always the case. Although a book entitled *The Principles of Automobile Body Design*, by Kingston Forbes, appeared as early as 1922, it was not until 1926 that General Motors introduced the concept of model styling changes each year and Americans became conditioned for the remainder of the century to expect, and to some extent demand, such modifications.

The most recent scholarly overview of this subject, and arguably the best, is David Gartman's *Auto-Opium: A Social History of American Automobile Design*, which combines business history with a social and cultural analysis of the significance of automotive aesthetics. Interestingly, Gartman maintains that the process of mass production generated class conflict that influenced car design as Americans sought to compensate themselves for the deprivations of capitalistic competition through the purchase of stylish and over-powered vehicles. More traditional in approach but also excellent is Paul C. Wilson's *Chrome Dreams: Automobile Styling since 1893*, which includes sections regarding the influence of popular tastes on automotive design up to the mid-1970s. Also very good and the most recent publication in this field is *A Century of Automotive*

Style: 100 Years of American Car Design, by Michael Lamm and Dave Holls, a heavily illustrated history of the evolution of the physical shape of the automobile and an exploration of the professional and personal lives of the men and women responsible for it. This volume is particularly strong on the contributions of the custom coach builders and corporate politics of the post–World War II years. Lamm is a former managing editor at *Motor Trend*, and Holls was director of corporate design at General Motors. A brief, popular overview of the same subject is available in *50 Years of American Automotive Design, 1930–1980*, by Dick Nesbitt and editors, which also attempts to explain the societal influences that inspired these changes. Finally, Strother MacMinn's "American Automobile Design," a chapter in *Automobile and Culture*, by Gerald Silk *et al.*, is worth examining both for its exploration of the significant impact that independent body/coach builders had on automotive design until the mid-1920s and for its discussion of the evolution of automotive styling as reflected in sports and luxury cars beginning in the 1930s.

Although the "hand-built" production car is now almost exclusively a European phenomenon, there were, and still are to a lesser extent, individuals and companies that made such cars in the United States. Probably the best introduction to this topic is Hugo Pfau's *The Custom Body Era*, a well-illustrated volume that is an authoritative source of information on custom body builders of the 1920s and 1930s. Pfau himself was a designer for LeBaron during the years 1928 to 1931. Much of the flavor and attraction of these unique cars can be extracted by reading *The Golden Age of the Luxury Car: An Anthology of Articles and Photographs from "Autobody," 1927–1931*, a selection culled by George Hildebrand from what was probably the premier trade magazine of the 1920s concerning custom coachwork.

Focus on one particular marque is provided by Hugo Pfau in his *The Coachbuilt Packard*, which describes and illustrates the custom-built bodies that were mounted on Packard chassis to create one-of-a-kind cars in the years 1906–1941. While this volume consists primarily of archival photographs and captions, the latter are especially precise and informative, and one gains a feel for the coach-building era as a whole. Among the builders described are Brewster, Darrin, Fleetwood, and LeBaron. In the same vein is Thomas E. Bonsall's *The Coachbuilt Lincoln*, which focuses on custom- and semi-custom-built Lincolns over the course of seventy years. More of an illustrated monograph than the Pfau volume, Bonsall's work covers the origins of this marque during the Edsel Ford years, the birth of the original Continental and other Zephyr-based custom cars of the 1940s, and the presidential limousines. One of the last vestiges of the custom-coach-built era disappeared in November 1996, when the last Cadillac Fleetwood was manufactured at the General Motors plant in Arlington, Texas.

A more contemporary practice, where professional customizers enhance the luxury and performance of assembly-line production cars, is described and illustrated in *Dream Cars*, by Ian Kuah.

Although the practice of modifying the engine and/or body of a factory-built automobile is as old as motor cars themselves, it reached a type of apogee with the "hot rods" of the postwar 1940s, 1950s, and 1960s, and has never completely disappeared. Indeed, the introduction in 1997 of the Plymouth Prowler, a car that might be termed the first mass-produced hot rod, has given new life to this movement. (See Karla A. Rosenbusch and Jeffrey I. Godshall's brief, forty-page *Plymouth Prowler: Anatomy of a New American* for the development of this car.) One of the earliest books on the hot rod phenomenon is Eugene Jaderquist and Griffith Borgeson's *Best Hot Rods*. Done in the early 1950s, it is useful today because it gives reference data about the beginnings of hot-rodding. A good, albeit brief, overview of this phenomenon is contained in Henry F. Robert Jr.'s "Hot Rods and Customs," a chapter in *Automobile and Culture*, by Gerald Silk *et al*. Probably the best enthusiast work in this regard is *Car Culture*, written by Paul Rambali and beautifully illustrated with photographs by Frances Basham and Bob Ughetti; it celebrates the custom car cult of hot rods, drag racers, and low riders.

Some of the earliest history is conveyed in two books by Don Montgomery: *Authentic Hot Rods: The Real "Good Old Days,"* a photo history of the 1930s and 1940s roadsters that became the fastest street machines, and *Hot Rods in the Forties: A Blast from the Past*, a work that also includes an intriguing collection of period photographs. For a general overview of the beginnings of the "golden era," readers are referred to Andy Southard Jr.'s *Hot Rods of the 1950s*, a compendium of now-"classic" cars that were shown or raced during that decade, plus coverage of hot rod memorabilia, and *Grease Machines: A Complete Guide to Hot Rods and Customized Cars of the Fifties*, compiled by the editors of *Consumer Guide*. See also Andrew Morland's largely pictorial *Street Rods* and *Street Machines*, which feature contemporary versions of pre-1948 and post-1950 cars, respectively, and Bo Bertilsson's similar *Classic Hot Rods* of the 1950s and 1960s.

Such cars continued to fascinate throughout the second half of the 20th century, as witnessed by the publication of *Showtime, the Story of the International Championship Auto Shows and the Hot Rod/Custom Car World: A Twenty-Year History*, by Michael Sheridan and Sam Bushala, which provides both a factual catalog and an appreciation of these "one-of-a-kind" cars during the period 1960–1980, and *Oakland Roadster Show: 50 Years of Hot Rods & Customs*, by Dain Gingerelli and Andy Southard Jr., a historical tribute to arguably the most prestigious event in hot-rodding, which began in 1949 and has been held annually ever since. Like other aspects of American culture, hot-rodders recently have experienced a fondness for what went before. In this regard, see Larry O'Toole's *Nostalgia Street Rods*, a 1998 publication that chronicles the fin-de-siecle return of customizers to the styling principles of the 1940s and 1950s. (For a treatment of hot rods as a social phenomenon, rather than as an aspect of automotive design, see the "Youth" section of Chapter 5.)

Automotive design has not always been an isolated phenomenon, unaffected by the artistic trends that influence American society. The earliest example of the latter would be the industrial design movement for streamlining and functionalism, which achieved a type of ascendancy in the late 1920s and throughout the 1930s. Two good overviews of this movement are Donald J. Bush's *The Streamlined Decade*, a general history that includes its automotive manifestations in the 1930s, including both aerodynamic vehicles that were actually built and ones that were merely proposed, and *Streamlining America*, a publication of the Henry Ford Museum and Greenfield Village that accompanied an interpretive exhibition of consumer objects, ranging from automobiles to furniture to household appliances. For the specific views of one of the initial leaders, see Norman Bel Geddes' *Horizons*, published in 1932, which contains a chapter describing his belief in the importance of aerodynamics to automotive styling and mechanical efficiency.

Streamlining was tried briefly in the 1930s by Chrysler with their Airflow models. In this regard, see Carl Breer's previously cited *The Birth of the Chrysler Corporation and Its Engineering Legacy* and Martin Simons' *Airflow*. While such cars proved to be unpopular with the consumer, they returned with much greater success in the 1980s. Contemporary instances of this phenomenon are presented in *Streamlined Cars in Europe/USA*, by Ralf J.F. Kieselbach. Recent experimentation with solar, electric, and ultralight automobiles has created new streamlining challenges for designers. For a technical description of those challenges, see Goro Tamai's *The Leading Edge: Aerodynamic Design of Ultra-Streamlined Land Vehicles*.

Contemporary observers have noted other examples of the link between automotive styling and popular artistic taste. For instance, see *Populuxe*, by Thomas Hine, with its emphasis on the relationship of design to consumerism in the period 1954–1964, including an analysis of automobile tail fins and the Ford Mustang, and *Art as Design, Design as Art: A Contemporary Guide*, by Sterling McIlhany, in which the author portrays the interaction between art and industrial design, using the automobile and its symbolism as one of its prime examples.

Individual Designers and Stylists

Although most designers work within the styling section of large automotive manufacturers and, as such, are relatively anonymous and their individual contributions unknown outside the company, there are a few significant exceptions to that rule. Some of them have already been cited in Chapter 2, and the reader should check the "Engineers and Designers" section there for biographies of Harley Earl, Gordon Buehrig, Raymond Loewy, Bill Mitchell, and others. While those works are primarily biographical in nature, they do contain significant information on the styling contributions of the individual involved. Some books, however, are predominantly concerned with the design achievements and work habits of a particular person or team, and they are more properly discussed here. The best work in this regard is Henry Dominguez's *Edsel Ford and E.T. Gregoire: The Remarkable Design Team and Their Classic Fords of the 1930s and 1940s*, which emphasizes Bob Gregoire's designs for Ford, Mercury, and Lincoln—including such classics as the Zephyr and the Continental—and analyzes his working relationship with Edsel Ford, then president of the Ford Motor Company. John Bridges' *Bob Bourke Designs for Studebaker* also is good, covering as it does the 1950–1955-model-year Studebakers and the 1956 Studebaker Hawks in detail, with some information on Bourke's contributions to the 1947 Studebaker and 1949 Ford. In addition, C. Edson Armi's *The Art of American Car Design: The Profession and Personalities* contains chapter-length interviews with nine American designers, including Gregoire, Bill Mitchell, and Gordon Buehrig. Finally, Rob de la Rive Box and Richard Crump's *The Automobile Art of Bertone* explores the worldwide influence of Italian designer Nuccio Bertone on automotive styling and the evolution of his work since 1912.

In addition to the "mainstream" designers featured above and in Chapter 2, the custom car culture, especially that of the hot rod, also has produced a number of legendary stylists. *Barris Kustoms of the 1950s* by George Barris and David Fetherston, is a photographic history of the legendary work of the Barris brothers (George and Sam) at a time when their shop produced some of the finest custom bodywork and paint designs. Dean Moon was another of the pioneers in this area, whose cars and high-performance parts were an important part of early drag racing. David A. Featherston's *Moon Equipped: Sixty Years of Hot Rod Photo Memories* offers a survey of the man, his company, and its products. For the work of arguably the best customizer of all, see Timothy Remus' *Hot Rods by Boyd Coddington* and Tony Thacker's similarly named *Hot Rods by Boyd*, both of which survey his work from his backyard days to his latest creations. Ed Roth is another in this genre who has received national recognition. *Hot Rods by Ed "Big Daddy" Roth*, written by Roth and Tony Thacker, is a photo history of the former's creations from the 1950s to the mid-1990s, including recollections from fellow customizers. Roth, with the assistance of Howie Kusten, is also the author of *Confessions of a Rat Fink: The Life and Times of Ed "Big Daddy" Roth*, a heavily illustrated autobiography. A more recent addition to the scene are the *Hot Rods by Pete & Jake*, which is the title of another photo history by Tony Thacker, as third author with Pete Chapouris and Jim "Jake" Jacobs, in which the latter two describe in word and picture their collaborative efforts since 1972 and their earlier individual work. For some of their creations, Chapouris and Jacobs have collaborated with Ed Roth and Boyd Coddington.

Not surprisingly, there also are anthologies devoted to automotive designers. The best work in this regard is G.N. Georgano's *Art of the American Automobile: The Greatest Stylists and Their Work*, the story of the impact of those individuals whose creative talents made a difference in the design of standard production car models and custom bodies since 1930. Among those discussed are Gordon Buehrig, Howard "Dutch" Darrin, Harley Earl, Raymond Loewy, Bill Mitchell, and Richard Teague. Also good is Armi's previously mentioned *The Art of American Car Design*, with its analysis of automobile designs and the people responsible for them, including Strother MacMinn, Bill Mitchell, Gordon Buehrig, and Bob Gregoire. Other books worth examining include *Automobile Design: Great Designers and Their Work*, a *Choice* magazine Outstanding Academic Book edited by Ronald Barker and Anthony Harding, which features the work of Henry M. Leland and Harry Miller, plus ten European engineers; *The World's Great Automobile Stylists*, by John Tipler, a geographically broader view that features the work of forty designers, including Harley Earl and Bill Mitchell; and *The Designers: Great Automobiles and the Men Who Made Them*, by L.J.K. Setright.

Concept and Dream Cars

The professional designers who work for major automotive companies are responsible for the so-called concept, prototype, or dream cars that manufacturers have been building since the late 1930s to test in-house and public reaction to styling innovations that are being considered for production vehicles. The resulting cars have been showcased in several collections, the best of which is Michael Frostick's *Dream Cars: Design Studies and Prototypes*, which, while international in coverage, does feature extensive sections on Chrysler, Ford, and General Motors. Another very good, worldwide survey is *The Automobile Year Book of Dream Cars: Their Design and Development*, by Frenchman Jean-Rodolphe Piccard, which combines a text that features commentary by the designers themselves with an impressive set of archival photographs and drawings. Similar to Frostick and Piccard, but less satisfying, are *Dream Cars: The Style for Tomorrow*, by Peter Vann and Serge Bellu, and *Prototype and Dream Cars*, by Dewar McLintock.

More American in focus are Jonathan Wood's *Concept Cars*, a brief (96-page), heavily illustrated survey of the evolution of such cars from the 1939 General Motors "Y-Job" to the late 1990s; and Henry Lent's *The X-Cars: Detroit's One-of-a-Kind Autos*, which, in addition to profiling the cars themselves, contains a chapter devoted to design and styling. Of historical interest is Fred Horsley's *Dream Cars*, a book published in 1953.

In at least three cases, we have printed collections of concept cars from a particular automotive manufacturer. In *Dodge Brothers/Budd Company Historical Album Photo Book*, John R. Velliky and Jean Maddern Pitrone present Dodge Brothers prototype automobile designs from the years 1915 through 1930 for cars that featured Budd Company bodies. In most cases, these cars were actually mass-produced with slight modifications. Additionally, for the concept cars, prototypes, clay studies, and drawings of one of the most innovative design studios of the postwar era, see Patrick R. Foster's *The Nash Styling Sketchbook*. This brief, eighty-five-page volume is particularly valuable for showing how and to what degree styling concepts become translated into actual production designs. Finally, Jesse Thomas' *Pontiac Dream Cars, Show Cars & Prototypes: 1928–1998 Photo Album* provides both interior and exterior photographs of early dealership, display-only automobiles, Motorama dream vehicles, Banshees, and contemporary concept cars for one of the longer-lived marques.

One reason for the development of concept cars is to display them at auto shows, wherein they both tempt the public and take the measure of the innovation's popularity. Although such shows now feature cars from a worldwide spectrum of manufacturers, this was not always the case. During the years 1949 to 1961, General Motors put together an annual show of its production and experimental cars that traveled to major American cities. The story of that public relations ploy is told by participant Bruce Berghoff in *The GM Motorama: Dream Cars of the Fifties*, which is a good source of information on one-of-a-kind concept cars from General Motors during that decade. The efforts of two of the GM divisions are portrayed in *Pontiac Show Cars, Experimentals & Special Editions*, by Dale Sass, and *Corvette Prototypes and Showcars: Photo Album*, edited by Wallace A. Wyss.

Obviously, not all concept cars reach production, even in modified form. Many were intended to be only "dream cars," others were scrapped for financial reasons, and some were stillborn in the world of managerial politics. A good introductory survey of these vehicles is Edward Janicki's *Cars Detroit Never Built: Fifty Years of American Experimental Cars*, which focuses on and illustrates over 140 prototype vehicles that the Big Three companies built from 1938 to 1995 to test new designs and technologies. In the same vein is *Cars That Never Were*, put together by the editors of *Consumer Guide* magazine and featuring photographs and descriptions of twenty-six different cars planned since World War II that never were manufactured.

Finally, some mention needs to be made of those cars that are just plain unique, intended to be individualized expressions of their creator's personality (or personalities). As might be imagined, book-length collections featuring such vehicles tend to be idiosyncratic. Nonetheless, readers interested in an introduction to this world may want to examine John A. Gunnell's *Weird Cars* and Adrianne Kessel's *The World's Strangest Automobiles*. The former ranges from the Batmobile to a zebra-striped Subaru to the Weinermobile, with every variation of chopped, channeled, and stretched vehicle in between. The latter contains its share of bizarre cars built by eccentrics but also some oddball designs from major automotive companies.

Riding comfort has always been an alleged goal of automotive design. Mention of it was present in some of the earliest car advertisements. Over the years, design considerations were usually limited to attempts to make the car as comfortable as possible. Little attention was given to how the configuration of the interior of the car also might protect the occupants' safety in the event of an accident. However, studies in this vein began to be undertaken in the early 1960s, and 1966 saw the publication of Stephen Black's *Man and Motor Cars:*

An Ergonomic Study, in which the author concludes that, up to then, the styling man paid little attention to the biological man. The last third of the century saw greater attention by designers and engineers to the interrelationship among design, comfort, and safety, as described by Jan P. Norbye in *Car Design: Structure & Architecture*. For more on the accusation that American automotive manufacturers frequently have placed styling ahead of safety in the design of their cars, see Chapter 11.

Decade-by-Decade Surveys

As one might expect, there are an incredible number of heavily illustrated "coffee-table" books that exist largely as tributes to the world of automotive design. Some of the more representative works in this genre are Quentin Willson's *Classic American Cars*, which features sixty uniquely designed automobiles produced since World War II; Bill Neely and John Lamm's *Cars to Remember*, an anthology of "In Retrospect" reviews from *Motor Trend* featuring thirty-seven diverse automobiles manufactured from 1911 on; and Richard Nichols' *Exotic Cars*, an international pictorial collection that includes the Cadillac V-16 and the Tucker Torpedo among the American entries. Chronologically more specific are works like D.B. Tubbs' *Horseless Carriages: A 19th Century Album of Early Designs* and Jerry Flint's *The Dream Machine: The Golden Age of American Automobiles, 1946–1956*, which is unusual in that it links social events of the time with corresponding developments within the world of motorization.

The 1950s is often referred to as the "golden era" of American automotive design and the "age of chrome." In addition, it was the period of the "tail fin," brought to perfection or outrageous excess, depending on one's perspective, by Harley Earl and Virgil Exner. As a result, that decade has spawned a greater number of works than any other. A good beginning point is *Fins and Chrome: American Automobiles of the 1950s*, by E. John DeWaard. What distinguishes this auto buff book from others is the attention that the author pays to the interaction between vehicular design and human personality traits, particularly in terms of customizing. Similarly, Mike Key and Tony Thacker's *Dream Cars of the Fifties* sees the origins of some of the designs in the pop culture of the period, especially the music, and American fascination with the new, jet-powered aircraft. Concentrating more exclusively on design are Brian Laban's *Chrome: The Glamour Cars of the Fifties*, a photographic tribute to thirty-four classic cars of the decade; *Fifties Stylish American Cars: Decade of Dazzle*; featuring the photography of Henry Rasmussen; and Jay Hirsch's *Great American Dream Machines: Classic Cars of the 50s & 60s*, similar to Laban but highlighting sixty memorable cars of that era.

Moving into the 1960s, one encounters the so-called muscle cars, which are the subject of special treatment in the next section. The 1960s is currently the last decade to be recognized by volumes devoted exclusively to car designs specific to it. Possibly it takes the passage of a generation to garner such recognition, or perhaps the aerodynamic emphasis in the last third of the century created a sameness that has limited unique car designs.

GENERIC DESIGNS

While particular models frequently fascinate us as automobile owners, collectors, or simply observers of the American scene, history is probably better traced by reference to generic design changes over the years. Thus, the transition from open cars to closed cars, the introduction of the hardtop and the convertible, and the appearance of such broad categories as "muscle" and "sports" cars mark significant developments in the use, function, and perception of the automobile in American culture and life. Described below, in alphabetical order, are a number of distinctive designs that have been studied by automotive historians and enthusiasts.

Air and Sea Cars

Perhaps the strangest forays in automotive design are those that have attempted to combine the motor car with the airplane or the boat. Throughout the first half of the 20th century, many people speculated that small, personal, hybrid air/road vehicles would soon replace the traditional motor car as the primary means of private transportation. There is only one book-length treatment of this surprisingly long-lived (given that no hybrid ever really got beyond the prototype stage) movement, and that, Daniel R. Zuck's *An Airplane in Every Garage*, was printed by a subsidy publisher. However, historian Joseph J. Corn has written a well-documented chapter on the history of this phenomenon, entitled " 'An Airplane in Every Garage?' The Gospel's Most Pervasive Promise" in his book *The Winged Gospel*. Similarly, Waldo Dean Waterman's autobiographical *Waldo, Pioneer Aviator: A Personal History of American Aviation, 1910–1944*, written with the assistance of Jack Carpenter, contains information on the development of the "aerocar." Unfortunately, there is nothing comparable on amphibious car/boats, such as the 1960s Amphicar, which, while manufactured in Germany, experienced most of its sales in the United States. However, Timothy Jacobs' *Lemons: The World's Worst Cars*, in addition to exploring "traditional" European and American examples, does include some information on seaworthy (and flying) cars.

The Convertible

Early autos generally were not permanently enclosed, and, in a sense, the motor car began as an open-air vehicle. Although they would be superseded in popularity by the closed sedan in the late 1920s, "touring cars," either without any top or with a foldable cloth one, and the sports car "roadster" dominated the market for almost three decades. One could argue that touring cars/roadsters were the predecessors to the modern "convertible," a term that was first standardized by the Society of Automotive Engineers in 1928, a recognition of the production of the first modern convertibles in 1927. Guiseppe Guzzardi and Luigi E. Rizzo's *Convertibles: History and Evolution of Dream Cars* offers a popular, heavily illustrated introduction to this subject, although with a decidedly European emphasis. Graham Robson's *The Post War Touring Car* and *Cabriolets*, by Jean-Paul Thevenet and Peter Vann, are similar in approach but more focused in content. Finally, Ken Vose's *The Convertible: An Illustrated History of a Dream Machine* is a contemporary, celebratory account of the evolution of the "ragtop" in Europe and the United States, both as a body type and as a cultural icon.

Beginning in the 1950s and continuing for approximately two decades, the convertible, with its mechanically retractable soft top, became a very popular body style in the United States. There are many enthusiast histories of the convertible, of which the following stand out. *The Great American Convertible: An Affectionate Guide*, by Robert Wieder and George Hall, chronicles its story in word and picture from 1910 to 1977 and is distinguished from similar works by its extensive reproduction of contemporary advertisements. The identically entitled *The Great American Convertible*, a heavily illustrated, decade-by-decade, encyclopedic treatment of the subject by Richard M. Langworth and the auto editors of *Consumer Guide*, contains photos and descriptions of all makes and models, production figures, and retail prices. John Gunnell's *Convertibles: The Complete Story* is more a collector's reference work than a true history, but it can be a valuable source of data for the years 1928 to 1983.

During the mid-1950s, Ford introduced its Skyliner model, a combination hardtop/convertible that featured a retractable metal roof that could be mechanically lowered into the trunk area. A brief photo history of this unique and ultimately financially unsuccessful attempt to combine the advantages of both open and closed cars is *Classic Motorbooks Ford Retractable, 1957–1959*, by Jerry H. Magayne. In the same vein but published a decade later is *Ford Fairlane 500 Skyliner, 1957–1959*, also by Magayne.

By the mid-1970s, the convertible had fallen on hard times in the United States. Safety considerations, air conditioning, and an unexplainable loss of public interest were all cited as reasons for such sluggish sales that all major American auto companies ceased production of that body style. For a while, the only new convertible available for purchase in the United States was produced by Volkswagen. By 1979 Warren Weith and Jay Hirsch's *The Last American Convertibles* was being billed as "a last, loving look" at such cars. Their fine tribute, covering four decades, proved to be premature, as consumer demand for convertibles returned in the late 1980s, almost as mysteriously as it had waned a decade earlier.

Luxury Cars

In each era of automotive history, there always has been a group of car marques and models that have been expensive to purchase, due to the superiority of their design and engineering. Aimed at wealthy buyers, such automobiles might generically be termed "luxury cars." In an article entitled "The Golden Age of the Luxury Car," written a decade ago, Paul Brennan notes that while there is ample literature concerning individual marques, there has been no systematic, scholarly analysis of the luxury car phenomenon itself. Thus, researchers interested in such cars must rely primarily on popular histories. Nonetheless, there are a number of outstanding volumes in this category, including Richard B. Carson's *The Olympian Cars: The Great American Luxury Automobiles of the Twenties and Thirties*, which won the McKean Award and is easily the best introduction to the topic with its excellent text and period photographs; Brooks Brierley's *Magic Motors 1930*, an illustrated history that is particularly strong when it explains the luxury car *business* in the 1930s; and John Bolster's *The Upper Crust: The Aristocrats of Automobiles*, which the scholarly journal *Technology and Culture* calls "very good."

Muscle Cars

Generally defined by their oversized engine, large bodies, and elaborate ornamentation, so-called muscle cars, such as the Pontiac GTO (developed by John DeLorean), the Mustang Boss 429, and the Hemi Plymouth Barracuda, were true "kings of the road" beginning in the 1960s and lasting until the early 1970s. For better or worse, their like will probably never be seen again. A good, general introduction to these behemoths is *Muscle Cars*, written by John McGovern. It covers not just the American fire-breathers but their foreign counterparts as well. More specific is Jim Campisano's heavily illustrated *American Muscle Cars*, which traces the complete history from concept to demise. J.G. Newbery's *Muscle Cars* is similar in nature, although it focuses on those vehicles that have become collector's cars and sees the newest Corvettes and Mustangs as a return to that era. More in the category of a "tribute" is Mike Mueller's *Motor City Muscle: The High-Powered History of the American Muscle Car*, although it does have the advantage of describing the technical development and corporate politics that brought such cars to production. Finally, Alex and Squire Gabbard's *Fast Muscle: America's Fastest Muscle Cars* is a good photo history of the era, heavy on technical data, that highlights approximately forty cars.

Numerous books concentrate on muscle cars produced by a particular manufacturer. While these tend to be largely pictorial in nature, their texts frequently are quite detailed and may contain background information that could prove useful to researchers concerned with societal impacts. Some of the better survey works within this genre are Phil Hall's *Fearsome Fords, 1959–73*, a good reference for Ford, Mercury, and Shelby models, in terms of both their "street" and racing performance; Wallace A. Wyss' *The Super Fords*, which covers DeTomasos, GTs, and Boss Series cars; Edrie J. Marquez's *Amazing AMC Muscle: Complete Development and Racing History of the Cars from American Motors*, featuring the AMXs, SS Ramblers, Javelins, and Rebels from 1968 through 1974; Anthony Young's *Mighty Mopars, 1960–1974*, on the monster machines from Chrysler, Dodge, and Plymouth, such as the Barracuda, Challenger, Road Runner, and GTS and the 400+-horsepower Hemi and Super Commando engines that powered them; the same author's more recent *Chrysler, Dodge & Plymouth Muscle*, which carries the story up to the contemporary Dodge Viper; and Thomas E. Bonsall's *Guide to GM Muscle Cars, 1964–1973*, which is similar in concept to the foregoing and includes the General Motors vehicles cited in the next paragraph.

There even are a number of books that describe the most significant marques in detail. For example, *Chrysler 300: America's Most Powerful Car*, the apt title given by Robert C. Ackerson to a vehicle first introduced in 1955, presents in words and pictures the early history of an automobile that many view as the progenitor of the muscle car. Powered by a 300-horsepower Hemi V-8 engine, it won an incredible number of NASCAR races and established a reputation for itself that continued in Chrysler advertisements throughout the century. Similarly, in 1964 Pontiac introduced the "GTO" model, essentially a medium-size Tempest powered by a big car engine (a 389-cubic-inch, 348-horsepower V-8). The brainchild of John Z. DeLorean, for over a decade it remained one of the most prestigious American muscle cars. Probably the best history of this legendary car is Albert Drake's *The Big "Little GTO" Book*, which covers the eleven year run (1964–1974) of this Pontiac model. ("Little GTO" is a reference to the popular hit of the same name sung by the Beach Boys.) Also very good is Thomas E. Bonsall's *GTO Resource Guide: 30th Anniversary Edition*, another comprehensive history that extends the story to include the GTO's descendants, most notably the Grand Am (1973–1980). The Pontiac GTO is generally viewed as the first of the true muscle cars.

The muscle car phenomenon was part of a larger effort by American automotive manufacturers to produce high-performance vehicles. In that vein, see Robert C. Ackerson's *The Encyclopedia of American Supercars*, a general survey of the years 1948 to 1970; Roger Huntington's *American Supercar: Development of the Detroit High-Performance Car*, which is similar in concept to the Ackerson volume but more extensive chronologically, extending from the 1911 Mercer Raceabout to the 1930s Duesenbergs and flathead V-8 Fords but concentrating on the 1960s and 1970s; and *Muscle Cars*, by the editors of *Consumer Guide*, which, despite its somewhat misleading title, chronicles the history of approximately forty-five of Detroit's "classic" 1949–1980 high-performance cars.

Off-Road Vehicles

The concept of an all-terrain passenger car that would not require an "improved" road surface is as old as the automobile itself. However, it was not until the middle of the 20th century that such a vehicle was mass-produced—the Jeep. Created originally for military service during World War II, it successfully made the transition to civilian use in the postwar years, and it and the International Harvester Scout were the harbingers of a variety of off-road and sport utility vehicles in the second half of the 20th century. While there is no scholarly account of the Jeep, there are numerous popular histories. Among the latter, the following three volumes provide a good starting point: Robert C. Ackerson's *Jeep: The 50-Year History*; Arch Brown et al.'s *Jeep: The Unstoppable Legend*; and David Fetherston's *Jeep: Workhorse, Warhorse & Boulevard Cruiser*. (For more on the functionality of the Jeep, see the "Motor Vehicles in Government Service" section of Chapter 10.)

The successor to the Jeep is the AM General Hummer, which from the outset was available in military and civilian versions. The story of its development and use in the Gulf War is told by Michael Green in *Hummer*, a heavily illustrated, brief volume that also contains technical data and specifications, and the same author's *Hummer: The Next Generation*, which also discusses its successes in off-road racing.

Sports Cars

While the traditional sports car—a two-passenger coupé or roadster built along racing lines—has a long and honored history in Europe, its adoption in the United States was slow in coming and to this day is not as thorough as might have been expected. There are a number of obvious explanations for this phenomenon, including the American penchant for bigness, the desire to have each vehicle capable of doubling as a "family" car, and the problems of owning a clearly upper-class car used solely for pleasure in a "classless" society that casts aspersions on the "idle rich." Nonetheless, interest in such vehicles was there from the beginning, as witnessed by the success of the legendary pre–World War I Mercer Raceabout and the Stutz Bearcat. The history of the latter is included in *The Splendid Stutz*, a Cugnot Award-winning book edited by Raymond A. Katzell that includes a section devoted to that marque's coachwork from the mid-1920s until its demise.

By the 1950s domestic manufacturers calculated that the demand was sufficient to warrant experimentation with homegrown sports cars, most notably General Motors' Corvette and Ford's 1955 Thunderbird. This was followed in the mid-1960s by the introduction of the Mustang by Ford and the Corvair Monza Club Coupe by Chevrolet. These two cars (or at least the former) ushered in the era of the enormously popular "pony cars"—small, sports car-like production vehicles aimed at the "baby boom" generation that was in its twenties.

The development of the sports car has been explored extensively by automotive aficionados. Charles L. Markmann and Mark Sherwin's *The Book of Sports Cars* is possibly the most comprehensive history through the late 1950s, featuring over 150 different marques. Another good historical survey of the subject to mid-century is provided by John E.G. Stanford's *The Sports Car: Development and Design*, which covers the period 1910 to 1955. Louis W. Steinwedel's *The Golden Age of Sports Cars* explores the considerable achievements of the interwar years, and Tom McCahill's *The Modern Sports Car* is a fascinating period piece, published in 1954 as an "initiation for Americans into this new cult." For a more general and pictorial treatment, see *The American Sports Car*, by the editors of *Consumer Guide*, and Richard Nichols' *American Sportscars: A Survey of the Classic Marques*, both of which bring the story up to recent Corvette models.

In addition, there are numerous global surveys of the sports car phenomenon, some of which contain significant segments devoted to American contributions. Probably still the best in this regard is G.N. Georgano's *A History of Sports Cars*, which is chronologically divided into five major parts, each of which has a section devoted to U.S. models. The Georgano volume was the cowinner of the SAH's first Cugnot Award in 1972. In the same vein is Rich Taylor's well-written *Modern Classics: The Great Cars of the Post War Years*, with separate sections covering selected American, British, and European automobiles. Also worthy of attention is *The Great Book of Sports Cars: Over 200 of the World's Greatest Automobiles*, written by Dean Batchelor *et al.*, which also concentrates on cars produced after World War II.

The Station Wagon and the Minivan

A final body style that is characteristically American is the "station wagon," sometimes called a "beach wagon," a vehicle that doubles as both a passenger and cargo vehicle. Although station wagons were available as early as the 1920s, they did not garner a sizable share of the market until after World War II. Given its longevity and important role in American automotive history, there are surprisingly few studies of this body type. The best overview is Ron Kowalke's *Station Wagon: A Tribute to America's Workaholic on Wheels*, a nostalgic, heavily illustrated work that covers the years 1946 to 1996 and includes first-person accounts by owners. Also worth examining is Bruce Briggs' very brief (88-page) *The Station Wagon: Its Saga and Development*, which goes beyond a survey of individual models to discuss the social significance of such vehicles.

Of all the station wagon variations, the "woodie" or "woody" has most fascinated automotive enthusiasts. It was so labeled because, prior to 1950, much of its exterior side panels was of wood, and after that date attempts were made to simulate such an appearance using plastics and composite materials. Donald J. Narus is responsible for two largely pictorial histories on this subject. *Great American Woodies and Wagons* covers developments from the early "depot hacks" to the mid-1970s, although the emphasis is on the postwar years. *Chrysler's Wonderful Woodie: The Town and Country* is a short account of probably the most famous station wagon model. David Fetherston's *Woodys: Classic Wood-Bodied Station Wagons, Custom Sedans and More* features an eclectic selection of wood-sided vehicles from the 1902 Stearns, steam-powered "wagonette," to the 1926 Ford Model T, boat-tailed racer, to the convertible of the 1990s. In addition to color photographs of the cars themselves, Fetherston has included contemporary advertising, cartoons, and other artwork. The same author's *American Woodys* is a heavily illustrated examination of the production of wood-sided station wagons by each of the Big Three manufacturers, featuring photographs, illustrations, and advertising from the years 1915 to 1960 and also including a chapter on collecting Woody toys. Finally, Bill Yenne's *Classic Woodies: A National Treasure* is, as the title implies, a celebration of this body type in word and picture, from the 1920s to the 1990s. One particularly meritorious aspect of this volume is the inclusion of many close-up photographs of design details, such as wood trim and door handles.

The combination of the gasoline embargoes and economic recession of the late 1970s created a market for more compact and less expensive vehicles and led to a downturn in station wagon sales. In addition, market research revealed that the traditional wagon was no longer exciting enough to attract young buyers. At this juncture, the Chrysler Corporation gambled and won on the 1983 introduction of the Plymouth Voyager and Dodge Caravan, the twin harbingers of the new era of the "minivan." With all of the advantages of the station wagon but none of its faults, Joseph Campana, Chrysler's vice-president of marketing at the time of the minivan introduction, could prophesy that "there's no question in my mind that it's the station wagon of the future." Other companies agreed, and by the early 1990s competition from Ford and Honda was seriously undermining the sales of the Chrysler minivans. In an attempt to dominate the market as it had done in the 1980s, and to help reverse corporate losses, Chrysler decided to redesign and reengineer its minivans. The story of this ultimately successful effort is well told by automotive journalist Brock Yates in *The Critical Path: Inventing an Automobile and Reinventing a Corporation.* Yates provides not only an insider's view of how the 1995 model minivans (*Motor Trend* magazine's Car of the Year) were physically developed but also insight into the predictable struggle between forward-looking managers and a corporate culture that resists change. (See the next chapter for a discussion of the SUV phenomenon.)

BIBLIOGRAPHY

Ackerson, Robert C. *Chrysler 300: America's Most Powerful Car.* Dorset, Eng.: Veloce Publishing, 1996.
Ackerson, Robert C. *The Encyclopedia of American Supercars.* Baltimore: Bookman, 1981.
Ackerson, Robert C. *Jeep: The 50-Year History.* Sparkford, Eng.: Foulis/Haynes, 1988.

Adams, G.E. *Bedtime Stories for Young Engineers: 40 Years in Product Design and Engineering at Ford Motor Company.* Green Valley, Ariz.: Adams Publishing, 1992.

Aird, Forbes. *Aerodynamics for Racing and Performance Cars.* New York: HP Books, 1997.

Aird, Forbes. *Race Car Chassis: Design and Construction.* Osceola, Wisc.: Motorbooks International, 1997.

American Technical Society. *Automobile Engineering.* 6 vols. Chicago: American Technical Society, 1920.

Armi, C. Edson. *The Art of American Car Design: The Profession and Personalities.* University Park: Pennsylvania State University Press, 1988.

Association of Licensed Automobile Manufacturers. *Hand Book of Gasoline Automobiles: For the Information of the Public Who Are Interested in Their Manufacture and Use.* New York: The Company, 1909.

Bacon, John H. *American Steam Car Pioneers: A Scrapbook.* Exton, Pa.: Newcomen Society of the United States, 1984.

Bamsey, Ian. *A History of the Turbo-Charged Racing Car.* Newbury Park, Calif.: Haynes, 1989.

Barker, Ronald, and Anthony Harding, eds. *Automobile Design: Great Designers and Their Work.* 2nd ed. Warrendale, Pa.: Society of Automotive Engineers. 1992.

Barris, George, and David Fetherston. *Barris Kustoms of the 1950s.* Osceola, Wisc.: Motorbooks International, 1994.

Batchelor, Dean, Chris Poole, and Graham Robson. *The Great Book of Sports Cars: Over 200 of the World's Greatest Automobiles.* New York: Portland House, 1988.

Bel Geddes, Norman. *Horizons.* Boston: Little, Brown, 1932.

Bell, Doug. *Cast Iron Wonder: Chevrolet's Fabulous Six.* Los Angeles: Clymer, 1961.

Bentley, John. *Oldtime Steam Cars.* New York: Arco, 1953.

Berghoff, Bruce. *The GM Motorama: Dream Cars of the Fifties.* Osceola, Wisc.: Motorbooks International, 1995.

Bertilsson, Bo. *Classic Hot Rods.* Osceola, Wisc.: MBI Publishing, 1999.

Black, Stephen. *Man and Motor Cars: An Ergonomic Study.* New York: W.W. Norton, 1966.

Blunsden, John. *The Power to Win.* London: Motor Racing, 1983.

Bolster, John. *The Upper Crust: The Aristocrats of Automobiles.* Chicago: Follett, 1976.

Bonsall, Thomas E. *The Coachbuilt Lincoln.* Baltimore: Stony Run Press, 1994.

Bonsall, Thomas E. *GTO: Resource Guide: 30th Anniversary Edition.* Rev. ed. Baltimore: Stony Run Press, 1993.

Bonsall, Thomas E. *Guide to GM Muscle Cars, 1964–1973.* Los Angeles: HP Books, 1991.

Borgeson, Griffith. *The Classic Twin-Cam Engine.* London: Dalton Watson, 1981.

Borgeson, Griffith. *The Golden Age of the American Racing Car.* New York: W.W. Norton, 1967.

Borgeson, Griffith, with the Smithsonian Institution. *Miller.* Osceola, Wisc.: Motorbooks International, 1993.

Boyne, Walter J. *Power behind the Wheel: Creativity and the Evolution of the Automobile.* New York: Stewart, Tabori, & Chang, 1989.

Breer, Carl. *The Birth of Chrysler Corporation and Its Engineering Legacy.* Edited by Anthony J. Yanik. Warrendale, Pa.: Society of Automotive Engineers, 1995.

Bridges, John. *Bob Bourke Designs for Studebaker.* Nashville: J.B. Enterprises, 1984.

Brierley, Brooks. *Magic Motors 1930.* Coconut Grove, Fla.: Garrett and Stringer, 1996.

Briggs, Bruce. *The Station Wagon: Its Saga and Development.* New York: Vantage Press, 1975.

Brown, Arch, and the Auto Editors of Consumer Guide. *Jeep: The Unstoppable Legend.* Lincolnwood, Ill.: Publications International, 1994.

Bush, Donald J. *The Streamlined Decade.* New York: George Braziller, 1975.

Campisano, Jim. *American Muscle Cars.* New York: MetroBooks, 1995.

Carson, Richard B. *The Olympian Cars: The Great American Luxury Automobiles of the Twenties and Thirties.* New York: Alfred A. Knopf, 1976.

Casucci, Piero. *Racing Cars.* Chicago: Rand-McNally, 1981.

Chapouris, Pete, Jim "Jake" Jacobs, and Tony Thacker. *Hot Rods by Pete & Jake.* Osceola, Wisc.: Motorbooks International, 1992.

Chase, Julian. *Motor Car Operation.* New York: Motor, 1910.

Clutton, Cecil, Cyril Posthamus, and Denis Jenkinson. *The Racing Car: Development and Design.* Cambridge, Mass.: Robert Bentley, 1962.

Clymer, Floyd. *Floyd Clymer's Historical Motor Scrapbook of Steam Cars.* New York: Bonanza Books, 1945.

Consumer Guide, Editors of. *The American Sports Car.* Skokie, Ill.: Publications International, 1979.

Consumer Guide, Editors of. *Cars That Never Were.* New York: Beekman House/Crown, 1981.

Consumer Guide, Editors of. *Grease Machines: A Complete Guide to Hot Rods and Customized Cars of the Fifties.* New York: Beekman House, 1978.

Consumer Guide, Editors of. *Muscle Cars.* Skokie, Ill.: Publications International, 1981.

Corn, Joseph J. *The Winged Gospel: America's Romance with Aviation, 1900–1950.* New York: Oxford University Press, 1983.

Corn, Joseph J., and Brian Horrigan. *Yesterday's Tomorrows: Past Visions of the American Future.* New York: Summit Books, 1984.

Cruikshank, Jeffrey L., and David B. Sicilia. *The Engine That Could: 75 Years of Values-Driven Change at Cummins Engine Company.* Cambridge, Mass.: Harvard Business School Press, 1997.

Cummins, C. Lyle, Jr. *Internal Fire.* Rev. ed. Warrendale, Pa.: Society of Automotive Engineers, 1989.

Cummins, C. Lyle, Jr. *Diesel's Engine: Volume One—From Conception to 1918.* Wilsonville, Ore.: Carnot Press, 1993.

Dark, Harris E. *Wankel Rotary Engine: Introduction & Guide.* Bloomington: Indiana University Press, 1974.

Day, John. *The Bosch Book of the Motor Car: Its Evolution and Engineering Development.* New York: St. Martin's Press, 1976.

Dees, Mark L. *The Miller Dynasty.* 2nd ed., rev. Moorpark, Calif.: Hippodrome, 1994.

Derr, Thomas S. *The Modern Steam Car and Its Background.* Rev. ed. Los Angeles: Floyd Clymer, 1957.

DeWaard, E. John. *Fins and Chrome: American Automobiles of the 1950s.* New York: Crescent Books, 1989.

Dominguez, Henry. *Edsel Ford and E.T. Gregorie: The Remarkable Design Team and Their Classic Fords of the 1930s and 1940s.* Warrendale, Pa.: Society of Automotive Engineers, 1999.

Drake, Albert. *The Big "Little GTO" Book*. Osceola, Wisc.: Motorbooks International, 1982.

Dyke, A.L. *Dyke's Automobile and Gasoline Engine Encyclopedia: The Elementary Principles, Construction, Operation and Repair of Automobiles, Gasoline Engines and Automobile Electric Systems; Including Trucks, Tractors, Motorcoaches, Automotive Diesel Engines, Aircraft Engines and Motorcycles*. 22nd ed. Chicago: Goodheart-Willcox, 1950.

Engelman, Roy A. *Autocraft*. Cincinnati: American Chauffeur Publishing, 1914.

Faith, Nicholas. *The Wankel Engine: The Story of the Revolutionary Rotary Engine*. Briarcliff Manor, N.Y.: Stein and Day, 1975.

Fetherston, David. *American Woodys*. Sebastopol, Calif.: Thaxton Press, 1998.

Fetherston, David. *Jeep: Workhorse, Warhorse & Boulevard Cruiser*. London: Osprey Automotive, 1995.

Fetherston, David. *Woodys: Classic Wood-Bodied Station Wagons, Custom Sedans and More*. Osceola, Wisc.: Motorbooks International, 1995.

Fetherston, David A. *Moon Equipped: Sixty Years of Hot Rod Photo Memories*. Sebastopol, Calif.: Author, 1995.

Flint, Jerry. *The Dream Machine: The Golden Age of American Automobiles, 1946–1965*. New York: Quadrangle/New York Times, 1976.

Forbes, Kingston. *The Principles of Automobile Body Design*. Philadelphia: Ware Brothers, 1922.

Foster, Patrick R. *The Nash Styling Sketchbook*. Milford, Conn.: Olde Milford Press, 1998.

Frostick, Michael. *Dream Cars: Design Studies and Prototypes*. London: Dalton Watson, 1980.

Frostick, Michael. *V8*. London: Beaulieu Books, 1976.

Gabbard, Alex. *Vintage & Historic Racing Cars*. Tucson: HP Books, 1986.

Gabbard, Alex, and Squire Gabbard. *Fast Muscle: America's Fastest Muscle Cars*. Lenoir City, Tenn.: Authors, 1990.

Gartman, David. *Auto-Opium: A Social History of American Automobile Design*. New York: Routledge, 1994

Georgano, G.N. *A History of Sports Cars*. New York: E.P. Dutton, 1970.

Georgano, G.N. *A Source Book of Racing and Sports Cars*. London: Ward Lock, 1974.

Georgano, Nick. *Art of the American Automobile: The Greatest Stylists and Their Work*. New York: Smithmark Publishers, 1995.

Gieck, Jack. *Riding on Air: A History of Air Suspension*. Warrendale, Pa.: Society of Automotive Engineers, 1999.

Gingerelli, Dain, and Andy Southard Jr. *Oakland Roadster Show: 50 Years of Hot Rods & Customs*. Osceola, Wisc.: MBI Publishing, 1998.

Gott, Philip G. *Changing Gears: The Development of the Automotive Transmission*. Warrendale, Pa.: Society of Automotive Engineers, 1991.

Green, Michael. *Hummer*. Osceola, Wisc.: Motorbooks International, 1992.

Green, Michael. *Hummer: The Next Generation*. Osceola, Wisc.: Motorbooks International, 1995.

Gunnell, John A. *Convertibles: The Complete Story*. Blue Ridge Summit, Pa.: TAB Books, 1984.

Gunnell, John A. *Weird Cars*. Iola, Wisc.: Krause, 1993.

Guzzardi, Guiseppe, and Luigi E. Rizzo. *Convertibles: History and Evolution of Dream Cars.* New York: Barnes and Noble, 1998.

Håard, Mikael, ed. *Automobile Engineering in a Dead End: Mainstream and Alternative Developments in the 20th Century.* Gothenburg, Sweden: Gothenburg University, 1992.

Hall, Phil. *Fearsome Fords, 1959–73.* Rev. ed. Osceola, Wisc.: Motorbooks International, 1987.

Harralson, Joseph, ed. *Design of Racing and High Performance Engines.* Warrendale, Pa.: Society of Automotive Engineers, 1995.

Henry, Alan. *Grand Prix Car Design and Technology in the 1980s.* Richmond, Eng.: Hazleton, 1988.

Henry, Alan. *The Quest for Speed: Modern Racing Car Design and Technology.* Sparkford, Eng.: Patrick Stephens, 1993.

Henry, Alan. *The Turbo Years: Grand Prix Racing's Battle for Power.* Marlborough, Eng.: Crowood, 1990.

Henry Ford Museum and Greenfield Village. *Streamlining America.* Detroit: Wayne State University Press, 1986.

Hildebrand, George, ed. *The Golden Age of the Luxury Car: An Anthology of Articles and Photographs from "Autobody," 1927–1931.* New York: Dover, 1980.

Hine, Thomas. *Populuxe.* New York: Knopf, 1986.

Hirsch, Jay. *Great American Dream Machines: Classic Cars of the 50s & 60s.* New York: Macmillan, 1985.

Hiscox, Gardner D. *Horseless Vehicles, Automobiles, Motorcycles: Operated by Steam, Hydro-Carbon, Electric and Pneumatic Motors.* New York: Norman W. Henley, 1900.

Holland, David. *Dashboards.* London: Phaidon Press, 1995.

Holmes, Howdy, and Don Alexander. *Formula Car Technology.* Santa Ana, Calif.: Steve Smith Autosports, 1980.

Homans, James E. *Self-Propelled Vehicles: A Practical Treatise.* New York: Theo. Audel, 1902.

Horsley, Fred. *Dream Cars.* Los Angeles: Trend Books, 1953.

Hughill, Peter J., and D. Bruce Dickson, eds. *The Transfer and Transformation of Ideas and Material Culture.* College Station: Texas A&M University Press, 1988.

Huntington, Roger. *American Supercar: Development of the Detroit High-Performance Car.* Tucson: HP Books, 1983.

Huntington, Roger. *Design & Development of the Indy Car.* Tucson: HP Books, 1981.

Incandela, Sal. *Anatomy and Development of the Formula One Racing Car from 1975.* 3rd ed. Newbury Park, Calif.: Haynes, 1990.

Jackson, Jack. *Four Wheel Drive.* Newbury Park, Calif.: Haynes, 1982.

Jackson, Terry. *Anatomy of Speed: Inside the World's Great Race Cars.* Edison, N.J.: Chartwell Books, 1996.

Jacobs, Timothy. *Lemons: The World's Worst Cars.* New York: Dorset Press, 1992.

Jaderquist, Eugene, and Griffith Borgeson. *Best Hot Roads.* New York: Arco, 1953.

Jamison, Andrew. *The Steam-Powered Automobile: An Answer to Air Pollution.* Bloomington: Indiana University Press, 1970.

Janicki, Edward. *Cars Detroit Never Built: Fifty Years of American Experimental Cars.* Rev. ed. New York: Sterling, 1995.

Kapadia, Behram. *The Turbo Decade.* London: Osprey, 1990.

Katz, John F. *Race Car Aerodynamics: Designing for Speed*. Cambridge, Mass.: Robert Bentley, 1995.

Katzell, Raymond A. *The Splendid Stutz: The Cars, Companies, People and Races*. Indianapolis: Stutz Club, 1997.

Kessel, Adrianne. *The World's Strangest Automobiles*. New York: Smithmark, 1996.

Key, Mike, and Tony Thacker. *Dream Cars of the Fifties*. Secaucus, N.J.: Chartwell Books, 1990.

Kieselbach, Ralf J.F. *Streamlined Cars in Europe/USA*. Stuttgart: Verlag W. Kohlhammer, 1982.

Kowalke, Ron. *Station Wagon: A Tribute to America's Workaholic on Wheels*. Iola, Wisc.: Krause Publications, 1998.

Kranzberg, Melvin, and Carroll W. Pursell Jr., eds. *Technology in Western Civilization*. New York: Oxford University Press, 1967.

Kuah, Ian. *Dream Cars*. New York: Crescent Books, 1986.

Kyle, Chester R. *Racing with the Sun: The 1990 World Solar Challenge*. Warrendale, Pa.: Society of Automotive Engineers, 1991.

Laban, Brian. *Chrome: The Glamour Cars of the Fifties*. Portland, Ore.: Gallery Press, 1982.

Lamm, Michael, and Dave Holls. *A Century of Automotive Style: 100 Years of American Car Design*. Stockton, Calif.: Lamm-Morada Publishing, 1996.

Langworth, Richard M., and the Auto Editors of Consumer Guide. *The Great American Convertible*. New York: Beekman House, 1988.

Lent, Henry. *The X-Cars: Detroit's One-of-a-Kind Autos*. New York: Putnam, 1971.

Levine, Gary. *The Car Solution: The Steam Engine Comes of Age*. New York: Horizon Press, 1974.

Ludvigsen, Karl E. *Wankel Engines, A–Z*. Pelham, N.Y.: Ludvigsen Publications, 1973.

MacKnight, Nigel. *Technology of the F1 Car*. Osceola, Wisc.: Hazleton, 1998.

Magayne, Jerry H. *Classic Motorbooks Ford Retractable, 1957–1959: Photofacts*. Osceola, Wisc.: Motorbooks International, 1983.

Magayne, Jerry H. *Ford Fairlane 500 Skyliner, 1957–1959*. Osceola, Wisc.: Motorbooks International, 1992.

Markmann, Charles L., and Mark Sherwin. *The Book of Sports Cars*. New York: G.P. Putnam's Sons, 1959.

Marquez, Edrie J. *Amazing AMC Muscle: Complete Development and Racing History of the Cars from American Motors*. Osceola, Wisc.: Motorbooks International, 1988.

McCahill, Tom. *The Modern Sports Car*. New York: Prentice-Hall, 1954.

McGovern, John. *Muscle Cars*. Secaucus, N.J.: Chartwell Books, 1984.

McIlhany, Sterling. *Art as Design: Design as Art: A Contemporary Guide*. New York: Van Nostrand Reinhold, 1970.

McLintock, Dewar. *Prototype and Dream Cars*. Secaucus, N.J.: Chartwell Books, 1989.

McShane, Clay. *Down the Asphalt Path: The Automobile and the American City*. New York: Columbia University Press, 1994.

Miller, Ray, and Glenn Embree. *The V-8 Affair: An Illustrated History of the Pre-War Ford V-8*. Oceanside, Calif.: Evergreen Press, 1972.

Milliken, William F., and Douglas L. Milliken. *Race Car Vehicle Dynamics*. Warrendale, Pa.: SAE International, 1998.

Montagu of Beaulieu, Lord, and Anthony Bird. *History of Steam Cars, 1770–1970*. New York: St. Martin's Press, 1971.

Montgomery, Don. *Authentic Hot Rods: The Real "Good Old Days."* Fallbrook, Calif.: Author, 1994.

Montgomery, Don. *Hot Rods in the Forties: A Blast from the Past.* Fallbrook, Calif.: Author, 1987.

Morland, Andrew. *Street Machines: '49 and On Custom Cars.* London: Osprey, 1984.

Morland, Andrew. *Street Rods: Pre-'48 American Rods in Color.* London: Osprey, 1983.

Mowery, David C., and Nathan Rosenberg. *Paths of Innovation: Technological Change in 20th-Century America.* New York: Cambridge University Press, 1998.

Mueller, Mike. *Motor City Muscle: The High-Powered History of the American Muscle Car.* Osceola, Wisc.: Motorbooks International, 1997.

Narus, Donald J. *Chrysler's Wonderful Woodie: The Town and Country.* 2nd. ed. Parma, Ohio: Venture, 1988.

Narus, Donald J. *Great American Woodies and Wagons.* Glen Ellyn, Ill.: Crestline, 1977.

Neely, Bill, and John Lamm. *Cars to Remember: 37 Great Automobiles in Retrospect.* Chicago: Regnery, 1975.

Nesbitt, Dick, and the Editors of Collectible Automobile. *50 Years of American Automotive Design, 1930–1980.* Skokie, Ill.: Publications International, 1995.

Newbery, J.G. *Muscle Cars.* San Diego: Thunder Bay Press, 1994.

Nichols, Richard. *American Sportscars: A Survey of the Classic Marques.* North Dighton, Mass.: JG Press, 1997.

Nichols, Richard. *Exotic Cars.* Greenwich, Conn.: Brompton, 1990.

Norbye, Jan P. *Car Design: Structure & Architecture.* Blue Ridge Summit, Pa.: TAB Books, 1984.

Norbye, Jan P. *The Complete Handbook of Front Wheel Drive Cars.* Blue Ridge Summit, Pa.: TAB Books, 1979.

Norbye, Jan P. *Modern Diesel Cars.* Blue Ridge Summit, Pa.: TAB Books, 1978.

Norbye, Jan P. *The Wankel Engine.* Radnor, Pa.: Chilton Books, 1971.

Nye, Doug. *Autocourse History of the Grand Prix Car, 1945–65.* Richmond, Eng.: Hazleton, 1993.

Nye, Doug. *Autocourse History of the Grand Prix Car, 1966–91.* 2nd. ed. Richmond, Eng.: Hazleton, 1992.

Nye, Doug, and Geoff Goddard. *Classic Racing Cars: The Post-War Front-Engined GP Cars.* Newbury Park, Calif.: Haynes, 1991.

Olney, Ross R., and Ron Grable. *The Racing Bugs: Formula Vee and Super Vee.* New York: G.P. Putnam's Sons, 1974.

O'Toole, Larry. *Nostalgia Street Rods.* Castlemaine, Australia: Graffiti, 1998.

Pagé, Victor W. *Questions & Answers Relating to Modern Automobile Design, Construction, Driving and Repair.* New York: Norman W. Henley Publishing, 1919.

Perrin, Noel. *Solo: Life with an Electric Car.* New York: W.W. Norton, 1992.

Peters, George, and Henri Greuter. *Novi—The Legendary Indianapolis Race Car: Volume One—The Welch Years (1941–1960).* Hazelwood, Mo.: Bar Jean Enterprises, 1991.

Pfau, Hugo. *The Coachbuilt Packard.* 2nd ed. London: Dalton Watson, 1991.

Pfau, Hugo. *The Custom Body Era.* Cranbury, N.J.: A.S. Barnes, 1970.

Piccard, Jean-Rodolphe. *The Automobile Year Book of Dream Cars: Their Design and Development.* New Orleans: Crescent Books, 1984.

Pomeroy, Laurence. *The Grand Prix Car, 1906–1953.* 2 vols. 2nd ed. London: Temple Press Books, 1954.

Powell, J. David, and Richard P. Brennan. *The Automobile—Technology and Society*. Englewood Cliffs, N.J.: Prentice-Hall, 1988.

Pratt, Clyde H. *Pratt's Automobile Instructor: The Standard Authority on the Construction, Operation, Care and Repair of the Gasoline Motor Car; A Home-Study Course and Reference for Amateur and Expert*. New and rev. ed. Chicago: Shrewsbury, 1917.

Rambali, Paul, Frances Basham (photographer), and Bob Ughetti (photographer). *Car Culture*. New York: Delilah Communications, 1984.

Rasmussen, Henry. *Fifties Stylish American Cars: Decade of Dazzle*. Osceola, Wisc.: Motorbooks International, 1987.

Remus, Timothy. *Hot Roads by Boyd Coddington*. Osceola, Wisc.: Motorbooks International, 1992.

Rive Box, Rob de la, and Richard Crump. *The Automobile Art of Bertone*. Sparkford, Somerset, Eng.: Foulis, 1984.

Robson, Graham. *The Post War Touring Car*. Chatsworth, Calif.: Haynes, 1977.

Robson, Graham. *Turbo: An A–Z of Turbocharged Cars*. Secaucus, N.J.: Chartwell, 1988.

Rosenbusch, Karla A., and Jeffrey I. Godshall. *Plymouth Prowler: Anatomy of a New American Roadster*. Kutztown, Pa.: Automobile Quarterly, 1997.

Roth, Ed, with Howie Kusten. *Confessions of a Rat Fink: The Life and Times of Ed "Big Daddy" Roth*. New York: Pharos Books, 1992.

Roth, Ed, and Tony Thacker. *Hot Rods by Ed "Big Daddy" Roth*. Osceola, Wisc.: Motorbooks International, 1995

Sakkis, Tony. *Anatomy & Development of the Indy Car: The Technical History and Evolution of Indy Cars and a Dissection of a Modern Race Car*. Osceola, Wisc.: Motorbooks International, 1994.

Sass, Dale. *Pontiac Show Cars, Experimentals & Special Editions*. Baltimore: Bookman, 1986.

Schiffer, Michael B., Tamara C. Butts, and Kimberly K. Grimm. *Taking Charge: The Electric Automobile in America*. Washington, D.C.: Smithsonian Institution Press, 1994.

Schmidt, Oscar C., ed. *Practical Treatise on Automobiles: A New, Complete and Practical Treatise on Gasoline, Steam and Electric Vehicles, Written Expressly for the Owner, Chauffeur, Machinist and Garage Man*. 2 vols. Philadelphia: American Text-Book, 1909.

Schneider, Roy A. *Sixteen Cylinder Motorcars: An Illustrated History*. Arcadia, Calif.: Heritage House, 1974.

Schorr, Martyn L. *Mopar: The Performance Years 1962–1972*. Osceola, Wisc.: Motorbooks International, 1984.

Schupack, Andrew L. *Formula Vee/Super Vee: Racing, History, and Chassis/Engine Prep*. Blue Ridge Summit, Pa.: TAB Books, 1981.

Seiff, Ingo. *The Great Classics: Automobile Engineering in the Golden Age*. New York: Gallery Books, 1986.

Setright, L.J.K. *The Designers: Great Automobiles and the Men Who Made Them*. Chicago: Follett, 1976.

Setright, L.J.K. *The Grand Prix Car, 1954–1966*. London: Allen and Unwin, 1968.

Shacket, Sheldon R. *The Complete Book of Electric Vehicles*. Rev. 2nd ed. Northbrook, Ill.: Domus Books, 1981.

Shelton, Mark. *The Next Great Thing: The Sun, the Stirling Engine, and the Drive to Change the World*. New York: W.W. Norton, 1994.

Sheridan, Michael, and Sam Bushala. *Showtime, the Story of the International Championship Auto Shows and the Hot Rod/Custom Car World: A Twenty-Year History*. Pontiac, Mich.: Promotional Displays, 1980.

Sherman, Joe. *Charging Ahead*. New York: Oxford University Press, 1998.

Shnayerson, Michael. *The Car That Could: The Inside Story of GM's Revolutionary Electric Vehicle*. New York: Random House, 1996.

Silk, Gerald *et al*. *Automobile and Culture*. New York: Harry N. Abrams, 1984.

Simons, Martin. *Airflow*. Blackbird, Victoria, BC: AE Press, 1984.

Society of Automotive Engineers. *GM Sunraycer Case History*. Warrendale, Pa.: Society of Automotive Engineers, 1990.

Society of Automotive Engineers [SAE] Historical Committee. *The Automobile: A Century of Progress*. Warrendale, Pa.: Society of Automotive Engineers, 1997.

Sorensen, Lorin. *The Classy Ford V8*. Reprinted ed. Osceola, Wisc.: Motorbooks International, 1990.

Southard, Andy, Jr. *Hot Rods of the 1950s*. Osceola, Wisc.: Motorbooks International, 1995.

Stanford, John E.G. *The Sports Car: Development and Design*. New York: Scribner, 1957.

Steinwedel, Louis W. *The Golden Age of Sports Cars*. Philadelphia: Chilton, 1972.

Suzuki, Takashi. *The Romance of Engines*. Warrendale, Pa.: Society of Automotive Engineers, 1997.

Tamai, Goro. *The Leading Edge: Aerodynamic Design of Ultra-Streamlined Land Vehicles*. Cambridge, Mass.: Robert Bentley, 1999.

Taylor, Rich. *Modern Classics: The Great Cars of the Post War Years*. New York: Charles Scribner's Sons, 1978.

Thacker, Tony. *Hot Rods by Boyd*. Sebastopol, Calif.: Thaxton Press, 1997.

Thevenet, Jean-Paul, and Peter Vann. *Cabriolets*. Osceola, Wisc.: Motorbooks International, 1986.

Thomas, Jesse. *Pontiac Dream Cars, Show Cars & Prototypes: 1928–1998 Photo Album*. Hudson, Wisc.: Iconografix, 1999.

Tipler, John. *The World's Great Automobile Stylists*. New York: Mallard Press, 1990.

Traister, Robert J. *All about Electric & Hybrid Cars*. Blue Ridge Summit, Pa.: TAB Books, 1982.

Tremayne, David. *The Science of Speed: Today's Fascinating Hi-Tech World of Formula 1*. Newbury Park, Calif.: Haynes North America, 1997.

Troyer, Howard W. *The Four Wheel Drive Story*. New York: McGraw-Hill, 1954.

Tubbs, D.B. *Horseless Carriages: A 19th Century Album of Early Designs*. Lausanne, Switz.: Edita, 1968.

Valkenburg, Paul van. *Race Car Engineering & Mechanics*. Seal Beach, Calif.: Author, 1992.

Vann, Peter, and Serge Bellu. *Dream Cars: The Style for Tomorrow*. Osceola, Wisc.: Motorbooks International, 1989.

Velliky, John R., and Jean Maddern Pitrone. *Dodge Brothers/Budd Company Historical Album Photo Book*. Detroit: Harlo, 1992.

Vose, Ken. *The Convertible: An Illustrated History of a Dream Machine*. San Francisco: Chronicle Books, 1999.

Wagner, William. *Continental: Its Motors and People*. Fallbrook, Calif.: Aero, 1983.

Wakefield, Ernest H. *History of the Electric Automobile: Battery-Only Powered Cars*. Warrendale, Pa.: Society of Automotive Engineers, 1994.

Wakefield, Ernest H. *History of the Electric Automobile: Hybrid Electric Vehicles*. Warrendale, Pa.: Society of Automotive Engineers, 1998.

Waterman, Waldo Dean, with Jack Carpenter. *Waldo, Pioneer Aviator: A Personal History of American Aviation, 1910–1944*. Carlisle, Mass.: Arsdalen, Bosch, 1988.

Weith, Warren, and Jay Hirsch. *The Last American Convertibles: A Last, Loving Look at the Original American Dream Machines*. New York: Collier, 1979.

White, George E. *Offenhauser*. Osceola, Wisc.: Motorbooks International, 1996.

Whitman, Roger B. *Motor Car Principles*. New York: D. Appleton, 1907.

Wieder, Robert, and George Hall. *The Great American Convertible: An Affectionate Guide*. New York: Doubleday, 1977.

Willson, Quentin. *Classic American Cars*. New York: DK Publishing, 1997.

Wilson, Paul C. *Chrome Dreams: Automobile Styling since 1893*. Radnor, Pa.: Chilton, 1976.

Wise, David Burgess. *Steam on the Road*. Twickenham, Eng.: Hamlyn, 1985.

Wood, Jonathan. *Concept Cars*. San Diego: Thunder Bay Press, 1998.

Wyss, Wallace A., ed. *Corvette Prototypes and Showcars: Photo Album*. Hudson, Wisc.: Iconografix, 1997.

Wyss, Wallace A. *The Super Fords*. Marina del Rey, Calif.: Zuma Marketing, 1979.

Yates, Brock. *The Critical Path: Inventing an Automobile and Reinventing a Corporation*. Boston: Little, Brown, 1996.

Yenne, Bill. *Classic Woodies: A National Treasure*. Cobb, Calif.: First Glance Books, 1997.

Yost, Stanley K. *They Don't Build Cars Like They Used To!* Mendolta, Ill.: Wayside Press, 1963.

Young, Anthony. *Chevrolet Big-Block Muscle Cars*. Osceola, Wisc.: Motorbooks International, 1993.

Young, Anthony. *Chevrolet Small-Block V-8: History of the Chevrolet Small-Block V-8 and Small-Block Powered Cars*. Osceola, Wisc.: Motorbooks International, 1992.

Young, Anthony. *Chrysler, Dodge & Plymouth Muscle*. Osceola, Wisc.: MBI Publishing, 1999.

Young, Anthony. *Ford Hi-Po V-8 Muscle Cars*. Osceola, Wisc.: Motorbooks International, 1994.

Young, Anthony. *Hemi: History of the Chrysler Hemi V-8 Engine and Hemi-Powered Cars*. Osceola, Wisc.: Motorbooks International, 1991.

Young, Anthony. *Mighty Mopars: 1960–1974*. Osceola, Wisc.: Motorbooks International, 1984.

Young, Clarence H., and Robert E. Tuttle. *The Years 1919–1969: A History of the General Motors Institute*. Flint, Mich.: General Motors Institute, 1969.

Zuck, Daniel R. *An Airplane in Every Garage*. New York: Vantage Press, 1958.

PART II

Specialized Sociological and Cultural Studies

CHAPTER 5

The Automobile and
Interpersonal Relationships

The automobile has changed the lifestyle of the average American more than any other 20th-century technological innovation, with the possible exception of television. The social and economic changes ushered in by the motor car have not only modified our daily routine but also altered the fundamental nature of personal relationships and the social institutions in which we interact.

We will be concerned with these changes in this chapter and the next. The emphasis here will be on how the automobile has affected the interpersonal behavior of people as individuals and members of small groups. In Chapter 6, we will view the resulting changes in the broader perspective of the community and society at large.

GENERAL LIFESTYLE MODIFICATIONS

Some of the most insightful and earliest writing on automotively induced lifestyle changes is embedded in larger sociological studies, as chapters or sections that contribute to the development of the broader theme(s) of the work. One of the best in this regard is Robert and Helen M. Lynd's classic study of Muncie, Indiana, in the 1920s: *Middletown: A Study in American Culture*. The Lynds' work is particularly good as a source for how people in a medium-sized town viewed the impact of the automobile on such varied aspects of family life as leisure and vacations, Sunday activities and church attendance, mealtimes, and personal finances. Their follow-up study, *Middletown in Transition: A Study in Cultural Conflicts*, published in 1937, is also worth investigating, particularly to see the cumulative effect of forces placed in motion a decade earlier.

While the Lynds were concentrating their attention on a "typical" American town, a federal task force, the President's Research Committee on Social Trends, was engaged in a somewhat similar nationwide study of *Recent Social Trends in the United States*. This two-volume work is a standard source of information for social change in the 1920s and early 1930s, and, although it has only a brief section devoted exclusively to motor vehicles, much information concerning the car's influence can be inferred and/or extracted elsewhere in the narrative.

Readers interested in a more popular approach to the era and many of the topics covered in the *Middletown* and *Recent Social Trends* volumes are directed to Frederick L. Allen's *Only Yesterday, Since Yesterday*, and *The Big Change*. Each of the these volumes examines a single decade, beginning with the 1920s, and Allen does an exceptional job of creating the mood and lifestyle of Americans in the interwar years by skillfully blending anecdotes with a historical narrative, including a fair amount of each devoted to the automobile. Unfortunately for the researcher, none of these volumes have an index.

Although a plethora of memoirs, reminiscences, and popular histories was published prior to World War II (see Chapter 1), many of which contain personal observations and statistical data concerning changing lifestyles, none of them have that topic as its primary focus. The first important book in that genre to do so is David L. Cohn's *Combustion on Wheels: An Informal History of the Automobile Age*. The title of this book is somewhat misleading, in that its "informal" approach is grounded in solid scholarship, complete with footnotes (but no bibliography). Cohn's work was a pioneering study of the interplay between the car and American society. Nonetheless, the book's 1944 copyright necessarily limits its observations to the first fifty years of automotive history, although this "contemporary" view may be of interest and/or value to some. Although popular histories of the automobile followed Cohn's book at regular intervals during the 1950s and 1960s, most notably M.M. Musselman's *Get a Horse!: The Story of the Automobile in America* (1950) and Frank Donovan's *Wheels for a Nation* (1965), these works returned to the earlier formula of mixing interesting sociological observations with what was essentially industrial history.

Surprisingly, the scholarly community led the way out of this lockstep. Having previously largely ignored the socioeconomic issues connected with the motorization of America, scholars began in the mid-1960s to seriously study the car's impact on American culture, beginning with John B. Rae's pioneering survey, *The American Automobile: A Brief History* (1965). Against an authoritative account of industrial developments, Rae shows how the automobile "has become a way of life," effecting social change and influencing cultural values. Rae's later *The Road and the Car in American Life* (1971) is a more in-depth study of the social and economic changes wrought by highway transportation. The author takes an essentially positive view of motorization and its societal impacts. Rae, incidentally, is generally recognized as the godfather of contemporary automotive history. A good counterpoise to Rae's second book is James J. Flink's *The Car Culture*, published in 1975. Flink develops a three-stage theory of American automotive history, with conclusions regarding the influence of "automobility" on American society that are much less positive than Rae's, namely, "technological stagnation, hazardous design, and urban strangulation." The same author's more recent *The Automobile Age* is probably the definitive work in this regard, providing a sweeping cultural history of the automobile industry and its social impact. Together, these books form a core of "must" reading for an introduction to how the car has influenced the American way of life in the 20th century.

Popular histories continued to be published in the 1960s, and 1970s, benefiting from concurrent scholarly research and evidencing much more concern with sociocultural questions than their predecessors. Among the more significant ones were Derek Jewell's *Man and Motor: The 20th Century Love Affair*, which attempts to show how our infatuation with the car has influenced every aspect of our lives, from literature to engineering; Leon Mandel's *Driven: The American Four-Wheeled Love Affair*, in which the author applies his version of social psychology to analyze what he sees as the multivariate impact of the car; and Stephen W. Sears' *The American Heritage History of the Automobile in America*, a lavishly produced and extremely well illustrated volume. Winner of the Thomas McKean Award, the Sears book has been judged by many to be the premier enthusiast overview available, and it contains much information of a sociological nature.

More recently, Christopher Finch, in his *Highways to Heaven: The Auto Biography of America*, shows how the car has influenced American culture while, at the same time, being shaped (both literally and figuratively) by it. Finch focuses primarily on the interplay of these influences in three areas: car styling, automotively induced spatial transformation, and the car as an environment in which activities, both in actuality and fantasy, take place. Similarly, but in a more popular vein, David Barry explains in *Street Dreams: American Car Culture from the Fifties to the Eighties* how the cars that Americans chose to drive (or aspired to own) reflected and changed in response to the culture of a particular decade. However, Barry maintains that throughout this forty-year period the American "dream car" was one that endowed its occupant(s) with power and glamour.

Also making its appearance in the post–World War II era was a new genre of travelogue books. While the newness of the automobile had generated a host of such books (see Chapter 1 for examples), wherein the motorized trip was given greater prominence than the locales visited, these later offerings were deliberate attempts to seek out what was unique about the culture and society of the United States. In such books, the car is more of a tool of discovery than the subject of the inquiry. Some of the more important works in this genre include William Least Heat Moon's *Blue Highways: A Journey into America*, in which the author travels some 13,000 miles of secondary roads (designated by the color blue on maps of the day) in search of what rural America still has to tell about the American spirit; Angus Kress Gillespie and Michael Aaron Rockland's *Looking for America on the New Jersey Turnpike*, an original and scholarly book that examines the 142-mile road unique both as a physical artifact and as an environment for interpersonal relationships, concluding that it reflects the traditional American struggle between the pastoral ideal of the colonial period and the industrialism of today; and K.T. Berger's *Where the Road and the Sky Collide: America through the Eyes of Its Drivers*, wherein the authors (brothers *K*evin and *T*odd) set out to discover how the car has managed to become such a large part of our lives and determiner of much of the man-made environment, how we try to reconcile our love for cars (or the "road") with the destruction that it causes our environment (or the "sky"), and how holistic thinking might allow both to survive and prosper in the future.

One important aspect of the automobile's cultural impact has been the way that it has achieved symbolic significance. That aspect was recognized early and interpreted in varying (and sometimes conflicting) ways during the first half of the 20th century. There are three interesting, contemporary studies in this area. *Driving Passion: The Psychology of the Car*, the work of two British psychologists, Peter Marsh and Peter Collett, is one of the first book-length works to concentrate exclusively on the psychological satisfactions associated with car ownership and driving in different cultures. As such, it has much to offer in terms of the car as a symbol in society, performing a diversity of roles, such as costume, icon, jewelry, weapon, and, generally, accessory to our fantasies. Less weighty, but nonetheless worthy of examination, is Stephen Bayley's *Sex, Drink and Fast Cars*. Using an eclectic approach, the author explores the various "meanings" of the automobile and how they are exploited by individuals and groups for social, economic, and political reasons. Finally, Marshall McLuhan's well-known study *Understanding Media: The Extensions of Man* analyzes how automotive driving has become an extension of our personality and beliefs. Although this book is difficult reading, and McLuhan's ideas no longer enjoy the vogue that they once did, the chapters on roads and the motor car (McLuhan subtitles the latter "The Mechanical Bride") are still full of stimulating, although debatable, ideas.

One result of the previously cited pioneering works by Rae and Flink was the creation of an air of respectability for the scholarly study of the social impact of the automobile. In consequence, the late 1970s can be seen as a watershed, with the first publication of specialized works investigating the car's influence on social relations in particular regions, states, cities, and towns. For instance, changes in the lifestyles of rural Americans caused by motorization were the subject of two important books: Reynold W. Wik's *Henry Ford and Grass-roots America* and Michael L. Berger's *The Devil Wagon in God's Country: The Automobile and Social Change in Rural America, 1893–1929*. Both works are valuable in that, together, they have individual chapters devoted to such topics as family life, religion, ecology, education, leisure-time pursuits, politics, and health. It should be remembered that not until 1930 did census data show that the United States was no longer predominantly a rural nation. See also Katherine Jellison's much more recent *Entitled to Power*, below.

More specific in focus were Howard L. Preston's *Automobile Age Atlanta: The Making of a Southern Metropolis, 1900–1935*, which analyzes how automobiles affected not only the spatial but the social development of that city, and Norman T. Moline's *Mobility and the Small Town, 1900–1930: Transportation Change in Oregon, Illinois*, with its discussion of how the car and improved roads created new patterns of travel and a new scale of distance, which, in turn, altered small town social and economic activity.

Not surprisingly, the book-length overviews and surveys spun off a number of shorter, more specialized, scholarly pieces. Some of the latter appeared in organized collections; others, as individual articles in scholarly journals. The best of the former is *The Automobile and American Culture*, edited by David L. Lewis and Laurence Goldstein, which includes a variety of pieces on lifestyle-related topics, such as the car's influence on American fashions, sexual relations, the architecture of the home, and the "quality of life." (Most of the chapters of that book appeared as articles in a special Fall 1980/Winter 1981 issue of the *Michigan Quarterly Review*, under the same title.) A second, earlier volume, *Automobiles in American Life*, edited by Charles L. Sanford, is also worth investigating. The essays therein emphasize the human dimensions of automotively related economic issues, with particular attention to the social costs and benefits involved. Containing articles by Henry Ford and other historical personages and intended to be a reader for college courses, the Sanford volume tends to be less scholarly and less topically diverse than Lewis and Goldstein. Individual chapters from both collections are cited elsewhere in appropriate chapters of this guide.

Of course, automotively induced lifestyle changes have not been limited to the United States. While studies of other nations are beyond the purview of this guide, cross-cultural investigations are not. Unfortunately, aside from works concerned with the industrial dimensions, there is very little significant writing of an international, comparative nature in automotive history. There are really only two pioneering, scholarly studies in the English language: *The Automobile Revolution: The Impact of an Industry*, by Frenchman Jean-Pierre Bardou *et al.*, and the previously cited *The Automobile Age*, by American James J. Flink. While both make significant contributions (see Chapter 1), neither is intended to be primarily a cross-cultural, *social* history, although Flink's work does contain chapters on changes wrought by the family car and automobile touring from the 1920s through the 1950s.

Thus, in terms of comparative studies, the best available works are popular histories. Among the more notable works in this genre are *Behind the Wheel: The Magic and Manners of Early Motoring*, by Lord Montagu of Beaulieu and F. Wilson McComb; *100 Years on the Road: A Social History of the Car*, by Raymond Flower and Michael W. Jones; and *Man & the Automobile: A Twentieth-Century Love Affair*, by Judith Jackson. All three of these coffee table books deliver what their titles promise, although with a decidedly British emphasis. A cut above is Julian Pettifer and Nigel Turner's *Automania: Man and the Motor Car.* The authors have produced one of the first books that explore automotively induced social and economic change from a truly global perspective, not just limited to the United States and Europe. In so doing, they offer an international overview and comparison of many aspects of the motorized lifestyle usually ignored in such volumes, for example, courtship, music, movies, and death.

Finally, before leaving this topic, mention should be made of a collection edited by Theo Barker and entitled *The Economic and Social Effects of the Spread of Motor Vehicles: An International Centenary Tribute.* Occasioned by the celebration of the 100th birthday of the 1885 Benz car, this volume consists of fifteen similarly structured chapters in which a historian describes developments in his native country. As such, it is not a truly comparative study, but it could have value for students needing national overviews as a starting point for cross-cultural research.

FAMILY LIFE

One of the more fascinating aspects of the automobile's impact on interpersonal behavior is the varying effects that it has had on the family as a group and on individual members within it. Until very recently, this topic was all but ignored by historians and sociologists. The significant exceptions were Robert Lynd and Helen M. Lynd, who, in their "Middletown" studies of Muncie, Indiana, in the 1920s and 1930s (cited in the previous section of this chapter), called attention to the importance of the automobile in changing the nature of communal family life. The Lynds unearthed the now-classic quotation of a farm woman who was asked by a government agent why her family had a car but not a bathtub. She replied: "Why you can't go to town in a bathtub." Other than the Lynds' studies, there was little analytical work in this area until the 1970s.

There were, however, a number of statistical compendiums published during this period that could be of assistance to the quantitatively minded historian. Representative of this genre are *Family Expenditures for Automobile and Other Transportation: Five Regions,* a comparative study done for the Federal government just prior to World War II by Day Monroe *et al.,* and *State per Capita Automobile Expenditures and Income: 1930, 1940, and 1950,* by Robert A. Bandeen.

The 1970s witnessed the first real wave of scholarly studies of the automobile. Of these, several that were mentioned in the "General Lifestyle" section above give considerable attention to family life. In this regard, see James J. Flink's *The Automobile Age* and Michael L. Berger's *Devil Wagon in God's Country,* both of which devote an entire chapter to the subject, plus Reynold W. Wik's *Henry Ford and Grass-roots America,* which is permeated with such discussion. Flink's is the most general treatment, with Berger and Wik concentrating on small town and farm families. These works were joined in the mid-1990s by

Clay McShane's *Down the Asphalt Path: The Automobile and the American City*, in which two key chapters discuss the car's impact on family relationships, especially in terms of changing patterns of gender identity.

The few works cited above explore the family as a functional unit, with individual members treated primarily in terms of their roles within it. Other books have focused on how the motor car has affected subgroups within the family, such as women, adolescents, and the elderly, and the remainder of this section is concerned with them.

Women

The impact of the automobile on the lives of women has been profound. Every aspect of their social and economic lives has been touched by it. In fact, it can be argued that motorization has had greater impact on their lives than on the lives of men. Nonetheless, there has been surprisingly little scholarly study of women motorists. The only published, comprehensive work devoted exclusively to that topic is Virginia J. Scharff's *Taking the Wheel: Women and the Coming of the Motor Age*. Professor Scharff does a fine job of documenting the interaction between women and the auto industry up to the depression years, showing how gender considerations both positively and negatively affected the design, engineering, and marketing of cars. In addition, she describes well how "the prospect of unleashing women on the American landscape deeply disturbed many observers who worried that mobile women would be beyond control, socially, spatially, sexually." In sum, Scharff helps explain how automobility was a strong contributor to women's liberation (for better or worse) from the home. Katherine Jellison's *Entitled to Power: Farm Women and Technology, 1913–1963* uses firsthand accounts to portray how the ready adoption of new technologies, including the automobile, brought increased economic freedom to farm women but did little to change the control of rural life, which remained in male hands. As such, this work makes a strong case against technological determinism.

Scholarly book chapters and articles treating the subject of female motorists are more numerous. For example, in a special thematic issue of *Research in Philosophy & Technology*, edited by Joan Rothschild and entitled "Technology and Feminism," Bayla Singer analyzes the interplay between "Automobiles and Femininity." She explores the social construction of technology and concludes that women's access to cars has been restricted by "the establishment of symbolic associations and . . . gender roles." Differing perceptions of the role of the car in the lives of men and women are also the subject of the "Gender Wars" chapter in Clay McShane's previously cited *Down the Asphalt Path*, a fine summation of the various gender-related issues that arose prior to World War I. McShane advances the interesting proposition that during this period only men wished to control the car culture.

A greater variety of topics can be seen in Charles L. Sanford's " 'Woman's

Place' in American Car Culture," a chapter in David L. Lewis and Laurence Goldstein's *The Automobile and American Culture* that explores the multifaceted nature of the interaction between women and cars, ranging from advertising to literature to racing. In that vein, see Virginia Scharff's "Putting Wheels on Women's Sphere," a chapter in *Technology and Women's Voices*, edited by Cheris Kramarae, which emphasizes the effects of the automobile on the nature and extent of interpersonal communications among women; Martha May's essay "The Historical Problem of the Family Wage: The Ford Motor Company and the Five Dollar Day," which appeared in a collection entitled *Families and Work*, edited by Naomi Gerstel and Harriet Engel Gross, an analysis of the impact of wage work on family life, with special attention to Ford's unprecedented salary increase of 1914, which effectively doubled the salary of industrial laborers while cutting their workday from ten to eight hours; and Sandra Rosenbloom's "Travel by Women," part of a volume of *Demographic Special Reports*, based on data from the 1990 Nationwide Personal Transportation Survey and published by the U.S. Department of Transportation in 1995.

While many of the pre-1970 popular histories mention women drivers in passing, only M.M. Musselman's *Get a Horse* has a discrete chapter devoted to it, entitled "Milady at the Wheel." Interestingly, in *Putnam's Automobile Handbook: The Care and Maintenance of the Modern Motor-Car*, written by H. Clifford Brokaw and Charles A. Starr and published in 1918, there is a chapter entitled "Women as Drivers." In it, the authors correctly predicted the replacement of the male professional chauffeur by wives and mothers, especially in suburbia, and noted women's abilities as drivers and mechanics.

A possible explanation for the relative paucity of serious literature is that the number of women licensed to drive was relatively small until around 1940. Between then and 1977, their numbers doubled! It also is a good indicator of how ingrained was the notion of motoring as essentially a male activity.

One set of reasons responsible for the relatively low number of women drivers prior to World War II centered on the nature of the vehicle, a piece of temperamental hardware far larger and more complicated than women had traditionally been expected to operate. Symbolic of this situation was the starting mechanism, which on most early cars required that one manually turn over the engine by means of a crank. Actually, this problem was technically solved as early as 1912, when an electric starter invented by Charles F. Kettering was installed in a Cadillac. However, the starting problem lingered on, since the Ford Model T (1908–1927), overwhelmingly the most popular car of the pre-depression era, never had a self-starter as standard equipment.

Given this situation, accounts of daring women drivers were noteworthy, and books began to appear around the time of the First World War describing motor excursions by one or more women. See, for example, Louise Closser Hale's delightful *We Discover the Old Dominion* (1916), in which she and a female friend explore what then passed for roads in the state of Virginia, and Beatrice Larned Massey's *It Might Have Been Worse: A Motor Trip from Coast to Coast*

(1920). Both adventures followed the historically more important 1909 journey of Alice Huyler Ramsey and three female passengers, described in her *Veil, Duster and Tire Iron*, the reminiscences of the first women to successfully complete a cross-country automobile trip.

Another reason discouraging female motoring was the evolution and maintenance of the "woman driver" stereotype, which not only denigrated the driving abilities of women but actually questioned the femininity of those who chose to drive. (See the book by Scharff and related chapters above.) While by mid-century belief in the alleged inferiority of women drivers seemed to be relegated largely to the realm of humor, as late as 1966 a large New York publishing house issued *Are You a Woman Driver?* Written by racing driver Denise McCluggage, it was a "how-to" book designed to bolster women's confidence behind the wheel and bring forth motoring skills that the author believed were equal or superior to those of men. Evidence that that goal may have been achieved by the 1990s can be found in Marilyn Root's *Women at the Wheel: 42 Stories of Freedom, Fanbelts and the Lure of the Open Road*, a collection of brief sketches in which women talk about their personal relationships with their cars, the freedom that motoring brings to their lives, and, most importantly, how their command of a motor vehicle has led to an improved sense of identity.

The bias against female motorists was mirrored in the treatment by the UAW union of women who began to work in the automotive industry during World War II and continued thereafter. Nancy Gabin and Ruth Milkman have both written important historical studies in this regard. For Gabin, see *Feminism in the Labor Movement: Women and the United Auto Workers, 1935–1975*, in which the author portrays how the collective action of women workers led to significant advances in gender equity in the workplace and even impacted on the development of the broader feminist movement.

Ruth Milkman's *Gender at Work: The Dynamics of Job Segregation by Sex during World War II* is an excellent, award-winning (Joan Kelly Memorial Prize) book, the central thesis of which again is that industrial structure and management strategies are the key factors responsible for the nature and type of opportunities available to women and the sexual division of labor. The presence of women on the assembly line was (and probably continues to be) a troubling phenomenon for many men. For additional studies of women and autowork, see the labor section of Chapter 3.

Youth

Almost every 20th-century biographic work contains some mention of the subject's youthful adventures with an automobile, as if such an encounter were a rite of passage to adulthood. See, for instance, 20th-century American novelist Mary McCarthy's description of how she lost her virginity in the autobiographical *How I Grew*. For some, their experiences were significant enough to form the central focus of a separate volume. In this regard, the reader is directed to the personal reminiscences described in the first section of Chapter 1 of this guide, such as Stephen Longstreet's *The Boy in the Model T: A Journey in the Just Gone Past*. In addition, there are countless works of fiction in which the automobile figures prominently, many with young protagonists, such as F. Scott Fitzgerald's *The Great Gatsby*. (The "Language and Literature" section of Chapter 7 treats this subject at length.)

Twentieth-century youth seemingly always valued having "wheels," in terms of both the mobility a car offers and the prestige that comes with its ownership. Unfortunately, no book-length, scholarly work deals exclusively with this relationship. However, some excellent book chapters and articles can provide an overview of the manifold aspects of this subject. For instance, *The Gang: A Study in Adolescent Behavior*, a 1958 book by Herbert A. Bloch and Arthur Niederhoffer, contains a brief, but suggestive, chapter exploring the role of the automobile within such teenage social organizations.

Probably the most visible manifestation of the bonding of young people with the automobile in the years since the depression of the 1930s has been the creation of the so-called hot rod vehicle and the concomitant activity of drag racing. (The professional sport of drag racing is explored in Chapter 9, and the commercial design of hot rods is a topic covered in Chapter 4.) While there is an abundance of coffee-table books that describe the individual cars and the uses to which they are put, there has been comparatively little serious scholarly study of the psychological and sociological factors involved in this phenomenon. The only book-length work is H.F. Moorhouse's *Driving Ambitions: An Analysis of the American Hot Rod Enthusiasm*. Although a disjointed amalgam of sociology and history, the author offers the fascinating proposition that the hot rod culture is a source of community, education, creativity, and craftsmanship for the participants. In this respect, he builds upon an earlier piece, entitled "The 'Work Ethic' and 'Leisure' Activity: The Hot Rod in Post-War America," which appeared as a chapter in *The Historical Meanings of Work*, edited by Patrick Joyce. In that chapter, Moorhouse explores how key elements of the "work ethic" have been carried over into the unpaid labor of a group of serious hobbyists. Nonetheless, most of the *Driving Ambitions* book is devoted to the evolution, commercialization, and eventual professionalization of the hobby/sport.

The best popular history is Dean Batchelor's *The American Hot Rod*, a survey of men and machines from the late 1920s to the early 1970s. While the emphasis is on racing (including the street variety), Batchelor captures the nature of the hot rod culture through his exploration of how and why enthusiasts modified the design and power plants of production vehicles and of the clubs they formed to support their "hobby." Tom Medley's two-volume *Hot Rod History: Tracing America's Most Popular Automotive Hobby* also describes hot-rodding in the early years (1920s through the 1950s), but with more attention to what was happening on the streets (as opposed to track and dry lakebed racing). Medley's books feature entertaining interviews with key personalities and hundreds of period black-and-white photographs—none, unfortunately, of particularly high quality. These are the first two in a projected multi-volume series. Albert Drake's *Hot Rodder!: From Lakes to Street, An Oral History* is similar in concept to the Medley volumes but is more concise and brings the story up to the 1990s. Drake is particularly adept at describing what it was like to "cruise" the streets in the 1920s and 1930s.

More specifically, Don Montgomery's *Hot Rod Memories: Relived Again* focuses on the 1940s in words and pictures, providing insight into the speed shops that made the hot rod and custom car classics of the day. *Cool Cars, Square Roll Bars: Photos and Recollections of Fifties Hot Rodding in New England*, compiled by brothers Arnold B. Shuman and Bernard Shuman, opens a window on the hot rod culture (drag races, club meetings, Autorama shows) in a place other than Southern California. Finally, William Carroll's *Muroc: When the Hot Rods Ran* is a brief (80-page) "history," focusing on a day (May 15, 1938) of racing at Muroc Dry Lake in California on which hot rodding "came of age" as 300 vehicles competed in a full-day event like nothing seen before. Carroll's book also includes additional facts regarding the early days of hot-rodding.

Although the practice of "customizing" the power plant and/or design of a factory-built automobile is as old as motor cars themselves, it reached a type of apogee with the "hot rod" phenomenon of the 1940s and 1950s. Spearheaded by the infinitely adaptable 1932 Ford Model A roadster—"the Deuce," a car that *Automobile Quarterly* has called the "quintessential hot rod"—a new creative aspect of American youth culture was born. The earliest designs and styles are well conveyed in three books by Don Montgomery: *Hot Rods in the Forties: A Blast from the Past*; *Hot Rods as They Were: Another Blast from the Past*; and the previously mentioned *Hot Rod Memories: Relived Again*, works that include an intriguing collection of period black-and-white photographs. For a general overview of the beginnings of the "golden era," readers are referred to Eugene Jaderquist and Griffith Borgeson's *Best Hot Rods*, written in the early 1950s, and *Grease Machines*, a guide to hot rods and customized cars of the 1950s by the Editors of *Consumer Guide*. See also Andrew Morland's largely pictorial *Street Rods* and *Street Machines*, which highlight contemporary versions of pre-1948 and post-1949 cars, respectively, as well as Andy Southard Jr.'s *Hot Rods of the 1950s* and *Hot Rods & Customs of the 1960s*, which showcase period photographs by the author taken at shows, on the street, and at the track. Mike Key's *Lead Sleds: Chopped and Low, '35 thru '54* is a more specialized work, focusing on one particular kind of customizing wherein the car was shortened and the front axle dropped. (A variation, called the "lowrider" was introduced in the mid- to late 1970s. Equipped with hydraulic jacks, the body of the car could be lowered to a few inches above the road. Fancifully painted lowriders have become very popular with Hispanic Americans, for whom they have come to symbolize cultural pride and individuality. For an enthusiast's description of this phenomenon, see Carmella Padilla's *Low 'n Slow: Lowriding in New Mexico*, with photographs by Jack Parsons of 100 original cars.)

Social critic Tom Wolfe attempted to capture this aspect of popular culture in his mid-1960s book *The Kandy-Kolored Tangerine-Flake Streamline Baby*, the title of which refers to a particularly gaudy customized car. Wolfe devotes one of twenty-four sketches to custom car devotees in a book full of references to the influence of the automobile on American society. For the story of one boy's participation in the West Coast origins of the hot-rodding craze, read Albert Drake's reminiscences in *Street Was Fun in '51*.

While such cars were frequently raced, both informally on the street and in organized amateur contests, they also were part of a larger teenage phenomenon called "cruisin'." An important part of the youth culture of the 1950s and 1960s was showing off your car (and, by association, yourself and your friends) by driving repeatedly up and down the main street in town (or city), stopped only by traffic lights. The latter, of course, provided an opportunity to prove that your car could accelerate faster than a rival's in the next lane over. A light-hearted look at this phenomenon and related activities is *Crusin': Car Culture in America*, by Michael Karl Witzel and illustrator Kent Bash, which, beside examining the "art" and practice of cruising in detail, also looks at its portrayal in popular music, motion pictures, and television. Similar in concept but with more emphasis on the cars and the roadside eateries that were frequented is Robert Genat and Robin Genat's nostalgic and heavily illustrated *Hot Rod Nights: Boulevard Cruisin' in the USA*.

Concluding that the popularity of hot rods meant that there was a market for a small, relatively inexpensive sports car aimed at the youth market, Ford in 1964 introduced its Mustang, a vehicle good enough to create a stable of imitators and to lend its name, albeit obliquely, to a new model designation— "ponycar." The best book on this subject is Gary L. Witzenburg's *Mustang!: The Complete History of America's Pioneer Ponycar*, part of the prestigious *Automobile Quarterly* Marque History series, thoroughly researched and well written. More in the coffee-table tradition, yet full of facts, is the *Complete Book of Mustang*, by the auto editors of *Consumer Guide*, which celebrates the first twenty-five years of that model in a full-color history. Other volumes worthy of examination include Ray Miller's *Mustang Does It!*, a heavily illustrated history through 1973, and Nicky Wright's *Ford Mustang: The Enduring Legend*.

In addition to ponycars, Detroit tried to capture past, present, and future hot-rodders with the introduction of a new generation of high-performance vehicles. Generally defined by their oversized engine, large bodies, and elaborate ornamentation, so-called muscle cars, such as the Pontiac GTO (developed by John DeLorean), the Mercury Eliminator, and the Plymouth Road Runner, were true "kings of the road" beginning in the 1960s and lasting until the early 1970s. For better or worse, their like will probably never be seen again. The most recent and probably best account of this phenomenon is Mike Mueller's *Motor City Muscle: The High-Powered History of the American Muscle Car*. Although the emphasis is primarily on technical developments and corporate competition, this heavily illustrated volume does capture the contemporary appeal of muscle cars through the reproduction of period posters, ads, and memorabilia. Another good, general introduction to these behemoths is *Muscle Cars*, written by John McGovern. It covers not just the American fire-breathers but their foreign counterparts as well. More specific in focus is *The Great Book of Muscle Cars*, by the editors of *Consumer Guide*, a detailed look at the cars of the 1960s and 1970s and the aspects that made them so attractive to teenagers of the period.

Given the tremendous influence that cars have exerted on teenage lifestyles, it should come as no surprise that such vehicles were/are frequently seen as a contributing factor to, if not the cause of, some socially unacceptable behavior. Even when the car is not seen as a contributor to negative behavior, there still is considerable concern for the safety of teenagers in such vehicles. While the subject of safety is treated in more detail in Chapter 11, mention should be made here of books that concentrate on the manner in which teenagers and young adults behave behind the wheel and the reasons for this behavior. Typical of one genre was John J. Floherty's *Youth at the Wheel: A Reference Book on Safe Driving* which, when it was published in 1937, was viewed as an important enough subject to be reviewed in the *New York Times*. Floherty's book is both a compendium of mechanical information regarding the car and advice on how to drive it safely and the consequences of not doing so.

However, *the* major problem concerning the safety of teenagers on the road is driving while under the influence of liquor and/or drugs. Unfortunately, there is no book-length work devoted exclusively to this subject, although much valuable information can be gleaned or inferred from Joseph R. Gusfield's *The Culture of Public Problems: Drinking-Driving and the Symbolic Order* and James B. Jacobs' *Drunk Driving: An American Dilemma*.

Before we leave this discussion of youth, some mention should be made of the long-standing practice of designing and building cars for children. Here we are discussing both the relatively inexpensive, usually nondescript, generic-type of automotive body shell that is foot-powered in one way or another and those costly vehicles that are downsized versions of the real things, complete with power plants that work. The best chronological survey of the miniature car phenomenon is Edoardo Massucci's *Cars for Kids*. However, it is largely a photo history with brief descriptive passages. See also Paul Pennell's *Children's Cars*, even though it is very brief and limited to pedal cars. (For a related discussion concerning the hobby of collecting toy cars, see Chapter 8.)

The Elderly

As American life has become increasingly motorized and public transportation less extensive and efficient, the lifestyle of the ambulant elderly, especially outside large cities, has become increasingly dependent on access to a car and the ability to drive it. Within the last two decades, this problem has become a subject of serious, scholarly research. See, for example, J. Peter Rothe's *The Safety of Elderly Drivers: Yesterday's Young in Today's Traffic*. Rothe combines sociological analysis with statistical detail to describe the daily experiences of a population that constitutes 28% of the North American driving public. Due attention is given to unique aspects of their driving styles, the importance of the automobile as a vehicle of mobility and expression of self-esteem, and their experiences with traffic violations and accidents as they cope with being older motorists in a transportation arena that increasingly lacks civility. Martin Wachs' conceptually broader *Transportation for the Elderly: Changing Lifestyles, Changing Needs*, a study of the travel patterns of senior citizens in Los Angeles County, reveals a serious mismatch between needs and public policy in terms of the provision of transportation services. More importantly, from the perspective of this guide, that policy tends to ignore the fact that the elderly are increasingly choosing to live in the suburbs, where the automobile is the transportation mode of choice.

Obviously, the elderly are not the only segment of the population that might find itself without cars; the poor and the disabled often suffer the same plight. Readers interested in placing the issue in broader perspective are urged to read Robert F. Paaswell and Wilfred Recker's *Problems of the Carless* and "The Transportation Disadvantaged" chapter of *Autos, Transit and Cities*, by John R. Meyer and José A. Gómez-Ibáñez.

MINORITIES

When one looks for books and even chapters devoted to the impact of the automobile on the lifestyle of American people of color, one discovers that there is surprisingly little available. In fact, one of the more obvious major voids in the literature is the lack of research undertaken in this area. The most significant scholarship to date has dealt with the relationships of African American workers to the automobile industry in general and to unions in particular. Although this topic is one of the main foci of Chapter 3, it deserves mention here to the extent that the primary emphasis of the work is on interpersonal relationships, as opposed to economic considerations.

Race and class issues permeate August Meier and Elliott Rudwick's 1979 *Black Detroit and the Rise of the UAW*, an excellent account of events in the 1930s and 1940s. The authors provide a pioneering and yet balanced study of the interplay between the fledgling UAW union, the black community and its workers, and local and federal government. (The latter, more often than not, allied itself with the discriminatory practices of industry during this period.)

During and after World War II, the absolute and relative number of African-American automobile workers increased significantly for socioeconomic reasons. This was particularly true of men and women on the assembly line. As a result, race relations became a more important part of personnel matters than they had been before, including recurrent worker allegations of "racism" on the part of management. These developments were followed by the broader civil rights movement, the subsequent period of "black power" activism, and attempts to organize African-American automobile workers as a separate group. The origins, activities, and demise of one such group are examined in James A. Geschwender's *Class, Race, and Worker Insurgency: The League of Revolutionary Black Workers*. The league was a Detroit organization of African-American intellectuals and autoworkers that espoused Marxist-Leninist principles during its brief life in the 1960s and early 1970s. In addition to Geshwender's work, Charles Denby provides a Marxist perspective on alleged racism within the UAW in *Indignant Heart: A Black Worker's Journal*. Partially in response to these developments, in recent years the UAW has followed a policy of promoting racial and economic justice in American society as a whole. (For an in-depth discussion of African Americans and the automobile industry, see the "Labor–Management Relations" section of Chapter 3.)

While much significant work still remains to be done in terms of analyzing the impact of the automobile on African-American social and economic life, still more research needs to be undertaken for other minority groups in our society. Pitifully little has been done on Native Americans and Hispanic Americans. Beyond some doctoral dissertations and a few articles, the only scholarly work devoted exclusively to the impact of the automobile on one of these ethnic groups is Luis F.B. Plascencia's "Low-Riding in the Southwest: Cultural Symbols in the Mexican Community," a chapter that appeared in *History, Culture, and Society: Chicano Studies in the 1980s*, edited by Mario T. Garcia *et al.* The Plascencia piece describes and analyzes a Mexican-American subculture that has evolved centering on the creation and ownership of customized cars with highly ornate decoration, a latter-day version of the "hot rod."

MORALITY, VALUES, AND SELF-IDENTITY

In a sense, the most significant changes wrought by the automobile have occurred in the area of American social and economic values and behavior. As such, the behavioral question permeates all topics covered in this guide and therefore is best discussed in relation to each of them as they are presented in specific chapters. At this juncture, we concentrate on how the motor car influenced those values associated with interpersonal relationships, beginning with moral standards.

Morals

While countless articles on this topic have appeared in mass-circulation magazines, serious study concerning cars and morality is only in its beginning stages. The pioneering scholarly work in this regard appeared in a 1974 issue of the *Journal of Popular Culture*, which contained a special thematic section on the automobile, edited by David J. Neuman. Within it, Glen Jeansonne's "The Automobile and American Morality" explored how and why the motor car became associated with sexual immorality, crime, and personal indebtedness, beginning in the 1920s.

Some of the more general works cited earlier in this chapter also contain sections devoted exclusively to the morality issue. See, for instance, Michael L. Berger's *The Devil Wagon in God's Country* and Julian Pettifer and Nigel Turner's *Automania*. Berger places the issue within the broader context of religion, while Pettifer and Turner concentrate on changes in courting habits. The latter subject is the focus of Beth L. Bailey's *From Front Porch to Back Seat: Courtship in Twentieth-Century America*, which traces the history of the social and economic conventions that have defined the courting behavior of young, middle-class Americans, with due attention to the automobile's role and the institution of "parking."

Probably the most specific attempt to analyze the car's impact on sexual morality is David L. Lewis' "Sex and the Automobile: From Rumble Seats to Rockin' Vans," which is part of a collection entitled *The Automobile and American Culture*, edited by David L. Lewis and Laurence Goldstein. While this relatively short essay lacks references, it nonetheless provides an excellent introduction to multiple aspects of a subject that is deserving of much additional scholarly work. Stephen Bayley's *Sex, Drink and Fast Cars* is a popular (as opposed to scholarly) study that has as one of its major themes the multifaceted role that the automobile plays as a strong sex symbol for both individuals and society at large. Although numerous other books and articles briefly touch on the linkage between moral standards and the automobile, the paucity of serious, in-depth research on this subject, as compared to the abundant attention given it in the mass media, is rather striking. Even admitting the difficulty of documentation, this is a topic that can and needs to be explored much further by social historians.

As noted above in regard to the Jeansonne article, as early as the 1920s there was a popular perception that the motor car was contributing to immorality. Since the best-selling car of that decade was the Model T Ford, an interesting aspect of automotive history is the degree to which Henry Ford tried to use his position as a national folk hero to reshape American values. Actions as varied as pushing old-fashioned square dancing in the era of the Charleston and the construction of the idealized Greenfield Village (See Chapter 2) are examples of his behavior in this regard. In the same vein was the appearance in 1928 of a small book written and published by "Mr. and Mrs. Ford," entitled *The Story of Mary and Her Little Lamb, as Told by Mary and Her Neighbors and Friends*.

During the first two decades of the 20th century, there were a number of attempts to legislate private morality. One of these, the Mann Act of 1910, while not owing its origins to the advent of the automobile, was certainly supported by the widespread adoption of the car. Under this federal law, any man could be accused of a felony for intending to commit an "immoral" act with a woman if she had crossed a state line either with him or to visit him. Since the auto became associated with such transportation, it and the Mann Act soon became intertwined in the public mind. For an excellent history of the origins, implementation, and impact of this act (which was in effect until 1986), see David J. Langum's *Crossing over the Line: Legislating Morality and the Mann Act.*

Values

While the connection between the car and morality would benefit from further research, what author Leon Mandel has termed the "American four-wheeled love affair" has been well documented. In many and diverse ways, from its role as a status symbol to its use as a recreation vehicle, the automobile has truly become a member of the American family. The best analysis of how this emotional attachment evolved is provided by James J. Flink in his article "Three Stages of American Automobile Consciousness," the themes of which formed the basis for his later book, *The Car Culture.* Flink maintains that during the second chronological stage (1910–1950) Americans developed a relationship with their cars that bordered on idolatry but that was subsequently undermined by the ecological and economic problems associated with the automobile.

In a more popular vein, several studies aimed at the mass-market audience have explored the affection of Americans for their cars. Contemporary examples of this genre would be such books as Leon Mandel's *Driven: The American Four-Wheeled Love Affair,* to which we previously alluded, and Peter Marsh and Peter Collett's *Driving Passion: The Psychology of the Car.* Mandel views America's relationship to automobiles as a dependence, bordering on an addiction, the negative psychological, social, and economic consequences of which are not fully understood or acted upon. He argues for a greater degree of rationality in approaching things automotive in the future. Marsh and Collett's work is a multicultural study, with emphasis on the American and British experience. It is an upbeat and well-written volume in which the authors emphasize the symbolic nature of the cars and their accoutrements, especially their usage as a means of self-expression in multiple aspects of American culture.

Many American families have experienced lives that center around the automobile, especially as a focus for leisure-time pursuits. Although the often all-consuming nature of being an automotive "buff" is discussed at length in Chapter 8, two representative works deserve to be mentioned here. Anthony Gibbs' *A Passion for Cars* describes his lifelong attachment to such vehicles, an infatuation that at times included a personification of the automobile. Roger Cutting's *Motor-Mania* is a similar autobiography, which the author states is "the story of a man's intoxication with the lure of the automobile and his association with fellow enthusiasts."

One measure of the degree of passion or addiction that Americans have regarding automobiles is their behavior in situations in which they are deprived of its use. The best recent example of such a situation was the oil embargoes of the mid- and late 1970s and the limitations on usage that were dictated by the resulting shortages. Given the widespread impact of those events on American society, they have been heavily studied.

The oil embargoes of the 1970s, together with increasing public concern regarding the car's multifaceted impact on the natural environment and personal safety, led to a national debate regarding the future role of the automobile in American society. The specifics of that debate, together with the writing concerning it, are extensively covered in Chapter 11. Here it should be noted that the views expressed often had their roots in the values dimension of the issues involved and, not surprisingly, ran the full spectrum of opinion. Thus, at one end, there were books like B. Bruce-Briggs' *The War against the Automobile*, an impassioned defense of the car and the way of life that it helped create. Attempting to balance the benefits and disadvantages of the car culture were studies such as *Running on Empty: The Future of the Automobile in an Oil Short World*, by Lester R. Brown *et al.* Finally, disenchanted by, if not outright critical of, the impact of the automotive industry and the car itself on American society were such works as James Flink's previously cited *The Car Culture*. Given the times in which all these works were written, there is a tendency toward polemic, although they still contain much valuable information worth reading.

Self-Identity

A final area that has been cause for considerable speculation is the use/place of the automobile as a status symbol. In 1906 Woodrow Wilson, then president of Princeton University, warned that nothing would spread socialism faster than the widespread adoption of the motor car by the wealthy. Although he himself later disowned this point of view, neither he nor other commentators on the social scene have questioned the automobile's symbolic value in American society. At first, just owning a motor vehicle was sufficient to elevate one's station in life. For descriptions of this phenomenon, see any of the general histories cited in Chapter 1.

As car ownership became more broadly based and car manufacturers began to produce individual makes and models aimed at members of specific socioeconomic classes, social status came to be associated more with a particular vehicle than ownership of a car per se. It did not take long for automobile manufacturers, in "collusion" with the car-buying public, to begin to differentiate among different makes and models. While price was usually the prime factor, styling, engineering, and even public opinion determined which cars had the highest and lowest status associated with them.

In each era of automotive history, there always has been a group of car marques and models that have been expensive to purchase, due to the alleged superiority of their design and engineering. Aimed at wealthy buyers, such automobiles might generically be termed "luxury cars." While there is ample literature concerning individual marques, there has been no systematic, scholarly book that analyzes the luxury car phenomenon itself. Thus, researchers interested in such cars must rely primarily on popular histories. Nonetheless, there are a number of outstanding volumes in this category, including Richard B. Carson's *The Olympian Cars: The Great American Luxury Automobiles of the Twenties and Thirties*, which won the McKean Award and is easily the best introduction to the topic; John Bolster's *The Upper Crust: The Aristocrats of Automobiles*, which *Technology and Culture* calls "very good"; *The Golden Age of the Luxury Car: An Anthology of Articles and Photographs from "Autobody," 1927–1931*, a selection culled by George Hildebrand from what was probably the premier trade magazine of the 1920s concerning custom coachwork; and Hugo Pfau's *The Custom Body Era*, a well-illustrated volume that focuses on coach-built bodies of the 1920s and 1930s. In addition, Brooks T. Brierley's *Auburn, Reo, Franklin and Pierce-Arrow versus Cadillac, Chrysler, Lincoln, and Packard* is a heavily illustrated book that features American luxury cars of the late 1920s and early 1930s, a period associated with the apogee of that type of car. The title refers to Errett Lobban Cord's 1934 plan to merge the first four marques, then the remaining independent luxury car makers, to better compete against the latter four Detroit makes.

For an interesting study of one dimension of the luxury car trade, see Donald F. Davis' *Conspicuous Production: Automobiles and Elites in Detroit, 1899–1933*, in which the author argues that the wealthy frequently invested in the manufacture of luxury cars to gain the social prestige associated thereby. Similarly, another book by Brooks T. Brierley, *Magic Motors 1930*, provides a photographic freeze-frame showing the impact of the depression on the luxury car market, both in terms of the industry itself and on the use of such cars for personal or business reasons. For another aspect of the broader issue, see the "Symbolic Landscapes" chapter in D.W. Meinig's *The Interpretation of Ordinary Landscapes: Geographical Essays*, which offers an analysis of the car as a symbol of affluence.

Another means of automotive self-expression has been the ownership of a sports car. While the traditional sports car—a two-passenger coupé or roadster built along racing lines—has a long and honored history in Europe, its adoption in the United States was slow in coming and to this day is not as thorough as might be expected. There are a number of obvious explanations for this phenomenon, including the American penchant for bigness, the desire to have each vehicle capable of doubling as a "family" car, and the problems of owning a clearly upper-class car used solely for pleasure in a "classless" society that casts aspersions on the "idle rich." Nonetheless, interest in such vehicles was there from the beginning, as witnessed by the success of the legendary pre–World War I cars like the Mercer Raceabout and the Stutz Bearcat, and continues to the present with the Corvette, among others.

The development of the sports car has been explored by automotive aficionados, if not scholars. A good historical survey of the subject to mid-century is provided by John E.G. Stanford's *The Sports Car: Development and Design*, which covers the period 1910 to 1955. Tom McCahill's *The Modern Sports Car* is a fascinating period piece, published in 1954 as an "initiation for Americans into this new cult." The publication date of the McCahill book roughly coincides with the introduction in 1953 of the Corvette, America's first true contemporary "sports car" with anything approaching decent longevity. The best introduction to this Chevrolet, which began as a model and is now really a marque in its own right, is Karl Ludvigsen's *Corvette, America's Star-Spangled Sports Car: The Complete History*, which has gone through four editions. Heavily illustrated, this volume is both a comprehensive history and a reference book, covering the years 1953–1977. Also good, although by its own admission a "nostalgic, evocative tribute," is *Corvette: A Piece of the Action: Impressions of the Marque and the Mystique, 1953–1985*, written by the *Automobile Quarterly* magazine staff with the assistance of William L. Mitchell and Allan Girdler. Mitchell was vice president for design at General Motors when the Corvette was introduced. There is no comparable volume bringing the story up to the contemporary ZR-1 model Corvette. However, there is an incredible number of books aimed at the enthusiast market, all of which might be termed "illustrated histories," with Noland Adams' multi-volume *Corvette: American Legend* being the best.

The muscle car phenomenon was part of a larger effort on the part of American automotive manufacturers to produce high-performance vehicles. Roger Huntington's *American Supercar: Development of the Detroit High-Performance Car* provides valuable insights into the technical evolution of such vehicles, beginning with the 1911 Mercer Raceabout but concentrating on the 1960s and 1970s, as do the editors of *Consumer Guide* in *Muscle Cars*, which, despite its somewhat misleading title, is similar in concept to the Huntington volume, except that it begins with the 1949 model year. For an in-depth view of an earlier generation of such cars, see Roy A. Schneider's *Sixteen Cylinder Motorcars: An Illustrated History*, which focuses on the Cadillacs, Marmons, and Peerlesses of the 1930s.

On the other end of the spectrum was the Model T Ford, the car that Henry Ford deliberately built for the masses. No other manufacturing company so dominated early American automotive history as the Ford Motor Company. Of the notable cars that Ford has produced, probably the most famous is the Model T, 15 million of which were sold during its nineteen-year (1908–1927) production run. Up until the late 1920s, the word "car" was synonymous with the Model T for most Americans. The most scholarly book devoted exclusively to the Model T is Philip Van Doren Stern's *Tin Lizzie: The Story of the Fabulous Model T Ford*. Although relatively brief (180 pages), this volume does a fine job of presenting the essential facts *and* capturing the flavor of what the "T" meant to America for almost two decades, including period photographs and original drawings by Charles Harper. There also are a number of well-researched and heavily illustrated popular histories. Probably the best of this genre is Ray Miller and Bruce McCalley's *From Here to Obscurity: A Look at the Changes in an Unchanging Car, the Model T Ford, 1909–1927.* Although best classified as a nostalgic coffee table book, Floyd Clymer's *Henry's Wonderful Model T, 1908–1927* is, nonetheless, full of factual information as well as excellent photographs and early advertisements. In the same vein is his earlier *Floyd Clymer's Historical Motor Scrapbook: Ford Model T Edition* and *Model T Memories and the Ubiquitous Model T.* Both contain Clymer's reminiscences of his experiences with that car, and the latter volume reprints Leslie Henry's well-known "Ubiquitous" essay as well. Joseph Floyd Clymer devoted most of his life to the automobile, and he could be viewed as one of its first historians.

The Model T was really more than a car; it was a true legend that directly touched the lives of millions of Americans for over two decades. Thus, it is not surprising that the demise of the Tin Lizzie brought forth an outpouring of eulogies, in much the same way that the death of a good friend would. Preeminent among such statements was *Farewell to the Model T*, by E.B. White and Richard Lee Strout, writing under the pseudonym Lee Strout White. "Obituaries" were published in almost all of the national periodicals and major newspapers, including *The New Yorker* and *The New York Times Magazine.*

In addition to the status associated with owning a particular marque, Americans have sought to express their self-identity through the purchase of a particular type of vehicle. As author Phil Patton notes in his book *Made in USA: The Secret Histories of the Things That Made America*, the car belongs to a class of objects that "assert the power and potential of the individual while possessing the generality of type." In addition to sports cars, discussed above, convertibles, station wagons, and off-road vehicles all have been used for such expression.

Convertibles. Early autos generally were not permanently enclosed, and, in a sense, the motor car began as an open air vehicle. Although they would be superseded in popularity by the closed sedan in the late 1920s, "touring cars," either without any top or with a foldable cloth one, dominated the market for close to three decades. One could argue that touring cars were the predecessors to the modern "convertible," a term that was first standardized by the Society of Automotive Engineers in 1928.

While convertible-type automobiles continued to be produced after the demise of the touring car, not until the 1950s did open cars come back into vogue. For approximately two decades, the modern convertible, with its mechanically retractable soft top, became a popular body style. *The Great American Convertible: An Affectionate Guide*, by Robert Weider and George Hall chronicles its story in word and picture from 1910 to 1977. The similarly named *The Great American Convertible* is a heavily illustrated, decade-by-decade treatment of the subject by Richard M. Langworth and the auto editors of *Consumer Guide.*

By the mid-1970s, the convertible had fallen on hard times. Safety considerations, air conditioning, and an unexplainable loss of public interest were all cited as reasons for such sluggish sales that all major American auto companies ceased production of that body style. For a while, the only new convertible available for purchase in the United States was produced by Volkswagen. By

1979 Warren Weith and Jay Hirsch's *The Last American Convertibles*, was being billed as "a last, loving look" at such cars. Their fine tribute, covering four decades, proved to be premature, as consumer demand for convertibles returned in the late 1980s, almost as mysteriously as it had waned a decade earlier.

The Station Wagon. Although the "station wagon" or "beach wagon," a vehicle that doubles as both a passenger and cargo vehicle, was available as early as the 1920s, it did not garner a sizable share of the market until after World War II. Its popularity then can be traced to the expansion of the American suburbs. The resulting dominant lifestyle required a car that could easily be handled by a woman, transport family and friends, and pick up and deliver the socioeconomic items (e.g., groceries and athletic equipment) associated with the mobile suburban existence. Given its longevity and important role in American automotive history, there are surprisingly few studies of this body type. The best overview is Bruce Briggs' very brief (88-page) *The Station Wagon: Its Saga and Development*, which goes beyond a survey of individual models to discuss the social significance of such vehicles. In addition, Donald J. Narus' largely pictorial history, *Great American Woodies and Wagons*, covers developments from the early "depot hacks" to the mid-1970s, although the emphasis is on the postwar years. These vehicles were nicknamed "woodies" because prior to 1950 much of the exterior body was made of wood.

Off-Road Vehicles. Developed for the U.S. Army during World War II by American Bantam and then Willys-Overland, the all-terrain "jeep" (from general purpose or GP vehicle) outlived its combat role to create a civilian niche for itself during peacetime. In fact, the postwar demand for surplus military jeeps was the harbinger of the significant market for off-road recreational vehicles and, more recently, SUVs. Because of its longevity and multi-purpose capabilities, the jeep has been the subject of numerous books, none of which are scholarly in approach. The best of the historical overviews written for the enthusiast market are (listed alphabetically by author) *Jeep: The 50-Year History*, by Robert C. Ackerson; *Jeep: Warhorse, Workhorse & Boulevard Cruiser*, by David Fetherston; *The Story of Jeep*, by Patrick R. Foster; *Jeep: A Challenge to Time*, by Jean-Gabriel Jeudy and Marc Tararine; and *The American Jeep: In War and Peace*, by Kurt Willinger and Gene Gurney.

Often associated with the jeep is the four-wheel-drive means of transmission that it helped popularize, and that has subsequently become a "standard option" on a broad range of vehicles. Two good general histories of the "4 × 4" drive and its applications are Jack Jackson's *Four Wheel Drive* and Howard W. Troyer's *The Four Wheel Drive Story*, although the latter carries the "story" only through the early 1950s.

By the late 1990s, elements from these means of conveyance had coalesced into the SUV. "Sport utes," formerly associated with blue-collar work, became enormously popular with white-collar America because they combined the roominess and versatility of a station wagon with the road-handling attributes of a four-wheel-drive vehicle. In addition, for reasons that are always difficult to explain, they became very trendy, possibly because of their sporty and off-road images. Given the relative newness of this phenomenon, it would be premature to expect a full spectrum of books on this subject. The best to date is David H. Jacobs' *Sport Utility Vehicles: The Off-Road Revolution.* Jacob observes that changing demographics and recreational interests have combined with technological advances to create the enormous popularity of SUVs. He also notes the enormous variety of SUVs, from the Jeep to the Ford Explorer to the Hummer, and the irony that a type of motor vehicle designed for off-road transportation has become one of the most popular on-road machines.

BIBLIOGRAPHY

Ackerson, Robert C. *Jeep: The 50-Year History.* Sparkford, Eng.: Foulis/Haynes, 1988.

Adams, Noland. *Corvette: American Legend.* 3 vols. Sidney, Ohio: Cars & Parts Magazine, 1996–1998.

Allen, Frederick L. *The Big Change.* New York: Greenwood, 1952.

Allen, Frederick L. *Only Yesterday.* New York: Harper & Row, 1931.

Allen, Frederick L. *Since Yesterday.* New York: Harper & Brothers, 1940.

Automobile Quarterly Magazine, Editors of, with William L. Mitchell, and Allan Girdler. *Corvette: A Piece of the Action, Impressions of the Marque and the Mystique, 1953–1985.* Rev. ed. New York: Automobile Quarterly, 1985.

Bailey, Beth L. *From Front Porch to Back Seat: Courtship in Twentieth-Century America.* Baltimore: Johns Hopkins University Press, 1988.

Bandeen, Robert A. *State per Capita Automobile Expenditures and Income: 1930, 1940, and 1950.* Ann Arbor: University Microfilms, 1959.

Bardou, Jean-Pierre *et al. The Automobile Revolution: The Impact of an Industry.* Translated from the French and edited by James M. Laux. Chapel Hill: University of North Carolina Press, 1982.

Barker, Theo, ed. *The Economic and Social Effects of the Spread of Motor Vehicles: An International Centenary Tribute.* Basingstoke, Eng.: Macmillan, 1987.

Barry, David. *Street Dreams: American Car Culture from the Fifties to the Eighties.* London: Macdonald Orbis, 1988.

Batchelor, Dean. *The American Hot Rod.* Osceola, Wisc.: Motorbooks International, 1995.

Bayley, Stephen. *Sex, Drink and Fast Cars.* New York: Pantheon Books, 1986.

Berger, K.T. *Where the Road and the Sky Collide: America through the Eyes of Its Drivers.* New York: Henry Holt, 1993.

Berger, Michael L. *The Devil Wagon in God's Country: The Automobile and Social Change in Rural America, 1893–1929.* Hamden, Conn.: Archon Books, 1979.

Bloch, Herbert A., and Arthur Niederhoffer. *The Gang: A Study in Adolescent Behavior.* New York: Philosophical Library, 1958.

Bolster, John. *The Upper Crust: The Aristocrats of Automobiles.* Chicago: Follett, 1976.

Brierley, Brooks T. *Auburn, Reo, Franklin and Pierce-Arrow versus Cadillac, Chrysler, Lincoln and Packard.* Coconut Grove, Fla.: Garrett and Stringer, 1991.

Brierley, Brooks T. *Magic Motors 1930.* Coconut Grove, Fla.: Garrett and Stringer, 1996.

Briggs, Bruce. *The Station Wagon: Its Saga and Development*. New York: Vantage Press, 1975.

Brokaw, H. Clifford, and Charles A. Starr. *Putnam's Automobile Handbook: The Care and Management of the Modern Motor-Car*. New York: G.P. Putnam, 1918.

Brown, Lester R., Christopher Flavin, and Colin Norman. *Running on Empty: The Future of the Automobile in an Oil Short World*. New York: W.W. Norton, 1979.

Bruce-Briggs, B. *The War against the Automobile*. New York: E.P. Dutton, 1977.

Carroll, William. *Muroc: When the Hot Rods Ran*. San Marcos, Calif.: Auto Book Press, 1991.

Carson, Richard B. *The Olympian Cars: The Great American Luxury Automobiles of the Twenties and Thirties*. New York: Alfred A. Knopf, 1976.

Carter, Thomas, and Bernard L. Herman, eds. *Perspectives in Vernacular Architecture, III*. Columbia: University of Missouri Press, for the Vernacular Architecture Forum, 1989.

Clymer, [Joseph] Floyd. *Floyd Clymer's Historical Motor Scrapbook: Ford Model T Edition*. Los Angeles: Floyd Clymer, 1949.

Clymer, [Joseph] Floyd. *Henry's Wonderful Model T, 1908–1927*. New York: McGraw-Hill, 1955.

Clymer, [Joseph] Floyd, and Leslie R. Henry. *Model T Memories and the Ubiquitous Model T*. Los Angeles: Floyd Clymer, 1959.

Cohn, David L. *Combustion on Wheels: An Informal History of the Automobile Age*. Boston: Houghton Mifflin, 1944.

Consumer Guide, Editors of. *The American Sports Car*. Skokie, Ill.: Publications International, 1979.

Consumer Guide, Editors of. *The Complete Book of Mustang*. Lincolnwood, Ill.: Publications International, 1989.

Consumer Guide, Editors of. *The Great Book of Muscle Cars*. New York: Beekman House, 1990.

Consumer Guide, Editors of. *Grease Machines*. New York: Beekman House, 1978.

Cutting, Roger. *Motor-Mania*. Boston: Rand Press, 1969.

Davis, Donald F. *Conspicuous Production: Automobiles and Elites in Detroit, 1899–1933*. Philadelphia: Temple University Press, 1988.

Denby, Charles [Matthew Ward]. *Indignant Heart: A Black Worker's Journal*. Boston: South End Press, 1978.

Donovan, Frank. *Wheels for a Nation*. [New York]: Thomas Y. Crowell, 1965.

Drake, Albert. *Hot Rodder!: From Lakes to Street, an Oral History*. Portland, Ore.: Flat Out Press, 1993.

Drake, Albert. *Street Was Fun in '51*. Okemos, Mich.: Flat Out Press, 1982.

Fetherston, David. *Jeep: Warhorse, Workhorse & Boulevard Cruiser*. Osceola, Wisc.: Motorbooks International, 1995.

Finch, Christopher. *Highways to Heaven: The Auto Biography of America*. New York: HarperCollins, 1992.

Fitzgerald, F. Scott. *The Great Gatsby*. New York: Charles Scribner's Sons, 1925.

Flink, James J. *The Automobile Age*. Cambridge, Mass.: MIT Press, 1988.

Flink, James J. *The Car Culture*. Cambridge, Mass.: MIT Press, 1975.

Floherty, John J. *Youth at the Wheel: A Reference Book on Safe Driving*. Philadelphia: Lippincott, 1937.

Flower, Raymond, and Michael W. James. *100 Years on the Road: A Social History of the Car*. New York: McGraw-Hill, 1981.

Ford, Mr. and Mrs. *The Story of Mary and Her Little Lamb, as Told by Mary and Her Neighbors and Friends*. Dearborn, Mich.: Mr. and Mrs. Ford, 1928.

Foster, Patrick R. *The Story of Jeep*. Iola, Wisc.: Krause, 1998.

Gabin, Nancy F. *Feminism in the Labor Movement: Women and the United Auto Workers, 1935–1975*. Ithaca, N.Y.: Cornell University Press, 1990.

Garcia, Mario T. *et al.*, eds. *History, Culture, and Society: Chicano Studies in the 1980s*. Ypsilanti, Mich.: Bilingual Press/Editorial Bilingue, 1983.

Genat, Robert, and Robin Genat. *Hot Rod Nights: Boulevard Cruisin' in the USA*. Osceola, Wisc.: Motorbooks International, 1998.

Gerstel, Naomi, and Harriet Engel Gross, eds. *Families and Work*. Philadelphia: Temple University Press, 1987.

Geschwender, James A. *Class, Race, and Worker Insurgency: The League of Revolutionary Black Workers*. Cambridge: Cambridge University Press, 1977.

Gibbs, Anthony. *A Passion for Cars*. New York: Scribner, 1974.

Gillespie, Angus Kress, and Michael Aaron Rockland. *Looking for America on the New Jersey Turnpike*. New Brunswick, N.J.: Rutgers University Press, 1989.

Gusfield, Joseph R. *The Culture of Public Problems: Drinking-Driving and the Symbolic Order*. Chicago: University of Chicago Press, 1981.

Hale, Louise Closser. *We Discover the Old Dominion*. New York: Dodd, Mead, 1916.

Heat Moon, William Least. *Blue Highways: A Journey into America*. Boston: Atlantic-Little, Brown, 1982.

Hildebrand, George, ed. *The Golden Age of the Luxury Car: An Anthology of Articles and Photographs from "Autobody," 1927–1931*. New York: Dover, 1980.

Howell, James W., and Jeanna Swanson-Howell. *Cadillac Eldorado*. Osceola, Wisc.: Motorbooks International, 1994.

Huntington, Roger. *American Supercar: Development of the Detroit High-Performance Car*. Tucson: HP Books, 1983.

Jackson, Jack. *Four Wheel Drive*. Newbury Park, Calif.: Haynes, 1982.

Jackson, Judith. *Man & the Automobile: A Twentieth-Century Love Affair*. New York: McGraw-Hill, 1979.

Jackson, Terry. *Corvette: Sports Car, America's Supercar*. Philadelphia: Courage Books, 1990.

Jacobs, David H. *Sport Utility Vehicles: The Off-Road Revolution*. New York: Todtri, 1998.

Jacobs, James B. *Drunk Driving: An American Dilemma*. Chicago: University of Chicago Press, 1989.

Jaderquist, Eugene, and Griffith Borgeson. *Best Hot Rods*. New York: Arco, 1953.

Jellison, Katherine. *Entitled to Power: Farm Women and Technology, 1913–1963*. Chapel Hill: University of North Carolina Press, 1993.

Jeudy, Jean-Gabriel, and Marc Tararine. *Jeep: A Challenge to Time*. New York: Frederick Warne, 1981.

Jewell, Derek. *Man and Motor: The 20th Century Love Affair*. New York: Walker, 1967.

Joyce, Patrick, ed. *The Historical Meanings of Work*. Cambridge: Cambridge University Press, 1987.

Key, Mike. *Lead Sleds: Chopped and Low, '35 thru '54*. London: Osprey, 1984.

Kramarae, Cheris, ed. *Technology and Women's Voices: Keeping in Touch*. London: Routledge & Kegan Paul in association with Methuen, 1988.

Langum, David J. *Crossing over the Line: Legislating Morality and the Mann Act*. Chicago: University of Chicago Press, 1994.

Langworth, Richard M., and the Editors of Consumer Guide. *The Great American Convertible*. New York: Beekman House, 1988.

Lewis, David L., and Laurence Goldstein, eds. *The Automobile and American Culture*. Ann Arbor: University of Michigan Press, 1983.

Longstreet, Stephen. *The Boy in the Model T: A Journey in the Just Gone Past*. New York: Simon and Schuster, 1956.

Ludvigsen, Karl. *Corvette: America's Star-Spangled Sports Car, Complete History*. 4th ed. Princeton, N.J.: Automobile Quarterly, 1978.

Lynd, Robert, and Helen M. Lynd. *Middletown: A Study in American Culture*. New York: Harcourt, Brace, & World, 1929.

Lynd, Robert, and Helen M. Lynd. *Middletown in Transition: A Study in Cultural Conflicts*. New York: Harcourt, Brace, & World, 1937.

Mandel, Leon. *Driven: The American Four-Wheeled Love Affair*. New York: Stein and Day, 1977.

Marsh, Peter, and Peter Collett. *Driving Passion: The Psychology of the Car*. Boston: Faber & Faber, 1987.

Massey, Beatrice Larned. *It Might Have Been Worse: A Motor Trip from Coast to Coast*. San Francisco: Harr Wagner, 1920.

Massucci, Edoardo. *Cars for Kids*. New York: Rizzoli International, 1983.

McCahill, Tom. *The Modern Sports Car*. New York: Prentice-Hall, 1954.

McCarthy, Mary. *How I Grew*. San Diego: Harcourt Brace Jovanovich, 1988.

McCluggage, Denise. *Are You a Woman Driver?* New York: Grosset and Dunlap, 1966.

McGovern, John. *Muscle Cars*. Secaucus, N.J.: Chartwell Books, 1984.

McLuhan, Marshall. *Understanding Media: The Extensions of Man*. New York: Signet Books, 1964.

McShane, Clay. *Down the Asphalt Path: The Automobile and the American City*. New York: Columbia University Press, 1994.

Medley, Tom. *[Tex Smith's] Hot Rod History: Tracing America's Most Popular Automotive Hobby*. 2 vols. North Branch, Minn.: CarTech, 1994.

Meier, August, and Elliott Rudwick. *Black Detroit and the Rise of the UAW*. New York: Oxford University Press, 1979.

Meinig, D[onald] W., ed. *The Interpretation of Ordinary Landscapes: Geographical Essays*. New York: Oxford University Press, 1979.

Meyer, John R., and José A. Gómez-Ibáñez. *Autos, Transit, and Cities*. Cambridge, Mass.: Harvard University Press, 1981.

Milkman, Ruth. *Gender at Work: The Dynamics of Job Segregation by Sex during World War II*. Champaign: University of Illinois Press, 1987.

Miller, Ray. *Mustang Does It!* Oceanside, Calif.: Evergreen Press, 1978.

Miller, Ray, and Bruce McCalley. *From Here to Obscurity: A Look at the Changes in an Unchanging Car, the Model T Ford, 1909–1927*. Oceanside, Calif.: Evergreen Press, 1971.

Moline, Norman T. *Mobility and the Small Town, 1900–1930: Transportation Change in Oregon, Illinois*. [Chicago]: University of Chicago, Department of Geography, 1971.

Monroe, Day *et al. Family Expenditures for Automobile and Other Transportation: Five Regions*. Washington, D.C.: U.S. Department of Agriculture, 1941.

Montagu of Beaulieu, Edward John Barrington Douglas-Scott-Montagu, Baron, and F. Wilson McComb. *Behind the Wheel: The Magic and Manners of Early Motoring*. New York: Paddington Press, 1977.

Montgomery, Don. *Hot Rod Memories: Relived Again*. Fallbrook, Calif.: Author, 1991.

Montgomery, Don. *Hot Rods as They Were: Another Blast from the Past*. Fallbrook, Calif.: Author, 1989.

Montgomery, Don. *Hot Rods in the Forties: A Blast from the Past*. Fallbrook, Calif.: Author, 1987.

Moorhouse, H.F. *Driving Ambitions: An Analysis of the American Hot Rod Enthusiasm*. New York: Manchester University Press, 1991.

Morland, Andrew. *Street Machines: '49 and on Custom Cars*. London: Osprey, 1984.

Morland, Andrew. *Street Rods: Pre-'48 American Rods in Color*. London: Osprey, 1983.

Mueller, Mike. *Motor City Muscle: The High-Powered History of the American Muscle Car*. Osceola, Wisc.: Motorbooks International, 1997.

Musselman, M.M. *Get a Horse!: The Story of the Automobile in America*. Philadelphia: J.B. Lippincott, 1950.

Narus, Donald J. *Chrysler's Wonderful Woodie: The Town and Country, 1941–1950*. Parma, Ohio: Marjac Enterprises, 1973.

Narus, Donald J. *Great American Woodies and Wagons*. Glen Ellyn, Ill.: Crestline, 1977.

Neuman, David J., ed. "Automobiles." *Journal of Popular Culture* 8 (Summer 1974): 121–184.

Nichols, Richard. *American Sportscars: A Survey of the Classic Marques*. New York: Gallery Books, 1988.

Paaswell, Robert F., and Wilfred Recker. *Problems of the Carless*. New York: Praeger, 1978.

Padilla, Carmella. *Low 'n Slow: Lowriding in New Mexico*. Santa Fe: Museum of New Mexico Press, 1999.

Patton, Phil. *Made in USA: The Secret Histories of the Things That Made America*. New York: Grove Weidenfeld, 1992.

Pennell, Paul. *Children's Cars*. Princes Risborough, Eng.: Shire, 1986.

Pettifer, Julian, and Nigel Turner. *Automania: Man and the Motor Car*. Boston: Little, Brown, 1984.

Pfau, Hugo. *The Custom Body Era*. New York: Castle Books, 1970.

President's Research Committee on Social Trends. *Recent Social Trends in the United States*. New York: McGraw-Hill, 1933.

Preston, Howard L. *Automobile Age Atlanta: The Making of a Southern Metropolis, 1900–1935*. Athens: University of Georgia Press, 1979.

Putnam's Automobile Handbook: The Care and Maintenance of the Modern Motor-Car. New York: G.P. Putnam's Sons, 1918.

Rae, John B. *The American Automobile: A Brief History*. Chicago: University of Chicago Press, 1965.

Rae, John B. *The Road and the Car in American Life*. Cambridge, Mass.: MIT Press, 1971.

Ramsey, Alice Huyler. *Veil, Duster and Tire Iron*. Covina, Calif.: Castle Press, 1961.

Root, Marilyn. *Women at the Wheel: 42 Stories of Freedom, Fanbelts and the Lure of the Open Road*. Naperville, Ill.: Sourcebooks, 1999.

Rothe, J. Peter. *The Safety of Elderly Drivers: Yesterday's Young in Today's Traffic.* New Brunswick, N.J.: Transaction, 1989.

Rothschild, Joan, ed. "Technology and Feminism." *Research in Philosophy & Technology* 13 (1993).

Sanford, Charles L., ed. *Automobiles in American Life.* Troy, N.Y.: Center for the Study of the Human Dimensions in Science and Technology, 1977.

Scharff, Virginia J. *Taking the Wheel: Women and the Coming of the Motor Age.* New York: Free Press, 1991.

Schneider, Roy A. *Sixteen Cylinder Motorcars: An Illustrated History.* Arcadia, Calif.: Heritage House, 1974.

Sears, Stephen W. *The American Heritage History of the Automobile in America.* New York: American Heritage, 1977.

Shuman, Arnold B., and Bernard Shuman. *Cools Cars, Square Roll Bars: Photos and Recollections of Fifties Hot Rodding in New England.* Sharon, Mass.: Hammershop Press, 1999.

Southard, Andy, Jr. *Hot Rods & Customs of the 1960s.* Osceola, Wisc.: Motorbooks International, 1997.

Southard, Andy, Jr. *Hot Rods of the 1950s.* Osceola, Wisc.: Motorbooks International, 1995.

Stanford, John E.G. *The Sports Car: Development and Design.* New York: Scribner, 1957.

Stern, Philip Van Doren. *Tin Lizzie: The Story of the Fabulous Model T Ford.* New York: Simon and Schuster, 1955.

Tast, Alan. *Thunderbird, 1955–66.* Osceola, Wisc.: Motorbooks International, 1996.

Thornburg, David A. *Galloping Bungalows: The Rise and Demise of the American House Trailer.* Hamden, Conn.: Archon Books, 1991.

Troyer, Howard W. *The Four Wheel Drive Story.* New York: McGraw-Hill, 1954.

U.S. Department of Transportation, Federal Highway Administration. *Demographic Special Reports, Nationwide Personal Transportation Survey.* 1990 NPTS Report Series, HPM-40. Washington, D.C.: U.S. Department of Transportation, 1995.

Wachs, Martin. *Transportation for the Elderly: Changing Lifestyles, Changing Needs.* Berkeley: University of California Press, 1979.

Wallis, Allan D. *Wheel Estate: The Rise and Decline of Mobile Homes.* New York: Oxford University Press, 1991.

Weider, Robert, and George Hall. *The Great American Convertible: An Affectionate Guide.* New York: Doubleday, 1977.

Weith, Warren, and Jay Hirsch. *The Last American Convertibles: A Last, Loving Look at the Original American Dream Machines.* New York: Collier, 1979.

White, Lee Strout [E.B. White with Richard Lee Strout]. *Farewell to the Model T.* New York: G.P. Putnam's Sons, 1936.

Wik, Reynold W. *Henry Ford and Grass-roots America.* Ann Arbor: University of Michigan Press, 1972.

Willinger, Kurt, and Gene Gurney. *The American Jeep: In War and Peace.* New York: Crown, 1983.

Witzel, Michael Karl, and Kent Bash. *Cruisin': Car Culture in America.* Osceola, Wisc.: Motorbooks International, 1997.

Witzenburg, Gary L. *Mustang!: The Complete History of America's Pioneer Ponycar.* Kutztown, Pa.: Automobile Quarterly Publications, 1979.

Wolfe, Tom. *The Kandy-Kolored Tangerine-Flake Streamline Baby.* New York: Farrar, Straus, 1965.

Wright, Nicky. *Ford Mustang: The Enduring Legend.* New York: Gallery Books, 1989.

CHAPTER 6

The Automobile and Community Change

While the modifications wrought by the automobile in the area of interpersonal relationships were relatively subtle, evolutionary, and privately experienced, changes in community structure and institutions were more obvious, sudden, and of public concern. In fact, the motor car was one of the major contributors, if not *the* major contributor, to the suburbanization of America during the years 1920 to 1960. That movement carried with it the seeds of the current urban decay and the widespread emigration from rural areas, as well as the demise of the family farm and the social and economic institutions that such farms supported and that supported them. In a larger sense, these developments were the result of community planning or lack thereof, and it is with that topic that we begin this chapter.

PLANNING

Concern for community planning certainly predates the appearance of the automobile. However, until the turn of the century, all such planning was based on the expectation of horse-drawn traffic, supplemented by the fixed-route, motorized transportation made possible by the railroad. The coming of the automobile added another variable to the equation that was to eventually be the most important of all.

By the time of the First World War, the automobile had become so widely accepted that scholarly articles began to appear analyzing the car's impact on community planning, development, and demise. Thus, as early as 1915, a paper delivered by Nelson P. Lewis before the annual National Conference on City Planning was entitled "The Automobile and the City Plan." In 1924 *The Annals* carried John Ihlder's "The Automobile and Community Planning" as part of a thematic issue called "The Automobile: Its Provence and Problems"; and in 1925, the *American Society of Civil Engineers Transactions* published George A. Damon's "The Influence of the Automobile on Regional Transportation Planning."

This early period of concern is well described by Blaine A. Brownell in "Urban Planning, the Planning Profession, and the Motor Vehicle in Early Twentieth Century America," a chapter in Gordon E. Cherry's *Shaping an Urban World*. For a broader perspective, see Mark S. Foster's *From Streetcar to Superhighway: American City Planners and Urban Transportation, 1900–1940*, an analysis of the shift from mass transit systems to the private automobile in which the author maintains that planners endorsed cars and the suburban movement out of professional conviction, not because they and certain business interests stood to gain financially. Finally, Edward Weiner's brief (122-page) *Urban Transportation Planning in the United States: An Historical View*, which begins with the highway planning of the 1930s and ends with an analysis of efforts to provide multi-modal transportation in the early 1980s, is a call for the continuing evolution of planning processes and institutions to meet the needs of planners, citizens, and decision makers.

While the coming of the automobile added a new variable to the city planning process, its influence was more apparent in the changing housing patterns that it made possible, especially the suburban "development," and the new commercial arrangements that it brought forth. Although much of the pre–World War II housing development that took place was relatively unplanned, there were individual examples of communities that were specifically designed to take into account the new means of transportation. Two of the most significant of these were Radburn, a model community designed for Bergen County, New Jersey, and billed as the "new town for the motor age," and J.C. Nichols' Country Club District, a suburb of 35,000 residents constructed outside Kansas City in the mid-1920s. Both later influenced the design and development of major residential areas elsewhere in the United States. The story of Radburn, the brainchild of architects Clarence Stein and Henry Wright, influential members of the Regional Planning Association of America, is well told in Daniel Schaffer's *Garden Cities for America: The Radburn Experience*. For the history of the Country Club District, see *J.C. Nichols and the Shaping of Kansas City: Innovation in Planned Residential Communities*, a combination biography and business/urban history, by William S. Worley, and *The J.C. Nichols Chronicle: The Authorized Story of the Man, His Company, and His Legacy, 1880–1994*, a biographical tribute by Robert Pearson and Brad Pearson.

Among other aspects, the Kansas City project contained Country Club Plaza, the first (1922) regional shopping center designed to cater to the automobile (two entire blocks were devoted to parking) and, as such, the harbinger of the geographic decentralization of American business.

By this time, the car was viewed as such an important part of American life that even "utopian" communities were designed with the assumption that it would be the paramount means of private transport. In this regard, see *New Towns and the Suburban Dream: Ideology and Utopia in Planning Development*, edited by Irving L. Allen, and, more specifically, Frank Lloyd Wright's *The Disappearing City*, published in 1932. Wright envisioned a decentralized, mobile community that he called "Broadacre City," where architecture and automobility functioned harmoniously. Although such communities were never built as planned, actual towns and cities did incorporate significant elements of the concepts proposed, such as Radburn (see above) and Greenbelt, Maryland, a garden city of the late 1930s planned and built by the federal government, and, later, the economically, socially, and politically self-sufficient communities of Reston, Virginia, Irvine, California, and Columbia, Maryland, constructed in the 1960s.

The influence of the passenger car on commercial, as opposed to residential, development is well described in *The Drive-In, the Supermarket, and the Transformation of Commercial Space in Los Angeles, 1914–1941*, wherein architectural historian Richard Longstreth analyzes how a desire to cater to automobility led to new spatial designs for retail space in car-dependent Los Angeles prior to World War II, setting precedents that were followed after the war throughout the country. Of particular interest to readers of this guide is Longstreth's focus on the development of automotive circulation patterns and parking for the service station and then the drive-in market that emerged in the 1910s and 1920s. The same author's earlier *City Center to Regional Mall: Architecture, the Automobile, and Retailing in Los Angeles, 1920–1950* is an award-winning historical survey that relates the spread of the automobile to changes in retail architecture, urban/suburban economics, and cultural issues, with the primary outcome being the development of the regional shopping center. As with his later book (see above), the importance of the automobile for personal transportation and the need to accommodate it (i.e., provide parking space) are seen as handmaidens for the decentralization of retailing.

These auto-induced residential and commercial changes were generally seen as positive developments through the first half of the 20th century. Typical of the prevailing views were those of Christopher Tunnard and Henry H. Reed, who were among those city planners who believed that urban areas always had reflected planning considerations and the changing needs and desires of the citizenry. They saw the current era (mid-20th century) as no different in principle from the past. Their *American Skyline: The Growth and Form of Our Cities and Towns* maintained that architects and engineers could plan contemporary cities that are both beautiful and efficient, even taking into account modern determinants of urban design, such as the automobile, highways, suburbs, and even parking lots.

Writing in the mid-1950s, Tunnard and Reed's *American Skyline* appeared at the height of the American love affair with the car. By the 1960s the socioeconomic influences of the automobile were beginning to be questioned, and this new, more critical perspective was reflected in books such as Jane Jacobs' *The*

Death and Life of Great American Cities, which has become somewhat of a classic since its publication in 1961. Jacobs brilliantly describes how real cities function, with special attention to what makes them safe. In that vein, she singles out streets and sidewalks as potential sources of vibrancy, while damning past efforts of city planners. She offers her ideas on how to revitalize the streets and neighborhoods in a lengthy chapter entitled "Erosion of Cities or Attrition of Automobiles," wherein she describes how American cities have been eroded, piece by piece, by accommodating the automobile. Jacobs advocates instead an approach whereby design considerations and policies will make the use of the automobile "less convenient," thus leading to a type of attrition as significant numbers of individuals decide not to use their cars in the city.

Criticism of the impact of the automobile on the vitality of the American city continued throughout the remainder of the 20th century. For example, in the mid-1980s *Access for All: Transportation and Urban Growth*, K.H. Schaeffer and Elliot Sclar contend that while improved transportation provided relief for the overcrowded cities of the 1800s by allowing for expansion, that process in the 20th century—abetted by the automobile—led to such unchecked growth and dispersion that individuals lost their sense of community. As a result, they recommend that future city developers reverse this trend by understanding the complexity of the processes that contribute to the growth of metropolitan areas and to the interaction of transport and land-use patterns and thus re-create an urban structure that functions effectively. A similar theme is the focus of James H. Kunstler's *The Geography of Nowhere: The Rise and Decline of America's Man-Made Landscape*, a 1994 polemic in which he claims that America has evolved from a nation of coherent, unique communities into one where every place is like every other and we have lost all sense of civic life and identity. Kunstler decries the creation of a man-made landscape of crass commercialism that ignores nature and human needs and has imposed enormous social costs and economic burdens on the individual and society. He blames a large share of these developments on the desire of Americans to accommodate the automobile and the lifestyle that it mandates. His solution lies in a return to sound principles of urban and suburban planning, ending our autocentric outlook, and assuring the ascendancy of public virtue over private rights.

HIGHWAYS AND COMMUNITY PLANNING

Although the major discussion of roads and highways is found in Chapter 10, mention needs to be made here of how consideration of highways influenced the thinking and actions of community planners. Three similarly titled monographs, from the 1960s and 1970s, provide a general introduction to this aspect of planning. They are, in chronological order, Eric Schenker's *An Inventory of the Economic Factors Influenced by a Highway Development Program*, which covers events from the depression up to the introduction of the interstate highway system; *Highways and Economic and Social Changes*, issued by the U.S.

Bureau of Public Roads, a data volume containing some good analysis but, even more important indicating several future research avenues; and the U.S. Federal Highway Administration's similarly titled *Social and Economic Effects of Highways*, which carries the story through the mid-1970s.

Highways were seen as generally positive influences in the first half of the 20th century, an observation supported by the views expressed by the books cited in the above paragraph and the passage of the Interstate Highway Act in 1956. In addition, *Future Highways and Urban Growth*, a 1961 study by the transportation consulting firm of Wilbur Smith and Associates, advocated "a continued and accelerated program" of superhighways, especially in urban areas. Not surprisingly, this volume was a publication of the Automobile Manufacturers Association. However, even government consultants supported such development at that time. For instance, *The Freeway in the City: Principles of Planning and Design*, a report prepared by the urban advisers of the U.S. Federal Highway Administration for the secretary of transportation, provides the mid-1960s perspective on how to approach the construction of such roads.

Yet, as with the automobile in general, the 1960s and 1970s marked the beginning of public disenchantment with the unrestricted construction of superhighways. Typical of the concern expressed, though by the author's own admission an "intensely personal interpretation," was Richard O. Davies' *The Age of Asphalt: The Automobile, the Freeway, and the Condition of Metropolitan America*, which explores the negative effects of federal transportation laws and decisions, especially during the Eisenhower years. Richard Hebert's *Highways to Nowhere: The Politics of City Transportation* has a similar focus, featuring descriptions of the chaotic transport systems in Atlanta; Dayton, Ohio; Flint, Michigan; Indianapolis; and Washington, D.C., in the early 1970s. Finally, Robert A. Caro's *The Power Broker: Robert Moses and the Fall of New York* analyzes urban expressway developments in that city and shows the incredible impact of the automobile on one urban area and, by implication, all other American cities.

One of the more controversial aspects of the development of urban superhighways has been their impact on old ethnic and racial neighborhoods. Some roads have permanently bisected such neighborhoods. In other cases, they have had the effect of creating an impassable barrier between the neighborhood and the rest of the city. *Rites of Way: The Politics of Transportation in Boston and the U.S. City*, by Alan Lupo *et al.*, in addition to describing the consequences to society and the individual of constructing expressways through urban areas, examines the successful effort in the late 1960s and early 1970s to impose a moratorium on further superhighway construction there. Similar in approach is Stephen H. Putnam's "Urban Impacts of Highway Systems," a chapter in *The Urban Impacts of Federal Policies*, edited by Norman J. Glickman.

More specifically, Richard O. Baumbach Jr. and William E. Borah have written a fine, scholarly study of *The Second Battle of New Orleans: A History of the Vieux Carré Riverfront-Expressway Controversy* that involved a proposal to construct a portion of an interstate highway through the historic French Quarter. It pitted downtown business interests against preservationists for over two decades (1946–1969). Finally, Alan Altshuler's *The City Planning Process: A Political Analysis* contains an excellent chapter on "The Intercity Freeway," which takes St. Paul, Minnesota, as a classic case study of city planning in the 1950s, showing the impact of such roads when they both bisect and circumnavigate a major urban area.

This concern over the potential disruption or destruction of the viability of urban neighborhood communities is a reflection of the long-standing belief (see Jacobs above) that streets carry the lifeblood of the "body metropolitan," that they are part of the infrastructure network that links the various communities together and allows them to function as a single economic (and social) entity. In this regard, see Donald Appleyard's *Livable Streets*, which uses San Francisco as a case study to compare and contrast the nature of life on streets with different types of traffic flow and to develop a program for creating more livable streets and protected neighborhoods. A brief, but insightful, historical survey of the importance of city roadways to the time of World War II is Clay McShane's "Urban Pathways: The Street and Highway, 1900–1940," a chapter in Joel A. Tarr and Gabriel Dupuy's *Technology and the Rise of the Networked City in Europe and America*, winner of the 1989 Abel Wolman Award.

SUBURBANIZATION

Unfortunately, there is no book-length work devoted exclusively to the history of the automobile's impact on suburban America. We do, however, have numerous studies of the phenomenon of suburbanization, which necessarily discuss the role of the car. Among these, the best is Kenneth T. Jackson's *Crabgrass Frontier: The Suburbanization of the United States*. Jackson won the American Historical Association's Bancroft Prize for this social history, which uses as one of its continuing threads the role that transportation played in the evolution of American suburbs. Of special interest to readers of this guide are the chapters on the "new age of automobility," suburban development between World Wars I and II, and the drive-in culture of contemporary America, plus the author's overall questioning of federal highway policies. (For an earlier synopsis of the ideas contained in this book, see Jackson's chapter entitled "The Crabgrass Frontier" in *The Urban Experience: Themes in American History*, edited by Raymond A. Mohl and James F. Richardson.) Also good, though briefer, is Peter O. Muller's *Contemporary Suburban America*. Particularly pertinent to this chapter is the attention that Muller gives to the role of the automobile in bringing about the demographic shifts that created the auto-centered suburb, which he correctly notes is no longer a satellite of the city but rather a self-sufficient social, political, and economic entity unto itself. Muller is also insightful regarding the impact of highway development on the form and substance of suburbs.

More recently, in *Bourgeois Utopias: The Rise and Fall of Suburbia*, a social history with an international perspective, Robert Fishman has argued not only that suburbs were well established before the automobile but that their roots lie more in middle-class ideals of property and familial privacy than in the means of transportation that abetted them. Finally, there is Barbara M. Kelly's *Suburbia Re-Examined*, an interdisciplinary and eclectic collection of twenty-six provocative essays that consider the changing nature and definition of suburbia, past and present (through the 1980s), and the processes that have influenced its development both physically and as an intellectual construct from various perspectives. The transportation revolution and its effect upon home, workplace, and community are among the issues explored.

Although we often view the emergence of contemporary suburbs as a post-1945 development, their historical roots are much deeper, going back at least to the turn of the century. At that time, they were largely dependent on commutation by train and streetcar. See Sam Bass Warner Jr.'s *Streetcar Suburbs: The Process of Growth in Boston, 1870–1900* for an excellent study of this phenomenon. Warner shows how the motorized (electric) street railway led to an era of city building that divided the metropolitan area into a center city consisting of commerce and residential slums and an outlying area of middle- and upper-class suburbanites who commuted to work. More recently, there is John R. Stilgoe's well-written and possibly definitive "prehistory," entitled *Borderland: Origins of the American Suburb, 1820–1939*, a work that is particularly strong in terms of describing in words and illustrations what life was like for the inhabitants of those areas that bordered Boston, Chicago, New York, and so on in the 19th and early 20th centuries. Neither work has much to say about suburbs abetted by the automobile.

The first serious studies of the automotively induced suburbs began to emerge in the mid-1920s. See, for example, *The Suburban Trend*, a 1925 book by Harlan Paul Douglass that focuses on developments in the communities surrounding New York City. Sparked by the establishment of the President's Research Committee on Social Trends and the 1933 publication of its two-volume report, *Recent Social Trends in the United States*, which historian Mark S. Foster calls "a standard source on pre–World War II suburban emergence," the 1930s witnessed more attention to the historical antecedents and future developments of these satellite communities. The report itself contained references to the automobile and commuting, the suburban movement, highway engineering, church interests, pleasure travel, and crime, among other issues. In fact, one of the supporting monographs written by Roderick D. McKenzie for the Committee on Social Trends was entitled *The Metropolitan Community* and was based on his "The Rise of Metropolitan Communities" chapter in the *Recent Social Trends* report.

Recent historiography also has focused on the interwar years as a "formative" period in the development of autocentric suburbs. In a nation where the government had not played a direct role in the planning and construction of residential communities, such developments were usually in the hands of real estate developers. In this regard, the Chicago suburbs are a prime example, as witnessed by the publication in the late 1980s of two scholarly monographs on this topic. In *Building Chicago: Suburban Developers and the Creation of a Divided Metropolis*, Ann Durkin Keating sees transportation, including the advent of the automobile, as a contributing force bringing about suburbanization, but not as the crucial determinant of the form of such residential areas. Exploring the same general topic, but taking a different approach, is Michael H. Ebner's *Creating Chicago's North Shore: A Suburban History*, a study that explains the origins and evolution of the North Shore as a distinctive region, while showing the unique social characteristics of the eight communities within it.

In addition, one book chapter is both worth examining and indicative of directions that future research might take. In his *America and the Automobile: Technology, Reform, and Social Change*, Peter J. Ling includes a chapter on the suburbs in which he maintains that, rather than providing a haven from work and market, the fully developed suburb has created a highway network that runs primarily from residence to workplace and thus has created on a grander scale that which existed in Warner's pre-streetcar city.

Before closing this section, two monographs in the field of labor studies deserve mention, both as valuable works in their own right and as exemplars of the need for similar scholarship in the future that focuses on the impact of the auto industry on community development. Clarence Hooker's *Life in the Shadows of the Crystal Palace, 1910–1927: Ford Workers in the Model T Era*, while essentially a study of the impact of scientific management and "Fordism" on the work and home lives of the company employees, provides insight into how and why the sleepy village of Highland Park, Michigan, was transformed from a small village into an industrial boomtown, becoming the first American community whose economic viability was completely dependent on the automotive industry. In a different vein, Bennett M. Berger's *Working Class Suburb: A Study of Auto Workers in Suburbia* tells the story of a group of 100 Ford workers from the city who, though forced to move in 1957 to suburban tract housing in Northern California as a result of a plant relocation, still retained their working-class views and lifestyle, thus showing that the physical community itself had very little impact on the factory workers' behavior.

THE CAR AND URBAN CHANGE

As urban historian Kenneth T. Jackson has argued, "the automobile . . . had greater social and spatial impact on cities than any technological innovation since the development of the wheel."[1] Interest in the impact of the road and car on urban life seems to have come into its own as a subject for serious study following World War II. Books in this area fall into two classes, overviews of urban transportation in general and specific studies of the interaction of the car and the city. Representative of books falling into the former category is Harlan

W. Gilmore's *Transportation and Growth of Cities*, a scholarly study completed in the early 1950s. Recommended among the more specific accounts are Wilfred Owen's 1959 *Cities in the Motor Age*, an exploration of whether we can be both urbanized and motorized, including discussion of city planning, the interstate highway system (the construction of which had just begun), the suburb versus the city, and proposals for the future, and a 1963 work by the eminent urban historian Lewis Mumford, entitled *The Highway and the City*, which is a collection of his essays on problems faced by American and European metropolitan areas as they undertake city and highway planning.

Not until the mid-1980s did good historical overviews of the specific impact of the car on urban America in general (as opposed to a specific city) appear. In 1986 David J. St. Clair's *The Motorization of American Cities* marked the first publication of a study that was national in scope. While qualitatively excellent, St. Clair's small volume is limited to an analysis of the auto industry's attempts to create an urban economic and political environment in which the private car would gain ascendancy over mass transit. Broader in coverage, Clay McShane's *Down the Asphalt Path: The Automobile and the American City* explores the multifaceted relationship between the car and urbanization prior to World War I as reflected in the struggle over who controlled city streets—those who lived on them or those who traveled through them. In the end, the desire to pass rapidly through the city prevailed over the need to use the streets for recreation and commerce, and the concept and physical design of the American city were changed to favor the commuter and to accommodate the motor car. Thus, McShane argues that the mass adoption of the automobile was due more to changes in urban culture than to advances in automotive technology, although he acknowledges that the two reinforced each other.

Of all the American cities, most scholars would agree that Los Angeles, for better or worse, has been the one whose design and functioning have been most affected by the motor car. An excellent introduction to that city's history and its transportation, within the broader context of the process of urbanization, is Robert M. Fogelson's *The Fragmented Metropolis: Los Angeles, 1850–1930*. Fogelson shows how the structure, character, and culture of Los Angeles in 1930 were the harbinger of developments in other American cities in the years following World War II. Those latter years are the subject of Greg Hise's *Magnetic Los Angeles: Planning the Twentieth-Century Metropolis*, in which the author puts forth the original proposition that metropolitan Los Angeles (L.A.) was the product of a "planned dispersion of jobs, housing, and services," not the result of a haphazard jumble of suburban developments. The most recent period is examined in *The City: Los Angeles and Urban Theory at the End of the Twentieth Century*, edited by Allen J. Scott and Edward W. Soja, which provides scholarly essays on that topic, many of which analyze the urban spatial configuration that has evolved and the social conditions that it has generated.

More specifically automotive in focus are Scott L. Bottles' *The Making of the Modern City: Los Angeles and the Automobile, 1900–1950*, with its explanation of how and why the motor car replaced public transit as the chief means of personal transportation there and the auto's role in transforming L.A. from a centralized city with a single business district into a decentralized metropolis with several important commercial centers, and *L.A. Freeway: An Appreciative Essay*, in which author David Brodsly explores the historic evolution and the very nature of the freeway system and, as the *Los Angeles Times* notes, sees it "as the source of feelings, experiences and unique life patterns for the urban driver."

Like Los Angeles, Detroit found itself transformed by the automobile, but in the latter, the changes had more of an effect on the nature of the city than on its physical appearance. Although it was not inevitable, metropolitan Detroit soon became the base for the Big Three auto makers. In fact, a 1913 article in *Automobile* magazine by L.V. Spencer was entitled "Detroit: The City Built by the Automobile Industry." For a broad survey of the city's history from its founding by Antoine de la Mothe Cadillac in 1701 to 1923, when it was the fourth largest city in the United States, see George B. Catlin's *The Story of Detroit*. A view of developments to the late 1930s is provided by Wessel Smitter in his 1938 book *F.O.B. Detroit*. Finally, two good books by Arthur Pound are worth examining. His 1940 *Detroit: Dynamic City* is both insightful and now historic in its observations. The more recent (1962) *The Automobile and an American City* further develops some of the points made in Pound's earlier, more general history of Detroit but focuses more on the impact of the early auto industry on the development of that city.

The history of Detroit and that of its diverse racial and ethnic population are inseparable. Although questions of race and automotive unionism are treated in more detail in Chapter 3, mention needs to be made here of books that analyze the impact of skin color and labor relations on the integrity of the community. For an introduction to that subject in the years immediately preceding World War II, see Richard W. Thomas' *Life for Us Is What We Make It*, an analysis of African-American community building in Detroit in the years 1815–1945 that concludes with a chapter that explores two conflicting strategies of black community building: unionization and (Ford) corporate paternalism in the period 1936–1941.

Foremost among the books focusing on the years after 1945 would be Thomas J. Sugrue's *The Origins of the Urban Crisis: Race and Inequality in Postwar Detroit*. In this prizewinning study, the author uses Detroit as symbolic of "rust belt" cities to show how de-industrialization and racial discrimination helped maintain and deepen the social and economic differences between black and white Detroit. As postwar automation and plant relocations diminished opportunities in the auto industry, the African Americans suffered most in terms of economic well-being, race relations, and access to the housing market, all of which were significantly worse for black people than they had been prior to the end of World War II. Still worth examining, though dated, is B.J. Widick's *Detroit: City of Race and Class Violence*, which relates those social issues to labor relations for the period 1920–1970. Widick was a former economist for the UAW, and his work reflects his background and the general (as opposed to scholarly) audience for which it was written. Finally, for a fascinating case study of the continuing power of the auto industry to shape the city to its needs, see Jeanie Wylie's *Poletown: Community Betrayed*, which relates the story of how an inner-city Detroit neighborhood was razed in the early 1980s over strong opposition from the multi-ethnic residents so that General Motors could build a Cadillac plant in that community.

Although Detroit was probably unique in the extent to which the motor car came to dominate its economic health, other Michigan cities experienced significant socioeconomic changes as local automotive manufacturing plants increasingly impacted on their lives. The city of Flint, Michigan, experienced many of the same developments as Detroit. Home to both General Motors and the UAW union, the histories of Flint and car manufacturing have been inseparably intertwined. For the story of both through World War II, see Carl Crow's *The City of Flint Grows Up: The Success Story of an American Community*. Approximately a decade later, George H. Maines' *Men, a City, and a Buick* appeared. Neither is a particularly scholarly work.

More directly related to the themes of this chapter are Ronald Edsforth's *Class Conflict and Cultural Consensus: The Making of a Mass Consumer Society in Flint, Michigan* and Steven P. Dandaneau's more recent *A Town Abandoned: Flint, Michigan, Confronts Deindustrialization*. The former uses Flint as a case study to show how the economy changed from a "producer-goods to a consumer-goods" one, which led to a significant transformation in which big business, big government, and a big union (the UAW) came to dominate local culture and politics. As a result, when the American auto industry began to suffer reverses in the 1970s, the city experienced economic recession and social disorganization. The latter picks up chronologically where Edsforth leaves off, analyzing how Flint responded to its economic and social decline in the context of class and culture in the United States in the last third of the 20th century. Dandaneau offers a Marxist critique of capitalism and concludes that rust belt cities like Flint are really powerless to combat problems that are international in scope and endemic to our economic system and that the best that cities can do is to offer public relations solutions until we are prepared to abandon the ideology of capitalism.

Similar in nature is anthropologist Kathryn Marie Dudley's *The End of the Line: Lost Jobs, New Lives in Postindustrial America*, another story of deindustrialization, in this case focusing on the 1988 closing of the Chrysler (formerly American Motors) assembly plant in Kenosha, Wisconsin, and the socioeconomic disruption that it caused. Dudley is particularly adept at portraying the difficult and often confusing process of change experienced by Americans—in this case auto workers—caught in the clutches of economic transition, wherein the concept of economic progress can come into direct conflict with that of financial security.

Some other major cities have been the subject of case studies in which the social and economic impact of the motor car is analyzed. Howard L. Preston's *Automobile Age Atlanta: The Making of a Southern Metropolis, 1900–1935*, was a pioneering study at the time of its publication and still deserves reading for its insightful analysis of how the car greatly influenced the physical development of one of the nation's key southern metropolitan areas. Joel A. Tarr's *Transportation Innovation and Changing Spatial Patterns in Pittsburgh, 1850–1934*, a pamphlet in the Essays in Public Works History series, examines first the streetcar's, and then the automobile's, effect on population distribution, journey-to-work patterns, and the growth of the central business district, including building development, industrial location, and traffic patterns. In *Resort City in the Sunbelt: Las Vegas, 1930–1970*, Eugene P. Moehring maintains that federal highway projects "were particularly crucial" to the emergence of Las Vegas as a major resort city and the evolution of its outlying suburban areas. Even with these case studies, this still is an area where much additional work needs to be done in the future, particularly of a comparative nature.

Finally, a few works attempt to study the impact of the car on a regional level. They are included in this section because they focus either directly or indirectly on the process of urbanization. Peirce Lewis' essay "The Unprecedented City" in *The American Land*, edited by Alexis Doster III *et al.*, explores the phenomenon of "galactic" cities that have grown up within metropolitan areas and that owe their genesis to the automobile. Unlike the old "nucleated" city, these new urban areas arrange their residential and commercial zones in loose, separated clusters, rather like galaxies in outer space. Lewis maintains that the galactic city is different from the traditional suburb in terms of its social and economic independence from the city center, although he admits that, culturally, its inhabitants still prefer the old downtown area. In a sense, the phenomenon described by Lewis is similar to the one posited more recently by Joel Garreau. In *Edge City: Life on the New Frontier*, Garreau analyzes the emergence of neighboring commercial structures (such as office buildings, parking lots, and shopping malls) that have grouped together on the periphery of most major American cities. Unlike suburbs, their function is seen as more commercial than residential; they are economically separate from the old central business district; and the automobile and major highways make access to edge cities both easy and a relatively short commute.

The same focus on metropolitanism, as opposed to suburbanization, can be found in *The Exploding Metropolis*, written by the editors of *Fortune* magazine, first published in 1958 and now generally regarded as a classic in urban history. Francis Bello's "The City and the Car" essay in this collection does a fine job of analyzing the role of the car in the "explosion" and the attendant problems connected with it, within the broader context of urban decline and suburban sprawl. More recently, Ray Suarez's *The Old Neighborhood: What We Lost in the Great Suburban Migration, 1966–1999* chronicles the outflow of millions of white, middle-class Americans from the nation's largest and oldest cities and bemoans the eviscerated neighborhoods that they left behind. He casts the automobile as one of the villains in this saga, since it undermined the dense space of the city that had contributed to easy social and economic intercourse, leaving behind a ragged collection of parking lots as its only legacy.

For two brief, though scholarly, overviews of the automobile's influence on one region of the United States, see David R. Goldfield and Blaine A. Brownell's "The Automobile and the City in the American South," in *The Economic and Social Effects of the Spread of Motor Vehicles*, edited by Theo Barker, and Thomas D. Clark's *The Emerging South*, especially the chapter entitled "The Road South," which explores the changes brought about by the construction of the interstate highway system and increased automotive tourism.

Finally, Horace J. Cranmer's *New Jersey in the Automobile Age: A History of Transportation* is a good example of the all-too-rare book-length analysis of the socioeconomic impact of the car on a statewide basis.

THE CAR AND RURAL CHANGE

When one considers the social and economic impact of the automobile in the years before the depression, the areas most affected were the rural, not the urban or suburban, ones. In the study of rural America one finds some of the best historical monographs concerning the impact of the automobile on community life. The pioneering work in this regard was Norman T. Moline's *Mobility and the Small Town, 1900–1930: Transportation Change in Oregon, Illinois*, published in 1971 as a University of Chicago geographical research paper. Moline's study is one of those little gems that appear without fanfare but earn themselves a permanent place in historical literature by the nature and quality of their presentation. This study is valuable in terms of its discussion of the automotively induced emergence of new travel patterns and concepts of time and distance. The author does a particularly good job of showing how the car and the concomitant improvement of rural roads altered the rhythm of town life and self-image of such communities.

Moline's study was followed by Reynold W. Wik's broader *Henry Ford and Grass-roots America*, with its insightful observations regarding rural responses to both Ford's inventions and his ideas. A "cousin" of the Wik book is Michael L. Berger's later *The Devil Wagon in God's Country: The Automobile and Social Change in Rural America, 1893–1929*, which contains a good chapter on how motorization changed community life during that time period and several others that discuss similar modifications in such social institutions as the family, schools, churches, and hospitals. In this regard, his work was path breaking, and these topics are deserving of further study. Finally, John A. Jakle's *The American Small Town: Twentieth-Century Place Images* shows how perceptions of various social and economic aspects of the small town were modified as the major mode of transportation changed from the railroad to the motor car. Jakle does an especially good job of showing how the imagery of townspeople changed as a result of that transformation.

More recently, the automobile has impacted on rural America in ways that it never had before. Starting in the mid-1970s, foreign and domestic car manufacturers began to chose small towns as the site for new manufacturing plants. Marysville, Ohio (Honda), Smyrna, Tennessee (Nissan), Georgetown, Kentucky (Toyota), and Spring Hill, Tennessee (Saturn), in turn, all found their economic, political, and cultural lives profoundly impacted by the introduction of such plants. The story of this phenomenon is convincingly told in Michele M. Hoyman's *Power Steering: Global Automakers and the Transformation of Rural Communities*.

There also are a number of studies of rural communities, which, while not having separate chapters devoted to the topic, nonetheless recognize the influence of the automobile at various points in the narrative. One of the best of this genre is John Baskin's *New Burlington: The Life and Death of an American Village*, a 200-year "history" of a small Ohio farming community told in the voices of the residents themselves, infused with numerous references to the impact that the coming of the motor car had on social and economic interactions within the village. In addition, see Lewis Atherton's *Main Street on the Middle Border*, a cultural and economic history of country towns of the Midwest from the Civil War to 1950, with special attention to their struggle to retain their belief in an essentially moral, ethical, and classless society, their small town intimacy, and their uniqueness in the face of encroaching industrialization, urbanization, and homogenization. The chapters entitled "The Horse Is King" and "Exit the Horse" are especially relevant to the concerns of this guide.

MOBILE HOMES

Before we leave the subject of urban and rural communities, some mention needs to be made of the development of what are now called mobile homes but were initially called "trailers," "house trailers," or sometimes "caravans." The mobile home has become a form of inexpensive, private housing in America that, despite the nomenclature, tends to remain stationary more often than not. The best general treatment of this subject is Allan D. Wallis' *Wheel Estate: The Rise and Decline of Mobile Homes*, a scholarly history, extensively illustrated, that firmly establishes the mobile home and its accompanying lifestyle as fitting subjects for scholarly research. Wallis offers a chronological account of the development of such housing from the mid-1920s through the 1980s and a theoretical framework for understanding the use, form, and meaning of the mobile home in American society. Older (1972) but still valuable is Margaret J. Drury's *Mobile Homes: The Unrecognized Revolution in American Housing*, which provides a concise introduction to the topic.

More specific in focus is Sheila K. Johnson's excellent *Idle Haven: Community Building among the Working-Class Retired*, a 1971 sociological work that focuses on interpersonal relationships within a typical mobile home park outside San Francisco, where people have fled from the problems of urban America to the perceived safety of a small, closed, homogeneous community of trailer dwellers, and David Rigsbee's *Trailers*, a fascinating study of 1990s trailer life in rural Montgomery County, Virginia, that treats the mobile home community as a legitimate and respectable residential choice, illustrated with strikingly realistic photographs by Carol Burch-Brown.

Such mobile home communities are primarily a post–World War II development. Prior to that, trailer owners tended to be more nomadic, alighting as transients at roadside parks before periodically returning home. David A. Thornburg's *Galloping Bungalows: The Rise and Demise of the American House Trailer* is a 1991 study of the transitional years of the 1930s and 1940s. Informal in approach and spiced with personal anecdotes, it treats house trailers, trailer parks, and the social life therein. One of Thornburg's key observations is that the nature of trailer life during those decades was often at odds with traditional American values. For contemporary views of the same period, see Blackburn Sims' *The Trailer Home, with Practical Advice on Trailer Life and Travel*, which provides insight into such activities in the mid-1930s, and Donald O. Cowgill's 1941 *Mobile Homes: A Study of Trailer Life*.

Interesting primarily for the authors and the philosophy that they espouse are two autobiographies: William B. Stout's *So Away I Went!*, the life of a 1930s inventor who developed a prototypic mobile home to go with his futuristic, streamlined, rear-engine Scarab automobile, and Wally Byam's *Trailer Travel Here and Abroad: The New Way to Adventurous Living*. Byam was the "guru" of such a lifestyle, having invented the Airstream trailer, the first commercially successful mobile home. A good popular account of that vehicle and the movement that it generated is *Airstream*, by Robert Landau and James Phillippi.

Such trailers evolved into the contemporary mobile home, which, as mentioned earlier, has become a semi-stationary installation, really a new form of inexpensive manufactured housing. For an explanation and justification for the popularity of such dwellings, see John Brinckerhoff (J.B.) Jackson's "The Mobile Home on the Range," an essay in his *A Sense of Place, a Sense of Time*, in which that pioneering interpreter of the American vernacular landscape celebrates the mobile home's practicality, low cost, and adaptability to the lifestyle occasioned by the finances of blue-collar workers and their families.

The true successor to the trailer is the "recreational vehicle," or RV, which has, to a greater or lesser extent, combined the car and the trailer into a single vehicle. Kay Peterson's *Home Is Where You Park It: A Guide to RV Living as a Life Style* is probably the best contemporary treatment of that topic. To the extent that RVs are the only domicile of some 10 million traveling Americans, one might argue that groups of them have become communities in motion. In that regard, see Michael A. Rockland's *Homes on Wheels*, which features the voices of people who have adopted a lifestyle that allows them to combine successfully the otherwise conflicting desires for individualism, mobility, and a sense of community (albeit transitory).

EDUCATIONAL INSTITUTIONS AND SERVICES

In this section, we are concerned with those community institutions that either directly provide education or serve as adjuncts to it. As such, the discussion is not limited to formal schooling. In addition, certain public services, such as libraries and mail delivery, are explored, since they frequently provide materials used in the educational process.

Schools

By far, the greatest changes in education occurred in rural areas. Unlike their urban counterparts, which had a sufficient number—and in many cases a superabundance—of pupils to allow for a variety of school types and sizes, rural schools tended to be of the one-room school type until the 20th century. Transportation to such institutions was usually accomplished by foot, although some teachers and even fewer pupils rode horses or used horse-drawn vehicles. In any case, such means limited the distance that could be traveled and meant that schools tended to remain small, similar, and isolated. For an overview of the automobile's impact on schooling in rural America, the "Education" chapter in Michael L. Berger's *The Devil Wagon in God's Country* is good. For one man's interest in, and impact on, such education, see "Ford and the Little Red School-house" in Reynold M. Wik's *Henry Ford and Grass-roots America*. Henry Ford was so interested in education that he secured permission from the city of Dearborn to run a public school on his property. It should also be noted in this regard that one of the first buildings that Ford had transported to his Greenfield Village outdoor museum was the one-room schoolhouse in which he was educated. In fact, the village itself was assembled to serve an educational function, as Ford used it to represent the values that he felt Americans should hold most dear. For more on this topic, see William A. Simonds' *Henry Ford and Greenfield Village* and the related discussion in Chapter 2.

Probably the greatest effect of motorization on education was the tremendous assistance that school buses and, to a lesser extent, passenger automobiles made to the rural schools' consolidation movement. Buses enormously expanded the geographic area that could be included in one school district, thus making possible larger student populations and broadening the course of study that could be offered. While buses as such are really beyond the purview of this reference guide, some mention of early developments in this area would seem necessary. Two "bulletins" published by what was then called the Bureau of Education, a component of the U.S. Department of the Interior, are worth examining. The first, by A.C. Monahan, was written in 1914 and is entitled *Consolidation of Rural Schools and Transportation of Pupils at Public Expense*. The second, in

1923 by J.F. Abel, was published under a similar title, *Consolidation of Schools and Transportation of Pupils*. The impact of motorization on the consolidation movement is clear from a comparison of these two bulletins. By way of summation, see Walter H. Gaummitz' *Availability of Public School Education in Rural Communities*, published in 1930, by which time the full impact of motorization would have been known.

In a similar vein, the increased mobility made possible much greater supervision of teachers within a local school system and of teachers and administrators by state authorities. In this regard, it might be said that the automobile brought to fruition the ideas first set forth by Horace Mann in the 1830s and 1840s. For a good review of conditions at a point where the car was just beginning to make its impact felt, see Katherine M. Cook and A.C. Monahan's *Rural School Supervision*, another bulletin of the Bureau of Education, published in 1917. Unlike the transportation of pupils, where passenger cars were always a supplementary means of conveyance (to horse-drawn wagons and then school buses), supervision work went directly from horse and buggy to the automobile and has remained there ever since.

Adult and Continuing Education

In addition to the education of traditional-age students, the car has figured, directly and indirectly, in a number of adult/continuing education efforts. For instance, it was quickly adopted by extension agents working for federal and state governments. (These agents, incidentally, frequently teamed up with traveling librarians [see below] for their "circuit ride.") Two early reviews of such work are contained in Grace E. Frysinger's U.S.D.A. circular *Home Demonstration Work, 1922* and Florence E. Ward's *Home Demonstration Work under the Smith–Lever Act, 1914–1924*, both published by the U.S. Department of Agriculture.

In addition, the U.S. Post Office, with its special rates for mailing magazines and books, has historically served as a type of bookstore. As a result, Americans, particularly those living in rural areas, received significant amounts of their reading matter through the mails. While the 1893 inauguration of rural free delivery (RFD) by the federal government and the testing of the Duryea brothers' first successful car that same year are obviously a coincidence, it is, nonetheless, symbolic, for the automobile really made RFD work and brought to the isolated not just news from family and friends but reading materials as varied as books that had been requested from town libraries and complimentary catalogs from Sears, Roebuck and from Montgomery Ward. The best general study of RFD is still Wayne E. Fuller's 1964 *RFD: The Changing Face of Rural America*, which includes reference to the automobile throughout.

Finally, back when the automobile was a relatively new invention, and its numbers were small, few people worried about how an individual learned to drive or to mechanically care for a car. One developed those fine arts through hands-on experience, sometimes assisted by an "expert" friend or relative and sometimes by written instructions. A book falling into the latter category, published originally in 1909, was Thomas H. Russell's *Automobile Driving Self-Taught: An Exhaustive Treatise on the Operation, Management, and Care of Motor Cars*, which, in addition to providing just what the subtitle promises, concludes with four separate lists of "don'ts" for motor car drivers and tire owners. Similar books appearing in the next decade include Julian Chase's *Motor Car Operation* (1910), H. Clifford Brokaw and Charles A. Starr's *Putnam's Automobile Handbook: The Care and Management of the Modern Motor-Car* (1918), and *Barney Oldfield's Book for the Motorist* (1919), attributed to the most famous race driver of his day.

By the 1930s cars had become numerous enough and the attendant safety problems serious enough to generate a movement for formal driver education/training in the schools. Symbolic of that movement was the publication in 1936 of a textbook entitled *Man and the Motor Car*, edited by Albert W. Whitney. Going beyond the mechanics of driving, this book is a serious attempt to change those habits and attitudes that are seen as endangering the public safety. Whitney concludes with a chapter entitled "The Automobile Millennium," a utopian view of what might be (or might have been) in the not-too-distant future.

This movement was further enhanced when insurance companies began to allow insurance rate discounts for drivers who had successfully completed driver education programs. It also provided an economic boost for private businesses specializing in driver training. An excellent, albeit brief (90-page) overview of these developments (up to the late 1960s) is provided by Frederick L. McGuire and Ronald C. Kersh in their *An Evaluation of Driver Education: A Study of the History, Philosophy, Research Methodology, and Effectiveness in the Field of Driver Education*. McGuire and Kersh ought to be the starting point for any inquiry in this area.

Finally, some mention should be made of those educational institutions that were created specifically to train men for work in the auto industry. One of the oldest was the School of Automotive Trades. Established in 1919, it became the Flint Institute of Technology in 1923 and part of General Motors in 1926, when it was renamed the General Motors Institute (GMI). Richard P. Scharchburg's *GMI: America's Co-Op College, The First 75 Years* is a fine history of the institute, which in 1982 became an independent entity as the GMI Engineering & Management Institute and is now called Kettering University.

Libraries

Libraries in the United States historically have been urban institutions. Although they were often among the first educational institutions to be founded in the American colonies, they seldom serviced the population in the surrounding rural area. Such a situation was unfortunate, particularly since the majority of Americans lived on farms and in rural towns until 1920.

A partial remedy for this situation emerged at the turn of the 20th century with the traveling library movement, with its horse-drawn "book wagons," the grandfather of today's motorized bookmobile, and "deposit stations," a form of untended branch libraries where books could be left and picked up by the borrowers. The coming of the automobile allowed initially for the expansion of both services and, ultimately, for a lessening of the demand for them. A number of early studies dealing with this phenomenon are interesting because of both the historical insights they provide and the missionary zeal that they espouse. In this regard, see the American Library Association's *Book Wagons: The Country Library with Rural Book Delivery*, published in 1922; Wayne C. Nason's *Rural Libraries*, a Farmers' Bulletin published in 1928 by the U.S. Department of Agriculture; and Ralph A. Felton and Marjorie Beal's 1929 *The Library of the Open Road*, jointly sponsored by the New York State College of Agriculture at Cornell University and the Library Extension Division of the New York State Department of Education.

The number of scholarly historical studies that discuss the impact of motorization on libraries is extremely limited. However, Michael L. Berger's "The Motorization of Library and Related Services in Rural America, 1912–1928," a chapter in *Roadside America*, edited by Jan Jennings, does provide a good introduction to developments during that period. Berger concludes that improvements in vehicular transportation led to increased library service, thereby expanding both the quantity and nature of books available, and multiplied the number of rural dwellers who could be classified as regular readers and that the availability of more material to read improved the quality of rural life. In addition, for a good overview of the bookmobile movement, see Eleanor F. Brown's *Bookmobiles and Bookmobile Service*. Unfortunately, Brown limits herself to a single-chapter historical introduction, with relatively little attention to the role that passenger automobiles initially played.

HEALTH CARE

In this section, we will examine community health care in the same generic way that we previously treated education. Since the focus of this chapter is on how the automobile impacted on social institutions, our primary concern here is with such entities as hospitals, community health services, and, of course, the general practitioner. In addition, this section deals only with the response to health problems caused by natural mental or physical ailments. Thus, material concerning highway accidents, drunk driving, and environmental pollution is found elsewhere in this guide.

To fully comprehend the changes in medical care abetted by the motor car, it is first necessary to know how that care was provided in pre-automotive days. For an insightful and lively autobiography of one doctor's life, see Arthur E. Hertzler's autobiographical *The Horse and Buggy Doctor*, a 1938 account of his professional experiences in Kansas. Despite the title, Hertzler does describe the transition to motorized transportation in a chapter entitled "I Go to the Patient."

As a group that depended on transportation for their effectiveness, physicians were among the first to embrace the automobile and to see its advantages over horse-drawn vehicles. (Possibly the first written testimonial by a physician appeared in a 1901 issue of the magazine *Horseless Age*, entitled "The Automobile in My Business," written by a Dr. H.L.S.) Two advantages frequently cited by doctors were the car's greater speed vis-à-vis the horse, which could often be translated into lives saved, and its mechanical nature, which meant that the physician did not have to be concerned about the condition of both his patient and that of his waiting steed. As early as 1906, the *Journal of the American Medical Association* published an extensive thirty-five-page article entitled "Automobiles for Physicians' Use," which consisted of numerous testimonials from satisfied doctors. Given the potential sales, from both doctors and the general public that trusted them, early automobile manufacturers were quick to dub versions of their cars as a "doctor's" or "physician's" model.

For the best contemporary views of how health care was affected by the automobile, readers are directed to studies and reports issued in, or concerned with, the 1920s. In this regard, *Rural Hospitals*, a brief (46-page) Farmers' Bulletin written by Wayne C. Nason for the U.S. Department of Agriculture is particularly worth examining. The relative isolation of farmers and small town residents from modern, well-equipped hospitals was a continuing concern at this time, and motorized transportation seemed to provide a way to minimize this problem. A broader perspective is taken by John C. Long in "The Motor's Part in Public Health," a chapter in a special thematic issue of *The Annals* entitled "The Automobile: Its Province and Its Problems." Finally, Michael L. Berger, in his *The Devil Wagon in God's Country*, has a two-part chapter devoted to the interrelationships between health care and motorization. The first explores how the automobile made possible the consolidation of services and abetted the rise of specialists. The latter is concerned with the environment and posits the interesting conclusion that the car initially *improved* the healthfulness of the environment by eliminating horse manure and dead horses from the streets, thereby reducing airborne disease. The popular press, particularly through the 1920s, contained numerous articles either crediting the automobile with improving the health of motorists or, conversely, blaming it for sickness or disease (caused by excessive motion or vibration). Such claims were largely unsubstantiated in terms of scientific research.

At first, there were few motorized vehicles specifically designed to transport severely injured or ill patients to hospitals or other medical facilities, although the doctor's car was sometimes used for that purpose. In fact, in the early days of the automobile, particularly in those areas with poor roads or severe winters, it was often common to rely on horse-drawn litters for such conveyance—what was lost in speed was gained in dependability. Nonetheless, by World War I, the motor car had evolved to the point where specialized ambulances were being commercially manufactured. In this regard, see Thomas A. McPherson's *American Funeral Cars and Ambulances since 1900*, a comprehensive, heavily illustrated history that takes the story to 1973. In the same vein, but primarily photographic, is Walt McCall and Tom McPherson's *Classic American Ambulances: 1900–1979 Photo Archive*. The late 1970s saw the sudden demise of ambulances based on a luxury car chassis (e.g., Cadillacs and Packards) with custom-built bodies. They became increasingly replaced by specially designed vehicles more akin to vans and light trucks.

Automobility for the individual doctor developed in a manner that probably would have surprised Hertzler and others of his generation. While the initial impetus was to make the physician more mobile, the final outcome was quite the opposite. Since it was felt that greater efficiency in numbers and effectiveness in care could be achieved by seeing patients in a modern office, the commutation roles were reversed, and the patient was expected to motor to the doctor's office or, in serious cases, be brought by ambulance to a centralized hospital. A significant aspect of this development is explored in *Journey to Labor: A Study of Births in Hospitals and Technology*, by Donnell M. Pappenfort. The "journey" in the title should be taken quite literally, as the focus of the book is on how attitudes toward, and methods of achieving, transportation of the expectant mother to a hospital have changed over time.

ROADSIDE BUSINESSES

Communities of all types also were affected by the growth of roadside business establishments that catered to the automobile. The two most important generic categories in this regard are facilities that provide fuel (the gas/filling/service station) and food (roadside/fast-food restaurants). In Chapter 7 the structures created to house these businesses are examined from an architectural or design perspective. Here, our primary concern is with the socioeconomic environment created therein.

Fuel

The preeminent work in terms of filling stations is John A. Jakle and Keith A. Sculle's *The Gas Station in America*, which traces the transformation of this necessity from its beginnings as curbside dispensers of gasoline in quart containers down to the electronic delivery systems and combination convenience stores of the mid-1990s. While comprehensive in approach, due attention is paid to the role that the gas station played in 20th-century American social history and popular culture and to its function as a mirror of an increasing mobile and consumer-oriented society. These themes are further reinforced by the inclusion of copies of over 150 vintage photographs and period advertisements to illustrate the text. Similar in approach but aimed more at the enthusiast than the serious scholar is Michael Karl Witzel's *The American Gas Station: History and Folk-*

lore of the Gas Station in American Car Culture. Witzel's unique contribution was soliciting anecdotal comments from former filling station owners regarding their remembrances of life on the "islands" and the folklore that grew up around the stations in the era when "full service" was the rule. Even more nostalgic, even celebratory, in approach are John Margolies' *Pump and Circumstance: Glory Days of the Gas Station,* which emphasizes the years 1920 to 1940, and William D. Jones' *Motor Cars and Serv-Us Stations.*

To the extent that social, cultural, and economic history can be read from period photographs, readers are referred also to *Gas Stations: Landmarks of the American Roadside,* by Wayne Henderson and Scott Benjamin; *Roadside Memories: A Collection of Vintage Gas Station Photographs,* by Todd P. Helms and Chip Flohe, covering the first seventy years of the 20th century; *American Service Stations, 1935 through 1943 Photo Archive,* edited by M. Kirn; and, more specifically, *Phillips 66, 1945 through 54 Photo Archive,* also edited by Kirn. All of the above feature vintage photos of stations, pumps and other equipment, related amenities, and their attendants (often in unique uniforms), some of them taken by such prominent photographers as Walker Evans and Dorothea Lange.

Food

Most of the early roadside eating establishments were sui generis, and thus we have little writing on them. This changed with the emergence of franchised restaurants in the mid-1920s. The standardized menu, food quality, and ambience created a lure that many families found hard to resist, and the spread of the automobile accelerated the growth of such restaurants and scholarly interest in them.

Anyone contemplating research on this subject needs to begin with John A. Jakle and Keith A. Sculle's *Fast Food: Roadside Restaurants in the Automobile Age,* easily the best book on this subject. The authors provide a 20th-century history of the origins and growth of what they call "quick-service" establishments, with particular attention to the car's impact on their commercial development and the emergence of a new category of food, the latter meant to be consumed quickly and easily, usually with the fingers. Unique coffee shops, diners, and drive-ins are studied, along with the early franchises and corporate chains of today, in individual chapters categorized by type of food served. Readers interested in a general introduction to the entire industry should see *Fast Food: The Endless Shakeout,* by Robert L. Emerson.

The oldest roadside restaurant franchise that has been examined in a book-length work is White Castle, which began in 1921 in Wichita, Kansas, and has remained primarily an urban institution. Nonetheless, it established many of the principles that have led to the success of the more recent, geographically more disparate, roadside, fast-food restaurants. David G. Hogan's *Selling 'Em by the Sack: White Castle and the Creation of American Food* is the story of the development of that chain, its founder, Edgar Waldo "Billy" Ingram, and its contribution to the emergence of the "carry-out" style of eating and the hamburger sandwich as *the* American fast food. (The "sack" reference in the book title refers to White Castle's unique merchandising approach of selling multiple, small, square burgers to a single customer in a paper bag.)

For a good introduction to the place of the hamburger in American popular culture and the chain-restaurant industry, see Jeffrey Tennyson's *Hamburger Heaven: The Illustrated History of the Hamburger*. A similar work by Ronald L. McDonald (really!), *The Complete Hamburger: The History of America's Favorite Sandwich*, is of interest primarily for its authorship (a nephew of the founders of the original restaurant), although the historical anecdotes are fascinating and offer some insight into contemporary American food culture.

While early roadside restaurants like White Castle were aided and abetted by the automobile, they did not owe their existence to it. That honor goes to the "drive-in" restaurant, which, while introduced in the 1920s, flourished in the twenty-five-year period following World War II. Volumes devoted exclusively to this phenomenon include Michael Karl Witzel's *The American Drive-In: History and Folklore of the Drive-In Restaurant in American Car Culture*, a heavily illustrated, nostalgic account that captures well the allure of such establishments, especially for young drivers looking for a respite from their "cruisin'," and Jim Heimann's *Car Hops and Curb Service: A History of American Drive-In Restaurants, 1920–1960*, similar in concept to the foregoing but with a heavier emphasis on the evolving design of such eateries. A unique aspect of the culture of such restaurants was service by "car hops" (waitresses) on roller skates.

In the last three decades, the nationally franchised fast-food restaurant has come to dominate the roadside eating scene, largely pushing aside such regional precursors as the Pig Stand, Richard's, and Howard Johnson's. Despite their relative newness, or possibly because of it, these fast-food establishments have become an acknowledged part of American culture and thus the object of scholarly inquiry—with McDonald's the leader on both counts.

John F. Love's *McDonald's: Behind the Arches* is the best work on that subject, explaining the complex organization of entrepreneurs and the marketing strategies that made possible the creation of a multibillion-dollar business that has become part of the very fiber of contemporary America. The incredible cultural influence of McDonald's in the late 1970s and early 1980s is examined in *The World of Ronald McDonald* and *Ronald Revisited: The World of Ronald McDonald*, respectively, both of which are collections of scholarly essays edited by Marshall Fishwick. (The former first appeared as a special thematic issue of the *Journal of American Culture.*) *Grinding It Out: The Making of McDonald's* is a history of the company written (with assistance) by Ray Kroc, the man who made it into a franchised phenomenon that changed the way we eat. Finally, *Big Mac: The Unauthorized Story of McDonald's*, by Maxwell Boas, is a highly critical account, based on investigative reporting, of everything from the quality of the food, to the company's hiring practices.

We have far less on the competition. James W. McLamore has written *The

Burger King: Jim McLamore and the Building of an Empire, an insider's account of the calculated rise of that company, with attention to the competition with McDonald's for the minds, hearts, and stomachs of America. R. David Thomas' *Dave's Way: A New Approach to Old-Fashioned Success* is a combination autobiography and business advice manual by the man who founded Wendy's in 1969, naming it after his daughter. Unfortunately, we are still waiting for similar auto/biographies and, eventually, comparative studies involving the other contemporary nationwide fast-food outlets.

Finally, some mention needs to be made of that form of roadside restaurant generically referred to as the "diner." Although architecturally similar, such establishments are individually (often family-) owned. While diners have tended to be primarily urban institutions, they have spread out along highways and thus have come to serve both townspeople and travelers. We lack a scholarly history of the subject, but a number of popular, heavily illustrated works provide a more than adequate introductory survey. Among the better ones are *The American Diner*, by Michael Karl Witzel, a cultural history of the diners of the past and present, with emphasis on their architecture and interior decor, their portrayal in films, television, and popular music, and the memorabilia associated with them; *American Diner: Then and Now*, by Richard J.S. Gutman, which traces its evolution from a horse-drawn wagon navigating urban streets in search of hungry night workers to the stationary stainless steel, glass-brick, and neon buildings that have achieved nearly cult status; *Diners*, by John Baeder, which features his watercolor paintings of both historic and contemporary diners from across the country, combined with a text that includes the history of each structure, anecdotes concerning it, culinary offerings, and the reminiscences of owners, managers, and patrons; and *Diners*, by Karen Offitzer, who maintains that food, architecture, and atmosphere define a diner and goes on to provide a historical survey of such eateries, with considerable attention to the roadside culture that has proven equally appealing to residents and travelers.

More specific are Robert O. Williams' *Hometown Diners* and Peter Genovese's *Jersey Diners*. The former is a tour of memorable diners of the Northeast (from Maine to Maryland), with the emphasis on the atmosphere created by the short-order cooks and waitresses who work there and the townspeople who form the regular patrons, all of whom provide Robert Williams with the type of anecdotes that distinguishes one diner from another. Peter Genovese's work is similar in approach, focusing on New Jersey, which has more diners (500+) than any other state. The author believes that such restaurants are more than places to eat and attempts to distill their essence. He sees diners as hangouts, community centers, and unofficial town halls where everyone meets on terms of equality—a true subculture of American democracy.

NOTE

1. Kenneth T. Jackson, "The Impact of Technological Change on Urban Form," in Joel Colton and Stuart Bruchey, eds., *Technology, the Economy, and Society: The American Experience* (New York: Columbia University Press, 1987), p. 160.

BIBLIOGRAPHY

Allen, Irving L., ed. *New Towns and the Suburban Dream: Ideology and Utopia in Planning Development*. Port Washington, N.Y.: Kennikat Press, 1977.

Altshuler, Alan. *The City Planning Process: A Political Analysis*. Ithaca, N.Y.: Cornell University Press, 1965.

American Library Association. *Book Wagons: The Country Library with Rural Book Delivery*. Chicago: American Library Association, 1922.

American Society of Civil Engineers. *American Society of Civil Engineers, Transactions*. New York: American Society of Civil Engineers, 1925.

Appleyard, Donald, with M. Sue Gerson and Mark Lintell. *Livable Streets*. Berkeley: University of California Press, 1981.

Atherton, Lewis. *Main Street on the Middle Border*. Bloomington.: Indiana University Press, 1954.

Baeder, John. *Diners*. Rev. ed. New York: Abrams, 1995.

Barker, Theo, ed. *The Economic and Social Effects of the Spread of Motor Vehicles: An International Centenary Tribute*. London: Macmillan, 1987.

Baskin, John. *New Burlington: The Life and Death of an American Village*. New York: W.W. Norton, 1976.

Baumbach, Richard O., Jr., and William E. Borah. *The Second Battle of New Orleans: A History of the Vieux Carré Riverfront-Expressway Controversy*. Tuscaloosa.: University of Alabama Press, 1981.

Berger, Bennett M. *Working Class Suburb: A Study of Auto Workers in Suburbia*. Berkeley and Los Angeles: University of California Press, 1960.

Berger, Michael L. *The Devil Wagon in God's Country: The Automobile and Social Change in Rural America, 1893–1929*. Hamden, Conn.: Archon Books, 1979.

Boas, Maxwell. *Big Mac: The Unauthorized Story of McDonald's*. New York: Dutton, 1976.

Bottles, Scott L. *Los Angeles and the Automobile: The Making of the Modern City*. Berkeley: University of California Press, 1987.

Brodsly, David. *L.A. Freeway: An Appreciative Essay*. Berkeley: University of California Press, 1981.

Brokaw, H. Clifford, and Charles A. Starr. *Putnam's Automobile Handbook: The Care and Management of the Modern Motor-Car*. New York: G.P. Putnam, 1918.

Brown, Eleanor F. *Bookmobiles and Bookmobile Service*. Metuchen, N.J.: Scarecrow Press, 1967.

Byam, Wally. *Trailer Travel Here and Abroad: The New Way to Adventurous Living*. New York: McKay, 1960.

Callow, Alexander B., Jr., ed. *American Urban History: An Interpretive Reader with Commentaries*. 3rd ed. New York: Oxford University Press, 1982.

Caro, Robert A. *The Power Broker: Robert Moses and the Fall of New York*. New York: Knopf, 1974.

Catlin, George B. *The Story of Detroit*. Detroit: Detroit News, 1923.

Chase, Julian. *Motor Car Operation*. New York: MoToR, N.Y., 1910.

Cherry, Gordon E., ed. *Shaping an Urban World*. London: Mansell, 1980.

Clark, Thomas D. *The Emerging South*. New York: Oxford University Press, 1961.

Colton, Joel, and Stuart Bruchey, eds. *Technology, the Economy, and Society: The American Experience*. New York: Columbia University Press, 1987.

Cowgill, Donald O. *Mobile Homes: A Study of Trailer Life*. Washington, D.C.: American Council on Public Affairs, 1941.

Cranmer, Horace J. *New Jersey in the Automobile Age: A History of Transportation*. Princeton, N.J.: D. Van Nostrand, 1964.

Crow, Carl. *The City of Flint Grows Up: The Success Story of an American Community*. New York: Harper, 1945.

Dahlheimer, Harry. *A History of the Mechanics Education Society of America in Detroit, from Its Inception in 1933 through 1937*. Detroit: Wayne University Press, 1951.

Dandaneau, Steven P. *A Town Abandoned: Flint, Michigan, Confronts Deindustrialization*. Albany: State University of New York Press, 1996.

Davies, Richard O. *The Age of Asphalt: The Automobile, the Freeway, and the Condition of Metropolitan America*. Philadelphia: J.B. Lippincott, 1975.

Doster, Alexis, III, Joe Goodwin, and Robert C. Post. *The American Land*. Washington, D.C.: Smithsonian Exposition Books, 1979.

Douglass, Harlan P. *The Suburban Trend*. New York and London: Century, 1925.

Drury, Margaret J. *Mobile Homes: The Unrecognized Revolution in American Housing*. Rev. ed. New York: Praeger, 1972.

Dudley, Kathryn Marie. *The End of the Line: Lost Jobs, New Lives in Postindustrial America*. Chicago: University of Chicago Press, 1994.

Ebner, Michael H. *Creating Chicago's North Shore: A Suburban History*. Chicago: University of Chicago Press, 1988.

Edsforth, Ronald. *Class Conflict and Cultural Consensus: The Making of a Mass Consumer Society in Flint, Michigan*. New Brunswick, N.J.: Rutgers University Press, 1987.

Emerson, Robert L. *Fast Food: The Endless Shakeout*. Rev. ed. New York: Lebhar-Friedman, 1982.

Felton, Ralph A., and Marjorie Beal. *The Library of the Open Road*. Ithaca, N.Y.: New York State College of Agriculture at Cornell, 1929.

Fishman, Robert. *Bourgeois Utopias: The Rise and Fall of Suburbia*. New York: Basic Books, 1987.

Fishwick, Marshall, ed. *Ronald Revisited: The World of Ronald McDonald*. Bowling Green, Ohio: Bowling Green University Popular Press, 1983.

Fishwick, Marshall, ed. *The World of Ronald McDonald*. Bowling Green, Ohio: Bowling Green University Popular Press, 1983.

Fogelson, Robert M. *The Fragmented Metropolis: Los Angeles, 1850–1930*. Cambridge, Mass.: Harvard University Press, 1967.

Fortune, Editorial Staff of. *The Exploding Metropolis*. Westport, Conn.: Greenwood Press, 1976 (originally published in 1958).

Foster, Mark S. *From Streetcar to Superhighway: American City Planners and Urban Transportation, 1900–1940*. Philadelphia: Temple University Press, 1981.

Fuller, Wayne E. *RFD: The Changing Face of Rural America*. Bloomington: Indiana University Press, 1964.

Garreau, Joel. *Edge City: Life on the New Frontier.* New York: Doubleday, 1991.

Genovese, Peter. *Jersey Diners.* New Brunswick, N.J.: Rutgers University Press, 1996.

Gilmore, Harlan W. *Transportation and Growth of Cities.* Chicago: Free Press, 1953.

Glickman, Norman J., ed. *The Urban Impacts of Federal Policies.* Baltimore: Johns Hopkins University Press, 1980.

Gutman, Richard J.S. *American Diner: Then and Now.* New York: HarperPerennial, 1993.

Hebert, Richard. *Highways to Nowhere: The Politics of City Transportation.* Indianapolis: Bobbs-Merrill, 1972.

Heimann, Jim. *Car Hops and Curb Service: A History of American Drive-In Restaurants, 1920–1960.* San Francisco: Chronicle Books, 1996.

Helms, Todd P., and Chip Flohe. *Roadside Memories: A Collection of Vintage Gas Station Photographs.* Atglen, Pa.: Schiffer, 1997.

Henderson, Wayne, and Scott Benjamin. *Gas Stations: Landmarks of the American Roadside.* Osceola, Wisc.: Motorbooks International, 1994.

Hertzler, Arthur E. *The Horse and Buggy Doctor.* New York: Harper & Brothers, 1938.

Hise, Greg. *Magnetic Los Angeles: Planning the Twentieth-Century Metropolis.* Baltimore: Johns Hopkins University Press, 1997

Hogan, David G. *Selling 'Em by the Sack: White Castle and the Creation of American Food.* New York: New York University Press, 1998.

Hooker, Clarence. *Life in the Shadows of the Crystal Palace, 1910–1927: Ford Workers in the Model T Era.* Bowling Green, Ohio: Bowling Green University Popular Press, 1997.

Hoyman, Michele M. *Power Steering: Global Automakers and the Transformation of Rural Communities.* Lawrence: University Press of Kansas, 1997.

Jackson, John Brinckerhoff [J.B.]. *A Sense of Place, a Sense of Time.* New Haven, Conn.: Yale University Press, 1994.

Jackson, Kenneth T. *Crabgrass Frontier: The Suburbanization of the United States.* New York: Oxford University Press, 1985.

Jacobs, Jane. *The Death and Life of Great American Cities.* New York: Random House, 1961.

Jakle, John A. *The American Small Town: Twentieth-Century Place Images.* Hamden, Conn.: Archon Books, 1982.

Jakle, John A., and Keith A. Sculle. *Fast Food: Roadside Restaurants in the Automobile Age.* Baltimore: Johns Hopkins University Press, 1999.

Jakle, John A., and Keith A. Sculle. *The Gas Station in America.* Baltimore: Johns Hopkins University Press, 1994.

Jennings, Jan, ed. *Roadside America: The Automobile in Design and Culture.* Ames: Iowa State University Press, 1990.

Johnson, Sheila K. *Idle Haven: Community Building among the Working-Class Retired.* Berkeley: University of California Press, 1971.

Jones, William D. *Motor Cars and Serv-Us Stations.* Aberdeen, Wash.: Jones Photo, 1998.

Keating, Ann Durkin. *Building Chicago: Suburban Developers and the Creation of a Divided Metropolis.* Columbus: Ohio State University Press, 1988.

Kelly, Barbara M., ed. *Suburbia Re-Examined.* Westport, Conn.: Greenwood Press, 1989.

King, Clyde L., ed. "The Automobile: Its Province and Problems." *The Annals of the*

Academy of Political and Social Science. 116 (November 1924): iii–279, 289–292.

Kirby, Ronald *et al. Para-Transit: Neglected Options for Future Mobility*. Washington, D.C.: Urban Institute, 1975.

Kirn, M., ed. *American Service Stations, 1935 through 1943 Photo Archive: Photographs from the Library of Congress and the Phillips Petroleum Company Corporate Archives*. Minneapolis: Iconografix, 1995.

Kirn, M., ed. *Phillips 66, 1945 through 1954 Photo Archive: Photographs from the Phillips Petroleum Company Corporate Archives*. Osceola, Wisc.: Iconografix, 1996.

Kroc, Ray, and Robert Anderson. *Grinding It Out: The Making of McDonald's*. New York: St. Martin's Press, 1990.

Kunstler, James H. *The Geography of Nowhere: The Rise and Decline of America's Man-Made Landscape*. New York: Simon & Schuster, 1994.

Landau, Robert, and James Phillippi. *Airstream*. Salt Lake City: Peregrine Smith Books, 1984.

Ling, Peter J. *America and the Automobile: Technology, Reform, and Social Change*. New York: Manchester University Press, 1990.

Longstreth, Richard. *City Center to Regional Mall: Architecture, the Automobile, and Retailing in Los Angeles, 1920–1950*. Cambridge, Mass.: MIT Press, 1997.

Longstreth, Richard. *The Drive-In, the Supermarket, and the Transformation of Commercial Space in Los Angeles, 1914–1941*. Cambridge, Mass.: MIT Press, 1999.

Love, John F. *McDonald's: Behind the Arches*. Rev. ed. New York: Bantam Books, 1995.

Lupo, Alan, Frank Colcord, and Edmund P. Fowler. *Rites of Way: The Politics of Transportation in Boston and the U.S. City*. Boston: Little, Brown, 1971.

Lynd, Robert S., and Helen Merrell Lynd. *Middletown: A Study in Contemporary American Culture*. New York: Harcourt, Brace, 1929.

Maines, George H. *Men, a City, and a Buick*. Flint, Mich.: Author, 1953.

Margolies, John. *Pump and Circumstance: Glory Days of the Gas Station*. Boston: Bulfinch Press/Little, Brown, 1993.

McCall, Walt, and Tom McPherson. *Classic American Ambulances: 1900–1979 Photo Archive*. Hudson, Wisc.: Iconografix, 1999.

McDonald, Ronald L. *The Complete Hamburger: The History of America's Favorite Sandwich*. Secaucus, N.J.: Birch Lane Press, 1997.

McGuire, Frederick L., and Ronald C. Kersh. *An Evaluation of Driver Education: A Study of History, Philosophy, Research Methodology, and Effectiveness in the Field of Driver Education*. Berkeley: University of California Press, 1969.

McKenzie, Roderick D. *The Metropolitan Community*. New York: Russell and Russell, 1967.

McLamore, James W. *The Burger King: Jim McLamore and the Building of an Empire*. New York: McGraw-Hill, 1998.

McPherson, Thomas A. *American Funeral Cars and Ambulances since 1900*. Glen Elyn, Ill.: Crestline, 1973.

McShane, Clay. *Down the Asphalt Path: The Automobile and the American City*. New York: Columbia University Press, 1994.

Moehring, Eugene P. *Resort City in the Sunbelt: Las Vegas, 1930–1970*. Reno: University of Nevada Press, 1989.

Mohl, Raymond A., and James F. Richardson, eds. *The Urban Experience: Themes in American History*. Belmont, Calif.: Wadsworth, 1973.

Moline, Norman T. *Mobility and the Small Town, 1900–1930: Transportation Change in Oregon, Illinois*. Chicago: University of Chicago, Department of Geography, 1971.

Muller, Peter O. *Contemporary Suburban America*. Englewood Cliffs, N.J.: Prentice-Hall, 1981.

Mumford, Lewis. *The Highway and the City*. New York: New American Library of World Literature, 1963.

Offitzer, Karen. *Diners*. New York: MetroBooks, 1997.

Oldfield, Barney. *Barney Oldfield's Book for the Motorist*. Boston: Small, Maynard, 1919.

Owen, Wilfred. *Cities in the Motor Age*. New York: Viking Press, 1959.

Pappenfort, Donnell M. *Journey to Labor: A Study of Births in Hospitals and Technology*. Chicago: Population Research and Training Center, University of Chicago, 1964.

Pearson, Robert, and Brad Pearson. *The J.C. Nichols Chronicle: The Authorized Story of the Man, His Company, and His Legacy, 1880–1994*. Lawrence, Kans.: Country Club Plaza Press, 1994.

Peterson, Kay. *Home Is Where You Park It: A Guide to RV Living as a Life Style*. Rev. ed. Livingston, Tex.: RoVers Publications, 1990.

Pound, Arthur. *The Automobile and an American City*. Detroit: Wayne State University Press, 1962.

Pound, Arthur. *Detroit: Dynamic City*. New York: Appleton-Century, 1940.

President's Research Committee on Social Trends. *Recent Social Trends in the United States*. New York and London: McGraw-Hill, 1933.

Preston, Howard L. *Automobile Age Atlanta: The Making of a Southern Metropolis, 1900–1935*. Athens: University of Georgia Press, 1979.

Rigsbee, David, and Carol Burch-Brown (photographs). *Trailers*. Charlottesville: University of Virginia Press, 1996.

Rockland, Michael A. *Homes on Wheels*. New Brunswick, N.J.: Rutgers University Press, 1980.

Russell, Thomas H. *Automobile Driving Self-Taught: An Exhaustive Treatise on the Operation, Management, and Care of Motor Cars*. Chicago: Charles C. Thompson, 1909.

St. Clair, David J. *The Motorization of American Cities*. New York: Praeger, 1986.

Schaeffer, K.H., and Elliot Sclar. *Access for All: Transportation and Urban Growth*. Hammondsworth, Eng.: Penguin Books, 1975.

Schaffer, Daniel. *Garden Cities for America: The Radburn Experience*. Philadelphia: Temple University Press, 1982

Scharchburg, Richard P. *GMI: America's Co-Op College: The First 75 Years*. Flint, Mich.: GMI Press, 1994.

Schenker, Eric. *An Inventory of the Economic Factors Influenced by a Highway Development Program*. East Lansing, Mich.: Highway Traffic Safety Center and the Department of Economics, 1960.

Schwartz, Barry, ed. *The Changing Face of the Suburbs*. Chicago: University of Chicago Press, 1976.

Scott, Allen J., and Edward W. Soja, eds. *The City: Los Angeles and Urban Theory at the End of the Twentieth Century.* Berkeley: University of California Press, 1996.

Sears, Steven W. *Hometown U.S.A.* New York: Simon & Schuster, 1975.

Simonds, William A. *Henry Ford and Greenfield Village.* Sunnyvale, Calif.: Stokes, 1938.

Sims, Blackburn. *The Trailer Home, with Practical Advice on Trailer Life and Travel.* New York: Longmans, Green, 1937.

Smitter, Wessel. *F.O.B. Detroit.* 3rd ed. New York: Harper, 1938.

Stilgoe, John R. *Borderland: Origins of the American Suburb, 1820–1939.* New Haven, Conn.: Yale University Press, 1988.

Stout, William B. *So Away I Went!* Indianapolis: Bobbs-Merrill, 1951.

Suarez, Ray. *The Old Neighborhood: What We Lost in the Great Suburban Migration, 1966–1999.* New York: Free Press, 1999.

Sugrue, Thomas J. *The Origins of the Urban Crisis: Race and Inequality in Postwar Detroit.* Princeton, N.J.: Princeton University Press, 1996.

Tarr, Joel A. *Transportation Innovation and Changing Spatial Patterns in Pittsburgh, 1850–1934.* Chicago: Public Works Historical Society, 1978.

Tarr, Joel A., and Gabriel Dupuy. *Technology and the Rise of the Networked City in Europe and America.* Philadelphia: Temple University Press, 1988.

Tennyson, Jeffrey. *Hamburger Heaven: The Illustrated History of the Hamburger.* New York: Hyperion, 1993.

Thomas, R. David. *Dave's Way: A New Approach to Old-Fashioned Success.* New York: Berkley Publishing Group, 1992.

Thomas, Richard W. *Life for Us Is What We Make It: Building Black Community in Detroit, 1915–1945.* Bloomington: Indiana University Press, 1992.

Thornburg, David A. *Galloping Bungalows: The Rise and Demise of the American House Trailer.* Hamden, Conn.: Archon Books, 1991.

Tunnard, Christopher, and Henry H. Reed. *American Skyline: The Growth and Form of Our Cities and Towns.* Boston: Houghton Mifflin, 1955.

Tunnard, Christopher, and Boris Pushkarev. *Man-Made America: Chaos or Control? An Inquiry into Selected Problems of Design in the Urbanized Landscape.* New Haven, Conn.: Yale University Press, 1963.

U.S. Bureau of Public Roads. *Highways and Economic and Social Changes.* Washington, D.C.: Government Printing Office, 1964.

U.S. Department of Agriculture. *Home Demonstration Work, 1922,* by Grace E. Frysinger. Dept. Circular No. 314. Washington, D.C.: Government Printing Office, 1924.

U.S. Department of Agriculture. *Rural Hospitals,* by Wayne C. Nason. Farmers' Bulletin No. 1485. Washington, D.C.: Government Printing Office, 1926.

U.S. Department of Agriculture. *Rural Libraries,* by Wayne C. Nason. Farmers' Bulletin No. 1559. Washington, D.C.: Government Printing Office, 1928.

U.S. Department of Interior, Bureau of Education. *Consolidation of Rural Schools and Transportation of Pupils at Public Expense,* by A.C. Monahan. Bulletin No. 30. Washington, D.C.: Government Printing Office, 1914.

U.S. Department of Interior, Bureau of Education. *Consolidation of Schools and Transportation of Pupils,* by J.F. Abel. Bulletin No. 41. Washington, D.C.: Government Printing Office, 1923.

U.S. Department of Interior, Bureau of Education. *Rural School Supervision,* by Katherine M. Cook and A.C. Monahan. Bulletin No. 48. Washington, D.C.: Government Printing Office, 1917.

U.S. Department of Interior, Office of Education. *Availability of Public School Education in Rural Communities*, by W[alter] H. Gaumnitz. Bulletin No. 34. Washington, D.C.: Government Printing Office, 1930.

U.S. Federal Highway Administration. *Social and Economic Effects of Highways.* Washington, D.C.: Federal Highway Administration, 1976.

U.S. Federal Highway Administration, Urban Advisors to the Federal Highway Administrator. *The Freeway in the City: Principles of Planning and Design.* Washington, D.C.: Government Printing Office, 1968.

Wallis, Allan D. *Wheel Estate: The Rise and Decline of Mobile Homes.* New York: Oxford University Press, 1991.

Ward, Florence E. *Home Demonstration Work under the Smith-Lever Act, 1914–1924.* Washington, D.C.: U.S. Department of Agriculture, 1929.

Warner, Sam Bass, Jr. *Streetcar Suburbs: The Process of Growth in Boston, 1870–1900.* Cambridge, Mass.: Harvard University Press, 1962.

Weiner, Edward. *Urban Transportation Planning in the United States: An Historical Overview.* Rev. and expanded ed. Westport, Conn.: Praeger, 1999.

Whitney, Albert W. ed. *Man and the Motor Car.* New York: National Bureau of Casualty and Surety Underwriters, 1936.

Widick, B.J. *Detroit: City of Race and Class Violence.* Rev. ed. Detroit: Wayne State University Press, 1989.

Wik, Reynold W. *Henry Ford and Grass-roots America.* Ann Arbor: University of Michigan Press, 1972.

Wilbur Smith and Associates. *Future Highways and Urban Growth.* New Haven, Conn.: N.p., 1961.

Williams, Robert O. *Hometown Diners.* New York: Harry N. Abrams, 1999.

Witzel, Michael Karl. *The American Diner.* Osceola, Wisc.: Motorbooks International, 1999.

Witzel, Michael Karl. *The American Drive-In: History and Folklore of the Drive-In Restaurant in American Car Culture.* Osceola, Wisc.: Motorbooks International, 1994.

Witzel, Michael Karl. *The American Gas Station: History and Folklore of the Gas Station in American Car Culture.* Osceola, Wisc.: Motorbooks International, 1992.

Worley, William S. *J.C. Nichols and the Shaping of Kansas City: Innovation in Planned Residential Communities.* Columbia: University of Missouri Press, 1990.

Wright, Frank Lloyd. *The Disappearing City.* New York: W.F. Payson, 1932.

Wylie, Jeanie. *Poletown: Community Betrayed.* Urbana: University of Illinois Press, 1989.

CHAPTER 7

The Automobile and American Culture

ARCHITECTURE, VISUAL ARTS, AND MUSIC

Given the profound effect that the automobile has had on American culture, it is not surprising that it has influenced the development of architecture, the visual arts, and music. Two books are highly recommended as introductions to this area of inquiry: *Automobile and Culture*, by Gerald Silk *et al.*, and *Roadside America: The Automobile in Design and Culture*, edited by Jan Jennings. More specific discussion of both works is included in the subsections that follow. In addition, Clay McShane's *Down the Asphalt Path: The Automobile and the American City* contains a good chapter on popular culture that explores the automobile's impact on ads, music, motion pictures, and children's literature.

Commercial Architecture

The automobile's impact on architecture has been profound. The motor car has contributed to the introduction of new architectural styles, such as "stream-lining" in the 1930s, and created the impetus for the development of certain building forms, such as the automobile garage and the gas filling station. How-ever, before there was change, there was adaptation. The commercial establish-ments constructed alongside motor highways in the first third of this century frequently echoed the architectural style of the colonial period. Architectural historian William B. Rhoads maintains that, in an era of rapid change abetted by the new means of transportation, Americans needed some reassurance that the bedrock cultural values of the country remained essentially traditional.

But while neo-colonial structures provided that reassurance, forces were at work that would ultimately radically alter the nature of the highway environment. An introduction to these developments can be found in the first two essays in Jennings' *Roadside America*. In "The Automobile: A Bridge between Engineering and Architecture," Folke T. Kihlstedt argues that the automobile created pressures for new building forms that forced architects and engineers to cooperate in ways that they had not done in the previous century. Robert M. Craig's "Transportation Imagery and Streamlined Moderne Architecture: A Case for a Design Typology" is more specific, theorizing that "the functional and aesthetic links to transportation and streamlining help to identify a unique building style, a style that mirrors an increasingly mobile American society" (p. 15).

Studies of the car's influence on architecture have focused on changes wrought in the design of commercial buildings, especially those that have come to be associated with roadside development. The first scholarly work in this regard is usually attributed to J.B. Jackson, who began writing for the journal *Landscape* in the 1950s concerning how the architectural environment of the roadside was being negatively affected by automotive traffic. An excellent collection of his work through the 1960s is contained in *Landscapes: Selected Writings of J.B. Jackson*, edited by Ervin H. Jube. See especially the essay entitled "Other-Directed Houses," in which Jackson laments the fact that commercial structures were being designed primarily to catch the motorists' attention, with minimal attention to questions of architectural integrity. A second essay in the same volume, "Life-Worship," similarly analyzes the architecture of the commercial highway strip.

Serious study of such roadside structures came of age in 1972 with the publication of *Learning from Las Vegas: The Forgotten Symbolism of Architectural Form*, by Robert Venturi *et al.* The authors take a much more positive view than Jackson regarding the commercial strip and celebrate it as a significant American contribution to architectural development. In their words, "Las Vegas is to the strip what Rome is to the piazza." In addition to analyzing such traditional elements of the commercial strip as restaurants, motels, and filling stations, the authors provide some pioneering observations on the nature of shopping centers, parking lots, and signage. Theirs is a pathmaking study of how our perceptions and the meaning that we assign to commercial space and structural form have been modified by automobility.

Contemporaneous with the Venturi *et al.* volume and probably equally significant is Reyner Banham's *Los Angeles: The Architecture of Four Ecologies*, one of which he designates as "autotopia," or the world of the freeway and its accompanying built environment. Given the symbolic view of Los Angeles as the prototype of an automotively centered city, Banham's pioneering observations and analysis concerning the physical development of the freeways and the accompanying sociological effects are must reading in this area of research. Chronologically more limited but nonetheless worthy of attention is *L.A. in the Thirties, 1931–1941*, by David Gebhard and Harriette Von Brenton, especially the sections concerned with the early "drive-in" establishments of that period and the development of the freeway system and the concomitant commercial strips. More building-specific but somewhat broader in geographic and chron-ological coverage is *A Guide to Architecture in Los Angeles & Southern California*, by Gebhard and Robert Winter, featuring notable establishments from the 1920s and 1930s.

More recently, Chester H. Liebs in *Main Street to Miracle Mile: American Roadside Architecture* offers the first comprehensive history of the development of roadside architecture. Interestingly written and well illustrated, Liebs' work is a serious cultural history that surveys a diverse collection of structures, in-cluding such research novelties as automobile showrooms, supermarkets, mini-ature golf courses, and drive-in movie theaters, and shows how these commercial structures mirror the national mood. A landmark book when first published in 1985, Liebs' work legitimized the scholarly study of the roadside landscape and is now generally viewed as a classic in this new field. More specific in focus is "The American Street" chapter in Spiro Kostof's *America by Design*, one of five chapters that explore how the design of the built environment has histori-cally reflected our needs and self-concept.

The most recent examination of how the automobile has influenced commercial architecture is *Roadside America: The Automobile in Design and Culture*, edited by Jan Jennings. Discrete chapters focus on filling stations, fast-food restaurants, diners, drive-in movie theaters, and parking lots. See especially Maggie Valentine's "Of Motorcars and Movies: The Architecture of S. Charles Lee" for the automobile's effect on the design of motion picture theaters; Daniel M. Bluestone's "Roadside Blight and the Reform of Commercial Architecture," with its emphasis on the early battles between roadside proprietors and reform-ers, a struggle that has continued throughout the 20th century; and R. Stephen Sennott's "Chicago Architects and the Automobile, 1906–1926," in which the author shows how buildings of the period were designed or adapted to accom-modate the new means of transportation.

A more personalized approach is provided by John Baeder's *Gas, Food, and Lodging: A Post Card Odyssey through the Great American Roadside*, which combines a collection of nearly 300 postcards drawn from the interwar period with the memories evoked by them in the author and others to create a journey through a roadside world of gas stations, diners, cafés, hotels, and main streets, a world that no longer exists. Similar in approach, though less successful, is John Margolies' *The End of the Road: Vanishing Highway Architecture in America*. Margolies is a photographer, and this thin volume is a collection of his pictures portraying motels, eating and drinking establishments, gas stations, and roadside attractions, together with a brief introduction. Although the objects photographed are more distinguished for their historical, rather than architec-tural, value, this is another interesting book for those who want to visualize the highway environment of a bygone era.

Roadside architecture in specific geographic areas also has been the subject of investigation. See, for example, the previously cited volume by Gebhard and Winter on Southern California and Thomas J. Schlereth's *U.S. 40: A Roadscape of the American Experience* for Indiana. The latter is an excellent study that examines changes in different building types, with special attention to service stations and diners. Will Anderson is the author/publisher of *New England Roadside Delights* and *Mid-Atlantic Roadside Delights*, two volumes that celebrate commercial architecture of the past and present in text and photographs. While obviously written for aficionados, these volumes can form an interesting introduction to the infinite architectural diversity of highway establishments, including gas stations, drive-in restaurants, motels, diners, and drive-in theaters. Finally, in a special issue of *The Historical Huntsville Quarterly of Architecture & Preservation* devoted to "Roadside Architecture," author Linda Bayer places the evolution of gasoline stations and motels in Huntsville, Alabama, in the broader context of the nationwide development of those service facilities.

In a more popular vein is *California Crazy: Roadside Vernacular Architecture*, by Jim Heimann and Rip Georges, primarily a photo-essay featuring *unique* and often bizarre West Coast buildings that have been constructed to service the myriad needs of the motorist. A fine essay by David Gebhard introduces the book. Broader in approach is Peter Genovese's *Roadside New Jersey*, in which that newspaper columnist goes beyond the superhighway to seek out quirky roadside attractions, including unique storefronts, signage, motel designs (both human and pet), and vernacular roadside art and messages.

These general works have been supplemented by studies of building forms that were developed, and have evolved, to fit specific needs generated by the automobile age. Chief among these forms are gasoline filling and service stations and the roadside restaurant. In regard to the former, Daniel I. Vieyra's *"Fill'er Up": An Architectural History of America's Gas Stations* is clearly preeminent. Vieyra combines a good historical narrative with excellent photographs in tracing the history of the filling station from its beginnings in the first decade of this century to the present. Michael Karl Witzel's *The American Gas Station: History and Folklore of the Gas Station in American Car Culture* includes a significant amount of information regarding the physical development of the stations. Witzel's book won the Thomas McKean Award for 1992 and a Cugnot Award of Distinction. John Margolies' *Pump and Circumstance: Glory Days of the Gas Station* is an illustrated history similar to the Witzel volume in concept but containing a valuable visual and print analysis of why and how oil companies used distinctive station architecture to attract business. Finally, Todd Helms and Chip Flohe offer *Roadside Memories: A Collection of Vintage Gas Station Photographs*, a visual record of the architecture of this "vehicular necessary" from the 1920s through the 1970s.

Although the motel as a form of tourist accommodation has been well studied (see Chapter 8), its architecture has been accorded far less attention. Several book chapters ought to serve as prototypes for more extensive works. "The Motel as Architecture" in *The Motel in America*, by John A. Jakle *et al.*, provides a chronological overview of the evolution of that building type, beginning with hotels and auto camps. (Portions of subsequent chapters describe the architecture associated with specific motel franchises.) Mary Ann Beecher's "The Motel in Builder's Literature and Architectural Publications: An Analysis of Design," a chapter in Jan Jennings' *Roadside America*, provides insights into the general design guidelines, aesthetic considerations, and suggested unit topologies and configurations that were recommended during the years 1930–1955. Finally, Elisabeth Walton's "Auto Accommodation" chapter in *Space, Style and Structure: Building in Northwest America*, edited by Thomas Vaughan and Virginia Guest Farriday, is a fine regional survey that traces the history of resort architecture (hotels, inns, lodges, etc.) built especially for the motorist during the decades between 1920 and 1950.

Besides the gasoline station and the motel, a third major building type that emerged to service the motorized traveler was the stand-alone roadside restaurant. While highway eating establishments existed as far back as the colonial period, they were usually adjuncts to inns and rooming houses and catered primarily to people on the move. The 20th-century version was quite different in form and function. The best and most recent work on this subject is John A. Jakle and Keith A. Sculle's *Fast Food: Roadside Restaurants in the Automobile Age*, a comprehensive survey that includes among its foci the architectural evolution of such restaurants during the past 100 years. The authors maintain that at first the primary need was to create a building and/or signage so unique that it caught the attention of the motorist so that he or she would stop and eat. With the advent of franchised restaurant chains and interstate highways, standardized architecture designed to reassure the out-of-town driver became the rule, and the company logo emerged as the most important design factor. Older, but still very good, is *Orange Roofs, Golden Arches: The Architecture of American Chain Restaurants*, by Philip Langdon, which provides an excellent history, well written and amply illustrated, of the design evolution of restaurants that owe their existence to the automobile, from (as the title indicates) Howard Johnson's to McDonald's.

More specific in focus are a number of books that concentrate on a particular franchise and/or type of restaurant. For instance, David G. Hogan's *Selling 'em by the Sack: White Castle and the Creation of American Food* pays due attention to the stand-alone urban buildings in the shape of a small castle, complete with turrets and battlements, that have served as that chain's symbol from the 1920s to today. *White Towers*, by Paul Hirshorn and Steven Izenour, is an earlier history of a similar chain, with a more decided architectural focus to it. Alan Hess' heavily illustrated *Googie: Fifties Coffee Shop Architecture* is the story of a restaurant style originated by a follower of Frank Lloyd Wright that featured radical, geometric lines, stainless steel, and expansive glass walls. Googies were part of the larger drive-in restaurant phenomenon. Jim Heimann's *Car Hops and Curb Service: A History of American Drive-In Restaurants, 1920–1960*, while primarily a photographic history, explores the architectural history of such restaurants and people responsible for them. In the same vein is Michael Karl

Witzel's *The American Drive-In: History and Folklore of the Drive-In Restaurant in American Car Culture.*

More specific in terms of food, but not necessarily of architecture, is Jeffrey Tennyson's *Hamburger Heaven: The Illustrated History of the Hamburger*, which, among other things, treats the design of hamburger restaurants and fast-food chains in a chapter entitled "Architecture and Signage." A broader perspective is offered in John F. Mariani's *America Eats Out*, wherein the author argues that restaurant architecture in general has evolved into an advertising device by which customers are attracted to a particular establishment, thus offering contemporary evidence to support the earlier views of J.B. Jackson.

Other building forms, while not called into being by the automobile, were nonetheless modified by its advent in terms of appearance and/or became associated with its lifestyle. The story of one of these, the diner, has been treated well in *The American Diner*, by Michael Karl Witzel, a cultural history of such establishments with substantial attention to the architecture, associated building materials (stainless steel, glass block, and neon accents), and interior decor; Gerd Kittel's *Diners: People and Places*, a photographic exploration of the exterior and interior architecture, as well as the patrons, of those few establishments that continue to exist; and *Diners*, by Karen Offitzer, who maintains in her historical survey that architecture is one of the defining qualities of a diner (the others being food and atmosphere). While the above studies and additional ones cited in the roadside restaurant section of Chapter 6 are interesting and valuable, the scholarly world would benefit from more analytical work on the phenomenon of the diner, especially as an architectural entity.

The motion picture theater and the industrial manufacturing plant also were modified by widespread acceptance of the automobile. In regard to the former, see Maggie Valentine's "Of Motorcars and Movies: The Architecture of S. Charles Lee," a chapter in Jan Jennings' *Roadside America*. Valentine shows how the design of the movie palaces of the 1920s, 1930s, and 1940s was influenced by the car styling of those decades and the culture that the automobile created. (She also includes a small section describing the architecture of the drive-in movie theater.)

In terms of industrial design, the most significant architect from the automotive perspective was Albert Kahn, who created an early building for Packard and then the pioneering Highland Park moving assembly line plant for Ford. Development of the latter is one aspect of Federico Bucci's *Albert Kahn: Architect of Ford*, the best book on the subject. More comprehensive introductions to Kahn's work can be found in *Designing for Industry: The Architecture of Albert Kahn*, by Grant Hildebrand, and *The Legacy of Albert Kahn*, by W. Hawkins Ferry. In addition, see Lindy Biggs' *The Rational Factory: Architecture, Technology, and Work in America's Age of Mass Production*, a scholarly study of the impact of changes in factory design on the modes of industrial production (and artistic expression), that uses the Ford plants at Highland Park and River Rouge as the primary examples.

Finally, although the literature describing their economic impact is discussed in Chapter 6, brief mention needs to be made here of the design and architecture of what has evolved into the contemporary, enclosed shopping mall. The best work in that regard is Richard Longstreth's *City Center to Regional Mall: Architecture, the Automobile, and Retailing in Los Angeles, 1920–1950*, a chronological analysis of the shift of commerce from the central business district to the outlying areas and the accompanying changes in retail architecture introduced to accommodate the automobile. Longstreth is particularly good at explaining the emergence of neighborhood and regional shopping centers and how the need for adequate parking determined the physical design and location of such autocentric retail clusters. Although he concentrates on Los Angeles as the prototypic experience, Longstreth also incorporates parallel developments elsewhere in the country. A different approach is taken by editor Robert D. Rathbun in *Shopping Centers & Malls*, a book that describes award-winning renovations that have been made to centers and malls that are at least fifteen years old. Although primarily an architectural reference manual (the third volume in a series), this book does contain "before and after" photos and drawings, along with data regarding tenant occupancy, merchandise mixes, and parking facilities that could be of use to the student of automotively related architecture. Scholarly articles analyzing individual malls, such as the pioneering County Club Plaza, developed outside Kansas City by J.C. Nichols in the 1920s, also contain some information on building and project design.

Before leaving this section, it should be noted that the commercial development of roadside architecture has not been without its critics. Probably the best work in this regard is the prizewinning (National Book Award) *Man-Made America: Chaos or Control? An Inquiry into Selected Problems of Design in the Urbanized Landscape*, by Christopher Tunnard and Boris Pushkarev. The authors describe the blight that results from unchecked development of the built environment and offer proposals for reversing that trend. See especially Part III: "The Paved Ribbon: The Esthetic of Freeway Design." Contemporaneous in time but much more of a highly negative polemic is Peter Blake's *God's Own Junkyard: The Planned Deterioration of America's Landscape*, with its criticism of commercial strips composed of fast-food restaurants, gas stations, motels, and so on. (Interestingly, within a decade, Blake had completely changed his view and was writing positive articles concerning commercial strips.) The architectural failings of roadside buildings are a subject also treated in "The Road," a chapter in Stephen A. Kurtz's well-received 1973 study entitled *Wasteland: Building the American Dream*. The topic of automotively related pollution of all types, including the contributions of the built environment, is treated in more detail in Chapter 11.

Domestic Architecture

It is not only commercial buildings that have developed or changed in response to the automobile; the design of the private house has been transformed as well. Some discussion of the car's impact on housing design and community development appears in almost every book concerned with the historical evolution of private dwellings in the United States. See, for example, Alan Gowans' *The Comfortable House: North American Suburban Architecture, 1890–1930.*

Although there is no book-length treatment devoted exclusively to the automobile's impact, there are a number of good book chapters and scholarly articles. Historically, the oldest of these may be Ernest Flagg's "A New Type of City House," which appeared in a 1907 issue of *Architectural Record.* Flagg was a New York architect who designed a home for himself that included a garage and a motor entrance. In the same vein is John F. Harbeson's 1924 short article entitled "The Automobile and the House of the Future," which contains some interesting prophecies regarding the size and function of individual rooms within private homes. It appeared in a special automotive issue of *The Annals,* entitled "The Automobile: Its Province and Its Problems," edited by Clyde L. King.

More scholarly and detailed are the contemporary articles and chapters that describe and analyze the evolution of the automobile garage. See, for instance, Jan Jennings' "Housing the Automobile" in *Roadside America,* in which she traces the early design decisions that led to the garage's becoming houselike or residential in character; Leslie G. Goat's "Housing the Horseless Carriage: America's Early Private Garages," an article in *Perspectives in Vernacular Architecture, III,* edited by Thomas Carter and Bernard L. Herman; and Folke T. Kihlstedt's "The Automobile and the Transformation of the American House, 1910–1935," a chapter in *The Automobile and American Culture,* edited by David L. Lewis and Laurence A. Goldstein. Kihlstedt analyzes the changes in domestic architecture, especially the addition or incorporation of a garage, that were introduced to accommodate the motor car and the way of life that accompanied it. Also good on the functional transformation of the garage is J.B. (John Brinckerhoff) Jackson's brief essay "The Domestication of the Garage," reprinted in his *Landscape in Sight.* For an exploration of the history and nature of a factory-made, metal garage, see "A Story of Prefabrication: How the Trachte Company Grew Up with the Roadside," by Carol Ahlgren and Frank E. Martin, a chapter in Jennings' *Roadside America.* Garages were among the structures manufactured by Trachte in the 1920s and 1930s.

Fine Art

Social realism has never been a very popular art form in American painting or music, and artistic paeans to technology have been few and far between. Nonetheless, the motor car still has been portrayed, either realistically or symbolically, in a considerable number of artistic works. The best and most complete book in this regard is John J. Zolomij's *The Motorcar in Art: Selections from the Raymond E. Holland Automotive Art Collection.* Drawing on items contained in the largest collection in the world, Zolomij presents paintings, lithographs, ceramics, metal sculptures, tapestry, and stained glass (and other forms of artistic expression) from the first third of this century. This volume was beautifully printed by *Automobile Quarterly* and won both the Cugnot and McKean Awards. Researchers should note, however, that the text is largely limited to informative captions and that the work is international in focus.

Possibly more satisfactory for the lay reader would be *Automobile and Culture*, by Gerald D. Silk *et al.* In the section "The Automobile in Art," Silk focuses on the symbolic portrayal of the motor car in art, and the emphasis is on painting, sculpture, photographs, and posters, principally drawn from the American scene. It is most successful when it treats the image of the automobile in modern art, less so when it attempts to show the interactions between that work and the society or culture in which it was created. Like the Zolomij volume, Silk's work is heavily illustrated, but beneficially not limited to works in a single collection. (The latter part of *Automobile and Culture* is concerned with questions of automotive design and is more appropriately discussed in that section of Chapter 4.)

Another good book on this subject is D.B. Tubbs' *Art and the Automobile.* Although it mixes European and American examples, Tubbs' profusely illustrated volume does explore an impressive range of artistic expression, from paintings of motor racing to 1920s custom coach building, from car mascots to photo realism. In addition, Germano Celant's *Auto Tattoo*, while essentially a photo album with a trilingual text, does present over 200 diverse examples of automotive art, with a decided preference for the bizarre. For a brief artistic overview of one aspect of motoring, see Thomas J. Schlereth's "The American Highway in Art," an illustrated essay in *The National Road*, edited by Karl Raitz. Finally, *50 Years of Road & Track: The Art of the Automobile*, edited by William Motta, is a visual history of that monthly magazine, featuring the best photographs, paintings, technical illustrations, cutaway drawings, and cartoons published therein from 1946 to 1996. Work by Charles Addams, Peter Helk, Walter Gottschke, John Lamm, Strother MacMinn, Toby Nippel, and Motta himself, among others, is included.

Probably the best-known works of art with an automobile theme are the Diego Rivera frescoes portraying the automotive industry in Detroit. Justifiably lauded as fine examples of worker realism in painting (Rivera was a Marxist), these frescoes have been the object of numerous studies and exhibitions. For a good contemporary (1939) introduction to the man and his work, see Bertram Wolfe's biographical *Diego Rivera: His Life and Times* and his later *The Fabulous Life of Diego Rivera.* Rivera himself has left us *My Art, My Life: An Autobiography*, written in 1960 with Gladys March. The best recent biography is Patrick Marnham's *Dreaming with His Eyes Open: A Life of Diego Rivera.*

Charles Sheeler is another internationally known artist whose interest in the industrial process led to works with automotive themes. A master of many media, including paintings, drawing, and photography, Sheeler was fascinated by the factories of the Ford Motor Company, and elements of them are depicted in many of his critically acclaimed pieces. For a scholarly analysis of his work in this regard, see Karen Lucic's *Charles Sheeler and the Cult of the Machine* and Mary Jane Jacob's essay "The Rouge in 1927: Photographs and Paintings by Charles Sheeler and Diego Rivera," which accompanies the Detroit Institute of Arts' exhibition catalog: *The Rouge: The Image of Industry in the Art of Charles Sheeler and Diego Rivera.*

Finally, Alfred Leslie is one of the few artists who have employed the medium of watercolors to portray American automotive culture. His *100 Views along the Road* is a collection of black-and-white paintings that were completed in the early 1980s. While the subjects of these realistic works will be familiar to anyone who has traveled the nation's highways, Leslie subverts this familiarity by using a number of artistic devices, most notably, through his representation of light.

Although the works of Rivera, Sheeler, and Leslie are important, they are individual pieces within a broader, essentially non-automotive corpus. More significant from the standpoint of this guide are those artists who devoted their entire lives to portraying the automobile artistically, usually in a racing setting. Paramount among these latter individuals in terms of two-dimensional art would be the late Peter Helck (1893–1988), whose work was internationally acclaimed for its vibrant realism. He collected his best work in *Great Auto Races*, which contains over 200 drawings and ninety paintings as illustrations for his history of motor racing from the turn of the century through World War II. He also was the author-illustrator of an earlier work, *The Checkered Flag*, covering the years 1895–1916.

Randy Owens is another artist who has devoted his creative efforts to motor sports. Clarence P. Hornung's *Portrait Gallery of Early Automobiles* contains over 100 color plates featuring the work of this artist, known for his brilliantly colored serigraphs. *Serigraphs: Ten Year Retrospective* is another collection of his Formula 1, Indy Car, and sports car racing prints by Randy Owens. A similar volume is *The Motorsport Art of Michael Turner*, which collects in one thin (96-page) volume some sixty-six of the renowned artist's black-and-white drawings and full-color paintings, created over a period of a half century. The accompanying anecdotes create a type of international, pictorial autobiography.

Photography

Photography has achieved increasing acceptance for itself within the artistic community, and at least four photographers of the automotive scene have achieved national recognition. *The Highway as Habitat: A Roy Stryker Docu-*

mentation, 1943–1955 is a catalog of his photographs depicting how our lives became increasingly intertwined with the roads that we traveled and the commercial establishments that evolved along them during the years in question. The catalog was compiled by Ulrich Keller, who also wrote an introduction. Similar in subject but different in approach is *Highway: America's Endless Dream*, featuring 100 contemporary color photographs by Jeff Brouws and thirty-seven black-and-white images by depression-era photographers, such as Dorothea Lange and Walker Evans, supplemented by cultural and historical essays by Bernd Polster and Phil Patton, respectively. The emphasis, both visually and narratively, is on the highway landscape as a cultural symbol of American freedom and mobility, the result of a synergistic relationship between that landscape and the people who motor through it.

In the mid-1950s, Robert Frank secured a Guggenheim grant to create a photographic portrait of life in the United States. The resulting photographs, first published in 1958 as *The Americans*, with an introduction by Jack Kerouac, were pioneering ones that established new directions for that art in the years ahead. Of special interest to us is the fact that more than a quarter of the photographs show the automobile and the road. More contemporaneous is Edward Ruscha, whose photographs in the 1960s portrayed the aesthetic dimensions of everyday objects. In this regard, see the following two collections by him: *Twenty-Six Gasoline Stations* and *Thirty-Four Parking Lots in Los Angeles*.

Additionally, Richard Ansaldi's *Souvenirs from the Roadside West* is an eclectic collection of over 100 photographs, with subjects ranging from unusual examples of the commonplace (neon and billboards, bars and restaurants, gas stations and motels), to nostalgic reminders of the "wild West" of the 19th century; *Vacant Eden: Roadside Treasures of the Sonoran Desert*, a similar photographic essay featuring the work of Abigail Gumbiner and Carol Hayden (with an introduction by author Jim Heimann), features images of automotive artifacts and architecture abandoned in the Sonoran Desert; Klaus F. Schmidt's *Signs of the Times* is a photographic collection that includes somewhat more mundane roadside objects, such as monuments, gravestones, mailboxes, and bus-stop signs; and *Car Culture*, edited by Marla Hamburg Kennedy, is an outstanding anthology of photographs from the turn of the 20th century through the 1960s. The work of such famous artists as Margaret Bourke-White, Dorothea Lange, and Ernest Haas provides a unique visual overview of the automobile's impact on American society and human behavior.

The art of photographing motor sports, especially of the Grand Prix variety, has become a genre unto itself. In that regard, see such collections as *Track Pass: A Photographer's View of Motor Racing, 1950–1980*, featuring the work of Geoff Goddard; *Track Record: The Motor Sport Photography of Maurice Rowe*, also for the years 1950–1980; *Formula One through the Lens: Four Decades of Motorsport Photography*, by Nigel Snowdon and Diana Burnett, covering the 1960s through the 1990s; and *Forty Years of Motorsport Photog-*

raphy, with images by Jesse Alexander. As might be expected, given the subject matter, all of the foregoing are heavily European in focus.

Closer to home are freelance photographer Stephen H. Baker's *Racing Is Everything: Images from the Track*, which includes candid shots of many of the great names in NASCAR and Indy car racing, together with the machines that they drive/drove; Chet Jezierksi's *Speed!: Indy Car Racing*, a photographic chronicle of the men and machines involved in the Indianapolis 500 and oval racing in general; and Craig McDean's *I Love Fast Cars*, a photographically brilliant (literally and figuratively) exploration of the much more mundane world of regional drag racing, with particular emphasis on the Rockingham Dragway in North Carolina.

Finally, some mention needs to be made of James E. Paster's "The Snapshot, the Automobile, and *The Americans*," another chapter in Jan Jennings' *Roadside America*. Paster provides an overview of the importance of the car as a subject for amateur photographers, presents a fivefold categorization of them, and then links his work to that of Robert Frank in the latter's aforementioned collection.

Folk Art

While the aforementioned literature analyzes fine art, there also have been studies of what might be termed folk art. Moira F. Harris' *Art on the Road: Painted Vehicles of the Americas* includes "kustom cars" as one of four major vehicle types drawn from this hemisphere, and Harrod Blank's *Wild Wheels*, a book written to accompany this artist-filmmaker's 1992 documentary about the "art-car" culture, visually portrays over forty cars along with the observations of the people who created them. Finally, Bill Gradante has authored a chapter entitled "Art among Low Riders," which appears in *Folk Art in Texas*, edited by Francis E. Abernethy. The "lowrider" phenomenon, described in more detail in Chapter 5, essentially is a Hispanic form of car customizing, the exterior designs of which are described in Gradante's brief chapter. (The professional customization of production cars is a topic explored in Chapter 4.)

If the automobile is indeed an object of folk art, then the vehicle itself can be treated as a piece of sculpture and, indeed, some automotive designers and stylists have considered it to be such. Readers interested in the artistic merits of *production* cars should see the "Design and Styling" section of Chapter 4. Here we are concerned with books that explore the professional customizing or physical reconfiguration of cars that created the "hot rods" of the late 1940s and the 1950s. The dominant names in that regard are Barris and Roth. An introduction to the work of George Barris and Sam Barris, at a time when they were the top customizing shop, is provided in *Barris Kustoms of the 1950s*, by George Barris and David Fetherston. *Hot Rods by Ed "Big Daddy" Roth*, by Ed Roth and Tony Thacker, features some of the former's more artistic creations. For a more general, illustrative history of the shops of Barris, Roth, and others see *Custom Cars of the 1950s*, by Andy Southard Jr. and Tony Thacker. A companion volume, *Hot Rods & Customs of the 1960s,* by Southard alone, photographically covers the next decade. Using the techniques of the trade, such customizers "chopped, scalloped, chromed, winged, lowered, louvered," and bizarrely painted their vehicles to become one-of-a-kind creations. Finally, the Silk volume mentioned above contains a more scholarly overview of this phenomenon in a chapter written by Henry Flood Robert Jr., entitled "Hot Rods and Customs."

The interesting and sometimes bizarre roadside sculptures that attract or accommodate the car's occupants are well treated and culturally analyzed in Karal Ann Marling's pioneering study *The Colossus of Roads: Myth and Symbol along the American Highway,* although one might have hoped for better illustrations of the mostly Minnesotan specimens that accompany the text; J.J.C. Andrews' *The Well-Built Elephant and Other Roadside Attractions: A Tribute to American Eccentricity*; the somewhat tamer in title, though not in content, *Roadside America,* by Jack Barth *et al.,* which also adds humorous commentary to the mix; *Only in America: Some Unexpected Scenery,* a collection of over eighty eclectic photographs by David Graham showing both the humorous and somber side of such architecture; and, most recently, *The New Roadside America: The Modern Traveler's Guide to the Wild and Wonderful World of America's Tourist Attractions,* a guidebook by Doug Kirby *et al.* Some of these attractions have developed "followings" significant enough to generate preservation movements after their economic viability has seemingly ended.

Automobile culture also has been an important presence in the comic strips throughout their history, the longest running and probably most famous of which is "Gasoline Alley," and the subject of countless individual cartoons. Unfortunately, there seems to have been no serious study of this phenomenon to date. What exists are primarily collections of the cartoon art, such as the pioneering 1905 *Auto Fun,* which contains cartoons, photographs, and commentary from the *Life* magazine of the period, and Jean Terry and Gerald A. Bennett's 1954 *Car-Toons.* An exception to this general rule is Elizabeth Moran's *Speed Racer: The Official 30th Anniversary Guide,* a tribute to the classic Japanese animated series that appeared on American television from 1967 to 1982 and that has attracted a cult following. (Books featuring cartoons primarily used for advertising and sales purposes are discussed under that heading in Chapter 3.)

Commercial Design and Advertising

While advertising as an aid in automotive sales is a subject treated in Chapter 3, it is appropriate to cite here works that focus on the artistic aspects of that profession. Prior to World War II, ad agencies often enlisted the assistance of artists of some note to create illustrations to accompany the text. The best collection of such work is Yasutoshi Ikuta's *The American Automobile: Advertising from the Antique and Classic Eras.* Coverage of another medium is provided by Jim Williams in his *Boulevard Photographic: The Art of Automobile Advertising.* Boulevard Photographic was the premier studio supplying car companies with distinctive ad photography from 1955 through the 1980s. Williams' book is a history of the work of photographers Jim Northmore and Mickey McGuire and a studio that used custom-built cameras and sets to raise automotive photography to a high art. In the same vein but more general in approach is *The Car and the Camera: The Detroit School of Automotive Photography*, a brief (96-page) survey by David Lanier Lewis and Bill Rauhauser that celebrates the work of those "shooters" who revolutionized automobile advertising in the second half of the 20th century, with due attention to the technological advances in photography and the interplay between American culture and marketing strategies.

Outdoor advertising is a sales genre that also has been transformed by the motor car, especially automotive tourism. Sally Henderson and Robert Landau maintain that there is something called *Billboard Art*, which mirrors the culture of a society and sometimes influences the other, more established arts. They trace the historical evolution of billboard advertising up to 1980, with examples drawn from the United States and Western Europe. *Billboard: Art on the Road*, a catalog for a museum exhibition organized by Laura Steward Heon *et al.*, can serve as another survey of this subject. In addition to a twenty-work retrospective of artist-designed billboards that were created in the last three decades of the 20th century and the introduction of five new billboards commissioned for the exhibition, the catalog contains small photographs and short descriptions of some 300 more billboards and three essays exploring the history, subject matter, physical creation, and siting of billboards. Narrower in focus is Steve Strauss' cleverly titled *Moving Images: The Transportation Poster in America*, which includes information on perhaps the greatest billboard designer of all—Otis Shepard. In addition, James Fraser's *The American Billboard: 100 Years* showcases approximately 200 examples of billboard art, including the work of Shepard and N.C. Wyeth. Finally, two collections by Wei Yew, *Gotcha!: The Art of the Billboard* and *Gotcha Twice!: The Art of the Billboard 2*, provide a broad range of examples through the early 1990s.

A precursor to the billboard was the practice of painting an advertisement on the side of a building. Such painted wall signs reached their apogee in the late 19th and early 20th centuries, although they continued to be in evidence until the 1950s. Cynthia Lea Haas' *Ghost Signs of Arkansas* documents in word and photographs (by Jeff Holder) this lost art which, as the title implies, tended to feature local products more than do contemporary billboards and was often viewed positively as breaking up the monotony of brick wall expanses. (Environmental issues related to outdoor advertising, including billboards, are a topic discussed in Chapter 11.)

More general in approach is *Signs of Our Time*, by John Margolies and Emily Gwathmey. Margolies' photographs record for posterity over 200 signs, ornaments, and vernacular structures, which, in turn, are grouped into five categories: transportation, main street, food and drink, roadside attractions, and motels. Both the text and the illustrations are heavily nostalgic, with little analysis of how these artifacts expressed meaning or attention to contemporary signage. John Baeder adds yet another dimension in his *Sign Language: Street Signs as Folk Art*, wherein the author/photographer showcases unusual signs that he has found in his travels across the United States and relates the circumstances under which he discovered them. Finally, in *Vanishing Roadside America*, Warren H. Anderson presents a collection of his full-color pencil drawings of motel, restaurant, and gas station signs prominent in the 1930s, 1940s, and 1950s, together with lengthy, descriptive captions, in an attempt to archive these signs as prime examples of a vernacular art form.

In addition, there are books that describe aspects of commercial or industrial design that have been influenced by the advent of the automobile. A broad theoretical introduction to this topic is provided in Ray Batchelor's *Henry Ford: Mass Production, Modernism and Design*, wherein the author does an excellent job of showing how the introduction of mass production led the "modernists" to believe that they could create perfectly designed commercial products that would bring happiness to the masses, only to be undone by the latter's yearning for the "style" of the past, such as Tudor-style suburban houses, and the power of consumers to determine the design choices from which they select.

In a more practical and down-to-earth vein, both literally and figuratively, is a series of books that concern the design of specific objects associated with motorization. Among these are Mimi Melnick and Robert A. Melnick's *Manhole Covers*, a volume including over 200 photographs (by Mr. Melnick) of interesting examples of these artifacts of the street drawn from across the country. An accompanying commentary describes the history of this form of urban industrial art, focusing on the design, manufacture, and use of manhole covers. Douglas A. Yorke Jr. *et al. Hitting the Road: The Art of the American Road Map* traces the origins (in the midteens), development, and disappearance (in the early 1970s) of the free oil company road map. Yorke *et al.* treat the illustrations that accompanied such maps as contemporary, artistic renderings of the landscape, architecture, and cars that inhabited the "roadscape" during different periods of American history. Yet another genre is the subject of *See the USA: The Art of the American Travel Brochure*, by John Margolies and Eric Baker. The authors present more than 200 examples of the eclectic graphics (and prose) designed to lure vacationists to a particular locale or site.

David Holland's *Dashboards* is a photographic history of dashboard design and instrumentation (and thus, indirectly, of motoring) from 1904 to 1973. Although the emphasis is European, American classics such as the Model T Ford and the Cord 812 are included. Finally, the ornaments (so-called "mascots") that have adorned the hoods of American automobiles have sometimes been viewed as a form of popularized metal sculpture. They are the subject of a heavily illustrated book for international collectors by William C. Williams, entitled *Motoring Mascots of the World*. Similar in concept and execution is Dan Smith's *Accessory Mascots: The Automotive Accents of Yesteryear, 1910–1940*, which is especially good in presenting the variety and diverse purposes of these objects. In addition, the Zolomij volume mentioned above discusses hood mascots.

Music

Aside from articles in periodicals, there is very little treatment of the automobile's influence on and portrayal in music. There is no book-length, scholarly treatment of the subject. In fact, only three volumes devote attention to it, and one of those is a reference work. Jan Jennings' *Roadside America*, oft-mentioned in this chapter, contains a chapter by E.L. Widmer entitled "Crossroads: The Automobile, Rock and Roll, and Democracy," in which the author maintains that "the automobile has exerted a hypnotic hold on the imaginations of popular songwriters" and traces that development from the beginning of the century to Chuck Berry and Elvis Presley. *The Popular Culture Reader*, edited by Jack Nachbar *et al.*, includes a chapter entitled "Croonin' about Cruisin'," in which author John L. Wright shows how the automobile from its inception was a "vehicle of musical inspiration" for popular songs, including blues, rock, and country music, and how that expression changed to mirror the times. In many respects, that brief chapter could serve as the outline for a full-blown monograph. *The Popular Music Handbook: A Resource Guide for Teachers, Librarians, and Media Specialists*, by B. Lee Cooper, devotes only one page to articles that discuss the interaction of cars and music.

This paucity of material on the subject is somewhat surprising, given the long association between motoring and musical composition. For instance, shortly after the turn of the century, songs such as "In My Merry Oldsmobile," with the memorable lyrics "Come away with me Lucille, in my merry Oldsmobile," were hits. Later, tunes like Bobby Troup's 1940s classic ballad urged us to "get your kicks on route 66" and, when popularized by Nat King Cole, added another dimension to the transformation of that highway into a piece of American folklore. Jackie Brenston's "Rocket 88," a reference to an Oldsmobile model of the 1950s and 1960s, was a song destined to reach first place on the rhythm and blues charts and to make a contribution to the birth of rock and roll. These songs were joined by such other popular hits as "Little Nash Rambler" and "Hot Rod Lincoln." Recognizing the influence of cars on popular music, the Ford Motor Company donated $250,000 to the creation of the Rock and Roll Hall of Fame Museum in Cleveland.

The automobile even has found its way into the world of classical music. For instance, Robert Moran, an avant-garde composer, has written a composition entitled "39 Minutes for 39 Autos," which, among other objects, calls for the use of thirty-nine auto horns and autos themselves, and another piece called "Titus," which requires an "amplified automobile and players." Similarly, one John Adams has composed "A Short Ride in a Fast Machine," a brief orchestral work. Others no doubt exist.

LITERATURE AND LANGUAGE

Of all the forms of cultural expression, it is in literature that the motor car has received the greatest degree of attention. Almost from its introduction, the automobile became a prime mover of fiction, in terms of both short stories and novels, and the subject of countless first-person narratives. In this section we examine works that offer insight into the varied impact of the automobile on fiction and poetry, its role in creating a non-fiction genre known as the "road book," and its use in folkloric writing.

Fiction

It is well beyond the scope of this guide to describe the countless number of fictional works that have made use of an automotive theme or setting in one way or another. However, mention needs to be made of the more significant works, if only to show the range of literature available.

Representative of early 20th-century novels with automotive themes published in the United States are C[harles] N. Williamson and A[lice] M. Williamson's *The Lightning Conductor* (1905); Harris Burland's *The Black Motor Car* (1905), possibly the first novel to mix crime (robbery and murder) with the automobile; Richard Harding Davis' *The Scarlet Car* (1907), which features the motorized kidnapping of a Tammany Hall lawyer; Edward S. Field's *A Six-Cylinder Courtship* (1907); C.N. Williamson and A.M. Williamson's *The Motor Maid* (1910); Victor Appleton Jr.'s *Tom Swift and His Electric Runabout, or The Speediest Car on the Road* (1910); Irving Bachellor's *Keeping Up with Lizzie* (1911); and Marvin West's *Motor Rangers through the Sierras* (1911).

By 1906 the motor car was well-enough established to form the basis for at least four multi-volume series for teenagers. Of these, the longest running was *The Motor Boys*, a twenty-two-volume series published between 1906 and 1924 and written by Clarence Young, a pseudonym for many different authors. Typical titles included *The Motor Boys on the Border* and *The Motor Boys over the Rockies*. In addition to cars, the boys' adventures included ones with motorcycles and boats. Purer in the sense of involving stories only about motor cars but less successful commercially was the five-volume *Auto Boys* series, written by James A. Braden and published between 1908 and 1913. See, for example, *The Auto Boys Vacation* and *The Auto Boys Big Six*.

Interestingly, although they started later, there actually were more books written with feminine main characters than males ones in this genre, if one includes only volumes in which the automobile figures prominently (as opposed to other forms of motorized transportation), for example, Laura Dent Crane's *The Automobile Girls along the Hudson*, the pseudonymous Margaret Penrose's *The Motor Girls*, and Katharine Stokes' *The Motor Maids by Palm and Pine* and *The Motor Maids School Days*, all which appeared in the two-year period 1910–1911. Subsequent volumes of these series found the girls/maids experiencing adventures in different geographic venues. For instance, see *The Automobile Girls at Washington, or Checkmating the Plots of Foreign Spies* (Crane, 1913) and *The Motor Girls in the Mountains, or, the Gypsy Girl's Secret* (Penrose, 1917). The *Motor Girls* series eventually was to include ten volumes; and the *Motor Maids* and the *Automobile Girls*, six each.

By 1916 automobiles had become important and numerous enough that they began to be linked with other American institutions, such as in *The Camp Fire Girls Go Motoring*, by Hildegard G. Frey, and to be embedded in other, longer-lasting, and better-known juvenile series books, such as the Franklin W. Dixon's Hardy Boys (beginning in 1927) and Carolyn Keene's Nancy Drew mysteries (beginning in 1930). Throughout these early juvenile series, one is struck by the degree of freedom enjoyed by the motorized teenage heroes and heroines in the post-Victorian period. For a good, though brief, introduction to this genre, see David K. Vaughan's "On the Road to Adventure: The Automobile and American Juvenile Series Fiction, 1900–40," a chapter in *Roadside America: The Automobile in Design and Culture*, edited by Jan Jennings.

Following World War I, automotive ownership among the vast American middle class was commonplace, and some of the more important writers of the interwar period began to include the car as an important symbolic element in their novels. Some of the more significant works in this regard are Booth Tarkington's *The Magnificent Ambersons* (1918), the Pulitzer Prize–winning novel in which one of the main characters becomes wealthy as an auto manufacturer; Sinclair Lewis' first novel, *Free Air* (1919), concerned with a post–World War I, cross-country "search for America" motor trip; F. Scott Fitzgerald's *The Great Gatsby* in 1925, with the automobile serving as the deus ex machina in this 1920s parable of social climbing; Louis-Ferdinand Celine's *Journey to the End of the Night* (1934), with its horrifying depiction of what it might be like to work in a Ford factory; John O'Hara's first novel, *Appointment in Sumarra* (1934), in which a car salesman commits suicide by carbon monoxide poisoning while in one of his vehicles; Upton Sinclair's *The Flivver King: A Story of Ford-America* (1937), which compares and contrasts the developing lives of Henry Ford and a worker in one of his factories—a deliberate attempt to aid the United Automobile Workers' organizing drive; and finally John Steinbeck's *The Grapes of Wrath* in 1939, the award-winning story of a migrant family whose lives are intimately connected with their automobile.

The automobile continued to be part of the literary scene in the years following World War II, including such novels as Henry Miller's *The Air Conditioned Nightmare* (1945–1947), a two-volume collection of stories and essays focused on the author's negative impressions of the United States as he motors through it; Flannery O'Connor's *Wise Blood* (1952), wherein the protagonist uses his Essex automobile not just as a means of transportation, but as his home and pulpit for the religion that he founds; Jack Kerouac's *On the Road* (1957), the "bible" of the counter-culture for almost a decade; John Updike's *Rabbit, Run* (1960), in which the main character "runs" away from reality in a lengthy motor trip through the South, interacting primarily with what he hears on his car radio; William Faulkner's *The Reivers* (1962), a Pulitzer Prize-winning novel of automotive adventures in Mississippi in 1905; John Steinbeck's *Travels with Charley in Search of America* (1962), which uses the familiar device of a cross-country automobile trip for the author's observations on contemporary America, as does the Kerouac book above; Erskine Caldwell's *Around about America* (1964), another book with a cross-country adventure theme; Tom Wolfe's *The Kandy-Kolored Tangerine-Flake Streamline Baby* (1966), which takes its title from a chapter devoted to custom car devotees and includes discussion throughout of the automobile's impact on American life; and William Saroyan's *Short Drive, Sweet Chariot* (1966), essentially an intercontinental motor adventure.

In addition, the car has played an important role in a number of contemporary novels of lesser literary quality but great popular appeal, such as James Jones' *Some Came Running* (1957), which features a significant driving lesson scene within it; Vladimir Nabokov's *Lolita* (1955), a large portion of whose action takes place while on a cross-country drive; Arthur Hailey's *Wheels* (1971), a novel concerning the lives of automotive tycoons and the industrial world that they inhabit; Harold Robbins' *The Betsy* (1971), similar in concept to Hailey's book; E.L. Doctorow's *Ragtime* (1975), which contains a satirical look at Henry Ford's religious beliefs; and Stephen King's *Christine* (1983), in which the automobile is personified as a monster.

A number of works, while not primarily concerned with automobility, contain a significant segment concerning it, such as Booth Tarkington's *Seventeen* (1916), in which the author uses the symbolic value of motor cars to convey status and to reflect upon the newfound freedom of youth; Sinclair Lewis' *Main Street* (1920), in which women use the automobile as a vehicle for escape; John Dos Passos' *The Big Money* (1936), which contains a chapter entitled "Tin Lizzie"; Robert Penn Warren's *All the King's Men* (1946), which shows how motoring is often used as an escape from reality in American society; Arthur Miller's award-winning play *Death of a Salesman* (1958), in which the protagonist earns (or does not earn) his living on the road; Joan Didion's *Play It as It Lays* (1970), which contains an excellent chapter concerning freeway driving in California; and, finally, *Brave New World*, Aldous Huxley's classic 1932 science fiction novel of a 25th-century dystopia, in which "Our Ford" is a type of godhead.

As might be expected, the novel is not the only literary genre affected by the adoption of the automobile by American society. One can see its impact in short stories written by such diverse authors as Isaac Asimov ("Sally"), Ambrose Bierce ("Moxon's Master"), Erskine Caldwell ("The Automobile That Wouldn't Run"), Arthur C. Clarke ("The Motor Car"), John Dos Passos ("Tin Lizzie"), Ralph Ellison ("Cadillac Flambé"), O. Henry ("While the Auto Waits"), William Saroyan ("1924 Cadillac for Sale"), and James Thurber ("The Car We Had to Push"). A brief collection of such writing is *Car Tales: Classic Stories about Dream Machines*, which contains pieces by F. Scott Fitzgerald, Jack Finney, and William Saroyan, among others. Similarly, *Road Trips, Head Trips, and Other Car-Crazed Writings*, edited by Jean Lindamood, is an eclectic collection of fiction, journalism, and poetry (see below) by the likes of Ernest Hemingway, John Steinbeck, S.J. Perelman, Allen Ginsberg, and P.J. O'Rourke. Finally, in *Ladies, Start Your Engines: Women Writers on Cars and the Road*, editor Elinor Nauen has brought together short fiction, non-fiction, and poetry written by 20th-century women, including Gertrude Stein, Joyce Carol Oates, Edna Ferber, and Emily Post.

Finally, the future of automobility and its past history have been the object of writing in the field of science fiction. For a good (though dated) overview of the treatment of this vehicle in such literature, the reader is directed to a text designed for secondary school teachers, *Grokking the Future: Science Fiction in the Classroom*, by Bernard C. Hollister and Deane C. Thompson. (Grokking refers to examining a topic with all one's senses.) Two of the more creative short stories with motoring themes can be found in *Alternate Histories: Eleven Stories of the World as It Might Have Been*, edited by Charles G. Waugh and Martin H. Greenberg. Steven Utley and Howard Waldrop's "Custer's Last Jump" has Benjamin Franklin inventing the internal combustion engine, and R.A. Lafferty's "Interurban Queen" presents a scenario in which the automobile loses out to rapid transit at the beginning of the century.

Fortunately, a number of books provide fine, analytical overviews of the subject of this section, with particular attention to the period after 1920. The most extensive and probably most often cited is Cynthia Golomb Dettelbach's *In the Driver's Seat: The Automobile in American Literature and Popular Culture*. Winner of the first Ralph Henry Gabriel Prize in American Studies, Dettelbach's work goes well beyond a narrative description of the motor car's appearance in fiction and the arts (including film and music) to offer the author's analysis regarding the cultural impacts of this form of transportation, especially in terms of formulating, undermining, and reformulating the American Dream. More specific in focus is Martha Banta's *Taylored Lives: Narrative Productions in the Age of Taylor, Veblen, and Ford*. Banta shows (not altogether successfully) how the quest for greater efficiency and productivity influenced an incredible range of literature, including novels, autobiographies, and fiction in women's magazines, and how these works often served as apologias for the concepts of system and order embedded in the management techniques of Frederick Taylor and Henry Ford. Finally, for an in-depth analysis of one aspect of the writing of a single author, see Dan Seiters' *Image Patterns in the Novels of F. Scott Fitzgerald*, wherein the author discusses transportation as one of five strands of imagery in those novels, with particular attention to *The Great Gatsby*.

Poetry

The automobile also has been the subject of poems by a number of nationally known American writers, such as e.e. cummings ("she being Brand/new" and

"XIX"), Joyce Carol Oates (*F---*), and Carl Sandburg ("Portrait of a Motor-Car"). Less known, though acknowledged to be one of the best poets of his generation, is Robert Phillips, whose fifth collection of verse, *Breakdown Lane*, contains the title piece and another poem, " 'Drive Friendly,' " with motoring themes. J.D. Reed's *Expressways* is a book of poems that, according to the author, concerns "the big middle of the country seen through a windshield." The best collection devoted exclusively to automotive poetry is *Drive, They Said: Poems about Americans and Their Cars*, edited by Kurt Brown, an anthology that includes the work of almost 100 contemporary poets, grouped thematically, including separate sections on "Men in Cars" and "Women in Cars." Among the well-known writers included are Elizabeth Bishop, Robert Bly, e.e. cummings, Rita Dove, Howard Nemerov, and James Tate. In the same vein but less extensive in coverage is *American Classic: Car Poems for Collectors*, edited by Mary Swope and Walter H. Kerr. In addition, *Working Classics: Poems on Industrial Life*, edited by Peter Oresick and Nicholas Coles, contains twenty-five poems that focus on the auto industry, written by generally lesser-known, but nonetheless distinguished, authors. Readers intent on seeing examples of doggerel are directed to Elsbery Reynolds' *Auto Line O'Type*, which is a collection of poems each of which mentions the Studebaker car in its final line. Laurence Goldstein's "The Automobile and American Poetry" is the pioneering study in this regard, which is a chapter in the collection that he and David L. Lewis edited on *The Automobile and American Culture*. For a broader perspective that does include the automobile, the reader is directed to Lisa M. Steinman's *Made in America: Science, Technology, and American Modernist Poets*.

The Road Book

The automobile also has been responsible for the emergence of a non-fiction genre that is often termed the "road book." Similar in nature to many of the early fictional accounts of cross-country motor trips, the road books are distinguished by their "search for America" and self-discovery themes. As such, they reinforce the observations of many that motoring is somehow conducive to self-analysis. While there are numerous works in this category, our concern here is with those written by prominent authors. The beginnings of this genre are usually attributed to Theodore Dreiser and his 1916 *A Hoosier Holiday*, an account of his drive, along with artist Franklin Booth, from New York City to Indiana. Given Dreiser's reputation as a novelist, this travel account helped legitimate the emotions that driving could engender and, more broadly, the automobile's role in serious fiction. In the same vein is James Montgomery Flagg's *Boulevards All the Way—Well, Maybe: Being an Artist's Truthful Impression of the USA from New York to California and Return, by Motor*, first published in 1925. The commercially most successful recent book in this genre is William Least Heat Moon's *Blue Highways: a Journey into America* (1982). The color blue is often used on maps to designate two-lane roads. Heat Moon traveled on 13,000 miles of them in thirty-eight states and subsequently wrote this celebratory account of the virtues of rural and small town America.

These and the similar fictional works cited earlier are the focus of Kris Lackey's *RoadFrames: The American Highway Narrative*. Drawing upon an incredible range of road novels and autobiographical accounts, the author concludes that this genre remains vital nearly a century after its inception. More importantly, he argues that the origins of the 20th-century road books lie in 19th-century American fiction, that the "open road" has yielded different experiences depending upon one's race and social class, and that it is curious, if not downright ironic, that a genre has grown up that uses a well-known polluter and consumer of our natural resources as a vehicle, both literally and figuratively, to criticize the environmental destruction of our industrialized society.

Folklore

A final area of literature and language that has been affected by the introduction of the automobile is folklore. To date, there is no book-length, published treatment of this subject. However, Jan Harold Brunvand's *The Vanishing Hitchhiker: American Urban Legends and Their Meanings* contains an entire chapter with citations entitled "The Classic Automobile Legends," from one of which the book's title is derived. Brunvand's goal is to discuss "the folk narrative stories that most people have heard as true accounts of real-life experiences." In addition, he notes that versions of these legends have often appeared in American fiction, for instance, in the work of such diverse novelists as Carson McCullers, Thomas Pynchon, and John Steinbeck. (*The Choking Doberman and Other "New" Urban Legends* and *Curses! Broiled Again!*, later books by the same author, also contains automotively related folklore.)

Humor has always been an important component of American folklore, and it should come as no surprise that automotive jokes emerged and developed along with the car itself. In the "Folk Art" section of this chapter, we briefly treat visual humor, primarily in the form of the comic strip and cartoon. Here, our attention is on motoring jokes that gained wide enough currency to be written down.

Unfortunately, there is no book-length scholarly study of this phenomenon. However, a number of books and articles are largely collections of automotive humor and jokes. Some of the earliest, published between 1905 and 1918, include *Motor Goose Rhymes for Motor-Ganders*, written by Herman Lee Meader and published in 1905; *The Automobile Joker*, containing both prose and poetry; *Automobile Jokes, Jests, and Joshes*, "told" by James the Chauffeur and described in its subtitle as "a literary joy ride"; and *Chauffeur Chaff or Automobilia: Anecdotes, Stories, Bonmots*, by Charles Welsh. Three of the earliest collections of humor devoted to a single manufacturer were the Presto Publishing Company's *Funny Stories about Ford* (1915), Joseph J. White's *Fun about Fords* (1915), and H.M. Russell's *Oh, That Funny Ford!* (1916). A recent example of the same genre is *The JokesWagon Book*, edited by Charles Preston. Given the enormous popularity of the Model T Ford and the Volkswagen "Beetle," it is not surprising that they should be the object of such attention.

While not a joke book per se, Jack Stevens' *Hooked on Old Cars* is a humorous account of the adventures of automobile collectors and restorers and, as such, is representative of the genre of narrative humor. Finally, it should be noted that almost any general survey of the automobile (see Chapter 1) contains at least a small section of automotive humor, especially jokes and anecdotes connected with the Model T Ford.

Before leaving this section, some mention should be made of a small genre of what might be termed "absurd" automotive literature. Included in this category would be such books as *Manifold Destiny: The One, the Only Guide to Cooking on Your Car Engine*, by Chris Maynard and Bill Scheller, which purports to show how one can prepare edible food by using the engine manifold as a stove top, and *The Original Road-Kill Cookbook*, by B.R. "Buck" Peterson, a thin volume that takes recycling perhaps a step too far.

Given the multitude of roles that the automobile has played in serious fiction, it is curious how little scholarly attention has been given to the impact of the motor car on the style and content of the English language. There has been no book-length treatment of the subject, although some related aspects of popular culture have been studied. For example, see Carol W. Gardner's *Bumper Sticker Wisdom: America's Pulpit above the Tailpipe*, wherein the author analyzes both the messages themselves and the motives of the people who display them.

FILM, RADIO, AND TELEVISION

In a 1980s article, Julian Smith refers to the relationship between the automobile and film as "a runaway match." His observation is an insightful one for two reasons. First, the motor car and the motion picture were invented and developed to the point of practicality at approximately the same time. In fact, as Smith notes, these two inventions were nourished by each other, with the automobile figuring as a protagonist in many early movies and film providing many Americans with their first views of the new means of transportation.

Second, the two inventions were matched most often in terms of stories involving a car chase, a scenario first popularized in the Keystone Cops comedies produced by Max Sennett and still very much a staple of contemporary motion pictures—witness such box office hits as *Thunder Road, American Graffiti, Greased Lightning, Smokey and the Bandit, Driving Miss Daisy*, and *Thelma & Louise*.

To date, there have been five noteworthy books on this relationship, only one of which can be termed "scholarly": *The Road Movie Book*, edited by Steven Cohan and Ina Rae Hark, a collection of sixteen insightful essays analyzing such films as *It Happened One Night, Easy Rider, Bonnie and Clyde, My Own Private*

Idaho, and *Thelma & Louise*. The road movie genre is seen as an artistic form for representing both the national psyche and aspects of personal identity (gender, race, class, etc.). Of the books aimed at the enthusiast, the best is Jack Sargeant and Stephanie Watson's *Lost Highways: An Illustrated History of Road Movies*, a collection of detailed essays on individual films as diverse as *The Wizard of Oz*, *The Wild Bunch*, and *Apocalypse Now*. Mark Williams, in *Road Movies: The Complete Guide to Cinema on Wheels*, provides brief, critical reviews of over 100 films produced since 1940 that have automotive themes. His introductory essay to that volume is insightful, and it does a good job of bringing order to an incredible mélange of motion pictures. More of a reference work is *Races, Chases & Crashes: A Complete Guide to Car Movies and Biker Flicks*, by Dave Mann and Ron Main, which describes some 500 films, their stars, and the cars, trucks, or motorcycles that are featured in them. Raymond Lee's *Fit for the Chase: Cars and Movies* is far less successful. Lee does little more than collate a large number of movie stills that happen to contain automobiles or portions thereof. While Lee does identify the make and year of the car, he does nothing to explain its relationship to the scene in which it is pictured.

The *Automobile and American Culture*, edited by David L. Lewis and Laurence Goldstein, contains the Smith piece mentioned earlier. In "A Runaway Match: The Automobile and Film, 1900–1920," Smith links the development of these two inventions, claiming a symbiotic relationship for the period under study. A second article, "Cars and Films in American Culture, 1929–1959," by Kenneth Hey, carries the story forward for another generation.

Although not explicitly *comparing* the development of film and cars, Marshall McLuhan's pioneering study, *Understanding Media: The Extensions of Man*, contains individual chapters on both. In addition, several of the themes that run throughout the book are applied to both automobiles and motion pictures, among other technological artifacts. One such idea is that some media are "hot," and others are "cool." The automobile is presented as an example of the latter, and film, of the former, and thus they might be viewed as complementary media (or forces). McLuhan may then provide a good, albeit unconventional, theoretical foundation for ideas such as those presented by Smith and Hey.

Finally, a number of literary works with automotive themes have been adapted with great success for presentation as motion pictures. Although these novels and short stories are treated in the "Literature" section of this chapter, they deserve mention here, largely because the film undoubtedly exposed more people to the story lines than did the original piece of literature. For example, see the screen adaptations of the following novels: William Faulkner's *The Reivers*, F. Scott Fitzgerald's *The Great Gatsby*, and John Steinbeck's *The Grapes of Wrath*.

Although less important from a literary perspective than the above motion pictures, a number of other post–World War II "box office hits" have had automotive themes. Among them would be *The Great Race* (1965), a transcontinental motor contest played for laughs; *Grand Prix* (1966), a story of the drivers' personal and professional lives; *Bullitt* (1968), which contains what is arguably the best car chase scene ever filmed; *The Love Bug* (1969), a Disney classic in which a Volkswagen Beetle is the hero; *Gumball Rally* (1976), the first and best cross-country, road race comedy; *The Car* (1977), a film in which the automobile, previously viewed as benevolent or an innocent tool, becomes a symbol of evil as a driverless vehicle terrorizes the countryside; *Tucker: The Man and His Dream* (1988), the biography of post–World War II independent auto manufacturer Preston Tucker; *Batman* (1989), with its Batmobile; and *Roger and Me* (1989), a documentary film that forcefully portrays the gap between Roger Smith, chairman of General Motors, and people affected by plant closings in Flint, Michigan.

Mark Smith and Naomi Black in *America on Wheels* list twenty-five memorable *racing* movies alone. One of these, *Le Mans* (1970), recently was the subject of in-depth analysis. In *A French Kiss with Death: Steve McQueen and the Making of Le Mans*, Michael Keyser and Jonathan Williams explore the complexities of producing such an action film, something that was made even more challenging given the ego and passion of the actor/racing enthusiast and the difficulties of blending actual race footage with simulated scenes.

In a different vein, there has been a continuing fascination with the individual cars that motion picture celebrities choose to drive and, in some cases, to have built for them. Although there has been no scholarly study of this interaction, a number of popular accounts indicate the direction that such investigations might take. The oldest of these, *Cars of the Stars and Movie Memories*, written and published by Floyd Clymer in 1954, is a scrapbook-like collection of pieces concerning both the vehicles that actors/actresses bought and the ones with which they starred in films. George Barris and Jack Scagnetti have written a similarly titled work, *Cars of the Stars*, which is a popular, descriptive account of individual movie (and television) stars and the motor cars that they owned, as well as the role of individual vehicles in motion pictures and television shows. Beki Adam's *Star Cars* is another book in the same genre that describes both American and European popular culture icons and the automobiles that they drove both in real life and on the screen. Most recently, there is John A. Conde's *Cars with Personalities*, a book covering the period 1896 to 1982. It blends brief, but informative, descriptions with contemporary photographs of over 500 notables, including movie stars, posed with the cars they owned or used in their careers. (It should be noted that at least two film stars achieved a certain degree of notoriety in terms of their avocational use of motor vehicles. Paul Newman won respect as professional race car driver, and the late Steve McQueen won kudos for his handling of motorcycles.)

In a related vein are those vehicles themselves that achieve a degree of stardom, such as the Batmobile. One of the chief designers of such custom cars has been George Barris, and his work is featured in David Fetherston's and his *Barris TV & Movie Cars*, which combines a history of the physical development and screen "role" of these cars with visual images drawn from studio archives, movie and television stills, and snapshots taken on location.

In addition, some related areas of the performing arts deserve serious, scholarly attention. For instance, relatively little has appeared on the phenomenon of the drive-in movie theater, which had a strong effect on American social life and mores for a quarter century before its recent eclipse. The best available work in this regard is Kerry Seagrave's *Drive-In Theaters: A History from Their Inception in 1933* (to 1992), a work that is aimed at the general audience. Don Sanders and Susan Sanders' *The American Drive-In Movie Theatre* is a heavily illustrated popular history which, besides the theaters themselves, features the design and function of marquees, snack bars, and playgrounds. Similar in concept to the Sanders volume, but less extensive in coverage, is *Cinema under the Stars: America's Love Affair with Drive-In Movie Theaters*, by Elizabeth McKeon and Linda Everett.

Similarly, there is no serious study of the use of automotive themes in plays and on the American stage. In 1929 Samuel French published Louise van Voorhis Armstrong's *Good Roads: A Play in One Act*. It is almost certain that there were earlier attempts to capitalize on this and other aspects of the motorization in the legitimate theater. It is well known that vaudeville and its predecessors often featured vignettes about automobiles, sometimes involving the operation of a real car onstage. Barney Oldfield, the legendary racing driver, appeared in at least one such skit. Although such props are generally associated with the period when cars were still novelties, the automobile was featured in at least one recent, long-running Broadway musical, *Grease*. Scholarship is this area would be welcome in its own right and as a base of comparison with developments in the motion picture industry.

Although radios were available as factory-installed equipment as early as 1923, there has been relatively little scholarly attention to that technological combination. For the time being, researchers will have to satisfy themselves with Donald W. Matteson's Moto Award-winning *The Auto Radio: A Romantic Genealogy*, a history that focuses on the years 1930 to 1942 and places the subject in the context of the sociocultural milieu of the times.

Finally, the interplay between television and motor cars is deserving of serious study. To date, only one scholarly work touches on this subject: Karal Ann Marling's *As Seen on TV: The Visual Culture of Everyday Life in the 1950s*. Marling maintains that how a particular person, product, or event was portrayed on television often determined the visual concept that the average American had of that entity and its role in society. She uses seven self-contained chapters to support her thesis, one of which focuses on the prominence of exceedingly long and extravagantly designed (e.g., tail fin-equipped) 1950s cars on television and at suburban curbsides.

There is a wide range of other possible subjects here, including the changes in the nature of holiday parades, such as that accompanying the Rose Bowl, occasioned by their motorization; the adaptation of best-selling novels with an automotive theme for television, such as *The Last Convertible* miniseries and *The Betsy*; and the use of nationally known personalities in car advertisements on television, such as Dinah Shore telling us to "see the U.S.A. in your Chevrolet" and Ricardo Montalban hyping the availability of "fine Corinthian leather" in Chryslers. Finally, the use of automobiles as characters in television shows— witness, most recently, "Kit" (a talking car!) in the very successful *Knight Rider* series and recall the Batmobile in the mid-1960s cult series *Batman* (and the more recent movie of the same name)—would be a productive area for further inquiry. In this regard, see Moran's previously mentioned book on the *Speed Racer* television cartoon show phenomenon.

BIBLIOGRAPHY

Abernethy, Francis E., ed. *Folk Art in Texas*. Dallas: Southern Methodist University Press, 1985.

Adam, Beki. *Star Cars*. London: Osprey, 1987.

Alexander, Jesse. *Forty Years of Motorsport Photography*. Santa Barbara, Calif.: At Speed Press, 1996.

Anderson, Warren. *Vanishing Roadside America*. Tucson: University of Arizona Press, 1981.

Anderson, Will. *Mid-Atlantic Roadside Delights: Roadside Architecture of Yesterday & Today in New Jersey, New York, and Pennsylvania*. Portland, Me.: Anderson and Sons, 1991.

Anderson, Will. *New England Roadside Delights*. Portland, Me.: Author, 1989.

Andrews, J.J.C. *The Well-Built Elephant and Other Roadside Attractions: A Tribute to American Eccentricity*. New York: Congdon & Weed, 1984.

Ansaldi, Richard. *Souvenirs from the Roadside West*. New York: Harmony Books, 1978.

Appleton, Victor, Jr. *Tom Swift and His Electric Runabout, or The Speediest Car on the Road*. New York: Grosset & Dunlap, 1910.

Armstrong, Louise van Voorhis. *Good Roads: A Play in One Act*. New York: Samuel French, 1929.

Auto Fun: Pictures and Comments from "Life." New York: Thomas Y. Crowell, 1905.

Automobile Joker, The: Complete Garage of Jokes in Prose and Poetry . . . in Which Is Depicted the Funny Side of Automobiling. New York: M.J. Avers, 1905.

Bachellor, Irving. *Keeping Up with Lizzie*. New York: Grosset & Dunlap, 1911.

Baeder, John. *Gas, Food, and Lodging: A Post Card Odyssey through the Great American Roadside*. New York: Abbeville Press, 1982.

Baeder, John. *Sign Language: Street Signs as Folk Art*. New York: Harry N. Abrams, 1996.

Baker, Stephen H. *Racing Is Everything: Images from the Track*. Bloomington: Indiana University Press, 1995.

Banham, Reyner. *Los Angeles: The Architecture of Four Ecologies*. New York: Harper & Row, 1971.

Banta, Martha. *Taylored Lives: Narrative Productions in the Age of Taylor, Veblen, and Ford*. Chicago: University of Chicago Press, 1993.

Barris, George, and David Fetherston. *Barris Kustoms of the 1950s*. Osceola, Wisc.: Motorbooks International, 1994.

Barris, George, and Jack Scagnetti. *Cars of the Stars*. Middle Village, N.Y.: Jonathan David, 1974.

Barth, Jack *et al. Roadside America*. New York: Simon and Schuster, 1986.

Batchelor, Ray. *Henry Ford: Mass Production, Modernism and Design*. Manchester, Eng.: Manchester University Press, 1994.

Bayer, Linda. "Roadside Architecture." *The Historical Huntsville Quarterly of Architecture & Preservation*. 9 (Fall 1982/Winter 1983).

Biggs, Lindy. *The Rational Factory: Architecture, Technology, and Work in America's Age of Mass Production*. Baltimore: Johns Hopkins University Press, 1996.

Blake, Peter. *God's Own Junkyard: The Planned Deterioration of America's Landscape*. New York: Holt, Rinehart, & Winston, 1964.

Blank, Harrod. *Wild Wheels*. San Francisco: Pomegranate Artbooks, 1994.

Braden, James A. *The Auto Boys Big Six*. Chicago: Saalfield, 1913.

Braden, James A. *The Auto Boys Vacation*. New York: Saalfield, 1913.

Brouws, Jeff (photographer), Bernd Polster, and Phil Patton. *Highways: America's Endless Dream*. New York: Stewart, Tabori, & Chang, 1997.

Brown, Kurt, ed. *Drive, They Said: Poems about Americans and Their Cars*. Minneapolis: Milkweed Editions, 1994.

Bruner, Michael. *Encyclopedia of Porcelain Enamel Advertising, with Price Guide*. Atglen, Pa.: Schiffer, 1994.

Brunvand, Jan Harold. *The Choking Doberman and Other "New" Urban Legends*. New York: W.W. Norton, 1984.

Brunvand, Jan Harold. *Curses! Broiled Again!: The Hottest Urban Legends Going*. New York: W.W. Norton, 1989.

Brunvand, Jan Harold. *The Vanishing Hitchhiker: American Urban Legends and Their Meanings*. New York: W.W. Norton, 1981.

Bucci, Federico. *Albert Kahn: Architect of Ford*. New York: Princeton Architectural Press, 1993.

Burland, Harris. *The Black Motor Car*. New York: G.W. Dillingham, 1905.

Caldwell, Erskine. *Around about America*. New York: Farrar, Straus, 1964.

Car Tales: Classic Stories about Dream Machines. New York: Viking Studio Books, 1991.

Carter, Thomas, and Bernard L. Herman, eds. *Perspectives in Vernacular Architecture, III*. Columbia: Published for the Vernacular Architectural Forum by the University of Missouri Press, 1989.

Celant, Germano. *Auto Tattoo*. Milano: Automobilia, 1986.

Celine, Louis-Ferdinand. *Journey to the End of the Night*. London: Chatto and Windus, 1934.

Clymer, Floyd. *Cars of the Stars and Movie Memories*. Los Angeles: Author, 1954.

Cohan, Steven, and Ina Rae Hark, eds. *The Road Movie Book*. New York: Routledge, 1997.

Conde, John A. *Cars with Personalities*. Keego Harbor, Mich.: Arnold-Porter, 1982.

Cooper, B. Lee. *The Popular Music Handbook: A Resource Guide for Teachers, Librarians, and Media Specialists*. Littleton, Colo.: Libraries Unlimited, 1984.

Crane, Laura Dent. *The Automobile Girls along the Hudson*. Philadelphia: Henry Altemus, 1910.

Crane, Laura Dent. *The Automobile Girls at Washington, or Checkmating the Plots of Foreign Spies*. Philadelphia: Henry Altemus, 1913.

Davis, Richard Harding. *The Scarlet Car*. New York: C. Scribner's Sons, 1907.

Dettelbach, Cynthia Golomb. *In the Driver's Seat: The Automobile in American Literature and Popular Culture*. Westport, Conn.: Greenwood Press, 1976.

Detroit Institute of Arts. *The Rouge: The Image of Industry in the Art of Charles Sheeler and Diego Rivera, in Recognition of the 75th Anniversary of Ford Motor Company*. Detroit: Institute of Arts, 1978.

Didion, Joan. *Play It as It Lays*. New York: Farrar, Straus, and Giroux, 1970.

Doctorow, E.L. *Ragtime*. New York: Random House, 1975.

Dos Passos, John. *The Big Money*. New York: Harcourt, Brace, 1936.

Dreiser, Theodore. *A Hoosier Holiday*. New York: John Lane, 1916.

Faulkner, William. *The Reivers: A Reminiscence*. New York: Random House, 1962.

Ferry, W. Hawkins. *The Legacy of Albert Kahn*. Detroit: Wayne State University Press, 1970.

Fetherston, David, and George Barris. *Barris TV & Movie Cars*. Osceola, Wisc.: Motorbooks International, 1996.

Field, Edward S. *A Six-Cylinder Courtship*. New York: Grosset & Dunlap, 1907.

Fitzgerald, F. Scott. *The Great Gatsby*. New York: Charles Scribner's Sons, 1925.

Flagg, James Montgomery. *Boulevards All the Way—Well, Maybe: Being an Artist's Truthful Impressions of the USA from New York to California and Return, by Motor*. New York: Doran, 1925.

Frank, Robert. *The Americans*. New York: Pantheon Books, 1968.

Fraser, James. *The American Billboard: 100 Years*. New York: Harry N. Abrams, 1991.

Frey, Hildegard G. *The Camp Fire Girls Go Motoring*. New York: A.L. Burt, 1916.

Gardner, Carol W. *Bumper Sticker Wisdom: America's Pulpit above the Tailpipe*. Hillsboro, Ore.: Beyond Words, 1995.

Gebhard, David, and Harriette von Brenton. *L.A. in the Thirties, 1931–1941*. 2nd ed., rev. and enlarged. Los Angeles: Hennessey & Ingalls, 1989.

Gebhard, David, and Robert Winter. *A Guide to Architecture in Los Angeles & Southern California*. Santa Barbara, Calif.: Peregrine Smith, 1977.

Genovese, Peter. *Roadside New Jersey*. New Brunswick, N.J.: Rutgers University Press, 1994.

Goddard, Geoff, with Doug Nye. *Track Pass: A Photographer's View of Motor Racing, 1950–1980*. Marlborough, Eng.: Crowood Press, 1990.

Gowans, Alan. *The Comfortable House: North American Suburban Architecture, 1890–1930*. Cambridge: MIT Press, 1986.

Graham, David. *Only in America: Some Unexpected Scenery*. New York: Knopf, 1991.

Haas, Cynthia Lee, with photographs by Jeff Holder. *Ghost Signs of Arkansas*. Fayetteville: University of Arkansas Press, 1997.

Hailey, Arthur. *Wheels*. Garden City, N.Y.: Doubleday, 1971.

Harris, Moira F. *Art on the Road: Painted Vehicles of the Americas*. St. Paul: Pogo Press, 1988.

Heat Moon, William Least. *Blue Highways: A Journey into America*. Boston: Little, Brown, 1982.

Heimann, Jim. *Car Hops and Curb Service: A History of American Drive-In Restaurants, 1920–1960*. San Francisco: Chronicle Books, 1996.

Heimann, Jim, and Rip Georges. *California Crazy: Roadside Vernacular Architecture*. San Francisco: Chronicle Books, 1980.

Heimann, Jim, Abigail Gumbiner, and Carol Hayden. *Vacant Eden: Roadside Treasures of the Sonoran Desert*. Los Angeles: Balcony Press, 1997.

Helck, Peter. *The Checkered Flag*. New York: Scribner, 1961.

Helck, Peter. *Great Auto Races*. New York: Henry N. Abrams, 1976.

Helms, Todd, and Chip Flohe. *Roadside Memories: A Collection of Vintage Gas Station Photographs*. Atglen, Pa.: Schiffer, 1997.

Henderson, Sally, and Robert Landau. *Billboard Art*. San Francisco: Chronicle Books, 1980.

Heon, Laura Steward, Peggy Diggs, and Lisa Dorin, organizers. *Billboard: Art on the Road*. Cambridge, Mass.: MIT Press, 1999.

Hess, Alan. *Googie: Fifties Coffee Shop Architecture*. San Francisco: Chronicle Books, 1986.

Hildebrand, Grant. *Designing for Industry: The Architecture of Albert Kahn*. Cambridge, Mass.: MIT Press, 1974.

Hirshorn, Paul, and Steven Izenour. *White Towers*. Cambridge, Mass.: MIT Press, 1979.

Hogan, David G. *Selling 'em by the Sack: White Castle and the Creation of American Food*. New York: New York University Press, 1997.

Holland, David. *Dashboards*. London: Phaidon Press, 1994.

Hollister, Bernard C., and Deane C. Thompson. *Grokking the Future: Science Fiction in the Classroom*. Dayton, Ohio: Pflaum Standard, 1973.

Hornung, Clarence P. *Portrait Gallery of Early Automobiles*. New York: Harry N. Abrams, 1968.

Horowitz, Helen Lefkowitz, ed. *Landscape in Sight: Looking at America/John Brinckerhoff Jackson*. New Haven, Conn.: Yale University Press, 1997.

Huxley, Aldous. *Brave New World*. New York: Harper & Brothers, 1932.

Ikuta, Yasutoshi. *The American Automobile: Advertising from the Antique and Classic Eras*. San Francisco: Chronicle Books, 1988.

Jackson, John B. *Landscape in Sight: Looking at America*. Edited by Helen Leftkowitz Horowitz. New Haven, Conn.: Yale University Press, 1997.

Jakle, John A., and Keith A. Sculle. *Fast Food: Roadside Restaurants in the Automobile Age*. Baltimore: Johns Hopkins University Press, 1999.

Jakle, John A., Keith A. Sculle, and Jefferson S. Rogers. *The Motel in America*. Baltimore: Johns Hopkins University, 1996.

James, the Chauffeur. *Automobile Jokes, Jests, and Joshes: A Literary Joy Ride, Originated, Gleaned, Garnered, and Compiled by James, the Chauffeur*. Baltimore: I. & M. Ottenheimer, 1918.

Jennings, Jan, ed. *Roadside America: The Automobile in Design and Culture*. Ames: Iowa State University Press, 1990.

Jezierski, Chet. *Speed!: Indy Car Racing*. New York: Harry N. Abrams, 1985.

Jones, James. *Some Came Running*. New York: Scribner, 1957.

Jube, Ervin H., ed. *Landscapes: Selected Writings of J.B. Jackson*. Amherst: University of Massachusetts Press, 1970.

Keller, Ulrich. *The Highway as Habitat: A Roy Stryker Documentation, 1943–1955*. Santa Barbara, Calif.: University Art Museum, 1986.

Kennedy, Marla Hamburg, ed. *Car Culture*. Layton, Utah: Gibbs Smith, 1998.

Kerouac, Jack. *On the Road*. New York: Viking Press, 1957.

Keyser, Michael, with Jonathan Williams. *A French Kiss with Death: Steve McQueen and the Making of Le Mans*. Cambridge, Mass.: Bentley, 1999.

King, Clyde L., ed. "The Automobile: Its Province and Its Problems." *The Annals of the*

American Academy of Political and Social Science 116 (November 1924): iii–279, 289–292.

King, Stephen. *Christine*. New York: Viking Press, 1983.

Kirby, Doug, Ken Smith, and Mike Wilkins. *The New Roadside America: The Modern Traveler's Guide to the Wild and Wonderful World of America's Tourist Attractions*. New York: Simon & Schuster, 1992.

Kittel, Gerd. *Diners, People and Places*. New York: Thames and Hudson, 1990.

Kostof, Spiro. *America by Design*. New York: Oxford University Press, 1987.

Kurtz, Stephen A. *Wasteland: Building the American Dream*. New York: Praeger, 1973.

Lackey, Kris. *RoadFrames: The American Highway Narrative*. Lincoln: University of Nebraska Press, 1997.

Langdon, Philip. *Orange Roofs, Golden Arches: The Architecture of American Chain Restaurants*. New York: Alfred A. Knopf, 1986.

Lee, Raymond. *Fit for the Chase: Cars and Movies*. Brunswick, N.J.: A.S. Barnes, 1969.

Leslie, Alfred. *100 Views along the Road*. New York: Timken, 1988.

Lewis, David Lanier, and Bill Rauhauser. *The Car and the Camera: The Detroit School of Automotive Photography*. Detroit: Wayne State University Press, 1996.

Lewis, David L., and Laurence Goldstein, eds. *The Automobile and American Culture*. Ann Arbor: University of Michigan Press, 1983.

Lewis, Sinclair. *Free Air*. New York: Harcourt, Brace, & Howe, 1919.

Lewis, Sinclair. *Main Street*. New York: Harcourt, Brace, 1920.

Liebs, Chester H. *Main Street to Miracle Mile: American Roadside Architecture*. New York: Graphic Society/Little, Brown, 1985.

Lindamood, Jean, ed. *Road Trips, Head Trips, and Other Car-Crazed Writings*. New York: Atlantic Monthly Press, 1996.

Longstreth, Richard. *City Center to Regional Mall: Architecture, the Automobile, and Retailing in Los Angeles, 1920–1950*. Cambridge, Mass.: MIT Press, 1997.

Lucic, Karen. *Charles Sheeler and the Cult of the Machine*. London: Reaktion Books, 1991.

Mann, Dave, and Ron Main. *Races, Chases & Crashes: A Complete Guide to Car Movies and Biker Flicks*. Osceola, Wisc.: Motorbooks International, 1995.

Margolies, John. *The End of the Road: Vanishing Highway Architecture in America*. New York: Penguin Books, 1981.

Margolies, John. *Pump and Circumstance: Glory Days of the Gas Station*. Boston: Bulfinch/Little Brown, 1993.

Margolies, John, and Eric Baker. *See the USA: The Art of the American Travel Brochure*. San Francisco: Chronicle Books, 1999.

Margolies, John, and Emily Gwathmey. *Signs of Our Time*. New York: Abbeville Press, 1993.

Mariani, John F. *America Eats Out: An Illustrated History of Restaurants, Taverns, Coffee Shops, Speakeasies, and Other Establishments That Have Fed Us for 350 Years*. New York: Morrow, 1991.

Marling, Karal Ann. *As Seen on TV: The Visual Culture of Everyday Life in the 1950s*. Cambridge, Mass.: Harvard University Press, 1994.

Marling, Karal Ann. *The Colossus of Roads: Myth and Symbol along the American Highway*. Minneapolis: University of Minnesota Press, 1984.

Marnham, Patrick. *Dreaming with His Eyes Open: A Life of Diego Rivera*. New York: Alfred A. Knopf, 1998.

Matteson, Donald W. *The Auto Radio: A Romantic Genealogy.* Jackson, Mich.: Thorn-ridge Publishing, 1987.

Maynard, Chris, and Bill Scheller. *Manifold Destiny: The One, the Only Guide to Cooking on Your Car Engine.* New York: Villard Books, 1989.

McDean, Craig. *I Love Fast Cars.* [New York]: powerHouse Cultural Entertainment, 1999.

McKeon, Elizabeth, and Linda Everett. *Cinema under the Stars: America's Love Affair with Drive-In Movie Theaters.* Nashville: Cumberland House, 1999.

McLuhan, Marshall. *Understanding Media: The Extensions of Man.* New York: Signet Books, 1964.

McShane, Clay. *Down the Asphalt Path: The Automobile and the American City.* New York: Columbia University Press, 1994.

Meader, Herman Lee. *Motor Goose Rhymes for Motor-Ganders.* New York: Grafton, 1905.

Melnick, Mimi, and Robert A. Melnick. *Manhole Covers.* Cambridge, Mass.: MIT Press, 1994.

Miller, Arthur. *Death of a Salesman: Certain Private Conversations in Two Acts and a Requiem.* New York: Viking, 1958.

Miller, Henry. *The Air Conditioned Nightmare.* 2 vols. New York: New Directions, 1945–1947.

Moran, Elizabeth. *Speed Racer: The Official 30th Anniversary Guide.* New York: Hyperion, 1997.

Motta, William A., ed. *50 Years of Road & Track: The Art of the Automobile.* Osceola, Wisc.: Motorbooks International, 1997.

Nabokov, Vladimir. *Lolita.* New York: Putnam, 1955.

Nachbar, Jack, Deborah Weiser, and John L. Wright, eds. *The Popular Culture Reader.* Bowling Green, Ohio: Bowling Green University Popular Press, 1978.

Nauen, Elinor, ed. *Ladies, Start Your Engines: Women Writers on Cars and the Road.* Boston: Faber and Faber, 1996.

O'Connor, Flannery. *Wise Blood.* New York: Harcourt, Brace, 1952.

Offitzer, Karen. *Diners.* New York: MetroBooks, 1997.

O'Hara, John. *Appointment in Sumarra: A Novel.* New York: Harcourt, Brace, 1934.

Oresick, Peter, and Nicholas Coles. *Working Classics: Poems on Industrial Life.* Urbana: University of Illinois Press, 1990.

Owens, Randy (photographer), and Larry Frenzel. *Serigraphs: Ten Year Retrospective.* Vienna, Va.: Randy Owens Originals, 1988.

Penrose, Margaret. *The Motor Girls.* New York: Cupples & Leon, 1910.

Penrose, Margaret. *The Motor Girls in the Mountains, or, the Gypsy Girl's Secret.* New York: Cupples & Leon, 1917.

Peterson, B.R. *The Original Road-Kill Cookbook.* Berkeley, Calif.: Ten Speed Press, 1987.

Phillips, Robert. *Breakdown Lane.* Baltimore: Johns Hopkins University Press, 1994.

Presto Publishing Company. *Funny Stories about Ford.* Hamilton, Ohio: Presto Publishing, 1915.

Preston, Charles, ed. *The JokesWagon Book.* New York: Bernard Geis, 1966.

Raitz, Karl, ed. *The National Road.* Baltimore: Johns Hopkins University Press, 1996.

Rathbun, Robert D. *Shopping Centers & Malls.* New York: Retail Reporting Corp., 1986.

Reed, J.D. *Expressways.* New York: Simon & Schuster, 1969.

Reynolds, Elsbery W. *Auto Line O'Type*. Chicago: Book Supply Co., 1924.

Rivera, Diego, with Gladys March. *My Art, My Life: An Autobiography*. Secaucus, N.J.: Citadel Press, 1960.

Robbins, Harold. *The Betsy*. New York: Pocket Press, 1971.

Roth, Ed, and Tony Thacker. *Hot Rods by Ed "Big Daddy" Roth*. Osceola, Wisc.: Motorbooks International, 1995.

Rowe, Maurice. *Track Record: The Motor Sport Photography of Maurice Rowe*. Queensgate, Basingstoke, Eng.: Macmillan, 1999.

Ruscha, Edward. *Thirty-Four Parking Lots in Los Angeles*. New York: Wittenborn, 1967.

Ruscha, Edward. *Twenty-Six Gasoline Stations*. Alhambra, Calif.: National Excelsior, 1963.

Russell, H.M. *Oh, That Funny Ford!* New York: Morris and Bendien, 1916.

Sanders, Don, and Susan Sanders. *The American Drive-In Movie Theatre*. Osceola, Wisc.: Motorbooks International, 1997.

Sargeant, Jack, and Stephanie Watson. *Lost Highways: An Illustrated History of Road Movies*. London: Creation, 1999.

Saroyan, William. *Short Drive, Sweet Chariot*. New York: Phaedra, 1966.

Schlereth, Thomas J. *U.S. 40: A Roadscape of the American Experience*. Indianapolis: Indiana Historical Society, 1985.

Schmidt, Klaus F. *Signs of the Times*. New York: Graphis Books, 1996.

Seagrave. Kerry. *Drive-In Theaters: A History from Their Inception in 1933*. Jefferson, N.C.: McFarland, 1992.

Seiters, Dan. *Image Patterns in the Novels of F. Scott Fitzgerald*. Ann Arbor: University of Michigan Research Press, 1986.

Silk, Gerald D. *et al. Automobile and Culture*. New York: Henry N. Abrams, 1984.

Sinclair, Upton. *The Flivver King: A Story of Ford-America*. Pasadena, Calif.: Author, 1937.

Smith, Dan. *Accessory Mascots: The Automotive Accents of Yesteryear, 1910–1940*. San Diego: Author, 1989.

Smith, Mark, and Naomi Black. *America on Wheels: Tales and Trivia of the Automobile*. New York: William Morrow, 1986.

Snowdon, Nigel, and Diana Burnett. *Formula One through the Lens: Four Decades of Motorsport Photography*. Richmond, Surrey, Eng.: Hazleton, 1998.

Southard, Andy, Jr. *Hot Rods & Customs of the 1960s*. Osceola, Wisc.: Motorbooks International, 1997.

Southard, Andy, Jr., and Tony Thacker. *Custom Cars of the 1950s*. Osceola, Wisc.: Motorbooks International, 1993.

Steinbeck, John. *The Grapes of Wrath*. New York: Viking Press, 1939.

Steinbeck, John. *Travels with Charley in Search of America*. New York: Viking, 1962.

Steinman, Lisa M. *Made in America: Science, Technology, and American Modernist Poets*. New Haven, Conn.: Yale University Press, 1987.

Stevens, Jack. *Hooked on Old Cars*. Haines, Ore.: Author, 1981.

Stokes, Katherine. *The Motor Maids by Palm and Pine*. Chicago: M.A. Donohue, 1911.

Stokes, Katherine. *The Motor Maids School Days*. Chicago: M.A. Donohue, 1911.

Strauss, Steve. *Moving Images: The Transportation Poster in America*. New York: Fullcourt Press, 1984.

Swope, Mary, and Walter H. Kerr. *American Classic: Car Poems for Collectors*. College Park, Md.: SCOP Publications, 1985.

Tarkington, Booth. *The Magnificent Ambersons*. Garden City, N.Y.: Doubleday, Page, 1918.

Tarkington, Booth. *Seventeen*. New York: Grosset & Dunlap, 1916.

Tennyson, Jeffrey. *Hamburger Heaven: The Illustrated History of the Hamburger*. New York: Hyperion Press, 1993.

Terry, Jean, and Gerald A. Bennett. *Car-Toons*. Los Angeles: Floyd Clymer, 1954.

Thornburg, David A. *Galloping Bungalows: The Rise and Demise of the American House Trailer*. Hamden, Conn.: Archon Books, 1991.

Tubbs, D.B. *Art and the Automobile*. New York: Grosset & Dunlap, 1978.

Tunnard, Christopher, and Boris Pushkarev. *Man-Made America: Chaos or Control? An Inquiry into Selected Problems of Design in the Urbanized Landscape*. New Haven, Conn.: Yale University Press, 1963.

Turner, Michael. *The Motorsport Art of Michael Turner*. Osceola, Wisc.: Motorbooks International, 1996.

Updike, John. *Rabbit, Run*. New York: Alfred A. Knopf, 1960.

Vaughan, Thomas, and Virginia Guest Ferriday, eds. *Space, Style and Structure: Building in Northwest America*. 2 vols. Portland: Oregon Historical Society, 1974.

Venturi, Robert, Denise Scott Brown, and Steven Izenour. *Learning from Las Vegas: The Forgotten Symbolism of Architectural Form*. Rev. ed. Cambridge: MIT Press, 1977.

Vieyra, Daniel I. *"Fill 'er Up": An Architectural History of America's Gas Stations*. New York: Collier Books, 1979.

Warren, Robert P. *All the King's Men*. New York: Harcourt, Brace, 1946.

Waugh, Charles G., and Martin H. Greenberg, eds. *Alternative Histories: Eleven Stories of the World as It Might Have Been*. New York: Garland, 1986.

Welsh, Charles. *Chauffeur Chaff or Automobilia: Anecdotes, Stories, Bonmots, Also a History of the Evolution of the Automobile*. Boston: H.M. Caldwell, 1905.

West, Marvin. *Motor Rangers through the Sierras*. New York: Hurst, 1911.

White, Joseph J. *Fun about Fords*. Chicago: Howell, 1915.

Williams, Jim. *Boulevard Photographic: The Art of Automobile Advertising*. Osceola, Wisc.: Motorbooks International, 1997.

Williams, Mark. *Road Movies: The Complete Guide to Cinema on Wheels*. New York: Proteus Books, 1982.

Williams, William C. *Motoring Mascots of the World*. Rev. and expanded ed. Portland, Ore.: Graphic Arts Center/Robert Ames, 1990.

Williamson, C[harles] N., and A[lice] M. Williamson. *The Lightning Conductor*. New York: Grosset & Dunlap, 1905.

Williamson, C[harles] N., and A[lice] M. Williamson. *The Motor Maid*. New York: A.L. Burt, 1910.

Witzel, Michael Karl. *The American Diner*. Osceola, Wisc.: MBI Publications, 1999.

Witzel, Michael Karl. *The American Drive-In: History and Folklore of the Drive-In Restaurant in American Car Culture*. Osceola, Wisc.: Motorbooks International, 1994.

Witzel, Michael Karl. *The American Gas Station: History and Folklore of the Gas Station in American Car Culture*. Osceola, Wisc.: Motorbooks International, 1992.

Wolfe, Bertram. *Diego Rivera: His Life and Times*. New York: Alfred A. Knopf, 1939.

Wolfe, Bertram. *The Fabulous Life of Diego Rivera*. New York: Stein and Day, 1963.

Wolfe, Tom. *The Kandy-Kolored Tangerine-Flake Streamline Baby*. New York: Noonday Press, 1966.

Yew, Wei, ed. *Gotcha!: The Art of the Billboard*. Edmonton, Alberta, Can.: Quon Editions, 1990.

Yew, Wei, ed. *Gotcha Twice!: The Art of the Billboard 2*. Edmonton, Alberta, Can.: Quon Editions, 1992.

Yorke, Douglas A., Jr., John Margolies, and Eric Baker. *Hitting the Road: The Art of the American Road Map*. San Francisco: Chronicle Books, 1996.

Young, Clarence. *The Motor Boys on the Border*. New York: Cupples & Leon, 1913.

Young, Clarence. *The Motor Boys over the Rockies*. New York: Cupples & Leon, 1911.

Zolomij, John J. *The Motorcar in Art: Selections from the Raymond E. Holland Automotive Art Collection*. Kutztown, Pa.: Automobile Quarterly, 1990.

CHAPTER 8

Personal Leisure and Recreation

This chapter begins an exploration of the role that the automobile has played in the leisure and recreational pursuits of Americans. Here, the emphasis is on activities in which people actively participate, such as touring, camping, and hobbies. Motor racing and other spectator sports are covered in the next chapter.

TOURING AND CAMPING

Some of the most significant socioeconomic impacts to result from the motorization of America are directly related to the extensive new travel (although some might say travail) that the automobile made possible. For the first time in human history, it was possible for the average person to travel where, when, and with whom he or she wanted, at a cost over which he or she had some control. The logistic, price, and privacy advantages over railway travel were clear, and at the time of the motor car's introduction, the former was the only real competition.

The starting point for any serious student of motorized touring has to be Warren J. Belasco's *Americans on the Road: From Autocamp to Motel, 1910–1945*. Belasco does a superior job of not only explaining the evolution of tourist accommodations in a recreation-oriented industry but also analyzing why Americans took to the road in cars and how the experience of tourism changed over a generation. A nice blend of business and cultural history, individual chapters investigate, in turn, the concept of "auto camping," the development of municipal auto camps, the introduction of pay camps, and the appearance of early motels.

After Belasco, the next obvious step is John A. Jakle's more recent *The Tourist: Travel in Twentieth-Century North America*. While Jakle's approach is a more comprehensive one, focusing on the evolution of the tourist industry and the businesses that emerged to serve (and attract) travelers, four chapters (approximately one-third of the total book) are devoted to an account of the chronological development of automotive travel and touring and the social revolution that accompanied it.

While Belasco and Jakle provide the most extensive coverage of this topic, books with a broader focus often still have valuable sections investigating the impact of the motor car. See, for example, William H. Marnell's *Vacation Yesterdays of New England*, which contains chapters devoted to auto touring and the evolution of motels in the broader context of vacationing in the 1920s and 1930s; *The Norton Book of Travel*, edited by Paul Fussell, a collection of travel writing (including fiction) from the Persian Wars to the mass tourism made possible by the automobile; and *In Search of the Golden West: The Tourist in Western America*, by Earl Pomeroy, which includes "motorists" among various groups that explored that section of the country during the latter years of the 19th century.

Naturally, many automotive histories contain sections on recreation and leisure. For instance, James J. Flink's comprehensive history *The Automobile Age* contains a chapter entitled "On the Road," devoted to this subject; Michael L. Berger in his *The Devil Wagon in God's Country: The Automobile and Social Change in Rural America, 1893–1929* writes in a chapter on leisure about how the car changed the travel habits of farmers and small town residents; and Raymond Flower and Michael Wynn Jones' *100 Years on the Road: A Social History of the Car* has two chapters on tourism, although the emphasis is heavily European.

Finally, even more general sociohistorical studies often examine some aspect of automotive travel. For example, in their *Middletown: A Study in American Culture*, Robert Lynd and Helen M. Lynd describe how cars changed social habits and family life in Muncie, Indiana, in the 1920s, including the length and frequency of visits to friends and relatives and the advent of the Sunday and after-dinner drive. A somewhat less extensive account of the same phenomena is provided for the 1930s in their sequel, *Middletown in Transition: A Study in Cultural Conflicts*.

Early Motor Touring and Auto Camping

In the very early days of motoring, extensive automotive travel was a newsworthy event, greeted with much the same hoopla and media coverage that we assign today to exploits in outer space. Credit for the first transcontinental motor trip is usually given to Dr. H. Nelson Jackson, and it has been ably chronicled in a book whose title says it all: *The Mad Doctor's Drive: Being an Account of the 1st Auto Trip across the U.S.A., San Francisco to New York, 1903: or, Sixty-Three Days on a Winton Motor Carriage*, by Ralph N. Hill. At least one earlier (1902), book-length account exists of an excursion that rivaled Jackson's in distance, Arthur J. Eddy's *Two Thousand Miles on an Automobile: Being a Desultory Narrative of a Trip through New England, New York, Canada, and the West, by "Chauffeur."* It is interesting to note the use of the preposition "on" in both titles, referring to a person's relationship to the car when driving it, possibly a holdover from the days when the horse was the primary motive power and reflective of the fact that most early cars were "open." By the end of the 1920s, the enclosed car had become more popular, and so had the use of the preposition "in" when referring to automotive travel.

Six years later, Florence Trinkle joined her husband, Fred, to travel *Coast to Coast in a Brush Runabout, 1908.* The next year, Alice H. Ramsey, accompanied by three female passengers/companions, became the first woman to drive across the country. Her own story of this adventure is contained in *Veil, Duster and Tire Iron.*

Mention of a specific marque in both the Hill and Trinkle books was not accidental. In the early years of motoring, successful transcontinental trips were often seen as providing evidence for the quality of the vehicle and thus good advertising. For citations of manufacturers' pamphlets describing such activities from 1903 through 1915, see Chapter 3. For a more complete listing, see Carey Bliss' *Auto across America: A Bibliography of Transcontinental Automobile Travel, 1903–1940.*

In addition, as one might imagine, there is a legion of personal narratives of touring and camping adventures in the early years of motoring. Among the better books fitting this description are Estella M. Copeland's *Overland by Auto in 1913: Diary of a Family Tour from California to Indiana*; Effie Price Gladding's *Across the Continent by the Lincoln Highway* (1915), the latter being the nation's first intercontinental road (see below and Chapter 10); Theodore Dreiser's *A Hoosier Holiday* (1916), written by the novelist famous for *Sister Carrie* and *An American Tragedy*; Louise Closser Hale's *We Discover the Old Dominion* (1916); Emily Post's *By Motor to the Golden Gate* (1917), published five years before her book on etiquette would make her the nationally known authority on proper behavior; Beatrice Larned Massey's *It Might Have Been Worse: A Motor Trip from Coast to Coast* (1920); Mary Crehore Bedell's *Modern Gypsies: The Story of a Twelve Thousand Mile Motor Camping Trip Encircling the United States* (1924), an unembellished account of an excursion primarily through the southern states; and Melville Ferguson's *Motor Camping on Western Trails* (1925).

Even in the late 1920s, publishers still thought there was a market for such volumes, attested by *The Family Flivvers to Frisco*, a 1927 alliterative account by Frederic F. Van de Water; *On Wandering Wheels: Through Roadside Camps from Maine to Georgia in an Old Sedan Car* (1928), by Jan Gordon and Cora J. Gordon; and *From Coast to Coast via the Old Spanish Trail* (1929), by J. Wadsworth Travers. (For additional early travelogues, see the personal accounts and reminiscences cited in Chapter 1.)

Organized tours and early touring in general were activities that, more often than not, were limited to the wealthy. The cost of early automobiles, together with the leisure time necessary to use them, was responsible for this situation. However, by the end of the First World War, motor travel had become widespread enough that one begins to see in print automotive guidebooks such as *The Complete Official Road Guide of the Lincoln Highway*, issued in 1915 and in subsequent years by the Lincoln Highway Association; the *Official Manual of Motor Car Camping* (1920), a publication of the American Automobile Association (AAA); the famous annual *Automobile Blue Books* produced by the AAA beginning in 1900 and the *ALA Green Books* of the American Legal Association first published in 1920; and a host of guides produced by state and local associations, magazines, and newspapers, such as E.V. Weller's *California Motorlogues: Suggestions for One-Day and Week-End Motor Trips on the Highways and Byways of California* (1921).

In the 1930s, one of the projects of the New Deal was a series of state travel guides written by the Federal Writers' Project of the Works Projects Administration (WPA). These were filled with facts, folklore, and history, focused on sights that were off the beaten track, and assumed that (despite the depression) one could travel about in an automobile. A scholarly overview of this effort is *The WPA Guides: Mapping America*, by Christine Bold, a book that uses the guides for Idaho, New York City, North Carolina, Missouri, U.S. Route 1, and the Oregon Trail as case studies to examine the cultural image of the United States that emerged from reading those guides. Typical of specific volumes in the WPA series were *Kansas, a Guide to the Sunflower State* and *Oklahoma, a Guide to the Sooner State*. Both were reissued as paperback editions in the 1980s, entitled respectively, *The WPA Guide to 1930s Kansas* and *The WPA Guide to 1930s Oklahoma*, along with similar volumes on Arkansas and Colorado. Since they capture life in pre–World War II America, they present a time capsule that is still worth examining today. This decade also saw the emergence of a number of guides specifically written to assist African American travelers, who frequently found themselves excluded from many hotels, restaurants, and other roadside amenities because of their race. *The Negro Motorist Green Book* was one such guide.

In addition, the period after 1910 also saw the emergence of the now ubiquitous auto road maps. The only book-length study of this phenomenon is *Hitting the Road: The Art of the American Roadmap*, by Douglas A. Yorke Jr. and John Margolies. Although the emphasis is on the artistic aspects of such maps, there is ample discussion of the changes in popular culture ushered in by the automobile, at least as viewed from the perspective of the companies distributing the maps from 1912 through the 1960s.

Motor Touring Comes of Age

As long-distance motoring became more common, the types of one-shot adventures described in the books cited in the previous section gave way to more regular and common trips to established historic and/or scenic sites. Of these, one of the most popular destinations became the national parks, which were relatively new creations at the time.

The coming of the motor car to the national parks was an event that was greeted with mixed emotions. On the one hand, it meant that more people from greater distances could enjoy the scenic beauty of the nation and visit various sites in less time. On the other hand, those increased numbers and the nature of the vehicle that brought them there meant new roads, different types of accommodations, and a general commercialization and, to some extent, a lessening of the quality of that parkland. This ambiguity (or challenge) of balancing enjoyment and preservation of the great outdoors has been analyzed in a number of general works concerning the development of the parklands, including Linda Flint McClelland's *Building the National Parks: Historic Landscape Design and Construction*, which focuses on the National Park Service, emphasizing the introduction of man-made things (including roads) that both accommodated visitors and minimized the damage to the natural setting; John Ise's *Our National Park Policy: A Critical History*, an account of legislative and administrative developments up to 1960; Alfred Runte's *National Parks: The American Experience*, especially the chapter entitled "Schemers and Standard Bearers"; Richard W. Sellars' *Preserving Nature in the National Parks: A History*, an award-winning critique of the National Park Service in which the author maintains that recreational interests and aesthetic concerns have prevailed over ecological management; and, most recently, Bob R. O'Brien's *Our National Parks and the Search for Sustainability*, which uses case studies of six western parks to illustrate the challenges faced by the Park Service when it tries to achieve a balance between protecting the wilderness and wildlife and allowing for visitation, recreational use of the land, and limited commercial development.

More specific are Richard A. Bartlett's *Yellowstone: A Wilderness Besieged*, which emphasizes its transition from essentially a nature preserve to this country's most popular national park for tourists; Stanford E. Demars' *The Tourist in Yosemite, 1855–1985*, a history of that national park within the socioenvironmental context of the period, with particular attention to changing interpretations of how such a park should/can be enjoyed; Alfred Runte's *Yosemite: The Embattled Wilderness*, which highlights the struggle between the preservationists and developers that has lasted for over a century and a third, with the latter seen as making significant inroads (both figuratively and literally); Anne F. Hyde's "From Stagecoach to Packard Twin Six: Yosemite and the Changing Face of Tourism, 1880–1930," a chapter in *Yosemite and Sequoia*, edited by Richard J. Orsi *et al.*, that does an especially good job of depicting the impact of the automobile, improved roads, and motor camping on tourism within that California park; and C.W. Buchholtz's *Man in Glacier* [National Park], a brief volume aimed at the general reader that includes the history of the transmountain Going-to-the Sun Road, completed in 1933, a significant engineering and aesthetic achievement that has since been designated a National Historic Landmark.

While there is much scholarly writing concerning motoring to and through national parks, the latter were clearly not the only destinations possible. More commercialized establishments began to appear in the 1920s that clearly catered to such traffic. One of the most significant undertakings in this regard, both in absolute terms and in regard to the subject matter of this guide, was Greenfield Village, Henry Ford's attempt to collect and display on a single site in Dearborn, Michigan, an incredible range of Americana artifacts, from the shards of ancient Indian pottery, to railroad locomotives, to the entire bicycle shop of the Wright Brothers. The ongoing history of this enterprise has been told several times, most memorably by H.F. Morton in *Strange Commissions for Henry Ford* (1934) and William A. Simonds in *Henry Ford and Greenfield Village* (1938) and, more recently, by the village and museum themselves, in Geoffrey C. Upward's *A Home for Our Heritage: The Building and Growth of Greenfield Village and Henry Ford Museum, 1929–1979*. All three are popular, essentially uncritical works.

Developments since World War II

As long-distance travel became increasingly a commonplace phenomenon, Americans began to show a decided preference for food, gas, and lodging franchises whose names they recognized and where an expected standard of service would be provided, regardless of where the establishment was found. Of late, these establishments have been joined by fast-food restaurants that have created, in Stan Luxenberg's phrase, "roadside empires."

In a sense, these commercial establishments signaled a new roadside environment, created partially by these franchises and partially by the interstate highway system. In some cases, roads were built through what had previously been "undeveloped" land, and thus these establishments were the first to be there. However, in many cases, these empires replaced an older, more variegated collection of roadside establishments that had existed alongside state and local highways that were now largely bypassed or incorporated into the new toll roads, expressways, and interstate highways. A good case study of roadside changes wrought by such development is Thomas J. Schlereth's *U.S. 40: A Roadscape of the American Experience* (see below). Evidence that significant sights still exist along selected stretches of interstate highway can be found in Eleanor Huggins and John Olmsted's *Adventures on and off Interstate 80: Natural and Human History along the Pioneer and Gold Rush Corridor from San Francisco's Pacific Shore to Nevada's Desert Sands*, a tour book published in the mid-1980s, and Peter Genovese's *The Great American Road Trip: U.S. 1, Maine to Florida*, a 1999 book that documents and describes the tremendous variety of attractions from Fort Kent, Maine, to Key West, Florida.

The years since World War II also have seen the full flowering of roadside amusements that have been designed for, or adapted to, the special interests of automotive tourists. For two extensive and enjoyable descriptions of the wide variety of attractions that can still be found alongside our nation's highways, see *The Colossus of Roads: Myth and Symbol along the American Highway*, by Karal Ann Marling, and *Roadside America*, by Jack Barth *et al*. Briefer, but still valuable, is John Margolies' *Fun along the Road: American Tourist Attractions*. For a tour of a state that seems to have more than its share of offbeat highway attractions, see Peter Genovese's *Roadside New Jersey*, a book that also offers the stories and people behind the strange signs and structures. Finally, in *Dixie before Disney: 100 Years of Roadside Fun*, Tim Hollis colorfully and nostalgically describes the "amateur" theme parks and attractions that lured people south to spend their vacations on the road there. (For more on the automobile and roadside attractions and the art/architecture that they have generated, see Chapters 6 and 7, respectively.)

The increasing specialization of American life during the last quarter of the 20th century affected this type of special-interest travel as well, yielding a host of "theme" tour guides. For example, see Richard E. Osborne's *Tour Book for Antique Car Buffs*; A.M. Nolan's *Rock 'n' Roll Road Trip: The Ultimate Guide to the Sites, the Shrines, and the Legends across America*; Jane Stern and Michael Stern's *Eat Your Way across the U.S.A.: 500 Diners, Farmland Buffets, Lobster Shacks, Pie Palaces, and Other All-American Eateries*; and Dale Peterson's *Storyville, USA*, which, while not technically a tour guide, is nonetheless a fascinating account of a 20,000-mile motor odyssey in search of the history and lore of curious small town place-names, such as Monkeys Eyebrow, Kentucky, and Deadhorse, Alaska.

In addition, there are a number of good contemporary books aimed at those who are interested in a motorized historical tour of a particular state or region. Included in this genre would be such books as *Touring New Mexico*, by Polly Arango *et al.*; John E. Miller's *Looking for History on Highway 14* (in Iowa); George Cantor's *Where the Old Roads Go: Driving the First Federal Highways of Arizona, California, Colorado, New Mexico, Nevada, and Utah* and the same author's *Where the Old Roads Go: Driving the First Federal Highways of the Northeast*; Angus Kress Gillespie and Michael Aaron Rockland's *Looking for America on the New Jersey Turnpike*; Eleanor Huggins and John Olmsted's previously cited *Adventures on and off Interstate 80*; Thomas Vale and Geraldine Vale's *Western Images, Western Landscapes: Travels along U.S. 89*; and Brian A. Butko's *Pennsylvania Traveler's Guide: The Lincoln Highway*, which provides a general history of the highway and a detailed guide to roadside attractions that once existed and still survive along the 360 miles of it that ran through Pennsylvania.

Before leaving this section, two unusual works deserve to be mentioned. In *Manifold Destiny: The One! The Only! Guide to Cooking on Your Car Engine!*, authors Chris Maynard and Bill Scheller provide a guide to cooking "road food" while you drive, complete with advice on how to prepare and wrap the edibles, where to place them under the hood, and how long to leave them there. While written in a tongue-in-cheek style, this is a serious work, the latter half of which contains a collection of unique recipes suitably titled, such as "poached fish Pontiac." The other book is *Flattened Fauna: A Field Guide to Common Animals of Roads, Streets and Highways,* by Roger Knutson, a "spotter's guide" to the roadkill frequently observed in passing by motor tourists. Knutson provides guidance on how to identify what you have seen, as well as information on the habits of the animals while alive. The publicity for this book suggests that such identification would be great for travelers weary of other car spotting games, such as license plates and historical markers.

Camping

While the automobile ushered in extended day trips of a type that was impossible with horse-drawn vehicles and gave new meaning to the concept of a "Sunday drive," the more revolutionary change was the twin developments of roadside campgrounds for motorists and the evolution of the motel. So swift was the development of the former that as early as 1924, the *Journal of Applied Sociology* was carrying an article entitled "The Auto Camp Community," by Harry B. Ansted, in which the mores and manners of such groups were analyzed.

In a sense, overnight auto trips became one of the vacation crazes of the 1920s, and the rich and famous participated along with the common folk. Probably the most celebrated trio of auto tourists was Henry Ford, Thomas Edison, and Harvey Firestone, who frequently went on opulent "camping" trips together. Most Americans, however, traveled on much tighter budgets and frequently stayed at free or inexpensive campsites with few amenities that were developed on the periphery of many towns and cities.

Camping in connection with motor touring grew in popularity during the interwar years, and there were numerous efforts by individuals to assist the would-be camper, such as Elon Jessup's 1921 *The Motor Camping Book,* a rationale for the practice and a practical guide for pursuing it; John D. and John C. Long's *Motor Camping* (1923), which is particularly good at describing the ingenious auto-related accessories that one could buy to make camping less of an adventure; and a series of volumes by Frank E. Brimmer, beginning in 1923, entitled *Autocamping, Autocamping Facts,* and *Motor Campcraft.*

Early overnight camping involved sleeping outside under the stars, in tents (both traditional and made to attach to the car), or in the vehicle itself. A significant improvement was the camp or folding-tent trailer, which, when pulled behind the car, freed up space in the latter and converted into a canvas shelter of one size or another. This was followed in the 1930s by the house trailer, which had the advantage of always being ready for occupancy and capable of being appointed as luxuriously as one could afford. In *Galloping Bungalows: The Rise and Demise of the American House Trailer,* David A. Thornburg traces the development of trailers and trailer parks in the 1930s and 1940s. Although more of a popular than scholarly work, it does provide a comprehensive overview and valuable insights into the social history of this movement during the years before trailers donned skirts and settled down.

More specifically, Blackburn Sims' *The Trailer Home, with Practical Advice on Trailer Life and Travel* offers insight into such activities in the mid-1930s. By the end of the decade, there were a number of good contemporary views of the significance of this new mode of traveling and living. See, for instance, Charles E. Nash's *Trailer Ahoy!*; Winfield A. Kimball and Maurice H. Decker's *Touring with Tent and Trailer*; and Kimball and W. Livingston Larned's *The Trailer for Pleasure and Business*, all published in 1937.

Sophisticated trailers began to replace the passenger vehicle as the preferred mode for overnight camping after World War II. Interesting primarily for the author and the philosophy he espouses is Wally Byam's *Trailer Travel Here and Abroad: The New Way to Adventurous Living*, written with David McKay. Byam is the "guru" of such a lifestyle, having invented the Airstream trailer, the granddaddy of them all. Here he offers advice to the would-be and current owner, as well as a description of guided caravan trips of which he has been a part. A good, popular account of the vehicle and the movement that it generated is *Airstream*, by Robert Landau and James Phillippi.

The postwar popularity of both the station wagon and motor camping led to a temporary resurgence of interest in ways that passenger vehicles could be adapted for camping. Thus, in 1957, the Ford Motor Company published *Station Wagon Living: A Guide to Outdoor Recreation, with a Directory of Over 1300 Campgrounds and Field Test Reports on 140 Items of Camp Gear*, which was compiled by Franklin Reck and William Moss. The station wagon was seen as uniquely designed, when supplemented by recreational gear, to provide the means of access to outdoor fun for the American family. (See Chapter 5 for additional books concerning this type of vehicle's impact on family life.)

Nonetheless, the true successor to the trailer is the "recreational vehicle," or RV, which has combined the car and trailer into a single vehicle. Michael Aaron Rockland's *Homes on Wheels* is probably the best contemporary treatment of that topic, treating the full variety of RVs (motor homes, vans, trailers, pickup campers, converted buses, and tent trailers) and the lifestyles of those people who prefer that their homes be mobile (either permanently or for vacations). Rockland correctly observes that such vehicles allow Americans to combine what traditionally were viewed as contending forces: wanderlust vis-à-vis permanent residence and the individualism of the RV vis-à-vis the communal life of the trailer park. Kay Peterson's *Home Is Where You Park It: A Guide to RV Living as a Life Style*, while less analytic than the Rockland volume, is similar in approach.

Motels

While outdoor camping was enjoying vast popularity, another means of overnight accommodation—the auto camp, tourist cabin, and/or motel—was developing and would eventually overtake the campground as the preferred locale for lodging by traveling Americans. Beginning in 1925 in San Luis Obispo, California, and developing during the 1930s throughout California and the West Coast, the motel took off in the two decades following World War II, crossed the Mississippi River, and became a truly national phenomenon. An unusual source for tracing this development is the Duncan Hines annual guides *Lodging for a Night*, which were published in a national edition beginning in 1938.

In the early 1960s, motels reached their apex, when approximately 61,000 motels were in business. The best source in this regard is *The Motel in America*, by John A. Jakle *et al*. Their comprehensive and scholarly work provides a solid history of this new style of lodging and is especially good in terms of the business and architecture (both interior and exterior) of motel chains, especially the Holiday Inns, from the 1950s on. It is less satisfying in terms of social history or the cultural context of the various developments described. Warren J. Belasco's *Americans on the Road* (cited earlier) is broader in scope but contains an excellent analysis of the social and economic history of the precursors to, and the evolution of, motels. Covering the chronologically earlier years 1910–1945, Belasco ought to be read prior to Jakle *et al*. Finally, Geoffrey Baker and Bruno Funaro's *Motels*, published in 1955, is worth examining as possibly the first serious, book-length study of the subject.

Written for a more general audience is John Margolies' *Home Away from Home: Motels in America*, a nostalgic account of the history and lore surrounding the development and evolution of this form of roadside accommodation, told in words and photographs, with particular attention to the visual aspects and physical idiosyncracies of pre-chain motel design.

In a more specific vein, Mary Ann Beecher looks at the physical aspects of motel forms in her "The Motel in Builder's Literature and Architectural Publications: An Analysis of Design," a chapter in Jan Jennings' *Roadside America* that examines builders' guidelines, aesthetic considerations, and the topology and configuration of individual units in the years 1930 to 1955. Another chapter in the Jennings volume, Keith A. Sculle's "Frank Redford's Wigwam Village Chain: A Link in the Modernization of the American Roadside," offers the history of one early motel chain (featuring a tepee motif) as a case study of the process of modernization applied to a roadside industry. Finally, Philip Abbott's *Seeking Many Inventions: The Idea of Community in America* studies the "community" that motels offer in comparison with that provided by four other inventions.

ROADS AND HIGHWAYS

As many historians have noted, the development of the automobile and, by association, motor touring and roadside camping was intimately linked with the improvement of the nation's road and highway system. John B. Rae provides an excellent historical overview of this phenomenon in his *The Road and the Car in American Life*, which should be the beginning point for any serious student of this subject. Howard L. Preston's *Dirt Roads to Dixie: Accessibility and Modernization in the South, 1885–1935* is a fine regional study of the same phenomenon that pays due attention to the economic potential of automotive tourism in creating a demand for highway development and improvements. Less scholarly in approach but valuable in its own right (a *New York Times* Notable Book of the Year) is Phil Patton's *Open Road: A Celebration of the American Highway.* While Patton's account of the development of the nation's highways is a fascinating one, the importance of his book for this chapter lies in his analysis of the social and cultural impact of such roadways. Finally, for a highly acclaimed, comprehensive history, see Albert C. Rose's *Historic American Roads: From Frontier Trails to Superhighways.*

The progress that was made prior to World War I in terms of upgrading local and state roadways was due largely to private organizations and the pressure that they brought to bear on each level of government. Philip P. Mason writes of the efforts of one such key group in his *The League of American Wheelmen and the Good Roads Movement, 1880–1905.* Among the significant factors discussed by Mason is the early conflict between rural and urban interests in terms of road development for pleasure as opposed to business, a topic also examined by John B. Rae's *The Road and Car in American Life* (see above). As its name indicates, the League of American Wheelman began as an interest group trying to influence local governments to improve roads for bicyclists, but it eventually became subsumed by the broader-based Good Roads Movement.

In addition to the League of American Wheelmen, the National Highways Association was another strong group advocating good roads, with particular interest in a national system of interconnecting highways. The first real attempt at an intercontinental highway was the so-called Lincoln Highway, designed to span the distance between New York and San Francisco. Portions were first opened for travel in 1915, and the route achieved true national proportions by the 1920s. The Lincoln Highway Association, a private group that lobbied for, and oversaw the construction of, that road published an official history in 1935 entitled *The Lincoln Highway: The Story of a Crusade That Made Transportation History*, focusing on the accomplishments of the association and Carl G. Fisher, generally viewed as the father of the transcontinental highway movement. In a sense this was a "final report" in that the route had been absorbed into the national route number system in 1927 and thus had lost most of its separate identity.

Over half a century later, Drake Hokanson's *The Lincoln Highway: Main Street across America* was the first book to provide the scholar with a well-researched and nicely illustrated history of this pioneering roadway and the changes that it wrought on the roadside landscape. As noted by a reviewer for the *Christian Science Monitor*, "Hokanson shows us how the West was won for the middle-class tourist, often in their own words." (Hokanson's book was a 1988 *Booklist* Adult Editors' Choice Award winner.) Finally, readers interested in vicariously experiencing what it was like to travel all 3,143 miles of the

Lincoln Highway in its heyday should peruse *The Complete Official Road Guide of the Lincoln Highway*, a periodic publication of the association. The 1915 edition was reprinted in 1984.

By the advent of the First World War, the Good Roads Movement as a separate entity had peaked. However, it had left a definite legacy of government interest in, and support for, highway construction. One tangible result of the agitation of the League of American Wheelmen, the National Highways Association, and the Lincoln Highway Association (see above) was the passage in 1916 of the Federal Aid Road Act, which established the (still) basic principle of federal–state cooperation in the construction of highways and, along with the Federal Highway Act of 1921, led to an interconnected system of state highways by the mid-1920s.

In 1925 highways that met certain restrictions were termed "U.S." highways, numbered, and joined together wherever possible. Many of these enjoyed success as auto touring routes prior to the construction of the interstate system in the 1950s. Arguably the most famous highway in American history was the 2,448 miles of Route 66. It captured the American imagination from 1926 to the mid-1960s and became associated with both fictional and true road adventures. As such, it has been extensively studied by both scholars and popular enthusiasts. In the former category would be Quinta Scott and Susan Croce Kelly, whose *Route 66: The Highway and Its People*, a comprehensive history by Kelly together with a photo-essay by Scott, emphasizes the road's impact on the people who lived beside it, on the small towns and countryside through which it passed, and on those who drove on it. It thus captures a way of life that no longer exists. In the area of popular literature are Michael Wallis' *Route 66: The Mother Road* and Michael Karl Witzel's *Route 66 Remembered*, both of which are nostalgic reviews, in text and photographs, of the roadside attractions and services that made this road from Chicago to Los Angeles so attractive to tourists. Wallis makes especially good use of interviews with people whose lives were intertwined with the vicissitudes of the highway. All three of these books also attest to the Route 66 mystique that has far outlived the integrity of the road itself. In this regard, also see "Sentimental Journeys: The Myths of Route 66," a chapter in Phil Patton's previously mentioned *Open Road*, and Arthur Krim's "Mapping Route 66: A Cultural Cartography," in *Roadside America*, edited by Jan Jennings, in which Krim explores the highway as a literary, musical, and cinematic icon.

Not surprisingly, a road with such appeal has generated numerous travel guides. Probably the best of the lot is Jack D. Rittenhouse's *A Guide Book to Highway 66*. First published in 1946 and still being reprinted four decades later, it provides a fine overview of the unique sights and towns along the way, while also noting the nature and location of necessary roadside amenities. Even after Route 66 ceased to exist, both as a continuous roadway and as a U.S. route number, travel guides continued to be published. For instance, see Tom Snyder's *The Route 66 Traveler's Guide and Roadside Companion* and Bob Moore and

Patrick Grauwels' *Route 66: A Guidebook to the Mother Road*, both of which provide documentation (in some cases, period maps) to assist with identifying the location of specific tourist attractions along what is left of the "Main Street of America" in the eight states that it traversed. (Incidentally, "the Mother Road" was the term used for Route 66 in John Steinbeck's depression-era novel *The Grapes of Wrath*.) Similar guides have subsequently been published for individual states, such as Jim Ross' *Oklahoma Route 66: The Cruiser's Companion*, Jill Schnieder's *Route 66 across New Mexico: A Wanderer's Guide*, and John Weiss' *Traveling the New, Historic Route 66 of Illinois*. A different approach is taken by Marian Clark in *The Route 66 Cookbook*, a tour of what the author considers to be the best-loved eating establishments along the road, together with nostalgia concerning them and their favorite recipes.

Another historic early-numbered motorway is the subject of a photo-essay by George R. Stewart. *U.S. 40: Cross Section of the United States of America* recounts a journey from Atlantic City, New Jersey, to San Francisco completed by him at the time that construction of the interstate system was just getting under way. Thirty years later, Thomas R. Vale and Geraldine R. Vale copied Stewart's route and methodology in *U.S. 40 Today: Thirty Years of Landscape Change in America*, thereby using the highway to show the physical and cultural changes that had occurred in the United States in the intervening generation. A more recent study of the same road is Thomas J. Schlereth's *Reading the Road: U.S. 40 and the American Landscape*, a 1997 revised edition of *U.S. 40: A Roadscape of the American Experience* (1985). While it covers only Indiana, the author explores in depth the changing service facilities (gas stations, diners, and other roadside businesses) that have catered to the traveler since the road's inception (see below). All three books treat U.S. 40 and its adjacent landscape and buildings as an "outdoor museum" whose study provides information regarding the changing nature of American society.

U.S. 40 incorporated the old National or Cumberland Road. When the latter was built during the first half of the nineteenth century, it became the first interstate highway built with federal aid. An excellent tour book for the original road is *A Guide to the National Road*, edited by Karl Raitz, which highlights the highway sites (and sights) that reflect the historical and cultural evolution of the roadside.

Possibly better known today is U.S. 1, a 2,500-mile-long highway that follows the coast from Maine to Florida. For many Americans, it was the road that they followed for vacations in the middle third of the 20th century, assisted in that regard by *U.S. One: Maine to Florida*, one of the 1938 American Guide Series publications of the Federal Writers' Project. More recently, Andrew H. Malcolm (text) and Roger Straus III (photographs), in *U.S. 1: America's Original Main Street*, recount and beautifully illustrate their travels as they traversed the entire length of the highway, from Key West, Florida, to Fort Kent, Maine, in the early 1990s, reflecting on sites of its past glory (possibly too nostalgically) and observing its current function and the socioeconomic changes that it wrought.

Despite the popularity of long-distance touring over interstate highways, local and state roads allowed for much more adventuresome day trips than had been possible before and provided a means to access relatively nearby vacation spots. For tourists, the various public and private parkways built during the 1920s and 1930s played a key role. In designing parkways, greater attention was paid to aesthetics, particularly landscaping, than had been true for the early numbered interstate highways. In addition, parkways generally excluded trucks and other commercial vehicles.

Several of these parkways have been the subject of book-length treatments, such as Bruce Radde's study of *The Merritt Parkway*, which runs from the New York state line to Stratford, Connecticut; Harley E. Jolley's *Blue Ridge Parkway*, a developmental account of the first fifty years of a roadway that follows the crest of the mountains through Virginia and North Carolina, specifically built for the pleasure of the motor tourist and part of the national park system; and Marilyn E. Wiegold's *Pioneering in Parks and Parkways: Westchester County, New York, 1895–1945*, the story of how an initial effort to clean up the pollution of the Bronx River led to the development of an extensive system of parks and aesthetically pleasing roadways. Wiegold's work is a forty-three-page pamphlet, separately printed as part of the Essays in Public Works History series. See also Gilmore Clark's "The Parkway Idea," reminiscences written by the man who oversaw the construction of the Bronx River Parkway, published in *The Highway and the Landscape*, edited by W. Brewster Snow. Finally, Sara Amy Leach's "Fifty Years of Parkway Construction in and around the Nation's Capital," a chapter in Jan Jennings' *Roadside America*, offers a short history and sociopolitical analysis of a more urban system of parkways that began as pleasure roads but soon were asked to serve the contradictory function of being commuter routes as well. (This development also was experienced by the Westchester County parkways.) For more on the parkway movement, see the section on highways in Chapter 10.

Many of the elements of such parkways (e.g., separation of opposing traffic, rest areas, concrete paving, etc.) were incorporated into the toll turnpike building boom that began before the United States entered World War II and accelerated after it. Motor turnpikes were America's first true superhighways and the precursors of (and often incorporated as part of) the interstate highway system of the latter half of the 20th century.

The first of these was the Pennsylvania Turnpike, opened in 1940. Built during the depression at the then-staggering cost of $60 million, it was a pioneering four-lane, divided, limited-access highway with no traffic lights, stop signs, or grade crossings—at a time when 99.7% of the public roads were only one or two lanes. The turnpike celebrated its golden anniversary in 1990, at which time Dan Cupper was commissioned to write *The Pennsylvania Turnpike: A History*, which, despite its brevity, is still the most comprehensive work available. Less successful is an earlier work by William H. Shank, entitled *Vanderbilt's Folly: A History of the Pennsylvania Turnpike*.

Turnpike travel represented a significant departure from all previous motor roads. Turnpikes were designed primarily to get the traveler from one location to another in the shortest time, and as such they bore a closer resemblance to the railroad than to the horse and buggy. While nature might be observed from one's windows, one had to get off the highway to enjoy the sights. What was between the point of departure and that of arrival began to be increasingly ignored.

A more in-depth study of highways, with an emphasis on the road as a conduit for business and the automobile as one among many forms of personal transportation, can be found in the "Roads and Highways" section of Chapter 10. Here, our focus is on those roads specifically built for the tourists and/or heavily used by them.

Finally, while the emphasis in this section is on how people use their own vehicles for touring and camping, it should be remembered that the fine art of hitchhiking predates the automobile and was easily adopted to it. In fact, the car presented an opportunity for a person to engage in a cross-country trip with no transportation costs and few of the dangers associated with hitching a freight train or stowing away on a plane or boat. Hitchhiking is one of those areas where, while one wishes for a more scholarly treatment of the phenomenon, one must accept the fact that the nature of the activity itself mitigates against the existence of an extensive historical record. However, there has been some attention to this phenomenon by students of folklore. See, for instance, the work of Jan H. Brunvand, including the aptly titled *The Vanishing Hitchhiker: American Urban Legends and Their Meanings*.

HOBBIES

Given the enormous impact that the automobile has had on American life, it should come as no surprise that a number of varied hobbies have grown up around it. The best overview of this subject is provided by *Automobile Quarterly's Complete Handbook of Automobile Hobbies*, edited by Beverly Rae Kimes, which is intended to be a reference work for the enthusiast and investor. In twenty-nine chapters, the *Handbook* covers everything from purchasing and restoring cars to collecting automotive art to the fun of touring and vintage racing—a book that truly defines the subject. Similar in approach but narrower in scope is John Gunnell's *A Collector's Guide to Automobilia*, an overview of many aspects of the hobby, including toys, hood ornaments, license plates, gas pump globes, dealer signs, sales literature and factory photos, clothing, art and posters, and so on.

Collecting and Restoring Automobiles

It is probably fair to say that any vehicle is fair game for the antique automobile collector. Even a cursory reading of some of the more popular "enthusiast" magazines, such as *Automobile Quarterly, Antique Automobile*, and *The Automobile*, makes this abundantly clear. Peter Sessler's *Car Collector's Handbook: A Comprehensive Guide to Collecting Rare and Historic Automobiles* is a good basic, albeit brief, reference to this hobby, covering the mechanics of acquiring and showing such a vehicle.

While some of these automobiles border on the esoteric, those of interest to sizable numbers of collectors and restorers have been highlighted in a number of encyclopedic anthologies. Although the treatment of individual cars is generally superficial, such volumes allow the potential collector to identify those (or that one) that most interests him or her. Included in this category of books would be *Buy an Antique Car*, an explanation of how to get into the old car hobby written in the late 1950s by L. Scott Bailey, who was subsequently to become editor of *Antique Automobile* and founding editor of *Automobile Quarterly*; the *Complete Book of Collectible Cars, 1930–1980*, compiled by the editors of *Consumer Guide*, which identifies over 700 good investments from the period indicated; *Restore and Drive: Collectible Cars of Postwar America*, by Bob Stubenrauch, a good introduction to the purchase and restoration of such cars, which features twenty-four of the most desirable ones; and *Marques of America: A Special-Interest Car Buyer's Guide*, edited by John Gunnell, in which he and others showcase those "out of the ordinary" vehicles from the 1930s through the 1960s that have proven to be most popular among collectors.

Three nationwide organizations—the Antique Automobile Club of America (AACA), the Horseless Carriage Association of America (HCAA), and the Veteran Motor Car Club of America—exist primarily to further the collecting and restoring interests and desires of their membership. (For a sixty-year [1935–1995] history of the AACA, see Robert C. Lichty's *The Official Book of the Antique Automobile Club of America*.) People who collect and restore cars often do so to exhibit them at local, regional, and even national meets and shows, usually for the purpose of winning awards in a manner similar to that of animal shows. Thus, although the original Glidden Tours of 1905–1913 (see Chapters 1 and 3) were abandoned once the mechanical "perfection" of cars was no longer in question, they were revived in 1946 by the Veteran Motor Car Club as a summer event at which vintage car collectors could motor and socialize together. Given the initial contribution of the Glidden Tours to improving automotive engineering and their subsequent popularity with auto buffs, they are deserving of book-length treatment by some future scholar. A somewhat similar activity is the Pebble Beach [California] Concours d'Elegance, where owners show their cars (and themselves) in a display of opulence. Robert T. Devlin offers a history of that event from 1950 to 1979 in the first half of *Pebble Beach, A Matter of Style*.

Display of a different type is featured in Michael Sheridan and Sam Bushala's *Showtime: The Story of the International Championship Auto Shows and the Hot Rod/Custom Car World*, a twenty-year, extensively illustrated history of custom and hot rod shows, with special attention to the International Champi-

onship Auto (ICA) Shows of 1960 to 1980. An annual event that is more ple-
beian in nature but probably of greater significance in terms of this hobby is the
focus of Rich Taylor's *Hershey: The World's Greatest Antique Car Event*. It
draws a quarter of a million people to a thirty-two-acre site in a small Pennsylvania town (best known for its chocolate company) in hopes of finding a
particular car, a hard-to-find part, or some automotive collectible.

Restoring antique automobiles can be more than a hobby; it also can be an
investment similar in nature to the purchase of a Victorian house that needs
considerable work. A number of authors have attempted to offer advice in this
regard. See, for example, two books by Richard H. Rush: *Automobiles as an
Investment*, a comprehensive "how to" manual for buying and selling cars, and
Investing in Classic Automobiles for Profit and Capital Gain, a similar volume
that also includes advice on restoration and maintenance; Bill Neville's *Real
Steel: An Investor's and Philosopher's Guide to the American Automobile*,
which concentrates on eighty-eight cars built between 1939 and 1969 that the
author thinks show the greatest "appreciation potential"; and Charles Webb's
more specialized *The Investor's Illustrated Guide to American Convertible and
Special-Interest Automobiles, 1946–1976*.

Probably the premier individual car collector in modern times was William
Fisk Harrah, who used part of a fortune amassed in Las Vegas gambling enterprises to purchase some 1,100 to 1,400 antique autos, restore them, and then
put them on display in a public museum that he founded. A good, recent biography of this man is *William Fisk Harrah: The Life and Times of a Gambling
Magnate*, by Leon Mandel. Another memoir by a motor vehicle collector is
Alan L. Radcliff's *Adventures of a Vintage Car Collector*. Radcliff describes
events connected with buying, restoring, and showing fourteen vehicles. Finally,
Great Car Collections of the World, by Edward Eves and Dan Burger, provides
a tour of the fifty major collections/museums in the world, some owned by
individuals and others by foundations and governments. For additional information on specific museum collections, see the "Automotive Museums" section
of Appendix 2.

Collectibles and Automobilia

The increasing cost of initial purchase, renovation, and upkeep of antique cars
has limited the number of people who can participate in this hobby. (It even led
the executors of Harrah's estate to sell off most of his vehicles in 1984.) The
collection of related artifacts, however, is within the financial means of most
people, depending, of course, on what is collected and how much is being
amassed. One cannot help but be impressed with the range and purported value
of such items as one peruses *American Automobilia: An Illustrated History and
Price Guide*, by Jim and Nancy Schaut, a fine overview of a hobby that includes
such collectibles as advertising, customizing, and service station items; automotive art; accessories; license plates; paper ephemera; toys; and auto club,

car show, and racing memorabilia. Similarly, *Automobilia: a Guided Tour for Collectors*, by Sotheby's motoring adviser Michael Worthington-Williams, covers car accessories and such items as motoring magazines, photographs, inkstands, paperweights, cigarette cards, and models, while offering guidance on what to collect and preserve, where to find it, and how to recognize it. Finally, *The Price Guide and Identification of Automobilia*, a well-illustrated work by Gordon Gardiner and Alistair Morris, includes accessories, instruments, clothing, badges, mascots, signs, globes, catalogs, postcards, trophies, novelties, pedal and toy cars, programs, and magazines. (Given the date of publication and its United Kingdom origins, the definition of the field provided by this last volume is much more valuable than the dated prices and individual items that are featured.)

The field of automotive collectibles has become so well established that books have begun to appear that differentiate not just by category (such as those described below) but by special-interest areas as well. See, for example, David Fetherston's *Hot Rod Memorabilia & Collectibles* and Ken Breslauer's *Fifty Years of Stock Car Racing: A History of Collectibles and Memorabilia*.

Most of the books cited in the following subsections provide a history and description of the particular collectible(s), including variations, availability, investment values, and the creation and identification of restorations and fakes.

Model and Toy Cars. A sizable group of collectors have decided that they do not want the actual automobile but rather a miniaturized version of it, and they collect what is generically termed "model cars." These vary in quality from the kind that have been available for decades as children's toys to ones that are hand-crafted or cast of rare woods or metals. The best overview history of this hobby in the United States and the collectibles themselves is Lillian Gottschalk's *American Toy Cars and Trucks, 1894–1942*. A former president of the Antique Toy Collectors of America, Gottschalk, supported by hundreds of exquisite photographs by Bill Holland, provides this definitive work for collectors of commercially built toy cars, trucks, and other vehicles, including tips on restoration and repairs. Also worthy of examination is the more specific *Detroit in Miniature: 400 Photos of American Diecast Models Made Worldwide*, by James Weiland and Edward Force.

These exclusively American works can be supplemented by information found in a number of good surveys with an international perspective. See, for instance, *The Collector's Guide to Toy Cars*, by Gordon Gardiner and Richard O'Neill, an all-inclusive guide that covers tin-plate and die-cast models, pedal cars, and powered play cars made worldwide since 1900; Ken Hutchison and Greg Nelson's *The Golden Age of Automotive Toys, 1925–1941*, which is similar in concept to Gardiner and O'Neill and covers European, Japanese, and American examples; *Collecting Toy Cars & Trucks: Identification and Value Guide*, by Richard O'Brien, which includes military as well as civilian vehicles, plus rubber, battery-operated, and pull toys; *Autohobby*, by Marco Bossi, a survey of the history of toy cars, one-fourth of which deals with pedal cars of the 1920s and 1930s; *Micro Cars: A Collector's Guide to 3-Inch Miniatures*, by Peter

Viemeister, a reference guide to 1/43rd-scale, die-cast models; and *The World of Model Cars*, by Guy R. Williams, a survey of the history, development, and manufacture of tin, die-cast, metal, and plastic models, plus slot and radio-controlled miniatures.

In addition, several books that cover the broader topic of toys have individual chapters or extensive material on cars. For instance, *The Warner Collector's Guide to American Toys*, by William S. Ayres; *Collector's Guide to American Transportation Toys, 1895–1941*, by Joe Freed and Sharon Freed; and *Toys in America*, by Inez McClintock and Marshall McClintock, contain such information.

Many of the companies that manufactured "static" automotive toys created sufficiently distinctive models that some individuals specialize in collecting just them. Listed below are a representative sampling of books that pertain to such specialization, although the books themselves describe not just cars but the full range of miniatures that a company produced. Most of these companies are European. They are included here since they sold significant numbers of their toys in the United States, and many of their models portrayed American cars. Listed alphabetically by company, they are *The Great Book of Corgi: 1956–1983*, a comprehensive 512-page history of this British die-cast toy maker written by its founder, Marcel Van Cleemput; *The Unauthorized Encyclopedia of Corgi Toys*, by Bill Manzke, which covers the ups and downs of four decades of die-cast production by this firm; *Corgi Toys*, by Edward Force, a history of the company and description of every model (over 1,000 of them) built from 1934 to 1984; *Dinky Toys*, also by Edward Force, a short history of all these 1/43rd-scale models, covering the period 1933 to the mid-1990s; and *Dinky Toys and Modelled Miniatures, 1931–1979*, by Mike Richardson and Sue Richardson, a more comprehensive reference work, including material and original design drawings from factory archives.

Continuing the list: *The Encyclopedia of Matchbox Toys, with Values*, by Charles Mack, which covers the years 1947 through 1996 and includes the die-cast vehicles of these internationally popular toys, so called because they were packaged in matchbox-like containers; *Matchbox Toys, 1948–1998: Identification & Value Guide*, by Dana Johnson, which also contains an illustrated history; *Matchbox Toys: A Guide to Selecting, Collecting, and Enjoying New and Vintage Models*, by Bruce and Diane Stoneback, which offers a history of the company and its products, "how-to" advice for the hobbyist, and, interestingly, an analysis of the yearly catalogs as "road maps across time"; *Greenberg's Guide to Tootsietoys, 1945–1969*, by Raymond R. Klein, which includes a detailed listings of the toy cars and trains produced by this manufacturer, together with a history of that firm (Dowst of the United States); *Tootsietoys: World's First Diecast Models*, a similar book by James Weiland and Edward Force; *Spot-On Diecast Models by Tri-ang: A Catalogue and Collector's Guide*, by Graham Thompson, which describes and illustrates every model and variation produced; *The Minic Book*, by Peter Bartock, which focuses on Tri-ang Minic toys; and

The Complete Book of Hot Wheels: With Price Guide, by Bob Parker, a guide to these die-cast miniatures and related accessories manufactured from 1968 to 1994. Of these, Meccano (Dinky), Corgi, Crescent, Spot-On, and Lesney (Matchbox and Dinky) are British firms. Mattel (Hot Wheels) and Dowst (Tootsietoy) are American, with the latter being the oldest to produce a full range of die-cast models, beginning in the years just before World War I.

Not everyone into collecting model cars purchases the work of others. There is a smaller group of hobbyists who fashion their own, to be included in their collections and/or sold to others. For them, there are books such as *Making Classic Cars in Wood*, by Joe B. Hicks, which provides directions for making such classics as the Model T, the Duesenberg SSJ, and the Corvettes; *The Complete Book of Model Car Building*, by Dennis Doty, a guide to various aspects of assembling and customizing vehicles from commercially prepared kits; two volumes by Frank Ross Jr., *The Tin Lizzie: A Model Making Book*, which explains how to make cardboard and paper models of the Ford Model T, and *Antique Car Models: Their Stories and How to Make Them*, which offers detailed instructions for constructing models of pre–World War I automobiles from scratch, including the Curved Dash Olds and the Stanley Steamer; *Scratchbuilding Model Cars*, by Saul Santos, a guide to creating large-scale (1/8th- and 1/16th-size) models from metal, wood, leather, and cloth; and *Model Car, Truck, & Motorcycle Handbook*, by Robert Schleicher, a guide to scratch-building models, assembling metal and plastic kits, and finishing the same. Finally, there is *The Complete Car Modeller* and *The Model Cars of Gerald Wingrove*, both by Gerald Wingrove, probably the foremost practitioner of the art alive today, a "model engineer" who produces incredibly detailed classics in 1/15th-scale.

Other books are aimed at both the builder and collector. Typical of this genre are *The Model Car Handbook*, by R.A. "Bob" Cutter, which emphasizes die-cast and plastic scale models and offers profiles of several model designers, and *The World of Model Cars*, edited by Vic Smeed, which describes the tools, materials, and methods of constructing and (where appropriate) operating the diverse range of model types, together with information on displaying them.

It should be noted here that from 1931 to 1968, General Motors sponsored the Fisher Body Craftsman's Guild Competition, an annual styling/design scholarship contest for youngsters eleven to twenty years of age who competed by submitting a scale model of the automobile of their dreams. For books on this topic, see the "Design and Styling" section of Chapter 4.

Another, related aspect of the model car hobby is the racing of such cars, which sometimes involves their construction as well. In this regard, see Robert Schleicher's *Model Car Racing*, which explores the building and engineering of such cars and the mechanics of racing on both indoor and outdoor tracks. Two contemporary guides to racing slot cars are *Greenberg's Guide to Aurora Slot Cars*, by Thomas Graham, which provides a history of the company and its racing vehicles, together with a complete listing of the cars produced to date, and *Vintage Slot Cars*, by Philippe de Lespinay, a nostalgic look at the era (ca.

1960–1975) of their greatest popularity, when commercial slot car tracks were common, and there even were professional slot car racers. (Slot cars get their name from the narrow grooves that run around the miniature track, into which the rudderlike "guide flag" located on the underside of the car is inserted and held in place.) Alan Harman's *The Basics of Radio Control Model Cars*, a brief (76-page) guide to the nature of radio-control (R/C) kits and racing classes and to building and racing such vehicles, and Bill Burkinshaw's *Buggy Racing Handbook*, which describes and offers advice regarding off-road radio-controlled cars, explore a different form of model racing. Finally, the phenomenal growth of the Internet has led to the development of simulated electronic stock car racing. In *The Beginner's Guide to League Stock Car Sim Racing*, Tim Kellebrew describes how to prepare for and participate in league-sanctioned competition in cyberspace.

Before leaving this section, some mention needs to be made of cars that were specifically manufactured for use by children. The definitive book in this regard is Edoardo Massucci's *Cars for Kids*, an international work (with side-by-side columns of text in English, French, German, and Italian) that traces their development from 1902 to the near present, a history that parallels that of the automobile in general. These so-called baby cars were and are exact replicas of the automobiles of their day, complete with motive power, detailed design features, and accessories. In the United States such cars have been produced by Chevrolet, Buick, Ford, Chrysler, Dodge, Studebaker, and Nash, among others. Today, they are also sought after as collector items by individuals and museums. Whether these are technically "toys" or not is an interesting question.

A very different type of vehicle designed for children is pedal cars, which tend to be generic in appearance and are driven by a bicycle-like mechanism. The best overview of these toys is Jane Dwyre Garton's *Pedal Cars: Chasing the Kidillac*, a work distinguished by its inclusion of oral histories by men and women who have worked in the factories that manufacture the toys and by enthusiasts who collect them.

Kit Cars. As noted in the previous sections, some hobbyists make their own miniature model cars. Others have taken to assembling full-size, working automobiles from commercially available kits. Such vehicles usually feature a custom body fitted to a standard American or foreign-made chassis. Kit cars have been available since the middle of the 20th century, and Paul North's *Kit Cars: A Source Book* reproduces factory literature for American models produced from 1950 to 1985. More contemporaneous in focus is *Performance Roadsters: The Enthusiast's Guide to Cars Inspired by the Classic Lotus 7*, by Monty Watkins *et al.*, essentially an appraisal of various sports cars that can be built from kit-form packages.

Automobilia. In addition to full-size and model cars, many Americans have chosen to collect ornamental parts of automobiles and sales literature. For a general introduction to this area, see Jack Martells' *Antique Automotive Collec-*

tibles, which discusses radiator nameplates, mascots, hubcaps, spark plugs, license plates, and literature, among other artifacts.

The nameplates or "badges" placed by car manufacturers on a car's radiator or hood have long been a serious collectible. See, for example, Brian Jewell's *Motor Badges and Figureheads*, a guide that not only catalogs the various types but also describes the materials and methods used in their production; *Car Mascots: An Enthusiast's Guide*, by Giuseppe de Sirignano and David Sulzberger, which focuses on three distinct types: specially commissioned, factory-produced, and mass-marketed; and Lynn Huntsburger's *U.S. Hood Ornaments and More . . .*, basically a photographic catalog of Huntsburger's collection that covers from the 1940s into the 1990s. The badges carried the name and most often the logo of the company and were usually made of metal. The mascots and figureheads normally adorned the front of the hood, frequently on top of the radiator filler, and generally were a personification of a given aspect of the company. Thus, a statuette of Mercury, the swift messenger of ancient Greece, was found on the car of the same name.

Other common collectibles are automotive license or registration plates, or "tags," as they are colloquially called in some parts of the United States. Uniform license plates were first issued in Massachusetts in 1903, although this practice was not adopted in all of the remaining forty-seven states until 1918. They are now issued by each of the fifty states to individuals and companies to identify specific cars that they own or lease. Thus, a given vehicle may have any number of "temporary" license plates during its lifetime. (A different practice has been followed in Europe, where the license plate is permanently affixed to the car and remains with it for as long as it is on the road.) Interest is strong enough in these objects to have generated the Automobile License Plate Collectors Association.

Generally acknowledged to be the best reference in this area is a comprehensive 800-page international guide to all contemporary plates, together with a historical summary, entitled *Registration Plates of the World*, a British publication written by Neil Parker *et al.* that has gone through multiple editions. For a broad survey of this collectible in its American context, see James K. Fox's *License Plates of the United States: A Pictorial History, 1903 to the Present*, which purports to illustrate and explain the history, graphics, and slogans of every license plate ever issued in this country and was nominated for the Cugnot Award in 1995. Also worthy of attention is the tenth edition of *The Official License Plate Book*, by Thompson C. Murray, which, in addition to picturing over 1,000 American and Canadian plates, explains how to read and decode them, including special tags such as government, Native American tribe, college alumni, and diplomatic ones.

More specifically, an in-depth look at American license plates for a limited chronological period is provided in Robert L. Gilber's *On Every Automobile and Truck, 1928–1931*; the history of the tags of one state is told in Richard E. Dragon's *Registered in R.I.: Motor Vehicle License Plates and the Registration of Motor Vehicles in Rhode Island since 1904*, a truly exemplary work, and in Josiah H.V. Fisher's *75 Years of New Hampshire License Plates, 1905–1979*; Jeff David and Chuck Westphal's *Florida Prestate License Plates* recounts the story of a state that required second, county plates in the early decades of the 20th century; and finally, for an account of one man's lifelong fascination with this particular hobby and specific tags, see automotive historian Keith Marvin's *Of Singular Fancy: The Romance of the License Plate.*

Other automotive-related collectibles have attracted the hobbyist's attention, especially those connected with the distribution and promotion of gasoline (sometimes referred to as "petroliana"). See, for instance, *Check the Oil: Gas Station Collectibles with Prices*, by Scott Anderson, which focuses on advertising memorabilia, signs, gas pumps, gas pump globes, and containers. In a similar vein is *Gas Station Collectibles*, by Mark Anderton and Sherry Mullen, which is essentially a collector's reference and price guide and includes the items in the Anderson volume, plus oil cans, promotional giveaways, uniforms, and car care products; *Petroleum Collectibles with Prices*, by Rick Pease, adds road maps, novelty giveaway items such as salt-and-pepper sets, dinnerware, and clocks, as well as substantial information on graphic designs used in advertising and accessory packaging; the *Value Guide to Gas Station Memorabilia*, by B.J. Summers and Wayne Priddy, is unique in its inclusion of catalog reprints from the 1940s and 1950s and a patent chart; and Michael Karl Witzel's *Gas Station Memories* appends patches and neon to the mix.

A more international approach can be found in Decio Grassi and Rossana Bossaglia's *Gasoline* where, in addition to many of the items cited above, one also can find information on the promotion of gasoline through the use of logos and brand identification. Picking up on the former subject is Wayne Henderson and Scott Benjamin's *Guide to Gasoline Logos*, a reference guide that includes a brief history of each company and illustrations of the chronological development of its logos over the years. This last named work also would be useful to those petroliana hobbyists interested in a method for assigning a date to a particular item.

Collectors of gasoline and oil memorabilia often limit themselves to one aspect of that hobby. Thus, some are interested in only one particular artifact, as witnessed by the publication of four books authored by Scott Benjamin and Wayne Henderson. *Oil Company Signs: A Collector's Guide* concentrates on those gas and oil signs made of tin, porcelain, and neon that have been used both within a filling station and as advertising along the roadside; *Gas Pump Collector's Guide* is designed for the hobbyist interested in collecting antique gas pumps and gaining information on the history of the manufacturers and their various models; and *Gas Globes: Amoco to Mobil & Affiliates* and *Gas Globes: Pennzoil to Union & Affiliates plus Foreign, Generic & Independent Oil Companies' Globes* are guides to thousands of gas pump globes that have been manufactured in the United States and abroad by various oil companies, the different types of originals, and the relatively recent emergence of reproductions.

Such globes also were the subject of an earlier book by Jeff Spanier, similarly entitled *Gasoline Pump Globes*.

Another subdivision within this area focuses on collectibles associated with one particular oil or gas company. For example, see Rick Pease's *A Tour with Texaco: Antique Advertising & Memorabilia, with Values*; Todd P. Helms' *The Conoco Collector's Bible*, featuring items produced by and for the Continental Oil Company; Rob Bender and Tammy Cannoy-Bender's *An Unauthorized Guide to Mobil Collectibles: Chasing the Red Horse*; Charles Whitworth's *Gulf Oil Collectibles*; and a volume by the ubiquitous team of Scott Benjamin and Wayne Henderson: *Sinclair Collectibles*.

There is also a booming business in collecting automotive "paper," such as sales brochures, manufacturer's stock certificates, postcards, magazines advertisements, sales literature, and other pieces of ephemera. An overview of the entire area is provided by Jimmie R.H. Evans in his *Collectors Guide to Automotive Literature*. The number of people who pursue this hobby is sufficiently large to justify the publication of *The International Directory of Automotive Literature Collectors*, a listing of those individuals worldwide who buy, trade, and sell such paper items.

It should come as no surprise that people also have begun to collect books concerning automobiles. Trade is particularly brisk in early "how-to" volumes, especially those written prior to 1930, and in accounts of pioneering motor adventures. An introduction to, and taxonomy for, this hobby have been provided by Charles Mortimer in his *The Constant Search: Collecting Motoring & Motorcycling Books*, although the specific works cited are exclusively British.

Others have taken to collecting stamps that portray automobiles or automotive personalities. John Hayne's *The World Automobile Stamp Album* is exactly what you would expect, with the Tin Type Press of Albuquerque publishing an annual supplement for new issues. Finally, there is also interest in collecting postcards that show cars and auto-related activities, as witnessed by sections of John M. Kaduck's *Transportation Postcards*. (See Appendix 2 for a description of the Curt Teich Postcard Collection, which is easily the finest in this regard.)

BIBLIOGRAPHY

Abbott, Philip. *Seeking Many Inventions: The Idea of Community in America*. Knoxville: University of Tennessee Press, 1987.

Adams, Noland. *Corvette: American Legend*. Vol. 5, *1958–60 Production*. Sidney, Ohio: Cars and Parts Magazine, 1999.

American Automobile Association. *Official Manual of Motor Car Camping*. Washington, D.C.: American Automobile Association, 1920.

Anderson, Scott. *Check the Oil: Gas Station Collectibles with Prices*. Lombard, Ill.: Wallace-Homestead Book, 1986.

Anderton, Mark, and Sherry Mullen. *Gas Station Collectibles: A Wallace Homestead Price Guide*. Radnor, Pa.: Wallace-Homestead, 1994.

Arango, Polly *et al. Touring New Mexico.* Albuquerque: University of New Mexico Press, 1995.

Ayres, William S. *The Warner Collector's Guide to American Toys.* New York: Warner Books, 1981.

Bailey, L. Scott. *Buy an Antique Car.* Los Angeles: Clymer, 1958.

Baker Geoffrey, and Bruno Funaro. *Motels.* New York: Van Nostrand Reinhold, 1955.

Barth, Jack *et al. Roadside America.* New York: Simon & Schuster, 1986.

Bartlett, Richard A. *Yellowstone: A Wilderness Besieged.* Tucson: University of Arizona Press, 1985.

Bartock, Peter. *The Minic Book.* London: New Cavendish, 1987.

Bedell, Mary Crehore. *Modern Gypsies: The Story of a Twelve Thousand Mile Motor Camping Trip Encircling the United States.* New York: Brentano's, 1924.

Belasco, Warren J. *Americans on the Road: From Autocamp to Motel, 1910–1945.* Cambridge, Mass.: MIT Press, 1979.

Bender, Rob, and Tammy Cannoy-Bender. *An Unauthorized Guide to Mobil Collectibles: Chasing the Red Horse.* Atglen, Pa.: Schiffer, 1999.

Benjamin, Scott, and Wayne Henderson. *Gas Globes: Amoco to Mobil & Affiliates.* Atglen, Pa.: Schiffer, 1999.

Benjamin, Scott, and Wayne Henderson. *Gas Globes: Penzoil to Union & Affiliates, plus Foreign, Generic & Independent Oil Companies' Globes.* Atglen, Pa.: Schiffer, 1999.

Benjamin, Scott, and Wayne Henderson. *Gas Pump Collector's Guide.* Osceola, Wisc.: Motorbooks International, 1996.

Benjamin, Scott, and Wayne Henderson. *Gas Pump Globes.* Osceola, Wisc.: Motorbooks International, 1993.

Benjamin, Scott, and Wayne Henderson. *Oil Company Signs: A Collector's Guide.* Osceola, Wisc.: Motorbooks International, 1995.

Benjamin, Scott, and Wayne Henderson. *Sinclair Collectibles.* Atglen, Pa.: Schiffer, 1997.

Berger, Michael L. *The Devil Wagon in God's Country: The Automobile and Social Change in Rural America, 1893–1929.* Hamden, Conn.: Archon Books, 1979.

Bliss, Carey. *Autos across America: A Bibliography of Transcontinental Automobile Travel, 1903–1940.* Austin, Tex.: Jenkins and Reese, 1982.

Bold, Christine. *The WPA Guides: Mapping America.* Jackson: University of Mississippi Press, 1999.

Bossi, Marco. *Autohobby: Autogiocattoli D'Epoca, Jouets Automobiles Anciens, Old Toy Automobiles.* Ivrea, Italy: Priuli & Verlicca, 1974.

Breslauer, Ken. *Fifty Years of Stock Car Racing: A History of Collectibles and Memorabilia.* Phoenix: David Bull, 1997.

Brimmer, Frank E. *Autocamping.* Cincinnati: Stewart Kidd, 1923.

Brimmer, F. Everett. *Autocamping Facts.* Chicago: Outer's Book, 1924.

Brimmer, F. Everett. *Motor Campcraft.* New York: Macmillan, 1923.

Brunvand, Jan H. *The Vanishing Hitchhiker: American Urban Legends and Their Meanings.* New York: W.W. Norton, 1981.

Buchholtz, C.W. *Man in Glacier.* West Glacier, Mont.: Glacier Natural History Association, 1976.

Burkinshaw, Bill. *Buggy Racing Handbook.* London: Argus Books, 1986.

Butko, Brian A. *Pennsylvania Traveler's Guide: The Lincoln Highway.* Mechanicsburg, Pa.: Stackpole Books, 1996.

Byam, Wally, and David McKay. *Trailer Travel Here and Abroad: The New Way to Adventurous Living.* New York: David McKay, 1960.

Cantor, George. *Where the Old Roads Go: Driving the First Federal Highways of Arizona, California, Colorado, New Mexico, Nevada, and Utah.* New York: HarperPerennial, 1992.

Cantor, George. *Where the Old Roads Go: Driving the First Federal Highways of the Northeast.* New York: Harper & Row, 1990.

Clark, Marian. *The Route 66 Cookbook.* Tulsa: Council Oak Books, 1993.

Consumer Guide, Auto Editors of. *The Complete Book of Collectible Cars, 1930–1980.* New York: Outlet Book, 1985.

Copeland, Estella M. *Overland by Auto in 1913: Diary of a Family Tour from California to Indiana.* Indianapolis: Indiana Historical Society, 1981.

Cupper, Dan. *The Pennsylvania Turnpike: A History.* Lebanon, Pa.: Applied Arts, 1990.

Cutter, R.A. *The Model Car Handbook.* Summit, Pa.: TAB Books, 1979.

David, Jeff, and Chuck Westphal. *Florida Prestate License Plates.* West Lake Panasoffkee, Fla.: Author, 1999.

Demars, Stanford E. *The Tourist in Yosemite, 1855–1985.* Salt Lake City: University of Utah Press, 1991.

Devlin, Robert T. *Pebble Beach, a Matter of Style: Racing through the Pines 1950–1956, Concours d'Elegance 1950–1979, a Complete History.* Costa Mesa, Calif.: Newport Press, 1980.

Doty, Dennis. *The Complete Book of Model Car Building.* Summit, Pa.: TAB Books, 1981.

Dragon, Richard E. *Registered in R.I.: Motor Vehicle License Plates and the Registration of Motor Vehicles in Rhode Island since 1904.* Providence, R.I.: Eastern Seaboard Press, 1998.

Dreiser, Theodore. *A Hoosier Holiday.* New York: John Lane, 1916.

Eddy, Arthur J. *Two Thousand Miles on an Automobile: Being a Desultory Narrative of a Trip through New England, New York, Canada and the West, by "Chauffeur."* Philadelphia: J.B. Lippincott, 1902.

Evans, Jimmie R.H. *Collectors Guide to Automotive Literature.* 2nd ed. Sioux City, Iowa: Larsen's Printing, n.d.

Eves, Edward, and Dan Burger. *Great Car Collections of the World.* New York: Gallery Books, 1986.

Federal Writers' Project, Works Projects Administration. *U.S. One: Maine to Florida.* New York: Modern Age Books, 1938.

Federal Writers' Project, Work Projects Administration for the State of Kansas. *Kansas, a Guide to the Sunflower State.* New York: Viking Press, 1939.

[Federal] Writers' Program, Work Projects Administration in the State of Oklahoma. *Oklahoma, a Guide to the Sooner State.* Norman: University of Oklahoma Press, 1941.

Ferguson, Melville. *Motor Camping on Western Trails.* New York: Century, 1925.

Fetherston, David. *Hot Rod Memorabilia & Collectibles.* Osceola, Wisc.: Motorbooks International, 1996.

Fisher, Josiah H.V. *75 Years of New Hampshire License Plates, 1905–1979.* Meredith, N.H.: Author, 1980.

Flink, James J. *The Automobile Age.* Cambridge, Mass.: MIT Press, 1988.

Flower, Raymond, and Michael Wynn Jones. *100 Years on the Road: A Social History of the Car.* New York: McGraw-Hill, 1981.

Force, Edward. *Corgi Toys, with Price Guide and Variations List.* West Chester, Pa.: Schiffer, 1984.

Force, Edward. *Dinky Toys.* 3rd ed. Atglen, Pa.: Schiffer, 1996.

Fox, James K. *License Plates of the United States: A Pictorial History, 1903 to the Present.* Jericho, N.Y.: Interstate Directory Publishing, 1994.

Freed, Joe, and Sharon Freed. *Collector's Guide to American Transportation Toys, 1895– 1941.* Raleigh, N.C.: Freedom Publishing, 1995.

Fussell, Paul. *The Norton Book of Travel.* New York: W.W. Norton, 1987.

Gardiner, Gordon, and Richard O'Neill. *The Collector's Guide to Toy Cars: An International Survey of Tinplate and Diecast Cars from 1900.* London: Salamander Books, 1996.

Gardiner, Gordon, and Alistair Morris. *The Price Guide and Identification of Automobilia.* Suffolk, Eng.: Antique Collector's Club, 1982.

Garton, Jane Dwyre. *Pedal Cars: Chasing the Kidillac.* Atglen, Pa.: Schiffer, 1998.

Genovese, Peter. *The Great American Road Trip: U.S. 1, Maine to Florida.* New Brunswick, N.J.: Rutgers University Press, 1999.

Genovese, Peter. *Roadside New Jersey.* New Brunswick, N.J.: Rutgers University Press, 1994.

Gilber, Robert L. *On Every Automobile and Truck 1928–1931.* Hollywood, Calif.: Dahlhousie Publishing House, 1976.

Gillespie, Angus Kress, and Michael Aaron Rockland. *Looking for America on the New Jersey Turnpike.* New Brunswick, N.J.: Rutgers University Press, 1989.

Gladding, Effie Price. *Across the Continent by the Lincoln Highway.* New York: Brentano's, 1915.

Gordon, Jan, and Cora J. Gordon. *On Wandering Wheels: Through Roadside Camps from Maine to Georgia in an Old Sedan Car.* New York: Dodd, Mead, 1928.

Gottschalk, Lillian. *American Toy Cars and Trucks, 1894–1942.* New York: Abbeville Press, 1985.

Graham, Thomas. *Greenberg's Guide to Aurora Slot Cars.* Waukesha, Wisc.: Greenberg Books, 1995.

Grassi, Decio, and Rossana Bossaglia. *Gasoline.* New York: Abbeville, 1995.

Gunnell, John. *A Collector's Guide to Automobilia.* Iola, Wisc.: Krause, 1994.

Gunnell, John, ed. *Marques of America: A Special-Interest Car Buyer's Guide.* Iola, Wisc.: Krause, 1994.

Hale, Louise Closser. *We Discover the Old Dominion.* New York: Dodd, Mead, 1916.

Harman, Alan. *The Basics of Radio Control Model Cars.* Hempstead, Herts, Eng.: Nexus Special Interests, 1995.

Hayne, John. *The World Automobile Stamp Album.* Albuquerque: Tin Type Press, 1994.

Helms, Todd P. *The Conoco Collector's Bible.* Atglen, Pa.: Schiffer, 1995.

Henderson, Wayne, and Scott Benjamin. *Guide to Gasoline Logos.* LaGrange, Ohio: PCM Publishing, 1997.

Hicks, Joe B. *Making Classic Cars in Wood.* New York: Sterling, 1990.

Hill, Ralph N. *The Mad Doctor's Drive: Being an Account of the 1st Auto Trip across the U.S.A., San Francisco to New York, 1903: or, Sixty-Three Days on a Winton Motor Carriage.* Brattleboro, Vt.: Stephen Greene Press, 1964.

Hines, Duncan. *Lodging for a Night*. Bowling Green, Ky.: Adventures in Good Eating, 1938.

Hokanson, Drake. *The Lincoln Highway: Main Street across America*. Iowa City: University of Iowa Press, 1988.

Hollis, Tim. *Dixie before Disney: 100 Years of Roadside Fun*. Jackson: University of Mississippi Press, 1999.

Huggins, Eleanor, and John Olmsted. *Adventures on and off Interstate 80: Natural and Human History along the Pioneer and Gold Rush Corridor from San Francisco's Pacific Shore to Nevada's Desert Sands*. Palo Alto, Calif.: Tioga, 1985.

Huntsburger, Lynn. *U.S. Hood Ornaments and More . . .* Sullivan, Ala.: Prairieland Publishing, 1994.

Hutchison, Ken, and Greg Nelson. *The Golden Age of Automotive Toys, 1925–1941*. Paducah, Ky.: Collector Books, 1997.

International Directory of Automotive Literature Collectors. Lancaster, Pa.: John E. Lloyd, 1970-date.

Ise, John. *Our National Park Policy: A Critical History*. Baltimore: Johns Hopkins University Press, 1961.

Jakle, John A. *The Tourist: Travel in Twentieth-Century North America*. Lincoln: University of Nebraska Press, 1985.

Jakle, John A., Keith A. Sculle, and Jefferson S. Rogers. *The Motel in America*. Baltimore: Johns Hopkins University Press, 1996.

Jennings, Jan, ed. *Roadside America: The Automobile in Design and Culture*. Ames: Iowa State University Press, 1990.

Jessup, Elon. *The Motor Camping Book*. New York: G.P. Putnam's Sons, 1921.

Jewell, Brian. *Motor Badges and Figureheads*. Kent, Eng.: Midas Books, 1978.

Johnson, Dana. *Matchbox Toys, 1948 to 1998: Identification & Value Guide*. 3rd ed. Paducah, Ky.: Collector Books, 1998.

Jolley, Harley E. *The Blue Ridge Parkway*. Knoxville: University of Tennessee Press, 1969.

Kaduck, John M. *Transportation Postcards*. 1st ed. Des Moines: Wallace-Homestead, 1976.

Kellebrew, Tim. *The Beginner's Guide to League Stock Car Sim Racing*. Santa Ana, Calif.: Steve Smith Autosports, 1998.

Kimball, Winfield A., and Maurice H. Decker. *Touring with Tent and Trailer*. New York: McGraw-Hill, 1937.

Kimball, Winfield A., and W. Livingston Larned. *The Trailer for Pleasure and Business*. New York: Whittlesey House/McGraw-Hill, 1937.

Kimes, Beverly Rae. *Automobile Quarterly's Complete Handbook of Automobile Hobbies*. Princeton, N.J.: Automobile Quarterly, 1981.

Klein, Raymond R. *Greenberg's Guide to Tootsietoys, 1945–1969*. Waukesha, Wisc.: Kalmbach, 1993.

Knutson, Roger. *Flattened Fauna: A Field Guide to Common Animals of Roads, Streets and Highways*. Berkeley, Calif.: Ten Speed Press, 1987.

Landau, Robert, and James Phillippi. *Airstream*. Salt Lake City: Peregrine Smith, 1984.

Lespinay, Philippe de. *Vintage Slot Cars*. Osceola, Wisc.: MBI, 1999.

Lichty, Robert C. *The Official Book of the Antique Automobile Club of America: A 60-Year History of Dedication to the Automobile*. Iola, Wisc.: Krause, 1999.

Lilliefors, Jim. *Highway 50: Ain't That America*. Golden, Colo.: Fulcrum, 1993.

Lincoln Highway Association. *The Complete Official Road Guide of the Lincoln Highway*. Detroit: Lincoln Highway Association, 1915.

Lincoln Highway Association. *The Lincoln Highway: The Story of a Crusade That Made Transportation History*. New York: Dodd, Mead, 1935.

Long, John D., and John C. Long. *Motor Camping*. Rev. ed. New York: Dodd, Mead, 1926.

Luxenberg, Stan. *Roadside Empires: How the Chains Franchised America*. New York: Viking, 1986.

Lynd, Robert, and Helen M. Lynd. *Middletown: A Study in American Culture*. New York: Harcourt, Brace, & World, 1929.

Lynd, Robert, and Helen M Lynd. *Middletown in Transition: A Study in Cultural Conflicts*. New York: Harcourt, Brace, and World, 1937.

Mack, Charles. *The Encyclopedia of Matchbox Toys, with Values*. Atglen, Pa.: Schiffer, 1997.

Malcolm, Andrew H., and Roger Straus III. *U.S. 1: America's Original Main Street*. New York: St. Martin's Press, 1991.

Mandel, Leon. *William Fisk Harrah: The Life and Times of a Gambling Magnate*. New York: Doubleday, 1982.

Manzke, Bill. *The Unauthorized Encyclopedia of Corgi Toys*. Atglen, Pa.: Schiffer, 1997.

Margolies, John. *Fun along the Road: American Tourist Attractions*. Boston: Bulfinch Press/Little, Brown, 1998.

Margolies, John. *Home Away from Home: Motels in America*. Boston: Bulfinch Press/ Little, Brown, 1995.

Marling, Karal Ann. *The Colossus of Roads: Myth and Symbol along the American Highway*. Minneapolis: University of Minnesota Press, 1984.

Marnell, William H. *Vacation Yesterdays of New England*. New York: Seabury Press, 1975.

Martells, Jack. *Antique Automotive Collectibles*. Chicago: Contemporary Books, 1980.

Marvin, Keith. *Of Singular Fancy: The Romance of the License Plate*. Troy, N.Y.: Author, 1993.

Mason, Philip P. *The League of American Wheelmen and the Good Roads Movement, 1880–1905*. Ann Arbor: University of Michigan Press, 1957.

Massey, Beatrice Larned. *It Might Have Been Worse: A Motor Trip from Coast to Coast*. San Francisco: Harr Wagner, 1920.

Massucci, Edoardo. *Cars for Kids*. New York: Rizzoli International Publications, 1983.

Maynard, Chris, and Bill Scheller. *Manifold Destiny: The One! The Only! Guide to Cooking on Your Car Engine!* New York: Villard Books, 1989.

McClelland, Linda Flint. *Building the National Parks: Historic Landscape Design and Construction*. Baltimore: Johns Hopkins University Press, 1998.

McClintock, Inez, and Marshall McClintock. *Toys in America*. Washington, D.C.: Public Affairs Press, 1961.

Miller, John E. *Looking for History on Highway 14*. Ames: Iowa State University Press, 1993.

Moore, Bob, and Patrick Grauwels. *Route 66: A Guidebook to the Mother Road*. Eagle Creek, Ore.: Innovative Publishing Group, 1994.

Mortimer, Charles. *The Constant Search: Collecting Motoring & Motorcycling Books*. Newbury Park, Calif.: Haynes, 1982.

Morton, H.F. *Strange Commissions for Henry Ford*. York, Eng.: Herald Printing Works, 1934.

Murray, Thompson C. *The Official License Plate Book: How to Read and Decode Current United States & Canadian Plates, Including Motorcycles, Trucks, Police Patches: A Registry of 1000 Color Illustrations*. Jericho, N.Y.: Interstate Directory Publishing, 1997.

Nash, Charles E. *Trailer Ahoy!* Lancaster, Pa.: Intelligencer Printing, 1937.

Negro Motorist Green Book. New York: Victor H. Green, 1938.

Neville, Bill. *Real Steel: An Investor's and Philosopher's Guide to the American Automobile*. Philadelphia: Running Press, 1975.

Nolan, A.M. *Rock 'n' Roll Road Trip: The Ultimate Guide to the Sites, the Shrines, and the Legends across America*. New York: Pharos Books, 1992.

North, Paul. *Kit Cars: A Source Book*. Baltimore: Bookman, 1986.

O'Brien, Bob R. *Our National Parks and the Search for Sustainability*. Austin: University of Texas Press, 1999.

O'Brien, Richard. *Collecting Toy Cars & Trucks: Identification and Value Guide*. 2nd ed. Iola, Wisc.: Krause, 1997.

Orsi, Richard J., Alfred Runte, and Marlene Smith-Baranzini, eds. *Yosemite and Sequoia: A Century of California National Parks*. Berkeley: University of California Press, 1993.

Osborne, Richard E. *Tour Book for Antique Car Buffs*. 2nd ed. Indianapolis: Riebel-Roque, 1994.

Parker, Bob. *The Complete Book of Hot Wheels: With Price Guide*. Atglen, Pa.: Schiffer, 1995.

Parker, Neil, John Weeks, and Reg Wilson. *Registration Plates of the World*. 3rd ed. Taunton, Eng.: EUROPLATE, 1994.

Patton, Phil. *Open Road: A Celebration of the American Highway*. New York: Simon & Schuster, 1986.

Pease, Rick. *Petroleum Collectibles with Prices*. Atglen, Pa.: Schiffer, 1997.

Pease, Rick. *A Tour with Texaco: Antique Advertising & Memorabilia, with Values*. Atglen, Pa.: Schiffer, 1997.

Peterson, Dale. *Storyville, USA*. Athens: University of Georgia Press, 1999.

Peterson, Kay. *Home Is Where You Park It: A Guide to RV Living as a Life Style*. Chicago: Follett, 1977.

Pomeroy, Earl. *In Search of the Golden West: The Tourist in Western America*. New York: Alfred A. Knopf, 1957.

Post, Emily. *By Motor to the Golden Gate*. New York: D. Appleton, 1917.

Preston, Howard L. *Dirt Roads to Dixie: Accessibility and Modernization in the South, 1885–1935*. Knoxville: University of Tennessee Press, 1991.

Radcliff, Alan L. *Adventures of a Vintage Car Collector*. New York: Bonanza Books, 1972.

Radde, Bruce. *The Merritt Parkway*. New Haven, Conn.: Yale University Press, 1993.

Rae, John B. *The Road and Car in American Life*. Cambridge, Mass.: MIT Press, 1971.

Raitz, Karl, ed. *A Guide to the National Road*. Baltimore: Johns Hopkins University Press, 1996.

Ramsey, Alice H. *Veil, Duster and Tire Iron*. Corvina, Calif.: Castle Press, 1961.

Reck, Franklin, and William Moss. *Station Wagon Living: A Guide to Outdoor Recreation, with a Directory of over 1300 Campgrounds and Field Test Reports on*

140 Items of Camp Gear. New York: Simon & Schuster and the Ford Motor Company, 1957.

Richardson, Mike, and Sue Richardson. *Dinky Toys and Modelled Miniatures, 1931– 1979.* London: New Cavendish, 1981.

Rittenhouse, Jack D. *A Guide Book to Highway 66.* Los Angeles: Author, 1946.

Rockland, Michael Aaron. *Homes on Wheels.* New Brunswick, N.J.: Rutgers University Press, 1980.

Rose, Albert C. *Historic American Roads: From Frontier Trails to Superhighways.* New York: Crown, 1976.

Ross, Frank, Jr. *Antique Car Models: Their Stories and How to Make Them.* New York: Lothrop, Lee, & Shepard, 1978.

Ross, Frank, Jr. *The Tin Lizzie: A Model Making Book.* New York: Lothrop, Lee, & Shepard, 1980.

Ross, Jim. *Oklahoma Route 66: The Cruiser's Companion.* Bethany, Okla.: Ghost Town Press, 1992.

Runte, Alfred. *National Parks: The American Experience.* Lincoln: University of Nebraska Press, 1979.

Runte, Alfred. *Yosemite: The Embattled Wilderness.* Lincoln: University of Nebraska Press, 1990.

Rush, Richard H. *Automobiles as an Investment.* New York: Macmillan, 1982.

Rush, Richard H. *Investing in Classic Automobiles for Profit and Capital Gain.* New York: Linden Press/Simon & Schuster, 1984.

Santos, Saul. *Scratchbuilding Model Cars.* Blue Ridge Summit, Pa.: TAB Books, 1983.

Schaut, Jim, and Nancy Schaut. *American Automobilia: An Illustrated History and Price Guide.* Radnor, Pa.: Wallace-Homestead, 1994.

Schleicher, Robert H. *Model Car Racing.* Radnor, Pa.: Chilton, 1979.

Schleicher, Robert. *Model Car, Truck, & Motorcycle Handbook.* Radnor, Pa.: Chilton, 1978.

Schlereth, Thomas J. *Reading the Road: U.S. 40 and the American Landscape.* Rev. ed. Knoxville: University of Tennessee Press, 1997.

Schlereth, Thomas J. *U.S. 40: A Roadscape of the American Experience.* Indianapolis, Ind.: Indiana Historical Society, 1985.

Schnieder, Jill. *Route 66 across New Mexico: A Wanderer's Guide.* 1st ed. Albuquerque: University of New Mexico Press, 1991.

Scott, Quinta, and Susan Croce Kelly. *Route 66: The Highway and Its People.* Norman: University of Oklahoma Press, 1988.

Sellars, Richard W. *Preserving Nature in the National Parks: A History.* New Haven, Conn.: Yale University Press, 1997.

Sessler, Peter. *Car Collector's Handbook: A Comprehensive Guide to Collecting Rare and Historic Automobiles.* Los Angeles: HP Books, 1992.

Shank, William H. *Vanderbilt's Folly: A History of the Pennsylvania Turnpike.* York, Pa.: American Canal and Transportation Center, 1973.

Sheridan, Michael, and Sam Bushala. *Showtime: The Story of the International Championship Auto Shows and the Hot Rod/Custom Car World: A 20 Year History.* Pontiac, Mich.: Promotional Displays, 1980.

Simonds, William A. *Henry Ford and Greenfield Village.* New York: Frederick A. Stokes, 1938.

Sims, Blackburn. *The Trailer Home, with Practical Advice on Trailer Life and Travel.* New York: Longman's Green, 1937.

Sirignano, Giuseppe di, and David Sulzberger. *Car Mascots: An Enthusiast's Guide.* New York: Crescent Books, 1977.

Smeed, Vic, ed. *The World of Model Cars.* Secaucus, N.J.: Chartwell Books, 1980.

Snow, W. Brewster, ed. *The Highway and the Landscape.* New Brunswick, N.J.: Rutgers University Press, 1959.

Snyder, Tom. *The Route 66 Traveler's Guide and Roadside Companion.* New York: St. Martin's Press, 1990.

Spanier, Jeff. *Gasoline Pump Globes.* Tulsa, Okla.: Author, 1979.

Steinbeck, John. *The Grapes of Wrath.* New York: Viking Press, 1939.

Stern, Jane, and Michael Stern. *Eat Your Way across the U.S.A.: 500 Diners, Farmland Buffets, Lobster Shacks, Pie Palaces, and Other All-American Eateries.* New York: Broadway Books, 1997.

Stewart, George R. *U.S. 40: Cross Section of the United States of America.* Boston: Houghton Mifflin, 1953.

Stoneback, Bruce, and Diane Stoneback. *Matchbox Toys: A Guide to Selecting, Collecting, and Enjoying New and Vintage Models.* Secaucus, N.J.: Chartwell Books, 1993.

Stubenrauch, Bob. *Restore and Drive: Collectible Cars of Postwar America.* New York: Norton, 1984.

Summers, B.J., and Wayne Priddy. *Value Guide to Gas Station Memorabilia.* Paducah, Ky.: Collector Books, 1995.

Tax Guide for Automotive Collectors and Restorers. Newport Beach, Calif.: Accelerated Trends, 1984.

Taylor, Rich. *Hershey: The World's Greatest Antique Car Event.* Phoenix: David Bull, 1997.

Thompson, Graham. *Spot-On Diecast Models by Tri-ang: A Catalogue and Collector's Guide.* Newbury Park, Calif.: Haynes, 1983.

Thornburg, David A. *Galloping Bungalows: The Rise and Demise of the American House Trailer.* Hamden, Conn.: Archon Books, 1991.

Travers, J. Wadsworth. *From Coast to Coast via the Old Spanish Trail.* San Diego: N.p., 1929.

Trinkle, Florence. *Coast to Coast in a Brush Runabout, 1908.* Los Angeles: Clymer, 1952.

Upward, Geoffrey C. *A Home for Our Heritage: The Building and Growth of Greenfield Village and Henry Ford Museum, 1929–1979.* Dearborn, Mich.: Henry Ford Museum Press, 1979.

Vale, Thomas, and Geraldine Vale. *Western Images, Western Landscapes: Travels along U.S. 89.* Tucson: University of Arizona Press, 1989.

Vale, Thomas R., and Geraldine R. Vale. *U.S. 40 Today: Thirty Years of Landscape Change in America.* Madison: University of Wisconsin Press, 1983.

Van Cleemput, Marcel. *The Great Book of Corgi, 1956–1983.* London: New Cavendish, 1989.

Van de Water, Frederic F. *The Family Flivvers to Frisco.* New York: D. Appleton, 1927.

Viemeister, Peter. *Micro Cars: A Collector's Guide to 3-Inch Miniatures, with Motor Vehicle Encyclopedia and Lore.* 1st ed. Bedford, Va.: Hamilton's, 1982.

Wallis, Michael. *Route 66: The Mother Road.* New York: St. Martin's Press, 1990.

Watkins, Monty, Ian Stent, and Peter Filby. *Performance Roadsters: The Enthusiast's Guide to Cars Inspired by the Classic Lotus 7*. Reigate, Surrey, Eng.: Firebird, 1995.

Webb, Charles. *The Investor's Illustrated Guide to American Convertible and Special-Interest Automobiles, 1946–1976*. San Diego: A.S. Barnes, 1979.

Weiland, James, and Edward Force. *Detroit in Miniature: 400 Photos of American Diecast Models Made Worldwide*. Litchfield, Conn.: Miniature Auto Sales, 1983.

Weiland, James, and Edward Force. *Tootsietoys: World's First Diecast Models*. Osceola, Wisc.: Motorbooks International, 1980.

Weiss, John. *Traveling the New, Historic Route 66 of Illinois*. Frankfort, Ill.: A.O. Motivation Programs, 1997.

Weller, E.V. *California Motorlogues: Suggestions for One-Day and Week-End Motor Trips on the Highways and Byways of California*. San Francisco: San Francisco Examiner, 1921.

Whitworth, Charles. *Gulf Oil Collectibles*. Atglen, Pa.: Schiffer, 1998.

Wiegold, Marilyn E. *Pioneering in Parks and Parkways: Westchester County, New York, 1895–1945*. Essays in Public Works History, No. 9. Chicago: Public Works Historical Society, 1980.

Williams, Guy R. *The World of Model Cars*. London: A. Deutsch, 1976.

Wingrove, Gerald. *The Complete Car Modeller*. New York: Crown, 1979.

Wingrove, Gerald. *The Model Cars of Gerald Wingrove*. London: New Cavendish Books, 1979.

Witzel, Michael Karl. *Gas Station Memories*. Osceola, Wisc.: Motorbooks International, 1994.

Witzel, Michael Karl. *Route 66 Remembered*. Osceola, Wisc.: Motorbooks International, 1996.

Worthington-Williams, Michael. *Automobilia: A Guided Tour for Collectors*. New York: Hastings House, 1979.

WPA Guide to 1930s Arkansas. Lawrence: University Press of Kansas, 1987.

WPA Guide to 1930s Colorado. Lawrence: University Press of Kansas, 1987.

WPA Guide to 1930s Kansas. Lawrence: University Press of Kansas, 1984.

WPA Guide to 1930s Oklahoma. Lawrence: University Press of Kansas, 1986.

Yorke, Douglas A., Jr., and John Margolies. *Hitting the Road: The Art of the American Roadmap*. San Francisco: Chronicle Books, 1996.

CHAPTER 9

The Sport of Motor Racing

In Chapter 2 we explored the available literature on men and women who have made a name for themselves as race car drivers. In Chapter 4 we examined books concerning the design and development of racing cars and the engines that power(ed) them. Here, our concern is with motor racing as a spectator sport, which began in the United States in 1895 with a road race sponsored by a Chicago newspaper. The history of that contest has been recounted many times, most notably by automotive pioneer J. Frank Duryea in *When Chicago Introduced the Automobile to America: My Chicago Race Winner*. The victory of the Duryea car and the press coverage thereof first aroused significant American interest in the automobile.

HISTORIC OVERVIEWS

General Surveys

Racing can be divided into different types of competition, for example, stock car, Grand Prix, drag racing, and so on. As we shall see, there are many books devoted to each type. However, researchers interested in motor sports may want to begin with one or more of the good general histories. Such volumes usually trace the development of this sport since the turn of the century and, as such, have a decidedly international focus to them. Typical of such volumes are two by Ivan Rendall: *The Power and the Glory: A Century of Motor Racing*, an evocative, best-selling history based on a BBC television series that gives equal attention to European Grand Prix and American oval racing, and, similarly, *The Checkered Flag: 100 Years of Motor Racing*, a comprehensive, year-by-year account of the evolution of international motor racing, with its twin themes of individual competition and engineering excellence; L.J.K. Setright *et al.*'s *With Flying Colours: The Pirelli Album of Motor Sport*, which is more European in emphasis; and William Boddy and Brian Laban's *The History of Motor Racing, 1894–1977*, a highly acclaimed, heavily illustrated survey. Finally, *The Automobile: The First Century*, by David Burgess Wise *et al.*, a popular, profusely illustrated, worldwide history, shows how the development of the car and that of motor sport have been inseparably intertwined, with each learning from and giving lessons to the other.

Less traditional in approach are *Motoring: The Golden Years*, a compilation by Rupert Prior that combines the recollections and anecdotes of the participants with artwork from London's Khachadourian Gallery to create an artistic anthology that recaptures the flavor of (mostly European) auto racing during its first forty years; *The Greatest Days of Racing*, by Peter Stevenson, an informal history composed of third-person stories of the events and personalities of motor racing from the beginning through the 1960s; and *Great Auto Races*, as told and painted by Peter Helck, a broad narrative and artistic survey of the diverse world of motor racing from its beginnings in the 1890s through the 1960s, an oversized book for which Helck won the AACA's 1975 McKean Award.

The above volumes tend to take an international perspective. The best historical overview of the domestic racing scene and winner of the 1974 Cugnot Award is Albert R. Bochroch's *American Automobile Racing: An Illustrated History*, which covers races, cars, and drivers for the period 1895 to 1973. Comprehensive in approach, Bochroch's work includes road, oval, and drag racing. Unfortunately, this book covers only the first three-quarters of the 20th century. Also worth reading is John Gunnell's *Race Car Flashback: A Celebration of America's Affair with Auto Racing from 1900–1980s*, an illustrated historical survey aimed more at the enthusiast market. Finally, *American Motorsports: The Definitive Illustrated Guide*, edited by David Phillips, begins with a brief history of the origins of the various forms of competition and then provides a survey of their contemporary manifestations, with due attention to the drivers and teams.

For an account of early (1910s through 1930s) domestic developments exclusively, readers are directed to Griffith Borgeson's comprehensive history of this period, *The Golden Age of the American Racing Car*. A revised edition of this McKean Award-winning 1966 classic appeared posthumously in 1998. Borgeson excels at the human side of racing, capturing the personalities and characteristics of pioneer designers, engineers, and drivers, including Fred Duesenberg, Louis Chevrolet, Harry Miller, and Fred Offenhauser, while providing an excellent history of the development of race car technology. Another good account of the same era is John C. Bentley's *Great American Automobiles: A Dramatic Account of Their Achievements in Competition*, which covers the years 1900–1932. The emphasis here is on the races themselves as Bentley describes such classic competitions as the Glidden Tours, the Vanderbilt Cup races, the New York-to-Paris Race, the first Indianapolis 500, and the "sand races" at Ormond-

Daytona Beach (Florida) and on the Bonneville Flats (Utah). Finally, Fred J. Wagner's *The Saga of the Roaring Road: A Story of Early Auto Racing in America* is the reminiscences (as told to John M. Mitchell) of probably the most famous automotive race starter of all time, first published in 1938 and good for insights into early racing.

Many early oval tracks in the United States had wooden surfaces, a unique aspect of international motor contests. The history of racing that took place on such banked (usually at forty-five to fifty degrees) tracks from 1910 to 1931 is told by Dick Wallen and twenty other motor sportswriters in the voluminous (434-page) *Board Track: Guts, Gold & Glory*, supported by hundreds of period photographs, other memorabilia, and extensive statistics regarding twenty-four individual tracks and the drivers that raced there. *Board Track* was selected as the Best Book of 1991 by the American Auto Racing Writers and Broadcasters Association (AARWBA).

Unfortunately, specific volumes do not exist for the general history of American motor racing in the 1940s, a not surprising development given that little racing took place during much of that decade because of World War II. For an in-depth (561-page), profusely illustrated look at the 1950s, see *Fabulous Fifties: American Championship Racing*, edited by Carol Sims, which provides a comprehensive survey of the National Championship races of those years and the men behind them. More specific is *American Sports Car Racing in the 1950s*, by Michael T. Lynch *et al.*, an account of the last decade before commercialization and technology revolutionized professional motor racing. This is the story of affluent teams like Cunningham and Scarab and individual owners like John Edgar, Johnny von Neumann, and Tony Parravano and the European cars that they drove. The same decade and the next are also the subject of Tom Burnside and Denise McCluggage's *American Racing: Road Racing in the 50s and 60s* (see below). Finally, Dick Wallen's *Roar from the Sixties: American Championship Racing* is another massive (593-page) survey, chronicling in words and photographs (1,400 of them) USAC Championship races during the years that witnessed the transition from front-engined roadsters to mid-engined Formula 1-type cars and the accompanying emergence of a new generation of drivers.

In addition to the historical approach, a number of works attempt to portray the "flavor" of contemporary professional motor car racing in the United States. The best of these are Sam Moses' *Fast Guys, Rich Guys and Idiots: A Racing Odyssey on the Border of Obsession*, wherein the motor sports writer for *Sports Illustrated* exposes the drama and personalities behind the public image; Leon Mandel's *Fast Lane Summer: North American Road Racing*, which, although brief (96 pages) offers some fine glimpses of what day-to-day life is like for members of a racing team during one season, as seen through the eyes of the owner, driver, manager, and crew; and Shaun Assael's *Wide Open: Days and Nights on the NASCAR Tour*, based on a year that the author spent on the Winston Cup stock car circuit, observing the lives of contemporary drivers and the culture of the sport in which they participate but also interviewing past legends to put today's events into historical perspective. More in the reference category is Johnny McDonald's *Under the Green: A Complete Guide to Auto Racing*, which contains sections on sanctioning organizations, track workers, racing teams, and the media (including track announcers), along with more traditional topics such as the cars and the drivers, all aimed at explaining what each does and how they make a race happen.

Road Racing

As noted earlier, the first American automobile race is generally acknowledged to be the one held on Thanksgiving Day 1895 and sponsored by the *Chicago Times-Herald*. It traversed the distance from Chicago to Evanston and back and thus, in contemporary terms, it may be said that motor racing in the United States began as open road (as opposed to track) racing. For the reminiscences of one of the participants in that 1895 contest, see Charles B. King's *Personal Sidelights of America's First Automobile Race*.

George N. Schuster and Tom Mahoney explore the American aspect of one of a number of early long-distance road races that were both intranational and international, the 1908 New York-to-Paris one, in their *The Longest Auto Race*, as does Alise Barton Whiticar in *The Long Road: The Story of the Race around the World by Automobile in 1908*. The 1908 race was a globe-circling contest that began in New York and traveled west. Cosponsored by Paris' *Le Matin* newspaper and the *New York Times*, it was concocted to publicize the automobile and to sell papers. It is also the focus of Dermot Cole's well-done *Hard Driving: The 1908 Race from New York to Paris* and Floyd Clymer's *New York to Paris, 1908*.

Organized road racing actually had begun in the United States in 1904, when the first contest for the Vanderbilt Cup was held on Long Island, just outside New York City. Accounts of the early Vanderbilt races can be found in the general histories mentioned earlier. In the same vein was a series of U.S. Grand Prize contests that were held in Georgia in 1908, 1910, and 1911, the subject of Julian K. Quattlebaum's *The Great Savannah Races*. Quattlebaum won the AACA's McKean Award for that book. See also Frank T. Wheeler's *The Savannah Races*, combining a wonderful collection of vintage photographs from the Georgia Historical Society with informative and relatively lengthy captions by the author. The Savannah site was such a good one for road racing that the sponsors of the Vanderbilt Cup were convinced to hold the 1911 competition there. Broader in focus is Peter Helck's *The Checkered Flag*, which describes in words and illustrations (Helck was a world-renowned automotive artist) American participation in early road racing (both home and abroad) from 1895 to 1916.

Road racing continued to generate interest in the years before World War I and the decade after. By the 1930s such racing reached a type of recognition with the formation of the Automobile Racing Club of America (ARCA), an organization for amateurs, and a renewal of the George Vanderbilt Cup races in 1936 and 1937. The latter were now Grand Prix-type races held on Long Island in an attempt to bring professional road racing to the United States. Brock W. Yates' *Vanderbilt Cup Race, 1936 and 1937* is a photographic study, accompanied by excellent captions, of the 300-mile contests held in those years at Roosevelt Raceway in New York. Designed to pit the best European cars against those from the United States, the race clearly showed the design and engineering superiority of the former at this time in a road-course format. Broader in focus, Joel E. Finn's *American Road Racing: The 1930s* provides an in-depth history of that period of motor sport development in the United States, making extensive use of the words of the participants, contemporary media accounts, ARCA archives, and over 600 black-and-white photographs. Similar in concept but more of an organizational history is John C. Rueter's *American Road Racing: The Automobile Racing Club of America in the 1930's*, which emphasizes the management of early Grand Prix-type competition in the United States.

After a hiatus during World War II, this form of racing returned in the early 1950s. In this regard, see *American Racing: Road Racing in the 50s and 60s*, by Tom Burnside and Denise McCluggage, a photographic chronicle featuring drivers like Carroll Shelby, Dan Gurney, Phil Hill, and Richie Ginther; open-wheel and sports racing cars; and the tracks (Sebring, Watkins Glen, and Elkhart Lake) that made history during those two decades.

Aspects of racing in the middle third of the century are examined in Allan Girdler's *American Road Race Specials, 1934–1970: Glory Days of Homebuilt Racers*. During these years "backyard" hybrid cars, with the names Scarab, Cunningham, and Chaparral, won races like the Can-Am series over the better-known and better-financed corporate competition and challenged the best that Europe could offer. Girdler's history of specific cars, of the men who created and drove them, and of the evolution from pure road racing to Grand Prix-like street courses is well researched and full of the author's enthusiasm for the sport.

Finally, Chris Jones' *Road Race*, a comprehensive, international history of such competition through the mid-1970s (when it effectively ended), contains a lengthy chapter on the Carrera Panamericana de Mexico. From 1950 to 1954, that race attracted American and European drivers to what was the last great, true road race in North America. The death of eight people in 1954 led to its demise.

CONTEMPORARY MOTOR SPORTS

Although the general public tends to think of baseball, football, and basketball as the big spectator sports in the United States, the truth is that professional motor sports garner an overall attendance that justifies their inclusion with them. In the mid-1990s, 5.3 million people watched one or more of the stock car races in the NASCAR Winston Cup Series, and it had become the fastest growing sport in the United States. Another 3.4 million attended Indy car events; 1.8 million paid to see The National Hot Rod Association (NHRA) drag cars compete; the World of Outlaw sprinters drew 1.6 million ("outlaw" because they are confined by few rules and have no restrictions on engine displacement); the SCCA (Sports Car Club of America) Trans-Am races drew 740,000; and 430,000 saw IMSA (International Motor Sports Association) GT/WSC cars compete. Thus, the professional side of motor sports attracted 13,270,000 spectators. In the following subsections, books on motor racing have been grouped by the generic type of cars involved: stock, Grand Prix, and dragsters.

Stock Car Racing

In stock car racing, standard, production cars are modified to improve their speed and handling; and the races are usually run on specially designed tracks. Although the title "stock car" is of relatively recent vintage, many (but not all) of the early road and "match" races involved such cars.

One very good book examines the origins of this type of motor sport. Sylvia Wilkinson's *Dirt Tracks to Glory: The Early Days of Stock Car Racing as Told by the Participants* offers the edited memories of such legendary figures as Bill France Sr., Bud Moore, Humpy Wheeler, Soapy Castles, Dan Gurney, and Linda Vaughan, in the days before rules and guaranteed prize money. In addition, the *Model T Ford in Speed and Sport*, edited by Harry Pulfer, shows that, with some modifications, the old black flivver had more than utilitarian virtues.

During the early years, the rules and regulations that governed American automobile racing emanated from the American Automobile Association (AAA), which was founded in 1902. The history of this relationship is a complex and fascinating one, deserving of book-length coverage. (For an introduction, see "The Coming of the AAA" chapter in Bellamy Partridge's *Fill 'Er Up!*) In late 1947, effective control of American stock car racing passed to the National Association for Stock Car Auto Racing (NASCAR). Basing its organization on that used for Grand Prix competition, NASCAR established circuits (initially in the South) and a rating system for drivers leading to the crowning of a yearly champion. The best history of this organization and the racing that it sponsors is Peter Golenbock's *American Zoom: Stock Car Racing—from the Dirt Tracks to Daytona*, which traces its origins back to southern moonshiners' efforts to outrun law enforcement officials and forward to the multimillion-dollar business known as the Winston Cup. Golenbock lets the drivers, mechanics, and promoters describe their exploits as they compete in races held at Daytona, Charlotte, and Watkins Glen. Similar in concept and almost equally good is Kim Chapin's *Fast as White Lightning: The Story of Stock Car Racing*. Chapin's work is entertainingly written, and the author is particularly adept at weaving together biographical information about the legends of stock car racing with a chronicle of how the sport evolved over half a century. First published in 1981, the updated 1998 edition explores the changes that increased media coverage, enlarged corporate sponsorship, and a new breed of drivers (e.g., Jeff Gordon) have had on the nature of stock car racing. Another good, though chronologically more limited, historical survey is *Stock Car Racers: The History and Folklore of NASCAR's Premier Series*, by Allan Girdler. The series in question is the Grand National Winston Cup, run on over thirty circuits. Girdler's well-written history of the people and the cars that have made this speedway sport won the 1988 MOTO Award for reporting.

In addition, Greg Fielden has compiled a four-volume reference work entitled *Forty Years of Stock Car Racing*, in which he provides information on the people, cars, and races that made history for forty seasons (1949–1989). His narrative is complemented by contemporary newspaper accounts, vintage photographs, and extensive statistics. Volume 1 covers the years 1949–1958; Volume 2, 1959–1964; Volume 3, 1965–1971; and Volume 4, 1972–1989. A supplement, *Forty Plus Four, 1990–1993*, can be considered a fifth volume in the series. Less ambitious, but nonetheless well done, is award-winning author Frank Moriarty's *The Encyclopedia of Stock Car Racing*, actually more a complete history than an encyclopedia, a book that traces its evolution from informal, rural, off-road contests into today's multibillion-dollar business of the Winston Cup Championship series. Similar in concept and content to the foregoing is Don Hunter and Al Pearce's *The Illustrated History of Stock Car Racing*. Finally, *NASCAR 50: The Thunder of America* celebrates in words and pictures the golden anniversary (1948–1998) of organized stock car racing.

Several well-illustrated volumes attempt to convey the "flavor" of stock racing by offering an insider's view of the sponsors, drivers, pit crew, and so on. Among these, the best are George H. Gilliam's *Racin': The NASCAR/Winston Cup Stock Car Racing Series*; Frank Moriarty and photographer Rick Farnkopf's *Sunday Drivers: NASCAR Winston Cup Stock Car Racing*; D. Randy Riggs' *Flat-Out Racing: An Insider's Look at the World of Stock Cars*; Frye Gaillard and Kyle Petty's *Kyle at 200 M.P.H.: A Sizzling Season in the Petty/NASCAR Dynasty*; Lyle K. Engel's *Stock Car Racing U.S.A.*; and W. Michael Lovern and Bob Jones Jr.'s *Grand National Stock Car Racing: The Other Side of the Fence*.

Finally, it should be noted that for a brief period of time convertibles competed against each other in sanctioned stock car races. Greg Fielden's *Rumblin' Ragtops: The History of NASCAR's Fabulous Convertible Division and Speedway Division* tells the story of this short-lived venture (1956–1959) in a heavily illustrated, yet fact-filled, volume.

Given that the NASCAR Winston Cup Series has become the most popular form of car racing in the United States by far, it should not be surprising to find that it is now being subjected to scholarly analysis. For instance, Mark D. Howell's *From Moonshine to Madison Avenue: A Cultural History of the NASCAR Winston Cup Series* explores the reasons for the popularity of this form of racing.

Grand Prix Racing

A second type of racing is usually referred to as "Grand Prix." More a series of races than a single event, Grand Prix driving involves street course (as opposed to oval track) competitions, held in a number of different countries. At the end of each racing season since 1950, a Drivers World Champion in Formula 1 is crowned based on the combined points earned during the tour. ("Formula 1" refers to the design and engineering specifications set by FIA [Federation Internationale de L'Automobile] that define the type of cars that can compete.) Always more popular in Europe than in America, Phil Hill in 1961 and Mario Andretti in 1978 are the only drivers from the United States to have won the world championship.

Nonetheless, the predecessors of Grand Prix competition have been present here since at least 1904, and Americans have been active participants throughout the 20th century. For instance, see Tim Considine's *American Grand Prix Racing: A Century of Drivers & Cars*, a heavily illustrated, thoroughly researched, and well-written history that highlights the 147 Americans and their cars that have driven in Grand Prix races in both Europe and America through 1993, beginning with George Heath and John Christie, who drove in the first such race in 1907 in France. Also very good, but more specific, is Albert R. Bochroch's *Americans at Le Mans: An Illustrated History of the 24 Hour Race from 1923 to 1975, with Emphasis on American Drivers and Cars.* Bochroch's comprehensive work begins with the first American victory (a Duesenberg in 1921), rejoices with the 1–2–3 finish of Fords in 1966, and notes that, in between, a Cadillac, Chevrolet, Chrysler, Cunningham, DuPont, Overland, Stutz, and Willys-Knight finished either second or third. Readers interested in a more general treatment of this subject should see *Grand Prix: The Cars, the Drivers, the Circuits*, by David Hodges *et al.*, which provides both a contemporary history of this type of racing and American participation in it.

Technically, though, Grand Prix racing did not come to the United States until 1950, when for a decade the Indianapolis 500 was an FIA-sanctioned Grand Prix contest, followed by more traditional street course racing in Long Beach (mid- and late 1970s), Detroit (1983–1989), and then Phoenix. Doug Nye's *The United States Grand Prix and Grand Prize Races, 1908–1977* is a good year-by-year reference in this regard, with the emphasis on the U.S. Grand Prix of the years 1959 to 1977.

There are numerous complete histories of Grand Prix racing. Given the European domination in this area, these works have relatively little to say about American drivers and cars. Nonetheless, five will be mentioned here to give some idea of the nature and variety of the books available. Adriano Cimarosti's *The Complete History of Grand Prix Motor Racing* is a season-by-season analysis of the performance of cars, drivers, and teams from 1894 through 1996, together with design and engineering developments and rule changes; Michael Frostick's ingenuously titled *Pit and Paddock* is an excellent photo history of

Grand Prix racing from 1894 to 1978; Alan Henry's *History of the Grand Prix* focuses on the drivers and the accompanying rivalries that developed; Doug Nye's two-volume *Autocourse History of the Grand Prix Car* covers the years 1945–1965 and 1966–1991 and emphasizes the design and engineering of the Grand Prix (GP) car during those periods; and Anthony Pritchard's *Grand Prix Racing: The Enthusiast's Companion* is a reference source that begins with the pioneering French road races of the 1890s, concludes with the events of the mid-1990s, and includes selections from the works of famous racing authors.

Partially to compensate for the necessarily limited American participation in the European-dominated Grand Prix circuit, North Americans created the Canadian–American Challenge Cup, the so-called Can-Am races, which were introduced in 1966, providing a regular taste of Grand Prix-like racing. Although some of the books cited above describe this series, several others are devoted totally to it. Karl Ludvigsen's *Group 7, the World's Most Powerful Road Racing Cars* provides a history of the first five years of Can-Am racing. The numerical designation refers to a class of cars on which there was no restriction regarding the size of the engine. Pete Lyons' *Can-Am* is a pictorial history of the sports car series that lasted until 1974, focusing on the racing teams that produced cars that were bold in design, driven by extraordinarily powerful engines, and thus capable of incredibly high speeds. Readers interested in placing the Can-Am series in historical perspective should examine Dave Friedman's heavily illustrated *Pro Sports Car Racing in America, 1958–1974*, wherein the author (and the participants) portray the emergence, development, and ultimate demise of this form of professional motor racing in North America, with the Can-Am series being viewed as its pinnacle.

For a time, Can-Am cars dominated SCCA racing. Those vehicles are the focus of David McKinney's *Can-Am Cars, 1966–1974*, an illustrated survey that features the American and international drivers and their innovative machines. Of the latter, the British Lola T70 was one of the most successful sports racers. Powered by Ford and Chevrolet V-8 engines, it was a winner both in Can-Am races and Daytona and Sebring endurance contests of the mid-1960s through the early 1970s. Its story is told in John Starkey's *Lola T70: The Racing History & Individual Chassis Record* and Dave Friedman's *Lola: Can-Am and Endurance Race Cars*. The former is particularly strong on the technical side, with detailed descriptions of the car's engineering and design characteristics. The latter is a photo history covering all the Lolas, not just the T70, supplemented by commentary from Lola drivers, mechanics, and team owners of the period, including Dan Gurney, Parnelli Jones, and Mark Donohue.

Drag Racing and Its Hot Rod Antecedents

While stock and Grand Prix car racing are best known and receive the greatest amount of publicity, professional drag racing continues to enjoy a significant amount of popularity, particularly on the local level. Dragsters are the fastest of all racing cars, capable of attaining speeds as high as 300 mph in the typical quarter-mile sprint. The definitive work in this area is Robert C. Post's *High Performance: The Culture and Technology of Drag Racing, 1950–1990*. Post, a curator at the Smithsonian Institution and a former drag racer himself, provides a scholarly yet highly readable and dramatic history of the sport, beginning with the first "legal" races on rural airfields down to the jet-powered professional spectator sport of today. With the enthusiasm of a participant, Post explores the personalities (including women), technological innovations, and organizational developments that have combined talent and technology to create a compelling sports event. At the same time, he pays due attention to how cultural factors (the commercial need to keep drag racing entertaining and competitive) have limited the application of technology (especially high-technology fuels and computers). Also worth examining is *Petersen's History of Drag Racing*, by Dave Wallace, a comprehensive, pictorial work that details the evolution of the sport in the United States from the 1950s to 1980. Finally, Bob Jackson explores the cultural aspects of top fuel and funny car (see below) dragster competition in *Top Fueler: Inside the World of Drag Racing*, with narrative descriptions and color photos of the action on the track and in the pits of vehicles powered by 5,000-horsepower engines.

For an in-depth look at drag racing's earliest years, see Albert Drake's *Flat Out: California Dry Lake Time Trials, 1930–1950*, wherein the author details the formalization of the sport, with the emergence of such sanctioning authorities as the Muroc Racing Association and the Southern California Timing Association (SCTA), and the "bootleg" racing that occurred during World War II. An additional work of historical interest is Wally Parks' *Drag Racing Yesterday and Today: The Story of the Fastest Sport in the World*. Parks was one of the pioneers in this area who founded the NHRA in 1951. He offers his historical observations from the vantage point of the mid-1960s.

By the late 1950s, drag racing had evolved and split into several different varieties or classes. An introduction to three of them is provided by Lyle K. Engel's *The Complete Book of Stock-Bodied Drag Racing*; Don Montgomery's *Those Wild Fuel Altereds: Drag Racing in the "Sixties"*; and David Fetherston and Steve Reyes' *Fabulous Funny Cars: A Pictorial History of the World's Fastest Automobiles*. Stock-bodied or "pro stock" cars, although they have been modified to enhance their speed, are most similar to the mass-produced vehicles that one finds in a dealer's showroom. The fuel altereds were short wheelbase coupés and roadsters that were introduced in response to the short-lived, 1957 ban on the use of either nitro or alcohol fuels in drag racing. Funny cars are stock automobiles that have been modified; for example, their hoods have been elongated, or there are body bulges in unexpected places, and thus they look somewhat "funny." Nonetheless, they are frequently capable of speeds of up to 285 mph.

More recently, we have seen the introduction of so-called top fuel dragsters, which are the fastest (and strangest-looking) of them all, powered by monster engines that deliver 5,000 horsepower to a vehicle that resembles a long, thin piece of pie. The "fuel" in question is a combination of methanol and nitromethane, a mixture much more powerful than gasoline. Probably the best introduction to this form of racing is Tony Sakkis' *The Anatomy & Development of the Top Fuel Dragster*, which traces the technical evolution of the cars and the growth of the sport, with due attention to their historic origins.

In a sense, professional dragsters emerged from the broader world of hot rod racing. A good introduction to this latter subject, intended for the general reader, is Dean Batchelor's *The American Hot Rod*. Batchelor, a former editor of *Road & Track* magazine and a hot rod enthusiast, traces the history of such cars (deuce [Ford Model A] roadsters, coupés, modifieds, dragsters, etc.) from their amateur beginnings in the 1920s, when they first appeared and raced on streets and western dry lakes, through the era of the 300+ mph professional drag races of the 1990s, with due attention to the associated clubs, timing associations, and publications. A different, more scholarly approach is provided by H.F. Moorhouse in his *Driving Ambitions: An Analysis of the American Hot Rod Enthusiasm*. Moorhouse goes beyond the history of the sport to analyze how a popular, though often illegal, activity was made respectable and commercially profitable by enthusiast magazines like *Hod Rod* and sanctioning organizations such as the NHRA. He also describes the accomplishments of women in drag racing.

More specific is Don Radbruch's *Roaring Roadsters:Track Roadsters from 1924 until 1956*, wherein the author explores the incredibly varied world of hot rod racing. Although centered in California and its paved oval circuits, roadsters also raced on dirt tracks in the East and South. In some cases, they were home-built, modified stock cars like the previously mentioned Ford Model A; in other instances, they were professionally built, technologically sophisticated machines for their time. It was in the latter that many Indy car drivers began careers that culminated with their winning the Indianapolis 500. The men and machines of those transitional years are the subject of Joe Scalzo's *Indianapolis Roadsters, 1952–1964*, an account of the Offenhauser-powered cars that dominated that era and of drivers such as A.J. Foyt, Rodger Ward, Bobby Unser, and Tony Bettenhausen.

For insight into the *amateur* world of drag racing, somewhat of a rite de passage in the 1950s, and the more general hot rod culture, see the "Youth" section of Chapter 5.

Other Types of Racing

At least three other types of racing—midget, sprint, and vintage—have attracted a significant following in the United States. (Car rallying never has and, therefore, is not covered in this guide.) Two of these popular types are the subject of Dan Owen's *Vintage and Historic Indianapolis Race Cars*, a brief (96-page) nostalgic history of midget and sprint cars that won championships throughout the country from the 1920s until the mid-1960s.

Although its origins go back to before World War I, midget racing did not become an organized sport until 1933. Midgets have the distinction of being the only cars designed specifically for racing and originally were powered by motorcycle engines and were miniaturized, home-built versions of full-size racers. Today, they are factory-built and usually powered by four-cylinder engines. The best available history is Jack C. Fox's *The Mighty Midgets*, which traces developments from 1933 to 1976 on both indoor and outdoor tracks. Also meritorious is Crocky Wright's *Midget Auto Racing Histories*, a 4-volume work that details in words and pictures the history of midget racing on the East Coast from 1934 through 1980, with due attention to the cars, drivers, and tracks of each era.

Jack C. Fox's *The Illustrated History of Sprint Car Racing. Volume 1: 1896–1942* is the best look at the evolution of this form of competition during the years that it laid the foundation for modern track racing. *USAC Sprint History, 1956–1980*, by Carl Hungness et al., a season-by-season, twenty-fifth-year anniversary history with statistics, is a good survey of the later years. The U.S. Auto Club (USAC) was one of a group of national organizations that sanctioned a variety of racing types, such as sprint cars, midgets, and stock cars. Their championship cars were the ancestors of today's Indy cars.

Although motor sports seem to be in a constant state of evolution, they have not been immune to America's fascination with nostalgia. Thus, George D. Lepp's *Vintage Automobile Racing* describes a world in which racing takes a step back in time. Once again, classic Corvettes, Mustangs, and Cobras, together with their contemporary European counterparts, compete on the track in what has become an increasingly popular spectator sport.

This might be an appropriate place to mention the racing history of Volkswagens in America. Formula Vee racing, which used the Beetle 1300 engine and suspension, was born in the United States in the early 1960s as a type of low-cost, entry-level competition. Formula Vee became popular enough to become part of the season at Daytona and other established racing venues. During the same period, Volkswagens became an established part of Class H drag racing, where their light weight allowed them to successfully compete against heavier, V-8-engined cars. Peter Noad's *VW Beetle in Motorsport: The Illustrated History, 1940s to 1990s* is the best source in this regard, providing a decade-by-decade account, although its focus is worldwide. Andrew L. Schupack's *Formula Vee/Super Vee: Racing, History, and Chassis/Engine Prep*, while primarily a technical guide, also contains a fair amount of historical information.

Team and Company Competition

Beginning in the 1960s, it became too expensive for one man or even a small group of people to successfully participate in motor racing and unwise to become tied to a single vehicle design or engine. Thus, the racing "team" has emerged, composed of drivers, designers, builders, mechanics, owners, and a plethora of corporate backers from ancillary industries and services, such as tires, motor oils, additives, and so on.

Such teams owe their origins to the pioneer mechanics who developed increasingly powerful engines in the decades following World War I, engines capable of being adapted to a variety of racing car designs. See, for example, Mark L. Dees' excellent *The Miller Dynasty: A Technical History of the Work of Harry A. Miller, His Associates and His Successors*, whose cars and engines dominated American oval track (dirt and board) racing during the years between World Wars I and II and whose successors remained important into the 1970s. Griffith Borgeson's more recent *Miller*, published in cooperation with the Smithsonian Institution, is similar in concept to the Dees book, with attention given to the man, his exceptionally engineered racing cars, and his engines. The latter were decades ahead of their time and were predecessors of the legendary Offenhauser engines. (For more on race car engineering and design, see those sections in Chapter 4.)

More specific to the emergence of the team approach to racing are Karl Ludvigsen's *Gurney's Eagles: The Exciting Story of the AAR Racing Cars*, a history of the Eagle All-American Racer (AAR) and the team that Dan Gurney assembled to race it during the years between 1966 and 1976; Andrew Ferguson's *Team Lotus: The Indianapolis Years*, which provides a comprehensive account of the technology and personnel that allowed a small British group to build twenty-five cars and successfully take on the "Indianapolis establishment" in the 1960s; and Carl Hungness' *Go!: The Bettenhausen Story*, a comprehensive history of an American racing family (Gary Sr. and Tony) that pursued the goal of winning the Indianapolis 500 through two generations and over more than fifty years.

More recently, there have been Doug Nye's *McLaren: The Grand Prix, Can-Am and Indy Cars*, which provides a complete history of the cars of another foreign team (Bruce McLaren was a New Zealander) that has had significant impact on American racing since the 1960s; and Alan Henry's *March: The Grand Prix and Indy Cars*, which covers twenty years in the history of this British team, with a significant segment devoted to their Indy car racing in the decade of the 1980s.

Probably the most famous American name in this regard is Carroll Shelby. For those unfamiliar with the significant achievements of the man and his team, a good place to begin would be with Dave Friedman's *Shelby American*, wherein the author provides a heavily illustrated historical overview of the varied American racing efforts of Carroll Shelby's company, both on the street and on the track, including the GT40 and the Cobra cars. The same author's *Remembering the Shelby Years, 1962–1969* is a tribute by the employees of Shelby American, ranging from drivers to mechanics to administrators, offered through eighty-five in-depth interviews. Richard J. Kopec's *Shelby American Guide*, although relatively brief, is probably the best developmental and technical history of these cars in the years 1962 to 1970, with special attention to the Cobra, Mustang, and GT40. Finally, Wallace A. Wyss' *Shelby's Wildlife: The Cobras, Mustangs and Dodges* is a comprehensive history (to 1987) of every model with which Shelby had been affiliated, with three chapters devoted to racing.

More specific are Trevor Legate's *Cobra: The Real Thing*, a detailed, comprehensive history (including racing) of the sports car born of a union between Shelby, Ford, and the English manufacturer AC; the similarly named, but less weighty, *Cobra* by Beki Adam, which is more American in focus and relatively more interested in the racing history of that car; and *Carroll Shelby's Racing Cobras: A Definitive Pictorial History*, by Dave Friedman and John Christy, an insider portrait of the Shelby Team in the mid-1960s, both well written and well illustrated. (For more on Shelby himself, see the biographies discussed in the "Engineers and Designers" section of Chapter 2.)

Jim Hall is another American engineer/designer whose cars and teams have enjoyed a lengthy period of racing prominence. Different models of his "Chaparral" pioneered in racing car technology in the 1960s and 1970s, defeating the likes of Ferrari, Jaguar, and Ford, and descendants of these vehicles were still being raced into the mid-1990s. Their story is well told in Richard Falconer and Doug Nye's *Chaparral*, wherein the authors provide an *authorized* account of Jim Hall and his team during the years 1961 to 1970. This book benefits from interviews with Hall and access to previously private records. It also suffers by virtue of the author's disinclination to probe into areas where negative revelations might be found, such as Chevrolet's alleged assistance to Chaparral. Also worth examining is *Chaparral: Can-Am and Prototype Race Cars*, by Dave Friedman, a photo history concentrating on the 1950s and 1960s and the Chaparral's performance in the Can-Am series. In addition to an excellent collection of photographs, this book contains extensive quotations from Hall and his drivers, including such legends as Roger Penske, Phil Hill, and Sam Posey.

Less well known today than Shelby and Hall but preceding them in terms of developing a successful, home-built racer was millionaire Lance Reventlow with his Scarab. Preston Lerner's *Scarab: Race Log of the All-American Specials, 1957–1965* tells the story of a marque that, in many respects, paved the way for the later track accomplishments of the Cobra and Chaparral.

The major American car manufacturers also have been sporadically involved in the racing scene. Originally, it was a way to prove the superiority of their vehicles vis-à-vis those made by the competition; lately it has become a means of testing advanced engineering concepts and advertising their products. The longest lived of these efforts are those of Ford and Chevrolet.

Ford's racing history is traceable to 1901, and Henry himself set the world land speed record in 1904, achieving a speed of 91.37 in his "999" car. The best overviews of this subject are Alex Gabbard's *Fast Fords* (1988), an excellent, decade-by-decade, illustrated history of the company's commitment to achieving success with racing and performance cars; Michael Frostick and Barrie Gill's *Ford Competition Cars: The Ford Motor Company in Competition* (1976), which examines some seventy years of such competition (both home and abroad), including the glory years of the 1960s and 1970s and the efforts to win at LeMans and Indianapolis; and Leo Levine's *Ford: The Dust and the Glory, a Racing History* (1968), the most detailed work of the three, which follows essentially the same approach as Frostick and Gill.

More specific and more contemporary in focus are Hans Tanner's *The Racing Fords*, which concentrates on the Indy-type and GT Fords, and Karl E. Ludvigsen's *The Inside Story of the Fastest Fords: The Design and Development of Ford GT Racing Cars.*

Having lost its racing preeminence following World War II, the Ford Motor Company attempted to regain it in the 1960s with the development of the Indy-engineered Shelby GT40 and succeeded with two victories at Le Mans over the previously dominant Ferraris. Michael L. Shoen's *The Cobra–Ferrari Wars, 1963–1965* is an extensive look at what was perhaps the most famous rivalry in racing history, that of Carroll Shelby versus Enzo Ferrari. Shoen's book is of a higher quality than most in this genre, as witnessed by its receipt of the 1991 Cugnot Award for "the best book in the field of automotive history." Also good and covering a broader range of events is Gordon Jones and John Allen's earlier *The Ford That Beat Ferrari: A Racing History of the Ford GT40*, a comprehensive, well-illustrated, competition history of every chassis built between 1964 and 1971, covering the efforts of the various teams and individuals that raced what was probably the most impressive of the Ford racing cars. Anthony Pritchard's *Ford versus Ferrari: The Battle for Le Mans* and David Hodges' *Ford GT40: An Anglo-American Supercar Classic* are also worth examining, covering the years 1964 to 1969, including the triumphal Ford victory in 1966.

Ford continued its involvement in Formula 1 (F1) racing in the early 1990s as part of a new team effort with Benetton. That story is told by Phil Drackett in *Benetton Ford: A Racing Partnership.*

Turning to Chevrolet's racing efforts, the literature is thin, except for books concerning the Corvette. This is true even when one considers that General Motors never bought into motor sports to the extent that Ford did. The most comprehensive work (600+ pages) is Robert Ackerson's *Chevrolet: High Performance*, which features the exploits of Corvettes, Chevelles, Camaros, and other models in NASCAR and NHRA drag races. Another good overview is Paul V. Valkenburgh's *Chevrolet-Racing . . . ?: Fourteen Years of Raucous Silence!!*, which, while surveying the earlier history, focuses on the years when Chevrolet appeared to have abandoned the track. From the late 1960s until the early 1970s, that company never built a complete competition race car. Nonetheless, it was heavily involved in the engineering side of racing, and its production cars benefited accordingly. Finally, a special 1995 issue of *Automobile Quarterly* devoted to the history of Chevrolet includes a chapter entitled: "Chevrolet Racing: A Tradition of Victory."

More specifically, there are *California Screamin': The Glory Days of Corvette Road Racing*, by Michael Antonick, a celebration of the success of "stock"

Corvettes and neophyte drivers in road racing during the years 1957 to 1965; *Corvette Racers*, by Gregory Von Dare, which is comprehensive in approach in terms of both types of competition and years covered (into the early 1990s); and Lowell C. Paddock and Dave Friedman's *Corvette Grand Sport: Photographic Race Log of the Magnificent Chevrolet Corvette Factory Specials, 1963–1967*. The Grand Sport was to have been the fastest American production car. However, only five were built and raced. Finally, it also should be noted that Thomas E. Bonsall's *Pontiac! They Built Excitement*, a comprehensive history of that marque, contains a chapter on racing.

There are even fewer books on the racing efforts of the Chrysler Corporation. Frank Moriarty's *Supercars: The Story of the Dodge Charger Daytona and Plymouth SuperBird* is a fascinating, inside account of the development of two Chrysler Corporation entrees into the NASCAR battles of 1969 and 1970. These were the so-called wing or aero cars, whose rear foils aerodynamically enhanced these coupés so effectively that NASCAR later banned such modifications. James A. Benjaminson's *Plymouth, 1946–1959* includes a section on achievements in racing and endurance competitions, as does Robert Ackerson's *Chrysler 300: America's Most Powerful Car*, whose 300-horsepower Hemi V-8 engine led to NASCAR domination for years. In addition, a special 1994 issue of *Automobile Quarterly* devoted to Chrysler includes a chapter entitled "On the Right Track: A Racing Heritage."

During the years 1966 to 1972, the Big Three manufacturers also became directly involved in "Trans-Am" stock car racing, as performance there was increasingly equated with dealer showroom sales. The subtitle of a recent book by Albert R. Bochroch, *Trans-Am Racing, 1966–1985: Detroit's Battle for Pony Car Supremacy*, sums up well the nature of those contests and indicates that that competition continued for a second decade despite decreasing direct company financial support for it. Bochroch's book provides a good historical survey of the cars and men of that era as well.

Not to be undone, the fourth largest U.S. company, American Motors, entered the fray during the muscle car era. The story of that adventure is recalled by Edrie Marquez in *Amazing AMC Muscle: Complete Development and Racing History of the Cars from American Motors*, which, in addition to detailing the history of the AMX, SS Rambler, Javelin, and Rebel models, has a special section on AMC racing cars.

The racing exploits of other recent American car manufacturers have been less well documented. However, there are a few books worthy of mention. Robert J. Neal's *Packards at Speed* is a beautifully produced volume that provides extensive information regarding the racing performance of Packards on the road and track, including the legendary Gray Wolf. (The same book also covers the use of Packard engines in boat racing and in aviation.) From a more historical vantage point, there are George P. and Stacey Pankiw Hanley's *The Marmon Heritage: More than 125 years of American Production of World Renowned Products*, an award-winning, definitive history that contains a considerable amount of material on the Marmon racing saga, and *The Splendid Stutz: Its Cars, Companies, People, and Races*, edited by Raymond A. Katzell, which, as part of a comprehensive company history, describes the racing cars, mechanics, and drivers that made the marque a track favorite prior to the depression. Katzell's book received the Cugnot Award for the best book on automotive history published in 1996.

Racing Tracks and Courses

While automotive competition in America began as road racing (e.g., the Vanderbilt Cup), it soon became limited to tracks, so much so that only since the mid-1970s have we seen the birth of true Grand Prix street racing in the United States. As a result, these tracks have been the sites for an infinite number of individual adventures and the subject of numerous book-length histories.

The best known and most thoroughly studied individual American track is the Indianapolis Motor Speedway, home of the Indianapolis 500 since 1911. The number of books related to that motor contest is legion. Some of the better "classic" volumes concerning the speedway and its Memorial Day competition include Floyd Clymer's *Indianapolis 500 Mile Race History*, a collection of articles and race reports describing every contest to 1941. Published in 1946, some readers may find this volume itself of historical value, since it provides an immediate postwar perspective and is the first in the Indy 500 yearbook series that continues to this day. Al Bloemker's *500 Miles to Go: The Story of the Indianapolis Speedway* is a good, but dated (1961), account by the publicity director of the speedway, valuable for its insights regarding the inception, ownership, and management of the track during its first fifty years. Jean Clavin's *Those Incredible Indy Cars*, despite its title, is really a history of the Memorial Day race down to 1960, with special attention to racing teams. Finally, Brock W. Yates' *The Indianapolis 500: The Story of the Motor Speedway* is a short, popularized history of the race, a revised edition of which appeared in 1961 to commemorate the speedway's golden anniversary.

More contemporary accounts include Ron Dorson's *The Indy 500: An American Institution under Fire*, which uses the accident-marred, never completed 1973 race as the basis for an excellent account of how the drivers and members of their teams prepare during the month of May so that the Memorial Day race "works"; Rich Taylor's *Indy: Seventy-five Years of Racing's Greatest Spectacle*, a comprehensive historical tribute written with the assistance of the Indianapolis Motor Speedway; Tom Carnegie's *Indy 500: More than a Race*, an encyclopedic work that covers everything from the initial financing of a new car to setting a new track record; and Dave Arnold's *Indy Race Cars: From behind the Garage Doors, the Month of May at Indianapolis*, which is similar to the Dorson volume in that it relates the story of how teams spend the entire month of May preparing and qualifying for the 500.

In addition to those books, there are a number of good popular histories, including *The Oily Grail: A Story of the Indy 500*, by Jack Albinson, which briefly (104 pages) emphasizes the evolution of safety devices while recounting the history of that race; *The Indianapolis 500: A Complete Pictorial History*, by John Devaney and Barbara Devaney, which provides an account of and photographs from each of the races through 1976, together with comments by the drivers; *The Illustrated History of the Indianapolis 500, 1911–1994*, by Jack C. Fox, which covers all the races in those years and thus provides an overview of the development of the sport over a period of eighty years; and *Indianapolis Racing Memories, 1961–1969*, by Dave Friedman, which explores in photographs and long, informative captions (often containing quotes from the participants) the nine Memorial Day races that many believe make the 1960s the most significant decade in the history of the 500.

Finally, at least three books investigate the history of those ceremonial cars that have set the pace for the thirty-three cars at the beginning of the Indianapolis 500 race since 1911. An overview of their evolution, in both print and photographs, is offered by L. Spencer Riggs in his *Pace Cars of the Indy 500* (through 1989) and the auto editors of *Consumer Guide* in their *Indy 500 Pace Cars*. More specific in focus is *The Official Chevrolet Indy Pace Car Book: From 1948 to 1990*, by D.M. Crispino and John R. Hooper, which provides all the details and technical specifications that one could want to know regarding the cars, beginning with the 1948 Fleetmaster and ending (at least for this book) with the 1990 Beretta, with an intermediate mix of Camaros, Corvettes, and even a Bel Air (in 1955).

Like Grand Prix racing, from which emerged the Formula 1 car, the competition at Indianapolis has given birth to a generic category called "Indy car" racing, which includes not just the Memorial Day race but others throughout the year on oval, street, and track circuits. Kris Perkins' *Indycar* provides a nice introduction to this variant, including a thorough introduction to the mechanics of the Indy car, descriptions of the circuits on which the cars compete, the complicated rules that govern the sport, and profiles of the teams and drivers involved, plus a series of data appendixes. (The technical development of such vehicles is covered in Chapter 4.)

Arguably the most successful competition series for Indy cars was organized in 1979 by Championship Auto Racing Teams (CART), a group of owners that split off from the U.S. Auto Club (USAC), which previously had been the sole sanctioning body for such races. Rick Shaffer's *CART: The First Twenty Years, 1979–1998* is an official history of that initiative, complete with profiles of drivers, owners, teams, and commercial promoters; explanations of the engineering and design developments that improved the cars; and a compilation of CART racing statistics and records.

Besides the Indianapolis Motor Speedway, several other nationally known race venues have been the object of book-length treatment. Probably the best known of these is Daytona and Ormond Beach, Florida, which has been the site of both "road" (actually sand) and track races. The subjects of William Neely's

Daytona USA, an "official history," are the cars and personalities that established Daytona and Ormond Beach as a prime racing site. This book has a nice symmetry to it, beginning as it does with Ransom E. Olds' "Pirate" in 1902 and concluding with Richard Petty's sixth Daytona 500 NASCAR victory in an Oldsmobile. Similarly, William R. Tuthill's *Speed on Sand* traces the history of Daytona/Ormond from 1902 to 1960, including Sir Malcolm Campbell's land speed record run of 330 mph in the mid-1930s. Chronologically more focused is Dick Punnett's *Racing on the Rim: A History of the Annual Automobile Racing Tournaments Held on the Sands of the Ormond-Daytona Beach, Florida, 1903–1910*, which effectively portrays a historic period when time trials and the repeated establishment of new speed records captivated the fledgling automotive world.

Greg Fielden's *High Speed at Low Tide* is an illustrated history of the years 1936–1958, with an emphasis on individual stock car races that are often seen as the precursors of the Winston Cup Series and on legendary drivers such as Lee Petty and Smokey Purser. *Daytona: The Quest for Speed*, a collection of historical articles and photographs from the *Daytona News-Journal*, compiled and edited by Tom Tucker and Jim Tiller, highlights key events in the development of Daytona and Ormond Beaches as a "road" course from 1902 to the mid-1990s, a site where the world's land speed record was set fifteen times during the period 1904 to 1935. The selections also cover the evolution of the Daytona Speedway, home to NASCAR Grand National stock car racing since 1959. Finally, Hal Higdon's *Showdown at Daytona*, winner of the AARWBA Best Book Award, describes the battle among six drivers for victory at the 1975 Daytona 500 race.

A more recent racing venue but one that may have surpassed Daytona in significance, is Sebring, Florida. Ken Breslauer's *Sebring: The Official History of America's Great Sports Car Race* is the best source on the "12 Hours of Sebring," a speed and endurance contest that has been run since 1950 and has attracted a constellation of legendary drivers (Hill, Andretti, and Foyt) and international racing teams (including Ford and Chevrolet). Note, however, that this is an authorized account by an employee of the Sebring International Speedway, with all the benefits and drawbacks that that entails. The founder of that race, Alec Ulmann, has left us *The Sebring Story*, in which he recounts his ultimately successful effort to establish Grand Prix sports car racing in the United States. In fact, the first U.S. Grand Prix was held at Sebring in 1959.

Books also have been published concerning several other venues that have figured prominently in racing history. They are briefly described below, in alphabetical order by track. Tom Kirkland and David Thompson's *Darlington International Raceway, 1950–1967* is essentially a photo history of the early years of NASCAR racing at that track, featuring the period photographs of Kirkland and quotations from personalities of the era. Gene Bryson's *Dover Downs NASCAR: The Monster Mile, Three Decades of Speed* provides an inside look at the drivers, cars, and competition that have contributed to the growing popularity of that track; Tom Schultz's *Road America: Five Decades of Racing at Elkhart Lake* in Wisconsin is a year-by-year history of the first road course specifically built for that purpose, home to Can-Am, Trans-Am, and Indy car races; Rich Taylor's *Lime Rock Park: 35 Years of Racing* describes the evolution of that Connecticut road racing track from its humble beginnings in the 1950s to national prominence in the 1960s and 1970s. Morris Stephenson's *From Dust to Glory: The Story of Clay Earles and the NASCAR Sanctioned Martinsville Speedway* is a heavily illustrated history of stock car racing at that Tennessee track from 1947 to 1991, with an emphasis on the men and machines that raced (and sometimes crashed) there.

Robert T. Devlin's *Pebble Beach, a Matter of Style*, a critically acclaimed volume, provides a history of early California racing and, more specifically, the Pebble Beach road races of 1950–1956, in addition to offering a complete, official history of the Pebble Beach Concours d'Elegance of 1950–1979 (see Chapter 8). The road races of the 1950s helped introduce European sports cars to the West Coast and were the predecessors of the Laguna Seca vintage races. Philippe Defechereaux's *Watkins Glen, 1948–1952: The Definitive Illustrated History* chronicles the first five years of a course generally credited with launching SCCA road racing, introducing Americans to the performance of European road cars like Ferraris and Jaguars, and showcasing legendary drivers such as Briggs Cunningham, Phil Hill, and John Fitch. Broader in focus is *Watkins Glen, from Griswold to Gordon: Fifty Years of Competition at the Home of American Road Racing*, by J.J. O'Malley and Bill Green, a survey of the Can-Am, Formula 1, Indy Car, Trans-Am, and Winston Cup races that took place there through 1997. In addition, Bob Latford's *Built for Speed: The Ultimate Guide to Stock Car Racetracks: A Behind-the-Wheel View of the Winston Cup Circuit* explores over twenty-five venues, including the Atlanta Motor Speedway and the Pocono International Raceway.

Finally, two natural sites have been the locales for automobile racing. Bonneville, Utah, has been the scene of most recent assaults on the land speed record (see below) in the United States. Its racing history is well chronicled in Louise Ann North's *Bonneville Salt Flats*, which describes in words and pictures the different types of competition that have occurred there since 1909, with emphasis on the years 1950 to 1980. Similarly, in *Bonneville Salt Flats: Speed Limit 1,000 MPH*, George D. Lepp explores the annual gathering of "speed freaks" from every type of racing as they challenge the record in their particular class. Interesting from a historical point of view is George Eyston and W.F. Bradley's *Speed on Salt: A History of the Bonneville Salt Flats, Utah, U.S.A.*, a brief (84-page) British account of record breaking there in the 1930s. (The American public's association of Bonneville with speed was taken advantage of by Pontiac, when it created a "muscle car" model with the same name.)

The other site is in Colorado, where the Pikes Peak Auto Hill Climb began in 1916 and continued for almost seventy-five years until environmental concerns led to its demise. Cars were challenged to climb twelve miles to a height of 14,100 feet. Given its longevity and the fact that it was a USAC-sanctioned race awarding points that counted toward the National Driving Championship, it is surprising to find no standard history of that race. In lieu of that, readers may want to investigate Stanley L. DeGeer's *Pikes Peak Is Unser Mountain*, a fact-filled, year-by-year account of all the races from 1916 to 1989. The book's title comes from the perennial participation of members of the Unser racing family in the annual climb. In addition, Marc Madow's *Pikes Peak: Race to the Clouds*, a brief (63-page), heavily illustrated volume provides another place to begin. It offers a historical overview of the vehicles and the participants, together with a photo album of the course and the races that have involved dirt track, sprint, and stock cars.

Before concluding this section, it should be noted that on countless "minor league" tracks a considerable amount of local motor racing still takes place. The nature of such racing can be gleaned from John Sawyer's *The Dusty Heroes*, which gives the flavor of racing on dirt tracks during the 1960s and 1970s; Harold L. Osmer's *Where They Raced*, a history of over 100 race courses and tracks that existed in the greater Los Angeles area since the early 1900s; and Donald Haener's *Hometown Stock Car Racing*, a brief (89-page), heavily illustrated look at the action and variety of drivers at small tracks in the eastern United States.

Quest for the Land Speed Record

Ultimately, the aim of all motor racing is to attain the highest speed possible while still controlling the vehicle. This goal appears in its purest form in the continual quest to establish new land speed records, and places like the Bonneville salt flats and cars such as the Bluebird, Spirit of America, Sonic 1, and Thrust have attained legendary status because of it. Four good historical overviews of this quest were published in the early and mid-1970s: Cyril Posthumus' *Land Speed Record: A Complete History of World Record-Breaking Cars from 39.24 to 600+ mph*; Frank Ross Jr.'s *Car Racing against the Clock: The Story of the World Land Speed Record*; Irwin Stambler's *The Supercars and the Men Who Race Them*, which includes individual chapters describing the exploits of such legends as John Cobb, Donald and Malcolm Campbell, Art and Walt Arfons, and Craig Breedlove; and Harvey Shapiro's *Faster than Sound*, which is similar to the Stambler volume in approach and content. More recently, Peter Holthusen's *The Land Speed Record: To the Sound Barrier and Beyond* emphasizes the rocket/jet-powered cars and the challenges created by supersonic speeds. Unfortunately, since this record is constantly being challenged, books on this subject are dated upon publication.

Reference Books

As might be expected, reference books are an important part of motor sport. Here, with the exception of stock car racing, it is impossible to avoid books that are international in coverage. Thus, we have Ivan Rendall's previously cited *The Checkered Flag: 100 Years of Motor Racing*, a year-by-year, authoritative, historical reference to racing worldwide, including Grand Prix, Indianapolis 500, Gordon Bennett, Targa Florio, and Mille Miglia, with due attention to the drivers themselves and the design and engineering of the cars they drove. Similar in approach is *The Guinness Guide to International Motor Racing: A Complete Reference from Formula One to Touring Cars*, by Peter Higham, a 543-page history of the various types of professional competition, incorporating information on the drivers and the teams, diagrams of the tracks, and even the rules of the individual types of racing.

Particular types of racing are the subject of János L. Wimpffen's *Time and Two Seats: Five Decades of Long Distance Racing*, a two-volume compendium that focuses on the World Sports Car, Grand Touring, and Manufacturers Championships, with coverage of every race, car, and driver from 1953 through 1998, including the "Triple Crown" endurance races of Le Mans, Daytona, and Sebring; *Autocourse: 50 Years of World Championship Grand Prix Motor Racing*, edited by Alan Henry, a celebration by *Autocourse* magazine of fifty seasons (1950–1999) of Formula 1 racing for the FIA Drivers' World Championship, featuring the different historical periods and the technical developments that characterized it; Adriano Cimarosti's previously mentioned *Complete History of Grand Prix Motor Racing*, a season-by-season, race-by-race compendium of cars, drivers, and teams from 1894 to 1996, together with a description of engineering developments during the same years; Bruce Jones' *The Complete Encyclopedia of Formula One: The Bible of Motorsport*, a 648-page volume with coverage from the beginning of F1 racing in 1950 through 1998, featuring worldwide data and information on the teams, drivers, and specific races, including season-by-season standings for Grand Prix, Drivers' World Championships, and the Constructors' Cup; and David Tremayne and Mark Hughes' *The Concise Encyclopedia of Formula One: A Complete Guide to the Fastest Sport in the World*, a celebration of the first fifty years of this form of motor racing, packed with the same type of information as the Jones work. *The Ultimate Encyclopedia of Formula One*, edited by Jones, is similar in concept to the foregoing, though much smaller in size (256 pages), with additional attention to technological innovations in Grand Prix racing, the business aspects of Formula 1, and, most interestingly, the attitudes of various nations toward such racing as a reflection of their culture.

The significance of Grand Prix and Formula 1 racing also has led to more specific compilations of data. Thus, the *Guinness Formula 1 Fact Book*, by Ian Morrison, combines a brief history of the sport with a compendium of race records and results and stats on the drivers and teams over the years. Similar in approach is the annual *IndyCar Record Book*, published by Championship Auto Racing Teams, Inc. (CART), the 1995 edition of which offers data on races run from 1909 through 1994 but focuses on the performance of teams and individual drivers during the last fifteen years of that period. (For additional reference works on Indy cars and the Indianapolis 500, see the discussion of the Indian-apolis Speedway in an earlier section of this chapter.) David Hayhoe and David Holland's *Grand Prix Data Book* covers the F1 World Championship Series from 1950 through 1994, with chapters on the races and the circuits, the con-structors and the drivers, and records of individual races in terms of lap times, grid positions, and results. Finally, the ubiquitous and never modest Bruce Jones is also the author of *The Best Book of Formula One Facts & Stats Ever!*, which attempts to be exactly what its title says it is.

Competition among stock cars is a type of automotive racing that has proven to be more popular than Grand Prix and Formula 1 racing in the United States and is the fastest growing motor sport in the world. *The Stock Car Racing Encyclopedia: The Complete Record of America's Most Popular Sport*, edited by Peter Golenbock and Greg Fielden, is a massive (984-page) compendium of data, statistics, and general information on arguably every race, driver, owner, designer, and car in NASCAR history, from 1949 through 1996. More recently, there is Bill Burt's *Stock Car Race Fan's Reference Guide: Understanding NASCAR*, a history through 1998 that combines the fundamentals of stock car performance with a survey of teams, drivers, and specific tracks and pertinent statistics. *The Official NASCAR Handbook: Everything You Want to Know about the NASCAR Winston Cup Series* takes a different tack. Aimed at the layperson, this handbook was created by NASCAR to provide an overview of the Winston Cup Series racing, with separate parts devoted to the nature of the competition; the people involved; the cars themselves; preparing for and participating in the race; and the history of the series.

As with Grand Prix and Formula 1 racing, there also are sports and stock car racing volumes that are primarily data compilations. For instance, *12 Hours of Sebring: The Record Book of America's Greatest Sports Car Race*, by Ken Breslauer, contains a complete statistical record of this annual contest for the years 1950 through 1989, including information on every car and driver, and *Stock Car Racing Record Book*, edited by Carol Aaronson, is a NASCAR pub-lication covering most of the first two decades of races sanctioned by that or-ganization.

Reference works on racing are not always as all-inclusive as the above books. For instance, David Hodges' *A–Z of Formula Racing Cars, 1945–1990* focuses on the design and construction of the vehicles themselves, ranging from the Formula 1 Grand Prix cars to the Formula 5000 and Formula Junior levels. Similarly, Mike Lawrence's *Grand Prix Cars, 1945–65*, is a reference source for the vehicles that ran in the early years of Grand Prix competition and also includes a brief, twenty-year history of that form of racing, and Anthony Prit-chard's "companion volume" *Directory of Formula One Cars, 1966–1986* is a comprehensive, data-driven history of cars (from Alfa to Zakspeed) and drivers during the decades indicated.

Finally, Joe Saward's *World Atlas of Motor Racing* is an example of a genre of books that serve as reference sources for the racing tracks themselves. Thus,

100 European, 50 North American, 30 Asian, and 5 African circuits are described and illustrated, with special attention to those that serve as venues for Formula Grand Prix racing. Going one step further, cosmologically speaking, is *A Racer's Guide to the Universe*, an annual published since 1992 that is designed to be a spectator's guide to some 300 tracks throughout the world, including information on the circuits, a schedule of the races, and advice on where to stay and eat in the area. More specific are Allan E. Brown's *The History of the American Speedway: Past & Present*, essentially a descriptive roster of approximately 4,500 tracks that have existed in the United States and Canada from the beginning of motor racing to the mid-1980s, including board and dirt tracks, and the *National Speedway Directory*, edited by Ross Ferguson and Nanette Ferguson, which lists and describes some 1,100 circuits here and in Canada, together with their track records, the last edition of which was published in 1985.

BIBLIOGRAPHY

Aaronson, Carol, ed. *Stock Car Racing Record Book*. Daytona Beach, Fla.: NASCAR, 1966.

Ackerson, Robert. *Chevrolet: High Performance*. Iola, Wisc.: Krause Publications, 1994.

Ackerson, Robert. *Chrysler 300: America's Most Powerful Car*. Dorset, Eng.: Veloce Publishing Place, 1996.

Adam, Beki. *Cobra*. London: Osprey, 1989.

Albinson, Jack. *The Oily Grail: A Story of the Indy 500*. Minneapolis: T.S. Denison, 1974.

Antonick, Michael. *California Screamin': The Glory Days of Corvette Road Racing*. Powell, Ohio: Michael Bruce Associates, 1990.

Arnold, Dave. *Indy Race Cars: From behind the Garage Doors, the Month of May at Indianapolis*. Osceola, Wisc.: Motorbooks International, 1989.

Assael, Shaun. *Wide Open: Days and Nights on the NASCAR Tour*. New York: Ballantine Books, 1998.

Automobile Quarterly 32 (April 1994).

Automobile Quarterly 34 (December 1995).

Batchelor, Dean. *The American Hot Rod*. Osceola, Wisc.: Motorbooks International, 1995.

Benjaminson, James A. *Plymouth, 1946–1959*. Osceola, Wisc.: Motorbooks International, 1994.

Bentley, John C. *Great American Automobiles: A Dramatic Account of Their Achievements in Competition*. Englewood Cliffs, N.J.: Prentice-Hall, 1957.

Bloemker, Al. *500 Miles to Go: The Story of the Indianapolis Speedway*. New York: Coward-McCann, 1961.

Bochroch, Albert R. *American Automobile Racing: An Illustrated History*. New York: Viking, 1974.

Bochroch, Albert R. *Americans at Le Mans: An Illustrated History of the 24 Hour Race from 1923 to 1975, with Emphasis on American Drivers and Cars*. Tucson: Aztex, 1976.

Bochroch, Albert R. *Trans-Am Racing, 1966–1985: Detroit's Battle for Pony Car Supremacy.* Osceola, Wisc.: Motorbooks International, 1986.

Boddy, William, and Brian Laban. *The History of Motor Racing, 1894–1977.* London: Macdonald Orbis, 1987.

Bonsall, Thomas E. *Pontiac! They Built Excitement: The Story of an American Automobile Company, 1926–1992.* Baltimore: Stony Run Press, 1991.

Borgeson, Griffith. *The Golden Age of the American Racing Car.* 2nd ed. Warrendale, Pa.: SAE International, 1998.

Borgeson, Griffith. *Miller.* Osceola, Wisc.: Motorbooks International, 1993.

Breedlove, Craig, with Bill Neely. *Spirit of America: Winning the World's Land Speed Record.* Chicago: Henry Regnery, 1971.

Breslauer, Ken. *Sebring: The Official History of America's Great Sports Car Race.* Cambridge, Mass.: David Bull Publishing, 1996.

Breslauer, Ken. *12 Hours of Sebring: The Record Book of America's Greatest Sports Car Race.* St. Petersburg, Fla.: Auto Racing Memories, 1989.

Brown, Allan E. *The History of the American Speedway: Past & Present.* Marne, Mich.: Slideways Publications, 1985.

Bryson, Gene. *Dover Downs NASCAR: The Monster Mile, Three Decades of Speed.* Rehobeth Beach, Del.: Portfolio Books, 1998.

Burnside, Tom, and Denise McCluggage. *American Racing: Road Racing in the 50s and 60s.* Verlagsgesellschaft, Ger.: Konemann, 1996.

Burt, Bill. *Stock Car Race Fan's Reference Guide: Understanding NASCAR.* Osceola, Wisc.: Motorbooks International, 1999.

Carnegie, Tom. *Indy 500: More than a Race.* New York: McGraw-Hill, 1986.

Chapin, Kim. *Fast as White Lightning: The Story of Stock Car Racing.* Rev. ed. New York: Three Rivers Press, 1998.

Cimarosti, Adriano. *The Complete History of Grand Prix Motor Racing.* Rev. ed. London: Aurum Press, 1997.

Clavin, Jean. *Those Incredible Indy Cars.* New York: Sports Car Press, 1973.

Clymer, [Joseph] Floyd. *Indianapolis 500 Mile Race History.* Los Angeles: Clymer Publishing, 1946.

Clymer, [Joseph] Floyd. *New York to Paris, 1908.* Los Angeles: Author, 1951.

Cole, Dermot. *Hard Driving: The 1908 Auto Race from New York to Paris.* New York: Paragon, 1991.

Considine, Tim. *American Grand Prix Racing: A Century of Drivers & Cars.* Osceola, Wisc.: Classic Motorbooks, 1997.

Consumer Guide, Auto Editors of. *Indy 500 Pace Cars.* Lincolnwood, Ill.: Publications International, 1996.

Crispino, D.M., and John R. Hooper. *The Official Chevrolet Indy Pace Car Book: From 1948 to 1990.* Westminster, Md.: J&D Publications, 1992.

Dees, Mark L. *The Miller Dynasty: A Technical History of the Work of Harry A. Miller, His Associates and His Successors.* Scarsdale, N.Y.: A.S. Barnes, 1981.

Defechereaux, Philippe. *Watkins Glen, 1948–1952: The Definitive Illustrated History.* Indianapolis: Beeman Jorgensen, 1998.

DeGeer, Stanley L. *Pikes Peak Is Unser Mountain: A History of the Pikes Peak Auto Hill Climb, 1916–1990.* Albuquerque: Peak Publishing, 1990.

Devaney, John, and Barbara Devaney. *The Indianapolis 500: A Complete Pictorial History.* Chicago: Rand-McNally, 1976.

Devlin, Robert T. *Pebble Beach, a Matter of Style: Racing through the Pines 1950–1956, Concours d'Elegance 1950–1979, a Complete History*. Costa Mesa, Calif.: Newport Press, 1980.

Dorson, Ron. *The Indy 500: An American Institution under Fire*. Newport Beach, Calif.: Bond, Parkhurst, 1974.

Drackett, Phil. *Benetton Ford: A Racing Partnership*. Swindon, Eng.: Crowood, 1990.

Drake, Albert. *Flat Out: California Dry Lake Time Trials, 1930–1950*. Okemos, Mich.: Flat Out Press, n.d.

Duryea, J. Frank. *When Chicago Introduced the Automobile to America: My Chicago Race Winner*. Albany, N.Y.: Argus, 1945.

Engel, Lyle K. *The Complete Book of Stock-Bodied Drag Racing*. New York: Four Winds Press, 1970.

Engel, Lyle K. *Stock Car Racing U.S.A.* New York: Dodd, Mead, 1973.

Eyston, George, and W.F. Bradley. *Speed on Salt: A History of the Bonneville Salt Flats, Utah, U.S.A.*. London: B.T. Batsford, 1936.

Falconer, Richard, and Doug Nye. *Chaparral*. Osceola, Wisc.: Motorbooks International, 1992.

Ferguson, Andrew. *Team Lotus: The Indianapolis Years*. Somerset, Eng.: Patrick Stephens/Haynes, 1996.

Ferguson, Ross, and Nanette Ferguson. *National Speedway Directory*. 6th ed. Comstock Park, Mich.: Allan E. Brown, 1985.

Fetherston, David, and Steve Reyes. *Fabulous Funny Cars: A Pictorial History of the World's Fastest Automobiles*. New York: Berkley Publishing Group, 1994.

Fielden, Greg. *Forty Plus Four, 1990–1993: First Supplement to the Forty Years of Stock Car Racing Series*. Surfside Beach, S.C.: Golfield Press, 1994.

Fielden, Greg. *Forty Years of Stock Car Racing*. 4 vols. Rev. ed. Surfside Beach, S.C.: Golfield Press, 1992.

Fielden, Greg. *High Speed at Low Tide*. Surfside Beach, S.C.: Golfield Press, 1993.

Fielden, Greg. *Rumblin' Ragtops: The History of NASCAR's Fabulous Convertible Division and Speedway Division*. Pinehurst, N.C.: Golfield Press, 1990.

Finn, Joel E. *American Road Racing: The 1930s*. Washington, Conn.: Garnett Hill Publishing, 1996.

Fox, Jack C. *The Illustrated History of the Indianapolis 500, 1911–1984*. 3rd ed. Speedway, Ind.: Carl Hungness, 1984.

Fox, Jack C. *The Illustrated History of Sprint Car Racing. Volume 1: 1896–1942*. Speedway, Ind.: Carl Hungness, 1985.

Fox, Jack C. *The Mighty Midgets*. Speedway, Ind.: Carl Hungness, 1977.

Friedman, Dave. *Chaparral: Can-Am and Prototype Race Cars*. Osceola, Wisc.: Motorbooks International, 1998.

Friedman, Dave. *Indianapolis Racing Memories, 1961–1969*. Osceola, Wisc.: Motorbooks International, 1997.

Friedman, Dave. *Lola: Can-Am and Endurance Race Cars*. Osceola, Wisc.: MBI, 1998.

Friedman, Dave. *Pro Sports Car Racing in America, 1958–1974*. Osceola, Wisc.: MBI 1999.

Friedman, Dave. *Remembering the Shelby Years, 1962–1969*. Los Angeles: Carroll Shelby Children's Foundation, 1998.

Friedman, Dave. *Shelby American*. Osceola, Wisc.: Motorbooks International, 1997.

Friedman, Dave, and John Christy. *Carroll Shelby's Racing Cobras: A Definitive Pictorial History*. Osceola, Wisc.: Motorbooks International, 1982.

Frostick, Michael. *Pit and Paddock: A Background to Motor Racing, 1894–1978*. Derbyshire, Eng.: Moorland, 1980.

Frostick, Michael, and Barrie Gill. *Ford Competition Cars: The Ford Motor Company in Competition*. Yeovil, Eng.: Haynes, 1976.

Gabbard, Alex. *Fast Fords*. Los Angeles: HPBooks, 1988.

Gaillard, Frye, with Kyle Petty. *Kyle at 200 M.P.H.: A Sizzling Season in the Petty/NASCAR Dynasty*. New York: St. Martin's Press, 1995.

Gilliam, George H. *Racin': The NASCAR/Winston Cup Stock Car Racing Series*. Charlottesville, Va.: Howell Press, 1989.

Girdler, Allan. *American Road Race Specials, 1934–1970: Glory Days of Homebuilt Racers*. Osceola, Wisc.: Motorbooks International, 1990.

Girdler, Allan. *Stock Car Racers: The History and Folklore of NASCAR's Premier Series, Tail Straight Out and Belly to the Ground*. Osceola, Wisc.: Motorbooks International, 1988.

Golenbock, Peter. *American Zoom: Stock Car Racing—From the Dirt Tracks to Daytona*. New York: Macmillan, 1993.

Golenbock, Peter, and Greg Fielden, eds. *The Stock Car Racing Encyclopedia: The Complete Record of America's Most Popular Sport*. New York: Macmillan, 1997.

Gunnell, John. *Race Car Flashback: A Celebration of America's Affair with Auto Racing from 1900–1980s*. Iola, Wisc.: Krause Publications, 1994.

Haener, Donald. *Hometown Stock Car Racing*. Erie, Pa.: Discovery Enterprise, 1975.

Hanley, George P., and Stacey Pankiw Hanley. *The Marmon Heritage: More than 125 Years of American Production of World Renowned Products*. Rochester, Mich.: Doyle Hyke Publishing, 1990.

Hayhoe, David, and David Holland. *Grand Prix Data Book: A Complete Record of the Formula 1 World Championship from 1950*. 2nd ed. Croyden, Eng.: D. Hayhoe, 1995.

Helck, Peter. *The Checkered Flag*. New York: Charles Scribner's Sons, 1961.

Helck, Peter. *Great Auto Races*. New York: Harry N. Abrams, 1976.

Henry, Alan. *History of the Grand Prix*. New York: Mallard Press, 1990.

Henry, Alan. *March: The Grand Prix and Indy Cars*. Richmond, Surrey, Eng.: Hazelton, 1989.

Henry, Alan, ed. *Autocourse: 50 Years of World Championship Grand Prix Motor Racing*. Richmond, Eng.: Hazleton, 1999.

Higdon, Hal. *Showdown at Daytona*. New York: G.P. Putnam's Sons, 1976.

Higham, Peter. *The Guinness Guide to International Motor Racing: A Complete Reference from Formula One to Touring Cars*. Osceola, Wisc.: Motorbooks International, 1995.

Hodges, David. *A–Z of Formula Racing Cars, 1945–1990*. Bideford, Devon, Eng.: Bay View Books, 1998.

Hodges, David. *Ford GT40: An Anglo-American Supercar Classic*. 2nd ed. Croyden, Eng.: Motor Racing Publications, 1998.

Hodges, David, Doug Nye, and Nigel Roebuck. *Grand Prix: The Cars, the Drivers, the Circuits*. New York: St. Martin's Press, 1981.

Holthusen, Peter. *The Land Speed Record: To the Sound Barrier and Beyond*. Newbury Park, Calif.: Haynes Publications, 1986.

Howell, Mark D. *From Moonshine to Madison Avenue: A Cultural History of the NASCAR Winston Cup Series*. Bowling Green, Ohio: Bowling Green State University Popular Press, 1997.

Hungness, Carl. *Go!: The Bettenhausen Story*. Speedway, Ind.: Carl Hungness, 1983.

Hungness, Carl, John Mahoney, and Jep Cadou. *USAC Sprint History, 1956–1980*. Speedway, Ind.: Carl Hungness, 1981.

Hunter, Don, and Al Pearce. *The Illustrated History of Stock Car Racing*. Osceola, Wisc.: MBI, 1998.

IndyCar Record Book. Troy, Mich.: Championship Auto Racing Teams, 1995.

Jackson, Bob. *Top Fueler: Inside the World of Drag Racing*. Osceola, Wisc.: Motorbooks International, 1987.

Jones, Bruce. *The Best Book of Formula One Facts & Stats Ever!* London: Carlton, 1998.

Jones, Bruce. *The Complete Encyclopedia of Formula One: The Bible of Motorsport*. London: Carlton, 1998.

Jones, Bruce, ed. *The Ultimate Encyclopedia of Formula One*. London: Hodder & Stoughton, 1999.

Jones, Chris. *Road Race*. New York: David McKay, 1977.

Jones, Gordon, and John Allen. *The Ford That Beat Ferrari: A Racing History of the Ford GT40*. London: Kimberley's, 1985.

Katzell, Raymond A., ed. *The Splendid Stutz: Its Cars, Companies, People, and Races*. Wilbraham, Mass.: Stutz Club, 1996.

King, Charles B. *Personal Sidelights of America's First Automobile Race*. Larchmont, N.Y.: Author, 1945.

Kirkland, Tom, and David Thompson. *Darlington International Raceway, 1950–1967*. Osceola, Wisc.: MBI, 1999.

Kopec, Richard J. *Shelby American Guide*. Rev. 2nd ed. Osceola, Wisc.: Motorbooks International, 1982.

Latford, Bob. *Built for Speed: Ultimate Guide to Stock Car Racetracks, A Behind-the-Wheel View of the Winston Cup Circuit*. Philadelphia: Courage Books, 1999.

Lawrence, Mike. *Grand Prix Cars, 1945–65*. Croydon, Eng.: Motor Racing Publications, 1998.

Legate, Trevor. *Cobra: The Real Thing*. Godmanstone, Eng.: Veloce, 1994.

Lepp, George D. *Bonneville Salt Flats: Speed Limit 1,000 MPH*. Osceola, Wisc.: Motorbooks International, 1988.

Lepp, George D. *Vintage Automobile Racing*. Osceola, Wisc.: Motorbooks International, 1990.

Lerner, Preston. *Scarab: Race Log of the All-American Specials, 1957–1965*. Osceola, Wisc.: Motorbooks International, 1991.

Levine, Leo. *Ford: The Dust and the Glory, a Racing History*. New York: Macmillan, 1968.

Lovern, W. Michael, and Bob Jones Jr. *Grand National Stock Car Racing: The Other Side of the Fence*. Richmond, Va.: Fast Company, 1982.

Ludvigsen, Karl. *Group 7, the World's Most Powerful Road Racing Cars: The Inside Story of the Can-Am Challenge, the Fastest and Most Exciting Road Racing in the World*. New York: World, 1971.

Ludvigsen, Karl. *Gurney's Eagles: The Exciting Story of the AAR Racing Cars.* Minneapolis: Motorbooks International, 1976.

Ludvigsen, Karl E. *The Inside Story of the Fastest Fords: The Design and Development of Ford GT Racing Cars.* Torino, Italy: Style Auto Editrice, 1971.

Lynch, Michael T., William Edgar, and Ron Parravano. *American Sports Car Racing in the 1950s.* Osceola, Wisc.: MBI, 1998.

Lyons, Pete. *Can-Am.* Osceola, Wisc.: Motorbooks International, 1995.

Madow, Marc. *Pikes Peak: Race to the Clouds.* [s.l.]: Author, 1979.

Mandel, Leon. *Fast Lane Summer: North American Road Racing.* Mill Valley, Calif.: Squarebooks, 1981.

Marquez, Edrie. *Amazing AMC Muscle: Complete Development and Racing History of the Cars from American Motors.* Osceola, Wisc.: Motorbooks International, 1988.

McDonald, Johnny. *Under the Green: A Complete Guide to Auto Racing.* New York: Peebles Press, 1979.

McKinney, David. *Can-Am Cars, 1966–1974.* Oxford, Eng.: Osprey, 1999.

Miller, Jerry. *Fast Company: The Men and Machines of American Auto Racing.* Chicago: Follett, 1972.

Montgomery, Don. *Those Wild Fuel Altereds: Drag Racing in the "Sixties."* Fallbrook, Calif.: Montgomery, 1997.

Moorhouse, H.F. *Driving Ambitions: An Analysis of the American Hot Rod Enthusiasm.* Manchester, Eng.: Manchester University Press, 1991.

Moriarty, Frank. *The Encyclopedia of Stock Car Racing.* New York: Metro Books, 1998.

Moriarty, Frank. *Supercars: The Story of the Dodge Charger Daytona and Plymouth SuperBird.* Charlottesville, Va.: Howell Press, 1995.

Moriarty, Frank, and Rick Farnkopf. *Sunday Drivers: NASCAR Winston Cup Stock Car Racing.* Charlottesville, Va.: Howell Press, 1994.

Morrison, Ian. *Guinness Formula 1 Fact Book.* Osceola, Wisc.: Motorbooks International, 1992.

Moses, Sam. *Fast Guys, Rich Guys and Idiots: A Racing Odyssey on the Border of Obsession.* Jamestown, R.I.: September Press, 1986.

NASCAR 50: The Thunder of America. New York: HarperHorizon, 1998.

Neal, Robert J. *Packards at Speed.* [s.l.]: Aero-Marine History, 1995.

Neely, William. *Daytona USA.* Tucson: Aztex, 1979

Noad, Peter. *VW Beetle in Motorsport: The Illustrated History, 1940s to 1990s.* London: Windrow & Greene, 1992.

North, Louise Ann. *Bonneville Salt Flats.* Osceola, Wisc.: MBI, 1999.

Nye, Doug. *Autocourse History of the Grand Prix Car, 1945–65.* Richmond, Eng.: Hazleton, 1993.

Nye, Doug. *Autocourse History of the Grand Prix Car, 1966–91.* 2nd ed. Richmond, Eng.: Hazleton, 1992.

Nye, Doug. *McLaren: The Grand Prix, Can-Am and Indy Cars.* 2nd ed. Richmond, Eng.: Hazleton, 1988.

Nye, Doug, *The United States Grand Prix and Grand Prize Races, 1908–1977.* Garden City, N.Y.: Doubleday, 1978.

Official NASCAR Handbook: Everything You Want to Know about the NASCAR Winston Cup Series. New York: HarperHorizon, 1998.

O'Malley, J.J., and Bill Green. *Watkins Glen, from Griswold to Gordon: Fifty Years of*

Competition at the Home of American Road Racing. Watkins Glen, N.Y.: Watkins Glen Raceway, 1998.

Osmer, Harold L. *Where They Raced.* Chatworth, Calif.: Author, 1996.

Owen, Dan. *Vintage and Historic Indianapolis Race Cars.* Osceola, Wisc.: MBI, 1998.

Paddock, Lowell C., and Dave Friedman. *Corvette Grand Sport: Photographic Race Log of the Magnificent Chevrolet Corvette Factory Specials, 1963–1967.* Osceola, Wisc.: Motorbooks International, 1989.

Parks, Wally. *Drag Racing Yesterday and Today: The Story of the Fastest Sport in the World.* New York: Trident Press, 1966.

Partridge, Bellamy. *Fill er Up!: The Story of Fifty Years of Motoring.* New York: McGraw-Hill, 1952.

Perkins, Kris. *Indycar.* London: Osprey, 1993.

Phillips, David, ed. *American Motorsports: The Definitive Illustrated Guide.* London: Carlton, 1997.

Post, Robert C. *High Performance: The Culture and Technology of Drag Racing, 1950–1990.* Baltimore: Johns Hopkins University Press, 1994.

Posthumus, Cyril. *Land Speed Record: A Complete History of World Record-Breaking Cars from 39.24 to 600+ mph.* New York: Crown, 1972.

Prior, Rupert, comp. *Motoring: The Golden Years.* London: Morgan Samuel Editions, 1991.

Pritchard, Anthony. *Directory of Formula One Cars, 1966–1986.* Bourne End, Bucks, Eng.: Aston Publications, 1986.

Pritchard, Anthony. *Ford versus Ferrari: The Battle for Le Mans.* Rev. ed. Marina Del Rey, Calif.: Zuma Marketing, 1984.

Pritchard, Anthony. *Grand Prix Racing: The Enthusiast's Companion.* Bourne End, Bucks, Eng: Aston, 1991.

Pulfer, Harry, ed. *Model T Ford in Speed and Sport.* Arcadia, Calif.: Post Motor Books, 1956.

Punnett, Dick. *Racing on the Rim: A History of the Annual Automobile Racing Tournaments Held on the Sands of the Ormond-Daytona Beach, Florida, 1903–1910.* Ormond Beach, Fla.: Tomoka Press, 1997.

Quattlebaum, Julian K. *The Great Savannah Races.* Athens: University of Georgia Press, 1983.

A Racer's Guide to the Universe. Hercules, Calif.: EVRAS Press, 1992-date.

Radbruch, Don. *Roaring Roadsters: Track Roadsters from 1924 until 1956.* Driggs, Idaho: Tex Smith Publishing, 1994.

Rendall, Ivan. *The Checkered Flag: 100 Years of Motor Racing.* Secaucus, N.J.: Chartwell Books, 1993.

Rendall, Ivan. *The Power and the Glory: A Century of Motor Racing.* Parkwest, N.Y.: BBC Books, 1993.

Riggs, D. Randy. *Flat-Out Racing: An Insider's Look at the World of Stock Cars.* New York: MetroBooks, 1995.

Riggs, L. Spencer. *Pace Cars of the Indy 500.* Ft. Lauderdale, Fla.: Speed Age, 1989.

Ross, Frank, Jr. *Car Racing against the Clock: The Story of the World Land Speed Record.* New York: Lothrop, Lee, and Shepard, 1976.

Rueter, John C. *American Road Racing: The Automobile Racing Club of America in the 1930's.* New York: A.S. Barnes, 1963.

Sakkis, Tony. *The Anatomy & Development of the Top Fuel Dragster*. Osceola, Wisc.: Motorbooks International, 1993.

Saward, Joe. *World Atlas of Motor Racing*. New York: Mallard Press, 1989.

Sawyer, John. *The Dusty Heroes*. Speedway, Ind.: Carl Hungness, 1978.

Scalzo, Joe. *Indianapolis Roadsters, 1952–1964*. Osceola, Wisc.: MBI Publishing, 1999.

Schultz, Tom. *Road America: Five Decades of Racing at Elkhart Lake*. Indianapolis: Beeman Jorgensen, 1999.

Schupack, Andrew L. *Formula Vee/Super Vee: Racing, History, and Chassis/Engine Prep*. Blue Ridge Summit, Pa.: TAB Books, 1981.

Schuster, George N., and Tom Mahoney. *The Longest Auto Race*. New York: John Day, 1966.

Setright, L.J.K., Derek Forsyth, and Robert Newman. *With Flying Colours: The Pirelli Album of Motor Sport*. New York: Summit Books, 1987.

Shaffer, Rick. *CART: The First Twenty Years, 1979–1998*. Richmond, Eng.: Hazleton, 1999.

Shapiro, Harvey. *Faster than Sound*. South Brunswick, N.J.: A.S. Barnes, 1975.

Shoen, Michael L. *The Cobra–Ferrari Wars, 1963–1965*. Vancouver, Wash.: CFW, 1990.

Sims, Carol, ed. *Fabulous Fifties: American Championship Racing*. Escondido, Calif.: Dick Wallen Productions, 1993.

Stambler, Irwin. *The Supercars and the Men Who Race Them*. New York: Putnam, 1975.

Starkey, John. *Lola T70: The Racing History & Individual Chassis Record*. Rev. ed. Dorchester, Eng.: Veloce, 1997.

Stephenson, Morris. ed. *From Dust to Glory: The Story of Clay Earles and the NASCAR-Sanctioned Martinsville Speedway*. Bassett, Va.: Bassett Printing, 1992.

Stevenson, Peter. *The Greatest Days of Racing*. New York: Charles Scribner's Sons, 1972.

Tanner, Hans. *The Racing Fords*. New York: Meredith Press, 1968.

Taylor, Rich. *Indy: Seventy-Five Years of Racing's Greatest Spectacle*. New York: St. Martin's Press, 1992.

Taylor, Rich. *Lime Rock Park: 35 Years of Racing*. Sharon, Conn.: Sharon Mountain Press, 1992.

Tremayne, David, and Mark Hughes. *The Concise Encyclopedia of Formula One: A Complete Guide to the Fastest Sport in the World*. North Vancouver, B.C., Can.: Whitecap Books, 1998.

Tucker, Tom, and Jim Tiller, eds. *Daytona: The Quest for Speed*. Daytona Beach, Fla.: Daytona Beach News Journal, 1994.

Tuthill, William R. *Speed on Sand*. Ormond Beach, Fla: Ormond Beach Historical Trust, 1978.

Ullmann, Alec. *The Sebring Story*. Philadelphia: Chilton, 1969.

Valkenburgh, Paul V. *Chevrolet-Racing . . . ?: Fourteen Years of Raucous Silence!!* Newfoundland, N.J.: Haessner, 1972.

Von Dare, Gregory. *Corvette Racers: Race History of America's Sports Car and the Drivers Who Pushed It to the Limit on Tracks from Sebring to Le Mans*. Osceola, Wisc.: Motorbooks International, 1992.

Wagner, Fred J., as told to John M. Mitchell. *The Saga of the Roaring Road: A Story of Early Auto Racing in America*. Los Angeles: Floyd Clymer, 1949.

Wallace, Dave. *Petersen's History of Drag Racing.* Los Angeles: Petersen, 1981.

Wallen, Dick. *Board Track: Guts, Gold & Glory.* Escondido, Calif.: Dick Wallen Productions, 1990.

Wallen, Dick. *Roar from the Sixties: American Championship Racing.* Glendale, Ariz.: Dick Wallen Productions, 1997.

Wheeler, Frank T. *The Savannah Races: Photographs from the Collection of the Georgia Historical Society.* Dover, N.H.: Arcadia Publishing, 1998.

Whiticar, Alise Barton. *The Long Road: The Story of the Race around the World by Automobile in 1908.* Fort Lauderdale, Fla.: Wake-Brook House, 1971.

Wilkinson, Sylvia. *Dirt Tracks to Glory: The Early Days of Stock Car Racing as Told by the Participants.* Chapel Hill, N.C.: Algonquin Books, 1983.

Wimpffen, János L. *Time and Two Seats: Five Decades of Long Distance Racing.* Redmond, Wash.: Motorsport Research Group, 1999.

Wise, David Burgess, William Boddy, and Brian Laban. *The Automobile: The First Century.* New York: Greenwich House, 1983.

Wright, Crocky. *Midget Auto Racing Histories.* 4 vols. Indianapolis: C. Wright Enterprises, 1979.

Wyss, Wallace A. *Shelby's Wildlife: The Cobras, Mustangs and Dodges.* 2nd. ed. Osceola, Wisc.: Motorbooks International, 1987.

Yates, Brock W. *The Indianapolis 500: The Story of the Motor Speedway.* Rev. ("Golden Anniversary") ed. New York: Harper and Row, 1961.

Yates, Brock W. *Vanderbilt Cup Race, 1936 and 1937: Photo Archive.* Osceola, Wisc.: Iconografix, 1997.

PART III

Political Analyses and Polemics

CHAPTER 10

Government Influences:
Regulations, Resources, and Roads

REGULATION

Today, there are multiple reasons for federal interest in the automobile and the automotive industry, including passenger safety; the desirability of developing more efficient engines, thereby reducing our reliance on foreign oil; and conservation of the environment. Each of these socioeconomic topics is explored in detail in the next chapter. Here, our concern is a broader one, with the reasons for and against government regulation of an automotive industry within a capitalist economy.

For a piece of machinery that has had such a profound impact on American history and life, there has been surprisingly little direct attempt on the part of the federal government to control its influence. While there are several notable, contemporary exceptions to this generalization (described in Chapter 11), the operating principle seems to be to interfere only in questions of public safety or economic instability. In addition, the automotive industry was generally viewed as primarily a domestic one, which, while it had significant sales abroad, was relatively impervious to foreign competition or international economic considerations.

Since the mid-1970s, however, there has been a decided change in the attitude of the federal government. The dependence of the economy on a healthy automotive industry has been publicly acknowledged in the face of the twin threats of the oil embargo and severe foreign competition (see Chapter 3 in regard to the latter). As a result, the government took direct action to prop up what was clearly an ailing industry, in short, to interfere openly with the free play of the forces in the marketplace. For a broad introduction to this area of concern, see *Government, Technology, and the Future of the Automobile*, a volume of papers presented at a 1978 Harvard Business School Symposium, edited by Douglas H. Ginsburg and William J. Abernathy. While the authors are, by design, an eclectic lot, their focus is on the varied impacts of technological change in the industry and of the domestic regulatory process and the role (if any) of the federal government in keeping American manufacturers competitive in an increasingly global marketplace. An international perspective can be found in Dennis Patrick Quinn's *Restructuring the Automobile Industry: A Study of Firms and States in Modern Capitalism,* a comparative study of Great Britain and the United States. Quinn argues that in democratic capitalist countries, the government's role is dependent on cyclical changes in the economy. The goal is always to promote economic growth at minimal cost to the government. Thus, when the economy is healthy, little assistance is offered, and public policy varies from one country to the next. However, when there is a recession or threat thereof, such governments favor subsidizing private firms to move them and the economy toward recovery. When the industry is a global, interconnected one, like the automotive one, nations also tend to adopt similar policies.

For insight into the multiple results of government intervention in the 1970s, as seen from two different perspectives, the reader is directed to the U.S. Department of Transportation's *Effects of Federal Regulation on the Financial Structure and Performance of the Domestic Motor Vehicle Manufacturers* and a study by H.C. Wainright & Company, entitled *The Impact of Government Regulations on Competition in the U.S. Automobile Industry.* A decade later, in *Blind Intersection: Policy and the Automobile Industry,* Clifford Winston *et al.* argue that government intervention is a negative factor and that the industry would be more likely to recover if free market forces were allowed to operate in an unfettered manner. Finally, a more comparative approach to one of the issues involved can be found in *Government and Technical Progress: A Cross-Industry Analysis,* edited by Richard R. Nelson, which contains a chapter on "The Motor Vehicle Industry," written by Lawrence J. White, that explores the influence of government policy (or lack thereof) on technological innovation.

The best-known example of the American government's departure from a laissez-faire stance was the so-called bailout of the Chrysler Corporation in the early 1980s, an action involving a $1.2 billion, low-interest federal loan to that automobile manufacturer. For books describing this event and analyzing the government's role therein, see the "Organization, Structure, and Competition" section of Chapter 3. In addition, all of the recent histories of the Chrysler Corporation (see Chapter 1) and biographies of Lee Iacocca (see Chapter 2) contain sections dealing with the bailout and the company's subsequent recovery.

While the government, by and large, has not seen fit to regulate the automotive industry, it has long recognized the car as a potential source of revenue, sometimes to be used for automotively related activities and sometimes to subsidize other, less profitable means of transportation, such as urban mass transit. Although the first attempt to generate such revenue was the implementation of a penny tax on gasoline in Oregon in 1919, it took the economic boom of the 1920s to make both the federal and state governments fully cognizant of this new source of funds. By 1932 the National Industrial Conference Board thought the issue was important enough to issue a 200-page report entitled *Taxation of Motor Vehicle Transportation*. While the proceeds from such taxes are usually applied to highway construction and maintenance, there are some notable exceptions. For example, in Indiana they have helped support education.

In addition, the need to set limits on who could drive and to control the flow of traffic increased with the number of cars on the road. Although not generally required until the second decade of this century, the issuance of state driver's licenses has effectively reduced the number of potential motorists for a variety of physical, psychological, age, and legal reasons.

Traffic laws are another means of regulation through which states (and sometimes localities) have tried to influence the impact of the automobile. While countless articles deal with contemporary problems and proposals, and a journal (*Traffic Quarterly*) is devoted to them, there is relatively little book-length, scholarly research on this subject from the sociohistorical point of view. Two exceptions to this generalization, both drawn from the 1920s, would be William P. Eno's *The Science of Highway Traffic Regulation, 1899–1920*, by the man generally recognized to be responsible for the American automotive rules of the road, and the September 1927 issue of *The Annals of the American Academy of Political and Social Science*, which was devoted to the theme of "Planning for City Traffic" and was edited by Austin F. MacDonald.

MOTOR VEHICLES IN GOVERNMENT SERVICE

Although no government agencies were involved in the introduction of the automobile to American society, they were among the first to see its potential for improving how they functioned. This was especially true for the armed forces, local police and fire departments, and the Office of the President of the United States. (Although motorization of government services involved much more than passenger vehicles, trucks, buses, weapons-carrying vehicles, etc. are beyond the scope of this guide.)

Military Applications

Unfortunately, this aspect of the car's impact on American society has not been subjected to the scholarly scrutiny that it deserves, particularly in terms of book-length treatments. Nonetheless, interest has been sufficient to generate a number of notable company and popular histories.

Several manufacturers have achieved both fame and profits by contributing to the country's war efforts. For example, during the First World War, Model T Fords were used in various military capacities. For one 1917 account of such activity, see William Y. Stevenson's *At the Front in a Flivver.* ("Flivver" was an affectionate nickname for the Model T.) The Cadillac Motor Car Company described its own *Participation in the World War* in a brief 1919 volume, as did White in *The White Record of Service in the World War*, also printed in 1919, which incidentally was the last year that company produced cars before turning to the exclusive production of trucks.

In addition, numerous books deal with the most famous of all military passenger vehicles, the four-wheel-drive "jeep," a name derived from "general purpose" or G.P. First introduced in World War II, during which some 660,000 were produced, it is still manufactured today by a division of Daimler-Chrysler. For the early history, see Herbert R. Rifkind's *The Jeep: Its Development and Procurement under the Quartermaster Corps, 1940–1942*, a publication issued by the corps itself. Rifkind traces the genesis of the jeep as a replacement for the combination motorcycle and sidecar, with due attention to the roles of manufacturers Bantam, Willys-Overland, and Ford and controversies over the letting of contracts by the Quartermaster Corps. Although not technically a sequel, Graham Scott's *Essential Military Jeep: Ford, Willys and Bantam Models, 1942–45* covers the models produced during that period, with a heavy emphasis on engineering specifications and performance characteristics. In addition, see Ray R. Cowdery and Merrill W. Madsen's encyclopedic (two-volume), primarily technical *All-American Wonder: The Military Jeep, 1941–1945*, which also contains anecdotal stories on the lighter side, and Wade R. Wells' *Hail to the Jeep: A Factual and Pictorial History of the Jeep*, a well-received account of the vehicle's exploits during World War II, first published in 1946.

Broader in approach, in that they cover the post–World War II years as well, and more in the category of popularized marque histories are (alphabetically by author) Robert C. Ackerson's *Jeep: 50 Year History*; Arch Brown's *Jeep: The Unstoppable Legend*, written with the auto editors of *Consumer Guide*; Englishman Michael Clayton's *Jeep*, probably the best in this category; Patrick R. Foster's *The Story of Jeep*, also excellent and cowinner of the AACA's 1998 McKean Cup; William Fowler's *Jeep Goes to War: A Pictorial Chronicle*, a heavily illustrated account of its military exploits through the Persian Gulf War of the early 1990s; Henry Rasmussen's *Jeep: Mechanical Mule to People's Plaything*; and Kurt Willinger and Gene Gurney's *The American Jeep: In War and Peace*, an exceptional photographic history. Also worthy of attention is Bart Vanderveen's *The Jeep*, a brief volume similar to that of Willinger and Gurney in concept. Despite their numbers, none of these jeep histories are very scholarly in nature. This is a vehicle deserving of serious study in terms of its widespread social, economic, and political effects.

Automotive companies also contributed to both 20th-century world wars by manufacturing matériel other than motor vehicles. In fact, during the Second World War, the automotive industry was *the* primary military supplier, providing several million motorized vehicles. That story is well told in V. Dennis Wrynn's *Detroit Goes to War: The American Automobile Industry in World War II*, which draws heavily upon magazine advertising of the period. Not only did the car companies convert to the production of heavy trucks, tanks, and planes, but they also were in the forefront of the conservation (especially gas) and recycling (rubber and scrap metal) efforts and leaders in patriotic advertising campaigns (copies of many of which are reprinted in Wrynn's book). More specifically, the story of the application by Henry Ford of his assembly line techniques to the manufacture of "Eagle" boats during the First World War is told by David A. Hounshell in "Ford Eagle Boats and Mass Production during World War I," a chapter in *Military Enterprise and Technological Change*, edited by Merritt Roe Smith. Similarly, the potential (eventually realized) for manufacturing aircraft during World War II is described in *500 Planes a Day: A Program for the Utilization of the Automobile Industry for Mass Production of Defense Planes*, written by a young Walter P. Reuther in 1940. In some respects, the changes in domestic industrial production, together with rationing, were the most visible symbols in the United States of a war that was raging in two theaters. Richard R. Lingeman has written a fine overview of this entire situation, entitled *Don't You Know There's a War On?: The American Home Front, 1941–1945*, which includes discussion of automobiles, the automotive industry, and the Detroit race riot of 1943.

The best reference on the group that eventually made wartime cooperation among the car manufacturers possible, together with the construction of thousands of tanks, jeeps, and other pieces of military hardware, is the Automobile Manufacturers Association's *Freedom's Arsenal: The Story of the Automotive Council for War Production*, wherein are included documents, speeches, and statistical data concerning the significant effort of the council. Keep in mind, though, that that volume was written and published in 1950 by the Automobile Manufacturers Association. There also is a government feasibility study prepared during the Korean War by Wilfred Owen, entitled *Automobile Transportation in Defense or War: A Report Prepared for the Defense Transport Administration*. Readers interested in the automotive industry's contributions to war efforts should also consult the histories of the individual companies described in Chapter 1, especially for Ford (e.g., see Nevins and Hill).

Finally, a number of books bring the story of military use to the contemporary period. Representative of these works would be Fred W. Crismon's encyclopedic *Modern U.S. Military Wheeled Vehicles*, a reference for all American-manufactured carriers and thus essentially heavily oriented toward trucks and tracked vehicles but also including information on ambulances, Humvees, and staff cars. In regard to the latter two, see also Michael Green's *Hummer: The Next Generation*, an enthusiast's account of the vehicle that militarily replaced the jeep but also has emerged in a popular off-road civilian version; and David Fletcher's brief (32-page) monograph on *Staff Cars*, an international survey of the broad range of types and models used to convey military people of importance since 1897, including Americans.

Domestic Law Enforcement

The introduction of the automobile into American society was followed almost immediately by local and state laws designed to regulate its use. Some of this legislation was logical and needed, even from today's standpoint. However, much of it was nonsensical, a naive response to a little-understood piece of machinery that seemed to threaten the "civilized" equestrian world. There exists an interesting collection of actual early laws, edited by Arthur C. Wyman in 1908. Entitled *Automobile Laws of the New England States, New York, New Jersey, and Pennsylvania*, this anthology gives the reader the advantage of being able to compare and contrast the laws of nine states in a single volume. For a brief, but chronologically broader and international, survey of initial legal attempts to curb the car, see the chapter entitled "Regulating the Car" in *Automania: Man and the Motor Car*, by Julian Pettifer and Nigel Turner.

The motor car's potential for widening the sphere of crime and delinquency was recognized early, both in fact and in fiction. Clyde Barrow's famous letter to Henry Ford, in which the bank robber thanks the manufacturer for producing one of the most dependable getaway cars, was simply confirmation of a well-known situation. In addition, the automobile's alleged contributions to immorality have already been discussed in Chapter 5. One book, however, deserves mention here as well, David J. Langum's *Crossing over the Line: Legislating Morality and the Mann Act*. Passed by the Congress in 1910 (and not effectively repealed until 1986), the Mann Act was a classic instance of a governmental attempt to legislate private morality. Aimed initially at prostitution, it soon was applied to any man and woman who crossed a state line with the intent to commit an immoral act. With the mass adoption of the automobile, more often than not it became the vehicle implicated in such activities.

Another legislative outcome of the same era was Prohibition, which also had its automotive dimensions. See, for instance, Derek Nelson's *Moonshiners, Bootleggers & Rumrunners*, a popular history emphasizing the years 1920–1933 that pays due attention to the role of the automobile in the transportation of illegal liquor. It is interesting to note that many early stock car drivers "apprenticed" for their careers by trying to outrun the "G-men" as they delivered their bootleg merchandise to distributors. In that vein, see Alex Gabbard's *Return to Thunder Road: The Story behind the Legend*, which is a history of the haulers of "white lightnin' " in Wilkes County, North Carolina, the self-proclaimed capital of such activities, in the 1930s, 1940s, and 1950s. (Incidentally, the book's title is a reference to the movie *Thunder Road*, a cult film released in 1958 that is viewed as the definitive moonshine motion picture.)

The automobile itself, as a piece of property, frequently has been the object of theft. Given the prevalence of this crime, surprisingly little research has been published in this area. As an indication of one direction that such research might take, see Gregg Hegman's "Taking Cars: Ethnography of a Car Theft Ring," which appeared as a chapter in *The Cultural Experience*, edited by James P. Spradley and David W. McCurdy. Another approach is represented by Donald Cressey's "Law, Order and the Motorist," a chapter in *Crime, Criminality and Public Policy*, edited by Roger Hood.

One of the early challenges for state and local officials was adopting and adapting the motor car as a tool for law enforcement. There never was much question that the transition from horse to automobile would occur in this area of government. Once the motorized criminal appeared on the scene, the advent of the police car was inevitable. Although there is no book-length, scholarly treatment of this subject, there are several good, heavily illustrated, popular histories of such cars. Probably the best is Edwin J. Sanow's *Encyclopedia of American Police Cars*, a chronological history from the 1930s to the 1990s, with an emphasis on technical specifications. Among the better, more specialized works are Sanow's *Vintage Police Cars*, which serves as a reference work for cars of the 1950s and 1960s, although the text continues to 1979, and what might be viewed as a companion volume, Robert Genat's *Modern Police Cars*, a pictorial celebration supplemented by technical specifications, with special attention to exceptional vehicles (e.g., Corvettes, Mustangs, and Cherokees). Monty McCord's *Cars of the State Police and Highway Patrol* is a photographic history of vehicles used by various state law enforcement agencies. Bruce W. Cameron's *Police Cars: A Graphic History* focuses on the progress made in lighting and graphics (door markings and color schemes) over time, a topic of special interest to enthusiasts.

In addition, several volumes authored or coauthored by Edwin J. Sanow deal with police cars by marque. *Chevrolet Police Cars* covers the years 1955 through 1996. In addition to giving the technical specifications of the available models and options, this book includes a sampling of true stories involving police and their cars. *Ford Police Cars, 1932–1997* is similar in concept but covers a broader chronological period since Ford's famous flathead V-8 engine was widely adopted by the police departments, and Ford was the first among the Big Three to offer special component packages for law enforcement work. *Dodge, Plymouth & Chrysler Police Cars, 1956–1978*, coauthored with John L. Bellah, describes the models available (invariably painted black and white), their specifications, and available options and accessories of these cars, known for their reliability and the performance of their big-block Mopar engines. A more recent companion volume, *Dodge, Plymouth & Chrysler Cars, 1979–1994*, covers the modern era, with experiential information from the California Highway Patrol and the Michigan State Police.

Before leaving this exploration of the interaction between motoring and law enforcement, it should be noted that many of the general works cited in Chapter 1 contain some discussion of the topic, although it is usually of a spotty nature. There is a clear need for substantial, scholarly studies in this area.

Presidential Motor Transportation

The Office of the President of the United States, state governors, and local mayors generally did not adopt the automobile as quickly as did members of the general public with similar incomes. While President William McKinley was the first American president to ride in a car, in 1900, it was not until the presidency of William Howard Taft that cars began to replace horses (1909) and the White House stable was transformed into a garage. Through World War II, the presidential cars were essentially showroom stock automobiles. Presidents generally were chauffeured about, although on occasion some presidents did their own driving, including the paraplegic Franklin Roosevelt. After 1945, security and communications concerns led to the purchase of the customized armored limousines still in use today.

A number of books deal with this topic, although none could be rightfully termed a scholarly treatment. Herbert R. Collins' *Presidents on Wheels* is a complete collection of carriages and automobiles used by the chief executive through 1970. Collins was an associate curator at the Smithsonian when this book was published. Broader in coverage is William D. Siuru Jr. and Andrea Stewart's *Presidential Cars & Transportation*, an illustrated history of those carriages, cars, trains, yachts, and planes that have carried the president, with special attention to the post-1970s limos. Finally, for a study of the automotive make that was long associated with the Office of the President, see Maurice D. Henry's *Lincoln: America's Car of State*.

Others

Before concluding this section, some mention needs to be made of several types of government vehicles which, while technically not passenger cars, are best placed in that category. For instance, since the early days of rural free delivery, the Post Office used cars to deliver letters and packages. In this regard, see James H. Burns' *Mail on the Move*, a well-illustrated, popular history.

Another type of vehicle to be included here would be the ambulance which, it would be well to remember, is essentially a passenger vehicle for those unable to drive. John S. Haller Jr.'s *Farmcarts to Fords: A History of the Military Ambulance, 1790–1925* is an excellent, scholarly, international study of the variety and evolution of transportation used to bring the wounded from the battlefield to hospitals and medical facilities behind the lines, with the emphasis on the American and British armies. Also very good is Arlen J. Hansen's *Gentlemen Volunteers: The Story of the American Ambulance Drivers in the Great War, August 1914–September 1918*, a heavily researched volume based on archival materials and the letters and diaries of the people who transported the wounded and gassed Allied troops from the carnage of the World War I trenches to medical care in non-combat areas. Drivers included such later legends as Ernest Hemingway, John Dos Passos, e.e. cummings, Dashiell Hammett, and even Walt Disney. Similarly, Virginia Scharff in her book *Taking the Wheel: Women and the Coming of the Motor Age* details the education that women received and the contributions that they made (including driving ambulances) in Europe and at home in a chapter entitled "Women Drivers in World War I."

Finally, although somewhat similar to the police cars discussed above, there is a distinct category of automobiles used by community fire departments. In *Fire Chief Cars; 1900–1997 Photo Album*, Donald F. Wood and W. Wayne Sorensen illustrate and describe the tremendous variety of vehicles, from specially built or modified cars to off-the-lot automobiles, that have been employed to get the chief to the site of the conflagration first so that he (or she) can establish a mobile command post.

THE AUTOMOBILE AND POLITICS

In addition to these direct applications, the automobile and the industry that it spawned have also been a vehicle, both literally and figuratively, for the exercise of political power, beginning with the depression of 1929. In *Organizing the Unemployed: Community and Union Activists in the Industrial Heartland*, James J. Lorence explores the efforts of activists in the fledgling United Automobile Workers (UAW) to mobilize the jobless in Michigan for mass action. His work is a valuable case study of the connection between the rise of industrial unionism in the 1930s and the political activism among the unemployed of that decade and of the common concerns that they shared both before and after the passage of New Deal legislation.

In 1933 Congress passed President Franklin D. Roosevelt's National Recovery Act (NRA). Included within the NRA was a so-called auto code, by which car manufacturers were to pledge themselves to voluntarily abide by guidelines for minimum wages and maximum hours. Of all the major companies, only Ford refused to enter into this agreement. The code and its impact on workers' interests are analyzed in Sidney Fine's *The Automobile under the Blue Eagle: Labor, Management, and the Automobile Manufacturing Code*, which also is valuable for its explanation of the labor policies of the Roosevelt administration and the activities of the UAW in the mid-1930s.

Without assessing blame, it probably is fair to say that militancy on the part of labor and management was an established fact by the late 1930s. Therefore, it should not come as a surprise that the auto industry's adaptation to the needs and demands created by the Second World War was a checkered one. On the one hand, the transition from the manufacture of automobiles to that of war matériel went reasonably well. On the other hand, a labor movement that had recently successfully expressed itself through militant action was frustrated by the restrictions that foreign policy developments placed on it, such as no wage increases or work stoppages during the duration of the war. For the resulting conflict within labor, the most complete work is Martin Glaberman's *Wartime Strikes: The Struggle against the No-Strike Pledge in the UAW during World*

War II. Also good are Nelson N. Lichtenstein's "Conflict over Workers' Control: The Automobile Industry in World War II," in Michael H. Frisch and Daniel J. Walkowitz's *Working Class America*, and Ed Jennings' "Wildcat!: The Wartime Strike Wave in Auto" and Martin Glaberman's "Epilogue," both part of a special thematic issue of the journal *Radical America* devoted to "Wartime Strikes in the Automobile Industry."

During the immediate post–World War II era, unionization firmly established itself within the automotive industry. As a result, the UAW broadened its concerns beyond workers' salaries and benefits and became involved in national social and economic issues. There are several excellent accounts of these efforts. In *The UAW and the Heyday of American Liberalism, 1945–1968*, Kevin Boyle presents a solid case against those who maintain that labor in the postwar years was a defender of the status quo. Instead, he argues that the UAW, under the leadership of Walter Reuther, was heavily engaged in the national political maneuvering that led to significant social democratic change during those years, including such struggles as civil rights, the War on Poverty, and other parts of President Lyndon Johnson's "Great Society." Martin Halpern's *UAW Politics in the Cold War Era* examines the political struggle within the union between those who favored a continuance of the center-left stance of the war years and others, led by Walter Reuther, who were eventually successful in leading the union to take a more conservative, pragmatic view of foreign and domestic issues. Stephen Amberg's *The Union Inspiration in American Politics: The Autoworkers and the Making of a Liberal Industrial Order* takes up after the period of Boyle's concern, focusing on the reasons for the demise of the New Deal coalition that had been so beneficial to labor. Amberg argues that a key reason for the breakdown was that labor became increasingly excluded from decision making in the workplace, as part of an unwritten agreement that guaranteed security, higher wages, and benefits in exchange for accepting an unequal partner status in the production process. Finally, for insight into the rise and fall of a 20th-century political alliance of which auto workers were a vital part, see *Organized Labor and American Politics, 1894–1994: The Labor–Liberal Alliance*, edited by Kevin Boyle. The essays by Bruce Nelson ("Autoworkers, Electoral Politics, and the Convergence of Class and Race: Detroit, 1937–1945") and Boyle ("Little More than Ashes: The UAW and American Reform in the 1960s") are particularly pertinent to this guide.

Although labor has, like other special interests, flirted with third-party movements, it has always been clear that influence within one or both of the major parties was the surest way to achieve labor's goals. Historically, the party of labor in the United States has been the Democrats. In this vein, there is a fine two-volume history covering almost a half century of the relationship between the state Democratic Party in Michigan and the UAW, from which the reader might extrapolate national implications. Written by Dudley W. Buffa, both books have the same main title, *Union Power and American Democracy*. The first volume, (misleadingly) subtitled *The UAW and the Democratic Party*,

1935–72, analyzes the interplay between that union and the party and what it meant for the democratic process in one state, with the emphasis on the late 1950s and beyond. Buffa concludes that by 1972 the UAW effectively controlled the Michigan Democratic Party. Volume 2, *The UAW and the Democratic Party, 1972–83*, continues the same themes, stressing the politics within the party during this period, especially the unusually strong position of union interests, and the lobbying efforts of the UAW to influence the passage of legislation that it favored and to hinder the implementation of those laws that it unsuccessfully opposed. In addition, Buffa analyzes the early 1970s abandonment of the Democratic Party by blue-collar workers and subsequent attempts to win them back. Of special note is the political role of African Americans in both time periods.

Automobile workers also have been the subject of broader studies of bloc voting, as witnessed by the publication of *When Labor Votes: A Study of Auto Workers* by Arthur Kornhauser, a 1956 book that labor historian Robert H. Ziegler calls "a pioneering electoral analysis."

ROADS AND HIGHWAYS

As many historians have noted, the development of the automobile was intimately linked with the improvement of the nation's road and highway system. Until there were reasonably good roads on which to travel, there was little point in developing vehicles capable of speeds faster than that of a horse. In addition, given the pounding that motor vehicles experienced on dirt roads, they had to be built to be particularly strong. So influential was the road that it even determined automotive design. An entire genre of cars, appropriately termed "high wheelers," emerged to cope with the rutted roads.

The focus of this section is on books that analyze how the actions of federal and state governments or lack thereof influenced the development of roads. Nonetheless, anybody interested in that subject should begin by reading several significant, general works that provide the broader context in which those developments took place.

Broad Historical Surveys

John B. Rae provides an excellent historical overview in his *The Road and the Car in American Life*, which should be the starting point for any serious student. Among the topics that Rae discusses that are pertinent to this chapter are the development of federal and state highway policies, the ongoing struggle between the private automobile and the public mass transit and rail systems, and the influence of roads and cars as a determinant of land-use patterns and population densities. James J. Flink's *America Adopts the Automobile, 1895–1910* and *The Car Culture*, two pioneering works in automotive history, are also good at explaining how and why the advent of the motor car stimulated road improvements and the evolutionary role of the federal and state governments in the development of automotive highways. A good, brief survey of the development of "Roads, Streets, and Highways" from the colonial period to the American Bicentennial is contained in the *History of Public Works in the United States*, edited by Ellis L. Armstrong for the American Public Works Association.

Howard L. Preston's *Dirt Roads to Dixie: Accessibility and Modernization in the South, 1885–1935* is a fine regional study, focusing on the evolution of the highway network, the economic changes made possible, and the cultural diversity introduced as the region moved literally from dirt roads to paved, divided interstate highways. Nonetheless, as Preston notes, this "progress" largely benefited urban business interests and was at the expense of rural areas and farmers, as money was funneled from the improvement of farm-to-market "good roads" to interstate highways to bring tourists into the region. See also Blaine A. Brownell's *The Urban Ethos in the South, 1920–1930* for the role of business organizations in the development of highways during that decade.

Less scholarly in approach, but valuable in its own right (a *New York Times* Notable Book of the Year), is Phil Patton's *Open Road : A Celebration of the American Highway*. While Patton's account of the development of the nation's highways is a fascinating one, the importance of his book for this chapter lies in his analysis of the social and cultural impact of such roadways. Similar in concept, *Highway: America's Endless Dream*, combines contemporary color photography by Jeff Brouws, classic black-and-white roadside images from the 1930s, and historical essays by Phil Patton and Bernd Polster to explore the highway as a symbol of the American way of life.

Chronologically More Limited Works

There are relatively few book-length treatments of the role that the federal or state governments played in early road building, perhaps because it had historically been viewed as a local concern, and that mind-set continued into the early automotive period. The one significant exception to this generalization was the National (or Cumberland) Road, the first interstate highway planned and funded by the federal government. Begun in 1808, periodic segments were added until 1850, by which time it stretched from Cumberland, Maryland, to Vandalia, Illinois, effectively linking the East to the traditional West. *The National Road*, edited by Karl Raitz, is an outstanding overview of that project, with chapters that not only describe the building of the highway but reflect upon its historic, cultural, economic, and demographic significance.

Probably the first pertinent work devoted exclusively to roads and highways in the United States was an 1886 book entitled *American Highways: A Popular Account of Their Conditions, and of the Means by Which They May Be Bettered*, by Nathaniel S. Shaler. Readers interested in a general survey of road development from the colonial period to the 20th century are referred to *Historic Highways of America*, a massive sixteen-volume work edited by Archer B. Hulbert, first published between 1902 and 1905 but available in relatively contemporary reprint editions. George R. Chatburn provides a good, single-volume survey of developments from colonial times to 1922 in his *Highways and Highway Transportation*. Finally, for a personalized view of the evolution of American roads and highways from the late 19th century through the 1920s, see Virginia Rishel's *Wheels to Adventure: Bill Rishel's Western Routes*, the story of a man who was part of that process.

The middle third of the 20th century, which includes the beginning of strong federal interest in highway construction, has been studied to a greater extent than the earlier period. Virginia Hart's *The Story of American Roads* and the second volume of Albert C. Rose's *Public Roads of the Past* (entitled *Historic American Highways*), published by the American Association of State Highway Officials, are works that take the road building story to midcentury; Philip P. Mason's *A History of American Roads* and Christy Borth's *Mankind on the Move: The Story of Highways*, a worldwide account with a significant portion devoted to the American experience, are late 1960s works; and Charles W. Wixom's *ARBA Pictorial History of Roadbuilding*, written for the American Road Builders' Association (ARBA), and Albert C. Rose's latest effort, the relatively brief (118-page), but highly acclaimed, *Historic American Roads: From Frontier Trails to Superhighways*, are mid-1970s publications of the same type. One interesting aspect of the Rose volume is the inclusion of a series of color illustrations done by an employee of the Bureau of Public Roads in the 1920s. Much of the factual information contained in the above books can be found in abbreviated form in the chapter entitled "Roads, Streets, and Highways" in *History of Public Works in the United States, 1776–1976*, edited by Ellis L. Armstrong.

Historical Developments to 1956

What progress was made prior to World War I in terms of upgrading local and state roadways was due largely to private organizations and the pressure that they brought to bear on each level of government. Philip P. Mason writes of the efforts of one such key group in his *The League of American Wheelmen and the Good Roads Movement, 1880–1905*. Among the significant factors discussed by Mason is the early conflict between rural and urban interests in terms of road development for pleasure as opposed to business, a topic also examined by John B. Rae's *The Road and Car in American Life* and Howard L. Preston's *Dirt Roads to Dixie* (see above).

As its name indicates, the League of American Wheelmen began as an interest group trying to influence local governments to improve roads for bicyclists, but it eventually became subsumed by the broader-based Good Roads Movement. For some early insights into the latter, read William H. Moore's *History and Purposes of the Good Roads Movement: Proceedings of the National Good Roads Convention, St. Louis Mo., 1903*, which was published that year by the federal Office of Public Road Inquiries. The progress that had been made on the eve of the mass adoption of the automobile can be gleaned from *The Official Good Roads Yearbook of the United States for 1912*, an annual publication of the American Association for Highway Improvement.

The Office of Public Road Inquiries had been established within the U.S. Department of Agriculture in 1893 as a result of the league's successful lobbying efforts and was to evolve into the Bureau of Public Roads. (Its placement within the agriculture department was a reflection of both the fact that most Americans lived in rural areas at the time and the fact that the roads there were in greatest need of improvement.) An important contemporary (1923) history and description of federal action up to that point is contained in W. Stull Holt's *The Bureau of Public Roads: Its History, Activities and Organization.*

In addition to the League of American Wheelmen, the National Highways Association was another strong group advocating good roads, with particular interest in a national system of interconnecting highways. For some insight into that association's programs and their rationale, see their *National Highways and Good Roads*, published in 1913.

By the advent of the First World War, the Good Roads Movement, as a separate entity, had peaked. However, it had left a definite legacy in government interest in, and support for, highway construction, which was to continue through midcentury. In that regard, see Bruce E. Seely's award-winning book, *Building the American Highway System: Engineers as Policy Makers*, in which he maintains that the professional expertise of federal highway engineers was frequently crucial in the promulgation of the policies of the Bureau of Public Roads and that that agency, in turn, greatly influenced local and state decisions regarding where and how roads would be constructed, resulting in profound social and economic change.

One tangible result of the agitation of the League of the American Wheelmen, the National Highways Association, and the Lincoln Highway Association was the passage in 1916 of the Federal-Aid Road Act, which established the (still) basic principle of federal–state cooperation in the construction of highways and, along with the Federal Highway Act of 1921, led to an interconnected system of state highways by the mid-1920s.

The first real attempt at an intercontinental highway was the so-called Lincoln Highway, designed to span the distance between New York and San Francisco, traversing 3,384 miles in thirteen states. Portions were first opened for travel in 1915, and the route achieved true national proportions by the 1920s. The Lincoln Highway Association, a private group that lobbied for and oversaw the construction of that road published an official history in 1935 entitled *The Lincoln Highway: The Story of a Crusade That Made Transportation History*, focusing on the accomplishments of the association and Carl G. Fisher, generally viewed as the father of the transcontinental highway movement. In a sense this was a "final report" in that the route had been absorbed into the national route number system in 1927 and thus had lost most of its separate identity.

Over half a century later, Drake Hokanson's *The Lincoln Highway: Main*

Street across America was the first book to provide the scholar with a well-researched and nicely illustrated history (actually a "photo-essay") of this pioneering roadway and the social and economic changes that it wrought on the areas through which it passed. (Hokanson's book was a 1988 *Booklist* Adult Editors' Choice Award winner.)

In 1925 highways that met certain restrictions were termed "U.S." highways, numbered, and joined together wherever possible. Many of these, such as U.S. 1, 40 (the National Road), and 66, enjoyed success as auto touring routes prior to the construction of the formal interstate system in the 1950s. (See the "Roads and Highways" section of Chapter 8 in this regard.) Despite the popularity of travel over U.S. routes, local and state roads allowed for much more adventuresome day trips than had been possible before and provided a means to access relatively nearby vacation spots. By the 1920s states had begun to build "parkways." Several of these parkways have been the subject of book-length treatments, and readers interested in their development and evolution should also see Chapter 8.

The stock market crash of 1929 and its aftermath meant doom for all but the most financially sound auto makers and considerably slowed new state highway construction. On the national level, however, some of the "make-work" legislation of the New Deal brought federal assistance in areas and amounts previously unknown. One agency, the PWA (Public Works Administration) became heavily involved in the construction and repair of highways and bridges. Especially noteworthy in the context of this chapter were its contributions to the construction of the Blue Ridge Parkway. A contemporary account of its work is contained in *America Builds!: The Record of PWA*. A more general treatment of government road initiatives and beneficiaries up to World War II is contained in economist Charles L. Dearing's *American Highway Policy*.

Given the economic depression of the 1930s, it was not surprising that considerable time and effort went into planning for what was hoped to be a better tomorrow. Thus, at the 1939–1940 New York World's Fair, the most popular exhibit was General Motors' "Futurama," with its depiction of eight-lane, limited-access highways and the introduction of cloverleaf intersections. Famed designer Norman Bel Geddes describes this show in enthusiastic terms in *Magic Motorways* in an effort to persuade others to join the crusade. Interestingly, opposition was expressed at the time by those who believed that such highways would benefit a few long-distance travelers while depriving the nation of much needed money for the improvement and construction of local roads. In any case, with the advent of World War II, plans for new highways were placed on hold.

For a decade after 1945, there was a significant increase in the sales of American passenger automobiles, fueled by the unsatisfied demand of the war years. The result was an unprecedented number of cars on the nation's highways and a renewal of the dialogue regarding the adequacy of the latter. Probably the most significant expression of professional opinion during this period was contained in *Highways in Our National Life: A Symposium*, the forty-six papers from which were edited by Jean Labatut and Wheaton J. Lane and published in 1950 by Princeton University's Bureau of Urban Research. Although chronologically, the topics of these analytical essays stretch from the precolonial period to mid-century, two are especially relevant to this chapter: Albert C. Rose's "The Highway from the Railroad to the Automobile" and Spencer Miller Jr.'s "History of the Modern Highway in the United States." In addition, the socioeconomic approach of many of the others provides a perspective not often found in collections of this type. As a reflection of the national mood, the issues raised and problems discussed at such symposia made their way to Washington, D.C., and were incorporated in the internal improvements agenda for Dwight D. Eisenhower's second term as president.

Interstate Highway System

Hailed as the greatest public works project in American history when President Eisenhower signed the law bringing it into existence, the construction of the interstate highway system has been the costliest project in human history and has had an impact far beyond that of the limited-access highways themselves. For a thoroughly researched analysis of the visions, politics, and economic considerations that led up to the passage of the Interstate Highway Act in 1956 and affected its aftermath, see Mark H. Rose's excellent *Interstate: Express Highway Politics, 1939–1989*. Rose is particularly insightful regarding urban highway planning (policy formation and political processes) and good at explaining how the United States reached a point where the federal government provided 90% of the costs of new superhighway construction. Also valuable is Tom Lewis' *Divided Highways: Building the Interstate Highways, Transforming American Life*, a detailed, comprehensive history of the evolution of that asphalt network. In addition to adeptly exploring the engineering questions, Lewis provides an in-depth analysis of the socioeconomic impact (and controversy) of the construction of such highways and their development as business corridors. He also includes case studies of specific projects, together with portraits of the individuals involved. Finally, for a different perspective, see *The States and the Interstates: Research on the Planning, Design and Construction of the Interstate and Defense Highway System*, published by the American Association of State Highway and Transportation Officials. An eclectic volume, it includes a history of modern highway building prepared by the Public Works Historical Society, intended to show the lessons learned by state highway officials during the planning and construction of the interstate system; the edited transcript from a symposium on the topic; the results of a survey of 300 national leaders in the state highway community; and selected quotations from 100 oral histories of state highway officials.

These comprehensive studies are supplemented by the existence of other good, but chronologically limited, works. For instance, in 1964 the Bureau of Public Roads, by then part of the U.S. Department of Commerce, produced its own interim history under the title *Development of the Interstate Highway System*. Ann F. Friedlaender's *Interstate Highway System: A Study in Public Investment*, published a decade after the act that inaugurated the system, provides a fine economic analysis of its development.

Books on this topic with a more specific geographic focus include David A. Ripple's four-volume, 892-page *History of the Interstate Highway System in Indiana*, which gives a detailed policy description of the planning, development, and funding of that program in one state from the late 1930s until 1972; John L. Haley's *Wooing a Harsh Mistress: Glenwood Canyon's Highway Odyssey*, the story of the building of Interstate 70 through a portion of Colorado, with attention to the attendant challenges of design, engineering, and construction, of environmentalists, and of the interests of individuals and lobbying groups; and Ronald Briggs' "The Impact of the Interstate Highway System on Nonmetropolitan Development, 1950–1975," a chapter in Rutherford H. Platt and George Macinko's *Beyond the Urban Fringe*, which explores changes in land use in rural and semi-rural areas through which such highways were built.

A prime motivation for the construction of this 45,500-mile system was to provide easy movement of troops and matériel in the event of war. In fact, the interstates were also known as the National Defense Highway. This is an important subject that has not been given adequate attention by scholars. In fact, the Alaska [Alcan] Highway, a more limited World War II project with the same purpose, has been the object of greater study. A defense artery of 1,500 miles constructed to link the military bases in Alaska with the continental United States, it, along with related projects, was built through the Canadian Northwest from 1942 to 1946 by over 40,000 American soldiers and civilians. There are several excellent studies of this engineering accomplishment, including Heath Twichell's *Northwest Epic: The Building of the Alaska Highway*; David A. Remley's *Crooked Road: The Story of the Alaska Highway*, differentiated by its extensive use of oral interview transcripts; and Kenneth S. Coates and W.R. Morrison's *The Alaska Highway in World War II: The U.S. Army of Occupation in Canada's Northwest*, a scholarly work that focuses on the socioeconomic and environmental impact of the construction. Finally, historical perspective is provided by *The Alaska Highway: Papers of the 40th Anniversary Symposium*, edited by Coates, with contributions examining the economic, political, and military impact of that route; and the same author's *North to Alaska! Fifty Years on the World's Most Remarkable Highway*, a golden anniversary celebration not just of the building of the highway but also of its long-term survival, the vitality of communities that have developed along its length, and the people who traverse it.

Despite their importance and successes, by the late 1960s interstate highways and their proponents were beginning to come under attack. See, for example, Helen Leavitt's *Superhighway—Superhoax*, in which the author claims that the Interstate Highway System provides substantial profits for business interests (a new breed of "highwaymen") and benefits to politicians at all levels but that its proponents are effectively preventing the development of an efficient system of mass transit, thus leaving the public no choice but to purchase and use automobiles for transportation; Ben Kelley's *The Pavers and the Paved*, which is critical of the lack of public involvement in highway policy making; A.Q. Mowbray's *Road to Ruin: A Critical View of the Federal Highway Program*; and John Burby's *The Great American Motion Sickness: Or Why You Can't Get There from Here*, a critique of our transportation policy (or really lack thereof) and the lobbyists responsible for it. Burby's entertainingly written work is in the tradition of the turn-of-the-century muckrakers and, as such, was an attempt (essentially unsuccessful) to create public pressure for remedial legislation and creation of a comprehensive transportation plan.

Each of the above owes its genesis, so to speak, to a 1963 book by Lewis Mumford, entitled *The Highway and the City*, in which the author is highly critical of the federally funded highway programs of the 1950s and bemoans what he believes to be the advent of a "one-dimensional transportation system" dominated by a vehicle (the automobile) that controls our lives. Much the same theme is also present in the author's earlier (1961) *The City in History*, wherein the automobile is seen as annihilating the city and undermining urban redevelopment.

Highway Funding

Although we tend to think of highway funding as becoming a national issue only after World War II, a 1924 issue of *The Annals of the American Academy of Political and Social Science* devoted to "The Automobile: Its Province and Its Problems," edited by Clyde L. King, contained a section on "The Building and Financing of Motor Highways," including essays on the taxation of motor vehicles and the financing of highways. By 1927 McGraw-Hill was publishing a textbook entitled *Highway Administration and Finance*, written by Thomas R. Agg and John E. Brindley. The latter, incidentally, contains several historical chapters focusing on the title of the book. Also during this period excise taxes on gasoline first began to be used to support highway construction and maintenance. Oregon was the first state to adopt such a tax in 1919, and the federal government introduced the same in 1932.

Another approach to highway financing has been to borrow, usually through bonds, the amount necessary for construction and then to pay off those bonds by charging drivers a toll to use the road (or bridge). There is a good early 1950s study of this approach by the University of California's Bureau of Public Administration entitled *Highway Planning by the Toll System in Pennsylvania, Maine, Connecticut, New Jersey, and New York, 1794–1951, Especially since 1937*, which focuses on the history and administration of pay roads in those states. In the same vein is Joseph Durrenberger's *Turnpikes: A Study of the Toll Road Movement in the Middle Atlantic States and Maryland*. Finally, *Toll Roads and the Problem of Highway Modernization*, written for the Brookings Institution by Wilfred Owen and Charles L. Dearing, provides a balanced discussion of the advantages and disadvantages of using the proceeds from such taxation not just to retire turnpike debt but also for the construction, maintenance, and improvement of toll-free roads.

Motor turnpikes were America's first true superhighways and the precursors of (and often incorporated as part of) the interstate highway system of the latter half of the 20th century. The first of these was the Pennsylvania Turnpike, opened in 1940. Built during the depression at the then-staggering cost of $60 million, it was a pioneering four-lane, divided, limited-access highway with no traffic lights, stop signs, or grade crossings—at a time when 99.7% of the public roads were only one or two lanes. The turnpike celebrated its golden anniversary in 1990, at which time Dan Cupper was commissioned to write *The Pennsylvania Turnpike: A History* which, despite its brevity, is still the most comprehensive work available. Less successful is an earlier work by William H. Shank, entitled *Vanderbilt's Folly: A History of the Pennsylvania Turnpike*.

Readers interested in a broader analysis of the funding problem should read Philip H. Burch Jr.'s *Highway Revenue and Expenditure Policy in the United States*, a 1962 study of policies pursued on the federal, state, and local levels, emphasizing the post–World War II emergence of state highway planning surveys and the political challenges associated with the allocation of limited funds. Also worthy of examination are *America's Highways 1776–1976: A History of the Federal-Aid Program*, a well-illustrated bicentennial publication of the U.S. Department of Transportation combining both descriptive and technical information on the evolution of this form of assistance, together with capsule biographies of significant personages; the same agency's 1984 *America on the Move!: The Story of the Federal-Aid Highway Program*; the Congressional Budget Office's *Highway Assistance Programs: A Historical Perspective*, a brief (86-page) background paper prepared by Porter K. Wheeler; and the American Association of State Highway Officials' (AASHO) *The History and Accomplishments of Twenty-Five Years of Federal Aid for Highways: An Examination of Policies from State and National Viewpoints*, a brief (31-page) publication first issued in 1944 and updated in 1965 by Sherwood K. Booth under the title "The History of Federal-Aid Legislation for Highways," as a chapter in the AASHO's *The First Fifty Years, 1914–1964*.

The above studies of federal aid can be supplemented by Norman Hebden and Wilbur S. Smith's *State–City Relationships in Highway Affairs*, an analysis of the growth and forms of state (including federal pass-through) financial assistance to cities for the construction and maintenance of urban roads, as seen from the perspective of midcentury. In much the same vein is a report from the Department of Commerce, entitled *A Quarter Century of Financing Municipal Highways, 1937–61*. For a study of funding in one state during the first half of the 20th century, see *Highway Finance in New Mexico*, which spans the period 1913–1950 and was written by a University of New Mexico research team headed by Julian S. Duncan.

Finally, the magnitude of the challenge of funding highway construction and maintenance periodically leads to innovative proposals for changing the traditional ways that things are done. For example, see *Road Work: A New Highway Pricing and Investment Policy*, by Kenneth A. Small *et al.*, a 1989 Brookings Institution study that recommends the use of targeted use taxes to control demand combined with greater investment in the type of technology that enhances the durability of the road surface, thereby reducing the public cost of providing highways. Alternatively, in the belief that government ownership of highways produces financial waste and mediocre roads, conservative transportation economist Gabriel Roth makes a case for their "privatization" in *Roads in a Market Economy*. He argues that the commercial provision, pricing, and management of roads, including charging for their use, will yield a more cost-efficient and superior system of highways through private enterprise.

The Automobile and Mass Transit

One aspect of the highway funding issue that continues to generate lively debate is the degree to which the automobile hindered the development of urban mass transit in the United States. The underlying assumption is that the economic and social costs of accommodating the privately owned car are considerably greater than providing public transportation. The best introduction to the beginning and growth of the competition between mass transit and the automobile can be found in Mark S. Foster's *From Streetcar to Superhighway: American City Planners and Urban Transportation, 1900–1940*. Foster's thesis is that, contrary to the view of some, city planners and traffic engineers initially urged accommodation of the motor car out of a genuine belief that it would be good for the city. Also good in regard to the early competition between mass transit and the car is Delbert A. Taebel and James V. Cornehls' *The Political Economy of Urban Transportation*.

The situation some forty years later is described in *Autos, Transit, and Cities*, a Twentieth Century Fund Report written by John R. Meyer and José A. Gómez-Ibáñez, wherein the authors describe past government efforts to revitalize and improve urban mass transportation and review some of the futuristic proposals that have been made in that regard. But the heart of their effort is an exploration of urban socioeconomic problems, such as air pollution and traffic congestion, caused by the automobile and the role of public policy in ameliorating them. (For more on this topic, see the next chapter of this guide.) Published at the same time was James A. Dunn Jr.'s *Miles to Go: European and American Transportation Policies*, an excellent comparative historical study in which the author argues that Americans' greater reliance on the automobile results from the lack of a unified, national policy regarding transportation, such as exists in most European countries.

There are also a number of solid case studies of specific urban areas. In *The Automobile and Urban Transit: The Formation of Public Policy in Chicago,*

1900–1930, Paul Barrett has done a fine job of analyzing transportation policy debate in that city for the first third of this century. Barrett maintains that unchallenged community assumptions regarding public transportation undermined professional attempts at unified planning and retarded innovations in mass transit. Howard Preston's *Automobile Age Atlanta: The Making of a Southern Metropolis, 1900–1935* is an excellent study of the multiple ways in which the car affected the development of the premier city of the new South, with extensive coverage of how it contributed to the demise of the street railways. Scott L. Bottles' *The Making of the Modern City: Los Angeles and the Automobile, 1900–1950*, offers a "pro-auto" explanation of why the car replaced public transit as the chief means of personal transportation. Richard Hebert's *Highways to Nowhere: The Politics of City Transportation* focuses on the negative effect of federal transportation laws and decisions, with descriptions of the chaotic transport systems in Atlanta, Dayton, Flint (Michigan), Indianapolis, and Washington, D.C., in the early 1970s. Finally, Robert Caro's *The Power Broker: Robert Moses and the Fall of New York* analyzes urban expressway developments in that city and shows the incredible impact of the automobile on one urban area and, by implication, all other American cities.

One controversial dimension of the early history of competition between cars and public transportation was the purchase by large automotive manufacturers, especially General Motors, of controlling interest in several urban bus and trolley lines. A strong case has been made by some scholars that the automotive interests then allowed these mass transit systems to decline so as to increase the importance of highways and cars. In this vein, see Stephen B. Goddard's excellent *Getting There: The Epic Struggle between Road and Rail in the American Century*. Goddard argues that road interests (contemporary "highwaymen") actually conspired to destroy efficient urban trolley systems. Goddard also emphasizes that "freeways" are a misnomer given the enormous cost of their construction and maintenance. Arguing against the existence of a conspiracy is the Bottles book cited above, wherein the author maintains that the preeminence of the automobile, vis-à-vis public transportation, was more the result of 20th-century urban developments and public desire than any "conspiracy" on the part of the auto companies to destroy mass transit. Taking more of a middle road is David J. St. Clair in his *The Motorization of American Cities*, a small volume that focuses on the auto industry's attempts to create an economic and political environment in which personal transportation would triumph over mass transit. In place of conspiracy, St. Clair sees a coherent and effective industrial strategy that was able to manipulate all levels of government to its advantage, especially in terms of building the infrastructure of an urban highway system.

For more general views of the subject of public versus private transportation in urban areas, see Wilfred Owen's insightful, mid-1960s *The Metropolitan Transportation Problem* and his later (1972) *The Accessible City*, both of which favor more reliance on metropolitan *systems* of public transit and less on automotive use in such areas, in a planned attempt to make cities more livable.

Another mid-1960s work is *Urban Transportation and Public Policy*, edited by Lyle C. Fitch, the chapters of which support the view that mass transit improvements would lead to significant increases in ridership and less use of the automobile. On the other hand, a work from the same period, *The Urban Transportation Problem*, by John R. Meyer *et al.*, examines the various alternative modes and concludes that a bus–automobile combination is preferable to a rail mass-transit approach for cities of that time and the future. Acknowledging some of the environmental problems associated with motor vehicles, the authors urge development of battery-powered, subcompact cars for urban areas.

More specific in focus are *The Technology of Urban Transportation*, by Donald S. Berry *et al.*, which provides an early 1960s cost-effectiveness study of the automobile and mass transit, and Theodore E. Keeler and Kenneth A. Small's *Automobile Costs and Final Intermodal Cost Comparisons*, a similar work published in 1975 by the Institute of Urban and Regional Development at the University of California, Berkeley.

During the last quarter of the 20th century, there was increasing recognition of the complexity of choosing among the various types of transportation for cities. Thus, Alan Altshuler *et al.* offer a more theoretical attempt to develop a framework for the appraisal of policy options in *The Urban Transportation System: Politics and Policy Innovation* (1979), which, as its Foreword indicates, "deals with the broad range of factors—economic, technological, political, and cultural—that must be considered in the analysis and evaluation of urban transportation systems and that ultimately dictate urban form." By 1992 Charles L. Wright was expressing the views of many in his *Fast Wheels, Slow Traffic: Urban Transport Choices* when he advocated combining the characteristics of different modes to create simple, low-cost, environmentally sound solutions that could be adapted to fulfill the needs of a variety of city types. (For the record, he prefers buses over automobiles and rail transit.)

Finally, when one thinks of competition between the private automobile and public transportation, the latter is usually thought of in terms of buses, streetcars, and commuter trains. However, it should not be forgotten that a variation of the private automobile is often classified as a form of public transportation, at least in urban areas, and that is the licensed taxicab. The best work in this regard is *The Taxicab: An Urban Transportation Survivor*, by Gorman Gilbert and Robert E. Samuels, a scholarly, sociological study of the industry. The authors explain its development to the early 1980s and show how it has adapted to changes in the urban environment over time. More importantly, they argue that it should be part of the urban transportation planning process since mass transit and it have the potential to help each other.

Gilbert and Samuels can be supplemented by several fine essays and chapters, such as: "Dial-a-Ride, Pooling, Taxis, and Futuristic Public Transportation," a chapter in John R. Meyer and José A. Gómez-Ibáñez' previously cited *Autos, Transit and Cities*; R.C. Cherry's "Computers, Taxis, and Grass Roots Transportation" and M. White's "Model Cities Jitney Transportation in Buffalo," two papers from the third *Conference on Demand-Responsive Transportation Systems*; and Martin Wohl's "Increasing the Taxi's Role in Urban America," an essay in *Urban Transportation*, edited by Herbert S. Levinson and Robert A. Weant. There also is at least one interesting popular study: D.L. Scrimger's brief (44-page) *Taxicab Scrapbook: A Pictorial Review of the Taxi* since 1922. Finally, Richard Hazard's *Hacking New York* is a fascinating period memoir of a New York City cab driver, published in 1930.

State Roads

The existence of organizations like the AASHO reflects the fact that highway construction and maintenance historically have been considered to be within the province of local government and, despite the development of the Interstate Highway System, continue to be largely the concern of the states. Founded in 1914, AASHO began publishing its monthly *American Highways* in 1921 and in 1965 issued *The First Fifty Years, 1914–1964*, a history of that organization and federal-aid highway legislation, with the addition of a historical chapter on early highway construction.

Given this local emphasis, it is not surprising that a number of good books, albeit dated, treat the history of highway development in a specific state. Although the investigator needs to always keep in mind that one state's experience may not be the same as another's, such histories do, at least, serve as case studies and provide possible starting points for additional research.

Representative of this genre of scholarship are the following works, listed alphabetically by state: Claus M. Naske's *Paving Alaska's Trails: The Work of the Alaska Road Commission*, a volume in the Alaska Historical Commission Studies in History series; Kenneth C. Adams' *From Trails to Freeways*, published by the California State Division of Highways; Ben Blow's *California Highways: A Descriptive Record of Road Development by the State and by Such Counties as Have Paved Highways*; Bayard H. Kendrick's *Florida Trails to Turnpikes, 1914–1964*, a history of its State Road Department and road construction in general, of a quality high enough to be listed in the *Harvard Guide to American History*; Sherry Lamb Schirmer and Thomas A. Wilson's *Milestones: A History of the Kansas Highway Commission and the Department of Transportation*; T. Harry Williams' biographical *Huey Long*, includes a good description of the program of highway development introduced by that legendary governor of Louisiana, as does Long's own *Every Man a King*; the Maine State Highway Commission's brief *A History of Maine Roads, 1600–1970*, a volume that surveys 370 years in thirty-nine pages!; and *The Development of the Minnesota Road System*, a well-done book by Arthur J. Larsen based on sound scholarship.

See also Capus Waynick's *North Carolina Roads and Their Builders*, which covers the years 1584 to 1952 and is strongest in terms of the biographical information that it provides on the people involved; Cecil K. Brown's *The State*

Highway System of North Carolina: Its Evolution and Present Status, a scholarly work that describes the development of that system through the 1920s; Robert L. Carlson and Larry J. Sprunk's *History of the North Dakota State Highway Department*; William H. Shank's *Indian Trails to Super Highways*, a brief (72-page) 300-year history of the evolution of intercity roads in Pennsylvania; John Hammond Moore's *The South Carolina Highway Department, 1917–1987*, which is best when describing the politics behind the formulation of state highway policies; and Ezra C. Knowlton's *History of Highway Development in Utah*.

BIBLIOGRAPHY

Ackerson, Robert C. *Jeep: 50 Year History*. Newbury Park, Calif.: Haynes, 1988.

Adams, Kenneth C. *From Trails to Freeways*. Sacramento: State of California Division of Highways, Department of Public Works, 1950.

Agg, Thomas R., and John E. Brindley. *Highway Administration and Finance*. New York: McGraw-Hill, 1927.

Altshuler, Alan *et al. The Urban Transportation System: Politics and Policy Innovation*. Cambridge, Mass.: MIT Press, 1979.

Amberg, Stephen. *The Union Inspiration in American Politics: The Autoworkers and the Making of a Liberal Industrial Order*. Philadelphia: Temple University Press, 1994.

American Association for Highway Improvement. *The Official Good Roads Yearbook of the United States for 1912*. Washington, D.C.: Waverly Press, 1912.

American Association of State Highway Officials. *The First Fifty Years, 1914–1964*. Washington, D.C.: American Association of State Highway Officials, 1965.

American Association of State Highway Officials. *The History and Accomplishments of Twenty-Five Years of Federal Aid for Highways: An Examination of Policies from State and National Viewpoints*. Washington, D.C.: American Association of State Highway Officials, 1944.

American Association of State Highway and Transportation Officials. *The States and the Interstates: Research on the Planning, Design and Construction of the Interstate and Defense Highway System*. Washington, D.C.: AASHTO, 1991.

Amstrong, Ellis L., ed. *History of Public Works in the United States, 1776–1976*. Chicago: American Public Works Association, 1976.

Automobile Manufacturers Association. *Freedom's Arsenal: The Story of the Automotive Council for War Production*. Detroit: Automobile Manufacturers Association, 1950.

Barrett, Paul. *The Automobile and Urban Transit: The Formation of Public Policy in Chicago, 1900–1930*. Philadelphia: Temple University Press, 1983.

Bel Geddes, Norman. *Magic Motorways*. New York: Random House, 1940.

Berry, Donald S. *et al. The Technology of Urban Transportation*. Evanston, Ill.: Northwestern University, Transportation Center, 1963.

Blow, Ben. *California Highways: A Descriptive Record of Road Development by the State and by Such Counties as Have Paved Highways*. San Francisco: Author, 1920.

Borge, Jacques, and Nicolas Viasnoff. *Les Voitures des Grands.* Paris: Balland, 1977.

Borth, Christy. *Mankind on the Move: The Story of Highways.* Washington, D.C.: Automotive Safety Foundation, 1969.

Bottles, Scott L. *The Making of the Modern City: Los Angeles and the Automobile, 1900–1950.* Berkeley: University of California Press, 1984.

Boyle, Kevin. *The UAW and the Heyday of American Liberalism, 1945–1968.* Ithaca, N.Y.: Cornell University Press, 1995.

Boyle, Kevin, ed. *Organized Labor and American Politics, 1894–1994: The Labor-Liberal Alliance.* Albany: State University of New York Press, 1998.

Brouws, Jeffrey T. (photographer), Bernd Polster, and Phil Patton. *Highway: America's Endless Dream.* New York: Stewart, Tabori, & Chang, 1997.

Brown, Arch, and the Auto Editors of *Consumer Guide. Jeep: The Unstoppable Legend.* Lincolnwood, Ill.: Publications International, 1994.

Brown, Cecil K. *The State Highway System of North Carolina: Its Evolution and Present Status.* Chapel Hill: University of North Carolina Press, 1931.

Brownell, Blaine A. *The Urban Ethos in the South, 1920–1930.* Baton Rouge: Louisiana State University Press, 1975.

Buffa, Dudley W. *Union Power and American Democracy: The UAW and the Democratic Party, 1935–72.* Ann Arbor: University of Michigan Press, 1984.

Buffa, Dudley W. *Union Power and American Democracy: The UAW and the Democratic Party, 1972–83.* Ann Arbor: University of Michigan Press, 1984.

Burby, John. *The Great American Motion Sickness, or Why You Can't Get There from Here.* Boston: Little Brown, 1971.

Burch, Philip H., Jr. *Highway Revenue and Expenditure Policy in the United States.* New Brunswick, N.J.: Rutgers University Press, 1962.

Burns, James H. *Mail on the Move.* Polo, Ill.: Transportation Trails, 1992.

Cadillac Motor Car Co. *Participation in the World War.* Detroit: Cadillac Motor Car Co., 1919.

Cameron, Bruce W. *Police Cars: A Graphic History.* Lincolnwood, Ill.: Publications International, 1997.

Carlson, Robert L., and Larry J. Sprunk. *History of the North Dakota State Highway Department.* Bismarck: North Dakota State Highway Department, 1979.

Caro, Robert. *The Power Broker: Robert Moses and the Fall of New York.* New York: Alfred Knopf, 1974.

Chatburn, George R. *Highways and Highway Transportation.* New York: Crowell, 1923.

Cheape, Charles. *Moving the Masses: Urban Public Transit in New York, Boston, and Philadelphia, 1880–1912.* Cambridge, Mass.: Harvard University Press, 1980.

Clayton, Michael. *Jeep.* North Pomfret, Vt.: David & Charles, 1982.

Coates, Ken. *North to Alaska!: Fifty Years on the World's Most Remarkable Highway.* Toronto: McClelland & Stewart, 1992.

Coates, Kenneth S., ed. *The Alaska Highway: Papers of the 40th Anniversary Symposium.* Vancouver: University of British Columbia Press, 1985.

Coates, Kenneth S., and W.R. Morrison. *The Alaska Highway in World War II: The U.S. Army of Occupation in Canada's Northwest.* Toronto: University of Toronto Press, 1992.

Collins, Herbert R. *Presidents on Wheels.* Washington, D.C.: Acropolis, 1971.

Conference on Demand-Responsive Transportation Systems. *Demand-Responsive Trans-*

portation Systems. Washington, D.C.: Highway Research Board, National Research Council, 1973.

Cowdery, Ray R., and Merrill W. Madsen. *All-American Wonder: The Military Jeep, 1941–1945*. 2 vols. Lakeville, Minn.: Northstar Commemoratives, 1986, 1990.

Crismon, Fred W. *Modern U.S. Military Wheeled Vehicles*. Osceola, Wisc.: MBI, 1998.

Cupper, Dan. *The Pennsylvania Turnpike: A History*. Lebanon Valley, Pa.: Applied Arts, 1990.

Daniels, George H., and Mark H. Rose, eds. *Energy and Transport: Historical Perspective on Policy Issues*. Beverly Hills, Calif.: Sage, 1982.

Dearing, Charles L. *American Highway Policy*. Washington, D.C.: Brookings Institution, 1941.

Duncan, Julian S., Harold Staus, and Katharine Nutt. *Highway Finance in New Mexico*. Albuquerque: University of New Mexico, Division of Research, Department of Government, 1952.

Dunn, James A., Jr. *Miles to Go: European and American Transportation Policies*. Cambridge, Mass.: MIT Press, 1981.

Durrenberger, Joseph. *Turnpikes: A Study of the Toll Road Movement in the Middle Atlantic States and Maryland*. Cos Cobb, Conn.: John E. Edwards, 1968.

Eno, William P. *The Science of Highway Traffic Regulation, 1899–1920*. Washington, D.C.: Brentano's, 1920.

Fine, Sidney. *The Automobile Under the Blue Eagle: Labor, Management, and the Automobile Manufacturing Code*. Ann Arbor: University of Michigan Press, 1963.

Fitch, Lyle C., ed. *Urban Transportation and Public Policy*. San Francisco: Chandler, 1964.

Fletcher, David. *Staff Cars*. Princes Risborough, Eng.: Shire Publications, 1990.

Flink, James J. *America Adopts the Automobile, 1895–1910*. Cambridge, Mass.: MIT Press, 1970.

Flink, James J. *The Car Culture*. Cambridge, Mass.: MIT Press, 1975.

Foster, Mark S. *From Streetcar to Superhighway: American City Planners and Urban Transportation, 1900–1940*. Philadelphia: Temple University Press, 1981.

Foster, Patrick R. *The Story of Jeep*. Iola, Wisc.: Krause Publications, 1998.

Fowler, William. *Jeep Goes to War: A Pictorial Chronicle*. Philadelphia: Courage Books, 1993.

Friedlaender, Ann F. *Interstate Highway System: A Study in Public Investment*. New York: Humanities Press, 1966.

Frisch, Michael H., and Daniel J. Walkowitz, eds. *Working Class America: Essays on Labor, Community, and American Society*. Urbana: University of Illinois Press, 1983.

Gabbard, Alex. *Return to Thunder Road: The Story behind the Legend*. Lenoir City, Tenn.: Gabbard Publications, 1992.

Genat, Robert. *Modern Police Cars*. Osceola, Wisc.: Motorbooks International, 1994.

Gilbert, Gorman, and Robert E. Samuels. *The Taxicab: An Urban Transportation Survivor*. Chapel Hill: University of North Carolina Press, 1982.

Ginsburg, Douglas H., and William J. Abernathy, eds. *Government, Technology, and the Future of the Automobile*. New York: McGraw-Hill, 1980.

Glaberman, Martin. *Wartime Strikes: The Struggle against the No-Strike Pledge in the UAW during World War II.* Detroit: Bewick Editions, 1980.

Goddard, Stephen B. *Getting There: The Epic Struggle between Road and Rail in the American Century.* Chicago: University of Chicago Press, 1994.

Green, Michael. *Hummer: The Next Generation.* Osceola, Wisc.: Motorbooks International, 1995.

Haley, John L. *Wooing a Harsh Mistress: Glenwood Canyon's Highway Odyssey.* Greeley, Colo.: Canyon Communications, 1994.

Haller, John S., Jr. *Farmcarts to Fords: A History of the Military Ambulance, 1790–1925,* Carbondale: Southern Illinois University Press, 1992.

Halpern, Martin. *UAW Politics in the Cold War Era.* Albany: State University of New York Press, 1988.

Hansen, Arlen J. *Gentlemen Volunteers: The Story of the American Ambulance Drivers in the Great War, August 1914–September 1918.* New York: Arcade, 1996.

Hart, Virginia. *The Story of American Roads.* New York: Sloane, 1950.

Hazard, Richard. *Hacking New York.* New York: C. Scribner's Son, 1930.

Hebden, Norman, and Wilbur S. Smith. *State–City Relationships in Highway Affairs.* New Haven, Conn: Yale University Press, 1950.

Hebert, Richard. *Highways to Nowhere: The Politics of City Transportation.* Indianapolis: Bobbs-Merrill, 1972.

Hendry, Maurice. *Lincoln: America's Car of State.* New York: Ballantine Books, 1971.

Hokanson, Drake. *The Lincoln Highway: Main Street across America.* Iowa City: University of Iowa Press, 1988.

Holt, W. Stull. *The Bureau of Public Roads: Its History, Activities and Organization.* Baltimore: Johns Hopkins University Press, 1923.

Hood, Roger, ed. *Crime, Criminality and Public Policy.* New York: Free Press, 1975.

Hulbert, Archer B., ed. *Historic Highways of America.* 16 vols. Cleveland: Arthur H. Clark, 1902–1905.

Keeler, Theodore E., and Kenneth A. Small. *Automobile Costs and Final Intermodal Cost Comparisons.* Berkeley: Institute of Urban and Regional Development, University of California, 1975.

Kelley, Ben. *The Pavers and the Paved.* New York: Donald W. Brown, 1971.

Kendrick, Bayard H. *Florida Trails to Turnpikes, 1914–1964.* Gainesville: University of Florida Press, 1964.

King, Clyde L., ed. "The Automobile: Its Province and Its Problems. *The Annals of the American Academy of Political and Social Science* 116 (November 1924).

Knowlton, Ezra C. *History of Highway Development in Utah.* Salt Lake City: Utah State Department of Highways, 1964.

Kornhauser, Arthur. *When Labor Votes: A Study of Auto Workers.* New York: University Books, 1956.

Labatut, Jean, and Wheaton J. Lane, eds. *Highways in Our National Life: A Symposium.* Princeton, N.J.: Princeton University Press, 1950.

Langum, David J. *Crossing over the Line: Legislating Morality and the Mann Act.* Chicago: University of Chicago Press, 1994.

Larsen, Arthur J. *The Development of the Minnesota Road System.* St. Paul: Minnesota Historical Society, 1996.

Leavitt, Helen. *Superhighway—Superhoax.* New York: Doubleday, 1970.

Levinson, Herbert S., and Robert A. Weant, eds. *Urban Transportation: Perspectives and Prospects.* Westport, Conn.: Eno Foundation for Transportation, 1982.

Lewis, Tom. *Divided Highways: Building the Interstate Highways, Transforming American Life.* 2nd ed. New York: Viking, 1999.

Lincoln Highway Association. *The Lincoln Highway: The Story of a Crusade That Made Transportation History.* New York: Dodd, Mead, 1935.

Lingeman, Richard R. *Don't You Know There's a War On?: The American Home Front, 1941–1945.* New York: G.P. Putnam's Sons, 1970.

Long, Huey P. *Every Man a King.* New Orleans: National Book, 1933.

Lorence, James J. *Organizing the Unemployed: Community and Union Activists in the Industrial Heartland.* Albany: State University of New York Press, 1996.

Maine State Highway Commission. *A History of Maine Roads, 1600–1970.* Augusta, Me.: State Highway Commission, 1970.

Mason, Philip P. *A History of American Roads.* Chicago: Rand-McNally, 1967.

Mason, Philip P. *The League of American Wheelmen and the Good Roads Movement, 1880–1905.* Ann Arbor: University of Michigan Press, 1957.

McCord, Monty. *Cars of the State Police and Highway Patrol.* Iola, Wisc.: Krause Publications, 1994.

MacDonald, Austin F., ed. "Planning for City Traffic." *The Annals of the American Academy of Political and Social Science,* 133 (September 1927).

Meyer, John R., and José A. Gomez-Ibáñez. *Autos, Transit, and Cities.* Cambridge, Mass.: Harvard University Press, 1981.

Meyer, John R., J.F. Kain, and M. Wohl. *The Urban Transportation Problem.* Cambridge, Mass.: Harvard University Press, 1966.

Moore, John Hammond. *The South Carolina Highway Department, 1917–1987.* Columbia: University of South Carolina Press, 1987.

Moore, William H. *History and Purposes of the Good Roads Movement: Proceedings of the National Good Roads Convention, St. Louis, Mo., 1903,* Bulletin No. 25. Washington, D.C.: U.S. Department of Agriculture, Office of Public Road Inquiries, 1903.

Mowbray, A.Q. *Road to Ruin: A Critical View of the Federal Highway Program.* Philadelphia: Lippincott, 1968.

Mumford, Lewis. *The City in History.* New York: Harcourt, Brace & World, 1961.

Mumford, Lewis. *The Highway and the City.* New York: Harcourt, Brace & World, 1963.

Naske, Claus M. *Paving Alaska's Trails: The Work of the Alaska Road Commission.* Lanham, Md.: University Press of America, 1986.

National Academy of Sciences, Highway Research Board. *Ideas and Actions: A History of the Highway Research Board, 1920–1970.* Washington, D.C.: Highway Research Board, 1970.

National Highways Association. *National Highways and Good Roads.* Washington, D.C.: National Highways Association, 1913.

National Industrial Conference Board. *Taxation of Motor Vehicle Transportation.* New York: National Industrial Conference Board, 1932.

Nelson, Derek. *Moonshiners, Bootleggers & Rumrunners.* Osceola, Wisc.: Motorbooks International, 1995.

Nelson, Richard R., ed. *Government and Technical Progress: A Cross-Industry Analysis.* New York: Pergamon Press, 1982.

Owen, Wilfred. *The Accessible City.* Washington, D.C.: Brookings Institution, 1972.

Owen, Wilfred. *Automobile Transportation in Defense or War: A Report Prepared for the Defense Transport Administration.* Washington, D.C.: Government Printing Office, 1951.

Owen, Wilfred. *The Metropolitan Transportation Problem.* Rev. ed. Washington, D.C.: Brookings Institution, 1966.

Owen, Wilfred. *Transportation for Cities: The Role of Federal Policy.* Washington, D.C.: Brookings Institution, 1976.

Owen, Wilfred, and Charles L. Dearing. *Toll Roads and the Problem of Highway Modernization.* Washington, D.C.: Brookings Institution, 1951.

Papademetriou, Peter C. *Transportation and Urban Development in Houston, 1830–1980.* Houston: Metropolitan Transit Authority of Harris County, 1982.

Patton, Phil. *Open Road: A Celebration of the American Highway.* New York: Simon & Schuster, 1986.

Pettifer, Julian, and Nigel Turner. *Automania: Man and the Motor Car.* Boston: Little, Brown, 1984.

Platt, Rutherford H., and George Macinko, eds. *Beyond the Urban Fringe: Land Use Issues of Non-Metropolitan America.* Minneapolis: University of Minnesota Press, 1983.

Preston, Howard L. *Automobile Age Atlanta: The Making of a Southern Metropolis, 1900–1935.* Athens: University of Georgia Press, 1979.

Preston, Howard L. *Dirt Roads to Dixie: Accessibility and Modernization in the South, 1885–1935.* Knoxville: University of Tennessee Press, 1991.

Quinn, Dennis Patrick. *Restructuring the Automobile Industry: A Study of Firms and States in Modern Capitalism.* New York: Columbia University Press, 1988.

Rae, John B. *The Road and the Car in American Life.* Cambridge Mass.: MIT Press, 1971.

Raitz, Karl, ed. *The National Road.* Baltimore: Johns Hopkins University Press, 1996.

Rasmussen, Henry. *Jeep: Mechanical Mule to People's Plaything.* Osceola, Wisc.: Motorbooks International, 1987.

Remley, David A. *Crooked Road: The Story of the Alaska Highway.* New York: McGraw-Hill, 1976.

Reuther, Walter P. *500 Planes a Day: A Program for the Utilization of the Automobile Industry for Mass Production of Defense Planes.* Washington, D.C.: American Council on Public Affairs, 1940.

Rifkind, Herbert R. *The Jeep: Its Development and Procurement under the Quartermaster Corps, 1940–1942.* Washington, D.C.: U.S. Army Quartermaster Corps, General Administrative Service, 1943.

Ripple, David A. *History of the Interstate Highway System in Indiana.* 4 vols. West Lafayette, Ind.: Purdue University and Indiana State Highway Commission, 1975–1976.

Rishel, Virginia. *Wheels to Adventure: Bill Rishel's Western Routes.* Salt Lake City: Howe Brothers, 1984.

Rose, Albert C. *Historic American Roads: From Frontier Trails to Superhighways.* New York: Crown, 1976.

Rose, Albert C. *Public Roads of the Past.* 2 vols. Washington, D.C.: American Association of State Highway Officials, 1952–1953.

Rose, Mark H. *Interstate: Expressway Highway Politics, 1939–1989.* Knoxville: University of Tennessee Press, 1990.

Roth, Gabriel. *Roads in a Market Economy.* Brookfield, Vt.: Avebury Technical, 1996.

Sanow, Edwin J. *Chevrolet Police Cars.* Iola, Wisc.: Krause Publications, 1997.

Sanow, Edwin J. *Dodge, Plymouth & Chrysler Police Cars, 1979–1994.* Osceola, Wisc.: Motorbooks International, 1996.

Sanow, Edwin J. *Encyclopedia of American Police Cars.* Osceola, Wisc.: Motorbooks International, 1999.

Sanow, Edwin J. *Ford Police Cars, 1932–1997.* Osceola, Wisc.: Motorbooks International, 1997.

Sanow, Edwin J. *Vintage Police Cars.* Osceola, Wisc.: Motorbooks International, 1996.

Sanow, Edwin J., and John L. Bellah. *Dodge, Plymouth & Chrysler Police Cars, 1956–1978.* Osceola, Wisc.: Motorbooks International, 1994.

Scharff, Virginia. *Taking the Wheel: Women and the Coming of the Motor Age.* New York: Free Press, 1991.

Schirmer, Sherry Lamb, and Theodore A. Wilson. *Milestones: A History of the Kansas Highway Commission and the Department of Transportation.* Topeka: Department of Transportation, 1986.

Scott, Graham. *Essential Military Jeep: Ford, Willys and Bantam Models, 1942–45.* Bideford, Devon, Eng.: Bay View Books, 1996.

Scrimger, D.L. *Taxicab Scrapbook: A Pictorial Review of the Taxi.* Charles City, Iowa.: Author, 1979.

Seely, Bruce E. *Building the American Highway System: Engineers as Policy Makers.* Philadelphia: Temple University Press, 1987.

Shaler, Nathaniel. S. *American Highways: A Popular Account of Their Conditions, and of the Means by Which They May Be Bettered.* New York: Century, 1886.

Shank, William H. *Indian Trails to Super Highways.* Rev. ed. York, Pa.: American Canal and Transportation Center, 1988.

Shank, William H. *Vanderbilt's Folly: A History of the Pennsylvania Turnpike.* York, Pa.: American Canal and Transportation Center, 1973.

Siuru, William D., Jr., and Andrea Stewart. *Presidential Cars & Transportation: From Horse and Carriage to Air Force One, the Story of How the Presidents of the United States Travel.* Iola, Wisc.: Krause Publications, 1995.

Small, Kenneth A., Clifford Winston, and Carol A. Evans. *Road Work: A New Highway Pricing and Investment Policy.* Washington, D.C.: Brookings Institution, 1989.

Smith, Merritt Roe, ed. *Military Enterprise and Technological Change: Perspectives on the American Experience.* Cambridge: MIT Press, 1985.

Spradley, James P., and David W. McCurdy, eds. *The Cultural Experience.* Chicago: Science Research Associates, 1972.

St. Clair, David J. *The Motorization of American Cities.* New York: Praeger, 1986.

Stevenson, William Y. *At the Front in a Flivver.* Boston: Houghton Mifflin, 1917.

Taebel, Delbert A., and James V. Cornehls. *The Political Economy of Urban Transportation.* Port Washington, N.Y.: Kennikat Press, 1977.

Twichell, Heath. *Northwest Epic: The Building of the Alaska Highway.* New York: St. Martin's Press, 1992.

U.S. Congressional Budget Office. *Highway Assistance Programs: A Historical Perspective.* Washington, D.C.: Congressional Budget Office, Congress of the United States, 1978.

U.S. Department of Commerce. *A Quarter Century of Financing Municipal Highways, 1937–61.* Washington, D.C.: Government Printing Office, 1961.

U.S. Department of Commerce, Bureau of Public Roads. *Development of the Interstate Highway System*. Washington, D.C.: U.S. Department of Commerce, Bureau of Public Roads, 1964.

U.S. Department of Transportation. *Effects of Federal Regulation on the Financial Structure and Performance of the Domestic Motor Vehicle Manufacturers*. Cambridge, Mass.: Transportation Systems Center, 1978.

U.S. Department of Transportation, Federal Highway Administration. *America on the Move!: The Story of the Federal-Aid Highway Program*. Washington, D.C.: Government Printing Office, 1984.

U.S. Department of Transportation, Federal Highway Administration. *America's Highways 1776–1976: A History of the Federal-Aid Program*. Washington, D.C.: Government Printing Office, 1977.

U.S. Department of Transportation, Federal Highway Administration. *Social and Economic Effects of Highways*. Washington, D.C.: Government Printing Office, 1976.

U.S. Public Works Administration. *America Builds!: The Record of PWA*. Washington, D.C.: Government Printing Office, 1939.

University of California, Bureau of Public Administration. *Highway Planning by the Toll System in Pennsylvania, Maine, Connecticut, New Jersey, and New York, 1794–1951, Especially since 1937*. Berkeley: University of California, Bureau of Public Administration, 1951.

Vanderveen, Bart. *The Jeep*. Osceola, Wisc.: Motorbooks International, 1981.

Wainright, H.C. & Co. *The Impact of Government Regulations on Competition in the U.S. Automobile Industry*. Boston: H.C. Wainright, 1979.

"Wartime Strikes in the Automobile Industry." *Radical America* 9 (1975): 77–114.

Waynick, Capus. *North Carolina Roads and Their Builders*. Raleigh, N.C.: Superior Stone, 1952.

Wells, Wade R. *Hail to the Jeep: A Factual and Pictorial History of the Jeep*. New York: Harper & Brothers, 1946.

White Motor Company. *The White Record of Service in the World War*. Cleveland: Author, 1919.

Williams, T. Harry. *Huey Long*. New York: Knopf, 1964.

Willinger, Kurt, and Gene Gurney. *The American Jeep: In War and Peace*. New York: Crown, 1983.

Winston, Clifford *et al*. *Blind Intersection: Policy and the Automobile Industry*. Washington, D.C.: Brookings Institution, 1987.

Wixom, Charles W. *ARBA Pictorial History of Roadbuilding*. Washington, D.C.: American Road Builders' Association, 1975.

Wood, Donald F., and W. Wayne Sorensen. *Fire Chief Cars: 1900–1997 Photo Album*. Hudson, Wisc.: Iconografix, 1998.

Wright, Charles L. *Fast Wheels, Slow Traffic: Urban Transportation Choices*. Philadelphia: Temple University Press, 1992.

Wrynn, V. Dennis. *Detroit Goes to War: The American Automobile Industry in World War II*. Osceola, Wisc.: Motorbooks International, 1993.

Wyman, Arthur C., ed. *Automobile Laws of the New England States, New York, New Jersey, and Pennsylvania*. Providence, R.I.: E.L. Freeman, 1908.

CHAPTER 11

Contemporary Socioeconomic Problems

Despite the automobile's mass appeal throughout the 20th century, its presence continues to pose unresolved problems for the American public. Chief among these are questions of safety, pollution, and traffic control. This chapter sequentially treats each of these problems and then touches on writings that explore future scenarios that might offer the necessary remedies. Before we begin that discussion, and lest the reader be left with the impression that these are new issues, mention should be made of Wilfred Owen's *Automotive Transportation: Trends and Problems*, a study published in 1949 by the Brookings Institution. In it, Owen discusses such contemporary-sounding concerns as our dependence on motor vehicles, highway design and safety, the need for technological improvements in automobiles, and the potential of traffic engineering for resolving auto-related problems.

SAFETY

Given the fact that more Americans have died on our nation's highways than in all of our wars combined and that deaths by automobiles (40,000–55,000 per year in the last quarter of the 20th century) exceed those attributable to any one disease, it should come as no surprise that at least one scholar claims that the traffic accident has long been a pervasive part of our national character.

As a result, one would think that automotive safety would be one of the chief concerns of the American government and people. Significantly, this was rarely the case in the past, and only recently has it received the type of attention that might be expected. The best "historic" survey on the subject is "Highway Safety and Traffic Control," edited by John W. Gibbons, a late 1950s volume in *The Annals of the American Academy of Political and Social Science* series. The authors therein cover the full range of topics that define automotive safety, including car design, traffic, highways, driver licensing, education, law (including police, prosecutors, and judges), public interest groups, and what is termed "Factor X"—human behavior. Interesting comparisons can be made between this work and an earlier 1924 volume of *The Annals*, entitled "The Automobile: Its Province and Its Problems," edited by Clyde L. King, which contains a section on "Safety on the Highway through Traffic Regulation," featuring such essays as "The Storage of Dead Vehicles on the Roadways," "Traffic Violations and the Court," and "Protective Measures for the Automobile and Its Owner."

In a similar vein but taking an international perspective is James Foreman-Peck's "Death on the Roads: Changing National Responses to Motor Accidents," a chapter in *The Economic and Social Effects of the Spread of Motor Vehicles*, edited by Theo Barker. Foreman-Peck examines the effectiveness of the legislative, administrative, and educational policies adopted to control motor accidents in the Western industrial countries during the period between World Wars I and II. During those years, according to the author, the ratio of highway deaths first garnered national attention in Britain and the United States, exceeding what he considers to be "the level of tolerance," a situation that would occur again in the 1970s in the States. For reactions to this phenomenon in other parts of the world, see a chapter entitled "The Car and Death" in Julian Pettifer and Nigel Turner's *Automania*, a book written to accompany a British television series of the same name.

Representative of post–World War II American thinking regarding cars and safety was a 1971 book by Robert F. Baker, entitled *The Highway Risk Problem: Policy Issues in Highway Safety*, in which the author argues that proposed traffic safety measures need to be balanced against the reduction in mobility that they may cause and should be made to compete with other lifesaving programs for the limited federal dollar. More recent attitudes are reflected in Paul W. Gikas' "Crashworthiness as a Cultural Ideal," a chapter in David L. Lewis and Laurence Goldstein's *The Automobile and American Culture*, where Gikas explores the increased interest in automotive safety that manifested itself in the last three decades of the 20th century. He also analyzes how Americans came to incorporate safety concerns into their list of factors that they consider when buying a car.

Safety and Car Design

There are multiple dimensions to the issue of cars and safety. The one that has captured the interest of the general public the most is that of the design and construction of the vehicle itself. Possibly the first two books devoted exclusively to the design/safety issue were Victor W. Killick's *Can We Build Automobiles to Keep Drivers Out of Trouble?* (1940) and Arthur W. Stevens' *Highway Safety and Automobile Styling*, published in 1941.

The best historical survey in this regard is Joel W. Eastman's *Styling vs.*

Safety: The American Automobile Industry and the Development of Automotive Safety, 1900–1966. Eastman maintains that competition within the industry, when combined with the lack of government regulation and consumer demand for increasingly complex vehicles, led to the production of automobiles with inherent safety problems for which the manufacturers took little responsibility. Among the specific topics that he considers are the safety deficiencies created by the introduction of the annual model change, the impact on automotive safety of the "horsepower race," the reaction of the automobile industry to the problem of traffic accidents and to the highway safety movement, and finally the origins of automobile design for crash protection. Also interesting from a historical perspective is *Passenger Car Design and Highway Safety*, the proceedings of an early 1960s Conference on Vehicle Design and Safety Research sponsored by the unlikely combination of the Association for the Aid of Crippled Children and Consumers Union. The purpose of the conference was to explore the then-current state of knowledge in the field, to discover whether there was discrepancy between what was known and what was applied in practice, and to identify areas in need of additional research. After an introduction to the general problem by the participants, most of the papers focus on the relationships between vehicle design and accident prevention, concluding with a discussion of the social, economic, and legal problems of implementing the research findings.

In addition, a good brief survey of the evolution of technical developments in regard to transportation safety from 1895 to 1995 is contained in chapters in *The Automobile: A Century of Progress*, a collection of articles compiled by the Society of Automotive Engineers (SAE) Historical Committee that first appeared in *Automotive Engineering* magazine. The authors approach their topic from a systems perspective, thus reflecting the way an automobile is engineered.

Joel Eastman used 1966 as the terminal date of his previously mentioned study since it allowed him to include discussion of what most historians and sociologists believe was a watershed event that occurred in 1965, the publication of Ralph Nader's *Unsafe at Any Speed: The Designed-In Dangers of the American Automobile*. Possibly one of the ten most significant "social conscience" books ever published, Nader's polemic did for auto safety what Rachel Carson's *The Silent Spring* did for the environmental movement. It established the author as the preeminent spokesman for consumerism by allegedly showing in the first chapter how General Motors had deliberately ignored safety considerations in the design of its then-new subcompact Chevrolet Corvair. (The omission of a fifteen-dollar stabilizing bar created a situation where the car tended to oversteer.) The remainder of the book was a general indictment of Detroit's insensitivity to safety concerns, favoring design and cost saving over safety engineering.

General Motors, without admitting the veracity of Nader's allegations, shortly thereafter ceased production of its Corvair model. A controversial decision at the time, it led to at least one book-length defense of the car, Andrew J. White's *The Assassination of the Corvair*, which concentrates on the court cases and adverse legal decisions involving that vehicle and others in the mid- and late 1960s. The controversy also found itself intruding into the usually all-positive world of enthusiast histories, most notably Mike Knepper's *The Corvair Affair*, which reviews the legal controversy and includes previously unpublished information in defense of that car.

Ralph Nader's testimony to a congressional committee chaired by Senator Abraham Ribicoff (D., Conn.) and the subsequent Corvair fight turned out to be the opening volley in what has become an ongoing concern for passenger safety, resulting in government agencies' being assigned watchdog and investigative responsibilities in this area. Although Nader's volume is the best known, its release coincided with the publication of another book that effectively took the automobile producers to task for allegedly putting profits before lives: *Safety Last: An Indictment of the Auto Industry*, by Jeffrey O'Connell and Arthur Myers. In addition to alleging that the auto manufacturers had fought legislation and public pressure to build safer cars, O'Connell and Myers maintain that the industry had tried to shift responsibility for the increasing number of accidents to driving behavior and the conditions of roads and highways.

The appearance of these and other similar books in the mid-1960s clearly was not coincidence and probably can be explained by the well-publicized safety problems connected with the Chevrolet Corvair and other so-called compact cars. In regard to the latter, see the chapter entitled "Small-Car Safety" in *Autos, Transit, and Cities*, written by John R. Meyer and José A. Gómez-Ibáñez. In any case, these writings created a public furor and led commentators like Elizabeth Brenner Drew to proclaim the advent of "the politics of auto safety."

Corporate Legal Responsibility

As might be expected, the publicity surrounding these books and the cars that generated them was not viewed as good news by the car makers. The latter had always been aware of the potential of being held legally liable for personal and property damage caused by their vehicles. In fact, in *Products Liability in the Automobile Industry: A Study in Strict Liability and Social Control*, a scholarly book published five years before Nader's, Cornelius W. Gillam had analyzed the law and legislation that regulated the automotive business at that time. Additionally, in an attempt to ascertain the nature and degree of the mid-1960s safety problem and to hopefully provide material for defense of the industry, the Automobile Manufacturers Association commissioned a study by the firm of Arthur D. Little, Inc. The result was *The State of the Art of Traffic Safety: A Critical Review and Analysis of the Technical Information on Factors for the Automobile Manufacturers Association*, published in 1966.

The issue of corporate liability for automotive engineering defects remained a lively one even after production of the Corvair ceased. Thus, a series of rear-end collisions in the 1970s in which Ford Pinto gas tanks exploded led to a much-publicized lawsuit against the Ford Motor Company alleging reckless homicide. The story of the resulting trial in 1980, in which Ford was acquitted, and its implications is told in *Corporate Crime under Attack: The Ford Pinto Case and Beyond*, by Francis T. Cullen *et al.*, and Lee P. Strobel's *Reckless Homicide: Ford's Pinto Trial*. The future significance of the Pinto trial lay in the fact that it established a precedent for the criminal prosecution of the manufacturer in a product liability case.

A related issue, present in all cases of corporate (and government) malfeasance, is the question of who has responsibility for reporting the problem(s) and how he or she is treated afterward. For a discussion of this issue in the Ford Pinto case, see Frank Camps' "Warning an Auto Company about an Unsafe Design," a chapter in Alan F. Westin's *Whistleblowing!: Loyalty and Dissent in the Corporation*. Finally, a relevant analysis of corporate social responsibility, more important for its authorship than its original ideas, is *The Human Environment and Business*, written by Henry Ford II and published in 1970.

The Corvair and Pinto cases, together with other somewhat less publicized ones, heightened the importance of the question of whether structurally and technologically safe vehicles would emerge from Detroit without government oversight. They also contributed to increased public scrutiny of the behavior of America's industrial giants. For example, in *Corporate Corruption: The Abuse of Power*, Marshall B. Clinard maintains that despite their economic success and public image, many of the Fortune 500 companies are guilty of abusing the public trust, their customers, their stockholders, and the environment. In a chapter entitled "Detroit Roulette," he singles out the auto industry as one of the four worst offenders.

The number of individual and class-action lawsuits brought against American and foreign manufacturers became so numerous that an annual publication entitled *Automotive Engineering and Litigation*, edited by George A. and Barbara J. Peters, was begun in the mid-1980s as a reference source for both engineers and lawyers in terms of contemporary issues and laws. Among the topics covered are product design, manufacturing defects, failure to warn, and user injury.

The best-known manifestation of these safety concerns is the occasional recalls issued by car manufacturers to correct problems that could lead to accidents and injuries. In addition, the engineering and design of cars are now regulated somewhat by legislation, government agencies, and consumer groups.

Driving Behavior

While obviously the above discussion shows that cars can indeed cause accidents, clearly the machine alone is not to blame in all cases. Much of the responsibility lies with the conduct of the person behind the wheel. Beginning in the mid-1930s, a plethora of solid studies of how drivers cause/avoid automobile accidents began to appear. Human culpability is a major theme in the broadly based *Sudden Death and How to Avoid It* (1935), by Joseph C. Furnas and Ernest M. Smith; Roy W. Sherman's *If You're Going to Drive Fast* (1935), which takes the interesting position that such behavior is inevitable despite the risks involved and, therefore, provides pointers as to how to drive safely at high speeds and how to handle emergency conditions; *Psychology and the Motorist* (1938), by Herbert A. Toops and S. Edson Haven, a scholarly study of automobile accidents that approaches its topic from a psychological perspective, criticizing pre–World War II highway conditions and driving practices and offering recommendations for improving them; *Seven Roads to Safety: A Program to Reduce Automobile Accidents* (1939), by Paul G. Hoffman (then head of the Automotive Safety Foundation) and Neil M. Clark, a brief work (87 pages) that proposes action in seven areas to reduce automotive accidents: legislation, motor vehicle administration, enforcement, engineering, education, technical personnel training, and research; and Harry R. DeSilva's 1942 book, *Why We Have Automobile Accidents*, which explores the role of such factors as speed, driving skill and incompetence, pedestrian behavior, driver training, and license examinations as contributors to and possible solutions for what is termed "our national highway accident problem." (For a brief examination of the literature concerning early driver education, see Chapter 6.)

These pioneering studies were followed by others and were still being published after World War II and well into the 20th century as interest in the prevention and control of traffic accidents continued unabated. See, for example, A[lvhh] R. Lauer's *The Psychology of Driving: Factors of Traffic Enforcement* (1960), with its emphasis on mental processes and the prevention and control of traffic accidents; Stephen Black's *Man and Motor Cars: An Ergonomic Study* (1966) which, despite its title, is as much concerned with human factors psychology, including unconscious attitudes toward driving and car design that the author obtained from study volunteers under hypnosis, as with chassis engineering; and Risto Naatanen and Heikki Summala's *Road-User Behavior and Traffic Accidents* (1976), which explores psychophysiological approaches to human information processing, especially in regard to attention.

Interest in human limitations in such areas as hand–eye coordination and sensation and perception has even led to studies of rather specific aspects of the safety problem. For example, see Ingeborg Schmidt and Paul L. Connolly's *Visual Considerations of Man, the Vehicle, and the Highway*, a study published by the Society of Automotive Engineers, and the six reports that constitute the *Highway Research Record*'s thematic issue on *Lighting, Visibility, and Driving*.

Nonetheless, by the 1990s some observers were beginning to question just how important considerations of engineering, psychology, and health were for safety on the highway. Thus, Leonard Evans in *Traffic Safety and the Driver* focused on prevention and control as the most significant factors. J. Peter Rothe in *Beyond Traffic Safety* took it one step further, arguing that *the* key element was that automotive traffic was fundamentally an instance of social interaction and that any measure designed to achieve greater safety needed to take that into account. In a sense, he was prophesying a new aspect of highway mayhem, something that later in the decade would have the appellation "road rage" applied to it.

Drunk Driving

While all of the above studies are important, the available data indicate that they concern only a minority of the accidents that occur each year. Clearly the most significant cause is driver intoxication. Approximately 40% of all motor accidents that occur in the United States are alcohol-related. The best scholarly overview of this problem is Joseph R. Gusfield's *The Culture of Public Problems: Drinking-Driving and the Symbolic Order*. Gusfield uses sociological analysis to show how a type of human behavior, in this case drinking and driving, becomes a public problem. In so doing, he shows the complexity of the issues involved, including the cultural milieu in which it occurs, the legal aspects that must be dealt with, and the cognitive framework that emerges in response to it. Also excellent is James B. Jacobs' *Drunk Driving: An American Dilemma*. Writing from the perspective of a law professor, Jacobs maintains that any assessment of the various strategies that society employs to control the problem requires an understanding of how the crime is defined in legal terms. As such, his work is both a synthesis of current (1989) research on the topic and an analysis of the origins and effectiveness of public policy aimed to control the behavior. Jacobs does a particularly fine job of assessing the various legal and mechanical strategies that have been proposed to stop drunk driving.

The continuing existence of the problem has led to an ongoing interest in ways and means of deterring intoxicated individuals from driving. Representative of the resulting literature are the National Transportation Safety Board's *Safety Study: Deterrence of Drunk Driving, the Role of Sobriety Checkpoints and Administrative License Revocations*; Gerald D. Robin's *Waging the Battle against Drunk Driving: Issues, Countermeasures, and Effectiveness*, a comprehensive overview of such efforts as legislation on the federal and state levels, together with grassroots citizen campaigns like MADD (Mothers against Drunk Driving); H. Laurence Ross' *Deterring the Drinking Driver: Legal Policy and Social Control* (1984), with its emphasis on prevention and control of intoxicated drivers so as to diminish the traffic accidents that they cause, and his later *Confronting Drunk Driving: Social Policy for Saving Lives* (1992), which focuses on the role of government policy and won the Society for the Study of Social Problems' Crime and Delinquency Division's award for outstanding scholarship in the year of its publication; and *Social Control of the Drinking Driver*, edited by Michael D. Laurence *et al.*, an international survey of what was known about the problem and ways to control it in the late 1980s. In addition, see David Scholl's legalistic "The Drinking Driver: An Approach to Solving a Problem of Underestimated Severity," a chapter in *Drunk Driving Cases: Prosecution and Defense*, edited by Brian Freeman, and Lilly Hoffman's study "Alcohol and Traffic Safety: Screening Out the Drunken Driver," a chapter report of which appeared in *Technological Shortcuts to Social Change*, edited by Amitai Etzioni and Richard Remp.

One aspect of the movement against drunk driving has involved administering one type of test or another to suspects to determine the level of alcohol in their blood. While in theory, almost everyone agrees with such practice, the legal issues involved remain unsettled after fifty years. A relatively early study of these issues, covering the years 1937–1950, is Robert L. Donigan's *Chemical Test Case Law: Legal Aspects of and Constitutional Issues Involved in Chemical Tests to Determine Intoxication*. Donigan's is a historical work, and, as such, it provides the contemporary reader both with a developmental framework with which to compare his or her own findings and with a perspective on how this issue was viewed at midcentury. Later editions of Dongian's study appeared in 1957 and 1966 under slightly different titles. Another difficult legal issue has been whether or not those hit by drunk drivers are entitled to sue for mental and physical suffering and permanent damage. In that regard, see Paul A. LeBel's *John Barleycorn Must Pay: Compensating the Victims of Drinking Drivers*, which provides proposals for doing just that. (John Barleycorn was a 17th-century personification of liquor.)

Other Aspects of Public Policy and Safety

Federal and state governments also have attempted to improve traffic safety through research and legislation aimed at making cars and highways safer places to be in/on. Such interest is largely traceable to a concern regarding the large number of automotive accidents that began to occur in the 1920s. Herbert Hoover, as secretary of commerce, shared that concern and was one of the prime movers behind the formation of the National Conference on Street and Highway Safety. The latter's *Ways and Means to Traffic Safety*, a summary of all its recommendations from meetings in 1924, 1926, and 1930, is an interesting and useful historical document in terms of later developments in the movement to regulate traffic through judicial actions and legislation and to prevent automobile accidents.

Contemporary relationships between government actions and highway safety are explored in *Public Policy Development: Linking the Technical and Political Processes*, by Robert F. Baker *et al.* They use highway safety as one of their prime illustrative examples in analyzing the interaction between technology and the state, with special attention to the social aspects of technology and to the decision-making process. Alan Irwin also wrestles with this issue in his cross-national study *Risk and the Control of Technology: Public Policies for Road Traffic Safety in Britain and the United States*, as does Jerome S. Legge Jr. in *Traffic Safety Reform in the United States and Great Britain*. More specifically, John D. Graham's *Auto Safety: Assessing America's Performance* provides a history of the thirty-year controversy regarding the placement and use of "occupant restraint systems" (seat belts) in cars. In so doing, he examines the role of government policymakers and lobbyists, corporate executives, consumer activists, and the courts as they struggle to resolve the controversy.

A very different perspective is presented in Gabriel J. Roth's 1996 *Roads in a Market Economy*, wherein the author criticizes government management of thoroughfares and advocates instead private ownership of express highways and intercity roads. Roth maintains that the same commercial principles that guide telecommunications and public utilities can be applied to roads and that such ownership would diminish problems of excessive congestion, pollution, and highway accidents, the latter by reducing drunk driving and weather-related accidents.

Mention also should be made here of an unintended highway safety benefit that arose from responses to the oil embargoes of the 1970s. At that time, there was a realization that there was a relationship between speed limits and the efficiency with which fuel was burned by a personal automobile. With that knowledge, the federal government moved for the first time in its history to establish a national speed limit (55 miles per hour). The results of that experiment are well told in a special report from the Transportation Research Board of the National Research Council, entitled *55: A Decade of Experience*. The report shows that highway safety was thereby enhanced, especially in terms of reducing automotive fatalities and injuries, while significant energy savings were achieved. The safety benefits led to continued support for the 55-mph limit until long after (1987) there was a perceived shortage in gasoline.

Finally, given that hundreds of thousands of motor accidents happen each year in the United States, a significant automobile insurance industry has developed to financially "protect" drivers and their passengers. This industry has been abetted by the state governments, which have felt it necessary to assure that each motorist carries a minimal amount of collision and liability insurance and that the cost of that coverage is reasonable. Edward J. Lascher Jr. offers a contemporary study of one aspect of this business is *The Politics of Automobile Insurance Reform: Ideas, Institutions, and Public Policy in North America*, in which he uses case studies from the United States and Canada to argue that politicians' beliefs in the efficacy of certain solutions and in the role of governmental institutions have influenced state/provincial control of insurance rates as much as the lobbying efforts of trial lawyers and the companies themselves.

A Concluding Note on Safety

Before ending this section, the American people's fascination with accidents needs to be noted. Anyone who has been involved in a traffic jam, only to discover that it was caused by rubbernecking drivers slowing down to observe an accident on the *other side* of a divided highway, can attest to this. Thus, it should come as no surprise that *Old Cars Weekly* regularly runs a feature entitled "Wreck of the Week," spotlighting photographs of highway mayhem. Over 200 of these photographs from the 1920s through the 1950s have been published in a collection entitled *Antique Car Wrecks*, edited by John Gunnell, which ostensibly reinforces the importance of driving safety. Similar in concept is Ron Kowalke's *Old Car Wrecks and the Vehicles at Accident Scenes, 1920s to 1960s,* which adds photographs of police cars, tow trucks, and ambulances doing their jobs in the aftermath of road accidents. In addition, Kowalke's work includes articles on auto crash testing and the evolution of automobile safety devices over time.

POLLUTION

Many of the early proponents of the motor car vis-à-vis the horse noted that it had the potential to improve the environment by eliminating horse manure from the roads and leading to the paving of roadways. Such developments promised a cleaner, quieter, healthier environment.

Nonetheless, in the years following the First World War, articles and reports began to appear associating the automobile with air, noise, and solid waste pollution. They questioned the health benefits of the car and claimed that the automobile was responsible for introducing new and potentially more dangerous forms of pollution into the environment. See, for example, "The Automobile as a Public Health Hazard," an article by A.J. Chesley that appeared in a 1924 issue of the *American Journal of Public Health.* Joel A. Tarr expertly describes this progression from remedy to problem in a 1971 article republished as a chapter in his *The Search for the Ultimate Sink: Urban Pollution in Historical Perspective.* That article/chapter is part of a broader thesis in which Tarr sees pollution problems repeatedly being "solved" by transferring them from one artifact and/or location to another.

Unfortunately, there is as yet no book-length survey devoted exclusively to a study of the relationship between the automobile and pollution in its many forms. The closest work in this regard is *The Automobile and the Environment: An International Perspective,* edited by Ralph Gakenheimer. The papers collected therein analyze mid-1970s data on transport-related environmental problems and government policy options for responding to them. The focus is decidedly international and urban. Of particular interest are the sections on traffic control in cities and air pollution and noise. In addition, a few monographs have chapters that discuss the relationship that existed or exists between cars and pollution. For instance, a Twentieth Century Fund Report, *Autos, Transit, and Cities,* by John R. Meyer and José Gómez-Ibáñez, contains chapters on land use, energy, air pollution, aesthetics, and traffic congestion in a section on issues and policies. Similarly, Michael L. Berger's *The Devil Wagon in God's Country* features sections examining environmental changes wrought by the automobile in rural America during the years 1893–1929. Finally, an offbeat "road book," K.T. Berger's *Where the Road and the Sky Collide: America through the Eyes of Its Drivers,* provides insights into how American drivers view their cars and the latter's impact on the environment. Embarking upon a nationwide investigative journey in the early 1990s, this self-professed "car biologist" interviewed drivers, auto industry executives and engineers, planners and transportation experts, and environmental activists trying to determine whether the car will evolve in ways that will be more environmentally friendly or whether it will continue to be an agent of degradation and destruction.

Air Pollution

In the 1960s literally tens of millions of tons of carbon monoxide, nitrogen dioxide, sulfur oxide, and lead were being released into the atmosphere, each of which posed a potentially toxic threat to human beings. Realization of the significant automotive contribution to the American air pollution problem led to both federal and state regulatory legislation. Most often, such legislation took the form of requiring catalytic converters and periodic car inspections.

By the early 1970s, regulations aimed at reducing air pollution from cars had been in place long enough to merit an assessment by experts in the field. Such a study was conducted by a group at Columbia University under a grant from the Legislative Drafting Research Fund. The resulting papers were published as *The Automobile and the Regulation of Its Impact on the Environment*, by Frank P. Grad *et al.*, a collection, not surprisingly, that emphasizes the use of law and legislation to control the negative environmental aspects of the motor car, with special attention to the air pollution caused by exhaust gases. The problems of regulation are viewed from legal, economic, and technological perspectives. Similar in approach but more specific and adding an interesting and valuable historical dimension is *Pollution and Policy: A Case Essay on California and Federal Experience with Motor Vehicle Air Pollution, 1940–1975*, by James E. Krier and Edmund Ursin.

Two signs of the coming-of-age of this wave of assessment were the appearance in 1974 of *Air Quality and Automobile Emission Control: A Report*, issued by the National Academy of Sciences and the National Academy of Engineering, with its emphasis on preventing and controlling air pollution caused by exhaust fumes, and David Harrison Jr.'s *Who Pays for Clean Air: The Cost and Benefit Distribution of Federal Automobile Emission Controls* (1975), in which the author employs mathematical models to analyze the economic aspects of automotive pollution control devices. In the same vein are two scholarly works from the same period by Donald N. Dewees: *Automobile Air Pollution: An Economic Analysis* and *Economics and Public Policy: The Automobile Pollution Case*, which analyze the economic benefits that could be derived from reducing automotive exhaust emissions, with special attention to the cost and effectiveness of various devices for reducing such air pollution. Dewees also explores the feasibility of achieving the same goal through curtailment of motoring.

Outcomes analyses continued to appear in books throughout the 1980s and 1990s. See, for instance, Lawrence J. White's *The Regulation of Air Pollutant Emissions from Motor Vehicles*, an evaluative study by the American Enterprise

Institute for Public Policy Research that focuses on the effectiveness of government controls on automotive exhaust gases; *Motor Vehicle Pollution Control—A Global Perspective*, a relatively technical volume from the Society of Automotive Engineers; *Air Pollution, the Automobile, and Public Health*, edited by Ann Y. Watson *et al.*, a publication sponsored by the Health Effects Institute that examines the toxicology and adverse physiological effects of motor vehicle emissions; Hilary F. French's *Clearing the Air: A Global Agenda*, a Worldwatch Paper that includes due attention to the automobile's role in this problem; Deborah Gordon's *Steering a New Course: Transportation, Energy, and the Environment*, which discusses the interplay of government policy, automotive fuel consumption, and environmental impact; and *Car Trouble*, by Steven J. Nadis *et al.*, a 1993 World Resources Institute guide that focuses on the environmental and social aspects of air pollution caused by exhaust fumes.

Although there was much debate throughout the last third of the 20th century as to the severity of the problem, there was no denying that the issue of automotive air pollution had become a political issue. Very good in this regard is *Approaches to Controlling Air Pollution*, edited by Ann F. Friedlaender, a highly regarded collection that explores the formulation of policy relative to air quality management and implementation through law and legislation, as well as the economics of determining the cost-benefit analysis of such controls. See especially the complex analysis in a chapter entitled "Government Policies toward Automotive Emissions Control," by Edwin S. Mills and Lawrence J. White.

Naturally, a key element in any attempt to make the automobile less of a threat to the environment has always been the response of the auto makers themselves to government regulations. While usually in theoretical agreement with the goals of the environmentalists, the corporate leadership often feels a more compelling obligation to preserve the financial health of its organization. As a result, these leaders have opposed a number of remedies, citing alleged prohibitive cost or lack of technological expertise. A recent and interesting overview of this subject is contained in *Government, Technology, and the Future of the Automobile*, papers from a Harvard Business School symposium edited by Douglas H. Ginsburg and William J. Abernathy. See especially Lawrence J. White's "Automobile Emissions Control Policy: Success Story or Wrongheaded Regulation?" in a volume that concentrates on industrial policy, especially as it relates to automotive construction and design.

Finally, for a non-traditional view of this topic, read Sudhir C. Rajan's *The Enigma of Automobility: Democratic Politics and Pollution Control*, in which the author maintains that mandatory pollution-control devices and emissions testing do *not* significantly reduce pollution and that current governmental policy blames the individual car makers and owners. Rajan argues that instead we need to accept the fact that shared ideologies and institutions are at the heart of the problem and that only they can be used to achieve a solution in a democratic manner.

Concurrent with the discussion of ways and means of limiting automotive air pollution was a related one concerning the development of an acceptable substitute for the spark-ignited, gasoline-fired, internal combustion engine. It was hoped that a new form of propulsion might neutralize the problem. An interesting, albeit very technical, volume to come out of this latter discussion was Douglas G. Harvey and Robert Menchen's *The Automobile, Energy, and the Environment: A Technology Assessment of Advanced Automotive Propulsion Systems*, a National Science Foundation-sponsored study published in 1974 that examines the impact of various systems on materials, energy, environment, economics, and society. The objective was to identify and compare alternative, low-polluting passenger cars of the near future and those policy options (government subsidization, taxation, and/or regulation) most likely to bring them into mass production by 1985. In the same vein, five years later, the U.S. Department of Transportation published the *Proceedings: Conference on Basic Research Directions for Advanced Automotive Technology*. While the government wished to explore means to limit pollutants emitted by cars, it was cognizant that such a change would have financial effects. Thus, the Department of Transportation also published *The Economic Impact of Conversion to a Nonpolluting Automobile*, a study by Edward Ayres that it commissioned.

At this juncture in history, some also looked back, not forward, for the "new" means of propulsion, fondly remembering the relative cleanliness of steam and electric cars. For instance, Andrew Jamison, in his 1970 *The Steam-Powered Automobile: An Answer to Air Pollution*, combines a history of the steam automobile from the turn of the 20th century through developments in the 1960s with a history of air pollution control legislation. He concludes that if we do not abandon the internal combustion engine, we will soon no longer have breathable air. Similar in concept is Gary Levine's *The Car Solution: The Steam Engine Comes of Age*, wherein, following a survey of its history, the steam-driven vehicle is offered as a 1974 remedy for air pollution, noise pollution, and the energy crises.

An example of the case for battery-driven automobiles is Daniel Sperling's recent (1995) *Future Drive: Electric Vehicles and Sustainable Transportation*, which takes increased travel as its point of departure and notes the accompanying adverse energy and environmental consequences thereof. Sperling then proposes electric propulsion as an environmentally more benign and sustainable transportation and energy system. Similarly, *Alternatives to the Internal Combustion Engine: Impacts on Environmental Quality*, by Robert U. Ayres and Richard P. McKenna, a Resources for the Future publication, pays considerable attention to environmental policy issues and the potential of electric automobiles.

See the "Engineering" section of Chapter 4 for additional books that explore contemporary proposals for electric and steam vehicles and other non-traditional forms of automotive propulsion, discussed primarily from a mechanical (as opposed to environmental) perspective.

Visual Pollution

While the car's role in fouling the air is probably the most serious type of pollution from a health standpoint, another group of critics has concentrated its attention on the built environment that has developed alongside roads and highways, pointing to what they term "visual pollution." Probably the best work in this area is the National Book Award-winning *Man-Made America: Chaos or Control? An Inquiry into Selected Problems of Design in the Urbanized Landscape*, by Christopher Tunnard and Boris Pushkarev, which analyzes the nature of the built environment based on a five-year study and offers remedies for the blight that befalls it. The authors maintain that by redesigning and rearranging man-made artifacts we can achieve an environment that is both functional and aesthetically pleasant, without damaging the American economy or standard of living. Contemporaneous in time but much more of a highly negative polemic is Peter Blake's *God's Own Junkyard: The Planned Deterioration of America's Landscape*, with its criticism of commercial strips composed of fast-food restaurants, gas stations, and motels; monotonous suburbs and subdivisions; congested cities; ugly and unnecessary roads; and, especially, billboards and how they degrade the environment in the name of "progress." The alleged pollution caused by poorly designed roadside buildings also is treated as part of Stephen A. Kurtz' well-received 1973 study entitled *Wasteland: Building the American Dream*. See, especially, the chapter entitled "The Road." Finally, for a brief overview of the entire problem, with special attention to the design of gas stations in the 1920s and 1930s, see Daniel M. Bluestone's "Roadside Blight and the Reform of Commercial Architecture," a chapter in Jan Jennings' *Roadside America*.

It should be noted that not all scholars have viewed the roadside built environment as necessarily bad or ugly. J.B. Jackson, a pioneer in landscape studies, viewed roadside architecture as reflecting American culture and, while admitting its ugliness (he called it a "longitudinal slum"), saw potential for cultural expression and beauty there. *Landscapes: Selected Writings of J.B. Jackson*, edited by Ervin H. Zube, contains two pieces that are particularly pertinent in this regard. "Other-Directed Houses" focuses on those roadside structures and accompanying lighting and signage that are deliberately designed to catch the attention of the passing motorist and draw him or her in. "Social Landscape" develops the idea that the resulting highway strips serve not just economic needs but a multitude of social functions as well. For Jackson, the challenge is to move away from viewing roads as ribbons of transportation efficiency and toward thinking of the highway as providing a new concept of leisure, its own art forms, and a legitimate claim to a share of the highway.

The specific problem of roadside signage and the challenge of enacting effective regulatory laws are well covered in *Highway Beautification: The Environmental Movement's Greatest Failure*, by Charles F. Floyd and Peter J. Shedd, and in Stephen Carr's *City Signs and Lights*, which, while being critical of the multiplicity of signs and the insufficient lighting often found in urban areas, places its emphasis less on pollution and more on creating a sensible plan to make the city more "legible and visible." While visual pollution caused by excessive roadside signage was present prior to the advent of the automobile, this pollution was intensified by the appearance of the motor car, especially alongside roadsides outside town and city limits.

A more specific dimension of the sign problem with a lengthy history of public concern is that of roadside billboards. Probably the best recent history is James Fraser's *The American Billboard: 100 Years*, which combines a brief, but well-done, account of developments from the late 1880s to the early 1990s with an outstanding collection of photographs. Insight into the development of this American contribution to outdoor advertising, prior to the depression, can be found in J. Horace McFarland's "The Billboard and the Public Highways," a chapter in the 1924 "The Automobile: Its Province and Problems," a special automotive issue of *The Annals*, edited by Clyde L. King; the "Health and the Environment" chapter of Michael L. Berger's *The Devil Wagon in God's Country: The Automobile and Social Change in Rural America, 1893–1929*; and *Outdoor Advertising—The Modern Marketing Force: A Manual for Business Men and Others Interested in the Fundamentals of Outdoor Advertising*, a "how to" manual published in 1928 by the Outdoor Advertising Association of America (OAAA).

By the end of the 1930s, the OAAA and its supporters had succeeded to the extent that the opposition felt compelled to publish a polemic against them: *The Billboard: A Blot on Nature and a Parasite on Public Improvements*, by Frederick S. Greene *et al.* Given the intensity implied in the title of the Greene book, it should come as no surprise that billboards and their placement became the subject of legal disputes. By 1958 the billboard problem had become complex enough to generate a special report by the Highway Research Board entitled *Outdoor Advertising along Highways: A Legal Analysis*. Agitation against roadside billboards continued into the 1960s, culminating in the passage of the Highway Beautification Act of 1965. This act limited the posting of signage along interstate highways and, thereby, reduced the number of billboards by two-thirds over the next thirty years. Enacted during the presidency of Lyndon Johnson, its history is told as part of Lewis L. Gould's *Lady Bird Johnson and the Environment*.

Before we leave this section, it should be noted that advertisers are not alone in their love of billboards. The latter have sometimes been viewed as an art form. For books that discuss that phenomenon, see the "Commercial Design and Advertising" section of Chapter 7.

The Highway Landscape

It has always been known that some highway and roadside landscapes are, or at least appear to be, prettier than others. Sometimes such developments seem to be the result of pure chance; other times, they are planned. Works regarding the latter began to appear in the 1920s. See, for instance, J.M. Bennett's *Roadside Development*, a 1929 technical manual by a Michigan county road superintendent that covers everything from preliminary field design through planting, seeding, and sodding, to maintenance. Bennett even has chapters on public utilities and comfort stations. Interest in this topic was enhanced by the formation of organizations such as the National Council for the Protection of Roadside Beauty, which was responsible for the 1931 *The Roadsides of California: A Survey* and similar works, and the publication from 1930 to 1950 of *Roadside Bulletin*, an illustrated journal devoted to roadside improvement and beautification. This concern was soon reflected in books such as Jac L. Gubbels' *American Highways and Roadsides*, a 1938 construction manual written by a landscape engineer that emphasizes how highways can be built and landscaped in such a manner that they preserve the roadside and promote safety. Less technical in approach and covering historical developments up to the late 1950s is *The Highway and the Landscape*, a collection of scholarly essays edited by W. Brewster Snow that focuses on the importance of planning and design. One outcome of this movement was the construction and landscaping of "parkways" during the 1920s and 1930s, a topic that is explored in Chapter 10. Worthy of special mention here is Bruce Radde's *The Merritt Parkway*, the story of a Connecticut roadway completed in 1940 that was hailed for its inherent beauty and respect for the natural environment.

The construction of aesthetically pleasing roads began to receive renewed attention in the mid-1960s. For instance, in *Freeways*, author Lawrence Halprin explores the aesthetics of freeway design in urban areas, arguing that they should be an integral part of the built environment through the use of tunnels, road depressions, and elevated highways, rather than barriers and dividers that need to be disguised through landscaping. Similarly, *The View from the Road*, by Donald Appleyard *et al.*, proposes a system whereby highway views would be rated according to their aesthetics and also makes recommendations for siting roads so as to maximize their aesthetic appeal.

One of the better historical overviews on this subject appeared in 1971, John Robinson's *Highways and Our Environment*. In what was then a timely perspective, Robinson argues that the car and the highway have done much to destroy our cities and degrade the natural environment. For him, the solution lies in redesigning our highways, both those internal to our cities and those that link one population area to another, so as to eliminate the accompanying pollution and make them more "scenic" and amenable to recreational use, including provision for pedestrian malls. All of this is to be done within the context of upgrading and expanding mass transit, to be paid for by taxes on the users and producers of motor cars. The 1970s was a period of great activity for public interest groups, and thus it was not surprising to see the publication in 1977 of *The End of the Road: A Citizen's Guide to Transportation Problemsolving*, edited by Robert J. Golten *et al.*, a publication of the National Wildlife Federation in which the author provides a "how-to" manual for community residents interested in affecting highway planning.

On a more specific level, *U.S. 40 Today: Thirty Years of Landscape Change in America*, by Thomas R. Vale and Geraldine R. Vale, examines the roadside environment (both physical and cultural) alongside that transcontinental route, comparing it with identical scenes recorded and analyzed in the 1950s by George R. Stewart in his pioneering *U.S. 40: Cross Section of the United States of America*.

For a broader view that places the highway within the context of a history of the American physical environment, see *The American Landscape*, by Christian Zapatka. Among the topics that he discusses are transportation within the national parks (see below), the Lincoln Highway, and New York's Jones Beach State Park and Parkway, built by Robert Moses. In the same vein, see the "Landscapes Redesigned for the Automobile" chapter in *The Making of the American Landscape*, edited by Michael P. Conzen, a collection that centers on the various impacts of human settlement (and movement) on the natural geography of the land.

Finally, some mention should be made of situations where the preservation of the natural environment competes with the desire and "right" of American citizens to view and enjoy it. An excellent overview of this topic is provided by Samuel P. Hays in his *Beauty, Health and Permanence: Environmental Politics in the United States, 1955–1985*, in which the author topically (as opposed to chronologically) analyzes the full gamut of issues: outdoor recreation, preservation of wilderness and open space, pollution control and ecology, and energy policy. More specifically, these issues have been the focus of several recent books that analyze the past history and current challenges faced by the federal government in the management of our national parks. See, for instance, Linda Flint McClelland's *Building the National Parks: Historic Landscape Design and Construction*, with its emphasis on early National Park Service (NPS) efforts to create buildings, roads, and hiking trails for visitors that were in harmony with nature, and, more recently, Richard W. Sellars' *Preserving Nature in the National Parks*, a comprehensive history of the NPS, critiques the ongoing internal struggle that has existed within the agency between the natural scientists and ecologists and the engineers and landscape architects, the latter more often prevailing with their advocacy of additional roads, parking lots, and buildings for park visitors. For additional books on this topic, see the section on motor touring in Chapter 8.

Government Responses to Automotive Pollution

The early 1970s decision of the Organization of Petroleum Exporting Countries (OPEC) to function as a cartel for the purpose of controlling the supply and price of crude oil showed the American government and its people how dependent its motorized lifestyle had become on foreign trade in general, energy imports in particular. The result was a number of relatively short-lived programs, such as the synfuels project to develop synthetic substitutes for petroleum (see below), the "downsizing" of American-made cars to achieve greater fuel economy, and the establishment of a nationwide speed limit of fifty-five mph for the same reason. Although the immediate crisis has long since passed, a true solution to the problem has never been found.

Nonetheless, the oil embargoes did generate renewed interest in analyzing the interaction among different types of energy, transportation, policy formation, and personal and societal values. For an early 1980s overview of this interaction, a good place to begin is *Energy and Transport: Historical Perspectives on Policy Issues*, a collection edited by George H. Daniels and Mark H. Rose. While the historical and topical range of the essays is broad, the book does include one essay on the social changes that accompanied the transition from trains to automobiles and another concerned with petroleum refining that shows the economic and political ties between the oil interests and the business of private transportation. Another collection, *The Dependence Dilemma: Gasoline Consumption and America's Security*, a set of symposium papers edited by Daniel Yergin, is more contemporaneous in approach and reflects the concerns and anxiety/urgency that accompanied the fuel shortages of the 1970s. As such, it explores alternative approaches to reducing demand, arguing that if we fail to take action, the social, economic, and military security of the United States will be at risk. More focused in coverage is Richard H.K. Vietor's *Energy Policy in America since 1945: A Study of Business–Government Relations*, which explores fossil-fueled energy policy from the end of World War II to 1980, with particular emphasis on the behavior and interaction of governmental agencies and private businesses, including the automotive industry. The author shows how both market forces and the inability of business and government to agree upon a uniform policy deepened the impact of dwindling domestic supplies of cheap energy resources.

In terms of the dependence on foreign oil, one proposed remedy was the idea that internal combustion engines could be made to run successfully on some fuel other than 100% petroleum. The example of the German use of alcohol during World War II was frequently cited to show the efficacy of that fuel. As a result, "gasohol," a combination of gasoline and ethyl alcohol, mixed in varying ratios containing up to 10% alcohol, was marketed in the late 1970s with the support of the federal government. For a 1979 bureaucratic report concerning the use of alcohol as a fuel and energy policy regarding it, see the U.S. Department of Energy's *The Report of the Alcohol Fuels Policy Review*. A more comprehensive overview of the obstacles faced by advocates of alcohol-driven vehicles is contained in *The Forbidden Fuel: Power Alcohol in the 20th Century*, by Hal Bernton *et al.*

Similarly, when the effects of the OPEC oil embargo were at their worst, the federal government funded attempts to develop a synthetic gasoline, in much the same way that synthetic rubber had been invented during World War II.

While most of the literature in terms of such efforts is hopelessly dated, fortunately an excellent retrospective collection of essays analyzing the phenomenon was published in 1987: *The Unfulfilled Promise of Synthetic Fuels: Technological Failure, Policy Immobilism or Commercial Illusion*, edited by Ernest J. Yanarella and William C. Green. Also good in this regard are *New Transportation Fuels: A Strategic Approach to Technological Change* and *Alternative Transportation Fuels: An Environmental and Energy Solution*, authored and edited, respectively, by Daniel Sperling. The emphasis in the former is on the synthetic fuels and transportation industries, especially in terms of the challenge of implementing technological innovation in the face of long-established practices. The latter is a collection of symposium papers that addresses transportation-fuel policy in regard to energy security, economic growth, and environmental quality, with special attention to such alternative fuels as methanol, natural gas, propane, and hydrogen.

Obviously, government interest in the motor car has not been limited to energy-related problems. In *Regulating the Automobile*, Robert W. Crandall *et al.* study the laws and regulations that have impacted the automotive industry in regard to safety and exhaust gas, with special attention to the issue of cost-effectiveness. In addition, an interesting case study from the late 1980s, John E. Beeker Jr.'s *Implementing Tailpipe Tests: What Factors Influence States to Respond to National Environmental Goals?*, explores a different dimension of the issue, namely, how internal socioeconomic and political forces influence a state's response to a well-intentioned federal environmental mandate, in this case the implementation of automobile tailpipe emission tests in 1982 for those states unable to meet the standards set by the Clean Air Act Amendments of 1977.

TRAFFIC CONTROL

It should come as no surprise that in a nation where there is approximately one car on the road for every person in the population, traffic control is one of our major challenges. Whether one is focusing on the social stresses experienced by the automotive commuter, the economic decline of inner-city businesses caused in large part by the lack of adequate parking, or the politics of effectively and efficiently moving millions of motorists day in and day out, the sheer magnitude of the challenges posed by our dependence on the automobile is overwhelming. Traffic engineer William Phelps Eno is generally credited with creating the rules of the road for the United States. In this regard, the reader may want to examine an early historical study by Eno entitled *The Science of Highway Traffic Regulation, 1899–1920* and his later *The Story of Highway Traffic Control, 1899–1939*. Eno espoused the theory of traffic flow and the use of rotaries to control it, and they underlay his work as described in these somewhat self-serving volumes.

Recognition of traffic control problems, particularly in urban areas, came early. By 1922, the situation had become serious enough for the Automobile

Club of Southern California to issue *A Report on Los Angeles Traffic Problems, with Recommendations for Relief.* Harold M. Lewis and Ernest P. Goodrich's *Highway Traffic in New York and Its Environs,* first published in 1925, was a regional survey of metropolitan New York and included a program for a study of all communication facilities within the area, written by Nelson P. Lewis. More general was Miller McClintock's *Street Traffic Control,* also appearing in 1925, which focused on the challenges posed by then contemporary American cities and presented solutions offered by experts of the day. Finally, a 1927 issue of *The Annals of the American Academy of Political and Social Science,* with its theme "Planning for City Traffic," edited by Austin F. Macdonald, included a series of chapters exploring traffic regulations within the context of city planning. Representative essays were John Ihlder's lead piece on the "Coordination of Traffic Facilities," Harold M. Lewis' "Routing through Traffic," and Burton Marsh's "Traffic Control."

For retrospective views of the "mechanical policeman" and other traffic control equipment during the early decades of the 20th century, see Gordon M. Sessions' *Traffic Devices: Historical Aspects Thereof,* a well-illustrated and thorough study based on material collected by the Institute of Traffic Engineers.

Pent-up demand and the prosperity of the post–World War II years led to a "golden era" for automotive sales in the 1950s and an accompanying increase in the associated highway traffic—hence, the publication in 1954 of *Modern Traffic Control,* by Joseph C. Ingraham, then the *New York Times'* traffic expert, a broad survey of the problems and possible remedies for the multiple aspects of this issue.

While subsequent years witnessed significant advances in the technology to control vehicle traffic, including the timing of lights at successive intersections, the problem became progressively worse as economic prosperity and the post–World War II baby boom increased the number of drivers on the road. As a result, two major research studies of traffic engineering in American cities were published in the mid-1960s: *The Urban Transportation Problem,* prepared for the Rand Corporation by John R. Meyer *et al.,* and a revised edition of *The Metropolitan Transportation Problem,* written for the Brookings Institution by Wilfred Owen.

Before developing this subject further, the human dimension should be noted in the form of *Traffic and the Police: Variations in Law-Enforcement Policy,* the title of a book by John A. Gardiner that explores possible explanations for why the traffic-ticketing behavior of the police varies from community to community, with special attention to Massachusetts. The author speculates on how things might be different if traffic law enforcement policy were public knowledge and the inequities did not exist. See also Robert L. Donigan and Edward C. Fisher's edited *Know the Law: A Compilation of Selected Articles on Various Phases of Law Applicable to Traffic Police and Traffic Court Activities* for a survey of enforcement in the late 1950s.

By the mid-1970s metropolitan areas in the United States were regularly experiencing a phenomenon that came to be known as "gridlock," a situation where the sheer number of vehicles overwhelmed our human and technical ability to move traffic through key intersections, and it came to a halt, at least temporarily. The nightmare that one day gridlock would not resolve itself and that people would abandon their "trapped" cars led to books such as *Stuck in Traffic: Coping with Peak-Hour Traffic Congestion*, by Anthony Downs, and *The Alternatives to Gridlock*, edited by Robert L. Deen. The magnitude of this problem became so great that it has generated at least one book that examines *Suburban Gridlock*, the title of a 1986 scholarly study by Robert Cervero that explores traffic flow and congestion in the American suburbs within the broader context of land use planning.

Gridlock, whether it occurs in cities or in the suburbs, is not just an inconvenience in terms of efficient movement of people. It also impacts on our use of energy, as literally billions of gallons of gasoline are consumed while the car remains stationary or moves at a crawl, and contributes to air pollution, in that exhaust fumes are produced in excess of what ought to be necessary. These topics, among others, were treated in two valuable national governmental studies in the late 1980s: the Federal Highway Administration's *Quantification of Urban Freeway Congestion and Analysis of Remedial Measures* and the U.S. General Accounting Office's *Traffic Congestion: Trends, Measures, and Effects*.

Nonetheless, it is unlikely that in the near future transportation planners will convince significant numbers of Americans to abandon their cars in favor of public transportation. The affection that Americans have for the automobile and the relative privacy that it affords are just too great. However, intermittent attempts to sell the idea of ridesharing or carpooling have shown some success when the proper incentives are provided, such as express lanes restricted to high-occupancy vehicles during rush hours. Here, too, there are problems, as evidenced by four reports done in the late 1970s and early 1980s for the U.S. Department of Transportation's Federal Highway Administration: *Incentives and Disincentives for Ridesharing: A Behavioral Study*, by Joseph B. Margolin and Marion Ruth Misch; *Legal Impediments to Ridesharing Arrangements* and *Legal Impediments to Ridesharing Arrangements: An Update*, both by Edward F. Kearney; and *Ridesharing: Meeting the Challenge of the '80s*, which was the final report of the U.S. Department of Transportation's National Task Force on Ridesharing. In the same vein are two 1981 reports by the Transportation Research Board: *Current Status of Ridesharing Activities*, which contains thirteen separate reports, and *Ridesharing Needs and Requirements: The Role of the Private and Public Sectors*.

For the most part, Americans have been granted the "right" to drive anywhere they want. The natural result has been the development of a related problem: where and how to store those vehicles until their drivers accomplish whatever it is they have come to do. Public parking is a perennial challenge for most large urban areas, one that is tackled by the municipality itself, private enterprise, or a combination of the two. Nonetheless, there are seemingly no contemporary books devoted exclusively to this challenge, although it does form sections of some. For instance, in his recent book *Edge City: Life on the New Frontier*, author Joel Garreau maintains that parking is *the* most important aspect of urban planning, since today's cities have become auto-dependent. He believes that this situation will continue until such time as another mode of transportation becomes more advantageous from the perspective of time and convenience, in much the same way that the car has largely replaced the passenger railroad.

Before concluding this section, one final aspect of the traffic control problem deserves to be mentioned: the multi-functional nature of roads and streets, especially those in towns and cities. Residents, pedestrians, and drivers of personal and commercial vehicles vie for space on thoroughfares and their abutments. Several provocative works explore the multiple aspects of this problem. Donald Appleyard's excellent *Livable Streets* examines the impact of traffic on neighborhood integrity in both the United States and Great Britain and offers proposals to recapture streets and protect neighborhoods from automotive traffic. He includes both historical and contemporary examples of the "politics of the street" and a chapter on traffic control devices and systems. In the same vein, *Public Streets for Public Use*, a collection of essays edited by Anne Vernez Moudon, offers a number of proposals for developing and managing streets so that they accommodate the diverse interests of their users. These proposals are supported by examples drawn from an international collection of case studies. For a good, general overview of the historical development of streets (and highways), see "The American Street" in Spiro Kostof's *America by Design*.

POSSIBLE SOLUTIONS

While the socioeconomic problems discussed in the preceding sections of this chapter existed to some extent from the earliest years of the automobile, post–World War II affluence and the accompanying "baby boom" intensified them. While acknowledging, and occasionally attending to, the problems of safety, pollution, and traffic congestion, most Americans never seriously contemplated any remedial action that would have been commensurate with the problems involved. Their dependence on—some would say love of—the car seemed to block any serious attempt to change the relationship that had developed over three-quarters of a century.

However, two major developments in the 1970s threatened to fundamentally alter the nature of the American automobile industry and the use of cars in the United States. These developments were the previously mentioned OPEC oil embargoes, with the subsequent realization of how dependent the United States was on foreign suppliers, and increased competition from foreign, especially Asian, manufacturers, leading to a relative diminishment of the American share of the world automotive market.

Those developments contributed to an unusual quantity of writing regarding the future of the car in American social and economic life. Although credit for the first, book-length criticism of the automobile in the post–World War II world goes to John Keats, who in 1958 published *The Insolent Chariots*, the 1970s ushered in a plethora of volumes that questioned the role and impact of the automobile in American society. In 1971 city planner Kenneth R. Schneider's polemic *Autokind versus Mankind: An Analysis of Tyranny, a Proposal for Rebellion, a Plan for Reconstruction* blamed the automobile for the destruction of the natural environment and the creation of unlivable urban areas, while offering suggestions for citizen action against both and advocating production controls on the manufacture of automobiles. In the same year, Tabor R. Stone's *Beyond the Automobile: Reshaping the Transportation Environment* provided a thorough analysis of alternatives to the car, with due consideration to the impact of each on the natural environment, to the type of built environment that it fosters, and to the challenges associated with converting to and implementing it. Stone concludes that the most promising future lies with a system of public, high speed ground transportation within and between cities.

Then, in 1972 came journalist Ronald A. Buel's *Dead End: The Automobile in Mass Transportation*, another polemic, but broader than Schneider's in that it takes on industry officials, highway engineers, and government officials, all of whom he sees as acting together to keep the environmentally destructive and relatively unsafe automobile as our chief means of transportation. Buel also presents his recommendations for creating an urban mass transportation system that can compete with the private motor car. Also published in 1972 was John Jerome's *The Death of the Automobile: The Fatal Effect of the Golden Era, 1955–1970* which, in addition to noting many of the same social and economic problems cited by Schneider, Stone, and Buel, criticizes the traffic laws, driver licensing procedures, and "unnecessary" horsepower of American automobiles and offers recommendations for remedying deficiencies in these areas. The chronological parameters of Jerome's work neatly dovetail with those of Keats. All four of these works pre-date the oil embargo and the serious challenge of Asian car manufacturers and thus represent deep-rooted dissatisfaction with the automobile per se rather than a questioning of its nature and role caused by changing economic conditions.

James J. Flink, one of the premier American automotive historians, was to later view these developments as significant enough to bring to a close what he termed the "Automobile Age." For the first time since the advent of the automobile, significant numbers of Americans began to discuss the possibility of alternative futures—ones in which the automobile would play a diminished role.

Keeping in mind that nothing becomes outdated as quickly as writings about the future, the books in this genre still should be of interest from a historical standpoint. This is especially true in that many of them consider the ongoing problem of finding that mix of public and private transportation that provides the most efficient delivery of people to their destinations. Typical of such writing in the late 1970s and 1980s were *Running on Empty: The Future of the Automobile in an Oil Short World*, by Lester R. Brown *et al.*, a study that investigates the complex political choices facing governments and the difficult personal choices that individuals will need to make in response to shrinking fuel supplies; *Rethinking the Role of the Automobile*, a report prepared by Michael Renner for the Worldwatch Institute nearly a decade later, which, in addition to the usual call for more efficient cars, alternative fuels, and improved and expanded mass transit, makes a plea for integrating urban design and planning with transportation planning to achieve needed diversity in transportation options and to reconcile the interests of the individual and society; and *How to Save Gasoline: Public Policy Alternatives to the Automobile*, a report prepared by Sorrel Wildhorn *et al.* of the Rand Corporation for the National Science Foundation that sees a much reduced role for the car vis-à-vis mass transit in future urban transportation networks. The federal government also contributed to this dialogue. See, for example, the U.S. Office of Technology Assessment's three-volume report on *Technology Assessment of Changes in the Future Use and Characteristics of the Automobile Transportation System*, which, as the title indicates, is an attempt to foresee automotive engineering advances and their social impact.

Yet, despite the dire warnings of the 1960s and 1970s and the plethora of suggested remedies, the nature and extent of American use of the automobile changed very little in subsequent years. Although some safety measures (e.g., air bags as standard equipment) were introduced and environmental measures implemented (e.g., the phasing out of leaded gasoline), critics of the "insolent chariots" realized by the early 1990s that, fundamentally, the situation had not improved. They continued to cite the negative effects of automobility and to offer solutions for it. Thus, Marcia D. Lowe's *Alternatives to the Automobile: Transport for Livable Cities* (1990), another Worldwatch Paper, emphasized the urban social and environmental problems caused by our continued dependence on cars and advocated measures to assure transport diversity, including mass transit, bicycling, and walking, and Wolfgang Zuckermann's *End of the Road: From World Car Crisis to Sustainable Transportation* (1991) also focused on the environmental aspects of automotive use, in addition to the questions of safety, cost-effectiveness, and the general quality of life, while providing over thirty different ways to reduce our dependence on the automobile and methods to assess related policies and programs.

As the new millennium approached, James H. Kunstler's *Home from Nowhere: Remaking Our Everyday World for the Twenty-First Century* (1996) identified the automobile among a group of factors responsible for the degradation of our environment. In that regard, he cites governmental policies that led to the construction of new and expanded highways as significant contributors to air pollution and the loss of farmland due to suburbanization. Nonetheless, Kunstler does offer a number of intriguing proposals for future urban planning. Similarly, in *Asphalt Nation: How the Automobile Took Over America and How We Can Take It Back* (1997), Jane Holtz Kay maintains that while the motor car has ravaged American cities and landscape, there still is a way to lessen our dependence on the automobile without seriously reducing our mobility. She notes examples from across the country where communities have become less auto-dependent through innovative architectural, political, and economic solutions that have enhanced mass transit and made walking easier and more pleasant. Peter Freund and George Martin approach the problems created by "auto-centered transport systems" from a sociological perspective in *The Ecology of the Automobile* (1993). The authors see such systems as having major negative impacts on cultural patterns, social relations, community, and options for social mobility, among other areas. Freund and Martin advocate lessening our dependence on the car by creating desirable alternatives as part of a diversified system of transportation. Finally, in *The City after the Automobile: An Architect's Vision* (1997), Moshe Safdie, the designer of Habitat, offers proposals for restructuring cities so as to make them more humane and economically attractive. Of interest to readers of this guide is his proposal for a fleet of rentable, electric "utility" cars that would replace the private automobile in urban areas.

Not surprisingly, after three decades of well-meant, but largely ineffective, criticism of the role of the automobile in American society, a revisionist view began to emerge. In late 1998 *Driving Forces: The Automobile, Its Enemies, and the Politics of Mobility*, by James A. Dunn Jr., appeared. Arguing that most Americans see the motor car as a positive good or at least a utilitarian necessity, Dunn maintains that attempts to regulate and/or replace the automobile are doomed to failure unless a superior means of mobility can be offered in its place. Pending that, he presents policies that he believes will preserve the benefits of the car while making it less of a threat to our environment and conserving energy. This book was followed early in 1999 by Richard C. Porter's *Economics at the Wheel: The Costs of Cars and Drivers*. While Porter acknowledges that cars and drivers cause problems, he argues that previous government policies and regulations have failed because they have ignored the external costs of operating automobiles. In other words, we have not attempted to solve those problems from an economic perspective. Porter sees driving as a "socially expensive habit" that can be broken or at least controlled by the implementation of policies that approach the problems of air pollution, highway safety, traffic congestion, and so on from the viewpoint of cost-effectiveness.

BIBLIOGRAPHY

Appleyard, Donald. *Livable Streets*. Berkeley: University of California Press, 1981.

Appleyard Donald, Kevin Lynch, and John R. Meyer. *The View from the Road*. Cambridge, Mass.: MIT Press, 1963.

Arthur D. Little. *The State of the Art of Traffic Safety: A Critical Review and Analysis of the Technical Information on Factors for the Automobile Manufacturers Association*. Cambridge, Mass.: Arthur D. Little, 1966.

Automobile Club of Southern California. *A Report on Los Angeles Traffic Problems, with Recommendations for Relief*. Los Angeles: Automobile Club of Southern California, 1922.

Ayres, Edward. *Economic Impact of Conversion to a Nonpolluting Automobile.* Washington, D.C.: International Research and Technology Corporation, 1969.

Ayres, Robert U., and Richard P. McKenna. *Alternatives to the Internal Combustion Engine: Impacts on Environmental Quality.* Baltimore: Johns Hopkins University Press, 1972.

Baker, Robert F. *The Highway Risk Problem: Policy Issues in Highway Safety.* New York: Wiley-Interscience, 1971.

Baker, Robert F., Richard M. Michaels, and Everett S. Preston. *Public Policy Development: Linking the Technical and Political Processes.* New York: Wiley, 1975.

Barker, Theo, ed. *The Economic and Social Effects of the Spread of Motor Vehicles: An International Centenary Tribute.* Houndmills, Basingstoke, Hampshire, Eng.: Macmillan, 1987.

Beeker, John E., Jr. *Implementing Tailpipe Tests: What Factors Influence States to Respond to National Environmental Goals?* New York: Garland, 1990.

Bennett, J.M. *Roadside Development.* New York: Macmillan, 1929.

Berger, K.T. *Where the Road and the Sky Collide: America through the Eyes of Its Drivers.* New York: Henry Holt, 1993.

Berger, Michael L. *The Devil Wagon in God's Country: The Automobile and Social Change in Rural America, 1893–1929.* Hamden, Conn.: Archon Books, 1979.

Bernton, Hal, Bill Kovarik, and Scott Sklar. *The Forbidden Fuel: Power Alcohol in the 20th Century.* New York: Griffin, 1982.

Black, Stephen. *Man and Motor Cars: An Ergonomic Study.* New York: W.W. Norton, 1966.

Blake, Peter. *God's Own Junkyard: The Planned Deterioration of America's Landscape.* New York: Holt, Rinehart, & Winston, 1964.

Brown, Lester R., Christopher Flavin, and Norman Cole. *Running on Empty: The Future of the Automobile in an Oil Short World.* New York: W.W. Norton, 1979.

Buel, Ronald A. *Dead End: The Automobile in Mass Transportation.* Englewood Cliffs, N.J.: Prentice-Hall, 1972.

Carr, Stephen. *City Signs and Lights.* Cambridge, Mass.: MIT Press, 1973.

Cervero, Robert. *Suburban Gridlock.* New Brunswick, N.J.: Rutgers University Press, 1986.

Clinard, Marshall B. *Corporate Corruption: The Abuse of Power.* New York: Praeger, 1990.

Conference on Basic Research Directions for Advanced Automotive Technology. *Proceedings of the Conference on Basic Research Directions for Advanced Automotive Technology.* 4 vols. Washington, D.C.: U.S. Department of Transportation, 1979.

Conference on Vehicle Design and Safety Research. *Passenger Car Design and Highway Safety: Proceedings of a Conference on Research.* New York: Association for the Aid of Crippled Children and Consumers Union of U.S., 1962.

Conzen, Michael P., ed. *The Making of the American Landscape.* Boston: Unwin Hyman, 1990.

Crandall, Robert W., Howard K. Gruenspecht, Theodore E. Keeler, and Lester B. Lave. *Regulating the Automobile.* Washington, D.C.: Brookings Institution, 1986.

Cullen, Francis T., William J. Maakestad, and Gray Cavender. *Corporate Crime under Attack: The Ford Pinto Case and Beyond.* Cincinnati: Anderson, 1987.

Daniels, George H., and Mark H. Rose, eds. *Energy and Transport: Historical Perspectives on Policy Issues.* Beverly Hills, Calif.: Sage, 1982.

Deen, Robert L., ed. *The Alternatives to Gridlock.* Sacramento: California Institute of Public Affairs, 1990.

DeSilva, Harry R. *Why We Have Automobile Accidents.* New York: John Wiley, 1942.

Dewees, Donald N. *Automobile Air Pollution: An Economic Analysis.* Cambridge, Mass.: Harvard University, 1971.

Dewees, Donald N. *Economics and Public Policy: The Automobile Pollution Case.* Cambridge, Mass.: MIT Press, 1974.

Donigan, Robert L. *Chemical Test Case Law: Legal Aspects of and Constitutional Issues Involved in Chemical Tests to Determine Intoxication.* Evanston, Ill.: Traffic Institute, Northwestern University, 1950.

Donigan, Robert L., and Edward C. Fisher, eds. *Know the Law: A Compilation of Selected Articles on Various Phases of Law Applicable to Traffic Police and Traffic Court Activities.* Evanston, Ill.: Traffic Institute of Northwestern University, 1958.

Downs, Anthony. *Stuck in Traffic: Coping with Peak-Hour Traffic Congestion.* Washington, D.C.: Brookings Institution, 1992.

Dunn, James A., Jr. *Driving Forces: The Automobile, Its Enemies, and the Politics of Mobility.* Washington, D.C.: Brookings Institution Press, 1998.

Eastman, Joel W. *Styling vs. Safety: The American Automobile Industry and the Development of Automotive Safety, 1900–1966.* Lanham, Md.: University Press of America, 1984.

Eno, William P. *The Science of Highway Traffic Regulation, 1899–1920.* New York: Brentano's, 1920.

Eno, William P. *The Story of Highway Traffic Control, 1899–1939.* Saugatuck, Conn.: Eno Foundation for Highway Traffic Control, 1939.

Etzioni, Amitai, and Richard Remp, eds. *Technological Shortcuts to Social Change.* New York: Russell Sage Foundation, 1973.

Evans, Leonard. *Traffic Safety and the Driver.* New York: Van Nostrand Reinhold, 1991.

Federal Highway Administration. *Quantification of Urban Freeway Congestion and Analysis of Remedial Measures.* Washington, D.C.: Department of Transportation, 1986.

Floyd, Charles F., and Peter J. Shedd. *Highway Beautification: The Environmental Movement's Greatest Failure.* Boulder, Colo.: Westview Press, 1979.

Ford, Henry, II. *The Human Environment and Business.* New York: Weybright and Talley, 1970.

Fraser, James. *The American Billboard: 100 Years.* New York: Harry Abrams, 1991.

Freeman, Brian, ed. *Drunk Driving Cases: Prosecution and Defense.* New York: Practicing Law Institute, 1969.

French, Hilary F. *Clearing the Air: A Global Agenda.* Worldwatch Paper 94. Washington, D.C.: Worldwatch Institute, 1990.

Freund, Peter E.S., and George Martin. *The Ecology of the Automobile.* Montreal: Black Rose Books, 1993.

Friedlaender, Ann F., ed. *Approaches to Controlling Air Pollution.* Cambridge, Mass.: MIT Press, 1978.

Furnas, Joseph C., and Ernest M. Smith. *Sudden Death and How to Avoid It.* New York: Simon and Schuster, 1935.

Gakenheimer, Ralph, ed. *The Automobile and the Environment: An International Perspective*. Cambridge, Mass.: MIT Press, 1978.

Gardiner, John A. *Traffic and the Police: Variations in Law-Enforcement Policy*. Cambridge, Mass.: Harvard University Press, 1969.

Garreau, Joel. *Edge City: a Life on the New Frontier*. New York: Doubleday, 1991.

Gibbons, John W., ed. "Highway Safety and Traffic Control." *The Annals of the Academy of Political and Social Science* 320 (November 1958): iii–141, 204–209.

Gillam, Cornelius W. *Products Liability in the Automobile Industry: A Study in Strict Liability and Social Control*. Minneapolis: University of Minnesota Press, 1960.

Ginsburg, Douglas H., and William J. Abernathy, eds. *Government, Technology, and the Future of the Automobile*. New York: McGraw-Hill, 1980.

Golten, Robert J., Oliver A. Houck, and Richard Munson, eds. *The End of the Road: A Citizen's Guide to Transportation Problemsolving*. Washington, D.C.: National Wildlife Federation, 1977.

Gordon, Deborah. *Steering a New Course: Transportation, Energy, and the Environment*. Washington, D.C.: Island Press, 1991.

Gould, Lewis L. *Lady Bird Johnson and the Environment*. Lawrence: University Press of Kansas, 1988.

Grad, Frank P. *et al. The Automobile and the Regulation of Its Impact on the Environment*. Norman: University of Oklahoma Press, 1975.

Graham, John D. *Auto Safety: Assessing America's Performance*. Dover, Mass.: Auburn House, 1989.

Greene, Frederick S. *et al. The Billboard: A Blot on Nature and a Parasite on Public Improvements*. New York: Moore, 1939.

Gubbels, Jac L. *American Highways and Roadsides*. Boston: Houghton Mifflin, 1938.

Gunnell, John, ed. *Antique Car Wrecks: From Old Car's "Wreck of the Week" Photo Album*. Iola, Wisc.: Krause, 1990.

Gusfield, Joseph R. *The Culture of Public Problems: Drinking-Driving and the Symbolic Order*. Chicago: University of Chicago Press, 1981.

Halprin, Lawrence. *Freeways*. New York: Reinhold, 1966.

Harrison, David, Jr. *Who Pays for Clean Air: The Cost and Benefit Distribution of Federal Automobile Emission Controls*. Cambridge, Mass.: Ballinger, 1975.

Harvey, Douglas G., and Robert Menchen. *The Automobile, Energy, and the Environment: A Technology Assessment of Advanced Automotive Propulsion Systems*. Columbia, Md.: Hittman Associates, 1974.

Hays, Samuel P. *Beauty, Health and Permanence: Environmental Politics in the United States, 1955–1985*. New York: Cambridge University Press, 1987.

Highway Research Board. *Outdoor Advertising along Highways: A Legal Analysis*. Special Report No. 41. Washington, D.C.: Author, 1958.

Hoffman, Paul G., and Neil M. Clark. *Seven Roads to Safety: A Program to Reduce Automobile Accidents*. New York: Harper and Brothers, 1939.

Ingraham, Joseph C. *Modern Traffic Control*. New York: Funk and Wagnalls, 1954.

Irwin, Alan. *Risk and the Control of Technology: Public Policies for Road Traffic Safety in Britain and the United States*. Dover, N.H.: Manchester University Press, 1986.

Jacobs, James B. *Drunk Driving: An American Dilemma*. Chicago: University of Chicago Press, 1989.

Jamison, Andrew. *The Steam-Powered Automobile: An Answer to Air Pollution*. Bloomington: Indiana University Press, 1970.

Jennings, Jan, ed. *Roadside America: The Automobile in Design and Culture*. Ames: Iowa State University Press, 1990.

Jerome, John. *The Death of the Automobile: The Fatal Effect of the Golden Era, 1955–1970*. New York: W.W. Norton, 1972.

Kay, Jane Holtz. *Asphalt Nation: How the Automobile Took Over America and How We Can Take It Back*. Berkeley: University of California Press, 1997.

Kearney, Edward F. *Legal Impediments to Ridesharing Arrangements*. Washington, D.C.: U.S. Department of Transportation, Federal Highway Administration, 1979.

Kearney, Edward F. *Legal Impediments to Ridesharing Arrangements: An Update*. Washington, D.C.: U.S. Department of Transportation, Federal Highway Administration, 1981.

Keats, John. *The Insolent Chariots*. Philadelphia: J.B. Lippincott, 1958.

Killick, Victor W. *Can We Build Automobiles to Keep Drivers Out of Trouble?* San Francisco: Reeves Publishing, 1940.

King, Clyde L., ed. "The Automobile: Its Province and Problems." *The Annals of the American Academy of Political and Social Science* 116 (November 1924): iii–279, 289–292.

Knepper, Mike. *The Corvair Affair*. Osceola, Wisc.: Motorbooks International, 1982.

Kostof, Spiro. *America by Design*. New York: Oxford University Press, 1987.

Kowalke, Ron. *Old Car Wrecks and the Vehicles at Accident Scenes, 1920s to 1960s*. Iola, Wisc.: Krause, 1997.

Krier, James E., and Edmund Ursin. *Pollution and Policy: A Case Essay on California and Federal Experience with Motor Vehicle Air Pollution, 1940–1975*. Berkeley: University of California Press, 1977.

Kunstler, James H. *Home from Nowhere: Remaking Our Everyday World for the Twenty-First Century*. New York: Simon & Schuster, 1996.

Kurtz, Stephen A. *Wasteland: Building the American Dream*. New York: Praeger, 1973.

Lascher, Edward L., Jr. *The Politics of Automobile Insurance Reform: Ideas, Institutions, and Public Policy in North America*. Washington, D.C.: Georgetown University Press, 1999.

Lauer, A.R. *The Psychology of Driving: Factors of Traffic Enforcement*. New York: Thomas, 1960.

Laurence, Michael D., John R. Snortum, and Franklin E. Zimring. *Social Control of the Drinking Driver*. Chicago: University of Chicago Press, 1988.

LeBel, Paul A. *John Barleycorn Must Pay: Compensating the Victims of Drinking Drivers*. Champaign: University of Illinois Press, 1992.

Legge, Jerome S., Jr. *Traffic Safety Reform in the United States and Great Britain*. Pittsburgh: University of Pittsburgh Press, 1991.

Levine, Gary. *The Car Solution: The Steam Engine Comes of Age*. New York: Horizon, 1974.

Lewis, David L., and Laurence Goldstein, eds. *The Automobile and American Culture*. Ann Arbor: University of Michigan Press, 1983.

Lewis, Harold M., in collaboration with Ernest P. Goodrich. *Highway Traffic in New York and Its Environs, Including a Program, by Nelson P. Lewis, for a Study of All Communication Facilities within the Area*. New York: Regional Plan of New York and Its Environs, 1925.

Lighting, Visibility, and Driving. Highway Research Record 216 (1968).

Lowe, Marcia D. *Alternatives to the Automobile: Transport for Livable Cities.* World-watch Paper 98. Washington, D.C.: Worldwatch Institute, 1990.

Macdonald, Austin F., ed. "Planning for City Traffic." *The Annals of the American Academy of Political and Social Science* 132 (September 1927): iii–249, 262–264.

Margolin, Joseph B., and Marion Ruth Misch. *Incentives and Disincentives for Ride-sharing: A Behavioral Study.* Washington, D.C.: U.S. Department of Transportation, Federal Highway Administration, 1978.

McClelland, Linda Flint. *Building the National Parks: Historic Landscape Design and Construction.* Baltimore: Johns Hopkins University Press, 1997.

McClintock, Miller. *Street Traffic Control.* New York: McGraw-Hill, 1925.

Meyer, John R., and José A. Gómez-Ibáñez. *Autos, Transit, and Cities.* Cambridge, Mass.: Harvard University Press, 1981.

Meyer, John R., J.F. Kain, and M. Wohl. *The Urban Transportation Problem.* Cambridge, Mass.: Harvard University Press, 1965.

Moudon, Anne Vernez, ed. *Public Streets for Public Use.* New York: Van Nostrand Reinhold, 1987.

Naatanen, Risto, and Heikki Summala. *Road-User Behavior and Traffic Accidents.* New York: Elsevier, 1976.

Nader, Ralph. *Unsafe at Any Speed: The Designed-In Dangers of the American Automobile.* New York: Grossman, 1965.

Nadis, Steven J., and James J. MacKenzie, with Laura Ost. *Car Trouble.* Boston: Beacon Press, 1993.

National Academy of Sciences and National Academy of Engineering, Coordinating Committee on Air Quality Studies. *Air Quality and Automobile Emission Control: A Report.* 4 vols. Washington, D.C.: Government Printing Office, 1974.

National Conference on Street and Highway Safety. *Ways and Means to Traffic Safety: Recommendations of the National Conference on Street and Highway Safety, including Findings of All Conference Committees and of General Meetings of Conferences Held in 1924, 1926 and 1930, as Summarized and Approved by the Third National Conference, May 27–28–29, 1930.* Washington, D.C.: Author, 1930.

National Council for the Protection of Roadside Beauty. *The Roadsides of California: A Survey.* New York: Author, 1931.

National Research Council, Transportation Research Board. *55: A Decade of Experience.* Special Report 204. Washington, D.C.: Author, 1984.

National Transportation Safety Board. *Safety Study: Deterrence of Drunk Driving, the Role of Sobriety Checkpoints and Administrative License Revocations.* Washington, D.C.: Author, 1984.

O'Connell, Jeffrey, and Arthur Myers. *Safety Last: An Indictment of the Auto Industry.* New York: Random House, 1965.

Outdoor Advertising—The Modern Marketing Force: A Manual for Business Men and Others Interested in the Fundamentals of Outdoor Advertising. Chicago: Outdoor Advertising Association of America, 1928.

Owen, Wilfred. *Automotive Transportation: Trends and Problems.* Washington, D.C.: Brookings Institution, 1949.

Owen, Wilfred. *The Metropolitan Transportation Problem.* Rev. ed. Washington, D.C.: Brookings Institution, 1966.

Peters, George A., and Barbara J. Peters., eds. *Automotive Engineering and Litigation.* New York: Garland Law, 1984–1994.

Pettifer, Julian, and Nigel Turner. *Automania.* Boston: Little, Brown, 1984.

Porter, Richard C. *Economics at the Wheel: The Costs of Cars and Drivers.* New York: Harcourt, Brace, 1999.

Radde, Bruce. *The Merritt Parkway.* New Haven, Conn.: Yale University Press, 1993.

Rajan, Sudhir C. *The Enigma of Automobility: Democratic Politics and Pollution Control.* Pittsburgh: University of Pittsburgh Press, 1996.

Renner, Michael. *Rethinking the Role of the Automobile.* Washington, D.C.: Worldwatch Institute, 1988.

Robin, Gerald D. *Waging the Battle against Drunk Driving: Issues, Countermeasures, and Effectiveness.* Westport, Conn.: Praeger, 1991.

Robinson, John. *Highways and Our Environment.* New York: McGraw-Hill, 1971.

Ross, H. Laurence. *Confronting Drunk Driving: Social Policy for Saving Lives.* New Haven, Conn.: Yale University Press, 1992.

Ross, H. Laurence. *Deterring the Drinking Driver: Legal Policy and Social Control.* Rev. and updated ed. Lexington, Mass.: Lexington Books, 1984.

Roth, Gabriel J. *Roads in a Market Economy.* Brookfield, Vt.: Ashgate, 1996.

Rothe, J. Peter. *Beyond Traffic Safety.* New Brunswick, N.J.: Transaction Publishers, 1994.

Safdie, Moshe, with Wendy Kohn. *The City after the Automobile: An Architect's Vision.* New York: Basic Books, 1997.

Schmidt, Ingeborg, and Paul L. Connolly. *Visual Considerations of Man, the Vehicle, and the Highway.* New York: Society of Automotive Engineers, 1966.

Schneider, Kenneth R. *Autokind versus Mankind: An Analysis of Tyranny, A Proposal for Rebellion, a Plan for Reconstruction.* New York: W.W. Norton, 1971.

Sellars, Richard W. *Preserving Nature in the National Parks: A History.* New Haven, Conn.: Yale University Press, 1997.

Sessions, Gordon M. *Traffic Devices: Historical Aspects Thereof.* Washington D.C.: Institute of Traffic Engineers, 1971.

Sherman, Roy W. *If You're Going to Drive Fast.* New York: Thomas Y. Crowell, 1935.

Snow, W. Brewster, ed. *The Highway and the Landscape.* New Brunswick, N.J.: Rutgers University Press, 1959.

Society of Automotive Engineers. *Motor Vehicle Pollution Control—A Global Perspective.* Warrendale, Pa.: Author, 1987.

Society of Automotive Engineers Historical Committee. *The Automobile: A Century of Progress.* Warrendale, Pa.: Society of Automotive Engineers, 1997.

Sperling, Daniel. *Future Drive: Electric Vehicles and Sustainable Transportation.* Washington, D.C.: Island Press, 1995.

Sperling, Daniel. *New Transportation Fuels: A Strategic Approach to Technological Change.* Berkeley: University of California Press, 1988.

Sperling, Daniel, ed. *Alternative Transportation Fuels: An Environmental and Energy Solution.* Westport, Conn.: Quorum Books, 1989.

Stevens, Arthur W. *Highway Safety and Automobile Styling.* Boston: Christopher Publishing House, 1941.

Stewart, George R. *U.S. 40: Cross Section of the United States of America.* Boston: Houghton Mifflin, 1953.

Stone, Tabor R. *Beyond the Automobile: Reshaping the Transportation Environment.* Englewood Cliffs, N.J.: Prentice-Hall, 1971.

Strobel, Lee P. *Reckless Homicide: Ford's Pinto Trial.* South Bend, Ind.: And Books, 1980.

Tarr, Joel A. *The Search for the Ultimate Sink: Urban Pollution in Historical Perspective.* Akron, Ohio: University of Akron Press, 1996.

Toops, Herbert A., and S. Edson Haven. *Psychology and the Motorist.* Columbus, Ohio: R.G. Adams, 1938.

Transportation Research Board. *Current Status of Ridesharing Activities.* Washington, D.C.: National Academy of Sciences, 1981.

Transportation Research Board. *Ridesharing Needs and Requirements: The Role of the Private and Public Sectors.* Washington, D.C.: National Academy of Sciences, 1981.

Tunnard, Christopher, and Boris Pushkarev. *Man-Made America: Chaos or Control? An Inquiry into Selected Problems of Design in the Urbanized Landscape.* New Haven, Conn.: Yale University Press, 1963.

U.S. Department of Energy. *The Report of the Alcohol Fuels Policy Review.* Washington, D.C.: Author, 1979.

U.S. Department of Transportation, Federal Highway Administration. *Ridesharing: Meeting the Challenge of the '80s.* Washington, D.C.: Author, 1980.

U.S. Department of Transportation. *Proceedings: Conference on Basic Research Directions for Advanced Automotive Technology, February 13 & 14, 1979.* Washington, D.C.: U.S. Department of Transportation, 1979.

U.S. General Accounting Office. *Traffic Congestion: Trends, Measures, and Effects.* Washington, D.C.: Author, 1989.

U.S. Office of Technology Assessment. *Technology Assessment of Changes in the Future Use and Characteristics of the Automobile Transportation System.* 3 vols. Washington, D.C.: Government Printing Office, 1979.

Vale, Thomas R., and Geraldine R. Vale. *U.S. 40 Today: Thirty Years of Landscape Change in America.* Madison: University of Wisconsin Press, 1983.

Vietor, Richard H.K. *Energy Policy in America since 1945: A Study of Business–Government Relations.* New York: Cambridge University Press, 1984.

Watson, Ann Y., Richard R. Bates, and Donald Kennedy, eds. *Air Pollution, the Automobile, and Public Health.* New York: Health Effects Institute, 1988.

Westin, Alan F. *Whistleblowing!: Loyalty and Dissent in the Corporation.* New York: McGraw-Hill, 1981.

White, Andrew J. *The Assassination of the Corvair.* New Haven, Conn: Readers Press, 1969.

White, Lawrence J. *The Regulation of Air Pollutant Emissions from Motor Vehicles.* Washington, D.C.: American Enterprise Institute for Public Policy Research, 1982.

Wildhorn, Sorrel, with Burke K. Burright, John H. Enns, and Thomas F. Kirkwood. *How to Save Gasoline: Public Policy Alternatives to the Automobile.* Cambridge, Mass.: Ballinger, 1976.

Yanarella, Ernest J., and William C. Green, eds. *The Unfulfilled Promise of Synthetic Fuels: Technological Failure, Policy Immobilism or Commercial Illusion.* Westport, Conn.: Greenwood Press, 1987.

Yergin, Daniel, ed. *The Dependence Dilemma: Gasoline Consumption and America's*

Security. Cambridge, Mass.: Harvard University Center for International Studies, 1980.

Zapatka, Christian. *The American Landscape*. New York: Princeton Architectural Press, 1996.

Zube, Ervin H., ed. *Landscapes: Selected Writings of J.B. Jackson*. Amherst: University of Massachusetts Press, 1970.

Zuckermann, Wolfgang. *End of the Road: From World Car to Sustainable Transportation*. Post Mills, Vt.: Chelsea Green Publishing, 1991.

PART IV

Reference and Research Sources

CHAPTER 12

Reference Works and Periodicals

REFERENCE WORKS

General References

Reference works of an encyclopedic nature are far fewer than one would expect given the significant impact of the automobile on American history and life. Until recently, the best available source was *The American Car since 1775*, a 1971 publication by the editors of *Automobile Quarterly* magazine. In addition to chapters on the history of the car and of the industry in the United States and Canada, this 501-page work included sections on coach built automobiles, the American influence on foreign cars, and the licensing of motor vehicles, together with descriptive lists of 5,000 cars produced in the United States and Canada, 165 vehicles that were planned but not produced, American automobile clubs, and American car museums and collections. Less ambitious but in some respects more useful is *Automobiles of America*, now in its fifth edition, produced by the American Automobile Manufacturers Association, containing a year-by-year description of "milestones" in the development of the automobile and the industry, biographical vignettes of the pioneers and other principal auto makers, the names and dates of 3,000 American manufacturers, and a plethora of historical and contemporary statistics. Historian James Flink called an earlier edition "an invaluable compendium of factual information."

As one might expect, reference books began to appear as soon as the popular acceptance of the automobile had been assured in the United States. Thus, there were a *Motor Query Encyclopedia* published in 1919, and a *Motor Encyclopedia*, in 1925, both published by the American Automobile Digest and essentially question-and-answer books, and *Dyke's Automobile Encyclopedia*, by A.L. Dyke himself, in 1927. A half century later, such works had expanded greatly in size and scope, as evidenced by the mid-1970s publication of *The World of Automobiles*, a twenty-two-volume encyclopedia that reflects both the complexity of the technology and the globalization of the industry.

By the late 1980s, more specialized versions of such scholarly encyclopedic works began to appear, as witnessed by the publication of *The Automobile Industry, 1896–1920* and *The Automobile Industry, 1920–1980*, both edited by George S. May and volumes in the Encyclopedia of American Business History series published by Facts on File. Designed for the non-specialist, both volumes consist of hundreds of entries, arranged alphabetically, on the individuals, companies, and professional organizations that created and developed the American automotive industry. Short biographies of inventors, entrepreneurs, business executives, and labor organizers are included, as are articles on specific engineering and design innovations, sales and marketing strategies, and management and labor techniques.

Focusing more on the cars themselves are four massive reference books intended for the enthusiast market. The *Encyclopedia of American Cars: Over 65 Years of Automotive History*, by the auto editors of *Consumer Guide*, is a 896-page volume featuring nearly fifty different major makes, 200 minor ones, and close to 24,000 individual models produced from 1930 to 1995, described in word-and-picture entries that list/show design and engineering changes on a year-by-year basis, together with information on road performance and sales. Similar in concept and from the same editors is *50 Years of American Automobiles, 1939–1989*. In this case, we have a 720-page work, illustrated with 2,000 photographs, covering the full gamut of cars manufactured during the years 1940–1990. This latter book does an especially good job of providing information (including specification tables) on "minor makes," such as the All-state, the Checker, and the Cunningham. Martin Rywell's *Directory of Every American Automobile Ever Manufactured* includes brief histories and illustrations of over 2,500 cars, together with a complete 1912 catalog. Finally, David Vivian's *Encyclopedia of American Cars* focuses more on the history of the automotive industry, with over 1,000 entries chronologically ranging from the Model T Ford to the Chevrolet Corvette.

More in the category of factual compendia would be the three-volume *Standard Catalog of American Cars*. Volume 1, spanning the years 1805–1942, was compiled by Beverly Rae Kimes and Henry Austin Clark Jr.; volume 2 focuses on the period 1946–1975, the most recent edition of which was edited by Ron Kowalke; and volume 3, with James M. Flammang and Ron Kowalke as editors, covers the years 1976–1999 in a third edition that is nearly 1,000 pages in length and illustrated with more than 2,000 photographs. Production figures, factory options, charts of specifications, chassis information, other technical data, serial numbers, and the history of each make and model are included in each volume. Kimes and Clark's effort won the SAH's 1985 Cugnot Award for the best book in the field of automotive history and the similar Thomas McKean Memorial Cup from the AACA. James Flammang also is the author of the *Standard Cat-*

alog of Imported Cars, 1946–1990 which, like the preceding volumes, offers paragraph-long descriptions for literally thousands of cars and individual models, usually accompanied by photographs and often including production statistics, engine and chassis specifications, factory options, and original prices.

"Standard Catalogs" also have been issued for individual companies or marques. Similar to the more general works cited above, each massive volume provides production figures, available options, body styles, engine configurations, chassis data and identification numbers, other technical specifications, historical facts, factory prices, and current values for every model manufactured each year, hundreds of illustrative photographs, and, in some cases, historical articles culled from the magazine *Old Cars Weekly*. Representative works in this series would include Pat Chappell's *Standard Catalog of Chevrolet, 1912–1990*; John Lee's *Standard Catalog of Chrysler, 1924–1990*; Ron Kowalke's *Standard Catalog of Ford, 1903–1998*, which covers not just the Ford marque but Lincoln, Mercury, and Edsel as well; John Gunnell's *Standard Catalog of American Motors, 1902–1987* which, in addition to Rambler, Nash, and Hudson, includes "ancestor" marques such as Essex, Jeffrey, Lafayette, and Terraplane; and Ron Kowalke's *Standard Catalog of Independents: The Struggle to Survive among Giants*, which features such significant companies as Auburn, Checker, Cord, Duesenberg, Hudson, Kaiser-Frazer, Nash, Packard, Pierce Arrow, Rambler, Studebaker, Stutz, and Willys.

Similar in nature would be works such as *The Cars of Lincoln-Mercury*, by George Dammann and James K. Wagner, featuring production data, specifications, factory options, engines, custom bodies, prices, and photographs of every Lincoln, Mercury, and Edsel from 1921 to 1987; and the *Identification Guide: Dodge, 1946–1985*, by Samuel A. Shields Jr., which provides photographs of each production model during those years, together with specifications, production and registration figures, engine options, and factory prices.

Volumes in another series, that of the "Car Spotter's," are like the "Standard Catalog" ones, in that they attempt to provide as much data as possible on the individual vehicles. The best of this series is Tad Burness' *Ultimate Car Spotter's Guide, 1946–1969*. A true identification guide, this volume is organized alphabetically by make and then by year and provides data on standard equipment, optional engine sizes and horsepower ratings, model variations, new features, and original costs for every American car manufactured during this period, plus illustrations from factory catalogs showing the front, side, and rear of each vehicle. (This is a revised and enlarged edition of the *American Car Spotter's Guide*, published in the 1970s.) A similar book by Burness, the *Monstrous American Car Spotter's Guide, 1920–1980*, features over 10,000 illustrations culled from sales brochures and advertisements. The same author also is responsible for a series of marque-specific volumes, including the *Chevrolet Spotter's Guide, 1920–1992* and the *Ford Spotter's Guide, 1920–1992*.

In the same vein but more pictorially oriented are the following works. The *Encyclopedia of American Cars, 1946–1959*, by James Moloney and George H.

Dammann, is a good reference for most makes and models. Volume 1 covers the years 1930–1942, and volume 2, 1946–1959. The latter contains a significant section devoted to approximately 250 cars that were financial failures. In addition, there is the similarly titled *The Encyclopedia of American Automobiles*, by G.N. Georgano, which contains extracts from a broader, international work cited below. Furthermore, *Chronicle of the American Automobile: Over 100 Years of Auto History*, by James Flammang and the auto editors of *Consumer Guide*, provides a heavily illustrated, comprehensive (576-page), year-by-year chronology of the cars and personalities that made the car *the* means of personal transportation in the United States, as does a "twin" volume entitled *100 Years of American Cars*, a decade-by-decade, model-by-model photographic history and identification book supplemented by accompanying design and engineering notes by John Gunnell on the cars and the companies that produced them.

Containing the same type of information found in the compendiums cited above, but presenting it in a gamelike format is *The Great Auto Trivia Book*, by Mitch Frumkin and the auto editors of *Consumer Guide* magazine, a collection of questions and answers, lists of facts and figures, photographs, and word-and-picture games. In a similar vein but without the question-and-answer format is *America on Wheels: Tales and Trivia of the Automobile*, by Mark Smith and Naomi Black. Finally, *Car Crazy: The Official Motor City High-Octane, Turbocharged, Chrome-Plated, Back Road Book of Car Culture*, by Dean D. Dauphinais *et al.*, is an eclectic collection of things automotive, from brief histories of individual cars to weird drive-in businesses.

Another group of books dealing with multiple marques takes a more selective approach, choosing cars for inclusion because of some distinction that they share in common. A sampling of such books would include John C. Bentley's *Oldtime Steam Cars*, which traces the fortunes of steam autos produced by eighty-four manufacturers, including Stanley, White, and Locomobile; Richard B. Carson's outstanding *The Olympian Cars: The Great American Luxury Automobiles of the Twenties and Thirties*, featuring in text and photographs the behemoths that dominated the classic car era, including the reasons for the ascendancy and decline of such vehicles; *The Encyclopedia of Sportscars*, edited by G.N. Georgano, an illustrated history up to the mid-1980s that celebrates legendary marques from around the world, including the American Corvette and Thunderbird; the *Standard Guide to American Muscle Cars: A Supercar Source Book, 1960–1995*, edited by Ron Kowalke, which not only features the classic muscle cars of the 1960s and 1970s but also includes other high-performance vehicles over a period of thirty-five years, for which complete specifications, production figures, and photographs are provided; and Edwin J. Sanow's *Encyclopedia of American Police Cars*, essentially a photo history of the unique features, capabilities, and options that have been incorporated into such cars from the 1930s down to the late 1990s, such as very high horsepower engines, quick-shifting transmissions, and bullet-proof transmissions, together with data on specific models.

Several book series consist of pictorial histories of individual marques. Such books usually follow a chronological, year-by-year, model-by-model approach, with a photograph of the exterior and/or interior of each car accompanied by minimal descriptive information, often in the form of captions. The pioneer in this type of publishing was Crestline, and representative volumes in its pictorial history series would be Dennis Casteele's *The Cars of Oldsmobile* and Don Butler's *The History of Hudson*. Over the years, Crestline produced similar works on Buick, Cadillac-LaSalle, Chevrolet, Chrysler, Dodge, Ford, Plymouth-DeSoto, and Studebaker, among others, each featuring some 1,500 to 2,000 photographs.

More recently, the staff of the National Automotive History Collection (NAHC) of the Detroit Public Library (see Appendix 2) has created a Photo Archive series using the factory photographs in their possession. Volumes in this series have included *Studebaker, 1933–1942 Photo Archive*, edited and with introduction by Howard L. Applegate, and *Packard Motor Cars, 1946–1958 Photo Archive*, edited and with introduction by Mark A. Patrick. Similarly, books based on the photographic libraries of the major American car manufacturers have begun to appear. For instance, advertising and production-line photos from the GM Media Archives from the basis of John D. Robertson's *A Pictorial History of Chevrolet, 1955–1957*; and *Imperial, 1964 through 1968 Photo Archive*, edited and with an introduction by P.A. Letourneau, features photographs from the Chrysler Historic Foundation and the Iconografix Collection of Automotive Images.

As might be expected, *many* reference works are international (mostly European) in focus, and these, necessarily, contain entries on American cars. The following volumes, listed alphabetically by author, give the American automotive scene its fair due: *The World Guide to Automobile Manufacturers*, by Nick Baldwin *et al.*, which analyzes and pictures 1,000 makes selected for their importance to the industry in terms of design, engineering, and/or production figures during its first century; *The Encyclopedia of the Motorcar*, edited by Phil Drackett, with chapters on industrial history, petroleum, how cars work, motor racing (four chapters, including one devoted exclusively to the United States), custom cars, road safety, and "100 Great Cars," as well as biographical sketches and annotated listings of museums, collections, and motoring organizations; *The New Encyclopedia of Motorcars, 1885 to the Present*, edited by G.N. Georgano, similar in approach to the Moloney and Dammann volume cited above, and claiming to contain "every make of car in the world," and now in its third edition (with title variations for each); *Guinness: The Book of the Car*, by Anthony Harding, which, in addition to the usual facts and figures, contains biographical information, anecdotes, and significant segments on racing; and The *New Illustrated Encyclopedia of Automobiles*, by David Burgess Wise, featuring entries on over 4,000 makes worldwide, manufactured from the 19th century to the mid-1990s, with notes on the history and contributions of each to the development of the motor car.

Data and Fact Books

Additionally, a genre of books provides production specifications for mass-produced automobiles, information that is useful for collectors, restorers, and enthusiasts. Included in this category (listed alphabetically by author or editor) would be Grace R. Brigham's *The Serial Number Book for U.S. Cars, 1900–1975*, which provides a year-by-year listing of such numbers by manufacturer, make, and model; the *Catalog of American Car ID Numbers, 1960–1969*, by the editors of *Cars & Parts Magazine*, containing engine and body numbers, paint and trim codes, and so on, and keys to unscramble them all; Jerry Heasley's *The Production Figure Book for U.S. Cars*, whose title is self-explanatory and which was last published in 1977; and two volumes edited by G. Marshall Naul, *The Specification Book for U.S. Cars, 1920–1929* and *The Specification Book for U.S. Cars, 1930–1969*, both of which include information on body types, engines, carburetors, ignitions, wheelbases, tires, car weights, and list prices. Curiously, such collections of specifications do not seem to appear after the late 1970s.

These books can become even more specific, as witnessed by the publication of Gail Rodda's two-volume *Model T Ford: Parts Identification Guide*, a heavily illustrated aid for identifying, and judging the authenticity of, such parts, including frames, timing gears, gas caps, and even battery boxes; Victor W. Pagé's *The Model T Ford Car, Its Construction, Operation and Repair: A Complete Practical Treatise Explaining the Operation Principles of All Parts of the Ford Automobile, with Complete Instructions for Driving and Maintenance*, published in 1917; and *The Ford Model A, as Henry Built It: A Color, Upholstery and Production Facts Book*, by George DeAngelis *et al.*

More contemporary in focus are the following works: the *Corvette Black Book, 1953–1999*, by Michael Antonick, a classic in this field, which features such data as production figures by color, factory options, engine specifications, and even month of manufacture for individual cars; the *Chevrolet: A Book of Numbers, 1953–1975*, eighty pages of serial numbers for every model manufactured during that period, plus identification codes for engines, rear axles, and transmissions; the *Mustang Red Book, 1964½–1990*, edited by Peter C. Sessler, similar to the preceding Corvette book and part of the larger "Red Book" series, containing production totals, serial numbers and engine codes, original specifications and options (including colors), and prices for each model (the Mustang was introduced halfway through the model year, hence the 64½); and another book by Sessler, the *Ultimate Guide to American V-8 Engines, 1949–1974*, in which the author provides bore, stroke, horsepower, torque, displacement, valve size, and other specifications for each engine, together with part numbers for manifolds, cylinder heads, and other essential engine components. Coverage includes the Big Three, American Motors, Packard, and Studebaker. While such books are only representative (there are *many* more!) and are published primarily for the collector and/or restorer of antique cars, they also contain data that can be of value to automotive historians involved in quantitative studies.

There also are a number of valuable data compilations on other topics related to the automobile. See, for example, *American Automobile Trademarks, 1900–1960*, for which C.H. Wendel has culled 800 different trademarks from 350 manufacturers that were registered with the U.S. Patent Office (and hundreds that were not) and provided brief descriptive captions for each illustration; the *Digest of U.S. Automobile Patents from 1789 to July 1, 1899, Including All Patents Officially Classed as Traction-Engines for the Same Period*, and the *Supplement to the Digest of U.S. Automobile Patents, July, 1899 to January, 1902*, both early 1900s volumes edited by James T. Allen; *Automobile Laws of the New England States, New York, New Jersey, and Pennsylvania*, a 1908 publication edited by Arthur C. Wyman; and the *List of Books on Automobiles and Motorcycles*, by Arthur R. Blessing, published in 1918 by H.W. Wilson, making it one of the first book-length bibliographies in the field.

Another category of books can best be described as automotive dictionaries. Included therein would be Greg J. Davis' *Automotive Reference: A New Approach to the World of Auto Related Information*, which defines *all* the words and phrases associated with cars and their repair and takes 460 pages to do it; I. McIntosh's *A–Z of Car Talk*, a comprehensive, 456-page dictionary of automotive language; and the Society of Automotive Engineers' *Glossary of Automotive Terms*, which is similar to the previous two but even more extensive (609 pages).

There also are works that consist of a chronological listing of developments in the field. Premier among such books would be Clay McShane's *The Automobile: A Chronology of Its Antecedents, Development, and Impact*, easily the most comprehensive of such lists, containing some 4,000 entries that go beyond industrial developments to include social, economic, and cultural changes abetted by the automobile. Douglas A. Wick's *Automobile History Day by Day* organizes similar information by the 365 days of the year, irrespective of the year in which the historical event occurred. While the variety of events that have occurred on a particular day can be quite fascinating, the value of such an organizational scheme for the serious researcher depends on the quality of the indexes. Unfortunately, they are not up to the task. Broader in coverage is Leonard C. Bruno's *On the Move: A Chronology of Advances in Transportation*, which covers developments from 30,000 B.C. to 1991! Nonetheless, a fair amount of coverage is devoted to the automobile, and the index in this regard is a good one.

Finally, on the most basic level are those books and chapters that attempt to list the names of all passenger cars that have been produced in the United States, usually with the date(s) of their manufacture. In this regard, see Plummer H. Riddle's *Cars of Today and Yesterday: A Cavalcade of Motor Car Names That Have Graced America's Highways since 1787*, a catalog with over 2,500 names; the "U.S. Vehicles Makes, Past to Present" section that appears regularly in

Hemmings' Vintage Auto Almanac and is updated every year or two; "5000 Marques: A Listing of Automobiles Produced in the United States and Canada," which appeared in the previously cited *The American Car since 1775,* by the editors of *Automobile Quarterly*; the "Roll Call" chapter of the American Automobile Manufacturers Association's *Automobiles of America,* which contains over 3,000 makes; the "Roster of Every U.S. Passenger Car," a list of almost 1,700 cars appended to *Esquire's American Autos and Their Makers*; and Philip H. Smith's *Wheels within Wheels: A Short History of American Motor Car Manufacturing,* which contains an extensive listing of cars and production dates. (Incidentally, probably the first such list appeared in the March 1909 issue of *MoToR* magazine. Entitled "MoToR's Historical Table of the Motor Car Industry," it delineated over 600 makes that had allegedly been produced from 1895 to 1909 and was compiled primarily by automotive pioneer Charles E. Duryea.)

Sourcebooks and Scrapbooks

Although there is no scholarly compendium of original source materials in the field of automotive history, there are a number of different types of "popular" collections that contain items that might merit inclusion in such a work. For instance, *Automobiles of 1904* is a collection of descriptions, illustrations, and prices of eighty-eight cars reprinted from the January 1904 issue of *Frank Leslie's Popular Monthly*; and *Motor Cars of 1906,* a compendium of reviews and accompanying photographs by the editors of *The American Magazine* that appeared in the February 1906 issue of that magazine. Similarly, *Motoring in America: The Early Years,* edited by Frank Oppel, is a 476-page volume of articles (most illustrated) describing personal journeys, technical innovations, trade shows, automobile races, and the car as a harbinger of socioeconomic change, all of which appeared in various magazines during the first decade of the 20th century.

Another type of collection is best described by the main title of a book by its foremost practitioner, *Floyd Clymer's Historical Motor Scrapbook.* Clymer's "scrapbooks" are heavily illustrated with photographs and reproductions of ads and sales literature concerning the car in question, supplemented by brief essays on its socioeconomic impact. The work cited above, subtitled *Ford Model T Edition,* also includes the personal experiences of the author in selling and racing automobiles and facsimiles of articles dealing with the Model T Ford. Clymer was responsible for a number of historical scrapbooks. Other noteworthy volumes in this "series" were *Historical Scrapbook: Early Advertising Art; Historical Motor Scrapbook: Steam Car Edition*; the *Scrapbook of Early Auto Supplies and Equipment*; and *Historical Scrapbook: Motor Cars and News of 1899: Historical and Technical Articles with Photos of Early Autos.* A brief, more recent volume in the same genre is D.L. Scrimger's *Taxicab Scrapbook: A Pictorial Review of the Taxi.*

Three other volumes by Clymer also might appropriately be included here:

Those Wonderful Old Automobiles, Treasury of Early American Automobiles, 1877–1925, and *Henry's Wonderful Model T*. All three are intended to "entertain" the reader and do so with a text that emphasizes the eccentric, illustrated with hundreds of photographs, advertisements, song lyrics, cartoons, and reminiscences by the author.

More specific in that they focus on parts and supplies are Gordon Schindler's *Ford Model T Catalog of Accessories*, a collection of advertisements for "aftermarket" products, including everything from parts to improve engine efficiency to grousers for converting the Model T into a farm tractor; Victor W. Page's similar *The Model T Ford Car, Truck and Tractor Conversion Sets*, published in 1918; and the *Ballou-Wright Automobile Supplies Catalog, 1906*, which has been reprinted by the Oregon Historical Society and features supplies for over ninety manufacturers of gasoline, electric, and steam automobiles.

Similar to the scrapbooks cited above, but more contemporaneous is a group of books that are designed to serve as compilations of ephemeral material regarding a specific make of car. Within this group would be the Source Book series from Bookman Publishing, which reprints factory and sales literature (including advertisements), specification and options sheets, performance data, and so on. There are over thirty of these now in print, each covering a particular high-performance make or model in approximately 145 pages. Representative works in this series would include Robert C. Ackerson's *Mustang: A Source Book*; Scott Campbell's *Javelin: A Source Book* (Javelin was a product of the American Motors Corporation); Samuel A. Shields Jr.'s *Barracuda & Challenger: A Source Book*; and Edward A. Lehwald's *Big Chevys: A Source Book*. Other books, such as *The Charger as Only Dodge Could Build It: 1966–1969* and *1961–1969 Cutlass F-85/4-4-2: A Book of Information*, take a similar approach.

Bibliographic Works

Prior to the publication of this guide, there was no book-length bibliographic reference work devoted to the automobile and its impact on American history and life. While there are other reference volumes, one must cull the automotive items from them. The broadest of these, *Technology and Values in American Civilization: A Guide to Information Sources*, by Stephen H. Cutcliffe *et al.*, is highly recommended. Composed of citations followed by brief, but information-laden, evaluative annotations, this volume contains references to over 2,400 significant books and articles up to 1980, all of which can be accessed through one of three indexes (author, title, or subject). A similar volume is James P. Rakowski's *Transportation Economics: A Guide to Information Sources*, which contains many titles not found in Cutcliffe *et al.* but unfortunately provides less descriptive information about the books and none on the articles included and is limited to the years 1960 to 1974. The *Handbook of American Popular Culture*, edited by M. Thomas Inge, contains a chapter entitled "The Automobile," written by Michael L. Berger and Maurice Duke. All of the works mentioned therein are included in this guide, and the style and approach are identical. However, individuals interested in the car as an icon of American popular culture may find the focus of the *Handbook* chapter more useful and the relatively limited number of works more accessible. Finally, *Manufacturing: A Historical and Bibliographical Guide*, edited by David O. Whitten and Bessie E. Whitten, includes a chapter entitled "Motor Vehicles and Equipment," by Robert M. Aduddell and Louis P. Cain. It contains a concise history of the automotive industry, a bibliographic essay, and a bibliography, using the Enterprise Standard Classification system.

More specifically, there is *Motorsports: A Guide to Information Sources*, by Susan Ebershoff-Coles and Charla Ann Leibenguth, which ought to prove valuable to researchers in that area, although the items tend to be less scholarly (possibly by virtue of the subject) than the Cutcliffe and Rakowski volumes in the same series. In addition, there are Bernard Mergen's *Recreational Vehicles and Travel: A Resource Guide*, similar in concept to this guide, which provides bibliographic essays on various aspects of the impact of RVs (and boats and aircraft) on American history and popular culture, while also identifying resources for further research, and the Detroit Public Library's *Labor Relations in the Automotive Industry: A Bibliography Tracing the Development of the Subject from Beginnings through the First Four Months of 1949*. Researchers interested in auto touring during the first third of the 20th century or simply early motoring should find Carey S. Bliss' *Autos across America: A Bibliography of Transcontinental Automobile Travel, 1903–1940* particularly useful with its listing of personal accounts of such travel.

Finally, some mention should be made of the series of Vance Bibliographies. While each item is brief (as few as five pages), it could prove to be a valuable starting point for researchers interested in the specific topic. Among the titles in the series are *Architectural Design of Parking Garages: A Revised Sourcelist*, by Anthony C. White; *Automobile Factories: A Bibliography*, by Mary Ellen Huls; and *Automobile Garages: A Bibliographical Overview*, by Coppa and Avery Consultants.

Two scholarly journals, *Technology and Culture* and *Isis* (from the History of Science Society), publish yearly indexes of recently published books and articles in their broadly conceived fields, sometimes with brief annotations. The former is called "Current Bibliography in the History of Technology" and is divided according to chronological and subject classifications. The latter, "Critical Bibliography of the History of Science and its Cultural Influences," is organized by subject discipline and time period. The *Technology and Culture* bibliography generally will prove to be more useful to automotive historians, essentially because of its disciplinary focus.

There is also an *Isis Cumulative Bibliography* of books, journals, serials, and book reviews pertaining to the history of science and its cultural influence. A compilation of listings (occasionally annotated) printed in the annual "Critical

Bibliography" section of *Isis*, it has appeared in four series, a five-volume one covering the years 1913–1965, edited by Magda Whitnow; two sets of two volumes, one set for the years 1965–1975 and the other for 1976–1985, both edited by John Neu; and, most recently, a four-volume work for 1986–1995, also edited by Neu. The major bibliographic divisions for all three series are persons, institutions, subjects, periods, and civilizations. Therefore, it may be necessary to examine several of these divisions to locate all the relevant citations for a particular research topic.

The remaining bibliographic works are limited to periodic literature, but they are well done and their annotations can be of great assistance to the researcher. They include *America: History and Life*, which is now available on-line for computer searches as well as in hard copy. The great advantage of this particular reference tool is that each bibliographic citation is followed by a full paragraph description of its contents. (Incidentally, similar information for doctoral dissertations can be found in *Dissertation Abstracts*).

In addition, *Writings on American History* and *Recently Published Articles*, both publications of the American Historical Association, can be useful sources of periodical citations. The former, published now on an academic year basis, began in 1902 as a listing of both books and articles but is now restricted, as its subtitle indicates, to being *A Subject Bibliography of Articles*. Separate multiyear index volumes have been published at periodic intervals, including a 1956 volume covering the years 1902–1940. *Recently Published Articles* (RPA) is issued three times a year and lists approximately 6,000 citations per issue, culled from some 4,000 journals worldwide. While its more frequent publication schedule makes RPA more current, *Writings on American History* probably is still the more prestigious of the two.

In addition, the following contemporary, specialized indexes regularly contain items that might be of interest to the automotive historian: *Abstracts of Popular Culture, Applied Science and Technology Index, Business Periodicals Index, Index of Economic Articles, Journal of Economic Literature, SAE [Society of Automotive Engineers] Handbook, Social Sciences Index* (see the *International Index to Periodical Literature* for pieces before 1960 and the *Social Science and Humanities Index* for 1960–1974), and *Sociological Abstracts*.

In addition, articles that have been published in auto enthusiast publications, magazines such as *Antique Automobile, Automobile Quarterly, Automotive History Review, Bulb Horn*, and so on, aimed at collectors and aficionados, can be of value to the student of automotive history. Although the articles usually lack citations, and the space devoted to the photographs often exceeds that of the text, the narrative is clearly research-based and can be of assistance to researchers interested in the impact of a particular person, vehicle, motor race, and so on. (See the "Periodicals" section of this chapter for brief descriptions of these and other magazines and journals.)

Access to these publications and mass-circulation auto monthlies like *Road & Track* and *Car & Driver*, both of which regularly carry articles of popular cultural significance, can be secured by using their own indexes or two privately printed periodical guides: *Automotive Literature Index*, compiled by A. Wallace, three volumes (1947–1976, 1977–1981, and 1982–1986) of which have appeared, and *The Auto Index*, which was published every other month between 1973 and at least the mid-1990s and in yearly compilations by volume. Care should be taken in using these indexes, since the placement of specific articles under the topical headings is sometimes questionable.

Finally, bibliographic listings also can be found in scholarly journals. In some cases, they appear on a regular basis, usually annually. Most relevant are those published in *Technology and Culture* and *Isis*, both of which already have been mentioned. The British *Journal of Transport History* provides the same service, through its "Bibliography of Transport History." It should be noted that both the *Technology and Culture* and *Isis* bibliographies also are available in electronic form on the World Wide Web, through the Research Libraries Information Network (RLIN). They both appear as part of the HST (History of Science and Technology) file on the RLIN and undoubtedly are a harbinger of more on-line bibliographies to come.

Pertinent items also can be found in journals whose research interests intersect with those of the automotive historian. For instance, *Labor History* compiles an "Annual Bibliography of Periodical Articles on American Labor History."

PERIODICALS

Given the degree to which the automobile is an integral part of American life, an article on it can appear in almost any magazine or journal. Nonetheless, the vast majority of serious work appears in four types of periodicals: (1) scholarly journals concerned with technology and its impact on society, (2) scholarly journals whose focus is a discipline that can be applied to automotive studies (e.g., see *Labor History* above), (3) auto "buff" or "enthusiast" publications that regularly contain historical selections, sometimes with references, and (4) general, mass-circulation magazines with an editorial interest in the interaction of science, technology, and society. The following selective list of periodicals includes all four types, suitably differentiated, in alphabetical order.

AFAS Quarterly (1987–date) is the publication of the Automotive Fine Arts Society. It covers all aspects of automotive fine art production and business, including collector trends, auctions, exhibitions, and recent automotive art releases. Regular features include representations of original fine art (paintings, photographs, and sculpture) by early automotive artists, stories about fine art galleries around the world, and profiles of the artists themselves.

American Heritage of Invention & Technology (1985–date) is published quarterly by American Heritage, although General Motors is its founding sponsor and chief advertiser. Written for the non-specialist and aimed at a general audience, this magazine regularly publishes articles concerning the car (not just GM ones) and road in American history.

Antique Automobile (1937–date) is the bi-monthly publication of the Antique Automobile Club of America, the largest of the enthusiast organizations. This beautifully illustrated magazine runs several multi-page articles each issue, usually at least one of which is historical in nature. A book review section also is a regular feature. A cumulative index was published in the late 1970s, covering volumes 1–42 (1937–1978).

Automobile (1987–date), published by a subsidiary of Rupert Murdoch's News Corp., is aimed at the "car connoisseur" market. High-end new and classic cars are featured in articles that critically examine design and performance of those vehicles and the socioeconomic and cultural factors associated with them, including vintage car collecting.

Automobile Quarterly (1962–date) is probably the preeminent magazine for "auto buffs"—collectors, restorers, and aficionados. It is a lavishly produced, beautifully illustrated, ad-free, *hardbound* quarterly. Although the articles usually lack citations, and the space devoted to the extraordinary photographs often exceeds that of the text, the narrative is clearly research-based and can be of assistance to individuals interested in the history and impact of a particular person, vehicle, motor race, design style, technology, and so on. *Automobile Quarterly* is indexed, and 1985 saw the publication of a cumulative index covering the first twenty volumes (1962–1982). An index covering the next five volumes (1983–1987) subsequently was published.

Automotive History Review (1973–date) is the research publication of the Society of Automotive Historians. Issued semi-annually, a typical issue consists of five or six relatively brief articles. Although these articles do not always contain footnotes and/or a bibliography, they often explore topics that previously have not received extensive coverage in print and, as such, they can serve as the starting point for researchers seeking new areas to investigate.

Auto Racing Memories and Memorabilia (1982–date) is devoted to antique race cars and auto racing history before 1965. Attention is also given to restoration and collecting memorabilia. Published five times a year, it carries brief, uncited articles, usually illustrated with black-and-white photographs. Nonetheless, it can be the source of analytical ideas and hard-to-find data.

Auto Week (1950–date) is the only weekly magazine for the auto enthusiast published in the United States. It includes reports on new car road tests and test drives, profiles of automotive personalities, features on classic cars from the past, racing news, and coverage of industrial developments worldwide.

Bulb Horn (1939–date), the quarterly magazine of the Veteran Motor Car Club of America (VMCCA), is similar in concept to *Antique Automobile* above, but is generally a less valuable source for social and cultural historians, lacks the color photography, and does not have a regular book review section. It was formerly called *The Bulletin of the V.M.C.C.A.*

Car and Driver (1961–date) is one of the three major, mass-circulation monthlies aimed at the automobile enthusiast included in this list, the other two being *Motor Trend* and *Road & Track* (see below). As one automotive historian has noted: "Of the three, *Car and Driver* is the only one willing to look at the automobile with anything resembling a critical eye." Occasionally, one of the features is historically based; profiles an important pioneer, stylist, or engineer; and/or touches on the cultural impact of the motor car. A book review section examines volumes not normally included in scholarly journals like *Technology and Culture*.

Car Collector (1997–date) focuses on the hobby of collecting cars (classic, nostalgic, and postwar) and related subject matter (e.g., restoration, legal matters, auction reviews) in each monthly issue. Billing itself as "for serious collectors & hobbyists," *Car Collector* features articles on the history of specific makes and models, with at least six in each issue. (This magazine continues a previous one entitled *Car Collector and Car Classics*.)

Car Styling (1987–date) is a bi-monthly that prints wonderfully illustrated (in color) articles, simultaneously published in both the English and Japanese languages, which cover the latest in automotive design worldwide, including considerations of aesthetics, aerodynamics, and interiors. The editorial emphasis is on individual models, auto shows, and thematic pieces.

Carrozzeria (1986–date) bills itself as "the only magazine dedicated to the art of automotive restoration, coach building, and panel beating." Essentially a quarterly information and "how to" periodical, it also regularly includes articles on motoring artists and photographers and their work.

The Classic Car (1953–date) is the bi-monthly magazine of the Classic Car Club of America. Similar in concept to the other car club magazines, it merits inclusion here for its publication of histories and book reviews concerning cars manufactured during the "classic" period, defined as 1925–1948.

Collectible Automobile (1984–date) contains articles on older cars, mostly American, built during the period 1930 to 1960 and is written for collectors of the same. The focus is mostly on the history and lore of the cars themselves, but this hardbound magazine also carries features on collectible automobilia, such as nameplates, license plates, and scale-model cars, and a section of brief book reviews.

Explorations in Economic History (1963–date), formerly *Explorations in Entrepreneurial History*, is a quarterly journal of research concerned with all aspects of applied economics in their historic context and, as such, has published a number of automotive articles over the years.

History and Technology: An International Journal (1983–date), based in France, explores the diverse relationships that have existed from antiquity to the present between science and technology and the cultural, economic, institutional, social, and political contexts in which it functions. As such, it is similar to *Technology and Culture* (see below), except that it is more international in focus, frequently publishing articles with contrasting views by American and European authors and trying to foster a transatlantic dialogue among scholars.

Horseless Carriage Gazette (1938–date) is the official publication of the

Horseless Carriage Club of America, which carries material similar to that in other American club magazines, although in a tabloid format.

Hot Rod (1948–date) is the premier magazine for Americans interested in building and racing technologically enhanced automobiles. Each issue contains performance information and technical data for aficionados of street, drag strip, and racetrack competition.

Isis: An International Review Devoted to the History of Science and Its Cultural Influences (1913–date) is the scholarly journal of the History of Science Society. There are five issues per year, the last of which primarily contains the Critical Bibliography described in an earlier section of this chapter. Although the vast majority of articles deal with science, there is an occasional technology piece, and the book reviews cover the latter topic as well.

Journal of Popular Culture (1967–date) is devoted to the analysis of the multiple aspects of contemporary mass culture. The quarterly journal of the Popular Culture Association, over the years it has published a number of articles on the automobile, including a special 1974 issue devoted to it. Articles tend to be written in a livelier style than most scholarly pieces, and the topics are more down-to-earth. The book review section also can be valuable.

Lost Highways (1994–date) is a full-color quarterly publication of The Lost Highways, The Classic Trailer and Motorhome Club and features articles from "old-timers" in the industry, reminiscences and photographs from club members, technical tips on restoration, and material from the Lost Highways Trailer Archives, together with news of club meets and rallies.

Mobilia (1993–date), a monthly periodical, claims to be the first major publication devoted exclusively to automotive collectibles and the only resource that systematically covers all types of automobilia. It includes articles on toys, models, gasoline company artifacts, racing memorabilia, automotive art, literature and paper ephemera, and so on, plus market and price reports on the same for the investor and/or the enthusiast.

Motor Trend (1949–date). The comments above under *Car and Driver* pertain here as well, although this publication is more consumer-oriented. The emphasis is on describing and testing new *domestic* cars, together with pieces on automotive technology in the same type of vehicles, with a decidedly upbeat view of the products of the American automobile industry.

Old Cars Weekly News & Marketplace (1971–date) is designed for hobbyists who collect, drive, and/or restore old cars and is issued as a tabloid newspaper. While its uniqueness lies in the timeliness of its news and advertising, *Old Cars Weekly* also publishes brief, undocumented, historical articles on individual marques, plus historical photographs, including a "Wreck of the Week" from the past.

Public Roads: A Journal of Highway Research and Development (1918–date). In addition to research articles on highways and their development, this periodical publishes scholarly manuscripts concerning highway safety, road surfacing, and related topics.

Road & Track (*R&T*) (1947–date). *R&T* is the oldest and possibly the classiest of the American enthusiast magazines. The emphasis is on exotic sports cars, both European and to a lesser extent American, and on automobile racing in all its forms. Otherwise, the contents mirror those that apply to *Car and Driver* (above).

Rodder's Journal, The (1994–date) is a coffee-table-style quarterly published for the custom car and hot rod enthusiast. This well-illustrated publication is strong on history, featuring articles on specific models, engines, and various locales where rodding has been/is popular. In addition, each issue contains an extensive interview with an important personage.

SAH Journal (1969–date) is really a newsletter for the Society of Automotive Historians and was so called until 1982. Nonetheless, each of the bi-monthly issues also carries short, historical articles and brief, but useful, book reviews. In addition, the exchanges in the letters-to-the editor section and the vintage photographs also can be of interest to the automotive historian.

Science, Technology, and Society (1977–date) is the bi-monthly *curriculum* newsletter of the Lehigh University STS Program and as such is of primary interest to college teachers in this interdisciplinary area. Nonetheless, its review sections include both books *and* articles that frequently pertain to the automobile and American life. In addition, the published course syllabi are a source of materials and ideas that could be of interest to researchers.

Smithsonian (1970–date) is the monthly magazine of the Smithsonian Institution and publishes articles on the intersection of science, technology, and socioeconomic history, occasionally including ones concerned with the automobile. More often than not, these latter articles are abridgments of chapters from forthcoming books. Nonetheless, the popular culture focus of the entire magazine is in harmony with the nature of this guide, and non-related articles can provide ideas for new approaches to automotive history.

Society for Commercial Archeology News (SCAN) Journal (1978–date) is the occasional publication of the Society for Commercial Archeology (SCA). SCA is dedicated to interpreting roadside architecture and landscapes and the preservation of suitable examples. This newsletter carries brief stories on the same, which can be the source of original approaches to the study of any historical artifact, especially the automobile. Book reviews also are a regular feature.

Special Interest Autos (*SIA*) (1970–date) is a bi-monthly magazine for collector car enthusiasts. Its "driveReports" include a detailed history of individual cars; "Half-Hour Histories" provide, in terms the lay reader can understand, information on the development of important mechanical components common to all collector cars; and it regularly runs interviews with, and stories about, stylists and engineers. *SIA* covers collector cars from the 1920s through the 1980s, and is probably the best of its genre.

Technology and Culture (*T&C*) (1959–date), the scholarly quarterly journal of the international Society for the History of Technology, occasionally publishes articles on automotive topics. More importantly, its excellent and extensive book review sections and its annual Current Bibliography in the History of Technology (described in a previous section) are very useful. More than any other publication, *T&C* mirrors the approach followed in this guide, in that the former is "concerned not only with the history of technological devices and processes, but also with the relations of technology to science, politics, social change, economics, and the arts and humanities."

Transportation Quarterly (1947–date) has always been a major source of articles on traffic flow, road engineering, and related safety issues. Known until 1982 as *Traffic Quarterly*, it changed its title that year and broadened the editorial focus to include consideration of the more general field of motor transportation.

Wheels (1983–date) is the occasional journal of the National Automotive History Collection of the Detroit Public Library. More on the order of a newsletter in format and content, *Wheels* does carry brief, sometimes multi-part articles on topics of interest to historians of the automobile. In addition, it provides information on the holdings and use of the best collection of automotive literature in the United States.

Some of the magazines described above have issued reprints of articles and, in some cases, entire issues in book form. These can be useful for gaining a historical overview of the topics covered and/or the nature of the magazine itself. For example, *Collector Car Digest: Old Cars*, edited by John Gunnell, presents stories, articles, and essays originally written for the collectors and restorers who read the weekly magazine *Old Cars*; the editors of Petersen's *Hot Rod Magazine* have published *Hot Rod Magazine: The First 12 Issues* and *50 Years of Hot Rod*, the latter featuring five decades of articles and archival photographs on the cars and personalities that have dominated the hot rod performance scene; *Fifty Years of Motor Trend*, by the editors of *Motor Trend Magazine* is similar in concept to the foregoing but with a broader focus on the evolution of cars and the auto industry since 1949; David E. Davis Jr.'s *Thus Spake David E.: The Collected Wit and Wisdom of the Most Influential Automotive Journalist of Our Time* is a collection of the author's columns written over the decades when he was editor in chief of *Car and Driver* and *Automobile* magazines; and *50 Years of Road & Track: The Art of the Automobile*, edited by William A. Motta, similar to the preceding but emphasizing artwork (photography, paintings, technical illustrations, and cartoons) and advertising as well, culled from more than 500 issues of a magazine that chronicled the last half century of motor racing, automotive performance and design, and car culture in general.

Finally, despite what might appear to be promising titles, several scholarly journals have *not* proven to be rich sources of information on the automobile and its various socioeconomic impacts. Among these publications would be the *Bulletin of Science, Technology & Society, Science as Culture, Science, Technology & Human Values*, and *Social Studies of Science: An International Review of Research in the Social Dimensions of Science and Technology*.

One other group of periodicals deserves to be mentioned: contemporary special interest magazines for aficionados of a particular type of automobile or a specific marque. This category literally includes hundreds of magazines. A representative sampling of these publications, showing the variety available, would include *Auto Racing Memories, Convertible Connection Magazine, Drag Racing Monthly, 4 Wheel Drive & Sport Utility Magazine, Keepin' Track of Vettes, Model Car Journal, Muscle Car Review, Mustang Monthly, Packard Cormorant Magazine,* and *Popular Hod Rodding.* A more complete list can be found in the periodicals section of each edition of *Hemmings' Vintage Auto Almanac.* On occasion, pieces in such magazines are meritorious enough to win writing awards from organizations such as the AACA.

Trade Magazines

Although the sheer number of articles that have appeared in them has prevented an inclusion of articles in "primary source" trade magazines, a guide such as this would be incomplete if it did not at least list the more prominent ones. They can be the source of invaluable information, particularly for the early years of automobile history. Please note that many of the magazines changed their names during their publication history, frequently more than once, and that volumes and titles are frequently confused in the secondary literature and sometimes by the publications themselves. The following alphabetical list is the product of an attempt to reconcile data derived from a number of different sources:

Accessory & Garage Journal (1911–1930)

American Automobile Digest (1918–1925)
  [Continued as *Automobile Digest*]

American Chauffeur (1913–1918)
  [Became *American Chauffeur and Automobile Digest*]

American Chauffeur and Automobile Digest (1918)
  [Became *American Automobile Digest*]

American Cyclecar (1913–1914)
  [Became *Carette*]

American Highways (1922–date)

American Motorist (1909–1930)

Automobile[1] (1899–1902)
  [Absorbed *Motor Review* and became *Automobile and Motor Review*]

Automobile and Motor Review (1902)
  [Resumed title as *Automobile*]

Notes 1 and 2 (on the following page) differentiate between two series of a single periodical interrupted by one or more name changes.

*Automobile*² (1903–1917)
 [Continued as *Automobile and Automotive Industries*]

Automobile and Automotive Industries (1917)
 [Title changed to *Automotive Industries*]

Automobile Dealer and Repairer (1906–1924)

Automobile Digest (1925–1942)
 [Continued as *Automotive Digest*]

Automobile Journal (1911–1922)
 [Merged into *Accessory and Garage Journal*]

Automobile Magazine (1899–1907)
 [Merged into *Automobile*]

Automobile Review (1899–1905)
 [Continued as *Motor Way*]

*Automobile Topics*¹ (1900–1948)
 [Continued as *Ward's Automobile Topics*]

*Automobile Topics*² (1951–date)

*Automobile Trade Journal*¹ (1912–1928)
 [Combined with *Motor Age* and became *Automobile Trade Journal and Motor Age*]

Automobile Trade Journal and Motor Age (1928–1930)
 [Resumed separate *Automobile Trade Journal* and *Motor Age* titles]

*Automobile Trade Journal*² (1930–1940)
 [Merged with *Motor Age*]

Automotive and Aviation Industries (1942–1947)
 [Resumed *Automotive Industries* title]

Automotive Digest (1942–1952)
 [Became *Automotive Service Digest*]

Automotive Engineering (?–1919)
 [Merged with the *Hub* to become the *Automotive Manufacturer*]

Automotive Exporter (1919–1922)

*Automotive Industries*¹ (1917–1942)
 [Became *Automotive and Aviation Industries*]

*Automotive Industries*² (1947–date)

Automotive Manufacturer (1919–1927)

Automotive Service Digest (1952–date)

Carette (1914–1915)

Carriage Monthly (1864–1915)

Cycle Age and Trade Review (1897–1901)
 [Also known as *Referee and Cycle Trade Review* (vols. 1–19). Merged into *Motor Age*]

Cycle and Automobile Trade Journal (1896–1911)
  [Became *Automobile Trade Journal*]

Cyclecar Age (1913–1914)
  [Became *Light Car Age*]

Cycle Trade Journal (1896–1899)
  [Became *Cycle and Automobile Trade Journal*]

Cycling West (1893–1900)
  [Absorbed by *Motor Field*]

Dealer and Repairman (1902–1904)
  [Absorbed by *Automobile*]

Good Roads (1910–1931)
  [Merged with *Roads & Streets*]

Highway Contractor and Road Builder (1914–1917)
  [Merged with *Good Roads*]

Horseless Age (1895–1918)
  [Merged with *Motor World, Automotive Industries*, and *Motor Age*]

Hub, The (1871–1919)
  [Merged with *Automotive Engineering* to form the *Automotive Manufacturer*]

L.A.W. [League of American Wheelmen] Bulletin (1885–1895)
  [Became *L.A.W. Bulletin and Good Roads*]

L.A.W. Bulletin and Good Roads (1895–1899)
  [Became *Good Roads*]

Light Car Age (1914–1915)

MoToR (1903–date)

Motor Age[1] (1899–1928)
  [Merged with *Automobile Trade Journal* to become *Automobile Trade Journal and Motor Age*]

Motor Age[2] (1940–date)
  [Also known as *Motor Age for Automotive Servicemen* and *Chilton's Motor Age*]

Motor Car (1908–1913)
  [Became *Motor Life*]

Motor Field (1892–1914)

Motor Land (1918–date)
  [Title was one word, 1946–1967]

Motor Life[1] (1913–1914)
  [Merged with *Motor Print*]

Motor Print (1906–1916)
  [Became *Motor Life*]

Motor Life[2] (1917–1927)

Motor Record (1917–1932)

Motor Review (1901–1902)
  [Absorbed by *Automobile*]

Motor Traffic (1906–1907)

Motor Vehicle Review (1899–1901)
  [Continued as *Motor Review*]

Motor Way (1905–1908)

Motor West (1914–1940)

Motor World (1900–1925)
  [Continued as *Motor World Wholesale*]

Motor World Wholesale (1925–1932)
  [Merged with *Automobile Trade Journal* in 1935 after suspending publication for three years]

New England Automobile Journal (1906–1910)
  [Continued as *Automobile Journal*]

Northwestern Motorist (1916–1918)

Referee and Cycle Trade Review (see *Cycle Age and Trade Review*)

Roads & Streets (1926–date)

Roadside Bulletin (1930–1950)

Ward's Automobile Topics (1948–1951)
  [Resumed *Automobile Topics* title]

As with contemporary magazines, one occasionally finds collections of articles from these historical trade journals published in book form. For example, *Highlights of History, Twenty-Five Years with MoToR* reprints items from the period 1904–1929 that appeared in that pioneering automotive industry publication. Such collections can be useful for gaining a historical overview of the topics covered and/or the nature of the magazine itself.

Annuals and Yearbooks

A number of annuals and yearbooks were intended to be reference works at the time of their publication and have taken on added historical value with the passage of time. Included among this group would be the *Official Automobile Blue Book*, published from the midteens to the mid-1940s, which was the standard guide for motor tourists of this period, with separate editions for different regions of the country; the similar *Official Manual of Motor Car Camping*, issued by the American Automobile Association; *Facts and Figures of the Automobile Industry*, which was published by the National Automobile Chamber of Commerce and appeared in yearly editions from 1920 to 1933 and then as *Automobile Facts and Figures* from 1934 to 1975, issued by the Automobile

Manufacturers Association (see also *Motor Vehicle Facts & Figures* below); and the *Floyd Clymer Indianapolis 500 Yearbook*, the original Indy 500 annual, which was published by Clymer for the races of 1946 to 1968 and followed a book entitled *The Indianapolis 500 Mile Race History*, in which he reproduced newspaper and magazine articles describing the races during the years 1909–1941. After a hiatus of four years, the *Indianapolis 500 Yearbook* appeared again, this time compiled by Carl Hungness, commencing with a volume that covered the races of 1969–1972 and then annually beginning with the 1973 issue. Finally, the *USAC Yearbook* reviewed the racing activities of the U.S. Auto Club, including the national championship contests, plus stock car, midget, and road racing and the Pike's Peak challenge, from the late 1950s to the early 1970s.

Examples of contemporary annuals or biannuals (listed alphabetically) would include:

Autocourse, the self-professed "world's leading grand prix annual," highlights the top drivers, analyzes team performance, provides reports and statistics on each Grand Prix race, and offers technical information on new chassis and engines of the previous Formula One season. It also includes a discrete section that reviews racing in the United States.

Automobile Year, which has been published since the mid-1950s and probably is the best overall annual available, focuses on developments in the automotive industry, including the year's best cars, innovative styling and engineering, interviews with, and stories about, the people responsible for them, and reviews of the various motor sport seasons—all on a worldwide basis.

Automotive Engineering and Litigation is a yearly legal volume that emerged in 1984 as result of the growth of legislation, government agencies, and consumer groups monitoring the safety performance of auto manufacturers in terms of the design and engineering of their vehicles.

Brickyard 400 Annual, an official publication of the Indianapolis Motor Speedway, offers in-depth coverage of the relatively new, high-profile NASCAR race created for that venue, with technical data on qualifying heats and running of the 400 itself, driver profiles, and color photographs of the action during the race.

CART Official Champ Car Yearbook, formerly known as the *Autocourse Indy Car Official Yearbook* and still published by Autocourse, includes biographical sketches of the Indy car race drivers, technical reviews, internal politics and players, and coverage of all the races that compose the Indy Car World Series during the year in question

Collector Car Annual, published by *Cars & Parts* magazine, is written for the hobbyist, with features on individual vehicles, antique automobile museums, and shows and tours, plus directories of products, services, and clubs.

The 500 Yearbook refers not to the now Indianapolis Racing League (IRL)-sponsored Indianapolis race but rather to the U.S. 500, a contest held at the Michigan International Speedway. The latter was created to compete with the Indy 500 on Memorial Day when the IRL adopted a "members only" policy.

Hemmings' Vintage Auto Almanac, the premier directory to the collector-car hobby, includes over 3,100 listings for and brief descriptions of clubs, dealers, appraisers, vendors, restoration shops, salvage yards, auction houses, and individuals serving the hobbyist. There also is a special section concerning private and public museums with vintage cars in their collections and one that focuses on automotive publications (book publishers, periodicals, newsletters, etc.). Finally, there is a unique listing of "legislative watch" organizations, groups that attempt to protect the interest of the collector car hobby/industry against government actions that would reduce or eliminate the supply of old cars and parts or impose additional costs or restrictions on the road use of vintage automobiles.

Indianapolis 500 Yearbook covers what at one time was arguably the "greatest spectacle in racing," with a text and photographs that cover the monthlong preparation and details of the race itself.

Indy Review has focused since 1991 on the yearly exploits of approximately thirty-five Indianapolis Racing League drivers as they compete not just at Indianapolis but throughout the country (Charlotte, Orlando, Las Vegas, Phoenix, etc.), with statistical coverage of everything from qualifying times to finishing positions.

International Directory of Automotive Literature Collectors contains the names, addresses, and collectible interests of individual enthusiasts, commercial literature dealers, clubs, and even museums. The *Directory* is intended to encourage interaction among people and organizations that follow this hobby.

Motorsports America: The Men and Machines of American Motorsport, the only annual devoted exclusively to the American scene, includes the events, teams, drivers, cars, and technologies that defined the previous year in Indy Car, Winston Cup, Trans-Am, and CART racing.

Rallycourse is a worldwide review of championship rallying, featuring profiles and assessments of the drivers, technical reports, and results and statistics for each national, European, and World Championship race.

Ward's Automotive Yearbook, issued annually by Ward's Communications of Detroit, is, with the 1998 demise of the American Automobile Manufacturers Association's *Motor Vehicle Facts & Figures*, probably the best source of statistics on the industry and individual companies within it.

BIBLIOGRAPHY

Ackerson, Robert C. *Mustang: A Source Book.* Baltimore: Bookman Dan, 1984.

Allen, James T. *Digest of U.S. Automobile Patents from 1789 to July 1, 1899, Including All Patents Officially Classed as Traction-Engines for the Same Period.* Washington, D.C.: H.B. Russell, 1900.

Allen, James T. *Supplement to the Digest of United States Automobile Patents, July, 1899 to January, 1902*. Washington, D.C.: American Patents Publishing, n.d.

American Automobile Association. *Official Manual of Motor Car Camping*. Washington, D.C.: American Automobile Association, 1920.

American Automobile Manufacturers Association. *Automobiles of America*. 5th ed., rev. Sidney, Ohio: Cars & Parts Magazine, 1996.

American Automobile Digest, Editorial Staff of. *Motor Encyclopedia: Questions and Answers*. Cincinnati: American Automobile Digest, 1925.

American Automobile Digest, Editorial Staff of. *Motor Query Encyclopedia: A Book of Ready Reference, Answering Over 400 Important Questions Constantly Confronting the Automobile Owner, Dealer, Garageman and Repairman*. Cincinnati: American Automobile Digest, 1919.

Antonick, Michael. *Corvette Black Book, 1953–1999*. Powell, Ohio: Michael Bruce Associates, 1999.

Applegate, Howard L., ed. *Studebaker, 1933–1942 Photo Archive: Photographs from the Detroit Public Library's National Automotive History Collection*. Minneapolis: Iconografix, 1995.

Automobile Club of America. *Official Automobile Blue Book*. New York and Chicago: Automobile Blue Books, ca. 1915–1943.

Automobile Quarterly, Editors of. *The American Car since 1775*. 2nd ed. New York: E.P. Dutton, 1971.

Automobiles of 1904. Maynard, Mass.: Chandler Press, 1987.

Baldwin, Nick *et al*. *The World Guide to Automobile Manufacturers*. New York: Facts on File, 1987.

Ballou-Wright Automobile Supplies Catalog, 1906. Portland: Oregon Historical Society, 1971.

Bentley, John C. *Oldtime Steam Cars*. Greenwich, Conn.: Fawcett, 1953.

Blessing, Arthur R. *List of Books on Automobiles and Motorcycles*. New York: H.W. Wilson, 1918.

Bliss, Carey S. *Autos across America: A Bibliography of Transcontinental Automobile Travel, 1903–1940*. Los Angeles: Dawson's Book Shop, 1972.

Brigham, Grace R. *The Serial Number Book for U.S. Cars, 1900–1975*. Osceola, Wisc.: Motorbooks International, 1979.

Bruno, Leonard C. *On the Move: A Chronology of Advances in Transportation*. Detroit: Gale Research, 1993.

Burness, Tad. *Chevrolet Spotter's Guide, 1920–1992*. 2nd ed. Osceola, Wisc.: Motorbooks International, 1993.

Burness, Tad. *Ford Spotter's Guide, 1920–1992*. 2nd ed. Osceola, Wisc.: Motorbooks International, 1993.

Burness, Tad. *Monstrous American Car Spotter's Guide, 1920–1980*. Osceola, Wisc.: Motorbooks International, 1986.

Burness, Tad. *Ultimate Car Spotter's Guide, 1946–1969*. Iola, Wisc.: Krause, 1998.

Butler, Don. *The History of Hudson*. Sarasota, Fla.: Crestline, 1982.

Campbell, Scott. *Javelin: A Source Book*. Baltimore: Bookman Dan, 1983.

Cars & Parts Magazine, Editors of. *Catalog of American Car ID Numbers, 1960–1969*. Rev. ed. Sidney, Ohio: Amos Press, 1994.

Carson, Richard B. *The Olympian Cars: The Great American Luxury Automobiles of the Twenties and Thirties*. 2nd ed. Minneapolis: Beaver's Bond Press, 1998.

Casteele, Dennis. *The Cars of Oldsmobile*. Sarasota, Fla.: Crestline, 1981.

Chappell, Pat. *Standard Catalog of Chevrolet, 1912–1990*. Iola, Wisc.: Krause, 1990.

The Charger as Only Dodge Could Build It: 1966–1969. Blairsville, Pa.: Crank'en Hope, 1984.

Chevrolet: A Book of Numbers, 1953–1975. Rev. and enlarged ed. Blairsville, Pa: Crank'en Hope, n.d.

Clymer, [Joseph] Floyd. *Floyd Clymer's Historical Motor Scrapbook: Ford Model T Edition*. Los Angeles: Floyd Clymer Publications, 1954.

Clymer, [Joseph] Floyd. *Floyd Clymer's Historical Scrapbook: Early Advertising Art*. New York: Bonanza Books, 1955.

Clymer, [Joseph] Floyd. *Floyd Clymer's Historical Scrapbook: Motor Cars and News of 1899: Historical and Technical Articles with Photos of Early Autos*. Los Angeles: Automobile Magazine, 1955.

Clymer, [Joseph] Floyd. *Floyd Clymer's Scrapbook of Early Auto Supplies and Equipment*. Los Angeles: N.p., 1954.

Clymer, [Joseph] Floyd. *Henry's Wonderful Model T*. New York: Bonanza Books, 1955.

Clymer, [Joseph] Floyd. *Historical Motor Scrapbook: Steam Car Edition*. Los Angeles: F. Clymer, 1945.

Clymer, [Joseph] Floyd. *Those Wonderful Old Automobiles*. New York: McGraw-Hill, 1953.

Clymer, Floyd. *Treasury of Early American Automobiles, 1877–1925*. New York: Bonanza Books, 1950.

Consumer Guide, Auto Editors of. *Encyclopedia of American Cars: Over 65 Years of Automotive History*. Rev. and updated ed. Lincolnwood, Ill.: Publications International, 1996.

Consumer Guide, Auto Editors. *50 Years of American Automobiles, 1939–1989*. Lincolnwood, Ill.: Publications International, 1989.

Coppa and Avery Consultants. *Automobile Garages: A Bibliographical Overview*. Monticello, Ill.: Vance Bibliographies, 1985.

Cutcliffe, Stephen H., Judith A. Mistichelli, and Christine M. Roysdon. *Technology and Values in American Civilization: A Guide to Information Sources*. Detroit: Gale Research, 1980.

Dammann, George, and James K. Wagner. *The Cars of Lincoln-Mercury*. Sarasota, Fla.: Crestline, 1987.

Dauphinais, Dean D., Peter M. Gareffa, and Don Boyden. *Car Crazy: The Official Motor City High-Octane, Turbocharged, Chrome-Plated, Back Road Book of Car Culture*. Detroit: Visible Ink, 1996.

Davis, David E., Jr. *Thus Spake David E.: The Collected Wit and Wisdom of the Most Influential Automotive Journalist of Our Time*. Troy, Mich.: Momentum Books, 1999.

Davis, Greg J. *Automotive Reference: A New Approach to the World of Auto Related Information*. 1987 ed. Boise, Idaho: Whitehorse, 1987.

DeAngelis, George, Edward P. Francis, and Leslie R. Henry. *The Ford Model A, as Henry Built It: A Color, Upholstery and Production Facts Book*. Allen Park, Mich.: Motor Cities Publishing, 1971.

Detroit Public Library. *Labor Relations in the Automobile Industry: A Bibliography Tracing the Development of the Subject from Beginnings through the First Four*

Months of 1949. Compiled by Roberta McBride. Detroit: Detroit Public Library, 1950.

Drackett, Phil, ed. *The Encyclopedia of the Motorcar.* New York: Crown, 1979.

Drake, Albert. *The Big Little GTO Book.* Osceola, Wisc.: Motorbooks International, 1982.

Dyke, A.L. *Dyke's Automobile Encyclopedia.* Chicago: Goodheart, 1927.

Ebershoff-Coles, Susan, and Charla Ann Leibenguth. *Motorsports: A Guide to Information Sources.* Detroit: Gale Research, 1979.

Esquire Magazine. *Esquire's American Autos and Their Makers.* New York: Esquire, 1963.

Flammang, James. *Standard Catalog of Imported Cars, 1946–1990.* Iola, Wisc.: Krause, 1992.

Flammang, James, and the Auto Editors of Consumer Guide. *Chronicle of the American Automobile: Over 100 Years of Auto History.* Lincolnwood, Ill.: Publications International, 1994.

Flammang, James M., and Ron Kowalke. *Standard Catalog of American Cars, 1976–1999.* 3rd ed. Iola, Wisc.: Krause Publications, 1999.

Frumkin, Mitch, and the Auto Editors of Consumer Guide. *The Great Auto Trivia Book.* New York: Beekman House, 1985.

Georgano, G.N. *The Encyclopedia of American Automobiles.* New York: Dutton, 1971.

Georgano, G.N. *The Encyclopedia of Sportscars.* New York: Exeter Books, 1985.

Georgano, G.N., ed. *The New Encyclopedia of Motorcars: 1885 to the Present.* 3rd ed. New York: E.P. Dutton, 1982.

Gunnell, John. *100 Years of American Cars.* Iola, Wisc.: Krause, 1993.

Gunnell, John. *Standard Catalog of American Motors, 1902–1987.* Osceola, Wisc.: Motorbooks International, 1993.

Harding, Anthony. *Guinness: The Book of the Car.* Enfield, Middlesex, Eng.: Guinness Books, 1987.

Heasley, Jerry. *The Production Figure Book for U.S. Cars.* Osceola, Wisc.: Motorbooks International, 1977.

Hemmings' Vintage Auto Almanac. Bennington, Vt.: Hemmings Motor News, 1976–date.

Hot Rod Magazine, Editors of. *50 Years of Hot Rod.* Osceola, Wisc.: MBI, 1998.

Hot Rod Magazine, Editors of. *Hot Rod Magazine: The First 12 Issues.* Osceola, Wisc.: MBI, 1998.

Huls, Mary Ellen. *Automobile Factories: A Bibliography.* Monticello, Ill.: Vance, Bibliographies, 1986.

Inge, M. Thomas, ed. *Handbook of American Popular Culture.* 2 vols. Rev. ed. Westport, Conn.: Greenwood Press, 1989.

Kimes, Beverly Rae, and Henry Austin Clark Jr., eds. *Standard Catalog of American Cars, 1805–1942.* 3rd ed. Iola, Wisc.: Krause Publications, 1996.

Kowalke, Ron, ed. *The Standard Catalog of American Cars, 1946–1975.* 4th ed. Iola, Wisc.: Krause, 1997.

Kowalke, Ron, ed. *Standard Catalog of Ford, 1903–1998.* 2nd ed. Iola, Wisc.: Krause, 1998.

Kowalke, Ron, ed. *Standard Catalog of Independents: The Struggle to Survive among Giants.* Iola, Wisc.: Krause, 1999.

Kowalke, Ron, ed. *Standard Guide to American Muscle Cars: A Supercar Source Book, 1960–1995.* 2nd ed. Iola, Wisc.: Krause, 1996.

Lee, John, ed. *Standard Catalog of Chrysler, 1924–1990.* Iola, Wisc.: Krause, 1995.

Lehwald, Edward A. *Big Chevys: A Source Book.* Baltimore: Bookman Dan, 1983.

Letourneau, P.A., ed. *Imperial, 1964 through 1968 Photo Archive: Photographs from the Iconografix Collection of Automotive Images and Chrysler Historical Foundation.* Minneapolis: Iconografix, 1994.

May, George S., ed. *The Automobile Industry, 1896–1920.* New York: Facts on File, 1990.

May, George S., ed. *The Automobile Industry, 1920–1980.* New York: Facts on File, 1989.

McIntosh, I. *A–Z of Car Talk.* London: Macdonald Orbis, 1988.

McShane, Clay. *The Automobile: A Chronology of Its Antecedents, Development, and Impact.* Westport, Conn.: Greenwood Press, 1997.

Mergen, Bernard. *Recreational Vehicles and Travel: A Resource Guide.* Westport, Conn.: Greenwood Press, 1985.

Moloney, James H., and George H. Dammann. *Encyclopedia of American Cars, 1946–1959.* Sarasota, Fla.: Crestline, 1980.

MoToR, N.Y. *Highlights of History: 25 Years with MoToR.* New York: Author, 1932.

Motor Cars of 1906: As Reviewed by the Editors of American Magazine, February, 1906. Marietta, Ga.: Brigham Press, 1977.

Motor Trend Magazine, the Editors of. *Fifty Years of Motor Trend.* Osceola, Wisc.: Motorbooks International, 1999.

Motta, William, A., ed. *50 Years of Road & Track: The Art of the Automobile.* Osceola, Wisc.: Motorbooks International, 1997.

National Automobile Chamber of Commerce. *Facts and Figures of the Automobile Industry.* New York: National Automobile Chamber of Commerce, 1920–1933.

Naul, G. Marshall, ed. *The Specification Book for U.S. Cars 1920–1929: A Complete Guide to the Passenger Automobiles of the Decade.* Osceola, Wisc.: Motorbooks International, 1980.

Naul, G. Marshall, and R. Perry Zavits, eds. *The Specification Book for U.S. Cars, 1930–1969.* Osceola, Wisc.: Motorbooks International, 1980.

1961–1969 Cutlass F-85/4-4-2: A Book of Information. Blairsville, Pa.: Crank 'en Hope Publications, 1985.

Oppel, Frank, ed. *Motoring in America: The Early Years.* Secaucus, N.J.: Castle Books, 1989.

Pagé, Victor W. *The Model T Ford Car, Its Construction, Operation and Repair: A Complete Practical Treatise Explaining the Operating Principles of All Parts of the Ford Automobile, with Complete Instructions for Driving and Maintenance; Includes the Most Thorough and Easily Understood Illustrated Instructions on Ford Repairing Ever Published; Based on Five Years' Experience of a Ford Operator—Invaluable to All Ford Owners, Dealers, Salesmen, Drivers and Repair Men—Every Phase of the Subject Treated in a Non-Technical Yet Comprehensive Manner.* New York: Norman W. Henley, 1917.

Pagé, Victor W. *The Model T Ford Car, Truck and Trailer Conversion Sets, Also Genuine Farm Tractor Constructions, Operation and Repair: A Complete Practical Treatise Explaining the Operating Principles of All Parts of the Ford Automobile, with Complete Instructions for Driving and Maintenance.* New York: Norman W. Henley, 1918.

Patrick, Mark A., ed. *Lincoln Motor Cars, 1946–1960 Photo Archive: Photographs from* the Detroit Public Library's National Automotive History Collection. Osceola, Wisc.: Iconografix, 1996.

Patrick, Mark A., ed. *Packard Motor Cars, 1946 through 1958 Photo Archive: Photographs from the Detroit Public Library's National Automotive History Collection.* Osceola, Wisc.: Iconografix, 1996.

Rakowski, James P. *Transportation Economics: A Guide to Information Sources.* Detroit: Gale Research, 1976.

Riddle, Plummer H. *Cars of Today and Yesterday: A Cavalcade of Motor Car Names That Have Graced America's Highways since 1787.* Salem, Ohio: Selma Press, 1951.

Robertson, John D. *A Pictorial History of Chevrolet, 1955–1957: As Told through Original Factory Photos from the GM Media Archives.* Sidney, Ohio: Cars & Parts Magazine, 1999.

Rodda, Gail. *Model T Ford: Parts Identification Guide.* 2 vols. Elgin, Ill.: Author, 1994.

Rywell, Martin. *Directory of Every American Automobile Ever Manufactured: History, Illustrations, Over 2500 Car Names Along with Year of Manufacture: Complete 1912 Catalog of American Cars with Detailed Descriptions and Cost.* Rev. ed. Harriman, Tenn.: Pioneer Historical Society, 1970.

Sanow, Edwin J. *Encyclopedia of American Police Cars.* Osceola, Wisc.: Motorbooks International, 1999.

Schindler, Gordon. *Ford Model T Catalog of Accessories.* Osceola, Wisc.: Motorbooks International, 1991.

Scrimger, D.L. *Taxicab Scrapbook: A Pictorial Review of the Taxi.* Charles City, Iowa: Author, 1979.

Sessler, Peter C., ed. *Mustang Red Book, 1964¹/₂–1990.* 2nd ed. Osceola, Wisc.: Motorbooks International, 1995.

Sessler, Peter C. *Ultimate Guide to American V-8 Engines, 1949–1974.* Osceola, Wisc.: MBI, 1999.

Shields, Samuel A., Jr. *Barracuda & Challenger: A Source Book.* Baltimore: Bookman, 1983.

Shields, Samuel A., Jr. *Charger: A Source Book.* Baltimore: Bookman Dan, 1982.

Shields, Samuel A., Jr. *Identification Guide: Dodge, 1946–1985.* Baltimore: Bookman, 1985.

Smith, Mark, and Naomi Black. *America on Wheels: Tales and Trivia of the Automobile.* New York: William Morrow, 1986.

Smith, Philip H. *Wheels within Wheels: A Short History of American Motor Car Manufacturing.* 2nd ed. New York: Funk & Wagnalls, 1970.

Society of Automotive Engineers. *Glossary of Automotive Terms.* 2nd ed. Warrendale, Pa.: Society of Automotive Engineers, 1992.

Vivian, David. *Encyclopedia of American Cars.* London: Grange Books, 1997.

Wallace, Angelo, comp. *Automotive Literature Index, 1947–1976: A Thirty-Year Guide to Car & Driver, Motor Trend, Road & Track.* Toledo, Ohio: Author, 1981.

Wallace, Angelo, comp. *Automotive Literature Index, 1977–1981: A Five-Year Guide to Fifteen American Automotive Journals.* Toledo, Ohio: Author, 1983.

Wallace, Angelo, comp. *Automotive Literature Index, 1982–1986: A Five-Year Guide to Seventeen American Automotive Journals.* Toledo, Ohio: Author, 1987.

Wendel, C.H. *American Automobile Trademarks, 1900–1960.* Osceola, Wisc.: Motorbooks International, 1995.

White, Anthony C. *Architectural Design of Parking Garages: A Revised Sourcelist*. Monticello, Ill.: Vance Bibliographies, 1983.

Whitten, David O., and Bessie E. Whitten, eds. *Manufacturing: A Historical and Bibliographical Guide*. Westport, Conn.: Greenwood Press, 1990.

Wick, Douglas A. *Automobile History Day by Day*. Bismarck, N.D.: Hedemarken Collectibles, 1997.

Wise, David Burgess. *The New Illustrated Encyclopedia of Automobiles*. Rev. ed. Leichhardt, New South Wales: Sandstone Books, 1997.

World of Automobiles: An Illustrated Encyclopedia of the Motor Car. Reference ed. Milwaukee: Purnell Reference Books, 1977.

Wyman, Arthur C., ed. *Automobile Laws of the New England States, New York, New Jersey, and Pennsylvania*. Legislative Reference Bulletin No. 2. Providence: E.L. Freeman Co., State Printers for the Legislative Reference Bureau of the Rhode Island State Library, 1908.

APPENDIX 1

Selected Chronology of American Automotive History Events

The chronology that follows highlights those events that contributed to and influenced the history of the automobile in the United States. It is not meant to be all-inclusive. Instead, items selected for inclusion are those that have the greatest relevance to the narrative of the preceding twelve chapters. Thus, the emphasis below is more on the impact of the car on American society than on the engineering accomplishments that accompanied it. Readers interested in a more comprehensive chronology should see Clay McShane's *The Automobile: A Chronology of Its Antecedents, Development, and Impact*.

Unfortunately, there exists a surprising amount of disagreement regarding the specific year of some automotive developments, especially in terms of the exact dates of an invention and its subsequent practical application. This issue was further complicated when American manufacturers began to market next year's model in the previous fall. Therefore, when there is an unreconcilable chronological discrepancy among historical sources, the event is listed below under the earliest plausible date for it. Thus, the reader should be aware that there may be a variation of a year or two in the "real" date of a specific development, particularly when it is one for which the public record might be unclear or even non-existent.

SELECTED CHRONOLOGY

1870   First roads paved with asphalt

1879   George B. Selden makes a model of his "road engine" and applies for a patent on it

1891   First street paved with concrete (Bellefontaine, Ohio)

1893   J. Frank Duryea drives the gasoline automobile that he built and his brother, Charles, designed (Springfield, Mass.)

U.S. Office of Road Inquiry, later the Bureau of Public Roads, is established

Good Roads Movement begins to have impact

An Olds gasoline-steam carriage becomes the first American car sold for export (to a customer in Bombay, India)

1894   A vehicle designed by Elwood Haynes and built by Elmer and Edgar Apperson is successfully driven on the streets of Kokomo, Ind.

1895   George B. Selden is granted a patent for the automobile

First automobile *road* race, in Chicago, won by a Duryea car with an average speed of 5 mph over fifty-two miles

First American automotive trade magazines (*Horseless Age* and *The Motorcycle*) begin publication

First illustrated automobile ad in an American magazine (for Benz in *The Motorcycle*)

First auto club formed, the American Motor League of Chicago

First recorded use of a car by a doctor for a house visit (Dr. Carlos Booth, Youngstown, Ohio)

1896   Henry Ford builds and operates his first car, the "Quadricycle"

Duryea Motor Wagon Company builds and sells multiple cars of the same design, thus establishing the American automobile industry

Ransom E. Olds completes and drives his first one-cylinder gasoline car

First American *track* (dirt) race at Narragansett Park, R.I.

First reported automobile accident

French word "automobile" used in print in the United States for the first time to describe motor cars

Technical developments include the introduction of the four-cylinder engine

1897   First automobile insurance policy issued for liability against horse-drawn vehicles (to Gilbert Loomis of Westfield, Mass.)

F.E. and F.O. Stanley construct their first steam car and establish company to manufacture it

Ransom E. Olds establishes first American automobile company in the state of Michigan

Pope Manufacturing Company holds first American model preview and open house for the press

Electric hansom cab service introduced in New York City

1898   First independent and franchised automotive dealerships established in the United States

First recorded woman driver (Genevra D. Mudge)

The "Motor Carriage Exposition" held in Boston is the first American auto show

Technical developments include the first air-cooled car, the use of aluminum alloys, and the introduction of the steering wheel instead of the tiller (by 1904 the latter would be obsolete)

1899   First American factory built specifically for automobiles (Olds Motor Works, Lansing, Mich.)

First Packard is manufactured

American Motor Company, New York City, opens first American garage devoted exclusively to automotive repairs

Back Bay Cycle and Motor Company established in Boston to *rent*, sell, store, and repair automobiles

Automobile Club of America organized

Boston parks closed to motor vehicles from 10:00 A.M. to 9:00 P.M. because of fear of runaway horses

First automobile showroom opens—for Winton cars (New York City)

First report of a person killed by an automobile (Henry H. Bliss in New York City)

First recorded automotive speeding citation (New York City)

U.S. War Department buys three cars, each fitted with devices making possible alternative animal propulsion if necessary

A.L. Dyke of St. Louis opens the first automobile parts and supply business

Mrs. John Howell Phillips of Chicago becomes first known licensed woman driver in the United States

First motorized mail vehicles placed in service (Buffalo, N.Y., Cleveland, Ohio, and Washington, D.C.)

First motorized police patrol wagon (Akron, Ohio)

1900   New York City issues first driver's licenses—"engineer's certificates" (Harold T. Birnie gets the first)

New York City buys first gasoline-powered ambulance

First automotive hearse placed in service (Buffalo, N.Y.)

First National Automobile Show, featuring 300 vehicles (New York City)

The *Saturday Evening Post* carries first national automobile advertising in a mass-circulation magazine

National Association of Automobile Manufacturers founded

Alexander Winton drives his car in the Gordon Bennett Race in France, the first American to participate in a foreign meet

William McKinley becomes first American president to ride in a motor car (a Stanley Steamer)

Technical developments include the first true transmission (manual), a front-wheel drive gasoline automobile, and the introduction of kerosene headlamps

1901   Curved-dash Oldsmobile (Model R) introduced, becomes world's first mass-produced automobile with sales of 450 cars

Connecticut is first state to enact a motor vehicle law (regarding speed)

Connecticut and New York become first states to register cars; license plates are required in the latter

Oldsmobile comes equipped with the first American odometer (a Jones)

Blue Books (travel guides with directions for motorists) begin to be published

Automobile Club of America starts posting the best motor route between New York and Boston

New York-to-Buffalo endurance run shows the feasibility of long-distance motoring

Oil discovered in Texas, leading to gasoline's becoming the primary fuel for motorized vehicles

First direct-service gasoline station using a bulk storage tank opens in New York City

A car (a Locomobile) "climbs" Pikes Peak in Colorado for the first time

U.S. Postal Department issues the first stamp featuring an automobile (a Baker Brougham electric taxicab)

Technical developments include the introduction of the shaft drive

1902   American Automobile Association (AAA) is founded in Chicago

Studebaker introduces its first car

Motor Mart in New York becomes the first establishment to buy and sell used cars

First car guarantee (for 60 days)

Packard introduces the advertising slogan "Ask the man who owns one," which remains in continuous use for over half a century (until 1956)

Technical developments include the introduction of the modern radiator and the running board, and the patenting of the "H" slot gearshift

1903   Ford Motor Company is incorporated and sells its first car, the original Model A

First Cadillac car built and sold

Packard introduces its first car

Buick Motor Company organized

Ford and others are sued as infringers of the Selden patent

First trans-continental automobile trip, from San Francisco to New York, accomplished in sixty-three days by Dr. H. Nelson Jackson and Sewall K. Crocker

MoToR magazine is founded

First motorized police vehicle (a Stanley Steamer) employed by a municipality (Boston)

First automotive fire engine placed in service (Newton, Mass.)

Enclosed cars are introduced

Barney Oldfield becomes the first person to break the mile-a-minute "barrier" (traveling 64 mph in the Ford-built *999* racer)

First reported speed traps

Other technical developments include the straight-eight cylinder engine, glass windshields, all-steel bodies, tilted steering posts, and shock absorbers

1904   U.S. Office of Public Roads established, which determines that there are 2 million miles of public roads in the country but that only 154,000 of them are surfaced

The United States surpasses France as the largest producer of automobiles in the world

Henry Ford becomes the first person to exceed 90 mph in an automobile (his Arrow racer)

First Vanderbilt Cup Race held (Long Island, N.Y.)

Prest-O-Lite Company markets acetylene gas automobile headlights, making night driving feasible

Demountable tire rims introduced, simplifying the process of fixing punctured tires

Canopy tops with glass-side windows on touring cars usher in the era of the convertible

The Detroit Young Men's Christian Association (YMCA) creates the first training school for auto mechanics

National Association of Retail Automobile Dealers is organized

Other technical developments include the first simple automatic transmission, power (air) brakes, and placement of the gearshift lever on the steering column

1905   Society of Automobile (later Automotive) Engineers (SAE) is organized

First Glidden (reliability) Tour run (continues until 1913)

Cars first sold on the installment plan

Roadster and touring bodies introduced

First stolen car reported (St. Louis)

Gus Edwards composes the song "In My Merry Oldsmobile," and it becomes an instant hit and a national standard

Other technical developments include the first four-wheel-drive American car, pneumatic tires (along with the concept of the "flat"), ignition locks, tire chains, spare wheels, and folding car tops

1906   First American automobile races on a circuit track held in Narrangansett Park, R.I.; all won by a Riker Electric Stanhope

A Stanley Steamer reaches a speed of 127.7 mph, a record for steam cars that would stand for eighty years

Technical developments include the first American six, V-8, and rotary engines; asbestos brake linings; air brakes; and spring front bumpers

1907   First parkway opened, the Vanderbilt (or Long Island Motor) Parkway, a privately owned toll road outside New York City

Association of Licensed Automobile Manufacturers (ALAM) announces a formula for figuring horsepower

First twenty-four-hour American motor race held (Philadelphia)

Speed bumps appear on the streets of Glencoe, Ill.

1908   Model T Ford introduced

General Motors Company organized by William Crapo Durant

William Howard Taft is the first American president to ride in a motorcade on the day that he is inaugurated

Cadillac becomes first American car to win the Royal [British] Automobile Club's Dewar Trophy, for its use of interchangeable, standardized parts

First family transcontinental motor trip, in a Packard by the J.M. Murdocks

George H. Robertson, driving a Locomobile, becomes the first American to win an international automobile race, the Vanderbilt Cup

New York-to-Paris, 20,000-mile automobile race (won by an American team in a Thomas Flyer)

Fisher Closed Body Company organized

Technical developments include the introduction of the first American eight-cylinder engine, left-hand steering, a practical, four-wheel-drive motor vehicle, baked enamel finishes, motor-driven horns, magnetic speedometers, the rumble seat, the non-skid tire, and vanadium steel

1909   Wayne County, Mich., builds the first mile of *rural* concrete road in the United States

Alice Huyler Ramsey becomes the first woman to drive across the United States

William Howard Taft is the first President to order an official White House automobile (a White steam car)

Indianapolis Motor Speedway opens

First AAA-sanctioned championship automobile races

Cadillac absorbed by General Motors

Technical developments include the introduction of electric headlights, hydraulic shock absorbers, the electric generator, four-door bodies, and dashboard oil gauges

1910   Central Oil Company constructs the first drive-in gasoline filling station (with an island for the pumps) in Detroit

Cadillac becomes first American company to offer enclosed bodies (by Fisher) as standard equipment

First (wooden) board racing track opens (Playa del Rey, Calif.)

Armored bank cars introduced

Technical developments include the introduction of torpedo bodies, the beginning of streamlining in design, modern battery ignition, and fuel injection

1911   Selden patent case decision: "valid but not infringed," thus allowing unimpeded development of American car manufacturing companies

Automobile stocks (General Motors) first listed on New York Stock Exchange

Chevrolet and Studebaker motor companies organized

First Indianapolis 500 motor race

Studebaker becomes the first auto maker to allow purchasers to buy on credit through the company

Painted white center stripes appear on streets in Wayne County, Mich.

Technical developments include the introduction of the all-steel body

1912   Modern electric starter introduced by Cadillac (invented by Charles F. Kettering)

Standardization of screw threads, parts, and materials by the SAE

Margaret Knight and Beatrice David become the first women to design an automobile, the K-D

First motorized bookmobile introduced

First commercial car wash opens for business

Technical developments include the engine temperature indicator (thermostat)

1913   Moving assembly line production of a complete car introduced by Ford Motor Company

The number of cars registered in the United States exceeds 1 million

National Automobile Chamber of Commerce (now the Automobile Manufacturers Association) organized

U.S. Good Roads Association comes into being

Lincoln Highway Association formed to lobby for a trans-continental motor road

New Standard Oil refining process significantly increases amount of gasoline derivable from crude oil

Gulf Oil Company becomes the first American gas company to distribute free road maps

1914   Ford Motor Company institutes five-dollar minimum wage for an eight-hour day

First American production car powered by a V-8 engine (Cadillac)

Dodge Brothers incorporate and become the first American company to conduct crash tests of their cars

First "stop" sign (Detroit)

First electric traffic lights—red only (Cleveland)

First midget auto race (Culver City, Calif.)

Other technical developments include headlights built into fenders and the adjustable driver's seat

1915   Accord reached on cross-licensing of automotive-related patents

William Durant gains control of General Motors again

The "jitney" automobile, with a five-cent fare, appears as a form of "public" transportation in cities

First American production cars (Packards) powered by a twelve-cylinder engine offered for sale

Dodge Brothers employ first automobile manufacturer's test track

Cars allowed to enter Yellowstone National Park

First visible gasoline pump introduced, allowing customers to check the amount delivered

Other technical developments include variable intensity (depressible-beam) headlights and a spare tire in the trunk

1916   Federal Aid Road Act adopted, providing for the establishment of a national highway system

Good Roads Act approved, with funding for the improvement of postal and farm-to-market roads

First round-trip, trans-continental motor trip

First use of automobiles in battle by American armed forces (by General John J. Pershing in Mexico against Pancho Villa)

First Pikes Peak hill climb contest

Technical developments include hand-operated windshield wipers, the slanted windshield, rear-view mirrors, and unitized body construction

1917   Automobile manufactures stop making cars to produce airplane engines and military vehicles for World War I

Non-driving days in various places to conserve gas for the war effort

Henry M. Leland resigns from Cadillac to found Lincoln

Technical developments include the introduction of optional car heaters, push-button windowsill door locks, and rumble seats

1918   Chevrolet acquired by General Motors

Red/yellow/green traffic signal installed for the first time (New York City)

Technical developments include the introduction of white sidewall tires

1919   All states now have highway departments

A military convoy under the direction of General John Pershing travels across the United States and reveals the poor quality of highway infrastructure

First state gasoline tax (Ore.)

General Motors Acceptance Corporation formed to handle installment sales

Rolls-Royce forms a division to manufacture cars in the United States

1920   Durant loses control of General Motors for the final time

Duesenberg and Lincoln marques introduced

Postwar recession creates fuel shortages and lines at filling stations

Automotive fatalities exceed 12,000 a year

Technical developments include the introduction of the first straight-eight engine in an American production car and four-wheel hydraulic brakes

1921   Federal Highway Act passed, providing for "primary" national highways and numbering thereof

Warren G. Harding becomes the first president to ride to his inauguration in a car

First American drive-in restaurant (Dallas, Tex.)

A play entitled *Six Cylinder Love* opens on Broadway

Technical developments include the introduction of turn signals and automatic back-up lights

1922   Ford purchases the Lincoln Motor Company for $8 million

Ford becomes the first car company to sell over 1 million cars (1,216,792) in a single year

Essex becomes the first mass-produced closed car

National Department Stores experiments with a branch store three miles outside St. Louis, inaugurating the suburban shopping center

First system of synchronized traffic lights introduced (Houston, Tex.)

Motorized snowplows used extensively for the first time during the 1922–1923 winter

Automobile insurance now calculated on the basis of actual value instead of purchase price

Other technical developments include the introduction of modern air filters, the dash-mounted gas gauge, chrome-plated bumpers and grills, and balloon tires

1923   Alfred P. Sloan Jr. becomes president of General Motors

Chevrolet becomes the first marque to offer a variety of car styles for a particular model (the Superior)

Bronx River Parkway, first limited-access public highway in America, completed

Anti-knock "ethyl" gasoline (containing tetraethyl lead) is developed and marketed

First all-steel enclosed chassis (Dodge)

First production station wagon manufactured by Star

Other technical developments include the introduction of power-operated windshield wipers and foot-controlled headlight dimmers

1924   First cars bearing the Chrysler name are produced

DuPont develops quick-drying enamel paint, thereby accelerating the manufacturing process

Purolator introduces replaceable, stock crankcase oil filters

Ford manufactures its 10 millionth car

There are no electric or steam cars at the annual New York Auto Show

Other technical developments include the introduction of the electric clock in cars and double-filament headlights

1925   Chrysler Corporation organized, an outgrowth of Chalmers and Maxwell

A uniform plan for signs and street marking on all federal highways is adopted

Lincoln Highway completed from New York City to San Francisco, the first trans-continental motor route

First nationwide chain of gas stations is created

More closed cars than open ones manufactured for the first time

The Ford Model T Runabout, selling for $260, becomes the lowest-priced, mass-produced American car ever

John D. Hertz establishes a chain of "driv-ur-self" rental car offices from coast to coast

Technical developments include the introduction of chrome plating (replacing nickel) and pyroxylin paint, the latter broadening color options available

1926   Ford inaugurates the five-day week in auto industry

General Motors establishes a separate design/styling department, the first in the industry (headed by Harley J. Earl)

Current scale for measuring octane in gasoline is established

SAE introduces oil viscosity ratings

A congressional law standardizes numbering on federal highways

General Motors introduces the Pontiac marque

Technical developments include the introduction of safety (shatterproof) glass and the one-piece tire rim as standard equipment and car heaters using the hot-water by-product of the engine's cooling system

1927   Production of Model T Ford halted after nineteen years and 15,007,033 cars (a world record that would stand until broken by the Volkswagen Beetle in 1972)

Stanley ends production of its steam cars

Massachusetts becomes the first state to require that automobile owners carry insurance

The first major underwater tunnel designed for motor traffic (the Holland Tunnel) opens in New York City

The first of the serial road signs advertising Burma Shave appear

1928   Ford introduces the Model A

Chrysler Corporation acquires Dodge Brothers, introduces Plymouth and DeSoto, and becomes the third largest automobile manufacturer in the United States

Herbert Hoover campaigns for president on a platform promising two cars in every garage

Texaco becomes the first oil company to have gasoline stations in all (then) forty-eight states

Technical developments include the introduction of synchromesh transmissions and factory-installed car radios

1929   Chevrolet introduces the "cast-iron wonder," a six-cylinder engine that continued to be produced in variations until 1953

Last production steam cars manufactured (Curran and Doble)

Approximately 90% of all passenger cars are now closed models, an 80% change from 1919

Aerocar introduces the commercially produced house trailer

General Motors purchases Opel, then the largest German auto maker

Other technical developments include the introduction of the first American diesel-powered car, front-wheel drive, body rustproofing, and taillights on both sides of the car

1930 First cloverleaf highway interchange constructed (Lincoln Highway at Woodbridge, N.J.)

Cadillac offers models with V-12 and V-16 engines

Death toll on the nation's highways reaches nearly 33,000 per year

Other technical developments include power brakes and the introduction of freewheeling, the oil cooling system, and use of stainless steel

1931 Production of six-cylinder cars in the United States surpasses that of four-cylinder ones

First standard new car warranty (90 days/4,000 miles)

Altoona (Pa.) Speedway closes, the last major board track

Technical developments include the multi-beam headlight and the introduction of adjustable shock absorbers and interior sun visors

1932 Ford replaces the Model A with the first mass-produced car with a V-8 engine

Congress approves a national one cent per gallon tax on gasoline, creating a new source of revenue for the federal government

Route 66, running from Chicago to Los Angeles, is opened for traffic

Maryland becomes the first state to require car safety inspections

Technical developments include the introduction of the first automatic choke and fender skirts as a design element

1933 First drive-in movie theater opens (Camden, N.J.)

Attempted assassination of President Franklin D. Roosevelt while riding in an automobile

First car ads touting miles per gallon appear

Technical developments include the introduction of "semi-automatic" transmission and independent, coil-spring, front-wheel suspension

1934 Federal Highway Act passed, marking the onset of true road planning on a national scale

Chrysler and DeSoto introduce the first American production cars with streamlined bodies (the Airflow models)

Chevrolet manufacturers its 10 millionth car

Technical developments include the introduction of automatic transmissions with overdrive and unitized (single-unit) body construction

1935 United Automobile Workers (UAW) chartered

First parking meters installed (Oklahoma City, Okla.)

Howard Johnson begins to franchise local roadside restaurants that will sell his products exclusively and be built according to a common design

The dates of the New York Auto Show are moved from January to November to spark sales during the winter doldrums

Paul G. Hoffman becomes Studebaker president

Antique Automobile Club of America (AACA) founded

1936   More than half of all American families own at least one car

UAW employs the technique of sit-down strikes to shut down General Motors

The San Francisco Bay Bridge opens, eliminating the need for 35 million daily commuters to take the ferry to/from Oakland

First drive-in restaurant (a Bob's Big Boy) opens

Technical developments include the introduction of the emergency brake, built-in windshield defrosters, and manually retractable headlights

1937   General Motors accepts UAW as the bargaining agent for its workers

Union organizers are physically attacked at Ford's River Rouge Plant

Ford Motor Company manufactures its 25 millionth car

Duesenberg ceases production

Gearshift moved from the floor to the steering column on many models

First bank to offer a drive-up window opens in Los Angeles

Waterman Arrowbile manufactured, one of the first "flying" automobiles

Other technical developments include the introduction of windshield washers and ashtrays

1938   Modern automatic transmission ("Hydra-Matic") pioneered by General Motors

Last Pierce-Arrow is manufactured

Other technical developments include the introduction of automotive air conditioning

1939   The General Motors building at the New York World's Fair includes "Futurama," an exhibit that predicts superhighways capable of handling cars traveling at speeds of 100 mph and cloverleaf intersections

Total American car production to date passes 75 million vehicles

Ford produces its 27 millionth car; and Chevrolet, its 15 millionth

Ford introduces the Mercury marque

Technical developments include the introduction of sealed-beam headlights, flashing turn signals, a hood lock operated from the passenger compartment, and reflective traffic signs

1940   Initial section of Pennsylvania Turnpike opens for traffic—the first limited-access, four-lane, divided, automotive toll road in the United States

First urban freeway constructed in Pasadena, Calif.

First modern turnpike restaurant (Howard Johnson's) opens on the Pennsylvania Turnpike

First "jeeps" built for the U.S. Army

General Motors discontinues the LaSalle marque

1941   Congress approves the Defense Highway Act, providing planning money to state governments for trunk highways

1942   World War II causes production of civilian passenger cars to be halted (until late 1945)

Gasoline and tire rationing introduced

National speed limit (35 mph) established to conserve fuel

1943   Non-essential driving banned in seventeen eastern states to aid the war effort

1944   Federal Aid Highway Act calls for the construction of rural and urban roads and a national system of interstate highways; the funding for the latter is not provided until 1956

Sports Car Club of America (SCCA) founded

1945   Civilian passenger car production resumes

Gasoline rationing ends

Henry Ford II takes over as president of the Ford Motor Company

Kaiser-Frazer Corporation becomes first of the new postwar car companies to go into production

The Willys Universal, a civilian version of the jeep, is introduced

1946   Federal government eliminates automotive industry price and wage controls implemented during World War II

Combination shock absorber/front suspension strut introduced by General Motors (developed by Earle McPherson)

Chevrolet becomes the first company to run network television ads

Radio telephones become operational in motor vehicles

Tucker Corporation is organized; introduces cars the next year

First automatic car wash opens (in Detroit)

Other technical developments include the introduction of self-adjusting brakes, fiberglass bodies, the first modern hardtop, and vacuum-operated power windows

1947   Henry Ford dies

National Association of Stock Car Auto Racing (NASCAR) formed

Driver education introduced in schools

Technical developments include the introduction of power seats

1948   First NASCAR (Daytona Beach, Fla.) and SCCA (Watkins Glen, N.Y.) races

100 millionth motor vehicle manufactured in the United States

Cadillac introduces the first "tail fin" as a rear body design element

Technical developments include the introduction of tubeless tires

1949   First Volkswagen is exported from Germany to the United States

Federal government eliminates regulation that limited the duration of a car loan to twenty-four months

Technical developments include the introduction of disc brakes and ignition requiring key switch only

1950   Rambler (Nash) and Henry J (Kaiser-Frazer) models inaugurate new era of small or compact cars

Korean War leads to a temporary cessation of auto manufacturing

Santa Ana (Calif.) drag strip opens

Technical developments include the introduction of the first seat belts in an American car and tinted glass and the development of the puncture-sealing tire

1951   National Hot Rod Association established

Technical developments include the introduction of power steering, padded dashboards, and the pop-out windshield

1952   First Holiday Inn motel opens (Memphis, Tenn.)

Technical developments include the introduction of ball-joint front suspension and four-way adjustable seats

1953   Kaiser-Frazer purchases Willys-Overland

Chevrolet introduces the Corvette sports car

Technical developments include introduction of warning ("idiot") lights as replacements for gauges as oil pressure and generator indicators on the dashboard

1954   General Motors manufactures its 50 millionth car

Nash and Hudson merge to form American Motors

Studebaker and Packard combine into one company

Ford's Thunderbird model is introduced

The Automotive History Collection of the Detroit Public Library is opened to the public

Technical developments include the gas-turbine engine and adoption of tubeless tires as standard equipment by all American manufacturers

1955   AAA Contest Board sanctions its last stock car race; United States Auto Club (USAC) is created to perform the functions of the defunct Contest Board

Ray Kroc inaugurates the fast-food restaurant movement with the opening of a McDonald's in Des Plains, Ill.

First solar-powered car runs successfully

1956   A new Federal Highway Act provides for the construction of a 41,000-mile, toll-free, national system of interstate and defense highways, to be funded by a one cent increase in gasoline and diesel oil taxes

A trip from New York to Chicago without encountering a stoplight is now possible using toll roads

Illinois is the first state to require seat belts on all new cars sold in its jurisdiction

American Motors announces that it will eliminate the Nash and Hudson nameplates after the 1957 model year

Technical developments include the introduction of safety electric door locks as standard equipment and six-way power seats

1957   Ford introduces the Edsel marque, which lasts but three model years, losing a record $250 million for the company

Ford also introduces the first production retractable hardtop. It, too, does not prove popular and is discontinued three years later

American auto companies account for over 80% of the cars produced in the world

Technical developments include the introduction of cruise control, paper (as opposed to oil bath) air filters, and dual headlights (four-headlamp systems)

1958   Packard ceases production

Big Three auto manufacturers withdraw from factory-sponsored racing activities

Federal law requires all new vehicles to have a window sticker showing complete specifications and manufacturer's suggested retail price (MSRP)

Toyota becomes the first Japanese manufacturer to market in the United States, introducing the Toyopet Crown Deluxe

Technical developments include an automobile engine cast in aluminum, the electric trunk lid release, and the introduction of day/night (non-glare) rearview mirrors and remote-controlled side-view mirrors

1959   For the first time, foreign vehicles account for more than 10% of the new car sales in the United States

California passes first exhaust emissions control law in the country

First U.S. Grand Prix held (Sebring, Fla.)

Daytona (Fla.) International Speedway opens

Ford Motor Company manufactures its 50 millionth car

Technical developments include the introduction of the anti-theft ignition switch

1960   Eighty percent of American families own automobiles

Chevrolet introduces its Corvair model to meet the challenge of foreign imports. It is the first American rear-engined, air-cooled car

Chrysler halts production of the DeSoto, which had been introduced in 1928

Ford becomes the first auto company to offer a 12,000-mile or full-year new car warranty

Technical developments include the introduction of the first all-weather anti-freeze/coolant

1961   National Driver Register Service begins to accumulate data on individual "serious offenders"

1962   First American car powered by a V-6 engine

Positive Crankcase Ventilation (PCV) emission control valves becomes standard equipment on American cars

General Motors manufactures its 75 millionth car

The Harrah Auto Museum opens in Reno, Nev.

Other technical developments include the use of amber-colored lights for turn signals, the first fuel-injected, turbocharged, V-8 engine, and the introduction of magnesium wheels

1963   President John F. Kennedy assassinated while riding in a motorcade (Dallas, Tex.)

Chrysler becomes the first auto company to offer a five-year/50,000-mile new car warranty on the engine and power train

Studebaker ceases production of cars in the United States

Kaiser-Jeep Corporation is formed

California becomes the first state to require emission controls on new cars sold within its borders

1964   Pontiac Tempest GTO, first of the "muscle cars," is marketed

Ford introduces its Mustang "personal sports car," which achieves record sales of 500,000 in eighteen months

Mandated by federal law, front seat belts become standard equipment on all American cars

1965   Motor Vehicle Air Pollution Control Act passed, requiring emission control devices on all cars beginning in 1968

Publication of Ralph Nader's *Unsafe at any Speed*, an exposé of the American auto industry that ushers in the consumer protection movement

The Federal Highway Beautification Act becomes law

Three million Chevrolets are manufactured, the first time that number of vehicles is produced for a single marque in one year

Craig Breedlove, in his jet-powered Spirit of America, becomes the first person to exceed 600 mph on land (Bonneville, Utah)

Introduction of the first front-wheel drive production car (the Oldsmobile Toronado) in the United States since the 1937 demise of the Cord

Shirley "Cha Cha" Muldowney is the first woman licensed to race dragsters by the National Hot Rod Association and goes on to become the second most successful driver in history (after Don "Big Daddy" Garlits)

1966   National Transportation and Motor Vehicle Safety Act passed by Congress

U.S. Department of Transportation established, with cabinet-level status

First twenty-four hours of Daytona race

First Trans-Am race (Sebring, Fla.)

Ford GT40s finish 1–2–3 at Le Mans

Technical developments include the introduction of collapsible steering columns and rear seat belts as standard equipment

1967   General Motors manufactures its 100 millionth American-made vehicle

1968   Mandated by federal law, all cars come equipped with engine exhaust emission control systems and front seat belts with shoulder harnesses

1969   Chevrolet discontinues production of Corvair; and American Motors, the Rambler model

Automobile accidents account for 54,895 deaths, the worst one-year total in American history

Mandated by federal law, all cars sold in the United States must have headrests as standard equipment

Society of Automotive Historians is founded

A Ford GT40 becomes the first to win France's 24 Hours of Le Mans in two consecutive years (1968 and 1969)

1970   American Motors purchases the Jeep Corporation from Kaiser-Willys

Passage of the Federal Clean Air Act, designed to reduce pollution from auto emissions by 90% in six years

Lee Iacocca becomes president of Ford

Four-cylinder cars outsell sixes for the first time since the 1920s

1971   Chrysler enters into a cooperative marketing agreement with Mitsubishi of Japan

General Motors acquires 34% of Isuzu of Japan

Introduction of engines designed to run on unleaded fuel

1972   Volkswagen Beetle surpasses the Ford Model T sales record for a single model

Mandated by federal law, all cars come with seat belt interlock ignition systems

Technical developments include the introduction of maintenance-free batteries and electronic ignition as standard equipment and the option of fiberglass radial tires

1973   Oil embargo (continuing into 1974) by the Organization of Petroleum Exporting Counties (OPEC) leads to a quadrupling of gas prices and creates apparent shortages in some areas of the country

Technical developments include the introduction of the air bag, although it will not become standard equipment for twenty more years

1974   OPEC oil embargo ends

National maximum speed limit of 55 mph becomes law to save gas and lives

1975   Energy Policy and Conservation Act mandates that the Environmental Protection Agency (EPA) establish average fuel economy standards for each auto manufacturer and a schedule for raising mpg on an annual basis

The number of registered cars in the United States tops 100 million

1976   "Last" American convertible built, an Eldorado model Cadillac

1977   Foreign imports total 2 million for the first time in U.S. history

Big Three manufacturers "downsize" the weight and engine capacity of some full-size models

Ford manufactures its 100 millionth car

As part of the effort to reduce air pollution, catalytic converters become mandatory on new cars, and leaded gas begins to be phased out

1978   Ford fires Iacocca, and he becomes chairman of the technically bankrupt Chrysler Corporation

Volkswagen becomes the first foreign car manufacturer to produce cars in the United States (Westmoreland, Pa.)

Championship Auto Racing Teams (CART) is formed to supervise Indy-type motor racing events

Technical developments include the introduction of the first modern American production car with a diesel engine

1979   Chrysler Corporation seeks federal loan guarantees to remain financially solvent (granted in 1980)

Second oil embargo by OPEC doubles gas prices

Japanese government voluntarily agrees to limit auto exports to the United States

American Motors enters into a cooperative arrangement to co-manufacture cars with Renault

1980   Japan surpasses the United States as the world's largest producer of automobiles

Eighty-seven percent of American households own or have access to at least one motor vehicle

1982   Chrysler is the first to reintroduce convertible models, after being the first to abandon them in 1970

Renault buys a controlling interest in American Motors

First car built in the United States by a Japanese company (a Honda Accord) is manufactured in Marysville, Ohio

Checker Motors abandons the body style that it had used since 1956 (primarily for taxicabs), making it the longest-lived American car design

1983   Chrysler pays off $1.2 billion in federally guaranteed loans (seven years early)

The Alliance, the first American model resulting from the 1979 agreement between AMC and Renault, is introduced and sets a precedent for later joint projects between American and Japanese companies

Nissan's Smyrna, Tenn., assembly line begins operation

1984   First solar-powered, automobile cross-country trip

Chrysler introduces the family "minivan" model as an alternative to the station wagon, creating a new segment in the car market

New York becomes first state to mandate the use of seat belts

New United Motor Manufacturing, Inc. (NUMMI), a joint-venture of General Motors and Toyota, begins manufacturing Toyota Corollas and Chevrolet Novas in California

1985   All states have passed laws requiring a child restraint safety belt or chair

General Motors announces its intent to create a new division, Saturn, in an attempt to "start from scratch" and challenge foreign imports with the newest production and management techniques

President Reagan allows the voluntary restraint agreement with Japan to expire in the interests of free trade

Ford and Mazda create AutoAlliance International, a joint-venture to manufacture cars in Flat Rock, Mich.

Hyundai Motor America is established

Technical developments include the introduction of the federally mandated center-mounted brake light and anti-lock brake systems (ABS) as standard equipment

1986   Honda introduces its Acura line into the American market, the first Japanese luxury cars to be sold here

1987   Chrysler Corporation purchases both American Motors, which becomes the Jeep/
        Eagle Division, and Lamborghini (sold in 1993 to an Indonesian firm)

        Subaru and Isuzu begin a joint-venture to manufacture cars in Lafayette, Ind.

1988   The first Toyota (a Camry model) rolls off its Georgetown, Ky. assembly line

        Chrysler and Mitsubishi open a joint manufacturing plant (Diamond Star) in
        Normal, Ill.

        A solar-powered automobile attains the speed of 48 mph

1989   Honda Accord is the best-selling car in the United States

        General Motors purchases a 50% interest in Saab of Sweden

1990   Introduction of the Ford Explorer marks the beginning of the sport utility vehicle
        (SUV) craze

        Ford buys Jaguar

1991   General Motors introduces the Saturn, first new American marque in thirty years

        Willy T. Ribbs is the first African American driver to qualify for the Indianapolis
        500

1992   Ford Taurus is the best-selling car in the United States for the year, thus ending
        the three-year domination by the Honda Accord in that category

        Lee Iacocca retires as chairman of the Chrysler Corporation

        The first product of a joint-venture involving Ford and Nissan rolls off the as-
        sembly line in Lorain, Ohio

        Chrysler and Steyr-Daimler-Puch form Eurostar to manufacture the former's cars
        for sale in Europe

        German auto maker BMW begins construction of an American assembly plant
        in Spartanburg, S.C.

1994   General Motors becomes the first American manufacturer to equip its cars with
        daytime running lights

        Other technical developments include the introduction of non-polluting air-
        conditioning coolants

1995   Repeal of the nationwide 55 mph speed limit law

        The U.S. Postal Service issues a postcard stamp commemorating the 1959 Cad-
        illac Eldorado tail fin

        Honda sells its 10 millionth car in the United States

        Technical developments include first use of halogen infrared headlights in a
        mass-produced car

1996   Ford Motor Company produces its 250 millionth vehicle

        A Chevrolet Cavalier becomes the first American-built car to be sold in Japan
        under a Japanese brand name (Toyota Cavalier)

        General Motors announces intent to market its EV1 electric vehicle in California
        and the Southwest

1997   Chrysler Corporation introduces the Plymouth Prowler, the first of a generation
        of "retro-styled" automobiles designed to look like cars from earlier eras

Ford Motor Company ceases production of its Thunderbird model, first introduced in 1954

1998   Chrysler Corporation announces merger with Germany's Daimler-Benz to become DaimlerChrysler

Chrysler announces that the Eagle marque will not be produced after the current model year

1999   The Dodge Viper, selling for a list price of $68,925, becomes the highest-price, mass-produced American car

Ford Motor Company purchases the automobile division of Sweden's AB Volvo

2000   The Toyota Prius and the Honda Insight, both combining a gasoline engine with a battery-powered electric motor, become the first mass-produced hybrid automobiles sold in the United States

After a hiatus of eight years, Formula 1 racing returns to the United States with the running of the United States Grand Prix at the Indianapolis Motor Speedway

General Motors announces plans to phase out its Oldsmobile Division, thus eliminating the oldest continuing American automotive marque

BIBLIOGRAPHY

Automobile Manufacturers Association. *Automobiles of America*. Detroit: Wayne State University Press, 1968.

Automobilia: Trivia-by-the Week. Rohnert Park, Calif.: Pomegranate Calendars and Books, 1996.

Baldwin, Nick *et al*. *The World Guide to Automobile Manufacturers*. New York: Facts on File, 1987.

Barry, David. *Street Dreams: American Car Culture from the Fifties to the Eighties*. London: Macdonald, 1988.

"A Brief Encyclopedia of Automotive Firsts." *Motor Trend* (November 1965): 114–126.

Bruno, Leonard C. *On the Move: A Chronology of Advances in Transportation*. Detroit: Gale Research, 1993.

Cleveland, Reginald M., and S.T. Williamson. *The Road Is Yours: The Story of the Automobile and the Men behind It*. New York: Greystone Press, 1951.

Dainton, Marianne, Jennifer Mintzer, and Lindsay Brooke. "Highlights of 100 Years." *Automotive Industries* (May 1985): 161–196.

Dauphinais, Dean D., and Peter M. Gareffa. *Car Crazy: The Official Motor City, High-Octane, Turbocharged, Chrome-Plated, Back Road Book of Car Culture*. Detroit: Visible Ink Press, 1996.

Denison, Merrill. *The Power to Go: The Story of the Automotive Industry*. Garden City, N.Y.: Doubleday, 1956.

Ikuta, Yasutoshi. *The American Automobile: Advertising from the Antique and Classic Eras*. San Francisco: Chronicle Books, 1988.

Jordan, Michael. "Milestones of Automotive Progress." *Car and Driver* (December 1986): 103–107.

McShane, Clay. *The Automobile: A Chronology of Its Antecedents, Development, and Impact*. Westport, Conn.: Greenwood Press, 1997.

Motor Vehicle Manufacturers Association of the United States. *Motor Vehicle Milestones*. Detroit: Author, [1986].

Partridge, Bellamy. *Fill 'er Up!: The Story of Fifty Years of Motoring*. New York: McGraw-Hill, 1952.

Preston, Howard L. *Dirt Roads to Dixie: Accessibility and Modernization in the South, 1885–1935*. Knoxville: University of Tennessee Press, 1991.

Rae, John B. *The American Automobile: A Brief History*. Chicago: University of Chicago Press, 1965.

Raitz, Karl, ed. *The National Road*. Baltimore: Johns Hopkins University Press, 1996.

"Recounting Some Automotive Milestones during the Industry's First 100 Years." *Cars & Parts* (February 1986): 26.

Road & Track. See especially the monthly "milestones" columns.

Smith, Mark, and Naomi Black. *America on Wheels: Tales and Trivia of the Automobile*. New York: Morrow, 1986.

SAH Journal. See especially the regular "It Happened Long Ago" columns.

Wick, Douglas A. *Automobile History Day by Day*. Bismarck, N.D.: Hedemarken Collectibles, 1997.

Wright, Karen. "The Shape of Things to Go." *Scientific American* 262 (May 1990): 92–101.

APPENDIX 2

Research Collections

MAJOR RESEARCH CENTERS AND ARCHIVES

There are two major automotive history collections in the United States, both located in public libraries. The preeminent one is the National Automotive History Collection (NAHC) of the Detroit Public Library, an operation large enough to publish its own periodical, *Wheels* (see Chapter 12). The other is the Automotive Reference Collection of the Free Library of Philadelphia. Both are described in more detail below.

The NAHC claims to be "the largest public automotive archive in the world" and certainly is the biggest in the United States. Established as a separate special collection in 1944, the holdings include some 440,000 cataloged items, mostly books, manuals, automobile literature, and photographs. Representative of the variety among the special collections in the NAHC are the former research library of the American Automobile Manufacturers Association, consisting of 407,000 sales brochures, 10,000 photographs, 10,000 owner's and service manuals, the Board of Director's Minute Books of the Association of Licensed Automobile Manufactures (the holders of the Selden patent), and 14,000 periodicals; the personal and business papers of Charles Duryea and Henry Leland, among others; the Nathan Lazarnick Collection, consisting of photographs taken by Lazarnick of early national automobile shows, Vanderbilt Cup races, and Glidden Tours; the archives of the Detroit Automotive Golden Jubilee; and the George Merwin Collection of racing photographs and programs, rally maps and navigation logs, and financial records and correspondence.

The Free Library's Automobile Reference Collection (ARC) owes its genesis to a 1948 donation of automotive books and trade literature by Thomas McKean, a Philadelphia socialite and antique car collector. In the following half-century, the holdings grew to be the second largest collection of automobile literature in the United States. ARC currently boasts 32,000 original sales brochures, beginning with one for the 1898 Duryea Motor Wagon; 9,000 owner's manuals, shop repair manuals, and illustrated parts books dating from the early 1900s; and 33,000 factory photographs in its Print and Picture Collection. Worthy of special mention is the Murray Fahnestock Collection, which includes the technical writings and pertinent correspondence of the man who was technical editor of the *Ford Dealer and Service Field Magazine* from the days of the Model T through the 1950s. In addition, its secondary source materials include 7,000 books (histories, biographies, technical works, cartoon books, annual industry statistical compilations, etc.), early trade magazines (such as *The Automobile, Horseless Age,* and *MoToR*), and contemporary trade and automobile club publications.

As might be expected, the Smithsonian Institution also is a major repository of primary and secondary sources concerning the automobile's impact on American life. The Smithsonian's libraries house approximately 1,200,000 books, 15,000 periodicals, and an extensive collection of manufacturer's trade literature and catalogs. One of the institution's self-proclaimed areas of strength is the history of science and technology, which obviously includes cars and roads/ highways. There also is a large collection of historic photographs in the Archives Center of the National Museum of American History, with 400 *cataloged* images featuring automobiles and *many* more in which librarians have not noted the motor car's presence.

Finally, mention needs to be made of the Still Picture Branch of the National Archives. A combination of records from federal departments, agencies, and bureaus, together with a relatively small collection of donated materials, forms probably the finest visual record of American life in the 20th century. Some 6 *million* images are on file. However, since the "record groups" are organized by government agencies, and none of the latter have been exclusively concerned with the motor car, the records do not readily lend themselves to easy access by researchers seeking pictures of automobiles. Nonetheless, some very valuable period photographs can be found by searching through the files of those agencies whose work is tangentially concerned with motorization, for example, the Records of the Bureau of Public Roads. Such photographs can be valuable not just for illustrative purposes but as historical artifacts that can be "read" as primary source materials.

CORPORATE COLLECTIONS

Each of the Big Three American auto makers has a significant collection of papers, photographs and illustrations, and memorabilia concerning the various marques that have been and are manufactured by their corporations. Unfortunately, access to these archival materials is not as easy as one might hope, although well-credentialed individuals are normally granted permission to use the collections. The reluctance on the part of the companies seems to stem from concerns regarding "investigative reporters" and the possibility of subsequent lawsuits in our increasingly litigious society. These concerns also sometimes manifest themselves in a company's insistence that its lawyers be allowed to review and edit manuscripts prior to publication that are based on material from their corporate archives. Nonetheless, the mere development and maintenance of archives by DaimlerChrysler, Ford, and General Motors augur well for future historians, and there are signs that company policies are becoming more accommodating in this regard.

For instance, in 1999 General Motors opened the Oldsmobile/GM Heritage Center in Lansing, Michigan. The first floor of that center features a chronological series of displays portraying Oldsmobiles produced in successive eras, each of which is illustrated by a representative car, artifacts, and documents from that time. Of greater value to the researcher is the second floor, which houses the Oldsmobile History Center with its vast company records, photographs, memorabilia, artifacts, and miscellaneous documents, including the 1880s papers of founder Ransom E. Olds.

In addition, the corporate archives of several companies that have ceased production still exist and are available to the researcher. For instance, the Studebaker Archives Center of the Studebaker National Museum, located in South Bend, Indiana, houses the records of a company that originally made horse-drawn carriages and was a major American automotive manufacturer until 1963. Its holdings include the corporate correspondence and papers of the various company presidents, the financial records, and legal documents, together with illustrative material (advertisements, photographs, and films) describing Studebaker products during its 114-year existence.

COLLEGE AND UNIVERSITY COLLECTIONS

College and university libraries can be rich sources of automotive literature. Notable automotive reference collections there are generally the outgrowth of the gift of items by one or more individuals, companies, or groups to the facility.

The best of these collections is the Archives of Labor and Urban Affairs at the Walter P. Reuther Library of Wayne State University in Detroit, which emphasizes the documentation of the history of automobile workers and their union. In addition to papers and collections dealing with the lives of the Reuther brothers (Roy, Victor, and Walter) and the emergence and growth of the United Automobile Workers (UAW), the archives have extensive material concerning issues affecting female and African American membership in the union, the study of workers in the context of community as shown in the records of Michigan UAW locals, and, ironically, the history of the auto companies themselves, among other topics. The archives also include an outstanding collection of oral histories, still photographs, audiotapes, and films that mirror the archives' manuscript holdings and date from the early 1900s to the 1980s. A library component of the archives houses related books and an extensive collection of labor journals and newspapers, including UAW publications on the national, regional, and local level.

The University of Michigan, as one might suspect, also has extensive holdings within the Transportation History Collection (THC) of its Special Collections Library in Ann Arbor. The THC consists of 70,000 items, including books, pamphlets, brochures, guidebooks, manuscripts, photographs, and prints, mostly from the late 19th and early 20th centuries. The subjects of automobiles and auto races are two of the strengths of the collection, which includes the archives of the Lincoln Highway Association and the Pierce-Arrow Company, together with the papers of Roy D. Chapin Jr.

The Popular Culture Library, one of the special collections housed in the Jerome Library of Bowling Green [Ohio] State University, describes itself as "the largest and most comprehensive research facility in the United States dedicated exclusively to the acquisition and preservation of primary research materials on 19th and 20th century American popular culture." Although automotive history per se is not one of the library's areas of strength, its extensive collections of popular and juvenile/young adult fiction; materials documenting recreation and leisure pursuits, including travel brochures; and literature concerning the performing arts could be of value to researchers interested in further pursuing the subjects covered in Chapters 7 and 8 of this guide.

Other notable, but more specialized, collections are located at Northwestern University (Evanston, Illinois), where the Transportation Library includes significant holdings devoted to highway and police administration, as part of a larger collection dealing with the socioeconomic aspects of the various types of transportation; the previously mentioned Wayne State Library, which also houses the System on Automotive Safety Information Collection, consisting of some 200,000 items related to, and analyzing the impact of, motor vehicles, drivers, and traffic engineering on automotive safety, together with material concerning the automobile's contribution to air pollution; Kettering University (Flint, Michigan), the depository for the ground vehicle papers of the Society of Automotive Engineers (SAE); the University of Wisconsin—Stout (Menonomie) library, which boasts two special collections that are pertinent to this guide: trade publications of (1) members of the American Hotel and Motel Association and (2) fast-food operations as part of a more general concentration in travel, tourism, and hospitality; and the University of Wyoming (Laramie), where the American Heritage Center includes an archival and research collection on transportation history.

Also of interest are two university media collections. One, the Ford Rouge Complex photographs housed at the Princeton University art museum in New Jersey, is a series of over 100 images taken between 1991 and 1995 by Michael Kenna. They were donated by the Ford Motor Company to the university in 1998 and feature views of the company's first manufacturing facility built for mass production, a complex designed by the preeminent industrial architect Albert Kahn. The other is the Oral History Research Center at Indiana University

(Bloomington), which contains tapes of Indiana autoworkers, especially those who worked at the Studebaker plant in South Bend.

Finally, as might be expected, the library holdings of major American universities can fulfill the reference needs of most researchers and occasionally provide specialist information as well. In this category would fall the resources of such facilities as the Widener Library of Harvard University, the Sterling Library at Yale, the Perry-Castaneda Library of the University of Texas at Austin, and the Young Research and Rosenfeld Management Libraries of the University of California, Los Angeles.

PUBLIC MUNICIPAL LIBRARIES

In addition to the major research collections of the Detroit Public Library and the Free Library of Philadelphia (described above), the public libraries of most large cities, especially in the Northeast, Midwest, and California, have significant holdings, though not necessarily special collections. Especially noteworthy in this regard are the New York [City] Public Library, the Los Angeles Public Library, and the Chicago Public Library. The Los Angeles County Museum of Natural History, besides displaying a small collection of historic cars, also has an impressive collection of research materials and photographs in the automotive history section of its library. In addition, the Indianapolis–Marion County [Indiana] Public Library has an Indianapolis 500 Auto Race Collection, which includes official programs and yearbooks from the Indianapolis Motor Speedway, covering the years 1909 to the present (with some gaps).

MUSEUMS

The evolution of the automobile as a cultural artifact has made it the focus of over 200 museums in the United States. Most of these display "only" a collection of antique cars and are of limited use to the researcher except in the sense of providing visual evidence in support of theories or conclusions that he or she wishes to make. The most complete listing of such facilities can be found in *Automobile Quarterly's Directory of North American Automobile Museums*, edited by John Heilig, which includes a brief description of each, including unique aspects of the collection.

However, some notable museums supplement their car displays with the type of archives that might prove more valuable to the automotive researcher. Arguably the best of this group is the Henry Ford Museum and Greenfield Village, a personal testament to the positive impact of industrialization and personal initiative on the development of American society. Not surprisingly, the museum owns one of the best (though not the largest) collections of automobiles in the United States. Numbering over 200 vehicles, these are displayed on a rotating basis in the transportation wing of the museum, along with a major exhibit entitled "The Automobile in American Life," which shows the multiple influences of the motor car on life in the United States.

The Henry Ford Museum's Library and Department of Archives contain extensive holdings in the broad area of popular culture, the primary one being the Automotive History Collection. The library has a large collection of books, trade catalogs, travel guides, and periodicals. The archives house the records of the Ford Motor Company through 1950; the correspondence and personal photographs of Henry and Clara Ford and other members of the family; the letters of Charles E. Sorensen; and the papers of several significant automotive designers. There also is an impressive collection of oral histories, consisting of interviews with employees, friends, acquaintances, and relatives of Henry Ford; automotive product literature from most American and some foreign companies; and automobile advertising and promotional material. Of special interest is the Prints and Photographs Collection of over 350,000 photographs, architectural drawings, and advertisements related to the Ford Motor Company and to Henry Ford himself in the period to 1950, as well as to the Autocar Company.

Second in importance to the Henry Ford Museum is the National Automobile Museum in Reno, Nevada, which shows some 220 historic vehicles (including the Thomas Flyer that won the 1908 New York-to-Paris race) and special-interest cars saved from William Fisk Harrah's original collection of over 1,500. Period street scenes and clothing displays are interspersed among automobiles that are arranged by decades. Visitors also can observe a working restoration shop, and there is a theater showing multi-media presentations on various aspects of American automotive history.

An extensive automotive research library, dating to the early 1950s, also is located in the National Automobile Museum complex. The library houses book monographs and automotive encyclopedias, trade journals, service manuals, owner's manuals, photographs and negatives, and miscellaneous historic records. In addition, there are a number of special collections, including 2,155 pieces of memorabilia from the aforementioned 1908 New York-to-Paris race.

The Blackhawk (formerly Behring) Auto Museum (Danville, California) like the National Automobile Museum, owes its origins to the collective efforts and financial support of a single individual—Kenneth Behring. Concentrating on unique and custom-built vehicles, some known for their owners and others for their feats, the Blackhawk Museum displays approximately 120 of these American and European cars. The museum is unique in that it now has a permanent exhibit entitled "Moving Inspiration: Artistic Interpretations of the Motor Age," in which portions of the most extensive collection (approximately 1,000 items) of automotive art in the United States are displayed on a rotating basis in a gallery specifically designed for it. Most of the pieces came from the Raymond E. Holland Automotive Art Collection, which was purchased in toto and moved from Allentown, Pennsylvania, to California to become the Blackhawk Automotive Art Collection in the mid-1990s. The museum also boasts the W. Everett Miller Automotive Research Library, one of the more extensive in the United

States. Its holdings are particularly rich in materials concerning American automotive styling and design in the custom coach building era (ca. 1925–1933).

Three of these combination museum/archives are more specifically focused on the history of one contemporary American manufacturer. The Walter P. Chrysler Museum, located at the DaimlerChrysler headquarters in Auburn Hills, Michigan, is the first museum to be owned and operated by an American car company. It was formally opened in 1999 as a tribute to the man who founded the Chrysler Corporation some seventy-five years earlier. It has a rotating exhibit of seventy-five vehicles (out of a total of 130 plus), as well as an archive and research area. The latter is particularly significant in that the Chrysler Archives are publicly accessible, something that none of the Big Three American manufacturers previously allowed. The holdings of the museum archives are particularly strong in terms of documents pertaining to the technical specifications and marketing of historic Chrysler vehicles. The archives are part of the DaimlerChrysler Corporate Historical Collection, the latter based in Highland Park, Michigan, and including documents, manuals, production information, photographs, advertisements, and audiovisual materials relating to Chrysler and its ancestor companies.

The Alfred P. Sloan Museum (Flint, Michigan) goes beyond Sloan's years at General Motors to showcase the full history of the company, especially as it relates to the city of Flint and the Chevrolets and Buicks produced there. In specially themed exhibits, such as "Flint and the American Dream," the museum portrays auto-related developments from the beginnings of the industry until now. In addition, the Sloan Museum possesses possibly the finest collection of prototype and experimental cars from General Motors, including the first in that category—the 1939 Buick Y Job. The museum also contains an archives of over 100,000 items, featuring sales literature, original factory photographs, blueprints, repair manuals, and other materials, primarily (but not exclusively) connected with the development of Buick and Chevrolet. Of special significance is the Perry Archives, home to an extensive collection of Buick engineering papers.

The R.E. Olds Transportation Museum (Lansing, Michigan) features cars constructed in that city since 1897 in displays that emphasize the importance of central Michigan in the development of the auto industry. Not surprisingly, Oldsmobiles and REOs dominate the collection. In fact, the museum claims to have "the largest collection of museum quality Oldsmobiles in the world." Nonetheless, there are other Lansing-manufactured makes on exhibit, including Star, Durant, and Bates. Nearby the museum complex is the Oldsmobile Heritage Center (see above), which houses Oldsmobile company records from its founding in the 1880s by Ransom E. Olds to the present, along with representative vehicles and related memorabilia.

The last museum in this category worthy of note is the National Corvette Museum (Bowling Green, Kentucky), a privately owned facility that displays some fifty Corvettes, dating from their introduction in 1953 to the present, in period settings, together with a collection of concept cars. In addition, the museum incorporates the Bill Mitchell Library, which has as its mission to become the prime repository of materials concerning the technical and stylistic development, historical evolution, and sociocultural impact of the Corvette.

There also are several museums devoted to displaying the automobiles of companies that have ceased to exist. Among the better ones is the Auburn-Cord-Duesenberg Museum in Auburn, Indiana. It is located in a former Auburn administrative building and factory showroom of 1930 art deco design, which is listed in the National Register of Historic Places. Beside exhibiting approximately 115 of the 1930s luxury cars that bore the Auburn, Cord, or Duesenberg nameplate, the museum has a collection of classic, antique, and special interest cars, clothing, and memorabilia. There are eight exhibit galleries, including re-created auto design and clay model studios and workers' offices. The Tri Kappa Collection of Automotive Literature contains over 50,000 items, primarily sales brochures and service manuals for Auburn, Cord, and Duesenberg and other cars built in Auburn. Furthermore, there are corporate correspondence and papers; styling drawings, watercolors, and photographs; and periodicals of the period. Finally, the Raymond Wolff Collection contains almost 1,000 original negatives from the Advertising Department of the Auburn Automobile Company, spanning the years 1925–1937.

Similar in some respects to the aforementioned is the Studebaker National Museum (South Bend, Indiana) which has over seventy vehicles on permanent display in two locations, one of which was constructed in 1919 at the site of the company's largest dealership. The collections span the company's rich and lengthy history, from 19th-century, horse-drawn wagons and carriages to Packards produced in the years of the ill-fated Studebaker–Packard merger. In addition, the Studebaker Corporate Archives are part of the museum, featuring one of the most complete collections of that type in the United States, including the company records, ledgers, notebooks, advertising materials, photographs, films, and audiotapes. In 1993 the museum won the SAH's James J. Bradley Distinguished Service Award for "exemplary efforts in preserving historical materials relating to the world's motor vehicles."

Finally, there is the Towe Auto Museum (Sacramento, California), a project of the California Vehicle Foundation. Its mission is "to serve the public by teaching automotive history and its socioeconomic influence through collecting, preserving, exhibiting, and interpreting automotive artifacts and memorabilia." In addition to displaying some 160 vehicles in thematic exhibits, the museum has a Research Library and Archive Center, featuring the Frank Klock Memorial Automotive Library (with 10,000 items), the Ford Life Photo Negative Files (containing 1,250 negatives), periodicals (1940s–present), new car brochures (1930s–present), car club publications, after-market supplier catalogs, and service and repair manuals.

Independent Thematic Museums

Of the remaining privately owned museums, most fall into the "parking lot" variety, existing primarily to display automobiles. However, some take their mission one step further, and in addition to providing data on the cars on exhibit, they attempt to show the collective influence of the motor car on American life. Probably the best in this category is the Petersen Automotive Museum in Los Angeles. The 1999 edition of *Hemmings' Vintage Auto Almanac* calls it the "largest, most definitive automotive museum in North America." Its self-proclaimed mission is "to explore the history of the automobile and its impact on American life, using Los Angeles as our primary example." As such, the first floor features seventeen dioramas (or scenes) that portray the car's evolving influence on the social, economic, and cultural aspects of American lives, with a special focus on those people residing in Southern California. The museum has identified five areas of automotive influence for special attention: how people travel, how people live, how people consume, how people play, and how government actions have affected motorists. In addition, there are smaller exhibits on a variety of more narrowly defined topics, ranging from correlations between population densities and mode of transportation, to the car's impact on the evolution of the roadside billboard, to cars owned by motion picture stars. A second floor is devoted to a more traditional display of automobiles from the museum's collection. The third floor features automotive artworks (paintings, sculptures, and collages) by members of the Automotive Fine Art Society and exhibits of petroliana.

A second museum in this category is the Frederick C. Crawford Auto-Aviation Museum in Cleveland. Run by the Western Reserve Historical Society, it has approximately 150 cars on display portraying the evolution of the automobile since 1895, plus a working restoration shop open to visitors and an extensive library of new car brochures, service manuals, photographs, and periodicals related to the evolution of both the car and the airplane. The emphasis throughout is on Cleveland and Ohio as centers of automotive production until the depression, home to such cars as Peerless and Winton, the Baker electric, and the White steamer. The Crawford Museum was the recipient of the SAH's 1998 James J. Bradley Distinguished Service Award.

In addition, there is the Museum of Transportation in Brookline, Massachusetts, a suburb of Boston, which is probably the best car museum in New England. Located in a Victorian carriage house that is listed in the National Register of Historic Places, its rotating exhibits are designed to show the automobile's impact on American lives in a particular era of U.S. history, in a setting that includes artifacts, music, photographs, and film from that period.

Arguably the best of the American museums devoted to motor racing is the gigantic (100,000-square-foot) Indianapolis Motor Speedway Hall of Fame Museum. Located in the infield of the two-and-a-half mile Indianapolis Motor Speedway oval track, it features 125 memorable racing cars from the past, an extensive collection of historical photographs pertaining to the speedway, and car and driver memorabilia from 1911 to the present. Other facilities in this category would include the Stock Car Hall of Fame and Museum (Darlington, South Carolina), which houses what purports to be the world's largest collection of stock car racers, organized to show their evolution, with special attention to those that achieved fame at the Darlington Raceway, and a special exhibit of NASCAR-designated illegal and outlawed parts and engines; the National Hot Rod Association's Motorsports Museum (Pomona, California), which showcases some sixty cars from Model T roadsters, to today's Top Fuelers, including many history-making vehicles, plus memorabilia, classic photographs, and period literature; and The Don Garlits Museum of Drag Racing (Ocala, Florida), which through design engineering exhibits, memorabilia, and a display of approximately 100 cars traces the evolution of a motor sport that "Big Daddy" made famous during his thirty-year career.

With a few notable exceptions, museums have not emerged to showcase the lives of automotive luminaries. The most significant one in this regard is the Elwood Haynes Museum (located in his former home in Kokomo, Indiana), a memorial to the life and career achievements of the multifaceted inventor that some view as having developed the first (1894) commercially successful automobile in the United States. In addition to displaying personal and business artifacts, the museum showcases a few significant Haynes and Haynes-Apperson cars and houses the papers and records of Haynes and his various companies.

In conclusion, it should be noted that car museums are numerous enough to have called into being a National Association of Automobile Museums (NAAM). The association's mission is to link such museums so that they can share exhibits, exchange information about the vehicles in their collections, and generally foster their educational objectives.

MISCELLANEOUS HOLDINGS

The widespread impact of the automobile on American life has led to the development of a number of atypical research facilities. Several of these are affiliated with associations of automotive enthusiasts. Premier among this group would be the Library and Research Center of the Antique Automobile Club of America (AACA), located in Hershey, Pennsylvania. Its collection includes over 4,000 books, thousands of early automotive periodicals and 210 current ones, sales literature, shop and owners' manuals, annual reports, photographs, automobiliana (e.g., sheet music, postcards, calendars, cartoons and jokes), and even color chips!

Another memorable collection is that of the Horseless Carriage Foundation, which has moved its Automotive Research Library to La Mesa, California, with holdings that focus on the years 1895 to 1943. Originally established in 1985 and located at the San Diego Automotive Museum, its goal is "to make automotive research and restoration information readily available to hobbyists, restorers, and scholars world wide." The library houses books, periodicals, business correspondence, sales literature, manuals, and original drawings. More specifically, it incorporates the Richard A. Teague Literature Collection, containing the papers of the renowned car stylist who worked for General Motors, Chrysler, Packard, and American Motors; the Art Twohy Collection of Pre-1916 Literature; and the archives of the Horseless Carriage Club of America.

One other enthusiast facility is the Automobile Club of Southern California's Corporate Archives. The archives are designed to preserve documents and illustrations that pertain to that organization, especially as they relate to socioeconomic and political developments that have impacted on the automobile and highways since the club was founded in 1900. The collection is composed of reports, studies, periodicals, tour books, photographs and films, maps, and memorabilia. It is especially strong in the area of road engineering and construction, housing the Ernest East Collection.

Two independent research facilities also are worthy of mention in this section. The American Automobile Association Library (Heathrow, Florida) focuses, as one might expect, on the history and development of this nation's highway system. Although the collection is a broad one, it is particularly strong in highway maps, historic photographs, and related periodicals such as the *American Motorist* and the *AAA Blue Books* series, both of which began in 1909. The Watkins Glen (New York) Motor Racing Research Library opened in 1999, with a reference collection of books and periodicals concerning drivers, cars, races, and the history of motor racing; photographs, films, videos, and oral histories pertaining to the same; and an archives for rare books, the personal papers of drivers, journalists, and authors, plus corporate and club records and race program and posters.

A resource of a different kind is the Automotive Hall of Fame (AHF) in Dearborn, Michigan. Founded in 1939, the AHF attempts to interpret the lives of people who have been instrumental in developing the global motor vehicle industry. Interactive exhibits focus not only on the "titans" associated with entire companies or significant vehicles, but also lesser-known people whose achievements in parts, processes, or concepts have warranted their induction. The Hall of Fame also houses a large collection of automotive literature and photographs, including the private papers of many of the inductees and the archives of several small, auto-related companies.

Finally, mention needs to be made of two specialized collections. The Curt Teich Postcard Archives, located at the Lake County Museum (Wauconda, Illinois), is the nation's largest public collection of postcards and related materials (over 375,000 cataloged images), built around the industrial archives of the Curt Teich Company of Chicago, which printed view and advertising postcards from 1898 to 1978. Among its special collections are ones dealing with Route 66 and the Lincoln Highway. There also is a reference library, with significant collections of books and periodicals concerning the American roadside and American popular culture. The combined Gilmore/Classical Car Club of America Museum

(Hickory Corners, Michigan) has what is probably the world's largest display of hood ornaments or "mascots." The Gilmore Car Museum collection features 532 of them, and the Classic Car Club of America Museum has 708. (This is in addition to over 140 vehicles on exhibit.)

NATIONAL HERITAGE AREAS

As a concluding note, Congress has the authority to designate a National Heritage Area, "where outstanding natural, cultural, scenic, aesthetic and recreational resources combine to form a nationally distinctive landscape, which tells the story of its residents." Such areas are affiliated with the National Park System and can be granted up to $10 million on a 50/50 match basis over a period of ten years. Thus, federal legislation was enacted in 1998 creating the Automobile National Heritage Area of Michigan. Dearborn, Detroit, Flint, Lansing, and Pontiac have been designated as constituting this area, in which efforts are being made to preserve, restore, and provide an interpretive educational program for structures and resources associated with the history of the American automobile. Among the facilities that are expected to be financially supported are automotive museums and historic manufacturing sites in the area. Similarly, in 1999 Congress approved the Route 66 Corridor Act with the goals of studying, preserving, rehabilitating, and restoring the cultural and commercial resources of the celebrated highway that ran from Chicago to Los Angeles. In a sense, it will become the nation's largest outdoor museum.

BIBLIOGRAPHY

Burger, Barbara Lewis, ed. *Guide to the Holdings of the Still Picture Branch of the National Archives*. Washington, D.C.: National Archives and Records Administration, 1990.

Eves, Edward, and Dan Burger. *Great Car Collections of the World*. New York: Gallery Books, 1986.

Geist, Christopher D. *et al. Directory of Popular Culture Collections*. Phoenix: Oryx Press, 1989.

A Guide to the Archives of Labor History and Urban Affairs, Detroit: Wayne State University Press, 1974.

Haeseler, Rob. *The Behring Collection: A Representative Selection*. Blackhawk, Calif.: Behring Educational Institute Press, 1988.

Heilig, John, ed. *Automobile Quarterly's Directory of North American Automobile Museums*. Kutztown, Pa.: Automobile Quarterly Publications, 1992.

Hemmings' Vintage Auto Almanac: 1999 Edition. Bennington, Vt.: Hemmings Motor News, 1998.

Lee, Allan E. *American Transportation: Its History and Museums*. Charlottesville, Va.: Hildesigns, 1993.

Modoc Press, comp. *Special Collections in College and University Libraries*. New York: Macmillan, 1989.

Oliver, Smith, H., and Donald H. Berkebile. *The Smithsonian Collection of Automobiles and Motorcycles*. Washington, D.C.: Smithsonian Institution Press, 1968.

Rasmussen, Henry. *A Century of Style: Imperial Palace Auto Collection, Las Vegas, Nevada*. Osceola, Wisc.: Motorbooks International, 1990.

Taylor, William R. *Auto Museum Directory USA Supplement, with Canadian Museums*. Butte, Mont.: Editorial Review Press, 1989.

Truesdell, Bill, comp. *Directory of Unique Museums*. Phoenix: Oryx Press, 1985.

Upward, Geoffrey C. *A Home for Our Heritage: The Building and Growth of Greenfield Village and Henry Ford Museum*. Dearborn, Mich.: Henry Ford Museum Press, 1979.

Wamsey, James S. *American Ingenuity: Henry Ford Museum and Greenfield Village*. New York: Abrams, 1985.

Author Index

Compiled by Marie T. Gallagher, Arcadia University.

Subject Index

Adams, G.E. ("Bud"), 116

Adams, John, 220

Advertising, xxiii, 21–22, 83–87, 89–90, 125, 130, 205, 210, 217–20, 231, 382, 431, 434, 436; roadside serial signs (Burma-Shave), 84; sponsorship of transcontinental trips by early manufacturers, 7, 86; and women, 150

Aero cars, 290

African Americans, xxiv, 89, 156, 319, 431; as auto industry workers, 79–80, 156–57, 182–83, 319, 431; automotive guide books for, 244; community building in Detroit, 182. *See also* Race relations

Air bags, 364

Air conditioning, 125, 163

Air pollution, xxv–xxvi, 15, 106, 109, 328, 350–53, 361, 364–65, 432; emissions testing, 359

Air suspension, 115

Airflow model cars (Chrysler), 119

Airstream (trailer), 187, 249

Alabama cites and state, 208

Alaska cities and state, 331; Alaska Road Commission, 331

Alaska (Alcan) Highway, 325

Alexander, Jesse, 216

AM General Hummer car. *See* Hummer vehicles

Ambulances, 192–93, 316–17, 350

American Association for Highway Improvement, 322

American Association of State Highway and Transportation Officials, 321, 324, 327, 331

American Automobile Association: Contest Board, 280; library, 439

American Automobile Manufacturers Association, 377; research library, 429

American Bantam car, 164

American culture. *See* Architecture, visual arts, and music; Film, radio, and television; Literature and language

American Enterprise Institute for Public Policy Research, 351–52

American Hotel and Motel Association, 432

American Motors cars, 86, 127, 290, 379, 385

American Motors Corporation, 13, 21, 24, 48, 86; attempt to produce Jeeps in China, 93; merger creating, 15

American Road Builders' Association, 321

American Technical Society, 106

About the Author

MICHAEL L. BERGER is Vice President for Academic Affairs at Arcadia University in Glenside, Pennsylvania. He serves as Secretary of the Society of Automotive Historians.